BOOK SALE
Solano College Library

HOAXES
AND
SCAMS

HOAXES
AND
SCAMS

*A Compendium
of Deceptions, Ruses and Swindles*

Carl Sifakis

Facts On File

Hoaxes and Scams:
A Compendium of Deceptions, Ruses and Swindles

Facts On File, Inc.
460 Park Avenue South
New York NY 10016
USA

Library of Congress Cataloging-in-Publication Data

Sifakis, Carl.
    Hoaxes and scams : a compendium of deceptions, ruses, and
swindles / Carl Sifakis.
        p.   cm.
    Includes bibliographical references and index.
    ISBN (hc) 0-8160-2569-X, (pb) 0-8160-3026-X
    1. Impostors and imposture.   2. Swindlers and swindling.
3. Fraud.   4. Deception.   I. Title.
HV6757.S57   1993
364.1′63—dc20   92-34347

A British CIP catalogue record for this book is available from the British Library.

Facts On File books are available at special discounts when purchased in bulk quantities for businesses, associations, institutions or sales promotions. Please call our Special Sales Department in New York at 212/683-2244 or 800/322-8755.

Jacket design by Catherine Hyman
Composition and Manufacturing by the Maple Vail Book Manufacturing Group
Printed in the United States

10 9 8 7 6 5 4 3 2 1

This book is printed on acid-free paper.

For Peter Kohlenberger

CONTENTS

Acknowledgments   viii
Introduction   ix
Entries A–Z   1
Selected Bibliography   293
Photo Credits   295
Index of Personalities   297
Index of Subjects   303

ACKNOWLEDGMENTS

The idea for this book was conceived by Ed Knappman when *The Encyclopedia of American Crime* was completed. As so happens, ideas for books may go onto the back burner for a time, and it was Gerard Helferich who made the idea work and Gary M. Krebs who saw it through to fruition. Special thanks go to Steven Ball for his kind assistance on the technical aspects of automotive matters, and of course to Joe Reilly and Paul Scaramazza for their copy editing work on the manuscript and to Shawna Kimber for diligent proofreading.

INTRODUCTION

"Everything that deceives may be said to enchant."
—Plato

One of the subjects of this book, Horace de Vere Cole—the brother-in-law of future Prime Minister Neville Chamberlain—was Britain's master hoaxer. His exploits are detailed in his entry, but we might well review one of the hoaxes not mentioned therein. According to Cole, he "perpetrated ninety-five major practical jokes during my career and have never once been caught out myself." Cole made a distinction between practical jokes and hoaxing (which he regarded as obsession with a profit motive in the form of some sort of swindle or confidence game). But, like most jokester-hoaxers, Cole need not be taken at his word, for in fact once he was more than simply found out. During his young dilettante days he had visited the island of Corsica and pulled a hoax on one of the locals. The humorless Corsican promptly shot him in the leg.

Undaunted, Cole remained the compulsive hoaxer, and like all who have that calling his main fear was not that he would be found out but that he himself might become the butt of a hoax. Then, in 1931, Cole married at the tender age of 48. He implored all of his friends not to engage in any horseplay at the expense of his bride or himself. His rascal friends honored his wishes, a somewhat remarkable forbearance considering that Cole had once hired an actress to interrupt a friend's wedding procession by throwing her arms around the petrified bridegroom and hysterically wailing about their grand past love.

Cole and his bride blissfully honeymooned in Venice and, on the night of March 31, the new Mrs. Cole decided to retire early, while husband Cole sat by the fire, apparently morose about something. The following day was All Fools' Day; for years Cole had never let such an occasion slip by without his special observance.

Finally, Cole quietly retrieved two large suitcases,

lined them with paper and headed for the nearest dock to catch a water taxi to the Lido across from Venice proper. There Cole found a horse stable and, waving a bank note, explained to the stableman his urgent requirements. His suitcases properly filled, Cole returned to the center of Venice, to the now deserted Piazza di San Marco.

When early-rising Venetians entered the piazza, they were greeted by an impossible—nay, a miraculous—sight. The "miracle of the dung," some called it. The piazza was decorated far and wide with the odoriferous booty Cole had purchased in the horse stable. But how, bewildered citizens wondered, had horses—not just one but clearly many—come there during the night when there are no horses or genuine paved thoroughfares in Venice? Were they ridden by angels? Who else could have brought them to the square so that they could leave their mark around the great St. Mark's Cathedral and the palace of the Doge?

Word spread throughout Venice and thousands came to marvel at the great happening. Horace de Vere Cole innocently left Venice with his bride, but the puzzle of the horses remained and is still spoken of in wonderment in that grand city of canals.

Cole was clearly a hoaxer just for the sheer deviltry of it. Others, as per his definition, become involved in it for the profit motive. Still others do it for more complex reasons than mere money, such as an art forger determined to get revenge on the critics who deny him fame. Certainly Hans van Meegeren demonstrated his own greatness by painting his own "Vermeers"—even inventing the artist's nonexistent "middle period"—which the experts hailed as masterpieces; Nazi leader Hermann Goering gladly handed over $256,000 for one such fake.

When one reads this volume, one may well find it

hard to understand why so many people seem to fall for an often preposterous hoax or fraud. In part, of course, a hoax is in the telling; told properly it will con hard-headed financial men and political figures, as well as the great unwashed or herd-instinct investors. Even men who have garnered fortunes in the business world have later bought a "franchise" that turns out to be nothing more than a chain-letter pyramid scheme, which, by the laws of mathematics, simply must collapse. But what of supposedly savvy New Yorkers who have fallen for many cons, including the classic "moon hoax," in which a supposedly new and powerful telescope spotted winged men inhabiting the lunar world? Or the "wild animal scare" that petrified the city with a front-page fantasy about all of the animals having escaped from the Central Park Zoo, ravaging the town, invading churches on Fifth and Park avenues and maiming and killing people? And, best of all, what of the thousands who turned out to labor on that great engineering project to saw Manhattan island in half, turn it around and then rehook the tip to the mainland—all because the island was supposedly sinking under the weight of all the buildings around the battery?

Most hoaxes and swindles succeed because of a great desire on the part of the victim to believe that which satisfies his or her ambition, chauvinism, prejudice or eagerness for financial—even if ill-gotten—gain. Con men say, not without considerable evidence on their side, that their only victims are the dishonest. As Yellow Kid Weil engagingly informed the famed 1950–51 U.S. Senate crime hearings, chaired by Senator Estes Kefauver, all his suckers were "only rascals."

The trouble with such a rationale is that as a con grows, many innocent persons are swept up as well, and they are left much poorer, if not impoverished, from the experience.

Beyond that, hoaxes can often produce an even more severe impact. Orson Welles' 1938 radio broadcast of "Men from Mars" ("War of the Worlds") threw the entire nation into turmoil, producing much violence and looting, as mobs roamed the streets and women and children huddled in churches. Even more grim was the aftermath of a Spanish radio adaptation of the broadcast put on in Ecuador the following year. Panic ensued, and when the public later discovered it had all been fiction, they burned down the radio station and a newspaper plant. Before order was restored, 21 persons had been killed, including six of the show's participants.

Many hoaxes have affected history; the infamous Zinoviev letter clearly sank the Labour Party in the 1924 British elections. Even more disastrous was the fake news story concocted in 1898 by four Denver newspaper reporter-barflies. The journalists re-ported that several American engineers had passed through town on their way to China on a project to demolish the Great Wall of China, as a gesture of the American government's goodwill and to encourage foreign trade. The report shot around the world and, upon reaching China, became the spark that ignited the great Boxer Rebellion.

It would be inaccurate to regard most hoaxers and swindlers as "geniuses" or anything close to that. It is astounding to discover how many got into the life after being first taken in themselves by other con men. This was true among the elite of American con men— Yellow Kid Weil, Oscar Hartzell and Fred Buckminster—and many others as well. Dapper Don Collins was a brilliant con man, but he was himself swindled round and round by "Count" Victor Lustig. It is precisely because these con men were victims themselves that they had an understanding of what will and will not work on other victims. Even the pros can learn an object lesson when they themselves are occasionally taken.

Once the Yellow Kid was working a transatlantic liner, swindling passengers, when he fell for a beautiful countess—so much so that he neglected his fleecing duties. When the ship docked, the countess tearfully confessed she needed a fast $10,000 to settle her alcoholic father's gambling debts. Weil gave her the cash and, on her insistence, took her valuable pearls to hold until she could meet him in a few hours. The "countess" never returned and the pearls turned out to be paste. Weil took the scam with good grace, saying of his lost love: "What a team we would have made."

The entries in this book should also be taken with good grace. Should the sober-minded really worry that some entries could be considered a "how-to" instruction method? No, since there is actually nothing new under the hoaxing sun, all schemes being but new wrinkles of age-old cons. For example, the pedigreed dog swindle, which worked so often on gullible barkeeps, is really no different from the stock swindle. In the latter, worthless securities are peddled to a greedy banker who thinks he has a customer willing to pay a higher price on property, gold, uranium or whatever has been found.

Hoaxes, scams, impostures come in so many varieties that they go beyond the pale of categorizing, and are best left in an alphabetical grab bag. Unfortunately, sources on hoaxes are not always the most impeccable, since the recorder of the tale—especially if it is the con man himself—frequently finds it impossible not to embellish the account. This problem is further discussed in the introduction to the Selected Bibliography.

Meanwhile, it is best to remember that anyone can be hoaxed in even the most absurd ways. There was the time a leading American hoaxer, Hugh Troy (see FLYPAPER REPORTS and VAN GOGH'S EAR), made a wager with friends that he could get some idiot verse he'd written published and credited to him in the *New York Times.* According to Troy profiler H. Allen Smith, Troy set his hoax in motion by writing the *Times'* Sunday book section under the name of "Miss Julia Annsbury, of Auburn, N.Y." that Miss Annsbury wanted help in identifying some verses of a poem that had "haunted [me] since long-gone childhood." It involved, said the phony Miss Annsbury, a gypsy girl taken sick on the roadway and abandoned by her fellow gypsies.

A few weeks passed and the book section offered a reader's response to Miss Annsbury's missive. It was signed "Poetry Lover, Rahway, N.J." and was, of course, another nom de plume for Hugh Troy.

Poetry Lover declared merrily, "I happen to remember the poem Miss Annsbury seeks. It is by Hugh Troy, and if memory does not fail me, its last lines run like this:

> So we leave her,
> So we leave her,
>   Far from where her swarthy
>   kindred roam,
> In the scarlet fever,
> In the scarlet fever,
>   Convalescent home."

Maybe it wasn't the finest verse the *Times* ever offered its readers—but hoaxer Troy had struck again!

ABRAMS, ALBERT *medical quack*

> The physician is only allowed to think he knows it all, but the quack, ungoverned by conscience, is permitted to know he knows it all; and with a fertile mental field for humbuggery, truth can never successfully compete with untruth.

These laudable words were written by a young San Francisco doctor, Albert Abrams (1864–1924). Dr. Abrams knew what he was writing about, as he became one of the most fantastic quacks in all medical history. One of his claims was that Henry Wadsworth Longfellow's handwriting proved the poet had syphilis. Abrams also professed that he could cure syphilis as well as many other diseases over the telephone.

In 1909 Abrams began expounding his first quack thesis, "spondylotherapy," his method for tapping on the spine as a way of finding the body's ailments. The tapping, he said, produced a spinal vibration that was distinctive for each specific ailment. Then Dr. Abrams came up with his new invention, the "dynamizer," which allowed him to do his diagnosis long distance. This was a metal box with all kinds of wires, levers, dials and switches and was attached to a stand-in for the patient. After a sample of the real patient's blood is placed in a box, Dr. Abrams would drum out his tattoo on the abdomen of this stand-in and get spinal vibrations that revealed not merely the illness of the long-distance patient, but also his age, sex and even religion.

Abrams followed this machine with his grandest contraption, which was based on the "Electronic Reaction of Abrams" (E.R.A.) and featured the "oscilloclast." Now the good doctor could vibratorily treat as well as diagnose a disease. And his "reflexophone" allowed the therapy to be done over the telephone!

What the magic of E.R.A. accomplished was all but eliminate the need for expensive hospital bills. The oscilloclast was leased, never sold, to other doctors with a $250 deposit and $200 for a course of instructions. Patients in turn paid $200 for a series of treatments. Abrams' sealed boxes were a huge success, and quacks, describing themselves as "electronic practitioners," set up banks of the boxes to handle all of the business. Abrams made them swear never to break the seals on the boxes and especially warned his quack customers not to try to operate them with a "skeptic" in the room, since the treatment would then prove useless.

Abrams' next quack breakthrough was a handwriting diagnosis method, which made even most blood samples unnecessary. Studying autograph letters he was able to label Samuel Johnson, Edgar Allan Poe, Samuel Pepys and Oscar Wilde as syphilitics, which did not stir too much opposition from the well informed; but when he added Longfellow to the list, there was quite a stir.

Dr. Abrams went on to accumulate over $2 million out of his quackery and enjoyed the support of some eminent personalities. One of his biggest boosters was Upton Sinclair, who absolutely refused to believe that Abrams was capable of deliberate deception. Sinclair was not the least bit moved when Abrams' methods failed after being subjected to tests by the medical profession. Sinclair noted that when Abrams was perfecting his devices, he had the air waves to himself. By the time the medical people were making their objections, the great muckraking writer said, "complex vibrations of I know not how many radio stations" were causing interference. One of the most incisive analyses of Sinclair's faith in Abrams was offered by H. L. Mencken in his book *Prejudices.* He pointed out that the same rebellious traits that produce a political radical frequently find a similar outlet in quack medical opinions.

Finally, in 1923, the American Medical Association brought Abrams down. The A.M.A. sent one of Abrams' quacks in Albuquerque blood samples from a "Miss Bell," which actually were those of a healthy male guinea pig. The quack's diagnosis: Miss Bell had "cancer to the amount of six ohms," a streptococcic infection of the left fallopian tube and an infection of the left frontal sinus for good measure. Another kind of blood sample was sent to Abrams himself and the chief quack said the patient was suffering from cancer, malaria, diabetes and V.D. Apparently, the patient was one sick Plymouth Rock rooster. A committee of experts opened one of the magic boxes and found nothing more than an ohm-meter, a rheostat, a condenser, magnetic interrupter and some other gadgets all wired together in ways that violated all scientific sense.

Defeated and exposed, Abrams was out of business; he died of pneumonia the following year.

ADAMS' NUDE PRESS CONFERENCE, JOHN QUINCY
See JOHN QUINCY ADAMS' NUDE PRESS CONFERENCE.

ADDRESSING ENVELOPES AT HOME *mail-order scam*
Each year thousands of persons in need of additional income are lured into answering advertisements that read: "HOW WOULD YOU LIKE TO MAKE BIG MONEY JUST BY ADDRESSING ENVELOPES AT HOME?" All they have to do is send $5 and they'll find out. For their money victims are supplied with a "sure-fire plan." They are instructed to address envelopes to persons listed in the telephone book offering them a sure-fire way they can make money addressing envelopes at home.

And the scheme does seem to have some sure-fire elements: After all, it did work on them in the first place.

ALCHEMIST CONS *making gold out of gold*
The main purposes of pseudoscientific alchemy in the 18th century were: to find a way to make gold and silver from base metals and, having done so, to find the "elixir of life," which would make man immortal. Neither aim was achieved. There were alchemist con men who masqueraded as having lived hundreds of years, but somehow they always seemed to end up dying within the life span of other living persons. While one could not fake life indefinitely, the alchemists were more successful—in their claims at least—at producing gold and silver, especially when dealing with superstitious people. Some managed to live handsomely with a royal or noble sponsor, milk-

ing them for years for upkeep and research costs, until some princes and lesser kings even bankrupted themselves.

The alchemists sought the so-called philosopher's stone, which would yield the secret of how matter was organized. Many claimed to have it, and that they simply needed more time to produce great wealth. Many alchemists did produce gold and silver with various deceptions that would do a modern magician proud. As related in 1722 by M. Geoffroy the elder at a sitting of the Royal Academy of Sciences at Paris, the most common con was the use of a double-bottomed crucible, a vessel for melting metals. The bottom surface was made of iron or copper, but the upper one was of wax, artfully painted to match the metal. The fakers would place gold or silver dust between the two. Then the pot was filled with lead, quicksilver or other base metals and placed on a fire. Before the eyes of astonished onlookers, the alchemists in time produced a small blob of valuable molten metal.

Another favorite dodge was the wand used to stir a molten brew. It was hollow and stopped up with wax or even butter at the end inserted in the hot metal. As the hot metal was stirred, the end of the wand opened and gold dust poured into the mixture.

Sometimes a lump of lead was doctored by drilling holes into it, filling the holes with molten gold and then resealing the holes with lead.

The problem for the alchemists was that the more successful they claimed to be, the less successful they were in soliciting rewards. A notorious faker, Albert Aluys, found it easy enough in 1726 to deceive the Duke de Richelieu—the ambassador in Vienna from the court of France—and appear to turn lead into gold a number of times. The duke wanted all his fire shovels and pokers to be made into silver and his pewter utensils into gold, and he felt Aluys should find the honor of his acquaintance as sufficient reward. After all, Aluys was a genius "who could not want wealth since he possessed so invaluable a secret." Sadly, Aluys decided it was time to bid adieu to his excellency and move on to lusher fields in Bohemia. But Aluys, as many of his crooked brethen, found it harder to explain his need for cash than to apparently produce gold.

These historic tales do not mean that alchemy is dead. Even in the 20th century it continues to thrive; the most notorious exponent was Franz Tausend who, in the 1920s, conned a number of wealthy Germans, including General Erich von Ludendorff, to invest in his secret process for producing gold from lead. Tausend's secret was flicking gold-dust from a cigarette into his vat.

See also TAUSEND, FRANZ.

In the alchemist's "kitchen," as depicted in a 16th-century work, there was an endless search for ways to make precious metals.

ANCIENT COIN FORGERY See BECKER, CARL WILHELM.

ANIMAL FARMING RACKETS

One of the constants in work-at-home schemes is small-animal raising—chinchillas, rabbits, foxes, minks, bullfrogs (as well as mushrooms)—which, on a commercial level, is almost always a guaranteed loser. The motive on the part of the gyp operators is to sell equipment at huge prices and then not fulfill their promise of buying the product of the victim's labor.

Chinchilla farming is perhaps the most constant of these swindles. The prices for getting started rise and fall not with the commercial demand for skins, but with how desperate victims become as the economic conditions of the time decline. In the 1990s, chinchilla cons enjoyed an explosive introduction in the former East Germany as it reunified with its western counterpart. As unemployment soared in that area, desperate East Germans grasped at any straw for in-

come, and many invested in the false promises of chinchilla swindlers.

A promoter might promise a victim that if he buys a pair of male and female chinchillas for $2,200 (again, the prices gyrate with whatever the market will bear at the time) and the necessary supplies, he can look forward to breeding four or six chinchillas a year. The operator promises to buy each pair for $1,100. So, the victim figures that four chinchillas—two male and two female—which will return most of his original investment. Nothing is said about buying the "skins."

And nothing is said of the possibility that there might be three of one sex or even four of one sex produced, which would drastically reduce the income—if the promoter has any intention whatsoever of keeping his promises. Then the victim would be left with the much more likely prospect of selling the furs for $25 or $30 each—or say a total of a little over $100—with deductions for skinning, tanning and shipping, etc. All of this is dependent upon whether he can find a market in an era of growing resistance to the purchase of fur coats.

"ANTIQUE" SMITH *Robert Burns forger*

Few literary men can boast of having a "personal forger" who almost single-handedly flooded the collector's market with faked documents. The extremely popular Scottish poet Robert Burns deserved that distinction in the person of Alexander Howland who, in the late 19th century, became infamous as "Antique Smith" for his countless Burns forgeries. Smith forged a huge amount of letters by Burns to Sir Walter Scott and other famous writers and by Scott and the other writers to Burns.

For a time Antique Smith's work enjoyed wide acceptance, even though it was somewhat sloppy. Fortunately for Smith, the art of document identification boasted very few true experts in that period. Smith frequently used the wrong kind of paper, simply ripped blank pages from old books, and folded and sealed his letters incorrectly.

Finally arrested and brought to trial in 1893, Smith was doomed by the testimony of George F. Warner, then assistant keeper of manuscripts at the British Museum, who pointed out his numerous faults. In addition to the paper problems, Smith was in the habit of dotting the letter "i" far to the right, while Burns always dotted his neatly, directly over the stem of the letter.

Sent to prison for a year, Antique Smith came out thinking he might be able to market what he called "facsimiles" of Burns' writings; but the public had had more than enough of alleged Robert Burns letters and Smith faded from sight.

APPLETON'S CYCLOPEDIA OF AMERICAN BIOGRAPHY *false entries*

To this day, *Appleton's Cyclopedia of American Biography* is regarded as a useful tool for researchers studying 19th-century personalities. The recommendation cannot be given without the caveat that the work is the greatest repository of faked pedigrees of any scholarly publication. The editors' policy of the 1886 and 1888 editions was to accept in good faith all material received by mail—a procedure that unwittingly (or inevitably) left the publication open to pranks. Although the subjects of these bogus biographies were supposedly well known in their particular profession or field of endeavor, every one of the phonies went undetected for 33 years. Finally, in 1919 Dr. John H. Barnhart, bibliographer of the New York Botanical Garden, published a finding that 14 of the biographies of scientists were false and that if they had lived at all, none had produced any of the works credited to them.

Later, Dr. Barnhart uncovered 15 additional botanists as nonexistent personalities. Other librarians joined in the hunt and, over the next two decades, a total of 84 fictitious entries were discovered. None of the pranksters who had submitted the original material were ever discovered, since the records of the 1886 and 1888 editions had been discarded before suspicions first arose.

ARTHRITIS CURE CONS *quack remedies*

Suffering from arthritis? Why not try the Slim-Twist Exerciser? This device is two pieces of wood connected by a ball-bearing swivel joint. The promoter claims all a person has to do is stand on the top piece, pretend to dance the "Twist" and the arthritis pain will be gone. Not only that, but the consumer will lose weight, cure heart and vascular problems, and find relief from asthma and diabetes.

That is just one of the items offered from the arthritis quack's bag of tricks. There are also things that vibrate, such as chairs and mattresses. These vibrators may produce what a spokesperson from the Food and Drug Administration calls "interesting sensations but they certainly are not harmless since the vibrations could further aggravate already inflamed joints."

Some quack gadgets are even more dangerous. Roy W. DeWelles, for instance, claimed that the Detoxacolon—a pressurized enema device—eliminated arthritis. In fact, he insisted it worked on all ailments known to man, including cancer, asthma, epilepsy, colitis, and high and low blood pressure. DeWelles theorized that all ailments were brought on by toxins in the colon and could be eliminated through irrigation with water and oxygen. What he failed to tell patients was that this Detoxacolon machine treatment could spread infection and even perforate the colon wall. On a number of occasions the FDA seized the machines, but DeWelles managed to stay out of jail for 20 years before being convicted of mail fraud.

Arthritis has been found in the bones of the Java Ape Man and Egyptian mummies. Today, more than 31 million Americans suffer from it and related diseases. There is no cure but, given the amount of sufferers, it is not surprising that prospecting quacks easily find many ripe victims for a "recent discovery" and a "miracle treatment that will at last end the misery of arthritis." In 1966, the annual price tag for quack devices and the like was estimated by the Arthritis Foundation at $310 million. Some 15 years later the estimate stood at $2 billion and growing. Today, for every dollar spent on arthritis research, $25 million is wasted by sufferers on unapproved devices, useless nostrums, unnecessary food supplements, and diet books.

The FDA states:

The various forms of arthritis have different causes, symptoms, and types of treatment. Medication, rest, heat, special exercises and surgery are all used to relieve the symptoms of these diseases. But what's best for the individual patients depends on an accurate diagnosis of the type of arthritis they have. Treatment programs also have to be tailored to fit the individual because the disease varies from patient to patient, and patients themselves vary in the way they react to different therapies.

Among the more audacious quacks are those who charge patients for sitting in abandoned mines to soak up the "curative" powers of uranium or for being buried up to their necks in horse manure.

Snake venom got a big boost as an arthritis treatment in 1979 after CBS's "Sixty Minutes" featured the work of a Florida doctor named Ben Sheppard, who had treated victims of multiple sclerosis and rheumatoid arthritis with a combination of cobra and other snake venom. The FDA's Bureau of Biologics held a public workshop on Sheppard's snake venom treatment, and experts felt that the product—incidentally named PROVEN—had not been proven effective and called for further laboratory testing. Dr. Sheppard died in 1980, but several other doctors jumped in and continued to offer the snake venom treatment.

Many quack arthritis treatment clinics are set up outside the United States, beyond the jurisdiction of U.S. authorities, but other alleged misrepresentative treatments have been found right in the local drugstore. Aspirin is considered a primary treatment for arthritis, but a number of experts have attacked the "glorification" of more expensive forms of aspirin as a sort of medical misrepresentation. So-called "arthritis strength" formulas are merely plain aspirin with a bit of caffeine or antacid added. The tablets are bigger than normal aspirin—and so is the price. One can get the same effect for less by taking regular aspirin and a quarter cup of coffee.

A few years ago an FDA panel of nongovernment experts recommended that "arthritis strength" or "arthritis pain formula" not be included on labels or advertising of aspirin products. The experts said ads suggesting that arthritis is a minor disease or that "extra strength aspirin" will control the disease could delay proper diagnosis and treatment. Experts also warn sufferers that pain relief and inflammation treatment are not the same. A product advertised as providing relief for minor arthritis pain does not necessarily treat inflammation.

Arthritis sufferers have to beware of products that claim "special" and "secret" formulas, that are said to produce quick or easy cures and that are promoted by testimonials and case histories rather than solid and accurate research. Because symptoms may well come and go—or the disease may temporarily go into remission—arthritis sufferers may actually believe, at least for a time, that some quack remedy has cured them. Such products and treatments are best ignored or left capped. There are no genies in a quack's bottle.

See also MEDICAL QUACKERY; SAFETY MILK CON; SEAWATER SWINDLES; URANIUM QUACKERY.

ART PRINT FRAUDS *mass-production cons*

The rich are not the only ones subject to art fraud. Art counterfeiters have found that middle-income people make excellent wholesale victims for fake prints sold either by mail order or through special telephone solicitations (with the usual money-back guarantees, which are not honored). This form of scam increased in the 1980s because of the public's general awareness of skyrocketing prices paid for the work of well-known artists. Even prints can soar in value if they are in limited supply—and genuine. But many are fakes, such as phony Salvador Dali prints, which came forth in a torrent after the famed artist's death. So many were sold in Florida that the Better Business Bureau of South Florida started referring to the wave of complaints as "Hello, Dali" calls.

ASHBY, JAMES *man who scammed the gamblers*

The pre-Civil War, golden era of the riverboat gambler on the Mississippi is replete with tales of chicanery as victims were skinned of their money, sometimes with the connivance of the riverboat companies. Less often remembered in gamblers' memoirs is a grizzled old sharper named James Ashby, who racked up a remarkable record with the gambling fraternity. Ashby was a dishonest gambler himself, but he operated with a certain ethic, concentrating on cheating the crooked gamblers who were trying to cheat him. The gamblers never did find out how old Ashby did it until he retired a very rich man in the 1830s.

Ashby used a young accomplice in his scam, which called for the pair to pose as father and son, allegedly coming home from the livestock market with a goodly sum of cash. The gamblers immediately zeroed in on the hick "son" as an easy mark to be trimmed at cards. The young man was easily lured into a game, while Ashby pretended to be an old coot just this side of senility. During the game old Ashby guzzled corn liquor and scratched out some tunes on his fiddle, stopping repeatedly as he forgot the notes.

In the game the son hardly played like the dimwit he appeared to be, winning hand after hand, despite the odds. When he was dealt cards that looked impressive, but would be beaten, he invariably dropped out without being suckered into big bets.

As one Mississippi historian put it, "Not for a long time did the gamblers learn that tunes were signals." By then it was too late and old Ashby left the river to live out his senior years in bountiful contentment.

ATAHUALPA STATUE *impostor monument*

Much the same way that Guayaquil, Ecuador, sports the fake OLMEDO STATUE, the town of Cuzco, Peru, does not offer a statue of Atahualpa—the last king of the Incas—but rather, for seemingly little logic, one of Chief Powhatan—Pocahontas' father. It seems the U.S. foundry had simply sent the town the wrong statue; but since the Peruvians lacked the finances to ship the statue back, they decided to make do with the "impostor statue," erecting it in the town square as a tribute to the Inca king.

ATLANTIS SEARCHES *discovery con*

Atlantis, a product of Greek mythology, was a large island said to be somewhere in the western sea. According to Plato, it was a utopia destroyed by an earthquake and swallowed up by the sea. Many modern believers in Atlantis have placed the mysterious island continent anywhere between South America and the Aegean (although by most accounts the island was too large to fit into that sea), but others do not exclude Asia or the Pacific. By the 19th century, Atlantis cults—many of them bizarre—thrived. People explored underground and underwater in search of Atlantis, while others posed convoluted theories to justify their beliefs. The Krupp family of German industrialists invested a half-million dollars of their steel fortune to finance an expedition to the Mato Grosso in Brazil to search for Atlantis. Nothing was found.

In 1911 Dr. Paul Schliemann, the grandson of Heinrich S. Schliemann (the famed archaeologist who had excavated what was believed to be Troy and Mycenae), came up with his startling Atlantis "find." That year he sold a story to the *New York American* entitled "How I Discovered Atlantis, the Source of All Civilizations." The younger Schliemann claimed he had been willed the secrets of Atlantis by his grandfather. These secrets allegedly were an old envelope full of papers and an ancient owl-headed vase. According to Paul, there was another piece of evidence, a bronze vase inscribed "From the King Chronos of Atlantis." Unfortunately, this was never shown to the public, and thus all Paul Schliemann had presented was a story.

In 1925 Percy H. Fawcett, a retired British army officer, set out with a party that included his son to find Atlantis in the depths of Brazil. The party vanished. Had Fawcett reached Atlantis? The mystery remained for 26 years until 1951, when the Calapalo Indians of the upper Xingu Basin confessed to hav-

The most commonly placed site of the legendary continent Atlantis is the middle of the Atlantic rather than the Aegean Sea, which is what the Greeks believed. According to its description, it would have been too big to fit into the latter.

ing killed the British explorers because of ill treatment they had suffered from them.

The most baldfaced false claim made by Atlantis hunters was made by Maxine Asher, a mystic with a longtime interest in the enigma. In 1973 she actually got Pepperdine University to sponsor a trip to Spain to search for the missing land. The university even agreed to give college credits to those students making the hunt, for a fee of $2,000 to $2,800 per student. On July 18, 1973, an ecstatic Asher announced the "greatest discovery in the history of the world." In a press release she claimed that three divers had located a sunken city 14 miles off the coast of Cadiz. She declared the city with streets and columns was at least 6,000 years old.

The Spanish government immediately launched an inquiry into Asher's claims and declared the story to be a hoax. One student had even seen the press release two days before the grand dive was supposedly made. Asher vanished. Eventually reporters traced her to Ireland, where she was blithely leading another expedition to Atlantis, this time near the Emerald Island.

For many years geologists have argued that whole continents cannot disappear overnight, and that it would take thousands or more probably millions of years for a continent to vanish. But this has not stopped the true believers and the hoaxers. As Martin Gardner states in *Fads & Fallacies in the Name of Science:*

> Until the last square mile of the oceans' depths is fully explored, those who are so inclined may continue to believe, in the words of John Masefield, that:
>
> > In some green island of the sea,
> > Where now the shadowy coral grows
> > In pride and pomp and empery
> > The courts of old Atlantis rose.

AUTOMOBILE PLOYS AND SCAMS *America's most common swindles*

There is a typical statement made about almost any occupational field—policemen, TV repairmen, lawyers, judges, dentists, etc. It is that most are honest, but that there are some bad apples in any group. However, if one adopts this view in the automotive field, including mechanics, service station operators, car salesmen and so on, "one might," as auto writer Steven J. Ball puts it, "just as well drive around with a license plate lettered SUCKER."

We spend hundreds of billions of dollars a year on car repairs, insurance, fuel and, of course, buying new cars and old heaps. Whatever the total investment the public makes in its love affair with the automobile, it is far greater than what the country spends on national defense. The sad truth is that we might well do better protecting motorists than protecting our borders and international interests. With only the tiniest tongue in cheek does one car expert declare, "The real enemy is within."

Item: A private, nonprofit group in New York City, the Citizens Committee for Metropolitan Affairs, did some minor doctoring on an Oldsmobile that was in perfect running condition. They reset the distributor points from the manufacturer's recommended specifications of 30 degrees up to 42 degrees. That produced a rough engine, hard starting and a loss of power. As the committee noted: "Even a kid in a high school mechanics class would recognize the cause as improper point setting." Yet out of 19 repair shops checked, only one mechanic recognized the fault immediately and adjusted the points without charge. Four others, more incompetent, eventually located the trouble after investigating everything back to the tailpipe. The 14 remaining mechanics diagnosed the car as needing work, quoting prices up to $40.

Item: Other investigators tried the same ploy in San Francisco with results almost as bad. They also reported a conversation in one garage:

> Investigator: I don't know the first thing about cars. What's the trouble?
> Mechanic: Valves, Mac. I don't know where I ever

run into a worse case of sticking valves. Probably burned all to hell, too, considering you've been running the car in this condition.
> Investigator: Oh, my. A man at a service station told me my sassifram was out of sync, whatever that means.
> Mechanic [without so much as changing his expression]: It could be, but I doubt it, Mac. This is valves; I know engines.

Perhaps some of the humor of this situation is lost when it is noted that the mechanic's estimate—which other garage mechanics had made for free—was $349.96!

Item: A noted car expert commissioned by a national publication to take specially doctored cars to repair shops all around the country concluded: "I ended my trip with a pretty low estimate of today's auto repair industry."

Item: Some years ago Glenn F. Kriegel, president of a Denver car-diagnostic center that did not do repair work itself but informed motorists what needed to be done, told a U.S. Senate subcommittee that his organization processed 5,000 car inspections, which called for an examination of the vehicles both before and after repairs were made. After the initial inspection and analysis, the autos went to various repair shops for servicing. On the recheck it was found that 50 cars—a mere 1%—had been adequately repaired. A great many of the automobiles showed no evidence that any work had been done, although the motorists had all paid for alleged repairs.

The above items reflect little difference from other rackets, or at the very least misleading ploys, perpetrated elsewhere in the entire automotive field, whether involving insurance fraud, other upkeep gyps or misrepresentations in the selling of autos. There is little difference between the mechanic who disassembles a car's parts and refuses to restore them unless the car owner meets his outrageous price demands for fancied repairs and the car salesman who holds onto a potential buyer's car keys so "we can evaluate its trade-in value while you look at some of our great buys"—and thus essentially keeps the customer a prisoner without wheels to make an escape.

The following items on various automotive scams represent a mere smattering of situations. To do full justice to the subject would require a separate book, with endless updates. Perhaps the best perspective on the enormous range of car gyps was offered by notorious swindler Yellow Kid Weil, who once defended his honor in a radio interview, noting that he did not prey on the innocent but on the greedy and dishonest who were most susceptible to a shady proposition if it afforded them a seemingly sure opportunity to cheat someone else. "It's not as though I was a used car salesman," the Yellow Kid proclaimed.

Adulterated Gas

Not long ago a leading oil company executive admitted privately that service station swindles increased during periods of economic stress because "a service station owner fears driving cutbacks. He actually will turn to gypping the public to soothe his worries, sort of making hay while he can."

One of the most common gyps unleashed during bad economic times is the adulterated gas racket. With premium gas netting more cents than regular, there's big money to be made with a doctored pump.

In New York City an official check was once made by authorities who tested samples from a number of service stations; their findings resulted in the conviction of 38 operators for selling adulterated gasoline. In many parts of the country, both regular and premium gasoline pumps have been found connected to the same tank. Since the tanks are underground, how can a motorist be sure there isn't just one big tank? According to motor club experts, the problem of doctored gas gets worse as one goes south. In one southern state, one very big station was found selling four different grades of gasoline at different prices; all of the pumps drew from the very same storage tank!

There is no real defense a car owner has against this dodge except buying gas from a station he has learned to trust. If a driver has a car that requires premium, and it suddenly seems to not be functioning well, experts suggest that before he blames the problem on a parts malfunction, he try switching gas stations for a while and determine if the new premium makes the car work better.

Air Bag Insurance Overpricing

The "air bag scam" has come to be used as a generic term for the failure of a number of auto insurance companies to pay discounts for cars equipped with safety and anti-theft devices. New York state law, typical of statutes around the country, requires insurance discounts for anti-theft devices and such safety features as anti-lock brakes, automatic seat belts and air bags.

In October 1991 it was announced that about one million New Yorkers would receive refunds of up to $225 each from five insurance companies that failed to pay the discounts. The settlement reached by the state attorney general's office and the five companies—State Farm Mutual, Allstate, General Accident, Travelers and Metropolitan—called for the companies to pay $110 million in refunds to an estimated 10 million customers around the country. At the time it was said that 200 other insurance companies were still under investigation, and it was estimated that a total of $500 million in refunds could eventually be due to customers.

The scandal began when a Rochester auto mechanic contacted the state attorney general's office after noticing that he had not received a discount for having an air bag in his automobile. According to Attorney General Robert Abrams, neither had 80% of the people who should have been awarded discounts.

The insurance companies offered a number of excuses for not having paid the discounts, one firm saying consumers had to specifically ask for them, another complaining its business was growing so fast it couldn't keep up with the discounts and so on. Besides making the refunds, the five companies also agreed to pay New York a total of $708,872 in order to avoid any prosecution.

Alley Treatment

Car buyers must understand that the car manufacturer writes the warranty, but it is the dealer who has to live up to it. The fact is many dealers don't want to do warranty work. They insist that 40% of their shop time is taken up with warranty replacement work, which is paid for by the auto maker at wholesale rates that are far below what the dealer can get for regular repair work. From the dealers' viewpoint, Detroit also mucks things up with a welter of paperwork and delays in payment to the dealer. A cynic might say the auto makers do this on purpose to encourage the dealers to go slow on warranty work, perhaps even to force a motorist to go elsewhere in disgust. After all, the less the dealer does, the less the company has to pay. Some dealers drag their feet so much that they end up giving "alley treatment" to warranty work, simply pulling the car into the back alley and leaving it there until the owner comes for it under the assumption that the trouble has been attended to.

Other dealers use a different method than the alley treatment to make warranty work—and the customer—pay. These dealers employ mechanics who are specialists at finding expensive non-warranty work that has to be done at the same time. One dealer has been quoted as bragging, "I have a man who can convince almost any customer that he needs at least a wheel-alignment job, even if the car is less than a month old."

Automatic Choke Cons

Motorists dread winter mornings, since they are the most inconvenient time for a faulty automatic choke to act up or, rather, not act up. Starting an engine can thus be murder, and once it does start up, it stalls time and again. The problem can be difficult to pinpoint, and many motorists are sold a bill of goods by their overfriendly mechanic and shell out for a complete tuneup. But that doesn't cure the problem. Automotive writer Simon Koch has said, "If you're having problems starting in the morning, invest in a new automatic choke and see if your problem doesn't disappear. It's a lot cheaper than buying a new carburetor, the crooked mechanic's favorite antidote to the hard-to-start-in-the-morning problem."

Automatic Transmission Con

When it comes to automatic transmission work, the sharpie mechanic has a standard patter. He shakes his head and shows a motorist metal filings fished out of the bottom of the transmission case. Most transmissions will, in fact, shed metal pieces—but it is not serious in reasonable amounts. However, many drivers fall for the act and are taken for the price of a rebuilt transmission. If the mechanic sizes up the motorist as a first-rate pigeon, the only transmission work done will simply be changing the fluid.

"Battery Boiling" Gyps

"Battery boiling" is one of the oldest and most effective methods of swindling by dishonest gas station attendants. All they have to do is slip a little baking soda into one of the cells and a chemical reaction occurs. The battery will foam, making it appear damaged or dead. The ploy is especially effective among women, who seem to imagine the battery is about to explode. Another method used is to drain the acid out of the battery cell and replace it with water. The attendant can then "prove" the battery is dead by making a hydrometer check.

Battery Test Scams

"You need a new battery." A sharpie car mechanic will say this—and even "prove" it—if a car owner is credulous enough. All he has to do is put the prods of his battery tester on the wrong electrodes and, of course, he gets a reading of a dead cell. Whenever a motorist asks for a voltmeter test, he must make sure the mechanic pushes the prongs below the surface of the battery contact points. Otherwise, the reading will *have* to be wrong.

Bird Dogging

Most car dealers have people who refer customers to them. Such a person is known as a "bird dog." The standard price in New York City for anyone referring a buyer to a dealer is between $25 and $50. It was $25 per sale in California until the practice was outlawed. Though illegal in a number of jurisdictions, bird dogging is still practiced.

Should you ever go to a dealer based on someone else's recommendation? Only if you are absolutely sure there's nothing in it for him. A person can be 100% honest in his recommendation of a dealer, but

a money payoff is certainly not going to cool his ardor. More importantly, car salesmen aren't about to give a customer referred by a bird dog an extra good deal. In the first place, that reward has to be remade. Car salesmen may say they are willing to give you a special deal because you know somebody, but there's very little room for sympathy in the car-selling game: It's strictly dollars and cents.

New car salesmen tell the standard story of the sharpie to whom a potential buyer was referred. The salesman promptly took him for almost list price, despite the fact that the customer had a trade-in that also netted the hustler an extra commission. The salesman also took the shopper for financing and insurance at very favorable terms—that is, for the car dealer. The kicker to the story showed up on the paperwork when the salesman filled in his contact for the sale. In the space naming the source, he'd written "Mother."

Brake Pedal Con

The average motorist is more conscious of the brakes than any other part of the automobile, since if they are faulty they can cause accidents. Gyp mechanics are aware of this, and if a car owner drives into the wrong station with brake problems, he or she is taking a good chance on being swindled.

One of the most common problems is caused by air getting into the hydraulic system. As a result, the brakes appear to be operating properly, but when the driver steps on the brake pedal it feels like a wet sponge under foot. The standard solution for this is bleeding the brakes to vent the air. However, if the condition returns, then it will be obvious that the situation is more serious. A car owner should be suspicious of a mechanic who says there's a need for a major brake overhaul before he's bled the brakes.

Breather Cap Con

The "breather cap con" may be described as the crooked service station operator's credo of "always kick a motorist when he's down." The routine starts when a motorist has been conned by a garage gouger into filling up with much more oil than he needs (see DIPSTICK DODGES). He drives along, then blue smoke issues from the engine. Panicky, he pulls into the next service station. The second operator looks at the smoking engine and realizes the motorist has been suckered into buying a lot of oil he didn't need.

Theoretically, the operator could say with all honesty, if not tact, "Hey, sucker, why do you let people swindle you like that?" He could say that, but usually he does not. Far more likely he will say to himself, "Once a sucker, always a sucker." Then he'll inspect the engine with a straight face and announce, "Breather cap trouble, that's what it is. Let me put on a new breather cap and it'll stop all the oil spray. Your trouble will be over once there's enough time for the oil to burn off."

The gullible driver is not told that excess oil will blow out of even a brand new breather cap. But the second service station operator sees no reason why he can't squeeze a few dollars out of the sucker for a new cap. This is the gyp service game's version of a chain letter.

Carburetor Con

A motorist has a problem with a carburetor, which is flooding all over the place. The standard line is: "What you need is a new carburetor. We can give you a rebuilt one cheap." Not, however, as cheap as what (the odds are) it really takes to fix the problem, namely a needle valve and seat. From the dishonest shop's point of view, the rebuilt carburetor is a better deal for them, not because of the extra money, but because it's so easy and profitable. All the operators have to do is steam-clean the motorist's own carburetor and take his money.

Car Insurance Misclassifying Trick

One way a shady auto dealer can make extra money is by juggling a car buyer's age on insurance forms. Hearings by the U.S. Senate Subcommittee on Automotive Marketing Practices disclosed that several insurance companies had been conniving with car dealers to misclassify car buyers as being under 25, thus putting them into the highest-charge category. When these findings were made public, a half-dozen companies immediately made refunds of close to a quarter million dollars to wrongly billed policy holders in order to cut off possible court action. Of course, this doesn't mean a dealer can't make an "honest mistake" today.

Car Insurance Trick Policies

Insurance men love to tell the tale of the trick operator who slipped a clause into a car insurance policy declaring it void if the automobile was used by an unauthorized driver. When a car was stolen, the trickster insisted the thief was an unauthorized party and declared the policy void! One should beware of such a policy and the specificity of the terms of such a clause—i.e., in case of a stolen car, the company will pay only for parts stripped off. In short, a consumer must read and completely understand a policy he or she buys. One should look out for "bargain" policies—especially in the high-risk field—and stay away from mail order car insurance. Always determine that the company is fully licensed to sell insurance in your state. Never take an agent's word for it; if ever in doubt, check with the BBB or a reputable insurance broker.

Car Owner Fraud Practices

Insurance companies are frequently the object of fraudulent practices from scam artists of all types, including "honest" car owners. A report in late 1991 indicated that the latter had become, in the words of Arnold Schlossberg Jr., director of the Insurance Crime Prevention Institute, "a growth industry, no question about it."

Besides staged auto accidents, there are many "lesser" capers that the public finds not entirely unacceptable, including:

- *Staged Claims.* The owner removes parts of a car, stores them away and reports they have been stolen. After the insurance company pays, the parts are put back in the car.
- *Owner Dumping.* A car owner reports his car is stolen and collects on the claim. The car's parts are peddled to auto shops and salvage yards.
- *Abandoned Vehicles.* Needing money, the owner abandons his car on the road or in a parking lot so that it will eventually be stolen or destroyed. The owner makes a report to the police and then files with the insurance company to collect on his policy.
- *Salvage Switches.* The vehicle indentification number—found on the dashboards of newer cars—is salvaged from a junked car and switched to a similar make and model, which the owner has reported stolen. The car with the false number is then re-registered and sold off, frequently in another state.

What can the average person do to avoid becoming innocently involved in such insurance frauds? The experts advise:

- Refuse to buy a car or an accessory, such as a radio, from an unknown party.
- When buying a used car, make certain the title is in the seller's name.
- Be wary when auto parts are offered at prices that are simply too good to be true.

"Dead Battery"

You hit your starter and all you get is a clicking noise. A dishonest gas station operator informs you that the battery is dead and you need a new one. But is it really dead? You can check to see if you are being told the truth. Does the horn still work? What about the radio and the lights?

If you are still getting power, chances are your real problem is badly corroded battery cables. In this case, the only thing the station operator needs to do is clean the cables and battery terminals with a wire brush. Whenever a service attendant or mechanic goes into mourning for your battery, check your cables before joining in.

Dipstick Dodges

A dipstick in the hands of a crooked service man comes close to being a stickup weapon. There is, for instance, the fast dipstick routine. As a car wheels up to the pump, the dipstick artist has the stick in to check the oil even before finding out what the customer wants. He'll take the order, pull out the dipstick and announce, "You're way short. Want some oil, too?" Naturally the motorist does. That is, the motorist should want some if he really is short of oil. But he will always be short of oil when the dipstick is flipped in a couple of seconds after the engine is turned off. It takes several minutes for oil trapped in the upper half of the engine to drain back into the crank. The heavier the oil, the longer it takes. A car owner who is not aware of this will get clipped for a quart of oil every so often.

Other dipstick artists use the filthy oil dodge, pulling out the dipstick and running a drop of oil between their fingers. "Filthy," they declare. See how gritty this is. Better let me change it." Actually, even if the oil was changed an hour ago, it will look gritty. All high-detergent oil color will fade from bright to dirty black within 60 minutes of pumping through any engine.

The true masters of the dipstick con art are the "short stickers." They are so good they can always avoid pushing the dipstick to its stop, just so they can show a driver an indication of a low oil level. They fill up a car and send it on its way, unconcerned that within an hour the engine will probably be covered with blue smoke from oil film that covers the entire engine.

Dirty Oil Dodge

A number of shady auto service stations are not above selling reprocessed old motor oil as new motor oil at current prices. The service station men save the discarded dirty oil they drain from cars and sell it in bulk to "refiners." Once the goo is "refined," the oil is shipped back in new cans to the gas stations to be peddled to unsuspecting customers.

The do-it-yourself service station gyp artist has his own refinement, running the entire scam himself and not sharing his illicit profits. He even has a machine that reseals cans from top brand names of oil. A motorist's only defense is to get out of the car and pick the can of oil he wants himself. A crimp on the lid will reveal if it's a refilled job. Reprocessed oil won't hurt a car's engine, but it still plays hob with the car owner's wallet.

"Fire Injectors"

"No," says the auto serviceman with guile, "you don't want ordinary spark plugs. What you really want are some 'fire injectors.' " A number of mail-order ads offer the items, and many garages also have

the ads posted on the wall. What do these marvelous fire injectors do? They give you a better spark, increase mileage, get the engine to start easily, save wear on your tires, and more. The prices in the ads are pretty steep, often quadruple the price of sparks. But the garageman is able to underprice the mail orders up to 25% percent less.

Yes, the consumer gets genuine fire injectors; the imported ones have the words "fire injector" printed right on them. All this is designed to convince the car owner that he hasn't bought some plain old sparkplugs—but that is exactly what he has bought.

Flat-Rate Manual Dodges

A car repair tab is determined by the *Flat Rate Manual,* which is issued annually and lists all standard repair jobs and the length of time they should require. When a car owner objects to the price of the work done, the boss will pull out this bible to back up the charge. As consumer car experts warn, this can be a plain hustle. The fact is that any reasonably good mechanic can beat the book time easily. Some mechanics can do two jobs in the time allotted for one, thus collecting double rate for each repair made. When this routine happens at your regular repair station, the experts recommend that you inform the boss you know the work can be done faster. Keep patronizing the garage and if your lecture has had any effect, your next bills will be smaller. If not, it is time to switch.

"Free Inspection" Car Repairs

Auto experts agree that a motorist should never accept repair garage offers for "free" inspections or diagnosis. One should not believe that mechanics who work on commission are going to spend their time gleefully making free inspections. If the garage offer is honest, the mechanics will soon be in revolt. The mechanic inevitably does get paid—but by the car owner, who is told that "urgent work" needs to be done on his car.

Freeway Runners

Some dishonest auto service stations, not satisfied with gouging whatever customers may drive in, actually use steerers or "freeway runners" to give chance a hand by hanging around highway exits befriending passing drivers. They flag them down and earnestly inform them their gas tank is leaking or one of their wheels is wobbly. The typical motorist is not only grateful for what seems to be the act of a good samaritan, but also eagerly accepts advice on the nearest place to get help.

Some freeway runners operate right on the road, pulling alongside a car at 60 miles per hour and shouting out a warning of imminent danger. Some crooked service station employees double as steerers during their off hours. The freeway runner generally receives a 50% payoff of whatever a gullible motorist is taken for.

Gasoline Brand Hoax

Do gasoline brands mean anything? According to gasoline companies, they certainly do and theirs is best. A more accurate picture is offered in a revealing letter to an auto hobbyist publication from a truck driver who works in an area where "one independent refinery sells, and I deliver to, no less than seven major-brand gasoline distributors and many private-brand outlets. A visit to a number of refineries will plainly reveal many major-brand tankers, along with common carriers, loading at the same platforms and taking on the same gas." Moral: Shop for your gas because you trust the man at the pump, the prices at the station, the quality of the repair work or for reasons other than a brand name.

Gas Pump Double-dipping

Ever wonder why virtually all phone booths in service stations are inside or around the corner—out of sight of the pumps? It could be a cute dodge known by gas jockey gypsters as double-dipping. When a motorist drives into a gas station and tells the attendant to fill it up while he makes an all-important phone call, he will come out to find his tank filled and the amount on the pump. He pays and drives off; the gas station, meanwhile, might just have put five gallons of gas in a can for servicing of emergencies—which the last customer just paid for.

Perhaps the baldest swindle of all was reported by a motor club in the South, which found a young attendant holding down a job only one day a week. He did it not only for the pay he drew, but for the "fringe benefits." Whenever a motorist left his car, the kid would run the nozzle into his own car and run a couple of extra gallons into his tank. "By the end of the day," the club's bulletin reads, "our young swindler had a full tank of gas and was set for a whole week's free driving."

Gas Pump Tumbler Scam

Are motorists being gypped at the gas pump? If this simple gimmick is employed, few drivers would notice. While the posted price might be 100.9 the tumblers on the face of the pump whiz around at 101.9 a gallon. In other words, the service station makes an extra penny a gallon. This might not seem like much but, considering the wholesale price of gas and the heavy taxes on it, the margins for the service station are small. Even if a station does a below-average 25,000 gallons of gas a month, the tumbler fix amounts to $250.

If the gyp operation does get nabbed at the scam every couple of years, the owner pays a small fine and forgets about it. (He says in his defense, "Whaddya gonna do, make a federal case outta it? So the tumblers were on the fritz and I charged a few people a few extra pennies. So what? I'm sorry. . . .")

Generally, the fines in such cases are mild because laws haven't been written in recognition of the fact that petty chiseling is the country's biggest racket. Some cynics warn that the fines had better be light, or the chiselers will just give those tumblers an extra whirl. In one week of tumbling the pumps for just an extra penny, the chiselers can easily make their money back.

How can the average motorist protect himself against the tumbler scam? Primarily, he can alter the way he buys gas. It should never be "fill 'er up" or even a specific dollar amount such as $6 or $8. An exception would be $10, since this leaves the exact price by simply moving the decimal point one digit. An exact gallon amount is also a better way, in that it becomes a simple exercise in multiplication. The customer should never fall for the lie that when the tumblers are off slightly, the money tumbler is the accurate measure.

It is very valuable for a motorist to spot a service station pulling the tumbler scam, since a shop that engages in such a practice is probably pulling other ripoffs as well.

Head Gasket Con

It looks and sounds terrible: The driver finds he is losing power; the motor sounds as though a muffler has blown and the engine overheats. If a motorist takes such a car to a crooked mechanic, he will probably be sold a motor job, being told he needs new valves because the compression on his motor is gone. The driver may well be falling for the head gasket con.

A head gasket protects a car's compression. Before a driver invests in a motor job, he should check the head gasket (located between the head of the motor and the motor) to see if the seal is broken. If so, a head gasket can be replaced in no time and at very little cost. Otherwise the car owner can be taken for a motor job costing hundreds of dollars.

"Hidden Load" Auto Insurance

What happens when car sales slump during adverse economic conditions? Prices are cut and dealers emphasize certain unrecognizable scams to add to their profits. A racket that is quite prevalent, especially on shady used car lots, is the "hidden load."

The dealer quotes a financing deal with some collision insurance, which he tells the customer is quite high but is required by the finance company. The customer signs. Later, the dealer dumps the contract to a finance company, which in turn peddles it to a bank. Eventually, the insurance company sends the customer a statement on the actual cost of the insurance, which is far less than the dealer said it was.

But the customer can prove nothing. His contract does not separately show the cost of insurance. Instead, the dealer has packed insurance and other fees in a single item. The buyer does not have anybody to complain to. The bank won't listen, even though one look at the contract will tell its officials that the buyers are being defrauded. Unfortunately, there are plenty of money-hungry banks that will do business with finance companies and dealers pulling the hidden load. In periods of bad loan portfolios gypped car owners are more dependable debtors than over-enthusiastic real estate operators or financial manipulators.

Honking

Honking—kicking a hole in a tire to cause a small leak—is probably the most vicious of all scams pulled by unscrupulous auto service station gyps on non-regular customers. It is relatively more common in small communities than in large cities, but it can be found almost anywhere.

There is no way a motorist can really protect himself from honking. The dirty work is done with a needle-sharp blade, implanted in a shoe, and a quick kick by a crooked attendant. Auto writer Simon Koch declared: "If you are ever victimized by honking, don't make a fuss, because the chances are that you're dealing with real desperadoes and anything can happen. As soon as you get away report the incident to the AAA, BBB, the police and anyone else you can think of."

In some small communities it does not pay to drive straight to the local police to report the gouge, since most crooked garages would not be pulling the stunt without "clearance." Instead victims should write letters to business leaders warning they will never again venture through their community until they get assurances the dirty work has ceased. In some cases, because of such pressure, state governments have cracked down on communities where honking, as well as other gouges, is perpetrated.

Ignition Wire Switch

One of the easiest ways to con motorists into a costly tune-up involves a quick-fingered attendant who switches a couple of ignition wires so that the motor will run roughly. A good time to pull this off is when the oil is being checked. The attendant goes into some fast talk to promote a tune-up job. Once the motorist agrees, all that is done is to switch the wires back the way they were.

This little racket demonstrates how important it is for car owners to know some basic facts about how a car operates. A wise motorist will protect himself from the sleight-of-hand scam by determining which sparkplugs his ignition wires should be connected to.

Light-bulb Con

This may be the smallest car repair gyp of all. There are some dishonest garages that won't think of letting a car off the premises without a little light-bulb gouge. Before the motorist shows up to pick up his car, the bulbs in some of the car fittings are loosened. When the driver gets behind the wheel he is asked to switch on the headlights, "just for a last check on the adjustment."

Usually the headlights are okay, but inevitably a tail-light, side-light or back-up light will always be out. The mechanic puts in a new bulb, holds the perfectly good one up for the driver to see it is burned out, smiles and takes his tip. Sometimes a bit of dirt on a mechanic's finger will smudge the bulb up enough to make it look burned out.

It is a very minor swindle, but many crooked shops figure it will add up to as much as $1,000 a year without any effort. Any defense against this little ripoff? As soon as a mechanic says a light isn't on, the response should be, "Gee, see if it got knocked loose." Usually that's enough to tell the gypster to wait for the next car.

Long-term Collision Policies

When providing financing for a car purchase, many dealers and insurance companies have come up with cute ways to pad their profits. One of the more popular and profitable is a three-year-collision policy on a new car. The premium for the entire period is simply added to the carrying charges. Thus a buyer is paying a huge interest on the cost of the second and third years of his insurance. Buy the same insurance separately from an insurance broker and you have to pay only one year at a time and eliminate the interest gouge to the finance company.

Lowballing and Highballing

The practices of "lowballing" and "highballing" are in most cases legal, but very unethical. They are used in a number of businesses, furniture and rug stores and the like, but are extremely prevalent in the used car business.

The car buyer may, for example, fall for a price offered by a car salesman that is too tempting to resist. The purpose is to keep the customer from shopping around and finding anything that can match the deal. The salesman even goes so far as to fill out a purchase order for the customer at this rock-bottom price. That has no meaning whatsoever, since a purchase order must be approved by an authorized representative of the firm to be binding. Meanwhile, the customer thinks his car is on order. But when he later finds himself stuck up for a higher price, he will often pay because by now it is too late to start looking elsewhere. Often he has also been bragging to family and friends about what a terrific bargain he had driven; if it now falls through, he would have to admit to them that he's been toyed with. To avoid that embarrassment, the customer ends up agreeing to the dealer's higher price.

The buyer can also be taken through "highballing." In this ploy the salesman offers a shopper a very high price for his old car. Of course, that price is subject to a reappraisal when the customer picks up his new car. At the last minute the dealer finds the old car not worth what he originally estimated. He may legally reduce his offer. The buyer is trapped, having wasted weeks on a deal that will now fall through unless he agrees to pay several hundred dollars more. Many buyers give in out of sheer exhaustion.

Mechanic's Lien

A car owner must never forget that if he starts dealing with a gyp mechanic he has very little recourse once work has begun on the automobile. The reason, known as "mechanic's lien," can best be explained in a complaint report filed by one victim:

> I let this repairman talk me into a motor job. I was shocked when he handed me the bill. I knew I was being taken and refused to pay. At this point he slapped a mechanic's lien on the car. I ran to my lawyer who was no help at all. According to him, no matter how brazenly you've been shafted by a crooked repair shop, the law gives it the right to lock up the car until you pay the bill in full. I told the lawyer I wanted to fight the matter but he only laughed. He told me the number of cases won by car owners against mechanics in a case like this probably could be counted on the fingers of one hand. After all, it's just your word against his, and almost any judge is going to take the word of an "expert" mechanic over yours. I still was stubborn and was considering fighting it out on principle until the lawyer warned me the legal costs would eventually mount up to far more than the total bill I was being soaked for. That took all the fight out of me.

Says auto writer Steven Ball, "About the only defense against a mechanic's lien is to insist on a bill in writing before any work is done. And it should be put in writing that no work on your car is to be done beyond that first written figure unless you are first notified and given the right to approve or disapprove."

Odometer Tricksters

Can you ever trust the mileage reading in a used car? The answer is no. If a dealer goes to all the trouble of improving an old car's general appearance, does

it make any sense for him not to alter the mileage to fit its new characteristics? Even relatively honest dealers almost automatically call in specialists known as "spinners" to reset odometers.

A good spinner can perform his task so well that nobody can find any trace of tampering. One California artist was so good that he was actually under "contract" to 10 or 11 dealers, charging $5 a fix and making about $2,000 a month. At those prices his work was a tremendous bargain to a used-car cheat, since that little spin could alter the price of a car by several hundred dollars.

Shortly after this particular spinner's activities were reported, California passed a law making the turning back of odometers absolutely illegal. Thereafter, the spinners' fee jumped to about $15 per job. Occasionally, odometer racketeers are nailed. In Baltimore, Maryland, a used-car shopper grabbed a real bargain with only 23,000 miles registered. Later, in an incredible coincidence, he ran into the original owner of the vehicle and discovered the correct odometer reading was 64,000 miles. A jury awarded the car buyer $25,600 in damages from the dealer who sold him the doctored vehicle. Incidents such as this are refreshing but few and far between.

If an odometer reading is not to be trusted, how can a buyer judge the car's true mileage? The dealer says 30,000 miles, but is there new rubber on a pedal or a new rug? Seat covers can keep the original upholstery looking new; always look underneath them for signs of heavy wear. If the seat covers look new, look up. There's something wrong when the downstairs is in good shape and the overhead upholstery is grimy and perhaps even worn in spots. Some other hints: Rust under the edge of the body or the condition of the exhaust pipe can indicate a car that has had heavier use. When such tell tales turn up, it would be prudent to double the odometer figure.

Padded Insurance Coverage

The standard motto of sharpie car insurance operators is: "Give 'em what they don't need, and charge plenty for it." Some agencies in Florida have been found selling their customers policies that include an extra premium for insurance against "partial or total auto destruction by snow storm." Dealers in states bordering Canada have been known to palm off protection against tropical hurricanes. Sometimes, however, matters boomerang. A few years ago a New York City driver on a camping trip had his expensive auto completely destroyed in an Alaskan earthquake. He collected on the full valuation of his automobile. Ironically, his claim sparked an inquiry, which determined that thousands of motorists were being sold padded-out insurance that covered earthquake damage.

Phantom Oil Scam

In the crooked service station field it's called "phantom oil" or in some areas the "Houdini oil trick." It works beautifully when a customer orders a complete oil change. The motorist is fortunate if he drives off with half the oil he should have.

The trick is actually so simple it can be pulled off before the victim's eyes. The motorist can watch the service man take the oil cans from the rack, punch holes in them and carefully pour the contents into the crankcase. After paying his bill, the motorist drives off, convinced he doesn't have to worry about his oil for some time. The service man scurries over to the trash can where he dumped the empties. He pokes around, pulls out several cans and returns them to the rack, the holes to the bottom so that it is not readily apparent that the cans are empty. Of course, he does not retrieve all the cans, as some are now totally useless. He can't easily reuse cans that have holes in the top and bottom.

This is one of the oldest swindles ever practiced around a gas station. When a regular customer orders some oil, it is quite possible he gets the full amount. But after he leaves, the empty oil cans are turned over and replaced on the rack until a sucker comes along.

Power Steering Garage Gyps

Except for the brakes, nothing makes the average motorist more nervous than when he thinks there is something wrong with his car's steering. In his mind's eye he visualizes himself doing 80 mph on a highway, unable to negotiate a turn.

The fact is most steering problems are caused by a lack of hydraulic fluid in the power unit. When this is the case, the unit will give off a high-pitched squeal, as, for example, when the driver turns the wheel as hard as he can while backing into a parking space. Auto expert Simon Koch says, "Less-than-honest gas station operators will try to talk you into buying a new power unit. In the vast majority of cases the condition is corrected by the simple procedure of adding a little fluid."

Premium Gasoline Con

"Naturally, any car will run better with premium." Ever heard that from a gas jockey? If you have, he was either a crook or a dummy. It has been estimated that approximately half the drivers using premium gasoline are giving their cars no better fuel than if they stuck with regular.

The car owner's manual clearly indicates whether a driver should use regular or premium. He or she should buy the kind of gas the manual says and forget the con from the gouger at the pump. Cost-conscious drivers can try to shave their gasoline expenditure. One oil company, which produces eight different grades of gasoline, advised customers to "try the recommended fuel; if it is satisfactory, try the next lower-priced blend; if that is also satisfactory, go another step lower; if the car knocks, then go up a blend."

Radiator Gyps

An expensive and often unnecessary car repair is the replacement of a radiator. Summertime—when highway traffic comes to a standstill on weekends—is when a radiator is most likely to overheat. The cause is usually a faulty thermostat or accumulated rust that cuts off circulation. Although it is hardly ever necessary, highway repair vultures will try to talk a motorist into buying a new and expensive radiator. Before doing so, automotive experts advise, check the body of the radiator with your hand. If some of the various points are cool, it is a sign that the circulation is blocked by rust deposits. But a new radiator is hardly necessary; a simple flush with a high-pressure hose will usually clear up the condition. Additional advice from automotive expert Simon Koch: "Have the thermostats removed (reinstall for the winter months) and see if this allows your engine to run cool again."

Repair Fixed Price Offers

Motorists should realize that auto shops advertising fixed prices such as for "any transmission resealed" seldom mean what they say. What they generally mean is that any work will cost more than the quoted price. Here's one account of what happens when a motorist is lured in with such an ad:

> A few days later I got a call from the place. They told me that extra parts were needed because the mating parts to which the seals attach are so worn that new seals will not stop the leaks. I had no choice but to pay the difference. Suddenly the whole job was no bargain.

It may well be that the story given the motorist was truthful. This happens, but advance warnings never make it into the advertisements, whose sole function is to bring the customers in.

Auto club and Better Business Bureau files bulge with complaints from car owners on offers for rebuilt engines. One East Coast driver was lured in by a stated flat rate of "$139.50 EXCHANGE." He described:

> I took that to mean that I would have my old engine pulled out and a new one installed for the stated figure. When they were all finished, I got socked with a bill that was almost double what I figured I was spending. I kicked, but it did a fat lot of good. They told me the "engine" meant only the engine block, with pistons and cylinders. I was told I still had to cough up for the carburetor, oil pan and spark plugs.

And to top that all off, labor was extra! I said I wasn't going to pay and they said, "Okay, we'll hold on to your car until you change your mind." So I paid.

Repair Gadgets

While the medical quack field is notorious for all sorts of phony medical devices, the quacks of the car repair field are not far behind with their own "scientific marvels." One fancy contraption, a "pulse suppressor," was said to "level off generator output peaks." Best of all, it could be installed for less than $150. One driver in Austin, Texas, who paid for the device later discovered the only thing wrong with his car was one cracked spark plug.

Then there is the "flutter-proof" battery. A typical victim was a New Orleans motorist who had a problem with a horn that bleeped on its own from time to time. A mechanic scamster diagnosed the problem as "battery flutter." Fortunately, he said, the "flutter-proof" battery solved that problem. "I went to another place," the car owner reported in his written complaint, "and the trouble was corrected for $4. It was a disconnected horn wire and occasionally the dangling wire made contact that caused the bleep."

Repair Shop Invoice Con

When paying for any car repair it is important to require that all invoices state specific conditions that were corrected. If a motorist's transmission would not go into reverse, the invoice should say "repair reverse," not some generalization such as "fix transmission." If the trouble crops up again, the motorist can claim the reverse wasn't repaired. If the work statement merely reads "fix transmission," the gyp shop can always claim something else was taken care of.

Shock Absorber Trickery

Far too many drivers are conned by unethical mechanics into switching shock absorbers much sooner than necessary—usually changes aren't necessary until 22,000 to 28,000 miles. A crooked shop can offer a variety of reasons for the switch—including making the car appear to spring loosely or claiming the oil reservoir is leaking—to frighten the driver into thinking the shocks are shot and that he'd better act before damage is caused to other parts of the car. Once a gullible driver swallows that line, the shop may not even bother to change shocks, but simply slap a coat of quick-drying paint on the old ones to make them look new.

Spark Plug Cons

Ask the reformed service station crook, and he'll admit that spark plugs are the number one parts con of them all. Crooked operators peddle more unneeded plugs than any other item, mainly because spark plugs are, as one says, "as good as gold." The standard operating procedure is to clean up old ones that are removed from cars and store them. These are put in the next customer's car for the same price as a new spark plug. And that customer's old plugs usually can be added to the "new battery" inventory.

Starter Deception

Whenever an automobile has problems, it actually talks, or at least makes all sorts of sounds. Recognizing what these sounds mean is the art of the diagnostician. One of the most distinctive sounds made by an auto occurs when the Bendix spring in the starter goes. The driver turns the ignition key and all he gets is a high-pitched whine. If the service station operator is out to gyp the car owner, he will go into a song and dance that both the starter and generator have to be replaced, since one affects the other. The car owner should not fall for that line and instead insist on just having the starter replaced. This repair is one that requires the motorist to watch the replacement being made to make sure he is getting what he is paying for. Gyp operators do a very profitable business selling rebuilt starters as new to victims.

Tire Wear Tricks

Tires wear unevenly when the tread doesn't roll on the road in a true and straight line. This could be the result of either faulty wheel alignment or a worn and loose front end. The difference in cost of repair is that the former runs about one-tenth of the latter. If a driver pulls into a strange service station and complains about uneven tire wear, it is obvious what the unscrupulous operator will recommend. Since it is impossible for the unsophisticated car owner to determine the cause of his tire problem, he should never have it corrected at a strange station. The problem is hardly critical, and the driver is best off in the hands of someone he can trust.

Tow Truck Thievery

Road calls are one of the lushest of all fields for the dishonest repairman. Quite a few garages issue standard orders to their men never to start a car on the road. In every case the vehicle is to be towed back to the shop. Since, in most cases, the motorists are not regular customers, they are ripe for plucking.

The lucrativeness of towing can be illustrated in the case of a Missouri driver on vacation in California. He skidded on a rain-slicked freeway and struck a guard rail with enough momentum to smash his front wheel. He had barely finished assessing the damage when a half-dozen tow trucks roared up and parked, boxing his car in. The unfortunate motorist found himself smack in the middle of a jurisdictional war. A fight broke out between the drivers over who had seen him first. Only the appearance of a state police car broke up the melee. The patrol car summoned a reliable tow operator whose charge was reasonable. Other drivers in California and elsewhere are not always so lucky.

Tow truck rackets are endless. There are crooked police who work on commission for crooked tow truck operators. Often, drivers are induced to sign a paper that may give the repair shop the right to make any and all repairs its mechanics find necessary. Armed with that kind of okay, there are truckers who will bang up a car some more if it has suffered too little damage.

Is it possible to be towed without being swindled? Being a member of a good auto club certainly helps. Honest cops know how to avoid the tow truck vulture. Instead of using their radio to summon a tow truck, an officer looking out for a motorist's welfare will often tell him to sit tight while he calls for aid from a nearby phone. This stymies the sharks who tune into police radio and ambulance calls. The real secret, of course, is to avoid signing anything. If the trucker insists, call another one. The police will help, as they've got to clear the mess off the road. Also, check if the tow man owns his own garage. If this is the case, insist that he tow you to another garage. If he refuses, you definitely know he's not right for you. Yell that you are going to report him if he refuses to take you where you want to go. He will usually wilt after that.

Transmission Tricks

By the time a driver puts 30,000 or so miles on his car, the pick-up is very apt to become sluggish. Service station bandits use the opportunity to frighten the unknowing motorist into thinking that the problem is most serious. The general pitch is that the gears are worn and a rebuilt transmission is needed. Rest assured they have the transmission available; chances are it was pulled out of a previous victim's car. To avoid falling for this transmission trick, do your own checking. When the pick-up is sluggish, smell the transmission oil. If the odor is bad, it needs only a new filter and fresh oil.

Trial-exchange Car-buying Hoax

On the surface the pitch seems to be to a car buyer's advantage. The used car salesman says: "Look, take it for a week, drive it around, then if you have any doubts about the car, come back and exchange it for full credit on another one."

What could possibly be wrong with that? The sad truth is that this pitch may be one of the most deceitful dodges pulled on trusting customers. A sample illustration:

John R. picks out a car on the lot with an asking price of $5,000, but of course asking prices on a used car lot mean nothing. He very easily bargains the price down to $4,200. Being cagey, John still says he has doubts about the purchase, so the salesman gives him the above pitch. John is satisfied that he's driven a hard bargain, got a good price and is even protected by a trial-exchange privilege.

John tests the car for a week and immediately detects problems. The fuel gauge turns out to be a sometime thing, reading empty when the tank is three-fourths full or perhaps half full when its almost out of gas. The turn signals work fine—as long as the headlights aren't on. And, during a rainstorm, the windshield wipers work perfectly—for about a minute.

John wheels the heap back to the lot and announces he is exercising his exchange privilege. He meets no resistance at all; the salesman assures him that's just fine.

John picks out a car tagged at $4,800, and asks how much it would cost. The salesman gives him a blank look and says, "$4,800."

Of course, John knows better. He haggles repeatedly, but the price is $4,800. John then discovers that all the cars on the lot have firm prices. Thus it finally dawns on him how valuable his trial-exchange privilege is—for the dealer. If John takes another car, the dealer makes a second profit, right on top of the one he's gotten for palming off the first heap on John. Yes, John could buy the second car for $4,800, which would go for $700 or $800 less to anyone else. But he's locked in. He can't bargain, since the lot has his money while he has only a piece of junk and a worthless exchange guarantee. He has to pay an extra $600 to get a car that is worth a couple of hundred less than his original buy.

However, one should not judge the car salesman too harshly. Magnanimously, he assures his luckless customer that if he wishes, he most certainly could exchange his second choice for yet another potential lemon.

Voltage Generator Dodges

When the red light on a motorist's dashboard indicates his battery is no longer taking a charge, chances are the problem is a defective battery, a loose or worn fan belt, or sometimes a faulty voltage generator. In any event, a competent mechanic can find the cause of the trouble in a few minutes. On very rare occasions the trouble will be caused by the generator. But if the mechanic says he will need several hours to find the problem, the logical assumption is that the driver is going to be taken for a sleigh ride no matter the season, and hit for a huge generator charge.

The motorist should drive on to another service station.

Wheel Wobble Con

"I'm warning you, buddy, your wheels could fly off anytime." A motorist would have a perfect right to be downright terrified if a garage mechanic told him that. And he'll get even more concerned when the mechanic shows him "proof."

A mechanic can show you a loose wheel on even a new car. He simply jacks up the front end of the car so that pressure is removed from the front spring. The wheel will appear to wobble badly, but this is only normal loose movement. The crooked mechanic will insist this is dangerous ball-joint wear, when actually the ball-joint is designed with a certain amount of clearance when the weight of the car is not on it. Many motorists react in panic and pay a hefty bill for new ball-joints. Sometimes the repair shop will actually provide new ball-joints (not a very expensive item for the shop), but it can just as well simply clean off the old ones.

White Smoke Trick

The "white smoke trick" is one of the grand catch-all cons used by dishonest service stations, especially on the elderly, women traveling alone or families with small children. All the crooked attendant has to do is surreptitiously spray a chemical substance on a hot engine, leading to a very scary eruption of smoke. What is the problem? Almost anything the attendant says it is. Women driving alone and motorists with young children are usually not about to take any chances.

Windshield Wiper Cons

Very often a motorist will fill up a tankful of gas and leave behind the price of the gas plus another $10 or so for a windshield wiper he didn't originally intend to buy. There are service stations in this country that sell five, eight, ten times the number of wipers that other places sell. The attendant needs to say only, "Wow, I sure wouldn't want to be driving this car the next time there's a driving rain." To demonstrate what he means he squirts some water on the glass and tells the driver to start the wiper. Unsurprisingly, it does a terrible job of wiping the windshield clean. Yes, the motorist figures he most certainly needs another wiper.

Some service station attendants can do wonders to a windshield wiper, ruining them right in front of a driver's face. All it takes is a quick squeeze between the thumb and two fingers to knock a wiper blade off line, so that poor contact is made with the glass.

B

BACON WAXING   *butcher overweighing trick*

It is fairly common for a butcher shop clerk to be indoctrinated early in his career in the art of "bacon waxing" or "giving the customer the bacon." In the old days the only thing needed was a scale that told lies; but government inspectors put a stop to that by dropping in with their sets of weights for unannounced tests. Crooked merchants took to new, more subtle ways of fixing a scale.

The bacon waxing technique is used when a customer makes a big purchase, such as a roast of five pounds or so. In this artful dodge the butcher places an eight-ounce package of bacon between two sheets of wax paper. Then, when a patron picks out the roast he likes, the butcher slaps it down on the top wax paper and nonchalantly puts the whole load, bacon and all, on the scale. He reads off the price (going by the bogus weight) and removes the load from the scale. As he wraps the meat behind the counter, he peels off the top sheet of wax paper, leaving the bacon to be used again and again for the same purpose.

BADGER GAME   *sex swindle*

Not long ago a 64-year-old New York widower answered a knock at his door and was confronted by a good-looking blonde who said she was a member of a Bible society. Lonely and eager for companionship, the man let her in and they talked and prayed together. The young woman left, agreeing to pay a return call soon. Several innocent visits followed until one evening session in which the door burst open and a man, raging with anger, charged in and accused the widower of engaging in sexual play with his daughter.

The "father" then demanded that the widower hand over a large sum of money or face exposure to his relatives, neighbors and fellow church members.

Frightened, the widower fell for the scam and hurried to his local bank where he withdrew $5,000 from his savings, almost all he had. Fortunately for the widower, the bank teller knew him well and noted his panicky behavior. The teller spoke to his superior and the police were notified, while the man was told he had to wait until the money was brought up from the vault. The police got to the scene just as the pair of blackmailers were in the act of receiving their loot.

However, this happy conclusion is an exception to the rule. If the victim can be strung along this far in the scheme, the con almost always succeeds.

The scam is nothing more than a variation of the old reliable badger game, an enduring sex swindle. Of course, it has been practiced in every country on earth. In America, perhaps the greatest practitioner of the racket was a New York criminal named Shang Draper, who also masterminded bank robberies and other crimes, but made much of his money from sex swindles. In the 1870s Draper operated a saloon on Sixth Avenue and 29th Street, which was a favorite haunt for big-time criminals. From there, Draper directed the activities of 30 women and girls in a combined badger and panel game operation that took place in a house in the area of Wooster and Prince streets.

The panel game was simple theft in which a thief would slip into a room where a prostitute was in bed with her customer and steal the man's money and other valuables from shedded clothing. The thief would enter through a hidden panel in the wall out of sight from the bed.

If a customer seemed prosperous, however, Draper used the badger game ploy, since the rewards were much greater. As a special Draper touch he used young girls from age nine to 14 as bait. Instead of an angry husband storming into the room, it would be the young girl's "parents." The "mother" would scream at the child and punch her in the face, her blows usually hard enough to cause bleeding from the mouth and nose. The act was very convincing and left the male victim stunned. Then the alleged father would shove his fist menacingly at the man's face and snarl, "I'm going to put you in prison for a hundred years!"

Men so threatened could often be induced to come across with thousands in hush money. Once Draper went to a telegraph office with a quaking out-of-town victim and waited with him until the man's bank wired $9,000 to pay for a badger frame-up.

By the time Draper's racket was finally suppressed in the 1880s, it was estimated he was conning up to 100 or more victims per month. By that time Draper had dozens of imitators.

Another colorful practitioner in more recent years was a Philadelphia con operator called "Raymond the Cleric," who posed as a minister-husband who was done wrong. In his act he prayed in a corner for divine forgiveness for his errant "spouse" (in on the scam) and her sinning lover when they were caught. While Raymond prayed, two burly "members of the congregation" would pressure the lover into repentance by demanding a sizable contribution to Raymond's "church."

The badger game continues unabated to this day. Whenever there is a sex scandal involving the exposure of some prominent man, the racket picks up immediately in that locality, since potential victims see the havoc exposure could wreak on their lives as well.

BAIT AND SWITCH *deceptive selling scams*

Bait and switch scams are extremely old, but they are always new to young buyers. They are used on all types of merchandise, from mattresses to household appliances to used cars. The mattress dodge is most common and is used even in some leading department stores.

A name-brand mattress is advertised at a very low price; but when the customer comes to the store it frequently isn't even on display, with only a catalog picture for viewing. If it is on display, it is dirty, lumpy and thin. Confidentially, the salesman says it's a piece of junk. As he does so, he glances around presumably to make sure no superior can hear him.

Then he offers another mattress at a higher price, but says it is "far, far, far better and will last years and years. That other one will be shot in six months."

Similar bait-and-switching is common on electric items. A new model offered at an excellent price sells out. "But," announces the salesman happily, "we have another model just as good and for less money."

The customer, who had wanted model XL3761 for $313, is offered a close resemblance called model XL3760. This one is available for just $303.

The difference in the last digit of the model number tells the real story. The "1" is the year's new model, while the "0" is from the previous year. Rather than selling it for $10 less, it should be at least $50 or $60 less than the newer model.

The same switch tactic is forever the rule in newspaper and radio ads for used cars. Unfortunately, it does little good to rush to the lot panting with money in hand for an advertised special. Somehow it's always gone. Another possible excuse: "Sorry, can't find the ignition key." "But," pitches the salesman, "here's another one just as good—a beautiful unadvertised special." This is when the high-pressure pitch starts. In one case, where the Better Business Bureau checked a lot's advertising, it found that seven of eight cars being plugged in ads were either not in shape for demonstration or were no longer available.

A standard part of a "bait" operation calls for the salesman to get hold of the prospect's own car. "So we can be checking on the trade-in value of your heap at the same time." Once the customer has given up his only means of escape, he will have to listen to one sales pitch after another until he finally weakens and gives in to a purchase he would otherwise never make.

BAKER, BOBBY *government wheeler-dealer*

During the early part of the Lyndon Johnson presidency, (1963–1969), Republican political charges were made that Robert Gene "Bobby" Baker (b. 1928)—a former U.S. Senate page boy from South Carolina who became a powerful legislative strategist on Capitol Hill—was guilty of gross improprieties that, in the words of Republican presidential candidate Barry Goldwater, "lead right straight into the White House."

In 1955, then Senate Majority Leader Johnson had hired Baker as his secretary for $9,000 a year. At the time, Baker's net worth was estimated at $11,000. Eight years later Baker's pay had climbed to $19,500, while his personal fortune miraculously stood at $2.25 million. Baker had by that time developed connections with high-level public officials; there were many charges of his giving and receiving numerous illegal payments. Baker was accused of improperly using influence in the Senate to win defense plant contracts for a vending machine firm and allegedly giving a $100,000 payoff to Johnson for pushing through a $7 million plane contract for General Dynamics Corporation. In 1964, testimony before the Senate Rules Committee revealed that Baker had allegedly helped a friend sell Johnson expensive life insurance policies in return for the friend's agreement to buy advertising on Mrs. Johnson's Texas radio station. There were also charges that Baker received an illegal $25,000 payment to be channeled into the 1960 Kennedy-Johnson campaign.

After President Johnson won the 1964 election, government investigators uncovered more evidence of Baker's wrongdoing. He was charged with seven counts of tax evasion, one count of conspiracy to defraud the government and another count of theft. Baker was convicted, but through appeals he kept out of jail until early 1971 when he started a one-to-three-year sentence in Lewisburg, Pennsylvania. He was released on parole in 1972 after serving 17 months, quite a comedown for a man regarded as one of the most effective wheeler-dealers in Washington history.

BAKER, NORMAN   See CANCER CURE CONS.

BAKER ESTATE SWINDLE   *heir racket*

For decades there was a saying among law-enforcement experts that "bakers fed more crooks than butchers." Actually, what was being referred to were persons named Baker. The Baker Estate swindle is one of the most lucrative and enduring swindles in American history; the Bakers certainly fed a lot of crooks between the 1860s and the 1930s. In that time no less than 40 different Baker Estate confidence groups were formed and gouged at least a half-million people out of a minimum of $25 million—or perhaps much more—for "legal expenses."

The first Baker Estate association was established in 1866 just after the Civil War. It was based on the alleged inheritance of one Colonel Jacob Baker, who died in Philadelphia in 1839. The claim was that the Baker heirs were entitled to thousands of acres of land in what is now Philadelphia, including the entire downtown area. Over the years, the value of this area had ballooned from an estimated $300 million to over $3 billion. The fortune was nonexistent, but one confidence operation after another roped in suckers—all persons named Baker (some operations included Beckers and Barkers)—with claims that the estate was just about to be settled and fees were necessary to assure the Bakers' legal claims.

For decades the estate swindle had little interference from the law, but in 1936 the federal government launched a determined drive to stamp out the racket. Dozens of arrests were made, among them one septuagenarian named William Cameron Morrow Smith, who had garnered millions from the swindle over a 30-year span.

Since the 1930s, similar con games have turned up from time to time, but none have been nearly as successful as those in the earlier years of the Baker Estate swindle.

BALFOUR, JABEZ   *swindler*

Jabez Spenser Balfour of the latter third of the 19th century was known as Britain's Napoleon of Finance. Besides being a pillar of his church, a justice of the peace and a member of Parliament from Burnley, he was a positive whiz at making money. And, with his financial acumen, he was certain eventually to become a member of the British cabinet. But Balfour's fortune was built on watered stock—not one phony company but many, with each supporting the other in a daring house of cards.

In 1868, Balfour set up the Liberator Building and Investment Society and followed up with several others, including the Lands Allotment Company, the House and Land Investment Trust, Building Securities Company, Hobbes & Company, George Newman & Company, and the Real Estates Company. Balfour's money-making scheme was simplicity itself. When money was needed to pay one shell company's dividends, Balfour got it from investments made in another company. Each company, allegedly independent of the others, would buy some property and then sell it to another at a big profit. That company then sold it to the next for another profit. The companies also lent each other money at high interest rates, so that all of the companies sported attractive balance sheets as needed. One could hardly blame the public for investing in a company that offered a 5% dividend and a 3% bonus annually—extraordinarily high interest for the era.

However, Balfour's juggling of accounts hit a point of no return in November 1892 when one of his firms failed with liabilities in the millions, more than double its stated assets. And most of these assets proved illusionary as well. The Napoleon of Finance did the only logical thing: He disappeared.

While he was gone, the losses for Balfour's lead company, Liberator, amounted to $41,804,020. Hiding out in Buenos Aires, Argentina, Balfour was recognized in January 1894 by the British consul and placed in custody. On his return to Britain in 1895, Balfour was convicted and sentenced to 14 years in prison. He was a broken man following his release. On February 23, 1916, Balfour was traveling on a train in England when he collapsed and died.

BALLOON BUSTERS   *carnival scam*

American circuses and carnivals of the 19th century were noted for many cheating operations, none too small if they netted operators a bit more revenue. The balloon concession was not a small operation; prices were inflated so that 90% of the sales price constituted sheer profit. The operators even hired assistants to blow tacks at balloons after purchase to create an instant demand from howling children for replacement of their busted balloons. In some cases, frustrated parents were forced to make a third purchase.

As some parents grew irate if more than one balloon popped, astute operators developed the custom of consoling a child by patting him on the back while filling the reorder. The operator's hand would be covered with chalk so that some would remain on the child's back. This mark informed the balloon busters that the child's balloon had been popped enough.

Oddly, this custom was the direct opposite of the practice of marking chalk on the back of a man who had been cheated in some crooked concession game. This indicated that he was a gullible "mark" who was ripe for the taking at other concessions.

See also MARK.

BALLOON HOAX *Poe's grand fiction*

The great "Moon Hoax" (see entry) perpetrated by the *New York Sun* and journalist Richard Adams Locke in 1835 probably had more of an effect on Edgar Allan Poe than on anyone. Reports of "moon people" and other astounding discoveries on that celestial body stopped Poe's writings dead. Poe later explained he had been forced to stop writing the second part of *"The Strange Adventures of Hans Pfaall"* because he felt he had been outdone. Then, with Locke's confession that it was all a hoax, Poe's admiration became unbounded, and he considered Locke to be a truly creative writer. Could Poe ever become as great as Locke?

On April 13, 1844, the *Sun* published a stunning news story once again. It was headlined: "Astounding News by Express via Norfolk; the Atlantic Crossed in Three Days; Signal Triumph of Mr. Monck's Flying Machine." The story featured a woodcut of the alleged craft.

It seemed that Mr. Monck's flying machine—more accurately a balloon—had transported Monck and seven others from England to a place near Charleston, South Carolina, in some 75 hours. The correspondent in South Carolina interviewed some of the intrepid participants of the flight. Included in the stirring dispatch were quotations from the journal of "Herman Ainsworth, British novelist," one of which read: "God be praised! Who shall say that anything is impossible hereafter?"

Poe, who had concocted the entirely faked report, caused considerable excitement for many days; but it was only a matter of time before authorities from South Carolina determined that there had been no strange flying machine, no Mr. Monck and no intrepid passengers landing in the area. Poe's hoax was doomed to be relatively short-lived since it was a little too close to home. South Carolina was merely hundreds of miles from New York, while Richard Locke's moon was 240,000 miles distant. Poe may have failed to match Locke, but he did run a credible second.

BALM OF GILEAD *infamous English quack medicine*

The Balm of Gilead was one of the greatest "health tonics" ever; it came with glowing testimonials, which would have put an American medicine show "professor" to shame. The elixir appeared in England around 1820 and came with this rhapsodic pitch: "Its composition has been sanctioned by the most learned physicians of the age, it has preserved its reputation from the period prior to the birth of Christ, growing in Gilead in Judea in 1730 BC."

Its uses were many: to relieve internal problems; to improve fertility and virility; and as an effective aphrodisiac when rubbed on the appropriate spots. Frederick the Great, it was said, found the balm most rewarding. It was also hailed as having been a great success in helping victims of the New York yellow fever epidemic in 1800. Some other ailments for which it rendered cures were: weak and shattered constitutions; hypochondria; horrors of the mind; intemperance; debauchery; and inattention to the necessary cares of health, luxury or the studious life.

Far from being of ancient vintage, the Balm of Gilead was a concoction produced by a former door-to-door boot-polish salesman named Samuel Solomon. For a number of years Solomon did a land-office business with some 400 agencies in Great Britain and 16 in America. He lived in great luxury in a mansion outside Liverpool, but despite his great wealth he was still available for personal consultations for which he charged one pound per visit (half-price for mail queries).

In time, however, complications developed. Quite a few users of the balm—especially many who were teetotalers—found they were growing addicted to the stuff. The ingredients, which reputedly included a minute amount of gold, actually consisted of nine parts pure brandy. The friends of one woman who had turned into a complete lush waylaid Solomon one night and beat him to a pulp. The Balm of Gilead probably did Solomon's injuries no good at all. Following further exposures, sales of the balm were on the way down.

BALSAMO, GIUSEPPE See CAGLIOSTRO, COUNT ALESSANDRO DI.

BANK EXAMINER *confidence game*

The "bank examiner" confidence game is an unusual swindle in that it relies on the innate honesty of the victim, rather than appealing to his dishonest instincts, as the average fraud does. Offhand, it might seem to be a flim-flam that wouldn't fool anybody, but it does work well in big cities or smaller towns, especially in recent years as the savings-and-loan scandals have left the public angered and highly motivated in stopping bank depredations.

The operation relies on flattery by involving the victim in an apparent plot to cooperate with law enforcement officials to catch an inside bank thief. The con man, who pretends to be an authorized "bank investigator," will either approach the victim on the bank's premises or contact him by phone and tell him that his cooperation could be vital in catching a dishonest teller. One or two men may even visit the victim's home and show what look like police badges or federal investigator identification. The patter is delivered in such a smooth, authoritative tone that the victim feels flattered in being picked for such a key role.

When this stage has been reached, the phony investigators tell the victim to withdraw a hefty sum of money from his account so that a check can be made on how the suspected teller handles the bookkeeping. He is to hand over the money to the investigators immediately and wait a few minutes while an out of sight bank executive supposedly "marks" or photographs the bills' serial numbers. Then the victim is told to redeposit the funds so the crooked bank employee's actions can be observed.

The victim turns over the funds as instructed. He is given a written receipt on the spot and told to wait. Naturally, neither the con men nor the money ever come back.

In New York City at least 50 or so such bank examiner swindles are investigated annually by the police; but these are only the cases reported. Hundreds of other such frauds may occur, but the victims are too humiliated to report their losses. Recently the city comptroller's office issued a special report on the bank examiner scam, warning: "You should be suspicious when strangers ask you to withdraw money from your bank and hand it over to them for any purpose, even for a brief moment."

Across the nation it is estimated that thousands are fleeced by this bald-faced scheme each year in communities of all sizes. Officials warn that the scam may be in the process of picking up steam because of the savings and loan exposures, and the fact that the public will have to pick up the tab has motivated citizens to try to stop banking depredations.

BARNUM, P.T. See CARDIFF GIANT; COLORADO MAN; EGRESS; FEEJEE MERMAID; GREAT UNKNOWN; HETH, JOICE; MISSING LINK.

BARON OF ARIZONA See REAVIS, JAMES ADDISON.

BARRIE, PADDY *racehorse fixer*

No racehorse "ringer" was more successful at fixing races than Peter C. "Paddy" Barrie (1888–1935), an "artist" born in Edinburgh, Scotland. According to the Pinkerton Detective Agency (which was charged with protecting many U.S. tracks), Barrie was responsible for swindling bettors out of between $5 million and $7 million from 1926 to 1934. Paddy's technique was simplicity itself. He bought two horses, one with an excellent record and another who was, in racetrack parlance, "a dog." Paddy simply "painted" the fast nag to resemble the other.

Paddy's first caper was against his employer, Lady Mary Cameron, who owned an estate near Edinburgh. He bought a fading old dapple-gray mare from Lady Cameron for $85 and later sold Lady Cameron a splendid spotted mare for $1,400. About a week after the mare joined the Cameron stables, the animal turned docile and listless and her color started to run. The departed Barrie had doctored the mare's gums and teeth, dyed her a bay and stimulated her for a short time with narcotics.

Later, in the United States, Barrie worked for racketeers, doping horses for $5,000 a mount and also "painting" good horses to resemble notoriously slow horses who deserved to go off at least 50 to 1. Since the ringer outclassed its opponents, it usually scored a "wake-up" win. Paddy's most famous ringer operation took place on October 3, 1931 at Havre de Grace in Maryland. He had bought a good sorrel stallion named Aknahton from the Marshal Field stables for $4,300, and another horse, named Sham, for $400. The latter had a poor record from a Long Island trainer. Barrie repainted Aknahton to look like Sham and entered him in a race at Havre de Grace. Mrs. Payne Whitney's Byzantine was a huge favorite in the race, while the lowly "Sham" was logically given odds of 52 to 1. The horse got out of the gate very poorly but had little trouble catching the field at the two-furlong pole and passed Byzantine to win by four lengths. Barrie and his gambling partners were estimated to have cleaned up more than $1 million on their wagers.

Barrie altered Aknahton's appearance at three other tracks—Bowie, Hialeah and Aqua Caliente—and made a total of five killings with him. His coups led crooked gamblers to refer to him as "Rembrandt." The Pinkerton Agency finally learned of Barrie's identity through drunken comments made by Nate Raymond, a leader of the crooked betting syndicate. Barrie was seized by police at Hialeah, but he escaped custody and continued his ringing operations for two more years by doctoring his own appearance as well.

Finally recognized at Saratoga racetrack in New York, he was bundled off to jail again. However, the laws on horse race gambling were rather loose at the time, and it was found that he was guilty of nothing more than having illegally entered the country. He was deported with a Pinkerton agent who rode out on the ship as far as Sandy Hook to make sure Barrie really went back to Scotland.

Six months later, in 1935, Barrie died. According to a sensational British tabloid, the cause was a "broken heart," due to the strain of the constant surveillance kept on him by Scotland Yard to make sure he did not ring another horse.

Because of Barrie's depredations, American racetracks adopted a number of precautions such as lip tattoos to make the ringing of other horses virtually impossible. However, since foreign horses are not so identified, they have been used as ringers in recent years. The disclosure of such fixes has led to closer checks on the identification of foreign horses.

BARRY, DR. JAMES *male impersonator*

In many respects Dr. James Barry (c. 1792–1865) had an illustrious life and military career. Barry entered Edinburgh University in 1808 at the age of 15 or 16 as a student of medicine. He joined the army upon graduation and served as a military surgeon in places throughout the world, including Canada, South Africa, India, the West Indies with lepers in Africa. In that time he rose to the rank of medical superintendent-general.

Both in college and later while on youthful duty on the Cape of Good Hope, Barry was known as an accomplished lady killer. As Mark Twain recounted in *More Tramps Abroad:* "There were plenty of pretty girls, but none of them caught him, none of them could get hold of his heart; evidently he was not the marrying man." Barry was, however, a fighting man who dueled with swords and in one case killed his foe.

Despite many scrapes, Barry escaped military censure and continued his otherwise distinguished career. Retired in London, Dr. Barry died on July 25, 1865. The army physician who examined the body then made an astounding discovery: Dr. James Barry was a woman.

This was particularly startling to the army doctor, since he himself had served several years under the inspector general in Africa. But his chagrin was matched by Barry's fellow students at Edinburgh, who

were contacted after her death. None had ever suspected her true sex. In fact, the only odd behavior they recalled was Barry's refusal to box. Her military servants had also suspected nothing during Barry's long career. How Barry managed to join the army and pass entrance physicals is a mystery. Most speculate that she had somehow enticed a male friend to pass muster for her.

Barry's actual identity was never uncovered by the British army, leading to speculation that certain high-level intervention in and out of the military was involved. After her death Dr. Barry was embraced by British feminists as a heroine, one tribute stating:

> In her numerous reports she proved herself a skilled doctor, and an enthusiast at her work. She wrote fearlessly and frankly, always ready to expose incompetence and charlatanism, even though it involved her in controversy and opposition. For high courage nothing could exceed the spirit of this woman who was so far ahead of her time that, to achieve her purpose, she renounced her sex.

For want of any other identification, the woman's tombstone is still inscribed "Dr. James Barry."

"BATTERY-FREE" FLASHLIGHT *nuclear age hoax*

Doesn't it make sense in the nuclear age when no marvel is too great? "This flashlight here, folks, will just work forever—without batteries!" This standard hoax product, peddled by fly-by-night stores and street hawkers, is not sold through the mail, because that would incur the wrath of postal inspectors. But it is amazing how many people fall for this fakery and pay out up to $10 or $15 for a batteryless flashlight, which allegedly lights on and on.

Of course, the flashlight does have batteries, but they are completely hidden in sealed plastic. When the light goes out, many suckers actually think to replace the bulb. When that doesn't work, the "light" finally flashes. Yes, there are batteries, but no, one can't replace them without completely destroying the flashlight itself. Maybe that "Made in China" label should have made the consumer suspicious.

Why the deception? Well how else can a $1 flashlight be sold for so much more?

BATTLE OF THE SOMME *faked film scenes*

During World War I, the most spectacular of all filmed battle scenes were those shown in a movie entitled *The Battle of the Somme*. The movie, shown to packed houses in England in 1916, pictured the chaos of attack in its dramatic climax, which was captioned: "The attack. At a signal along the entire 16 mile front, the British troops leaped over the trench parapets and advanced toward the German trenches, under heavy fire of the enemy."

The impression on the public was searing. Lloyd George's secretary, Frances Stevenson, recorded in her diary: "I am glad to have seen the sort of thing our men have to go through, even to the sortie from the trench and the falling in the barbed wire. . . . It reminded me of what Paul's last hours were: I have often tried to imagine to myself what he went through, but now I *know:* and I shall never forget. . . ."

G. H. Malins, the cameraman who provided the sequence for the film, offered a graphic account of how he had accomplished it in his book *How I Filmed the War* in 1920. However, in 1922 the Imperial War Museum convened a panel of experts to view the film and then pronounced the climactic sequence a fabrication. Another cameraman later said he found a soldier who had "died" for Malins in a mortar school trench well behind the front lines.

The film, mostly because of its vivid climax, had enjoyed enormous popularity during the war and was viewed as a key rallying point for the public. But it does appear that there were doubts about the authenticity of the key sequence from the beginning. Thus, when a sequel film, *The Battle of the Ancre and the Advance of the Tanks,* was released in 1917, it opened with: "General Headquarters is responsible for the censorship of films and allows nothing in the nature of a 'fake' to be shown. The pictures are authentic and taken on the battlefield."

It would seem any official doubts about the authenticity of elements of *The Battle of the Somme* during the war would have been counterproductive.

A complete account of this is offered in "A Wonderful Idea of the Fighting: The Question of Fakes in *The Battle of the Somme,*" by·R. Smither, *Imperial War Museum Review,* III (1988).

BBC RIOT PANIC *men from mars predecessor*

It happened on the evening of January 16, 1926, 12 years before Orson Welles' "Men from Mars" ("War of the Worlds") radio broadcast that panicked America. This, however, was the BBC, the staid, calm British Broadcasting Company. Millions of radio listeners were immersed in a speech being broadcast from Edinburgh when it was interrupted by an eyewitness account of startling events in London. Some of the actual report went as follows:

> The Houses of Parliament are being demolished by an angry mob equipped with trench mortars. The clock tower 320 feet in height has just fallen to the ground, together with the famous clock, Big Ben, which used to strike the hours on a ball weighing nine tons. . . . One moment, please. Fresh reports announce that the crowd has secured the person of Mr. Wurtherspoon, the minister of traffic, who was attempting to make his escape in disguise. He has

> now . . . been hanged from a lamp post in Vauxhall. London calling. That noise you heard just now was the Savoy Hotel being blown up by the crowd.

Additional news flashes served only to rile up the radio listeners all the more. People rushed to their telephones and jammed telegraph offices to try to contact relatives. Newspaper and government officials were flooded with anxious inquiries. Callers to the Admiralty demanded that the navy proceed up the Thames to stem the violence. Denials by officials failed to calm the public—after all, people had heard it on the radio.

Obviously, few of the listeners in their panic remembered the early portion of the broadcast, which had announced that all that followed was a "burlesque." The listeners did not doubt for a moment the authenticity of reports from Trafalgar Square that the unemployed were rioting, led by a Mr. Popplebury, secretary of the National Movement for Abolishing Theater Queues.

To calm nerves the BBC had to interrupt its programs with an official explanation of the broadcast and repeat the introductory text of the program. Once public calm had been restored, there was a storm of criticism of the radio company, and no such hoax was repeated on radio in Britain thereafter. In the United States, the story resulted in considerable amusement at the gullibility of Britons. That situation was reversed in 1938 when Orson Welles' radio "War of the Worlds" produced a panic even greater than the one caused by the BBC's sorry attempt at satire.

See also MEN FROM MARS PANIC.

BEAUTY CONTEST FIXING *fakery in the first competition*

It has long been suspected that many beauty contests, especially the smaller ones in the United States, are either fixed or the judges are unfairly influenced. Considering the history of the first American beauty contest, this view is not easily dismissed. In 1881 Adam Forepaugh, showman rival of the likes of P. T. Barnum and James A. Bailey, scored a coup on his rivals by announcing a $10,000 contest to discover "the handsomest woman in America." In keeping with the honored tradition of the early American circus, the result was fixed.

The winner was Louise Montague, a variety actress of bosomy proportions—the epitome of female pulchritude at the time. It must be reported that the lovely Miss Montague did not get the $10,000. Instead, by prior agreement, she received a relatively meager $100 a week to lead Forepaugh's street pageant in each city visited and then take the part of "The Lovely Oriental Princess, Lalla Rookh" in the circus's opening spectacle of the royal beauty's "Departure from Delhi." In the fictional *Thief of Baghdad* a princess of renowned beauty is carried through the streets in a grand parade, but soldiers ride ahead of the pageant, shooting deadly arrows at windows left unshuttered. In Forepaugh's "Departure from Delhi," the public could relive the tale with no fear of fatal results—almost. The fighting in Chicago was so great to view the "handsomest woman in America" that windows of offices and shops were shattered in the crush. One man trying to gain an unfettered view of Miss Montague fell from a second-floor window and broke his neck. Needless to say, the fatal mishap was a circus publicity agent's dream come true.

The enthusiasm in other cities was just as unrestrained, and Forepaugh made an estimated half-million dollars in 1881 and 1882, thanks largely to his beauty contest brainstorm—not at all bad for a non-investment of $10,000. Despite Forepaugh's deceit, he still must be recognized as the "Father of the Beauty Contest," which rapidly became a distinctly American art form.

BECKER, CARL WILHELM *ancient coin forger*

The most prolific forger of ancient coins was a scholarly Austrian, Carl Wilhelm Becker (1772–1830). Becker became a coin forger apparently after being sold a fake coin by another collector. When Becker learned he had been cheated, the crooked collector derided him for his ignorance on the subject. Becker thereupon took up the study of ancient coins with a vengeance and had the satisfaction of unloading a number of fakes on the collector who had once victimized him.

Becker's output soon found its way into a great many of the leading and private collections in Europe. Becker's biographers called him a most complicated individual, moving in learned circles of scholars and collectors who included Goethe, Count Rasumovsky and Count Wiczay. He was a close friend of Prince Carl von Isenburg and copied the prince's Visigothic coins.

Becker was a skilled engraver and did not use mechanical methods of reproduction, cutting all of his dies freehand. When the notion struck him, Becker mischievously made up new coins that fooled expert collectors. To age his coins, Becker placed them in boxes filled with iron filings and attached them to the axle of his carriage. Thus, while Becker took pleasure rides, his coin counterfeiting racket was continuing at full pace.

Becker insisted he was not a criminal, that what he was doing was imitating rare coins of all periods in history so that collectors could have copies that would otherwise be beyond their ability to obtain. He insisted that if others passed them off as originals, it was their evildoing not his. That was hardly accurate: Becker maintained a network of agents in many European cities who sold the coins as originals.

When Italian numismatist Sestini exposed Becker's counterfeiting, Becker shifted the distribution of his coins to Turkey so that they could return to western Europe later with a more credible source of origin. Perhaps Becker's greatest compliment was when Caprara, a brilliant contemporary forger who worked in Syros and Smyrna, made skilled imitations of his work. Even today Becker and Caprara fakes continue to fool the experts, still appearing in scholarly publications, such as Ernest Babelon's *Traité* and, by admission of the institution itself, several of the British Museum's catalogs.

BEGGING COUNTERFEIT RACKET *passing technique*

In the 1990s there has been a return to what was long referred to as the "beggar counterfeit racket," which victimizes small lunch rooms and diners. In bad economic times business owners can be a good source for a man pleading he is down on his luck. When a man claiming to be out of work asks for a simple meal, nothing fancy, he is often given a plain meat sandwich and coffee. The man gobbles the food down as though he hasn't eaten in days, and it makes the proprietor feel good that he has provided someone a helping hand.

At the end of the meal the man thanks the proprietor profusely and carelessly reaches into his pocket, pulling out a rumpled handkerchief to wipe his mouth. As he does so, a folded bill plops onto the counter.

Hurriedly, he tries to retrieve it, but the proprietor grabs his wrist and takes it away, glaring at him. When he unfolds the bill, he really explodes. "Fifty bucks! You've got fifty bucks and mooch a free meal claiming you haven't eaten in three days!"

In disgust, the proprietor rings up $1.50 on the cash register, throws the exact change at the beggar and angrily escorts him from the establishment.

The proprietor is still smoldering about it the next morning when he deposits the previous day's receipts at the bank. That's when the teller won't accept the $50, declaring it counterfeit.

The proprietor starts screaming for everybody—the police, the Secret Service, the Marines. He demands that the beggar be found, arrested and forced to return the $48.50.

The police patiently explain the sad facts to him. Even should the beggar be found, he could not be arrested, having not committed a crime. He had not even tried to pass the counterfeit bill. Strictly speaking, the proprietor stole it from him, forcibly taking it to pay for the food. The proprietor is told that all he can do is swallow his loss.

See also BEGGING SCAMS.

BEGGING SCAMS *ageless capers*

For a number of years she has been a 14-year-old runaway trying to raise the plane fare to get back home. Her beat: Chicago's O'Hare Airport. Her real background: She's in her twenties, a graduate from Oberlin with an M.A. in fine arts. Her take: about $1,000 a week.

He patrols the area around New York's Lincoln Center with a phony bruise on his forehead and a catsup stain on his designer shirt. He claims to have been a mugging victim. His take: about $700 a week.

The practice—and profession—of begging undoubtedly goes back to prehistoric times. Begging started in America with the first arrivals from the Old World. Some had been beggars there and were hardly about to stop in virgin territory.

The two more recent practitioners above were graduates of something called "Fagin Prep" by *Money* magazine. The "institution" was opened in New York by a resourceful entrepreneur after years of successful panhandling to teach the art to others. Here are a couple of lessons:

> To be successful, you have to be glib, inventive, patient, fast, and aggressive. And you have to be well-dressed, well-groomed, and well-spoken. . . . The most effective pitches involve a medical emergency situation. Everyone can identify with an emergency situation, and they don't want you to die at their feet. It's a nuisance. They give you money to get you out of their lives.

Fagin Prep had special instructions for subway beggars. It was suggested that one target be picked out, and that the beggar should stand before him and loudly whine, "Please!" If that does not produce results, the pannie should drop to one knee and continue to plead until the victim gives.

There have been many legendary beggars in America. One of the princes of the 1920s was New York's "Breadline Charlie," who eschewed the use of a harness or any other equipment to make him appear crippled or helpless. Instead, he kept small chunks of stale bread and, when in a crowd, he would drop a piece of the bread on the sidewalk. He would see it, let out a scream of ecstasy and gobble it down as though he hadn't eaten in a week. It was an act that quickly tapped the hearts and purses of passersby.

An earlier faker was George Gray who had earned by his own estimate more than $10,000 a year for many years around the turn of the century—a most significant sum for the day. He made his living through his ability to feign an epileptic fit or a heart attack, generally in front of the residences of well-to-do Manhattanites. Following one of his many arrests, Gray was taken by police to Presbyterian Hospital and was diagnosed by medical experts as "a curiosity of nature in that he possesses the power of accelerating or retarding his heart action at will." One prominent citizen, Jesse L. Strauss, gave the police a terrible argument when they tried to roust Gray as he lay writhing on the pavement. Strauss had his money in hand and was ready to give it to the unfortunate man to get medical attention. Gray was at the time wanted as the era's most professional "fit thrower" by police in a dozen cities.

Then there was Robert T. Ingles, also known as Joseph E. Addeison, who toured the nation for years on a regular begging beat until he died in a charity ward in New York in the 1950s. On his person he had a bank book showing he had $2,500 on deposit. In time authorities turned up accounts in 42 other banks—from Maine to California—showing his total assets totalled over $100,000.

A very popular ploy today is a beggar in a business suit who embarrassedly tells victims he has lost his wallet and needs commuter fare home. Since home is a far way off, a minimum bite is $10. He offers victims his business card (one of many he has collected) and vows to mail them a check the next day (which he won't).

But the best begging scams involve health problems. There was one New York beggar who used to pose as a leper. He was a tall, gaunt, olive-skinned man who'd haunt shadowy alleys and emerge only when a likely sucker came along. "Mister . . . I'm a leper . . . Will you drop some money on the sidewalk for me? . . . Will you please? . . . For a poor leper." During this time the "leper" kept coming forward, arms outstretched; many a poor victim was known to have dropped his wallet in panic and raced for safety. Some of the current crop of pannies have tried the AIDS approach, but have not been too successful. "Too much prejudice out there," one observed.

See also BEGGING COUNTERFEIT RACKET; BLINKIES; PHONY CRIPS; POSTAL IMPOSTORS.

BERINGER'S STONES *fossil fraud*

One of the most amazing scientific hoaxes of the 18th century victimized Dr. Johannes Beringer (1667–1738), dean of the medical school at the University of Würzburg. One historian described the episode as "a devastating comment on the effects of professional competition in science," which required a

Dr. Johannes Beringer, one of the preeminent scholars of the 18th century, gullibly accepted these stones as the "capricious fabrications of God"—including one signed by Jehovah himself.

"tremendous amount of work, expense and time" on the part of the hoaxers.

Although autocratic in his beliefs, Beringer was regarded as one of the preeminent scholars of the day. He seemingly achieved even greater fame with his 1725 discovery of hundreds of fossils that he claimed were actually pure stone and "capricious fabrications of God" in their minute representation of varied life forms. Also unearthed were grotesque clay tablets, including one signed by Jehovah.

In 1726 Beringer published *Lithographia Wirceburgensis,* a book about the finds and his theories. Beautifully illustrated with finely engraved studies of the famed stones, it was a huge success and was enthusiastically accepted by scholars; soon all of Europe was agog over Beringer's figured stones. Then rumors surfaced that the stones had all been planted by students of the pompous professor. Beringer reacted with outrage at such stories, believing them to be an attempt to deprive him of his glory. Actually, the Beringer stones were fakes, but not concocted by students, although some of them may have been involved in burying the stones. The real conspirators against Beringer were J. Ignatz Roderick, professor of geography, algebra and analysis at the university, and Georg von Eckhart, the university librarian and librarian to the prince-bishop of Würzburg. They had both previously denounced Beringer's theories and now had manufactured some figured stones, which they managed to get Beringer to buy through an 18-year-old intermediary. Then they made a public confession to forging some of the stones. They had not manufactured all of them; many were true fossils of animal and plant life forms.

For a time Beringer held his ground and denounced his scholarly foes for circulating "vicious raillery, false rumors and gossip." But suddenly Ber-

inger fell silent. Some of the stones he had found turned out to have his own name inscribed on them in obscure spots. Beringer realized the truth and tried to buy up all the copies of his book, which he had printed at enormous personal expense. When the public learned the truth, the book became a treasured collector's item and owners would not part with their copy at any price. In fact, in 1767 the demand for the book was so enormous that a German publisher brought out a second edition, clearly labeled as a humorous curiosity. Happily for Beringer, he had died years earlier and thus did not have to relive his disgrace. Beringer's detractors did not fare much better. Von Eckhart, the librarian, died not long after the scandal broke. Professor Roderick was forced to leave the university in disgrace and move on to Cologne.

While the hoax left a once-renowned scholar to be remembered only for his gullibility, there was an upside to the destruction of his stone theory. Scholars began more and more to embrace Leonardo da Vinci's suggestion that fossils were the remains of a former age; this helped in the establishment of the theory of the antiquity of the world.

BERNERS STREET HOAX *prank turned nightmarish*

For nearly two centuries the "Berners Street Hoax" has been regarded as the most inventive and chaotic practical joke in history and, say some film historians, the inspiration for the hilarious stateroom scene in the Marx Brothers' movie, *A Night at the Opera.*

It all began as a wager made by a notorious author and hoaxer named Theodore Hook, who was described as possessing "quick intelligence, and brilliant with an unfailing flow of animal spirits."

One day in 1809, while strolling along a quiet London street with another author, Sam Beazeley, Hook declared he could make a nondescript row house at 54 Berners Street the most famous house in the city. Beazeley agreed to a wager, and Hook learned that the residence belonged to an elderly widow named Tottingham. He proceeded to write hundreds of letters in Mrs. Tottingham's name asking for certain goods and services to be provided at a certain time and day.

At 9 o'clock that morning a dozen chimney sweeps appeared at Mrs. Tottingham's front door, each announcing they were there "upon your esteemed request" to clean the chimney. The sweeps jostled for position and were outraged when the widow insisted she had summoned none of them. Then a wagonload of coal drew up before the house. This was followed by a van of furniture, then a hearse with a coffin and a train of mourning coaches. Two doctors arrived, as did a dentist and a midwife, all in separate coaches. Berners Street was getting clogged up.

However, the chaos had only begun. There followed a shipment of several kegs of beer, a wagon carrying a pipe organ (with six hardy men to unload it) and a cartload of potatoes. Also on hand were: confectioners and bakers carrying their wares; wigmakers; hairdressers; butchers; opticians; repairmen; machinists; and various curiosity dealers, all with samples of their merchandise. Next, footmen, coachmen, cooks, housemaids and nursemaids all turned up to apply for positions.

This was followed by a parade of most illustrious personages—the archbishop of Canterbury, a cabinet member, the governor of the Bank of England, the lord chief justice, the lord mayor and finally the duke of York. The lord mayor had come ostensibly to receive the depositions of a dying person who wished to make a most revealing confession. The duke of York, commander in chief of the army, had responded after being informed that one of his officers lay dying at 54 Berners Street and had to see him. The others most likely showed up for similar reasons.

By now Berners Street resembled a frenzy. The police were unable to maintain order as wagon wheels locked together and vehicles started turning over. Fights broke out and even some of the dignitaries were insulted and shoved about.

The bedlam took on a life of its own, with Hook and Beazeléy enjoying the mad spectacle from behind a curtain in a nearby boarding house. Chaos continued all day and only after some hours of darkness did the participants finally start fading away in sheer exhaustion. Hook also left the scene and London as well, hiding out in the country until public indignation died down. The lord mayor who knew Hook for his "boisterous buffooneries" correctly surmised that he was the villain; but suspicion was not enough and Hook was never prosecuted, although he admitted to the deed long before his death in 1841.

BETTER BUSINESS BUREAU CONS *deceptive selling methods*

Nothing more pacifies leery victims about goods and services offered them than assurance that the firm the hustler represents is a member of the Better Business Bureau. This is more than enough reason not to sign anything or pay for anything until checking with the BBB. Under the bylaws of the Better Business Bureau, no member firm or anyone else is permitted to refer to the BBB in sales promotions, either written or verbal. When a salesman makes representation of BBB approval of a product, two facts are certain: The salesman is lying and the product needs lying about.

BIBLE SCAM *selling con*

A perennial in unordered merchandise scams is the "deluxe Bible" selling pitch. In its most recent form, operators obtain the names of devoted religious persons and send them an unordered Bible with a bill for $24.99 "for the leatherette cover edition." A cover letter informs the recipients that a deluxe, full-leather, gold-lettered edition is available for $49.95; should they prefer that, they may simply return the cheaper version with a check for the larger amount and it will be sent by return mail.

Of course, the deluxe version has been sent "by mistake" and even some of the most religiously minded persons cannot resist mailing in a payment at the lower price (which happens to be the true price for the deluxe edition). Sometimes the mail-order con man really hits the jackpot when some ethical customer calls attention to the error and sends a check for $49.95.

BIGAMY BY THE DOZEN *female marriage scam artist*

Something of a record in bigamy was established by a 24-year-old English lass named Theresa Vaughn (b. 1898) who was brought to trial in Sheffield in December 1922. Theresa confessed that without divorcing her first husband at 19, she flitted about Great Britain, Germany and South Africa, marrying 61 other men in a five-year period. This made her average stay with a spouse approximately 30 days, a dizzying pace that left just enough time for gathering up the booty from the marriage before moving on to a new relationship. After a short prison stint, Theresa disappeared; it has not been ascertained if she did, in fact, live happily ever after in marital bliss.

BIGFOOT FAKES

Most monster stories are deeply imbedded in legend and are a prime target for the hoaxer out for profit or for the sheer devil of it. The so-called Bigfoot or Sasquatch of the Pacific has been "sighted" since 1840 and was a staple of Indian legends for centuries earlier. Most accounts describe him as a "hairy man" with thick fur and long arms, standing up to nine feet tall and weighing 600 to 900 pounds.

In 1982 an 86-year-old, devil-may-care ex-forest ranger named Rant Mullens of Toledo, Washington, laid claim to being "Bigfoot's father." Mullens admitted he had been planting phony evidence of Bigfoot's existence while on the job since 1928. Mullens began by whittling a pair of oversized wooden feet, putting them on and stomping all around the woods near Mt. St. Helens. Excited hikers reported finding Bigfoot's footprints. Over the succeeding decades Mullens said he carved a half-dozen more big feet

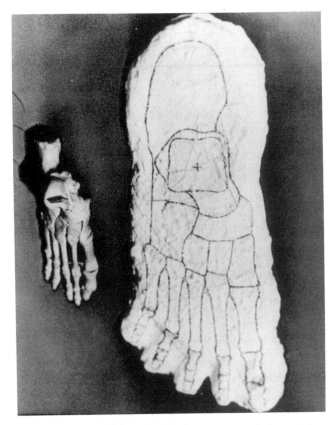

A plaster cast of a footprint attributed to Bigfoot. A human foot is at its left for comparison.

and, with the aid of accomplices, spread tracks throughout the Northwest.

"I tell you, people will believe just about anything," Mullens glowed mischievously.

BIG 6-BIG 8   *casino craps scam*

While some observers might view all casino gambling as essentially a scam, it must be noted that some of the action is more suspect than others. A case in point would be the "Big 6" or "Big 8" bets on craps at Las Vegas casinos. While these are outlawed in casinos in Atlantic City, the Big 6 and Big 8 bets are extremely prominent on Nevada layouts.

The principle of the bet is that if one bets on Big 6, for example, one wins if a 6 is thrown before a 7, and loses if the 7 comes up first. Winners are paid off at even money, which represents a huge edge for the casinos, since the 7 can come up six different ways and the 6 (or 8) only five ways. Of course, no casino will pay off on true odds, but in Atlantic City the state-mandated payoff is 7 to 6. This is done by making a "place bet" on the appropriate number on the layout. As a matter of fact, the similar place bet can be made on 6 or 8 in Las Vegas as well with the payoff at 7 to 6; but the place bet is much less prominent on the layout than Big 6 or Big 8. How do Nevada casino operators justify this

bit of flimflammery, which allows them an edge of 1.5% from "smart" bettors and 9.09 from the uninformed? As one representative of Las Vegas casinos put it: "If a man doesn't know what he's playing, he deserves to be taken." In other words, regardless of state supervision, "Let the Sucker Beware."

BIG STORE   *major confidence game operation*

Until the end of the 19th century, most swindles in the United States were, with few exceptions, essentially "short cons" in which victims were taken for a few dollars, a few hundred or a few thousand. The problem was keeping the victim in tow long enough to take him for really big money, even to "put him on the send" to go home, sell some securities or other properties, or take a mortgage on his home to hurry back for a "sure thing." This was impossible in the so-called dollar stores that sprang up all across the country. Customers were lured in by bargains on all sorts of items selling for $1 and then skinned with such gambling games as three-card monte, the shell game and smack.

One ingenious con man, Buck Boatright, made a small fortune in western dollar stores, preying on passing pioneer wagon trains and cheating many settlers out of their family's nest egg. Boatright was a con artist who thought big. He concocted plans to set up a permanent base of operations, either an office or a store with seemingly authentic trimmings, including many employees and "customers."

The operation required the participation of some of the best con men in the country, and a completely protected territory with payoffs to both police and politicians, sometimes granting the latter a percentage of the profits on individual coups. In such an operation the sucker could be skinned with meticulous precision.

This concept, known as the "Big Store," was not completely new. Back in 1882 Oscar Wilde, while on a speaking tour in the United States, was trimmed in a New York "skinning dive" and taken for several thousand dollars in a banco game in which everyone save the illustrious writer was in on the scam. But these early Big Store versions lacked the scope of Boatright's dream.

In 1900 Boatright found his scam paradise in Webb City, Missouri, the town in which he opened his fake gambling club. Boatright's biggest operation involved fixed sporting events (generally foot races or fights). The atmosphere was so convincing that Boatright could truthfully boast that no mark ever became suspicious that he was losing his money in a completely play-act arena. Business got so good that the ingenious con man soon set up a branch in Council Bluffs, Iowa.

The Boatright style called for letting the sucker win a few small bets; but most times even that money was held by the "roper"—the swindler who brought in the victim and pretended to be his partner in the bets. Finally, the victim was induced to come up with several thousand dollars to wager on a contest that he was assured was fixed. But something went wrong. The contestant the sucker bet on might suddenly "drop dead," triggering a false panic as everyone stampeded from the arena, since such sporting contests were illegal at the time and could lead to prosecution of everyone present. In other cases the victim would be "given the kiss-off" by two con men who suckered him into the plot and presumably lost a fortune along with him. These two worthies got into a vicious argument, each blaming the other, until one pulled a gun and shot the other "dead." The plugged man, actually shot with blanks, sank to the floor with blood gushing from his mouth. The gory but most effective performance involved the use of a "cackle-bladder" (see entry), a small pouch of chicken blood that was bitten open with the first shot. This act was to put the sucker "on the run," since up until then the only law he'd broken was illegal betting; but now he believed he was an accessory to murder. (This ploy is enacted in the 1973 movie *The Sting*, which is set in what appears to be a plush gambling parlor.)

Boatright's Big Store concept quickly spread around the country, since the acting and atmosphere was so convincing that men of wealth and business made the typical victims. They never suspected a swindle, but rather viewed their experience as being one of incredibly bad luck. The con men filed away the names of many victims and often approached them a few years later with a proposition to recoup their losses; the suckers would be taken again with a different wrinkle to the same or similar swindle. This was especially carried out in what became the "con capital of America," Denver, Colorado, where master-fixer Lou Blonger operated with impunity for four decades.

See also CACKLE-BLADDER; DOLLAR STORE.

BILL STUMP'S STONE *pickwickian hoax*
Few cases of life imitating art can match the 1838 discovery of a mysterious stone tablet in the Grave Creek Mound at Moundsville, in what is now West Virginia. It was inscribed with a form of hieroglyphics that defied translation by linguists and academicians for the next 92 years. Not that there was any shortage of theories. In 1856 a French scientist deciphered the inscription as reading: "The Chief of Emigration who reached these places has fixed these statutes forever." In 1872 another scientist told the Congress of Americanists at Nancy, France, that the

inscription was Canaanite and said, "What thou sayest, thou dost impose it, thou shinest in thy impetuous clan and rapid chamoid." Yet another theory held that it meant: "The grave of one who was assassinated here. May God avenge him, strike his murderer, cutting off the hand of his existence."

Some 50 other linguists divided on the language of the inscription as being: Etruscan (4); Runic (5); Phoenician (10); ancient Greek (1); Old British (14); and Celtiberic (16). The common thread to all these translations was that the stone proved the existence of other civilizations in America before Columbus.

Then, one day in 1930, Andrew Price, president of the West Virginia Historical Society, chanced to glance sideways at the tablet and thought he made out "1838." Turning the tablet to an angle, Price could make out a complete phrase in English: "Bill Stump's Stone, October 14, 1838."

The mystery was solved. In Charles Dickens' 1837 novel *Pickwick Papers*, an ancient Roman inscription discovered by one of Dickens' characters was subsequently declared by an irreverent rogue to be nothing more than being "Bill Stumps His Mark." In Grave Creek Mound some joker had decided to have life imitate art. Though remaining silent at the time, he stumped generations of linguists.

BILLIES AND CHARLIES *forged medieval metals*
In the mid-19th century England was caught up in a craze for medieval metal objects. These metal objects, chiefly plaques, were later to be called Billies and Charlies after the forgers who made them. They were cast in lead or "cock metal"—an alloy of copper and lead—and then artificially pitted with acid. In 1847–48 William Smith and Charles Eaton (Billy and Charley) turned out thousands of the objects and then planted some in excavation sites in and around London. Englishmen proudly sought to gain ownership of such remnants of the country's history, while Billy and Charley sold their wares to "simple folk and the more naive collectors," as a contemporary account states. Finally, the British Archaeological Association exposed the Billies and Charlies as fakes and the hoax trade collapsed, leaving some speculators impoverished.

BLACK SOX SCANDAL DOUBLECROSS *cheating the cheats*
Most accounts of the infamous Black Sox Scandal— the fixing of the 1919 baseball World Series—attributed it to the crooked genius of the underworld mastermind Arnold "the Brain" Rothstein. In point of fact, Broadway Arnold did not concoct the plot, although he profited immensely from it, thanks most likely to a devious hoax within a hoax that he had masterminded.

Apparently it was Chicago player Charles Arnold "Chick" Gandil who first approached gamblers Joe "Sport" Sullivan of Boston and William "Sleepy Bill" Sullivan of New York and told them he could recruit several other White Sox players to throw the series against the Cincinnati Redlegs if the price was right. The two gamblers felt they needed more financial backing to pull off the coup, and Rothstein, the nation's top gambler, was propositioned to bankroll the operation. The plot was outlined to Rothstein who, according to later Broadway gossip, put the stall on the plotters by saying he would have to think about it.

The rest of Rothstein's maneuvering was said to have been as follows. The gamblers, faced with a shrinking time frame, finally went ahead without the Rothstein bankroll, using Abe Attell, the former featherweight boxing champion, as the lead man in the plot. As the opening game approached, Rothstein tracked certain monies being bet in Boston and New York, which told him the fix was indeed in. Rothstein bet the $60,000 he would have invested in bribing the players and garnered a profit of $270,000. How many more thousands he made betting through fronts is not known. Rothstein's scam outsmarted the plotters and he apparently made much more out of the coup than they did, without investing a penny of his own.

BLACK WIDOW OF MARLOW *masquerading murderess and con woman*

In Marlow, New Hampshire, the folks have yet to forget Audrey Marie Hilley. In 1980 they knew her as Robbi Hannon Homan and later, incredibly, as her own twin sister. At the time Robbi Homan was a pleasant-looking married woman who worked as a secretary in nearby Keene. Then, in 1982, she went off to visit her sister in Texas. The Keene newspaper reported that she had died there suddenly.

Shortly thereafter, Robbi's sister—allegedly her twin—Terri Martin turned up in Marlow and moved into the home of her grieving brother-in-law. It seemed they would soon marry. Unfortunately for Terri Martin, detectives back in Texas discovered that Robbi Homan had not died but had faked her death. She was now Terri Martin continuing Robbi's life in Marlow.

But Terri Martin was not Robbi Homan either. She was finally identified as Audrey Marie Hilley, who had been convicted in Alabama of murdering her husband. Audrey was also suspected of poisoning her daughter. It turned out she had escaped from prison in Alabama and continued her deadly con woman career by adopting other identities. Dubbed the "Black Widow" by the press, she was returned

to Alabama. She died there in 1987 while attempting once more to escape prison.

BLINDMEN'S DINNER See EULENSPIEGEL, TILL.

"BLIND" WILLIAMS See POSTAL IMPOSTORS.

BLINKIES *fake blind beggars*

His normal beat is New York's Fifth Avenue, but not every day. As soon as he builds up a stake, he's off to Aqueduct or Belmont to bet on the nags, religiously studying the *Daily Racing Form*. Knowing horseplayers will sidle up to him and ask, "See anything good?" There is considerable racetrack humor in the question since he happens to be a "blinkie," a beggar who feigns blindness to get his coin cup to overflow with human kindness.

He simulates his blindness by pasting down his eyelids with collodion, used as protective coating over photographic film. After a hard day on the street, he will step into a secluded alley, pull out a small bottle of alcohol and a swab of cotton from his pocket and wipe the collodion from his eyelids.

One New York study found that 56% of all beggars fake their ailments and the figures for blinkies were much higher. An official for the New York Lighthouse, an organization that aids the blind, once stated that New York is such a soft touch for blinkies that many of them commute to the city from Pennsylvania and New Jersey and return home, their pockets bulging.

Perhaps the New York Police's favorite blinkie was "Blind Charley," who for years stationed himself outside Macy's department store bearing a sign: "I AM BLIND. PLEASE HELP ME."

Charley made out well enough to buy four apartment houses, but sadly he eventually did go blind (the result of many years of standing in the street keeping his eyes well open toward the sun) and retired. As he explained to a policeman who ran into him some time later, "You can't expect me to go on working in this disabled condition, could you?"

BLUE LAW HOAXES

Every so often a popular journal will present a list of zany laws that at one time or to this day are on the law books. It would take a massive effort to verify the facts in each case, but suffice it to say that many and most likely most are hoaxes and fabrications. Many of the so-called blue laws trace back to the Puritans, at least as narrated by some dubious historians. If we are to believe these accounts, there are laws that enjoined parents from kissing their children on the Sabbath; that forebade the baking of mince pies; that outlawed the playing of any musical instrument save for the trumpet, drum or Jew's harp; and that in sundry ways placed drastic limitations on people's freedom of action on weekdays.

Many of these early blue laws were first stated by Daniel Neal in his *The History of New England,* published in London in 1747. Many of these were restated a half-century later by the Reverend Samuel Peters in his *General History of Connecticut.* Peters added many more blue laws to the list, which by general consensus now are regarded as being figments of his imagination. Diligent historians have failed to uncover the slightest trace of these bizarre laws in the records. So many errors and outright fabrications occur in Peters' writings that he was later referred to in scholarly circles as the "lying Episcopalian parson."

See also PETERS, SAMUEL ANDREW.

BLUFFSTEIN, SOPHIE   See RENTED FLAT SCAMS.

BOBBED HAIR TAX   *German hoax*
In Leipzig in 1920, a crowd of women surrounded city hall to pay a supposed "bobbed hair tax." This practical joke would later be cited both within and without the country as having been a result of the Germans' reputed attitude toward accepting any government edict, no matter how ludicrous, without thinking. They had all received florid pronouncements on an official-looking government document that they had failed to pay the tax levied on bobbed hair and faced severe penalties unless they brought their tax status up to date. Most women, cash in hand, all insisted to puzzled officials they were not tax dodgers but had simply not been aware of the new levy.

It should be noted that the undiscovered joker had made many prominent and sophisticated members of Leipzig society the butt of his hoax.

BOESKY, IVAN   *"Ivan the Terrible" of Wall Street*
Up until the mid-1980s Ivan Boesky (1937–   ) was considered perhaps the most controversial high-rolling stock speculator on Wall Street, bearing the sobriquet of "Ivan the Terrible" as he gambled tens of millions on risky security deals. Later, when the secrets of his methods were uncovered, he was regarded as the biggest crook in the financial world.

Son of a Russian immigrant in Detroit, Boesky was graduated from law school in 1962 and moved to New York four years later. After working for an investment firm and then a brokerage house, Boesky was attracted to the wild world of risk arbitrage—risking huge sums buying and selling stocks that appeared to be merging or about to be taken over by other firms. Boesky started his own arbitrage firm with some $700,000 in capital. Eleven years later, Boesky's financial empire was worth some $2 billion. He lived with his wife and four children in a 10-bedroom mansion on a 200-acre estate in suburban Westchester County and maintained a lavish riverview apartment in Manhattan. He was invited to join the boards of several companies and gave huge sums to charities, while making increasing sums on his stock deals.

Unfortunately, Boesky did it all by bending and breaking the rules, seeking out insider tips and paying generously for the illegal information. In May 1986, Dennis Levine, one of Boesky's best illegal sources and a wheeler-dealer in his own right, was trapped by government investigators and started "singing." The trail led to Boesky, and in November he was forced to make an agreement with the government to pay a $100 million penalty for breaking security laws. To cut his potential prison sentence, Boesky started to outwarble Levine and turn in his fellow violators. He even let investigators tape his phone conversations as he carried out his stock deals. Numerous heads rolled as a result, and Drexel Burnham Lambert, one of the giant financial institutions on Wall Street, plunged to near collapse, turning into a shell of its former self.

In a plea bargain Boesky got off with a three-year sentence. He said he was "deeply ashamed" for what he'd done. Many observers thought he had paid a very small price for the ruined financial fortunes of so many shareholders; even his $100 million penalty—albeit the largest of its type in history—left him a most wealthy man. The only comfort to Boesky's victims was that, after his release from prison, Boesky faced a host of ex-partner and shareholder lawsuits that would drain his fortune considerably in future years.

BOILER-ROOM OPERATIONS   *swindlers' favorite tactic*
Boiler-room operators may well be the best business swindlers in operation today. Certainly the boiler-room professionals consider themselves a branch of show business in a field that allows them to emote for an audience of one, with their success measured by how much they can clip their victims for one-on-one.

Boiler-room specialists who engage in charity drives move from city to city while others, such as those peddling fraudulent investment plans, tend to stay rooted in one spot for a time until it seems wise to move on before authorities locate them. This means setting up shop in a new address under a new name, but with a vital bank of telephones.

Investment boiler-room operators and their sales squads look to rapidly contact a large pool of potential victims. The investment swindler considers his time well-spent, even if it takes 50 or 100 or 200 phone calls to locate one prize "mooch"—the swindler's term for suckers—since the swindler is shooting for that person's entire savings.

These swindlers usually supplement their hunt with bonafide mailing lists—names and addresses of persons subscribing to particular investment publications. They may use a mail pitch at first, but because they are fearful that postal authorities will take notice, they often do not make an immediate pitch for the victim's money. Instead they seek to get a written or phoned response for more information. Then victims get the boiler-room call or calls to close the swindle. Often they also try phone appeals to those who don't respond to the original mailing.

Sometimes the approach appears extremely low key. The telephone pitchman merely informs the client that he wishes him to be acquainted with the firm's services. The salesman declares a certain commodity is going up soon. He tells this to a number of potential mooches. Then he tells an equal number that the same commodity is soon going to drop. All the members of whichever group got the right prediction get a second call with the same ploy—half that another commodity will go up and half that it will go down. The half that again got the right answer (one-quarter of the original sucker list) are now most impressed; within that group there are many who are ripe for picking. The boiler room boys have no more interest in guessing about commodities. They get the mooch's money and in nothing flat his investment is wiped out. And the mooch's phone stops ringing.

See also INVESTOR FORECASTING SWINDLE.

BONNIE & CLYDE'S DEATH CAR IMITATIONS
In March 1934, Jesse Warren, a roofing contractor in Topeka, Kansas, bought a tannish-gray ("Desert Sand") Ford V-8 for $785. In late April, the car was stolen by a notorious pair of criminals, Bonnie Parker and Clyde Barrow. For the next 23 days Bonnie and Clyde crisscrossed the Midwest for a total of 7,500 miles, committing crimes and eluding police capture. Then, on May 23, Bonnie and Clyde were ambushed at Gibland, Louisiana, near the Texas border, by a group of lawmen. Apparently without offering the criminal pair a chance to surrender, the lawmen let loose a barrage of gunfire, hitting the Ford 107 times and killing both occupants. They dug 25 bullets out of Clyde and 23 out of Bonnie.

The Warren V-8 thus became the best known car in America. When it was returned to the owner, he leased it out to a number of "showmen" who exhibited the car at fairgrounds and carnivals. It brought in a goodly amount of money, considering the Depression and the fact that there were at least five fakes on the exhibition trail at the same time. Enough pictures had been printed of the death car that fakers had little trouble doctoring up other V-8s to pass off as the "Genuine Bonnie & Clyde Death Car."

By the late 1940s interest in the death car had petered out and it was packed away. In 1952 a carnival showman named Ted Toddy bought the car for $14,500 to publicize a documentary about gangsters. Again the fakers emerged with their bogus versions and everyone made some more money at fairs, carnivals and shopping centers. When the hit film *Bonnie and Clyde* starring Warren Beatty and Faye Dunaway appeared in 1967, showman Toddy brought his car out of retirement and began exhibiting it again with "bloodied" dummies placed inside the car. Toddy made considerable profits, but he had to begin a practice of prosecuting the owners of the fake death cars. However, these imitators proved hard to catch as they flitted off after only a two- or three-day stint in any community. Whenever they were questioned if their car was the authentic death car, they indignantly whipped out old newspaper pictures to demonstrate that their car was the real thing, with every bullet hole matching.

As a result, the Bonnie & Clyde death car, real or fake, continued to be profitable. In the late 1970s it was estimated that the authentic death car had grossed over $1 million—and the fakes had taken in a similar sum. By contrast, the biggest "job" Bonnie and Clyde themselves ever pulled was $3,500 and their total career-criminal take was only about $20,000.

BORDER-JUMPING SCAMS *victimizing Mexican immigrants*
The *pollos*, or chickens, are among the most pathetic of any scam victims. These impoverished migrants attempting to slip into the United States from Mexico were branded *pollos* by the vicious brutes who victimize them. The crooks view the desperate migrants as nothing more than chickens to be plucked and, on occasion, killed.

The main entry way for *pollos* is a corridor along the California border, some $5\frac{1}{2}$ miles from the San Ysidro-Tijuana port of entry and the Pacific Ocean. The chain-link fence cannot be kept in proper repair and has so many holes that three times as many illegals get in as are caught by the border patrol.

But the border patrol is not always the main problem for the *pollos*. The border bandits, young Chicanos who ambush the migrants in the corridor at night, represent a larger menace. They seize their money

U.S. border patrolmen must constantly rescue "pollos" stranded in the desert by crooked alien smugglers.

and whatever pitiful possessions they may be carrying, safe in the knowledge that the *pollos* cannot appeal to the law for protection.

The *pollos* are victimized even before they leave their native country. First they must pay a "coyote" in Mexico to provide them with transportation and for a guide (known as a "mule") to lead them. The coyote often collects an extra bounty from California growers to deliver his merchandise directly to their farms where they are put to work for wages well below the legal minimum. Once again the *pollos* lack legal redress, being subject to deportation if they come forward.

The *pollos* can face even worse treachery from the mule. He may lead them into an ambush by the border bandits first and pick up a percentage of the loot as his share. Then the mule will continue to guide the victims to the farms for the next stage of their victimization—provided they survive the robberies, which are generally brutal affairs involving bone-breaking, pistol whipping and at times fatal knifing. In one two-year period 251 robberies, seven rapes and seven murders were reported in the corridor. No one doubts the unreported crimes are several times greater.

BOSTON MARATHON HOAX See RUIZ, ROSIE.

BOTTOMLEY, HORATIO *the friend of the poor*
Few con men could match the saga of rags to riches to rags as experienced by Horatio Bottomley (1860–1933) who, in the early 20th century, exercised tremendous political, social and economic influence over the English masses and literally terrified the king of England into following his agenda. Born in London's East End and orphaned as a youth, Bottomley started out as an errand boy and became a solicitor's clerk.

His first business venture was putting out a small suburban paper, which failed to deliver the number of subscribers promised to advertisers. He ended up in bankruptcy and was charged with fraud. Bottomley defended himself at his trial and beat the charge, the judge being so impressed with his histrionics that he urged the young man to become a barrister. The judge also suggested that Bottomley would be wise to stay out of the business world. Young Bottomley ignored the advice and started his sensational climb to success.

Soon Bottomley became a millionaire, most of his fortune coming from the promotion of Australian gold mines, both real and of his fancy. By 1897 he was worth more than £3 million. His companies were worth much less, and during the first five years of the new century he was hit with 67 legal actions. None of this bothered Bottomley, who ignored such trivial matters. He lived on a lavish manorial scale, complete with a number of homes and estates, as well as the almost obligatory racing stable. However, Bottomley knew how to woo the support of the common people with a sort of crude eloquence and well-trumpeted philanthropic activities. He used that popularity to get elected to the House of Commons. Meanwhile, he founded the *Financial Times*, bought *The Sun* and launched a jingoist newspaper called *John Bull*, which was to become the bible of British soldiers during World War I.

In 1909 Bottomley beat yet another fraud charge, but three years later, despite all of his twists and turns, he was forced into bankruptcy. In 1914 Bottomley returned to patriotism and filled *John Bull* with saber-rattling editorials and stories. He terrified King George into removing the Garter banners of the German kaiser and crown prince from St. George's Chapel at Windsor by threatening to lead a mob of his adherents to do the job forcibly. Bottomley became so powerful that he was the one man the Asquith cabinet demanded personal approval of before it dared to introduce conscription.

Within a few years, Bottomley extricated himself from bankruptcy and in 1918 was reelected to Parliament. Because of his great public following he was seriously viewed as a future prime minister.

Immediately after the war Bottomley concocted his grandest swindle—the Victory Bond Club. The government had issued bonds at a price that Bottomley declared was too high for the little man, and his club was to answer their needs. The public was invited to subscribe in any sum—nothing was too small—

and Bottomley ("The Friend of the People") would make large investments with the overall money. In six months the fund took in about a half-million pounds. Bottomley did buy some Treasury bonds and as an added incentive to the public the club even staged a lottery for the shareholders. Later it was revealed that Bottomley skimmed off £150,000 for himself.

Bottomley operated many other businesses in like manner. Many times he appeared before angry shareholders who had seen their investments swallowed up in his ventures; somehow, with his uncanny oratorical powers, he turned their threats into apologies and even got them to take new subscriptions.

However, even the patented Bottomley snake oil could not go on forever. In late 1921, the Chancery Court launched a major investigation into Bottomley's affairs. That broke the bubble, and one of his former partners accused Bottomley of swindling shareholders. Bottomley filed a suit for criminal libel but dropped it when it became evident that the Chancery probe was leading to a prosecution.

Bottomley was brought to trial in 1922 and tried to seize control by dictating procedures. The court even bowed to his demand that he was entitled to an adjournment each morning at 11:30 for some champagne for "medicinal" purposes. In the end, however, a jury in Old Bailey found him guilty, and Bottomley was branded the worst fraud and charlatan in England. He was sentenced to seven years penal servitude and, as a convicted felon, he was expelled from the House of Commons. Burly, corpulent, ruddy-faced, a living image of John Bull when he entered prison, he came out five years later a broken man, with a drawn face and white hair. He was 57 years old, but looked 80 to observers.

With the same audacity that had marked his entire career, Bottomley tried to reinsert himself in public life, starting a new paper called *John Blunt*. But by this time the public had had enough and the newspaper flopped. He sold his memoirs, *Five Years of Hell*, to the sensationalist press and, desperate for funds, sank to making pathetic personal appearances on stage at the Windmill Theatre, an institution best noted for females who appeared totally naked.

In May 1933 Bottomley, flat broke and facing a serious internal operation, petitioned the government for an old-age pension. It was denied the day Bottomley entered the hospital. He died of complications of the operation on May 26.

BOUNTY JUMPING *Civil War racket*

Because a bounty was paid in the American Civil War for men to enlist in the Union army, it became a common practice for men to enlist, desert, then re-enlist elsewhere and so on. In one case a man was caught after no less than 32 enlistments and desertions, an activity that netted him a four-year prison term. However, the apprehension rate for such desertions was extremely low, and organized gangs of bounty jumpers thrived. In all, it has been estimated that bounty jumping may have accounted for half the total desertions from the Union army, or about 135,000 of 268,000.

A young gambler and fixer, Mike McDonald became "King of the Bounty Jumpers," heading up a gang of hoodlums who garnered bounties varying from $100 to $1,000 for each enlistment. McDonald shuttled his bogus soldiers from one area to another and kept track of their enlistments on a large war map of Illinois. Profits from these operations gave McDonald a treasury that made him the most important criminal operator in Chicago for four decades after the war.

BOVAR, ORIC *false messiah*

One of the most charismatic false messiahs of recent years, a mystic named Oric Bovar established a cult following of about 200 devoted adherents in the 1970s. If the number was small, the membership was impressive, stretching from learned circles in New York to wealthy Hollywoodites in California. Among the show business celebrities attracted to Bovar were Carol Burnett and Bernadette Peters.

Bovar was an apostle for clean living, with strong warnings against evils such as smoking, drinking, drugs and extramarital sex. As Bovar gained more influence over his followers, he picked mates for them to marry. He issued strong prohibitions against doctors, which caused several of his followers to have babies without medical attention.

By 1976 Bovar was assuring his followers he was Jesus Christ and ordered his followers to observe Christmas on his own birthday, August 29, rather than on December 25. By this time some of his followers, including Peters and Burnett, had left him, and Bovar issued orders that the devoted break off all friendship with such defectors.

As Jesus, Bovar announced, he could raise the dead. Thus when a New York Bovarite named Stephanos Hatzitheordorou died of cancer, Bovar set about bringing him back to life. Bovar and five of his flock—a college teacher, a writer, a Wall Street clerk, a railroad employee and an Evelyn Wood speed-reading instructor—spent a two-month vigil over the corpse, chanting "Rise, Stephan, rise." They even paid the dead man's rent so they could raise the dead without outside, mundane distractions.

Finally, the police broke in on the scene and charged Bovar and his followers with failing to re-

Charismatic false messiah Oric Bovar told his dedicated cult followers he could do almost anything—including raise the dead—since, after all, he was Jesus Christ.

port a death. While awaiting a court appearance on the charge, Bovar faced a flock that had increasing doubts about his claims. Bovar announced he could demonstrate his great powers by stepping out a window, fluttering about for a time and coming back inside. On April 14, 1977, Bovar stepped out of his 10th-floor apartment window and plunged to his death.

BOY WITH HIS FINGER IN THE DIKE *made-in-America hoax*

Near the Spaarndem lock, Haarlem, the Netherlands, stands a statue to one of the most fabled boys in Dutch history. It is that of the urchin who saved the country from the sea by plugging his finger in a hole in the dike. Not only is the story apocryphal, but the statue itself is a hoax.

This classic tale of old Holland was actually born in America, appearing in 1865 in *Hans Brinker, or the Silver Skates* by Mary Mapes Dodge. The story was idolized by American schoolchildren and was soon accepted as an authentic Dutch tale. Quite naturally, American tourists took the story to the Netherlands and very earnestly inquired of the Haarlem citizens

the precise spot where the heroic urchin had plugged the dike with his finger. For many years the Dutch tried to explain the tale was pure fiction—and imported at that.

Finally, in 1950, the Dutch were forced to give up their losing battle and erect the statue near the Spaarndem lock. The result was happy tourists and even happier shopkeepers in the area. It is also happy for all that there is little need for the Dutch to inform American tourists that the heroic boy could more readily have kept himself out of harm's way by simply plugging the hole with a stone instead of his finger.

BRAWLEY, TAWANA *sexual assault claimant*

Few cases of alleged sexual assault have proved as divisive as the Tawana Brawley case. On Thanksgiving of 1987 black, 15-year-old Tawana Brawley turned up "missing" from her home in Wappingers Falls, New York. When she was found, her hair had been cropped short, she'd been smeared with dog feces, and someone had used a felt-tipped pen to write "KKK" and "NIGGER" on her body. According to Tawana, her attackers were all white men, including one white law enforcement officer.

The Brawley case galvanized the black community, which saw in it not only another incident of white exploitation but also a deliberate effort by law enforcement to dismiss the case. Among whites there was an overwhelming inclination to disbelieve the charges; this was a simple case of a teenager improvising a tale to alibi her absence from home and the punishment she would likely face. It was said that her mother, Glenda Brawley, and the man she lived with, 40-year-old Ralph King, had a reputation for "fast hands." King had served a seven-year prison term for the manslaughter death of his first wife. A New York newspaper, the *Daily News*, later claimed that Tawana had sometimes been beaten for staying out all night. Television reports offered witnesses who said they had seen Tawana partying part of the time she later claimed she was being brutalized by the white attackers.

Acknowledged black leaders such as Jesse Jackson were described as "tiptoeing" around the case, which was in the hands of three black spokesmen: the Reverend Al Sharpton and two lawyers, C. Vernon Mason and Alton H. Maddox Jr.

These advisers began a campaign attacking the local prosecutors in the case as being unwilling to prosecute white men. The following February, Governor Mario Cuomo appointed the state attorney general, Robert Abrams, to act as a special prosecutor. With the alleged "crackers" off the case, Abrams and his staff of 430 lawyers took over, a situation that was applauded by the Brawley side. However, within a few days the three advisers turned their fire on Abrams as well, charging him with being biased. Sharpton eventually attacked Abrams as being little better than Hitler. Attorney Maddox added his own bit of obscenities to the affair by suggesting that the state attorney general masturbated over a photo of Tawana Brawley.

The drumbeat of attacks continued with Sharpton insisting there was an Irish Republican Army "link" to the case, since many of the supposed perpetrators were of Irish descent. Undeterred, Abrams continued his investigation. After one of the largest probes in state history—including testimony from almost 200 experts and witnesses—a grand jury produced a 170-page report declaring "that Tawana Brawley was not the victim of a forcible sexual assault." The judge who approved the report concurred in the finding, which he said was "based on clear and convincing evidence . . . beyond any doubt."

While investigations of the three advisers were continued, the general opinion was that the Brawley affair had been a hoax and that friends had aided the girl in concocting the tale to avoid certain punishment.

However, the significance of the Brawley hoax may run far deeper. As Stanley Diamond, distinguished professor of anthropology and the humanities on the graduate faculty of the New School for Social Research, noted:

> In cultural perspective, if not in fact, it doesn't matter whether the crime occurred or not. Tawana Brawley's handlers—the Rev. Al Sharpton and lawyers C. Vernon Mason and Alton Maddox—must know this. They simply reversed the predicament black Americans find all too familiar: the use of false charges to rationalize the maiming and murder of countless blacks in the United States; the mass creation of victims. Tawana Brawley herself has a history of being abused. She understands evasion, the need to dissimulate for the sake of survival, a mark not only of the oppressed but a familiar style in white-collar American society as well. . . . What is most remarkable about this faked crime is that traditional victims have re-created themselves as victims in a dreadfully plausible situation. Although oppressors have imprisoned and murdered designated victims throughout history—rationalizing their acts with false charges, fake trials and manufactured evidence—the Brawley case is the opposite and is rare if not unique. It may be asking too much of the white community to excuse the Brawley deceit; but they misunderstand it at their peril.

BRAZILIAN CARD SMUGGLING SCAM *outwitting customs*
Today in a lavish villa atop a hill in Rio de Janeiro lives a brilliant smuggler, now a millionaire and free of all chance of prosecution. He became rich by the very implausible method of smuggling in *worthless* decks of cards. Smuggling cards into Brazil is a very rewarding pastime, since the local product is notoriously inferior with many imperfections that make cheating easy. However, Brazil, long obsessed with the idea of maintaining an overall favorable balance of trade as well as protecting the domestic card industry, has banned the importation of quality cards.

This cunning smuggler ignored government policy and imported one million decks of U.S. playing cards. As the smuggler expected, the cards were seized by Brazilian customs. Then, also as the smuggler anticipated, the government auctioned off the seized cards. Normally, the cards would have been destroyed, but the government saw no reason to do so since the decks were valueless, as they were all lacking the ace of spades. The shrewd smuggler had previously arranged for his U.S. supplier to remove all of the aces of spades from the decks. Several months earlier the smuggler had then conspired to get the aces admitted to Brazil without any problem. At the time he posed as a furniture maker and explained to Customs that the aces were to be laid into cocktail furniture tops for sale primarily to the U.S. market. Naturally, the government had approved that deal since it meant considerable foreign exports.

In the auction for the incomplete decks, the smuggler now entered a miniscule bid for the cards. Not surprisingly, there were no other bids. The government was quite pleased to get something for the seizure. Now the smuggler reinserted the aces into the decks, which were then sold at black market prices of $4 and up retail. His profits were estimated to have been somewhere between $1 million and $2 million.

BRINKLEY, "DR." JOHN R. See GOAT GLAND SEX REJUVENATION.

BROOKLYN BRIDGE See PARKER, GEORGE C.

BROOMING *supermarket overcharging scam*
It is not a well-kept secret that supermarket executives know they are at the mercy of the store manager in the actual running of each store. Shady managers are known to pocket anywhere from $500 to $1,000 a week in scams that gyp the customers. Some time ago in St. Louis, Missouri, one manager—with the aid of a single dishonest cashier—quickly grabbed $11,000. The pair mainly utilized the tried-and-true "broom racket."

All they did was place a new broom against the checkout counter. Whenever a big-order customer came along, especially mothers minding small children, the cashier would distract them for a moment and ring up $1.69, $2.69 or $3.69 depending on the size of the broom. Often the manager would do the distracting by coming to the checkout counter to make change or say something to the clerk.

After totaling the sale, the clerk would package all the purchases—except, of course, the broom. It would stay right where it was, waiting for the next likely victim.

On the rare occasions that a customer spotted the overcharge, the cashier would excuse himself, saying he'd assumed the customer was buying the broom. Since the manager had money in the register that had not reduced the store's inventory, there was no need for him to risk altering the receipts. He had his pick of any disposable merchandise in the store, and took out in cases of cigarettes the equivalent of what had been stolen from customers.

That eventually led to his downfall. Inspectors never got wise to him—never even receiving a complaint against the store—but the chain's central office noticed an abnormal increase in cigarette sales, out of line with other stores. The manager had picked cigarettes because they can be disposed of closer to the retail price than any item in a store.

BROTHERS AND SISTERS OF THE RED DEATH   fatal doomsday hoax

The bloodiest doomsday hoax occurred in 1900 in the Kargopol district of Russia. It was carried out by a 200-year-old sect called the Brothers and Sisters of the Red Death, a group long noted for its unusual beliefs, including a firm ban on marriage. Sexual intercourse could be practiced provided the lovers immediately submitted themselves to possible death by being subjected to possible suffocation with a large red cushion.

Having determined that the Earth would end on November 13, 1900, the leaders of the sect convinced the members that God would be most pleased if they first sacrificed themselves to death by burning. When news of the planned mass suicide reached St. Petersburg, 400 miles away, czarist troops were dispatched to prevent the holocaust. However, by the time the soldiers arrived, more than 100 members had already perished. When the day of doom passed without incident, disillusioned members disbanded the sect.

BUCKINGHAM PALACE HUNGER MARCH   Hearst newspaper fake

In the early 1930s, as well as on a few other occasions, newspaper publisher William Randolph Hearst was a champion of labor. He typically thought nothing of faking stories to support his positions. In 1932 his *New York Mirror* published an article that alleged that hunger marchers were storming Buckingham Palace, which allowed him to cater to two of his own biases of the moment, pro-labor and anti-British. To substantiate its report, the *Mirror* ran a picture of great crowds surrounding the palace. It was later learned that the photo was from 1929, as crowds gathered to anxiously await news during the illness of King George V.

BUCKMINSTER, FRED   con man

As a confidence man Fred Buckminster (1863–1943) stands out as one of the most daring of that fabled flock. Not only did he rob the boobs, but he delighted in swindling other swindlers as well. It might be said that Buckminster—more so than even the notorious Yellow Kid Weil (see entry) would con anyone still breathing and not have the slightest qualm about coming back to hit them again.

Buckminster took to the "bunco life" when still a teenager and, as he put it, "never looked back." He discovered early on that no one made an easier victim than another thief—amateur or professional. Buckminster sought out dishonest bankers (of which there was "an endless supply"), especially those "marked" as having been accused of cheating their customers. He would pretend to be a new depositor with some stocks that he would leave for safekeeping, and would then let himself be "swindled" out of the worthless certificates by the banker after seeing he was fed false information that the stock had suddenly soared in value. "When I see a crook, I see nothing but dollar signs," Buckminster remarked.

For more than 20 years Buckminster worked with the Yellow Kid, and they pioneered some of the grandest con games ever, such as the "pedigreed dog" scam (see entry), variations on the "fixed" prizefight and horse race swindles. They operated out of a "big store," or phony betting shops to take the suckers. Once in a while the boys victimized a genuine betting parlor by "past posting." One of them would get the results at the Western Union office while the other placed a bet before the bookie joint received the results. They took "Palmer House" Ryan, who ran a huge betting establishment in the woods outside of Chicago, by having a railroad engineer signal the winner with his train whistle in code as the train passed the gambling joint.

Buckminster's most lucrative swindle of other swindlers was a scam concocted by himself and Kid Dimes, a "gimmick mechanic" who fixed roulette wheels (see entry) to take advantage of dishonest gambling houses. The pair became the first to fix a fixed roulette wheel. In 1918 Kid Dimes fixed the wheel at the King George Club, a Chicago loop joint where gullible big bettors were steered to be swindled. The Kid's standard routine was setting up three numbers so the croupier could steer the ball to avoid any payoffs. By utilizing these three numbers the croupier could control the color, even-odds and the set of winning numbers or the actual number. All the croupier did was press a button that magnetized the number he preferred and the little ball would end up there.

Dimes and Buckminister also had a hidden button that could be used to negate the number the croupier wanted and instead hit number 8. Then Buckminister breezed into the joint, posing as a wild-spending Texas oilman looking for action. After a few small bets Buckminister plunked $10,000 on the numbers 7 through 12, which called for a payoff at 5 to 1. Then, at the last moment, he tossed $1,000 more on number 8 "for luck." The croupier pushed his button and Buckminister pushed his. Number 8 came out and pandemonium broke loose as the bogus Texan won $85,000 on the spin. Because there were so many honest bettors in the house, the gambling joint was forced to pay off. Buckminister hung around, dropping a few thousand dollars and then leaving, vowing to come back the next night and really clean up. He didn't return.

Naturally, the crooks hauled Kid Dimes in to explain under pain of very bad consequences what had gone wrong. The Kid coolly dove under the table and switched batteries, coming up with a bad one. "Why don't you people change batteries at least once a week to be safe? At a dime a throw you ought to even be able to afford to change batteries every night."

Buckminster and Dimes worked that racket dozens of times for more than a decade. Buckminster estimated they cleared three-quarters of a million from the scam.

As good as Buckminster was, he spent many years in prison for his cons. The trouble was, he said, the police had a huge edge over the con man. "A copper can make a thousand mistakes but a crook only one to get put away." When he finished his last prison sentence in 1938, he informed reporters that he was finished with cons. He was—but not quite. In 1941 he wrote a series of memoirs for a detective magazine, earning $100 each time his byline was used. Buckminster promptly raised one of the checks from $100 to $1,000 and cashed it. The publishing house took it with good grace, as it seemed a little late in the game to get a 78-year-old con man with one foot in the grave to reform. Buckminster died two years later, a "reformed" con man.

BUSHEL BASKET TOSS   *carnival con*

"Step right up, folks, and try your luck at tossing three baseballs in the basket for a mere dollar. Get all three to stay in and win a portable TV, get two in and take your choice of an electric toaster-oven, mixer

or blender. One or none in and you lose. But it's not hard. Just watch me, folks." At this point the operator of the game easily lobs three baseballs into the bushel basket.

In the old days the con commonly utilized a mechanism in the basket bottom that is triggered when the first ball is tossed in. The next two inevitably popped back out. But because many communities now police carnival games (at least in areas where the fix is not in), carnival cons have simplified the procedure, eliminating any traceable cheating procedure. But while the operator can sink baseballs that don't bounce, the customers still can't get them in. Reason: The baskets have solid, wood-reinforced bottoms that cause the ball to bounce back. The baskets are tipped toward the player at an angle; the greater the angle, the more inviting the target appears to the customer and the more likely the balls will bounce out. This will happen much more often when the balls hit the upper half of the basket bottom, which they do 90% of the time.

Meanwhile, the operator baits suckers by popping in balls to stay. His advantage is that his angle is on the other side of the counter. He can toss in balls that don't hit the upper half of the bottom of the basket, but rather hit down low or else hit the sides of the bushel, bounce to the other side and settle at the bottom.

BYRON'S ILLEGITIMATE SON   *obsessive forger*

Major George Gordon De Luna Byron appeared on the London scene in the 1840s, beginning a grand imposture as the illegitimate son of the celebrated poet Lord Byron. He insisted his mother, a Spanish lady known as the Countess De Luna, had contracted a secret marriage with the great poet. The major's title, he averred, resulted from service with the East India Company. He even affected a superior military air, and he did bear some resemblance to Byron in looks and bearing; but he was studiously ignored by the poet's family.

The major announced his ambition to become legitimized as Byron's son and to clear the latter's name of the slights that had descended upon him after death. The major took pen in hand and forged hundreds of letters and other communications from Lord Byron to other writers and friends.

Among his forgeries were very extensive correspondences between Byron and poets Shelley and Keats. The major, an expert raconteur, had familiarized himself with the minutiae of his "father's" life, and he dropped many phrases into the correspondence to draw attention to his own alleged origin and, partly, to earn money to support himself while pressing his claims. The major labored arduously over his forgeries, netting only about one pound per letter, not a trivial sum at the time but certainly no grand fortune. The major was shooting for bigger game, however, seeking to convince a number of publishers of his own legitimacy and to publish his claims. Unfortunately, the major's letters were not up to the literary quality of Byron and Shelley, and thus he took to lifting his "father's" keenest observations from old published articles of others. The editor Robert Palgrave recognized some of these long passages, which led to the major's unmasking in 1852.

Major Byron and his wife decamped for New York, where, he announced before departure, he intended to produce a biography of his "father" based on an alleged 1,000 unedited letters and the journal of the poet. Nothing more came of that, and history relegated Major George Gordon De Luna Byron to the role of an infuriating, if most energetic, forger and impostor.

C

THE CABBY COUNT *shortchanging gyp*

It has been estimated by police bunco experts that an accomplished cabby can easily increase his income by $100 a week or more with a simple short-changing tactic. It's known as the "cabby count" and comes in two basic forms: the hesitation and the split pay (which is also a hesitation dodge). The first method, and the one used less frequently, is simple hesitation when a customer pays with a large bill. The driver starts talking like crazy, complaining about the city and whatnot. He pockets the bill, repeats the amount off the meter, makes a big show of handing over the silver change and then hesitates. If the passenger is in a hurry or has been sufficiently distracted by the cabby's spiel, there is a fair chance he will leave before getting his paper change. If, on the other hand, he stays put, the driver counts out the bills. The entire delay is only a second, and most passengers are not even aware they are being stalled, so the driver is not at risk.

The "split pay" method is more common. The spiel is basically the same. If, for example, a customer pays a $4.75 charge with a $20 bill, he tells the cabby to make it $5.50. The driver thanks the passenger copiously, handing over two quarters. He then digs out four $1 bills, which he also hands over. He proceeds to make a big show of tucking away the $20 bill at the other end of his money wad in his wallet. This is the stall he does as he fishes for the $10 bill. Again the hesitation is short, but quite often the passenger is gone with only part of his change.

The best thing about the cabby count is that it requires the driver to fool his victim for only a brief instant until he gets out of the cab. After the taxi drives off, the customer can do nothing if he suddenly remembers he has been shorted. The "cash register" has gone.

CACKLE-BLADDER *murder hoax*

As portrayed in the hit movie *The Sting*, con men since the 19th century concentrated on setting up phony gambling establishments in which all the participants other than the mark, or victim, are part of the swindle. In the con the "cackle-bladder" played a vital role in "blowing off the mark"—that is, getting rid of the mark after taking his money and then involving him in an apparent homicide.

After being conditioned by a few small wins, the mark is informed that a big fix is in on a horse race. Naturally, the fixed horse—the "sure winner"—loses because of some mix-up in signals; but before the mark can remonstrate, another supposed loser turns on the con man companion of the mark, screaming that he has been ruined. He pulls a gun and shoots the con man dead. It is a gory act, with blood gushing from the murdered man's mouth.

Panic ensues as bettors, tellers and cashiers rush for the door. The mark does the same since he is a man of considerable prominence in his home town and, even worse than the money he has lost, he faces personal disgrace if he is involved in a murder. Often the con man who did the shooting flees with the mark, and they leave the city together, sometimes even moving on together to another city or two before the mark figures out he is an accessory to murder and decides in self-preservation to separate from him.

Needless to say, the con men have no fear of hearing from the terrified sucker ever again.

Of course, no murder has occurred. Blanks were used in the shooting and the spouting of blood came from the cackle-bladder, a tiny pouch of chicken blood concealed in the mouth and bitten open by the supposed victim when the shooting starts.

The cackle-bladder was used not only in fake betting parlor shoot-outs, but also at boxing matches, foot races and sporting events that were illegal at the time. The mark was lured to these staged events with the assurance that one of the athletes was guaranteed to win in a fix. However, during the event—and before the rehearsed loser could lay down—the would-be winner suddenly keeled over and died, with the appropriate flow of blood, an obvious victim of some sort of unexpected stroke or other physical mishap. Naturally, the usual flight followed since all the bettors themselves, including the gullible mark, faced imprisonment for attending and wagering on an outlawed event.

Today the cackle-bladder is rarely used in confidence operations, but it remains a mainstay among insurance accident fakers, who use the dramatic spurt of blood to convince witnesses they have really been injured.

See also BIG STORE.

CAESAR'S MARBLE HEAD *long-honored forgery*
Throughout the 19th and much of the 20th century, the most famous and idealized portrait of Julius Caesar was a marble head of the great Roman statesman housed in the British Museum. Today, pictures of the head are still offered as a contemporary view of "the noblest Roman of them all." But by the mid-20th century, experts were having their doubts, and in 1961 it had been conclusively labeled a forgery by Bernard Ashmole, who declared that the surface of the head had been artificially weathered—most likely by pounding with a nail-studded block of wood—and then stained to give an impression of age. Ashmole concluded that the head had been produced in Rome in about 1800—at the dawn of the century that would be the golden age of art forgeries.

CAGLIOSTRO, COUNT ALESSANDRO DI *adventurer, impostor and wandering Jew*
In the 18th century he was the oldest man alive, having been around since the time of Jesus. He was known, in fact, as the "Wandering Jew." How had he managed to live so long? He claimed he had discovered the elixir of everlasting life, and all who could pay for it could enjoy its benefits. His name was Count Alessandro di Cagliostro, and in this incredible mountebank guise he captivated one capital or royal house after another with his magnetism, magical deception and false prophecies. He made a fortune with his quack cures and his celebrated elixir. And if his 1,800 years were not proof personified as to the secret elixir's potency, one could take his wife, who at times was the Marchese de' Pellegrini and at others the Countess Seraphina. He explained that while his wife looked like a lovely girl in her early 20s, she was actually an old woman with a son who was 50.

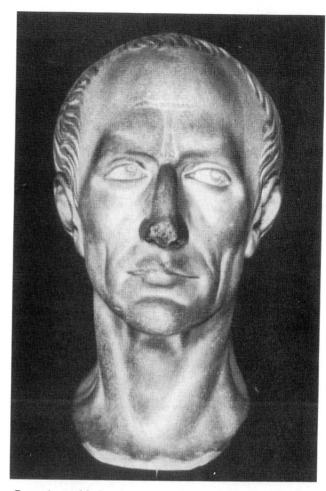

Caesar's marble head—owned by the British Museum and long regarded as the best contemporary portrait of "the noblest Roman of them all"—was conclusively determined in 1961 to be a forgery dating back to only about 1800.

Alas, the count's wife was in her early 20s, and Count Alessandro di Cagliostro was certainly not 1,800-odd years old. Actually he was Giuseppe Balsamo, born in Palermo, Sicily, in 1743, the son of a shopkeeper. Before he developed his Cagliostro imposture, he was an accomplished thief, forger, pimp, counterfeiter, fortune-teller and magician.

His depredations became so notorious that Balsamo was forced to flee Palermo for Messina, then cross to Reggio Calabria and finally onward to Naples and Rome, where he met and married Lorenza Feliciani. He moved with her to Venice, Marseilles, Paris and London. Balsamo prospered by putting his wife's body up for sale; in London he adopted his own version of the badger game, arranging to catch a wealthy Quaker in his wife's bed so that the couple lived many months on the blackmail money. It was in London that Balsamo put on whiskers and the uniform of a Prussian colonel and rechristened himself Count di Cagliostro.

Giuseppe Balsamo, alias Count Alessandro di Cagliostro, was one of the most audacious fakers of the 18th century. He claimed to have found the elixir of everlasting life and said he was some 1,800 years old.

He ventured fully into alchemy and worked on a number of cures and elixirs, some drugs to flatten wrinkles and others to set passion ablaze. Then he went wholehog into rejuvenation and claimed he had lived for centuries on the "wine of Egypt," along with constant purges of his body. His rejuvenation course was available to the big spenders of Europe, who underwent a 40-day course of purges, sweats, root diet, phlebotomy and theosophy. The count never lost a client—at least not in those 40 days.

As soon as he was exposed in one city he moved on to another. He was a particular hit in St. Petersburg, where he practiced as a doctor, treated the poor without charge and was received by the statesman Potemkin. However, the personal physician of Catherine the Great analyzed some of Cagliostro's elixirs and found them worthless. Catherine gave him 24 hours to leave.

Cagliostro was exposed again in Warsaw in 1780 in a booklet called *Cagliostro demasque;* but before it could catch up with him he moved on to Vienna, Frankfurt and Strasbourg. There he met Cardinal Prince de Rohan, a cleric who stands as one of the prize marks of all time. Cagliostro completely bamboozled this cardinal, who brought him to Paris and placed in his palace a bust of "the divine Cagliostro." Rohan was also the victim in the affair of the DIAMOND NECKLACE HOAX, a caper often credited with speeding the French monarchy to its destruction. Cagliostro was hurled into the Bastille for his suspected involvement in the affair, but he was later freed as innocent, certainly one of the few times he was not guilty of a fraud.

He was ordered out of France and settled for a time in London. Then he made the mistake of going to Rome. He was arrested there by the Inquisition in 1789 for his involvement in the Grand Egyptian Lodge, a modified form of freemasonry. His true identity was established and he was sentenced to life imprisonment. He died in papal captivity in the castle of San Leo near Pesaro in 1795. He was 52—a mere 1,748 years short of living 1,800 years.

CALAVERAS SKULL   *fossil hoax*

It was a momentous discovery in 1876, one that would establish Calaveras County, California, as the cradle of mankind, a sort of New World Eden. What was found was the skull of "Calaveras Man," so identified by James D. Whitney, chief geologist of the California Geological Survey. Whitney was convinced that the skull was genuine and proved that humans had inhabited central California two million years ago; it was much older than human fossils found anywhere else in the world.

Actually, the skull had been planted as an innocent hoax in Marson's Mine by a couple of miners—at the instigation of John C. Scribner, the local Wells Fargo agent, druggist and operator of a general store at Angels Camp where the miners lived. The skull actually came from the skeleton of a Digger Indian whose grave had been flushed out by floodwaters. Scribner just wanted to confound his friends and especially the local doctor who collected fossils and other curiosities. Before the pranksters realized what was happening, the enthusiastic physician sent the skull off to his friend, geologist Whitney, who in turn made his exuberant announcement. Authorities immediately flocked to Calaveras to investigate and engage in scientific debate. The pranksters decided their only course was to remain silent and escape censure for a joke that had gotten out of hand.

The scientific debate continued for 35 years, during which time druggist Scribner held his peace. He revealed the truth only to his sister and the Reverend Mr. Dyer, rector of the Episcopal Pro-Cathedral of Los Angeles, who were barred from saying anything about it until he was dead. By 1911 both Scribner and Whitney were dead and the bearers of the secret disclosed the story, but not with any ease. The *Los Angeles Times* refused to print their account, explaining, "History seems to stick to the delusion."

Finally, however, scientific research exploded the Calaveras Man myth. The earth matrix found inside the skull did not at all match the gravels of the mining pit, confirming druggist Scribner's private confession.

CALISTOGA SPRINGS WATER SCAM *gold flour salting plot*

A decade or so after the initial discovery of gold in California in 1848, the finds were still coming in strong, although perhaps not in as many guises as fraud among the gullible. One of the most outrageous frauds was a promotion originating in Calistoga Springs, California, which claimed the local waters were so rich with tiny particles of gold that the promoter was extracting from $5 to $10 worth from each barrel of water. While it is true that flour gold can sometimes be so fine that it will float in water, Calistoga Springs definitely had no flour gold, other than what the promoter had filtered into his samples. It was Mark Twain, a notable hoaxer in his own right (and deflator of others' hoaxes) who burst the bubble of Calistoga gold. Responding to an account concerning the claim, Twain wrote:

> I have just seen your dispatch from San Francisco in Saturday evening's Post. This will surprise many of your readers but it does not surprise me, for once I owned those springs myself. What does surprise me, however, is the falling off of the richness of the water. In my time the yield was a dollar a dipperful. I am not saying this to injure the property in case a sale is contemplated. I am saying it in the interest of history. It may be that the hotel proprietor's process is an inferior one. Yes, that may be the fault. Mine was to take my uncle (I had an extra one at that time on account of his parents dying and leaving him on my hands) and fill him up and let him stand fifteen minutes, to give the water a chance to settle. Well, then I inserted an exhaust receiver, which had the effect of sucking the gold out of his pores. I have taken more than $11,000 out of that old man in less than a day and a half.
>
> I should have held on to those springs, but for the badness of the roads and the difficulty of getting the gold to market, I consider that the gold-yielding water is in many respects remarkable, and yet no more remarkable than the gold-bearing air of Catgut Canyon up there toward the head of the auriferous range. This air, or this wind—for it is a kind of trade-wind which blows steadily down through 600 miles or richest quartz croppings—is heavily charged with exquisitely fine, impalpable gold.
>
> Nothing precipitates and solidifies this gold so readily as contact with human flesh heated by passion. The time that William Abrahams was disappointed in love he used to sit outdoors when the wind was blowing, and come in again and begin to sigh, and I would extract over a dollar and half out of every sigh.
>
> I do not suppose a person could buy the water privileges at Calistoga now at any price, but several good locations along the course of Catgut Canyon gold-bearing trade-winds are for sale. They are going to be stocked for the New York market. They will sell, too.

Needless to say, the great Calistoga Springs water scam drowned in a sea of laughter.

CANCER CURE CONS *quack treatments*

The cruelest—and certainly the most lucrative—of all medical quack cures are those for cancer. Charlatans offer marvelous "new" discoveries to treat this fatal disease, something medical science has been unable to do. The appeal works on the desperately stricken who grasp at any straw for a cure. They abandon the competent doctor for these frauds who often claim they are being harassed by a vindictive medical establishment. The seriously ill spend thousands of dollars on phony treatments that do nothing to relieve their suffering or the disease itself. Frequently, the quack cancer treatment clinic is set up just across the U.S. border, beyond the jurisdiction of American authorities.

Experts warn that before a patient enters any cancer clinic, he should consult his own physician. The experts add there is no one remedy or device that can diagnose or treat all types of cancer, nor can it be detected or treated solely through the use of any machine. No one medical test conducted one time can definitely diagnose cancer, nor can a machine operated by a medical faker cure it.

Postal inspectors regard Norman Baker as perhaps the greatest cancer charlatan they ever had to deal with. Baker defended himself against the authorities with every known legal weapon for nine years before he was finally put out of business. Baker's operations were so prosperous that he even operated hospitals and radio stations and published an Iowa newspaper.

The Baker cancer cure involved feeding patients huge doses of acids and flavored waters. Baker kept his overhead amazingly low by the expedient of serving no substantial foods to his patients. Quite naturally, many patients died, but this in no way prevented Baker from accumulating $4 million in profits from his operations. The paltry penalty he had to pay—four years imprisonment and a $4,000 fine—was nothing by comparison.

Postal inspectors point out that one of the main reasons so many cancer quacks remain in business is that many of their victims, the chief witnesses, die before the case can be brought to trial.

"CANNED GOODS" *Nazi plot to start World War II*

At 10 o'clock on the morning of September 1, 1939, Adolf Hitler addressed the German Reichstag and the German people to justify the German invasion of Poland. He railed about "numerous Polish attacks on German territory, among others an attack by regular Polish troops on the Gleiwitz transmitter."

There had indeed been an attack on the transmitter, as well as a number of other incidents—all deadly hoaxes—which brought on World War II. They were all part of "Operation Canned Goods."

The "canned goods" were concentration camp prisoners who were dressed in Polish army uniforms and left for dead at the scene; they were drugged and shot after allegedly attacking German troops. In the case of the attack on the Gleiwitz transmitter, there had been a change in plans, and it was decided to use SS troops to stage the violence as Polish soldiers. The SS men took the transmitter and broadcast a speech prepared by SS higher-ups declaring the time had come for Poland to attack Germany. The SS attackers left an appropriate canned-goods corpse and departed.

Operation Canned Goods was a smashing success for the Nazis. The one untidy element in the hoax was the SS men who wore the Polish uniforms in the simulated attacks. Their fate was revealed in testimony at the Nuremberg Trials by General Erwin Lahousen of the Abwehr. All the SS men were, as the general described it, "put out of the way."

CAPONE GRAVE HOAX *gangster's double grave*
Some tourists still come to Plot 48 in Chicago's Mount Olivet Cemetery, where there is a marble shaft and a headstone that reads:

QUI RIPOSA
Alphonse Capone
Nato: Jan. 17, 1899
Morto: Jan. 25, 1947

The only problem with Plot 48 as a tourist attraction is that the grave does not contain a body. It is a unique hoax to mislead the public. The Capone family had originally buried Al Capone—the underworld boss of gangster-infested Chicago—in the family plot in Mount Olivet along with other members of the family. But the family realized, probably almost from the start, that the public would come to the gravesite to gawk. So the family secretly arranged to have Al's casket—as well as all other members of the family—moved to a new family plot at Mount Carmel Cemetery in Hillside, a West Side suburb about 40 minutes from downtown Chicago. The new graves are clustered around a giant slab, and the flat headstones are all inscribed "My Jesus Mercy." Al's headstone is slightly larger than the rest.

There are published guides that now direct tourists to the real Capone grave. (Enter the first gate of the cemetery on Roosevelt Road, west of Wolf Road. Turn right immediately. The Capone plot is on the right about 150 feet from the gate.) But perhaps as many visitors are still decoyed to Mount Olivet. Even in death, America's most notorious gangster continues to be involved in deceit.

CAPONE'S SOUP KITCHEN FRAUD *publicity con*
When the Great Depression reached its low point in the 1930s, Chicago's mob boss Al Capone saw it as the time to play the role of a "socially responsible" gangster, taking care of the city's unemployed. Capone opened a storefront on State Street to provide food and warmth for the destitute. Capone informed reporters he considered it his civic duty to help the jobless. His Loop soup kitchen dispensed 120,000 meals at a cost of $12,000. On Thanksgiving Day Capone proudly declared he was donating 5,000 turkeys.

The soup kitchen was a wonderful publicity ploy by Capone, especially since it hardly cost him a dime, and in fact allowed for some skimming of supplies by the mob. Coffee roasters and blenders were leaned on to supply brew. The packinghouses were required to furnish hearty meat dishes. Bakeries furnished day-old doughnuts and pastries, and the South Water Market Commission merchants came though with potatoes and vegetables. They were all assigned strict quotas, and any who complained that the amount was too much were informed by mob musclemen that the "Big Fellow is very worried that your trucks might be wrecked or their tires slashed."

Good publicity was one thing for Capone, but the ganglord wanted a more tangible return for his good deed. In December 1930, the price of beer (produced at an estimated $4 a barrel) to speakeasies was raised from $50 to $60, supposedly to produce more aid for the poor. Speakeasy owners were informed by Capone's salesmen, "The Big Fellow says we've all got to tighten our belts a little to help those poor guys who haven't got any jobs." It proved, said writer Ben Hecht, "good deeds provide their own rewards."

CAPTAIN OF KÖPENICK *celebrated German imposture*
In Prussia in 1906, Wilhelm Voigt (1849–1922) became famous for concocting the boldest military impersonation ever. Voight, a 57-year-old cobbler by trade, was an unsuccessful criminal who had spent a total of 27 years in prison for various petty crimes. Now, however, he had masterminded a most delicious caper. Voigt understood that in Germany of that day nothing was more respected than a military uniform. He went out and bought a secondhand captain's uniform of the Prussian Guards, one of the most illustrious of all units.

With merry abandon Voigt wore his uniform about Berlin, perfecting his official style. He attended a brewery exhibition and, as he strolled through the stands, soldier after soldier sprang to attention as he passed.

Then Voigt polished his Prussian officer's "bark." On October 16, 1906, he marched into an army barracks, rounded up 10 grenadiers and yelled for them to follow him on an important mission. It never occurred to any of the soldiers to question Voigt's authority, his uniform sufficing. Voigt marched them to the railway station and entrained them for the small town of Köpenick outside the capital.

On their arrival, the domineering captain quick-marched his men to the town hall, placed guards on all entrances, and ordered the burgomeister, or mayor, placed under arrest. When the mayor asked the reason, the bogus captain informed him, "I am acting under orders." Then he ordered the local police official to see to it that order was maintained while he completed his assignment, which was to check on municipal irregularities that had been noticed by Berlin officials. Voigt ordered the treasurer brought to him and demanded not only the town books but the entire cash treasury as well. He signed a receipt for the money—a bit over 4,000 marks (a considerable sum at the time)—as "von Alesam, Capt. Guards Reg.," and then commandeered two carriages. He ordered the treasurer in one and the mayor in the other and ordered them off under military guard to be presented to General Moltke for further interrogation. When the mayor's wife became hysterical, the captain gave her permission to accompany her husband.

Voigt himself returned to Berlin, but when he emerged at the railway station, he was no longer wearing his Prussian uniform. He did, however, still have all the loot.

Meanwhile, when the "prisoners from Köpenick" arrived at military headquarters, no one had the slightest idea what to do with them. General Moltke was quite bemused. When it was determined what had happened, a 25,000 mark reward was posted for the impostor captain.

Voigt was captured when he injudiciously attempted to get a passport to attempt to flee Germany. But by then the entire world knew that an unimportant little man had managed to pull off a grand hoax. One German paper said that Prussians "all lie on their bellies before a uniform."

Voigt was tried and convicted and sentenced to four years in prison, but in quick time he was pardoned by Kaiser Wilhelm. It was said that the kaiser himself was most amused by the merry imposture, but others surmised he pardoned the hoaxer because the Prussian military corps complained his imprisonment was giving the army a bad name.

While he was behind bars Voigt received hundreds of marriage proposals from women entranced by his performance. He rejected all of the offers and instead "the Captain of Köpenick"—as the world's newsmen and cartoonists dubbed him—departed for America to perform an autobiographical cabaret act in various German-American communities.

Later he returned to Germany for more public appearances. He retired to Luxembourg on a generous pension from a wealthy Berlin dowager who regarded him as a "national treasure." He died in 1922.

In later years, Voigt's imposture was retold in play and movie comedy form many times.

CARABOO OF JAVASU, PRINCESS *exotic impostor*

The strange girl, lost, dazed, wearing a turban and what appeared to be some sort of oriental garb, was found and taken in by a wealthy family in Almondsbury, England, in April 1817. The master of the house, Samuel Worrall, the recorder of Bristol, was unable to communicate with the girl as she spoke some unknown language. Worrall summoned leading linguists of the area, but all were baffled by the young stranger's tongue. The girl did not respond to spoken words, but reacted to pictures in travel books that Worrall showed her. When she saw a picture on the wall that showed bananas, the girl uttered the word "caraboo" several times, pointing to herself.

Finally, a Portuguese sailor turned up in Bristol and announced he understood the girl's strange dialect. He proceeded to translate her story. The girl was "Princess Caraboo of Javasu who had been kidnapped from this island off Sumatra, sold to pirates and recently shipwrecked on the coast of England."

The story made Princess Caraboo the pride of Bristol, and she was feted by society. Gala parties were held for her and milliners and mantuamakers pressed her with exquisite hats, dresses and laces, to acquaint her with their wares and in the hope of her future patronage. Jewelers lent her gorgeous gems to wear and likenesses of her were done in sketches, engravings and oil paintings, which were sold throughout England. Scholars tried to fill in the missing gaps of her story about Javasu. Many published learned papers on the subject.

Then plans were laid for the Princess Caraboo to be taken to London, even to be presented to George III to promise him the "unobstructed commerce and friendship of her realm," as one report put it.

These grandiose plans did not come about. A newspaper story mentioned a peculiar scar the princess had on her back, and Caraboo was recognized by a woman who once knew her as Mary Baker. It turned out the princess was born in 1795, the daughter of a Devon village cobbler. She ran away at 18 and worked in London for three years as a maid until she was dismissed for stealing. Then she married a man named Baker who had traveled in the Orient. Baker told her much about the area until he deserted her and apparently returned to the Far East.

It was then that the young woman devised her plan to become—with the aid of her Portuguese sailor acquaintance—the exotic Princess Caraboo. When she was exposed, Mary Baker finally confessed all. Yet, incredibly, her appearances continued to draw crowds, people being amazed, or perhaps delighted, that this barely literate girl had been able to fool for more than a year not only the cream of society but also men of learning. Very few tradesmen and the like sought the return of their merchandise, or else they failed to act quickly enough. The bogus Princess Caraboo and her translator decamped, taking with them an estimated £10,000 in booty. Before anyone was aware, Mary Baker sailed for America.

For a number of years thereafter Bristol and its inhabitants were unmercifully ridiculed throughout Britain. Burlesque songs and plays immortalized the Caraboo hoax for many theatrical seasons.

Remarkably, Mary Baker returned to England in 1824, and even tried to show herself as "the former Caraboo." But everyone had had enough and she faded into obscurity. Mary married and spent several decades of her life with her husband in the leech trade—something that great master of humbuggery, P. T. Barnum, saw as "an occupation not without a metaphorical likeness to her early and more ambitious exploit." She died in 1865.

CARDIFF GIANT *most brazen scientific hoax in history*

There is some question as to whether the perpetrators of the infamous Cardiff Giant find—labeled by Richard Milner in *The Encyclopedia of Evolution* as "the most brazen scientific hoax in history"—intended it as a hoax or as a swindle, which it inevitably became. The brain of the operation was one George Hull, a former cigar maker in Binghamton, New York, who appears to have been something of a freethinker. In 1868 he heard a fire-and-brimstone preacher, the Reverend Turk, orate on *Genesis*, stating "There were giants on the earth in those days."

Exasperated with such sermonizing, Hull determined to give the clergyman and others of his kind the giant they deserved. Hull obtained a five-ton block of gypsum in Iowa and shipped it to Edward Salle, a stonecutter in Chicago, who shaped it into a man of giant proportions. Salle aged the figure with sand, ink and sulfuric acid and used darning needles to punch pores into his creation.

Hull proceeded to take his giant baby in hand and had it transported to the farm of his cousin, William Newell, near Cardiff, New York. After it was planted in the ground for about a year, the alleged fossilized remains of an authentic giant was "discovered" by farmer Newell. Here, at last, was proof of the huge men who had in ancient times walked the earth!

The figure, 10 feet 4½ inches tall and 2,990 pounds in weight, became an overnight sensation. A Syracuse newspaper heralded the find "A WONDERFUL DISCOVERY," and Hull and Newell pitched a tent and began exhibiting the giant for five cents a view. As news of the find spread around the country and the world, thousands descended on Cardiff to see fossil evidence of human evolution. The hoaxers raised the admission price to 50 cents and then to $1. Meanwhile, the scientific community divided on the find, but most tended to believe it. Two Yale professors, a chemist and a paleontologist, agreed it was a true fossil. The director of the New York State Museum thought the giant was really a statue, but said it was indeed most ancient and "the most remarkable object yet brought to light in this country." Others, including Ralph Waldo Emerson and Oliver Wendell Holmes, agreed. Cornell's president labeled the giant a gypsum forgery, and paleontologist O. C. Marsh pronounced it "remarkable—a remarkable fake."

However, nothing stopped the crowds. In New York the great showman and humbug, P. T. Barnum, offered $60,000 for a lease on the giant for three months. When the offer was rejected, the undeterred Barnum hired a sculptor, Professor Carl C. F. Otto, to fashion an exact copy of the giant. When Hull and Newell brought the Cardiff Giant to New York City in 1871 for exhibit, they were chagrined to discover the showman was already displaying his version in Brooklyn, thus giving the public a multiple choice in giants.

Newell and Hull took Barnum to court. While the legal case was pending, newspapermen were busy tracking Hull's activities and discovered his purchase of gypsum in Iowa and its consignment to Chicago. Salle, the stonecutter, was unearthed and confessed all. Hull in turn confessed his fraud but insisted his aim had not been profits but rather to ridicule the clergy. With Hull's confession, Barnum escaped legal consequences by claiming all he had done was exhibit a hoax of a hoax. Hull and Newell had spent about $2,200 to make their fake and said their profits were $33,000. Other estimates placed their loot between $44,000 and $110,000. Barnum actually made out better, garnering a profit of at least $150,000. He continued to display his "authentic fake" for many years.

The original fake is today displayed in an earthen pit at the Farmer's Museum in Cooperstown, New York.

CAR RESALE SWINDLE *false-arrest scam*

Few business people are more attuned to dealing with "deadbeats" than a car dealer. They especially worry about turning over an expensive automobile in a payment by check. This shouldn't be a worry when a customer has established credit with a bank, so that he can pick up his car on a Saturday morning (when the banks are closed). But this is precisely when the

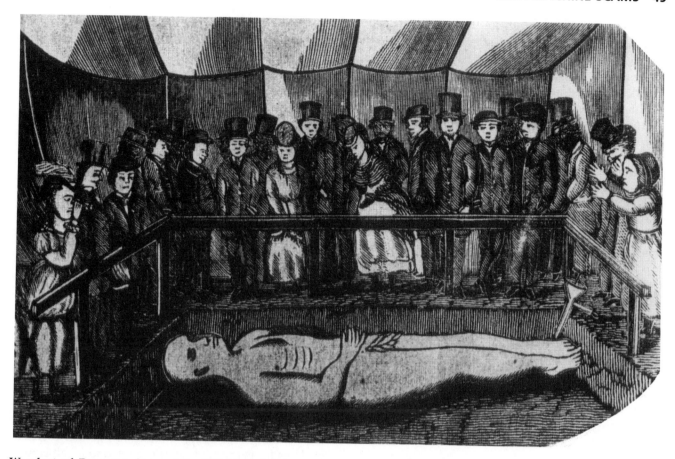

Woodcut of Barnum's bogus "Cardiff Giant." Purported to be the fossil remains of an authentic giant man, it was actually cut out of gypsum and planted near Cardiff, New York, for later discovery.

car resale swindler shows up. He pays for a car in full by check and drives off.

A few hours later, he drives his new car into a used car lot and offers to sell it for half what he just paid for it. Let us say he pays $12,000 and then offers the car to the used car dealer for $6,000. He makes all kinds of silly excuses to explain why he needs money in a hurry, but the dealer, who notices the bill of sale was made out the same day, is naturally highly suspicious. Under some pretext he excuses himself for a few minutes and puts in a fast call to the car dealer who made the sale. The car dealer, holding a check for $12,000, is panic-stricken and races over with a policeman.

"Trying to push off a rubber check on me," he snarls at the car owner. "Officer, place this man under arrest."

The officer obliges and the car dealer breathes a sigh of relief at how close he came to losing $12,000. However, on Monday morning the car dealer is feeling much differently. It turned out the check is fully covered by the buyer.

The car dealer has caused the arrest of an innocent person. There is nothing in the law permitting the jailing of a man just because he tries to sell a $12,000

item for $6,000. Now the vindictive car buyer is in a rage. He declares he had gotten a tip on a sure thing at Belmont race track and wanted to bet the entire $6,000 on the "C" horse in the 9th race. He says the horse won at 4 to 1 so "you cost me $18,000 in profits besides throwing me in the can."

It goes without saying the car dealer will have to pay far more than $18,000 in damages in what is an unprovable swindle.

CASH MACHINE SCAMS

The explosive growth of bank cash machines has inevitably been accompanied by theft techniques concocted by ingenious scam artists. Recently, in New York City, a bank card customer approached a cash machine during evening hours and found a handwritten sign reading: "Sorry for the inconvenience. Minimum withdrawal $300."

The card holder had wanted to withdraw much less but decided to take the full $300, the maximum allowed on this particular machine. He inserted his card, punched out his code and saw the money drop into a withdrawal slot. However, when he tried to raise the slot cover, he found he could not open it. Bewildered for a time, he finally noticed two tiny screws inserted in the slot cover, one on each side. They had effectively sealed the cover. The man left the outer bank lobby in search of a police officer. Returning after going only one block, he found the screws removed and his $300 gone.

Bank card machines are designed to thwart thieves, but for every safety method, the scam artists design a new stealing technique. The bank announced it would alter the slot cover design on its machines, but this was regarded by experts as offering little hope for success. The slot covers on some machines were designed to replace certain types of money dispensers that dropped the cash through an open slot. These were plugged by the scam artists using various wax sprays and the like. The money could in turn be cleared out by the thieves at their leisure after the customer left. Most cash machines have a special telephone connection to the bank machine's main office for a customer to call on the spot when such a caper is in the works. The crooks generally put the communication system out of service as well.

Police advise bank card customers to be wary when using cash machines, and to walk away from any machine that seems to have any sort of unusual problem. It is recommended that a card user frequent only a machine that has been observed in good working order for another customer first.

CATALOG CONS   *fake salesmen*
They present themselves as "catalog representatives" who make personal house calls to exhibit several glossy catalogs put out by large reputable retailers. They explain that mail order costs have become so high that many catalog firms are now shifting much of their business to personal representatives. And, since they are doing so, they save an enormous amount on catalog printings and mailings.

As a result, the salesman declares that the catalog firms can offer a special 10-and-10 bargain deal. "You pay ten percent down," the salesman explains, "and we can give you ten percent off the price listed in the catalog and there are no shipping charges."

The salesman takes the down payment. He will never return, and the ordered goods never arrive either. The con may seem transparent, but the thought of getting a bargain on catalog purchases is enticing to many victims who think they are getting a special deal without having to leave their homes.

CAT AND RAT RANCHES   *journalistic hoax*
Some journalistic hoaxes start out with at least some mitigating motive or intent, but, satire, alas, is seldom understood for what it is by much of the public and a rather large segment of the press. In 1875 Willis B. Powell, editor of the Lacon, Illinois, newspaper, had become so tired of the flood of fraudulent

moneymaking offers appearing in newspaper ads that he produced and published a hilarious scheme of his own, intended to be what a later era might call "The Mother of All Get-Rich-Quick Satires." The ad Powell created read:

> Glorious Opportunity to Get Rich—We are starting a cat ranch in Lacon with 100,000 cats. Each cat will average 12 kittens a year. The cat skins will sell for 30 cents each. One hundred men can skin 5,000 cats a day. We figure a daily net profit of over $100,000. Now what shall we feed the cats? We will start a rat ranch next door with 1,000,000 rats. The rats will breed 12 times faster than the cats. So we will have four rats to feed each day to each cat. Now what shall we feed the rats? We will feed the rats the carcasses of the cats after they have been skinned. Now Get This! We feed the rats to the cats and the cats to the rats and get the cat skins for nothing.

The Associated Press picked up the story and it was printed in newspapers from coast to coast. And, needless to say, eager investors from all parts of the country sought to get in on the cat and rat ranches.

CAT-WANTED HOAX
An advertisement in a Chester, England, newspaper in 1815 made an urgent call for cats and offered "sixteen shillings for every athletic full-grown cat, ten shillings for every adult female puss, and a half crown for every thriving kitten that can swill milk, pursue a ball and thread or fasten its young fangs in a dying mouse."

The felines were needed, alleged the advertiser, to battle a rodent plague on St. Helena, where Napoleon Bonaparte was exiled. Sadly, this was all a hoax with tragic consequences, as 3,000 people converged on the address listed in the newspaper and found only a vacant house. Five thousand hapless cats ended up being flung into the Dee River by their owners.

The same sort of hoax was perpetrated on New Yorkers during World War I, ostensibly for cats needed by American prisoners of war held in Germany to combat rats. But in this case the cats happily did not become the victims of the cruel joke.

CELEBRITY SCAMS
One of the prices of fame is that celebrities are constantly besieged by fans and admirers for some kind of souvenir. The incorrigible rogue, Bat Masterson—about whom it has been said there have been more lies told about his alleged gunfighting than any other Wild West character—turned that predicament into a money-making scam. In his final years as a New York sportswriter Masterson took to notching guns he picked up at hock shops and junk stores with 20 or more carvings and peddling them to the more gullible members of his admiring legions. As west-

Bat Masterson, a notorious western rogue. His gunfighting exploits were more vastly exaggerated than those of any other character of his era.

ern encyclopedist Denis McLoughlin has noted, "It is quite conceivable that dozens of 'this was Masterson's' sixgun are still going the rounds."

Johann Strauss hoaxed his admirers not for profit but for pure self-preservation. When he visited the United States in 1872, accompanied by his black long-haired retriever, Strauss was mobbed everywhere, since his "Blue Danube" waltz was at the time nearly as popular as "Yankee Doodle." It became the rage among his female admirers to seek a lock of hair from the composer's distinctive black mane.

Strauss distributed these gifts by the hundreds during his tour and by all rights should have ended up bald, but amazingly his head was unscathed. The mystery remained unsolved for Strauss watchers until the day of the composer's departure from New York. According to an observer, his retriever (kept out of sight much of the time) "now looked more like a well clipped poodle."

CHADWICK, CASSIE *impostor and swindler*

One of this country's most daring swindles began one day in New York City when Mrs. Cassie Chadwick (1857–1907), the wife of Leroy Chadwick of the socially prominent Cleveland Chadwicks, ran into a lawyer who was a friend of her husband. She asked him if he would please drive her over to her father's house. The lawyer was startled when she gave the address as that of Andrew Carnegie, the millionaire and philanthropist. The lawyer waited in his car-

riage while Mrs. Chadwick blustered her way inside the mansion, asking to speak to the housekeeper, whom she had telephoned earlier in the day for an appointment. Cassie explained that she wanted to check on the reliability of one Hilda Schmidt, whom she was thinking of hiring as a maid, now that she had left the Carnegie employ.

"Why I never heard of her," the housekeeper said.

Cassie exchanged a surprised look with the housekeeper, and the women engaged in an amused conversation about the "deception of some people." Mrs. Chadwick asked if she might use a table to do a bit of writing, as the lack of a maid would cause her some problems. The housekeeper graciously permitted her to do so, and it was some 25 minutes later that Cassie left the mansion, with a wave back to the housekeeper who came to the door with her.

When Mrs. Chadwick reached the lawyer's carriage she was stuffing the contents of a large envelope back into it; but the lawyer noted that one of the papers was a note signed by Andrew Carnegie, giving her the rights to draw on a half-million dollars. The lawyer now had no doubts whatsoever that Cassandra Chadwick truly was Carnegie's daughter, even though he was a renowned bachelor. Swearing the lawyer to secrecy, Cassie informed him that she was Carnegie's illegitimate daughter to whom he had given millions to appease his guilt. Cassie said that he had given her some $7 million over the years, but it was nothing compared with the $400 million she would inherit. If the lawyer had kept Cassie's secret she would have been both amazed and disappointed.

Cassie had been born Elizabeth Bigley on a Canadian farm in 1857 and had always been a girl on the lookout for something better. While in her teens she had printed up business cards that read: "Miss Bigley—Heiress to $15,000." The act was good enough to let her fleece a number of gullible storekeepers by running up huge credit balances until she left town. In her 20s she was an accomplished con woman and mulcted numerous railroad travelers out of considerable sums of money with a number of tales of woe. She also got into blackmail until finally arrested and sent to prison for three years in Ohio.

After her prison stint, Cassie became a resident of a plush New York brothel where she met her husband-to-be, whom she assured she was on the premises only to lure the women back to the good and proper life. Chadwick believed her tale and married her.

In the late 1890s Cassie thought up her Carnegie caper. Shortly after her performance with the lawyer she showed up at a leading Cleveland bank, where the president's cloying attitude clearly indicated he had heard from the lawyer. Cassie then turned over to the banker some $7 million worth of allegedly valid securities for safekeeping. She implored him to keep her relationship to Carnegie secret, which meant, of course, that the news spread throughout banking circles and among the city's social set. Cassie Chadwick was now really somebody, and she won invitations to the leading social functions. Bankers also offered their services without being asked. And yes, Mrs. Chadwick allowed, she might be able to use a loan or two against future payments from her tycoon father.

She made a practice of taking out "small loans"—all under $100,000—and repaying them promptly by taking out other loans from different banks and private lenders. Then Cassie really got busy and borrowed millions at high interest, but considering all that Carnegie money behind her, the bankers were sure she was good for it.

Cassie's scheme was so outrageous that it was above question. Certainly no one was going to approach the great Carnegie for confirmation. The Chadwicks expanded their activities further, traveling regularly to Europe and entertaining lavishly whenever they returned to Cleveland. Mrs. Chadwick became a public benefactor too, but she could well afford it, having suckered the banks out of upwards of $20 million.

The bubble finally burst in 1904, when the *Cleveland Press* became aware of a Boston creditor who had doubts that he would get his money back. The *Press* dug into Cassie's background and found she was Elizabeth Bigley, a convicted forger who had been pardoned in 1893 by Ohio Gov. William McKinley. When the news broke, Charles T. Beckwith, president of the Citizens National Bank of Oberlin (to whose institution Cassie owed $1.25 million), promptly swooned of heart failure. There was a panicky run on the bank and on dozens of others that had made loans to Cassie.

Cassie had been on a New York shopping spree when the story surfaced. She was arrested and shipped back to Cleveland. She was tried and sentenced to 10 years in prison. She died there in 1907. Despite Carnegie's angry statement that he was not Cassie's father, there were many who firmly believed that the steel magnate would someday admit all and make good on her debts. As such it was a powerful affirmation of the fact that there's a sucker reborn every minute.

CHAIN LETTERS See PYRAMID SCHEMES.

CHAKHVASHVILI, "PROFESSOR" DAVID *scientific impersonator*

For years in the 1960s and '70s a Moscow janitor named David Chakhvashvili found it highly profit-able to supplement his income by masquerading as a science professor. Although totally unschooled in science, Chakhvashvili successfully lectured university students on such subjects as "The Atom," "Modern Medicine," "The Technical Revolution" and various other technical topics. Finally arrested by Soviet police, Chakhvashvili was said to have disappeared from detention. The pre-glasnost public record does not appear to reveal if the learned janitor ever surfaced again.

CHARITY CONS *gouging the giving*

The cause sounds worthy and the solicitor seems to be so sincere. However, one should beware of a charity one has never heard of or one that has a name that sounds similar but is not exactly the same as some well-known charitable group. Some swindlers start their own charity—one that helps only themselves—to take advantage of the natural instinct people have to aid the unfortunate.

One fake operating under the name of "Ex-GI Plastic," starting in the 1940s and throughout the 1950s, sent out cheap crucifixes or a plastic "four-way medal" and asked donations to aid "the partially disabled veteran who is making this effort of seeking to succeed." If the statement made little sense it worked on many people who thought they were helping disabled veterans. The operator, the sole beneficiary of the operation, was an ex-GI, with a 10% disability owing to a nervous condition. He was hauling in $50,000 a year from the operation until he was put out of business by postal authorities.

Another character a few years later mailed out St. Christopher medals along with small circulars stating that, as the Religious Distributing Company, with drops from Florida to Pennsylvania, he was operating for his own benefit. However, because of the company name, which clearly presented a religious appeal, postal authorities checked the venture and interviewed scores of addressees who said they had not noticed or paid any attention to the disclaimer. The suckers sent in money to the tune of $1,200 a day, thinking it was for religious purposes. Criminal action was taken to put this operation out of business.

There are ways one can make sure that money one gives gets into the right hands. Always ask for identification of both the solicitor and the charity, and find out the charity's specific activities, how funds are expended and if contributions are tax deductible. Mailed appeals should address all of these questions. If the answers are unsatisfactory or leave matters in doubt, don't give, or at least not until checking with the Better Business Bureau. Generally, the best rule is to give to charities that you know.

CHASTITY BELT FORGERIES

While there is evidence of the use of chastity belts since around 1400 when they were apparently invented in Italy, the frequency of their employment has been greatly exaggerated. A publication of the British Museum notes: "The evidence for their use in the Renaissance period, however, is largely anecdotal or in burlesque fiction. It is probable that the great majority of examples now existing were made in the eighteenth and nineteenth centuries as curiosities for the prurient, or as jokes for the tasteless."

By the 20th century, the few genuine chastity belts that existed were salted away in private holdings, and frustrated collectors fell victim to unscrupulous dealers who fabricated supposedly ancient devices. The late, exiled King Farouk of Egypt supplemented his fabled private collection of pornography with dozens of chastity belts, later regarded as spurious. Perhaps the most compulsive collector was Ned Green, the profligate son of American millionaire eccentric Hetty Green. Green was a sucker for chastity belts, but insisted on only having those that were diamond-encrusted (which few, if any, originals were). After Green's death, his collections were auctioned off, and it was revealed that just as the belts themselves were faked, many of the diamonds were badly flawed as well.

Perhaps the saddest blow of all to the chastity belt myth was delivered by the Cluny Museum in Paris in 1950, when it stopped displaying all but one of its famed collection, having concluded all of them were fakes. One remained on public view to serve merely as a curiosity.

CHASTITY FRAUDS

Generally speaking, chastity fraud court cases are less prevalent than the public believes. They were long associated with seduction and divorce cases, but court rulings have narrowed the parameters of such cases, especially in matters of seduction. In recent years, seduction prosecutions—e.g., persuading a chaste female to have sexual intercourse under a promise of marriage or by means of a fraudulent representation—have greatly declined as a result of the sexual revolution. The crime is effectively and legally erased if the man marries the woman. When a man has taken this escape hatch, however, the courts have been loath to release him from the commitment even if he subsequently is able to prove chastity fraud. In cases where the man develops the proof that he was not the only recipient of the woman's favor, the courts today almost always rule that only a fool involved in an illicit relationship would believe he was the sole individual so favored.

Chastity fraud no longer is very effective in divorce cases either. In New Jersey an ex-prostitute convinced a man to marry her by claiming that she had been chaste and that he had seduced her. The man learned the truth after the marriage, but he failed to convince the court to dissolve the marriage. The court declared:

> Certainly it would lead to disastrous consequences if a woman who had once fallen from virtue could not be permitted to represent herself as continent and thus restore herself to the rights and privileges of her sex, and enter into matrimony without incurring the risk of being put away by her husband on discovery of her previous immorality. Such a doctrine is inconsistent with reason and a wise and sound policy.

Obviously, in cases of chastity fraud, let the lover beware.

CHATTERTON, THOMAS *literary forger*

There are many distinguishing characteristics in the tragic career of Thomas Chatterton (1752–1770) as a literary forger. It was one of the shortest (he lived only 17 years and nine months), yet one of the most prolific.

Chatterton's career as a forger was to give him lasting fame, praised by a number of great poets for his contributions to our appreciation of medieval poetry. Among those who have hailed him are Coleridge, Shelley, Keats, Crabbe, Byron, Scott and Rossetti. In France, the Romantics cheered his example. Yet virtually everything he wrote was a fraud.

Born in 1752 in Bristol, England, and raised by his widowed mother, Chatterton created his first literary forgery at the age of 11, the duologue of "Elinoure and Juga," allegedly a 15th-century poetic work. Already Chatterton had begun to "medievalize" himself by brooding over old parchments his uncle had found in a Bristol church. Sensitive, imaginative, hard to manage and often obnoxious, he lived in a private world of his own historic fantasies. He wrote some poetry in the English of his own time but found little interest in it by publishers and critics, who regarded it as undistinguished. But when Chatterton wrote in 15th-century style he was a genius. His greatest work was the legend of Thomas Rowley, supposedly a priest of the Parish of St. John in the City of Bristol during the reign of Henry IV. After first trying to sell the material to a London bookseller (who ignored it), he sent some of his Rowley manuscript to Horace Walpole. This was not a bad choice considering Walpole himself had published *Otranto* as a medieval original five years earlier before admitting his authorship in the second edition.

Walpole was greatly taken by the Rowley tale and asked Chatterton to submit more. The prolific youth complied, having no shortage of material. Unfortu-

Two portraits of poet Thomas Chatterton, who died by his own hand before he was 18 years old. Chatterton remains a tragic figure now regarded as a forger, hoaxer, liar, impostor—and genius.

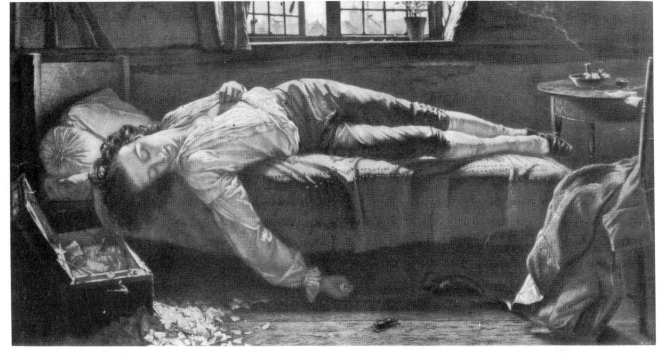

nately, Walpole passed them on to Thomas Gray and William Mason, who both declared them forgeries— only for the reason that the form and meter were not those of the 15th century. Walpole wrote a severe letter to Chatterton, advising him to seek some sort of commercial employ instead of being a poetic forger. By this time it was not clear if Chatterton even believed he had created a fake, so complete was his identification with the fictitious Rowley.

Frequently despondent, Chatterton headed for London in April 1770, ignoring Walpole's admonishment. He sold a few Rowley poems to various periodicals but was paid so poorly that he was soon on the edge of real starvation. Failing to get a post on an African trader, the morose Chatterton—literally without food—penned a farewell poem and then killed himself by drinking arsenic. He was buried in a pauper's grave.

Today his poems fill two volumes, and many literary experts agree that had he labeled his writings as imitations instead of originals, he would have gone on to achieve fame as a great poet if he had not killed himself. (This is hardly true since had he not committed suicide he would have starved to death within a few days.)

When Chatterton's remaining manuscripts were published in 1777, his editor held Walpole partly responsible for Chatterton's death. Walpole countered he had no duty to help an impostor. Oliver Goldsmith, with his usual warmheartedness, felt the Rowley poems were genuine. Dr. Samuel Johnson laughed at his friend for that, adding: "This is the most extraordinary young man that has encountered my knowledge. It is wonderful how the whelp has written such things." Wordsworth described him as "the marvelous boy" and Coleridge wrote a "monody" to him. Shelley commemorated the boy in "Adonais" and Keats dedicated *Endymion: A Poetic Romance* to him and was himself greatly influenced by Chatterton's works.

Ironically, one English writer recently included him in a catalog of the 600 greatest criminals of all time. Chatterton might have been a forger, hoaxer, liar, impostor and even a genius, but he hardly could be called a criminal.

CHECK-PASSING "DRUNKS" *con game*
The successful art of passing rubber checks generally involves the criminal's ability to inspire the victim's trust. However, another routine, the act of appearing to be drunk, is so rewarding that almost every professional rubber check artist has used it many times in his career. The check passer walks into a bar and proceeds to drink enough so that he appears to have gotten cockeyed. He acts careless with his

change and, apparently without noticing, even knocks a coin or two behind the bar.

Having properly set the stage, he then asks the bartender to cash what appears to be a valid payroll check. Normally a bartender might seek proof for the check's authenticity, but now he is more taken by the tippler's apparent lack of alertness and sees an opportunity to shortchange him. The bartender eagerly accepts the check, cashes it and shorts the tippler $10 or $20. Sometimes the check passer's routine is so convincing that another patron will volunteer to cash the check for him—and similarly seek to beat him. Some professionals have admitted this scam is good for $25,000 to $50,000 a year as they move from city to city and bar to bar.

CHESS-PLAYING AUTOMATON *mechanical hoax*
In many respects Johann Nepomuk Maelzel (1772–1838), the Austrian impresario and showman, was a forerunner of Rube Goldberg. He started out as a music teacher, but found that boring and devoted his full time to eccentric musical instruments and other useless inventions. Among these were an automatic trumpeter, speaking dolls, tiny mechanical birds that flew out of boxes and an exhibit that depicted the "Conflagration of Moscow." Maelzel's first great success was the panharmonicon, a device he touted as a mechanical orchestra. It consisted of a connected assortment of wind instruments through which a bellows blew, the notes governed by a revolving brass cylinder with pins. Maelzel even talked Ludwig van Beethoven into composing *Wellington's Victory* for it in commemoration of the duke's triumph over Napoleon. Maelzel made plans to tour the Continent with Beethoven to put the musical machine through its paces. After a few performances, Beethoven accused Maelzel of cheating him and withdrew the piece. (It is still played today by human musicians, to mixed opinion among music lovers.)

However, Maelzel is better remembered for an even more bizarre contraption known as "The Turk," a supposedly mechanical chess player that could easily beat any human competition. This mechanical nonwonder, which Maelzel did not invent, nevertheless draped him with the mantle of charlatan extraordinaire.

The Turk was a machine fashioned in the form of a massive Turkish man, carved in wood and complete with turban, robes and a bevy of jewels. He was seated behind a wooden chest with a chess board carved on its top. Maelzel had bought the Turk from its French inventor and took it on tour in the United States in the 1820s. At the Turk's New York premiere, Maelzel opened a series of doors in the wooden chest to expose the machine's mechanical innards to

A variation of Maelzel's "Turk," a supposedly mechanical chess player.

the audience. Then, after Maelzel opened and closed each door in turn, he asked for a volunteer to compete against the chess-playing contraption. Several in the audience volunteered and the first opponent stepped forward. The Turk disposed of him in a half hour, the audience cheering wildly.

"Nothing of a similar nature has ever been seen in this city that will bear the slightest comparison with it," glowed the *New York Evening Post*.

However, in reality it had not been a case of man vs. machine, but rather man vs. machine and man or, more accurately, a woman who squeezed into the innards of the Turk—shifting about as doors were opened—and made the Turk's moves. She was a French woman who filled in until Maelzel imported a French chess player to take over.

The Turk was a smash hit as it toured a number of cities. Then, in May 1827, near-disaster struck in Baltimore. Two boys who had sneaked backstage saw the human chess player emerge from the Turk. The story was on the front page of the next day's issue of the *Baltimore Gazette*. Maelzel brazened it out, calling the boys little fibbers. He decided to put the Turk in storage for several months until things blew over. The Turk's cover was blown for good in 1837 when a down-and-out former chess-playing pal of Maelzel told the Paris magazine *Pittoresque* how the Turk really worked.

Maelzel decided it was time to leave the east coast and ventured into the middle of the country and then down to New Orleans. The Turk's appeal waned, however, as increasingly speedy communications of the day exposed the hoax. He tried Cuba but the Cubans stayed away in droves after learning the truth. Then Maelzel's chess-playing "inside man" died in Havana in 1838. The depressed impresario, down to

his last few dollars, booked passage to Philadelphia aboard the *Otis*. He locked himself in his stateroom and guzzled down endless bottles of cheap wine to drown his grief. A week later Maelzel was found dead in his bunk.

CHICAGO MAY *queen of the con women*

Clear proof that swindling is not the exclusive preserve of men is the career of the fabulous Chicago May (1876–1935), known alternatively as Queen of the Con Women and Queen of the Badger Game.

Of course, May Churchill Sharpe did not invent the badger game, in which a gentleman is invited to a lady's room on the promise of being "done for" and ends up being "done out" of his money through blackmail or straight robbery at gunpoint. While not the first practitioner, Chicago May was the racket's greatest exponent in the 1890s.

Her real name was Beatrice Desmond, and she was born near Dublin in 1876. Her Irish family, like many of the day, was large, poor, religious and hard-working. Not one of these attributes met with the girl's approval. When she was 13, she pilfered £60 from her father's strongbox—the family's entire savings—and ran off to America. She was still only 13 when she met and became the mistress of Dal Churchill. Within a few months Churchill, so entranced by the girl, married her. Churchill was hardly a wholesome sort, being in Chicago May's words "a robber, highwayman, safecracker, cattle rustler and general all-around crook." Churchill took the girl west and reached new esteem in her eyes as a member of the notorious Dalton gang. It was not a long-lived feeling. Within a year Dal was caught in a train robbery and strung up by vigilantes in Arizona.

A beautiful widow at 15, May headed for Chicago where she gained her great fame as the Queen of the Badger Game. She used the name of May Churchill Sharpe, but became known as Chicago May. May's technique was to victimize the man in a hotel room by robbing him and stealing his papers. Later she would write her victims and remind them of their "good time" with her and demand more money. If they didn't send money, May threatened to take up the matter with their wives. Invariably, the men handed over money to May's pickup man and retrieved their papers. May felt she was very ethical throughout, since she never tried to take a victim a third time. It was one robbery, one blackmail pitch and out.

Later May refined her act with male accomplices and an older woman who posed as her mother. "Mom" would happen across May and her victim and start screaming for help, which would appear on the scene in the form of a hulking "relative" or "neighbor." The victim would pay through the nose or be faced with the likelihood of having a bloody one.

Later, in her autobiography, May would claim she had accumulated $100,000 by the time she was 16 and $300,000 at 17.

In the mid-1890s May decided the real money was to be found in New York. Her favorite haunt there was Considine's, a famous watering hole and slumming spot for literary, theatrical and sporting folk. In her search for victims, Chicago May once spotted an interesting bushy-haired man and inquired who he was. Informed he was Mark Twain, May made a point of reading up on Tom Sawyer and Huck Finn before approaching Twain. She introduced herself to the author as Lady May Avery of London. She gushed that she so admired Twain's work that she just had to meet him. The next evening Lady Avery and Twain dined together. May had learned that Twain was not a man averse to the more spicy things in life and invited him to join her in Connecticut for a weekend. Twain's eyes lit up but he declined the offer.

"I'm sorry, dear lady," he said, "but I'm off to Washington in the morning and then am going West for an extended period."

May was disappointed by his refusal, but it was nothing compared with Twain's parting words. He kissed her hand and whispered, "I cannot thank you enough for a most amusing time. Of course, I don't believe a word of your story that you are an English noblewoman."

Although that was one of Chicago May's non-triumphs, she became the queen of the New York con, especially after forming an alliance with one of the city's most corrupt police officers, Sergeant Charles Becker, who fed her victims in exchange for 25% of the take.

Later, reform was to hit New York and May got out just in time to head for London. Officer Becker years later went to the electric chair for murder.

In England May became the lover of the brilliant bank robber Eddie Guerin and took part with him in the $250,000 heist of the Paris American Express office. Later the lovers had a falling out, and both were caught by French police. Guerin was shipped to Devil's Island, from where he later made a sensational escape. May was convicted only of transporting the American Express loot to London; she did a stint in an English prison and was then ordered out of the country.

May came back to New York in her 40s and found she was no longer the Queen of the Badgers. Her career thereafter plummeted. She engaged in any number of smaller confidence games with only limited success. Without the needed police protection, she ended up arrested a number of times and served short stints for theft and petty larceny. Only when

May opened what she called a "nice house" in Philadelphia did some of the grandeur return, for a time. Prostitutes vied to work for her and listen to her accounts of the golden days of Chicago May. Then postwar reform hit Philadelphia and May was out of business.

In 1928 Chicago May announced that she had come to the conclusion that crime did not pay, and she produced her autobiography. Although some parts of her book were less than totally accurate, it was still an account of a unique life and era. She wrote: "My old friends, in the police write me letters of encouragement. Christians feel called upon to send me platitudes. Professional crooks berate and praise me. Beggars importune me. Sycophants lather me with adulation. The rich . . . and others . . . patronize me."

The book was at best a modest success, and by the 1930s May could no longer survive by living on her past. The last, withered news clipping about Chicago May is sad and disheartening. She was arrested in Detroit for soliciting male pedestrians, offering them a "good time." Her price: $2. Two years later, in 1935, Chicago May died.

CHIMNEY GYPS See FIREPLACE FIXERS.

CHRISTMAS CARD ENVELOPE SWITCH *cheating a cashier*

The "Christmas card envelope switch" can work at other times of the year with birthday cards, but scam artists prefer the Yuletide season, since many stores hire inexperienced cashiers at that time. The gypster buys a Christmas card for a dollar, paying for it with silver. As the cashier counts up the change, the gypster puts a postage stamp on the envelope and pulls out a wad of dollar bills and says, "Could I have a $20 bill for this? I want to put it in with the card for my mother." The cashier hands over a $20 bill and the gypster stuffs the bill in the envelope with the card and places it in his jacket pocket or her purse.

When the cashier finishes counting the singles, she finds that there are only 19. The gypster takes back the money and counts it as well. He or she is very embarrassed and darned if that isn't all the cash the gypster has. But luckily his or her spouse is outside in the car. "I'll go get another dollar."

The gypster retrieves the sealed envelope and Christmas card and hands it to the cashier, saying, "Here, hold this in your register until I get back." The gypster leaves with the 19 singles and the $20 bill, which is still in his or her possession. The cashier has been given a similar envelope that, when opened (because the customer never returns), yields a piece of paper instead of a $20 bill. The store does not suffer a total loss. The postage stamp on the envelope is perfectly good.

CHRISTMAS CAROL KILLINGS *the deadliest ruse*

One of the deadliest tricks used by murderous criminals first developed in Norway centuries ago. To gain entrance to Christian homes during the Yuletide season, criminal bands would gather in front of such a home and sing Christmas carols. When the residents opened their door to wish the carolers well, the robbers pounced on them, slayed them and proceeded to loot the house.

This bloody scam has endured through the centuries and was used in the 1960s and 1970s in the Philippines by criminals who slaughtered scores of victims.

CHUNG, JOHNNY   See FOOTBALL HOAXES.

CIGAR-FILLED STATUES *smuggling scam*

Five statues in the famed Austria Fountain in Vienna stand today as a tribute to a sculptor's illegal scam to take in a few extra shillings. Working outside Austria, sculptor Ludwig von Schwanthaler (1802–1848) designed hollow bronze statues for the fountain and hid cigars in them to smuggle past customs for resale. However, von Schwanthaler grew ill and died before he could remove the contraband. The statues were erected in the fountain with the cigars still hidden inside them.

CIRCUS GRIFTING *the greatest scam on earth*

Despite much nostalgia today for the American circus, the institution's history is one that rightfully deserves the title of "The Greatest Scam on Earth." The 19th-century American circus employed "performers" and "exhibits" that were short on talent but long on nefarious know-how. One of the chief sources of revenue of the old-time circus was crooked gambling, typically in the form of three-card monte and the shell game (see entries). Circus management often claimed that such evildoers infested the grounds despite their earnest efforts to rout them; in actuality, many of these scam artists were either employed directly by the circus or charged a percentage of their take for the right to operate.

Circus grifting was big business and to operate efficiently required the work of talented con men, dishonest circus management, public and police officials open to bribery and lots of gullible victims. There was never a dearth of supply in any of these categories.

Placards announcing the arrival of a circus in town produced instant excitement in the average community, along with very predictable warnings from church pulpits of the pitfalls awaiting the unwary. The sermons were singularly ignored by the public, who flocked to the circus to be sheared with cold-blooded efficiency by crooks of all sorts. The short-changers and pickpockets grabbed whatever the crooked gambling artists didn't get. As late as the beginning of the 20th century it was common among many smaller circuses to charge shortchangers $35 a week (without salary) to handle ticket booth sales. Using the "rip" and other techniques, shortchangers could well afford the tariff and made out handsomely clipping the "rubes" eager to rush into an exhibit. The lucrative pickpocketing franchise was awarded to professional "dips"; to assist these light-fingered crooks, the master of ceremonies would make it a point to warn patrons to beware of pickpockets. Instantly, most men would quickly feel for their wallets and thus tip off watchful thieves to the pocket in which they had their cash.

The development of the crooked American circus varied notably from the much more honest European version mainly in its mobility. In England for instance, the circus rooted itself in one spot for much longer periods of time, which obviously tempered the larcenous inclinations of the operators. The very footloose nature of the American circus, often in town for only a day or so, inevitably created a criminal business thrust. Knowing they would be in town only a brief time, circus workers and grifters stole from farms, barns and clotheslines. Circus managements left no scam, large or small, unutilized. Balloon stands had special assistants who acted as "balloon busters" (see entry), blowing tacks at balloons to create an instant demand by bawling children for a second or third purchase. In the smaller circuses, many of the exhibits were total frauds. "Siamese Twins," for example, were simply two individuals bound together with a flesh-colored belt. As soon as that particular show closed, the twins separated to handle other exhibits or to take part in some cheating activity.

When a circus pulled up stakes, the grifters were assigned to ride out of town in the "privilege car," one lined with steel plates to protect them from angered victims taken in by the circus' many scams. Many circuses changed their names from year to year, or even from town to town, so that word of their activities could not warn the next community. When a circus returned to a community that had been angered the previous time around, it always sported a new identity, if the same old scams.

Circus grifting was an acceptable practice in virtually all circuses until the 1880s and probably in all except Ringling's until 1900 or a bit thereafter. Most big circuses got rid of the grifters not out of altruism, but rather because they realized the identity and reputation of their circus had become more important than the revenue brought in by grifting. Small-circus grifting died in the Great Depression of the 1930s only because attendance fell off and the circuses could no longer afford to pay the tribute demanded by public officials. Thereafter, and in some places today, such grifting exists only in crooked carnivals.

See also REDLIGHTING.

CITY INSPECTOR SCAM *quick repair confidence game*

There is probably no city in America that has not been plagued by the so-called city inspector scam. Flashing impressive but phony identification, the so-called city inspector says he is making required safety checks of some vital feature of a home, such as the furnace, heater, plumbing, wiring, trees or whatever. The inspector comes up with an allegedly serious defect—the furnace is liable to explode, trees outside the house could snap electrical wires and cause a serious fire, and so on.

Under such circumstances all the inspector can do is issue an on-the-spot injunction calling for the emergency cutting off of electricity or perhaps of the heating system (a ploy very popular during a cold spell) until necessary repairs are made and inspected. However, the inspector says, because the city realizes this will inconvenience homeowners, it has made up a list of emergency repair service firms and contractors who are on call for quick work. If the homeowner wishes, the inspector will summon one.

The repairman who shows up does the unnecessary work quickly and shoddily (if at all) and charges an exorbitant fee. Most homeowners are too terrified and thankful to complain. The clear defense to this racket as advocated by consumer protection groups is to insist on ironclad identification of the inspector and to call the city department the inspector claims to represent. Such telephone numbers should be obtained from the telephone book and not from the inspector.

CIVIL WAR GOLD HOAX *journalistic market coup*

The tribulations of Abraham Lincoln during the Civil War were many, but—according to one White House witness—almost nothing angered Lincoln more than an illegal money scheme aimed at inflating the price of gold. Behind the plot was Joseph Howard, city editor of the *Brooklyn Eagle,* who fabricated a proclamation by President Lincoln.

Along with a reporter named Francis A. Mallison, Howard forged an Associated Press dispatch concerning the supposed proclamation, which began, "In all seasons of exigency it becomes a nation carefully to scrutinize its line of conduct, humbly to approach the Throne of Grace, and meekly to implore forgiveness, wisdom, and guidance." Lamenting the military stalemate in Virginia and disastrous news from Louisiana, the president supposedly called for a national day of "fasting, humiliation and prayer" eight days hence, on May 26, 1864. The bogus proclamation then announced that 400,000 additional men were to be drafted.

The plotters knew that such a draft announcement would jolt financial circles and the stock market and send the price of gold soaring. Thus, several days before the pair launched their hoax, Howard purchased a huge amount of gold on margin, under a variety of names. One can only guess by how many thousands he profited in the coup.

The hoaxers sent young boys out to deliver the phony AP dispatch to various New York newspapers. The information was so shocking that several of the newspapers sought confirmation of the story before printing it. But Howard and Mallison timed the release of the dispatch to newspaper deadlines so that the *World* and the *Journal of Commerce* had to go right to press without checking. The markets were in turmoil when the news hit, and instantly gold started to rise, moving up 10%; fortunes were made and lost in a matter of minutes before the hoax could be exposed.

Receiving reports of the hoax, Lincoln, Secretary of State William H. Seward and Secretary of War Edwin M. Stanton ordered the two newspapers seized because they regarded the report as being politically inspired by enemies of the administration. Only two days later, on May 20, the investigation pointed to Howard and Mallison. In the meantime, however, the two newspapers had been closed and their owners and editors imprisoned. This now led to a firestorm of protest about the Lincoln administration's disregard for free speech, an embarrassing charge for Lincoln who was in the midst of seeking reelection. Almost forgotten in the controversy were Howard and Mallison, who were being held in confinement at Fort Lafayette.

The pair remained imprisoned for three months until Howard's father, an elder in Henry Ward Beecher's church, enlisted the famed minister to petition Lincoln for mercy. Beecher pictured the 35-year-old Howard as "the only spotted child of a large family" who had acted in "the hope of making some *money.*" Seeking to end the entire affair, Lincoln released the culprits.

Lincoln had actually special reason for feeling grateful to the hoaxers. Besides being a crook, Howard was perceptive in his understanding of the political and military situation. A new draft was very much needed. In fact, at the very time the phony proclamation was released, Lincoln had a real one on his desk, calling for the drafting of 300,000 men. When the president saw the impact of the false proclamation on the public and the financial markets, he delayed the real call-up for 60 days until the situation cooled.

COCKROACH EXTERMINATOR   *mail-order gyp*
The so-called cockroach exterminator kit, said to be "100% effective against cockroaches when used as directed," is a frequently used mail-order con. Victims sending money for the kit receive a package containing wooden blocks generally numbered I and II, plus a short sheet of instructions.

The instructions read: "Put Block I on a flat surface. Place cockroach on Block I. Now take Block II and strike down on Block I with force." The kit's purveyors are indeed accurate: When used as directed, the extermination equipment is 100% effective.

When this scam first appeared, authorities adhered to the concept of "Let the Buyer Beware." In recent decades, however, the authorities and the courts have taken a less benign view of the con and have sent practitioners to jail. However, the scam continues to be worked by hit-and-run fraudsters who open and close up shop quickly, hoping to stay ahead of the law.

COLD POKING   *hoaxing female pickpockets*
Pickpockets are easily the most chauvinist criminal group. Female "dips" are never accorded much honor among practitioners, being regarded as capable "lush workers" (stealing money from drunks) or "moll buzzers" (pocketbook thieves), but little else. It is true, in the sense that women make poorer pickpockets, since they can seldom jostle or fondle a man in any way without attracting attention.

However, once in a while a female pickpocket will loudly proclaim her abilities as the equal of any man's, which frequently leads to her being a victim of "cold poking."

A male pickpocket will point out an older man in a nightclub as being loaded and challenge the woman to lift his wallet. The woman does so, but as the older man (actually another pickpocket, in on the hoax) tumbles to her, he screams, "Thief!"

The woman races out of the place and doesn't stop running for a dozen blocks or so until she is sure she has eluded all pursuers. Then she examines the wallet. It is loaded all right, not with money but rather with cut-up pieces of paper decorated with obscene messages and insults.

COLE, HORACE DE VERE   *Britain's master hoaxer*
Horace de Vere Cole (1883–1936) was a young dilettante who studied art, wrote poetry and played outlandish pranks at every opportunity. He was the brother-in-law of later Prime Minister Neville Cham-

berlain, and by contrast bore a close resemblance to Labour Party leader Ramsay MacDonald. As such he frequently appeared among crowds of workingmen and, when called upon to make a speech, he would suddenly start denouncing all of the things MacDonald stood for. He damned the labor unions and heaped praise on the Tories and declared that from that moment on he was having nothing more to do with the depraved Labour Party. His listeners would be stunned for a while, which happily gave Cole sufficient time to make a getaway before a class war erupted.

During his undergraduate days at Cambridge, Cole and a number of students masqueraded as African princes visiting England. Cole, as the Sultan of Zanzibar, made a visit to Cambridge with his friends, whereupon they were given a champagne dinner by university and city officials. In return, Sultan Cole offered "the dorsal fin from the Sacred Shark of Zanzibar—a token of everlasting remembrance."

On another occasion Cole and five students masqueraded as Abyssinian princes, with Cole as Mr. Herbert Cholmondly of the Foreign Office, who escorted them on various tours of England, including being shown through the H.M.S. *Dreadnought* by naval officers in full regalia. In addition to Cole, the other culprits included blackface author-naturalist Anthony Buxton, artist Duncan Grant, the son of a prominent judge named Guy Ridley and a brother-sister team of Adrian and Virginia Stephen (who later gained fame under her married name of Virginia Woolf). Virginia was fearful of being spotted as a woman and limited her words to merely an occasional "Chuck-a-choi, chuck-a-choi." Some of the others went in for "bunga, bunga" or else recited passages of Vergil's *Aeneid*, happily mispronouncing the words so they would not be recognized as Latin or any other known language.

When the hoax became known, the government and the navy were outraged. But the public remained enchanted. "Bunga, bunga" became thereafter a popular phrase for an expression of delight.

Cole could enjoy a good hoax even when he never learned the final outcome himself. Once he was home hanging pictures when he ran out of twine. He hurried to a shop to buy some and on the way back it happened that a most proper Englishman approached. Overwhelmed with the hoax fever, Cole stopped the gentleman and said with proper deference, "I say, I'm in a bit of a spot. We're engaged in surveying this area in order that we may realign the curb, and my assistant appears to have vanished. Could I prevail upon your time for just a few moments?"

It was hardly a proposal a proper gentleman could decline. Cole gave him the end of the twine and proceeded to march off backward around the corner, unwinding the twine as he went. When he ran out of twine, Cole thought to tie it to a lamppost or a doorknob when fortune in the form of another Englishman appeared. Cole made a like request of him and left that gentleman holding the other end of the twine.

Cole went off to purchase a new ball of twine and returned to his picture-hanging chores, deliciously wondering of the outcome to his ruse.

COLORADO MAN *Barnum hoax*

When the Cardiff Giant hoax (see entry) of the 1860s and 1870s had run its course, the incorrigible showman P. T. Barnum was determined to come up with a similar exhibit. He therefore put up $2,000 to have another "ancient man" built in Elkland, Pennsylvania. It was an ambitious effort and, unlike the Cardiff Giant, was not made out of gypsum. Instead it was provided with real bones and "human ingredients" concocted from clay, plaster, stone and dried eggs. To make it seem more ancient, the "man" was given arms that were longer than its legs. The entire mold was baked for two weeks.

Barnum arranged to have it shipped to the Rocky Mountains, where it was found and dubbed "Colorado" man. It just so happened that a traveling "geologist" found the body there while the great Barnum was on a temperance lecture tour. Barnum said he was awestruck by the great discovery and announced he would pay $20,000 for this monumental find. But, in the wake of the Cardiff Giant hoax, scientists descended on the find immediately to determine its genuineness. It was Yale paleontologist O. C. Marsh (who had exposed Cardiff) who now punctured Barnum's Colorado Man as well. The scientist took one look at the figure and declared its very rotundity did not fit with the results of one who had died and fossilized. In such a situation, Professor Marsh pointed out, the abdomen would have collapsed.

Even Barnum did not have the audacity to promote Colorado Man to any great extent after that. While it enjoyed some notoriety and display in the West, the fake never made it to the big time.

COMPANY FOR CARRYING ON AN UNDERTAKING OF GREAT ADVANTAGE, BUT NOBODY TO KNOW WHAT IT IS *grand 18th-century swindle*

In his classic book *Extraordinary Popular Delusions and the Madness of Crowds*, Charles Mackay recounted the hoaxes and manias that gripped much of Europe in especially the 15th to early 18th centuries, such as alchemy and a belief in witches, wolf-men and haunted houses, and such financial frauds as the Mississippi and South Sea bubbles. However, the most incredible hoax of all was one that would not

have been accepted as possible by Mackay's 19th-century readers were it not for scores of credible witnesses. At the height of the Mississippi Bubble and South Sea Bubble crazes (see entries), an even more audacious unknown adventurer announced "A company for carrying on an undertaking of great advantage, but nobody to know what it is."

As Mackay summarizes the colossal caper:

> The man of genius who essayed this bold and successful inroad upon public credulity, merely stated in his prospectus that the required capital was half a million, in five thousand shares of £100 each, deposit £2 per share. Each subscriber, paying his deposit, would be entitled to £100 per annum per share. How this immense profit was to be obtained, he did not condescend to inform them at that time, but promised that in a month full particulars should be duly announced, and a call made for the remaining £98 of the subscription. Next morning, at nine o'clock, this great man opened an office in Cornhill. Crowds of people beset his door, and when he shut up at three o'clock, he found that no less than one thousand shares had been subscribed for, and the deposits paid. He was thus, in five hours, the winner of £2,000. He was philosopher enough to be contented with his venture, and set off the same evening for the Continent. He was never heard of again.

COMPUTER SCAMS *high-tech swindles*

Computer scams are very probable because computer technology is still in its infancy and a smart, fast-moving scam artist can find a weakness in almost any program. The inherent problem is that a swindler can easily commit fraud once he learns the code or password that will activate the system. All the scam artist has to do is link up a keyboard terminal to a touchtone telephone and start issuing orders to the computer.

In one case a bank employee developed a computerized money diversion to steal more than $1 million, money he sorely needed to play the horses. He worked out a computerized handicapping system, but unfortunately it was not nearly as good as his stealing operation.

In another scheme, a bank employee programmed the institution's computer to shift $120,000 from various depositors' accounts to those belonging to a couple of friends. One programmer simply set up a computer to deduct sums from many accounts and pay them into dummy accounts, which the programmer then emptied.

Computer scams are also a headache to the Internal Revenue Service. One IRS programmer set up a system that funneled unclaimed tax credits to the account of a relative. Another simply set up his system so that checks being held for taxpayers whose mailing addresses could not be determined were transferred to his own account.

Some computer scams reach monumental levels, such as the great Equity Funding Corporation swindle, which worked between 1964 and 1973. That looting involved some $2 billion.

Banks remain the most vulnerable institutions for computer frauds. In the pre-computer era it was estimated that there were at least 200 ways to embezzle money from a bank without danger of immediate exposure. Now, in an era of ever advancing technology, experts say it is senseless to even attempt to count the ways. Computer scams remain the ultimate growth industry.

See also EQUITY FUNDING CORP. FRAUD.

COMPUTER VIRUSES AND OTHER FRAUDS

Since the late 1980s the vulnerability of computers to "viruses" has produced a number of actions by hoaxers and fraudsters that threatened various computer networks in the United States and, in some instances, worldwide. In May 1990 Robert Tappan Morris Jr., a former Cornell University graduate student, was sentenced to three years' probation, fined $10,000 and ordered to perform 400 hours of community services for creating a computer virus program that had disrupted a nationwide network. He was the first person sentenced under the federal Computer Fraud and Abuse Act of 1986. The judge refused to give Morris a prison term because he said he could not find "fraud and deceit" in Morris's actions. The defendant had argued he had not intended to close down the Internet Computer network, but had simply set up a program that had gotten out of control and paralyzed or slowed down computers as it made its way along the network.

The greatest computer panic produced was the so-called Michelangelo virus, which terrified computer users around the world in 1992. It was set to be triggered March 6, the birthday of the great Renaissance painter. The threat was that Michelangelo, spread through floppy disks used in personal computers compatible with IBM design, would erase a computer's hard drive.

The perpetrator of Michelangelo set up viruses that were likely to produce whimsical pictures or messages; others were created that would destroy any legitimate data encountered. Virus experts were fearful that over one million computers could have their memories wiped out, and computer users in several countries scrambled to neutralize the anticipated plague with special software.

In the end Michelangelo produced more panic than damage. There were some scattered reports of computer outages in the United States, but there was no link confirmed to Michelangelo. There were some scattered cases of the virus in Europe and South America, while South Africa proved the hard-

est hit. In all about 1,000 computers, most run by pharmaceutical companies, were affected in that country.

If the so-called virus threat proved more heralded than actual, law enforcement in the United States remained more concerned about computer hackers engaged in real fraud activities. In April 1992 California authorities smashed a nationwide fraud network of about 1,000 loosely affiliated young computer hackers who had been able to break into the electronic files of an Atlanta-based credit rating company and, as a result, made millions of dollars worth of fraudulent credit card purchases. The setup was exposed accidentally when San Diego police investigated a local credit card fraud case. In the resultant sweep arrests were made and computer equipment seized in New York, Seattle and the Philadelphia area.

COOK, DR. FREDERICK A. *explorer and business fraud*

Dr. Frederick A. Cook (1865–1940) is infamously known for his false claim of having been the first man to reach the North Pole. The feat was actually accomplished by Robert E. Peary in 1909, about a year after Cook claimed to have done so. At first Cook was celebrated worldwide for his so-called accomplishments, but in due course virtually all scientific findings turned against Cook, who became disheartened and disgraced.

It was not Cook's only fraudulent attempt to seek fame. In 1899, while part of the Belgian Antarctic expedition, Cook borrowed a Yahgan grammar and dictionary compiled by the Reverend Thomas Bridges, who had served as a missionary among the barbarian tribes of Tierra del Fuego. Try as they might, neither the missionary nor his son could pry the manuscript loose from Cook; in due course, there was an announcement that a Yahgan grammar and dictionary was to be published by Dr. Cook. Charles H. Townsend of the New York Aquarium, who knew the facts, intervened with the Belgian Commission and caused the cancellation of the publication plans.

Frustrated in his literary and exploratory claims, Cook turned to other fields, becoming a Wyoming geologist and then an oil promoter near Fort Worth, Texas. He took part in creating the Petroleum Producers' Association and sold its stock through the mails. In 1923 the government found the land worthless, and Cook was convicted of using the mails to defraud. He served seven years in prison and was released from Leavenworth penitentiary in 1930.

Cook spent the last 10 years of his life in poverty, cared for by his daughter Helene, who frantically supported him in all his past claims—the North Pole and the scaling of Mount McKinley. Cook was unsuccessful in filing a lawsuit against the *Encyclopaedia*

Britannica, which stated that his McKinley claim was "universally rejected."

Ironically, the act that landed him in prison had a bizarre twist. By the 1930s the "worthless" lands he had sold were developed by later owners and were worth more than what Cook had charged for them. While this was not a result that Cook could have contemplated, it did appear unseemly to continue holding him responsible. President Franklin Roosevelt granted Cook a pardon in 1940 when the 75-year-old reprobate was on his deathbed.

COOLIDGE HOAXES THE SECRET SERVICE

Among Secret Service agents guarding U.S. presidents, there has never been any doubt as to which man had been their most difficult assignment. Although it is hard for the general public to believe, the dour and unspeaking Calvin Coolidge was the hardest to watch over. Coolidge liked to hide in the White House shrubbery and then jump out and scare his unsuspecting Secret Service guards. Eventually the Secret Service got its revenge.

It all started when Coolidge poked behind some curtains in his office and noticed a button on the wall. He pressed it and sat down at his desk to await developments. Suddenly, the door flew open and a horde of agents charged into the room. The president looked up innocently and inquired as to the meaning of the rumpus. The agents mumbled their apologies and departed.

Coolidge had happened on an alarm the Secret Service had installed throughout the White House to signal imminent danger. Coolidge immediately pressed the button again and the hectic scene was replayed. Over the next week—a time now legendary in the service as an utter nightmare—the president tormented his guards, causing agents to charge and recharge into his office while he kept a straight face.

Finally, a suspicious agent stayed behind out of sight and watched Coolidge do his act again. The agent said nothing, but the wires to the button were cut and, thereafter, whenever Coolidge pushed the button during his two terms, nothing happened. As Secret Service folklore has it, that is the reason Silent Cal never smiled again during the rest of his White House years.

COPPOLA, ROBERTO *priestly impostor*

In 1975, 19-year-old Roberto Coppola (1956–   ) was arrested in Rome, where he had been impersonating a priest for some two years. In the course of his "religious duties," the teenager had performed weddings, heard confessions and celebrated masses by the hundreds. The revelation of Coppola's impersonation sent Italian couples in a scrambled renewal of vows and left the church in considerable turmoil. Coppola's overall judgment of his own activities: "I liked it."

CORNELL'S MYSTERY RHINO *campus hoax*

A hoax of the 1920s at Cornell University concerned a rhinoceros that appeared on campus following a snowfall. At least there were tracks in the snow, which indicated this to be the case. The campus awakened one morning to find the strange tracks, which zoology professors—to their own amazement—identified as rhinoceros tracks.

The trail of the rhino was followed across the campus and down to Beebee Lake. The lake was frozen and the tracks led out across the ice about 15 yards from shore where there was a large gaping hole. It was obvious what had happened: The misplaced rhino—wherever it came from—had ventured out on the ice, crashed through and apparently drowned.

Since Beebee Lake was the source of Cornell's water supply, half the people stopped drinking tap water. Those who continued to drink it insisted they could definitely taste a "rhino flavor" to the water.

Actually there was no rhino, merely a rhinoceros foot wastebasket. A Cornell student, Hugh Troy—who was to become a leading illustrator and throughout his life an accomplished practical joker—had happened across the wastebasket fashioned from a rhino foot, in the home of a friend. He borrowed it and, together with another friend, filled the foot with scrap metal to give it weight and attached a long clothes line to either side. They took positions some 30 feet on each side of the rhino foot and gingerly raised and lowered the line so that the tracks appeared at the logical intervals in the snow.

When the hysteria reached its peak, Troy revealed anonymously in writing—with no identification of the culprits—how the hoax had been worked. The revelation left several red faces in the school's science department. After that the people decided the water at Cornell tasted just fine.

COSTER, F. DONALD See MUSICA, PHILIP.

COUNTERFEIT FAKE SCAMS *passing con*

The age-old counterfeit bill swindle works with many different wrinkles. A common one calls for a young man to enter a store and make a small purchase, such as a pack of cigarettes or candy, and pay with a crisp new $20 bill. He pockets the change, opens the package, makes a remark about the weather to the merchant or clerk and leaves. The store person thus has had an opportunity to take more than passing notice of him.

A few minutes later, an older man dashes into the store, flipping back his coat to show a badge and snaps something like "federal case." He says, "I'm tracing a young man about 27, wearing a blue cap and dark leather jacket. Slender, dark hair. Was he just in your store?"

The cash register person recognizes the description, whereupon the "officer" gets excited. "Did he leave you a $20 bill, a new one with the number — _____?"

There is a fresh $20 bill in the register. The serial number matches. "Counterfeit!" the supposed officer mutters. "He's flooding the area with them. Let me take this. I'll be back in a few minutes. He can't get away. We've got a net around the block."

There is no net around the block and neither the "officer" or the $20 bill come back. He's a phony, although the bill is not.

A middle-aged man-and-woman team particularly adept in the fake counterfeit scam operated for many years in the South. The woman, very bulky in stature—and thus readily remembered—specialized in passing good $50 bills only to have her mate appear as a "Treasury man," flash his spouse's picture, pronounce the $50 bill as bogus, sign a receipt for it (the law requires that counterfeit bills be seized immediately) and leave.

Once the pair hit a total of 18 shops in a Southern town in a single day, passing and requisitioning 17 $50 bills and one $100 bill. Thus the total loot for the day was a tad over $1,000 plus the merchandise.

COUNTERFEIT MONEY BY MAIL

Even an advertisement that might be literally correct can be a swindle and as such punishable by law. This was established in the 1950s by a hard-fought legal case against a small-town Arkansas postmaster who went into the mail-order business with an ad he placed all over the country that read: "Counterfeits? No! Confederate $20.00 sample bill sent by mail for $2.00."

The ambitious postmaster was deluged with responses and made more than a small fortune until the U.S. Postal Service intervened. The postmaster was arrested for fraud, the Postal Service arguing that his intent was to make his victims believe that they would receive a counterfeit $20.00 bill. In federal court the defendant responded that he had sent exactly what he had promised, a $20.00 Confederate bill for $2.00; his advertisements plainly stated that it was not a counterfeit.

The court found that the postmaster was liable for what he intended his victims to believe, and that the wording of his advertisements was beside the point. It was held that the postmaster, by raising the point about counterfeits, had obviously intended to make the uninitiated believe he would send a $20 counterfeit bill.

The decision opened the floodgates for prosecution of a number of mail-order scams previously regarded as immune from prosecution.

See also DETECTIVE LESSONS BY MAIL.

COUNTERFEIT-PASSING SCAMS

While much is made of the perils of counterfeit money, the fact remains that most bills reproduced today are easy to spot as phony. Passers therefore have to find a way to get rid of a bill so that it avoids any close scrutiny. Since the favorite counterfeit bill today is the twenty, one of the more common ploys is to enter a store and make a purchase for a couple of dollars and pay with a fifty. Passers like to zero in on young unsophisticated cashiers, even though they are more likely to be required to call the manager to verify the authenticity of a bill of that denomination.

The bill is confirmed to be genuine (since it is), and the cashier then makes change and packs up the purchase. Meanwhile, the passer makes it look as though he is putting away the change, when on second thought he asks for change of one of the twenties he's just been given. In change for $50 there is almost always at least one $20 bill. The passer asks for a ten and two fives instead, and the cashier obliges, taking back the twenty without giving it a second glance. Of course, the passer has simply switched to a counterfeit bill he'd been palming all along and walks out with a good twenty for a bad one.

CREDIT MOBILIER RAILROAD SCANDAL   *first great robber baron plot*

The construction of the Union Pacific Railroad led to what was called the Credit Mobilier Scandal, a scam that tarnished the reputation of Congress more than any other in the 19th century. Credit Mobilier was the financial unit charged with financing the construction of the railroad, and it was decided by Oakes Ames (1804–1873)—the key figure within Credit Mobilier and a congressman from Massachusetts— that some inventive lobbying would be necessary to get favorable legislation on land grants and rights-of-way. Ames accomplished this in 1867 by "selling" company stock at half-price to key congressmen where, in Ames' own words, it "will do the most good for us."

Things went well for Credit Mobilier for five more years, until the *New York Sun* came into possession of letters that exposed the entire scam. Discovered among the beneficiaries of Credit Mobilier's "good-will" purchasers were Vice President Schuyler Colfax (speaker of the House at the time of Ames' sales pitch), Senator Henry Wilson and Republican James A. Garfield. A congressional investigation concluded that Credit Mobilier stockholders, including members of Congress, had reaped $23 million in illegitimate profits on the deal. Ames was censured by the House and went home broken-hearted, still insisting he was innocent. He died shortly thereafter of a cerebral hemorrhage. Garfield narrowly survived the scandal and was later elected president.

Oakes Ames is regarded as having fathered the concept of the "robber baron," although there have been some efforts to rehabilitate him by a few economic historians who claim the Credit Mobilier take was "only $13 million to $16 million," which they declared was not "excessive" for the standards of the day. As for the payoffs to congressional figures, this was merely a "grievous error of judgment." Most historians remain unimpressed by this view and consider the robber-baron tag richly deserved, even though the tactics used by Ames were probably followed by other railroad managements as well. Historian Robert Schick says that the Southern Pacific Railroad, for instance, managed to avoid an investigation along similar lines only because a fire just "happened" to destroy its financial records.

CREDIT SCAMS *guaranteed loans for bad credit risks*

Probably no group of people is more eager for credit than those who have been denied it because of a poor credit rating. They are bombarded by direct mail, newspaper ads and television commercials all assuring them that loans and grants are available to people who have bad credit histories. A typical con ad stated that all consumers had to do was telephone (900) USA-LOAN for the information. According to the New York attorney general's office, callers to that particular New York City service "only got the list of Federal agencies that offer housing loans and project grants." And if that was a disappointment, "perhaps the biggest surprise was that the calls cost each consumer $50 or more."

CROWN JEWELS THEFT *royal hoax*

On May 9, 1671, Colonel Thomas Blood, a notorious adventurer, and two confederates, all dressed as clergymen, entered the Tower of London to see the English crown jewels, which had only recently been opened to public view by King Charles II. It was 7 A.M. and Blood had arranged the early showing before the normal viewing times because his two companions were to leave London on an early coach. Blood proceeded to pull a mallet from under his coat and slug the custodian.

The thieves tried to file the big scepter in half but were unsuccessful, and they settled for fleeing with the orb and ceremonial crown. They almost got away, but were apprehended at the outer gate of the tower.

What punishment fit the crime of crown-stealing? Torture? The gibbet? The stake? Exile? Incredibly, none of the above. Instead, King Charles seemed so taken by the extraordinary daring of the plot that he granted the perpetrators a royal pardon. Blood was even rewarded with a position at court! That was the official line, but there was a much more believable explanation for this leniency. The king was always in need of money and it was taken for granted in court circles that Charles himself had been the brains behind the plot. This was so widely understood that no one was in the least surprised when Blood was also granted deeds to rich tracts of land in Ireland.

While none of this grand hoax theory was absolutely proved at the time, history does record that when Charles died in 1685, shocked officials discovered a terrible fact about the coronation crown. The precious jewels had been removed and replaced with worthless imitations. And, for some years thereafter, former mistresses of the late king kept turning up with a valuable jewel or two. The stealing of the crown jewels was a daring hoax, whether it had succeeded or not, and was fully worthy of a rogue like Blood—or of a playboy-king who could really use the money.

THE CRUCIFORM MONUMENT *pious fraud*

The stone cruciform monument from Sippar, southern Mesopotamia (now a part of Iraq), is one of the oldest forgeries uncovered by archaeologists and certainly one of the most ancient "pious frauds." A pious fraud is one that seeks to advance a religious tenet by means of forgery. In Christendom the most famous—or infamous—example is the spurious DONATION OF CONSTANTINE.

The cruciform monument was found in 1881 in excavations on behalf of the British Museum. The 12 sides of it are covered with inscriptions, dealing mostly with the renovation of the temple of Shamash and the very substantial revenues advanced to the temple at the time by the king of Akkad, Manishtushu, who ruled from about 2276 to 2261 B.C. Various scientific and archaeological studies determined that the monument was not inscribed during Manishtushu's reign but forged several centuries later. It was apparently the work of the temple priests seeking to establish the long-standing right to privileges and revenues for the temple. The inscription on the cruciform monument concludes: "this is not a lie, it is indeed the truth. . . . He who will damage this document let Enki fill up his canals with slime. . . ."

CUNNING MEN *19th-century quack spell-fighters*

In much of England in the 19th century, especially in the north, belief abounded not only in spells cast by the devil but also in cures effected by rather amazing fellows known as "cunning men."

On June 23, 1838, the *Hertford Reformer* felt obliged to publish an expose of the cunning men and told the case of a man who was afflicted for two years with a painful abscess that numerous doctors had failed to treat. Urged by friends, the man's wife traveled to New St. Swithin's to consult a cunning man. She was informed by this quack that her husband's disorder was an infliction of the devil, occasioned by his next-door neighbors using Satan-supplied charms. The cunning man knew exactly what the neighbors were doing—molding some wax by a fire into a form of her husband and then piercing it with pins on all sides. The neighbors repeated the Lord's Prayer backward and offered prayers to the devil that he would aim his vicious stings into the person the figure represented.

Now that the cause of the husband's ailment was clear, it was possible to counter the diabolical process.

In his seminal 19th-century work, *Extraordinary Popular Delusions and the Madness of Crowds*, Charles Mackay relates that the cunning man "prescribed a certain medicine, and a charm to be worn next the body, on that part where the disease principally lay. The patient was to repeat the 109th and 119th Psalms every day, or the cure would not be effectual. The fee that he claimed for this advice was a guinea.

"So efficacious is faith in the cure of any malady, that the patient actually felt much better after a three weeks' course of this prescription. The notable charm which the quack had given was afterwards opened, and found to be a piece of parchment covered with some cabalistic characters and signs of the planets."

Of course, there was still the newfound problem of facing the next-door neighbors. They had a right to be alarmed that the cunning man was prescibing means for punishing them for their supposed witchcraft. To escape such a fate, the neighbors consulted another cunning man who furnished them with a charm that would preserve them from malice inflicted by their enemies. The *Hertford Reformer* then offered the charming conclusion of the tale by noting that the first cunning man, "not long after he had been consulted, wrote to say, that he had discovered that his patient was not afflicted by Satan, as he had imagined, but by God, and would continue more or less in the same state till his life's end."

The *Reformer*'s expose did not do much to curb the belief of the credulous in cunning man hoaxers.

D

DARSEE, DR. JOHN *medical research faker*

"Dr. Darsee is clearly one of the most remarkable young men in American medicine. It is not extravagant to say that he became a legendary figure during his year as chief resident in medicine at Grady Memorial Hospital."

This was the exuberant commendation offered by cardiologist Paul Walter of Georgia's Emory University in endorsing the selection of his former colleague, Dr. John Darsee, for one of the highest rewards offered in academic medicine, an appointment to the Harvard Medical School faculty.

It had been a meteoric rise for Darsee from modest origins in Huntington, West Virginia. He was on the dean's list as an undergraduate at Notre Dame and had an M.D. from Indiana University. When he moved on to Emory University he was remembered there by one colleague as "extremely smart, incredibly hard working. I never had any reason to doubt his character or integrity."

That opinion would later change. Darsee arrived at Harvard in 1979 at the wunderkind age of 31 and went into heart research. Within two years of his arrival, he had an astounding near-100 papers and abstracts to his publishing credit. The only problem was that Darsee was a research cheater, and his unmasking was to rock Harvard, Emory and, in fact, the world of medical research.

The first hint of fraud in connection with Darsee's work came in 1981 when fellow researchers spotted him getting rid of a dog's carcass without first removing the heart—the very research his work was based upon. His colleagues retrieved the canine's heart and held it as evidence. Not long afterward, Darsee was observed clearly fabricating an electrocardiogram tracing on another dog.

Remarkably, Darsee talked his way out of trouble. When his actions were reported to superiors, he convinced them it was only an isolated act brought on by having to show his raw data to a man a year his junior and that his fabrication "was a destructive way to show my anger." He also said he was under considerable stress, never having taken a day of vacation in six years and being worried about the health of his hospitalized mother. Darsee's mentors seemed unwilling to destroy the career of "an apparently brilliant researcher."

However, in time the National Institutes of Health found the results of Darsee's work to have been at total variance with studies elsewhere. The truth emerged: Darsee had been faking data for years. In 1983 the National Institutes of Health barred him from receiving federal grant funds and contracts for 10 years, the harshest penalty for fraud it had ever imposed. His supervisors were rebuked for failing to keep close enough watch on his work.

At the time Darsee insisted he had "no recollection" of committing any abuses, but later issued a statement "asking forgiveness for whatever I have done wrong," and declared, "I want to continue to contribute to the medical system."

Darsee took a two-year fellowship with a Schenectady, New York, hospital. According to a hospital spokesperson, Darsee had been "completely honest" in discussing his past and "we feel he has a lot to offer." Darsee was not assigned any research work.

DAUDET'S ESCAPE *hoax pardon*

For many years right-wing journalist-politician Léon Daudet (1867–1942) was a thorn in the side of the French government, frequently characterizing state officials as unthinking machines. He went on to prove it in a way that amused France after he was slapped into prison in 1927. Daudet was confined in Santé Prison from which only five prisoners had escaped since it was built in 1867. Daudet became the sixth man with the most baldfaced of tricks. He simply had a friend make a telephone call, pretending to be the minister of the interior and saying that Daudet had been pardoned. The credulous warden unthinkingly set Daudet free without even checking the call. The escape proved so embarrassing to officials it was decided not to return Daudet to prison, in a sense making a fake pardon good.

DE ANGELIS, ANTHONY "TINO"   See GREAT SALAD OIL SWINDLE.

DEBT CONSOLIDATION SCAM *preying on desperate borrowers*

Many people get so deeply in debt that they cannot keep up with payments as they come due. Their best hope is to reach an agreement with their creditors on a new schedule of payments. This can be done with the assistance of debt consolidation or adjustment services, some of whom are nonprofit or even religious organizations licensed or approved by local governments. However, the field has attracted a goodly number of con artists. Debt consolidators do not lend debtors money, but simply collect regular payments from them and apportion the money to creditors who hold off on foreclosures, attachments and the like.

Unlike the public-spirited nonprofit groups, the debt tricksters charge a whopping fee for their services, often hidden from their clients and guaranteed by a new time-contract that the franctic debtor has to sign. If nothing else, these debt scam artists place themselves first in line for the debtor's money; some real fly-by-night operators simply keep all the money they receive until various bill collectors start going after the debtor once again. When the debtor tries to contact the service, he finds it is gone. But sometimes these debt charlatans sign their hapless victims to a shady third party. Now the unfortunate debtor has all of his old bills and is saddled with this contract—the biggest debt of all—and a new set of repossessors.

This can be avoided if the debtor sticks with authorized consumer debt-counseling services and checks legal associations and the Better Business Bureau before dealing with any private debt consolidation service.

DEFENBACH, MARIE   See FAKE MURDER FAKES.

DE HORY, ELMYR   *art forger*

Clifford Irving (see entry), of faked Howard Hughes autobiography fame, has described Elmyr de Hory (1906–1976) as "probably the greatest and certainly the most prolific art forger of all time." Considering Irving's expertise, this must be regarded as the earnest appreciation of a colleague. De Hory, a Hungarian Jewish emigre, was an unsuccessful expressionist painter who turned to imitating the works of the great world painters—Picasso, Gauguin, Matisse, Chagall, Cezanne, Modigliani, Dufy, Braque and others. Hundreds of de Hory's phonies still considered to be genuine hang in museums and thousands more in private collections.

The de Hory bubble burst in 1967 when two "agents" for de Hory's fakes sold 44 Postimpressionist canvases to a Texas millionaire. They were found to be bogus.

Since the early 1960s, de Hory had done his forging on the Spanish island of Ibiza. After he was exposed, his biography, *Fake!*, was written by another Ibiza resident of the time, Clifford Irving. The critical success of *Fake!* opened up the publishing field to Irving and provided him with the opportunity of working on his own Hughes fraud. As for de Hory, he was later the subject of a full-length documentary film by Orson Welles. But by 1976 his mental state had deteriorated into one of growing fear. He was constantly harassed by the two sellers of his fakes and faced extradition to France and a likely long prison term. De Hory committed suicide.

To this day some of de Hory's works are valued at over $30 million—as genuines rather than the fakes they are.

DE LOYS' APE   *evolutionary fake*

In 1920 a Swiss oil geologist, François de Loys, and his son were exploring the Venezuelan wilderness when, as de Loys would later claim, they happened across some apes. This was remarkable because there had never been any report of apes in South America. When the apes saw the members of the expedition they "were very angry." Standing upright, they screamed wildly, tore branches from trees and heaved them at the geologists. Then they defecated in their hands and hurled their excrement at the men. When it looked like the two apes were about to start an all-out attack, de Loys quickly leveled his rifle and fired. "The female," he later said, "covered the male with her body and fell dead; the male then took to his heels and disappeared into the undergrowth of the jungle."

De Loys approached the fallen creature cautiously to confirm that the female primate was dead. He beckoned the native members of the expedition to look at it, and all said they had never seen an ape like that. It was almost five feet tall, covered with reddish hair and was more human in appearance than any monkey in the jungles of South America.

De Loys said he realized he had a major zoological find, which should be brought to the outside world for further study. But he had no way to embalm the creature, and in the jungle heat the body would decay and decompose in a few days. Thus de Loys did the next best thing. He seated the body on an oil can, propping it up with a stick under the lower jaw and took a photograph. Then he had the creature skinned, putting the hide in a box filled with salt in an effort to preserve it. The ape's head went into another box.

The expedition continued on its oil hunt until the explorers reached the Tarra River region, when they were attacked by some wild Montilones Indians. De Loys was hit by an arrow and the party barely escaped. In the confusion the ape hide box was lost. They still had the skull, but by the time they reached civilization, it had dried up and was lost bit by bit. All de Loys had was the photograph.

On the basis of this single picture, anthropologist Georges Montandon declared that de Loys had found a new species, which he dubbed *Ameranthropoides loysi*. An article published under de Loys' byline in the *Illustrated London News* was headlined "A Gap Filled in the Pedigree of Man." After much consideration the vast majority of scientists, including those of the Paris Academy of Science, rejected de Loys' ape as a crude hoax; it was merely a dead spider monkey sitting on an oil can with its tail either hidden or amputated. (Apes do not have tails.)

Nevertheless, others tried to confirm the existence of de Loys' ape, but with no success. Seasoned zoologists tracking de Loys' path found nothing. Then, in 1951 Roger de Courteville, a mining engineer and explorer, announced he had visited de Loys' country many times and had twice seen a red-haired, manlike ape who walked on its hind legs. He said one sighting had occurred in 1938 and another in 1947. Courteville said he had made sketches of the creatures and also produced a photograph taken by one Dr. de Barle. Scientists found holes in Courteville's description of the creature. As for the photograph— Dr. de Barle was apparently just a jungle traveler who dispensed the picture and never, as far as was known, emerged from the jungle—it was even more fraudulent than the de Loys photo. In fact, it was nothing more than a doctored-up copy of the original shot. The stick that propped up the dead ape had been air-brushed out and the oil can covered up with a jungle backdrop.

De Loys' ape has never been seen since.

DEMARA, FERDINAND WALDO, JR. *busiest impostor*

With little doubt, Ferdinand Waldo Demara Jr. (1921–1982) was the busiest impostor in American history. Just as soon as he was exposed in one guise, he merrily charged off to find another. Demara was exceptionally skilled at his calling, carrying off so many

Perhaps the most active, and frequently charming, impostor in American history, Fred Demara was a successful naval surgeon, a Trappist monk, a cancer researcher, a law student, a college psychology teacher, a soldier, a sailor, a hospital orderly, a deputy sheriff, a prison guidance counselor and more.

hoaxes and impostures and fooling so many experts in so many fields that he became known to many as the Renaissance Man reborn. Demara showed a remarkable ability to teach himself advanced concepts so well that he was readily accepted as a brilliant scholar in whatever field he chose.

A high school dropout, Demara masqueraded while in his 20s as a doctor of philosophy named Robert L. French and taught college psychology classes. Later, he successfully transformed himself into Cecil Boyce Haman, with a doctor's degree in zoology. Demara was also a Trappist monk in a Kentucky monastery, a biologist involved in cancer research in an institution near Seattle, Washington, a law student, an American soldier, a hospital orderly, a sailor, a deputy sheriff and a guidance counselor in a Texas maximum-security prison.

Although born a Roman Catholic, he twice "converted" to that religion. Demara's greatest feat of impersonation took place during the Korean War when he served as a lieutenant-surgeon in the Canadian navy. Boning up on medical texts, he pulled teeth, removed tonsils and amputated limbs. His crowning achievement under severe battle conditions was removing a bullet from within a fraction of an inch of a South Korean soldier's heart. Those assisting him in the harrowing operation gave a lusty cheer when he successfully completed the procedure. Although totally unqualified for his medical service, Demara never lost a patient, and doubtless saved several lives.

Demara's downfall as a wartime surgeon followed news stories about his medical exploits. Back in Canada, eager newsmen tried to do follow-up stories on his background and determined that his identity was faked. Demara was ordered back to Canada and drummed out of the service, but with all pay due him. It was assumed he had simply enlisted under a false name. Nobody doubted he was a doctor.

When a Demara imposture was uncovered, he was almost always banished with deep regret by his victims. The Trappist monks hated to have such a dedicated individual leave their monastery. Texas prison officials wondered where they would ever find another expert who gained so much respect from convicts.

In 1956 Demara answered the siren call of academia—a longtime weakness of his—and became Martin D. Godgart. He served under this name as the English, French and Latin teacher in a Maine island high school. When unmasked, he served a few months in jail charged with "cheating by false premises."

Demara's exploits brought him lasting fame in a best-selling book by Robert Crichton called *The Great Impostor* and a 1960 movie by the same name, with Tony Curtis in the title role. Hollywood thought Demara was so charming an impostor that after the film they put him to work as a doctor in a minor epic called *The Hypnotic Eye.*

Demara was frequently asked to explain his odd compulsion. His answer: "Rascality, pure rascality." It was not an answer that would have satisfied many psychiatrists. Demara faded from sight in the mid-1960s. In the late 1970s he turned up as a hospital chaplain in California, a properly ordained minister under his rightful name. What happened in between is not known. Demara died of heart failure in 1982 at the age of 60.

DE ROUGEMONT, LOUIS *king of the cannibals*

In 1898 *Wide World* magazine, a reputable London publication, electrified England with the serialized, harrowing experiences of one Louis de Rougemont, who had spent 30 years among Australian cannibals and eventually became their king.

It seemed de Rougemont had been shipwrecked by a gale in the 1860s, while pearl fishing in the Pacific. The ship's dog pulled the exhausted de Rougemont the final bit of distance by its tail to the shore of a small island. There de Rougemont and his loyal canine companion lived in true Robinson Crusoe style. De Rougemont robbed pelicans of their fish, lived in a hut of pearl shells with a shark-hide hammock and

used 600-pound turtles as "taxis" to negotiate sand and surf.

One day another storm blew in four naked aborigines, a couple and their two young children. They were very friendly, especially the woman named Yamba. Together they all built a boat and reached the mainland. De Rougemont was ceremoniously met by the aborigines, who in time asked him to be chief of the tribe. De Rougemont's queen was Yamba, who left her husband. De Rougemont told of cannibals feasting on the tribe's enemies, consuming meals of worms and emus, his own courageous battle with a giant alligator and his discovery of a new strain of flying wombat.

When the first of the series appeared, the British Association for the Advancement of Science invited de Rougemont to address it at Bristol. The Association, and the Royal Geographical Society, accepted his fantastic tales at face value, and the bizarre anecdotes continued in ensuing issues of *Wide World.*

In these de Rougemont told of pining for civilization until he and Yamba started an arduous overland trek to civilization. Part way de Rougemont came down with malaria, and Yamba was forced to kill her newborn baby since it was impossible for her to nurse both child and husband. The still weak de Rougemont described killing a big bull buffalo:

I determined to test the efficacy of a very popular native remedy for fever—for shivering fits still continued to come upon me at most abnormal times—usually late in the day. No matter how much grass poor Yamba brought me, I never could get warm, and so now I thought I would try some animal heat.

Scarce had the life left the body before I ripped the buffalo open between the fore and hind legs, and then crawled into the interior, fairly burying myself in a deluge of warm blood and intestines. My head, however, was protruding from the animal's chest. . . . Next morning to my amazement, I found I was a prisoner, the carcass having got cold and frigid, so that I had literally to be dug out. As I emerged I presented a most ghastly and horrifying spectacle. My body was covered with congealed blood, and even my long hair was all matted and stiffened with it. But never can I forget the feeling of exhilaration and strength that took possession of me as I stood there looking at my faithful companion. *I was absolutely cured*—a new man, a giant of strength.

This incident more than most roused some suspicion about the so-called cannibal chief's tale. The *Daily Chronicle* launched a sweeping investigation and soon uncovered the real truth, which was accompanied by de Rougemont's confession. He was a Swiss named Grin, had never been a cannibal chief but had at one time been a butler to a Lady Robinson in Australia. He had also once served as a footman and courier for Fanny Kemble, the English actress. He had gleaned most of his material about Australia—enough to con a number of experts—by research at the British Museum. *Wide World* published an embarrassed apology, while de Rougemont made a prudent retreat with the considerable amount of money he had earned from public appearances.

However, some years later, a tall but stooped bearded man was seen selling matches in Piccadilly or Shaftesbury Avenue. He wore a ragged overcoat over the top of which lay his thinning hair, framing a calm, philosophical and intelligent face. It was Grin, the former Louis de Rougemont, the cannibal king of Australia.

DETECTIVE LESSONS BY MAIL

For many years one of the worst mail frauds was "Be a Detective" advertising that appeared in many newspapers and magazines. The ads assured readers that there was a gaping need for detectives in almost every neighborhood and offered a course of lessons on how to become a detective. Each month students were sent a detective lesson, and at the end of one year they were rewarded with a tin badge.

Even with the passage of a law against using the mails to defraud in the 1950s, the United States district attorney in Kansas declined to present a case to the grand jury against the detective-agency swindlers. He felt they could not be convicted since they had sent their clients everything they promised. However, U.S. postal inspectors pursued the case on their own and went before the grand jury in Leavenworth, claiming that the swindlers had convinced their victims they would be qualified detectives and could make a handsome living arresting lawbreakers and collecting rewards.

The detective-lesson operators were indicted, tried and convicted. The landmark decision in this case opened up the opportunity to drive many similar petty fraudsters out of business. Typical were those who offered readers a good coat hanger and upon receipt of cash mailed back a nail. Another was one that offered victims a chance to "learn something valuable" for a small fee. The hopelessly curious then received the keen advice: "Do not answer advertisements of this kind."

See also COUNTERFEITS BY MAIL.

DIAMOND-COUNTING CONTESTS *sales con*

The friendly neighborhood jeweler sends out an announcement that he is sort of in the bean contest business. The setup is the same as the game in which players estimate how many beans are in a jar, except in this case the "beans" are a phial of diamond chips

in his window. If you guess the total within a certain margin of error, you automatically win an honest-to-goodness genuine diamond. If you guess 50, you will be within the margin of error. If you say 500, you will also be within the margin of error.

Yes, the player does win a diamond. But the winner must abide by the rules of the contest, such as stipulations requiring that all diamonds have to be suitably mounted in gold or platinum settings. A nice setting is offered for $40, $50, $60, $100, $200 or more. The dealer claims it's still a marvelous bargain since the buyer is getting the diamond "free."

The jeweler has an endless source of diamonds—that is, chips or commercial diamonds, which can be worth less than $1.

DIAMOND NECKLACE HOAX *scandal that helped destroy the French monarchy*

Speaking of the execution of Marie Antoinette, Napoleon later said, "The Queen's death must be dated from the Diamond Necklace Trial." Most historians agree. Ironically, the queen was innocent of any nefarious dealings in the matter, but she was nevertheless blamed for it by the French populace.

Involved was a notorious profligate cleric, Cardinal Prince de Rohan, who sought to regain favor with the queen after years of having attacked her and her mother, Maria Theresa of Austria. If he could garner the queen's good graces, Rohan felt he might win the post of first minister of the Crown.

The necklace in question was one that the late Louis XV had ordered for his mistress, Madame du Barry. It was worth then about a half-million dollars and was still in the hands of the jewelers, Boehmer and Bassenge, when Louis died.

The idea of the cardinal gaining favor with the queen originated with Rohan's mistress, Jeanne, Countess de la Motte, an adventuress who claimed descent from Henry II of France by a mistress. She had advanced her fortunes by sleeping around, finally hooking the profligate cardinal. She then worked on a plot to gain herself a fortune and sold the cardinal on the lie that she was close to the queen and could improve his relations with her. She forged affectionate letters from the queen and passed them to Rohan. Finally, Marie Antoinette granted a private meeting with the cardinal. It took place in the "Grove of Venus" at Versailles, in the dark of night. It was not the queen, of course, but the "Baroness" d'Olive, a prostitute hired by la Motte to impersonate Marie Antoinette. The cardinal kissed the "queen's" foot and received from her a rose as a sign of their reconciliation.

With the gullible cardinal now dreaming of making Marie Antoinette his mistress, la Motte forged another letter from the queen authorizing Rohan to buy the diamond necklace in her name for a price of 6 million livres. The cardinal presented the letter to the jewelers, obtained the necklace and passed it on to the Countess de la Motte to give to the queen. Instead, the necklace went to the countess's husband who immediately headed for England, where it was said the diamonds were sold off piece by piece.

When the bill for the first quarter-payment came due on July 30, 1785, the queen denied ordering or receiving the necklace and said she had never written the letter that bore her signature. The letter was shown to the king who immediately recognized the signature as a forgery. Rohan was summoned for interrogation as to his involvement. The king was certain that Rohan was involved in a conspiracy with the crown's many enemies. The king ordered the cardinal to the Bastille and issued an arrest order for Countess de la Motte. She hid out in a number of places but was finally apprehended, as was d'Olive (the impersonator) and the forger who had written the letters. "Count" Cagliostro (see entry), the master mountebank of the day—who was involved with Cardinal Rohan and was in the process of swindling the cleric in a number of cons—was also arrested.

As word of the scandal spread, Marie Antoinette felt only a public trial could clear her name. Following a sensational trial, Rohan was freed as innocent.

Nevertheless, the king stripped him of his offices and exiled him to an abbey. The forger and the prostitute drew prison terms. Only Cagliostro, cleared of all charges, was released.

The worst punishment was reserved for Jeanne de la Motte. She was stripped and publicly whipped before the Palace of Justice and branded with a V (for *voleuse*, "thief") and sent to the notorious Salpetriere women's prison for life. After a year she escaped and joined her husband in London. Before her death in 1791 she wrote an autobiography, which told her story of the necklace affair.

Public opinion continued to blame Marie Antoinette for bringing the affair to a public trial. The French felt the queen's well-known insatiable appetite for diamonds had been reason enough for the cardinal to fall for the gigantic hoax. As Will and Ariel Durant state in *Rousseau and Revolution*, "she had preserved her virtue and suffered damage to her reputation."

DIAMOND SWITCHERS *superstar shoplifters*

They aren't exactly shoplifters, since they do leave something of value in return for what they take. These are the diamond switchers, who use sleight-of-hand expertise to flinch expensive diamonds and rings. The best operators are women, and the greatest superstar of all—because she has never been caught—is

Left: A contemporary illustration of the gorgeous diamond necklace. Right: Jeanne, Countess de la Motte, the chief plotter of the scandal that, more than anything else, brought Marie Antoinette into disrepute with her French subjects.

the Persian lamb-clad switch artist who took both Tiffany's and Harry Winston on New York's Fifth Avenue in the 1970s.

First she sauntered into Tiffany's and studied a tray of rings. She plucked out one going for $19,800 and put in its place a look-alike $7,500 item. Then the lady moved on to Harry Winston and dumped the $19,800 ring into a tray in exchange for one costing $38,500.

The quickie caper took place on a Saturday afternoon. Nothing was noticed until Monday morning when a Winston salesperson took a tray of rings from the safe and was struck by something very wrong. In place of a 5.30-carat marquise diamond, he found a 3.69 one. In addition, the ring had a Tiffany marking.

Winston informed Tiffany's of their find. A Tiffany salesman remembered the first part of the three-ring switch—a lady sporting Persian lamb reviewing a tray that contained a 3.69-carat marquise diamond. She had left without buying anything.

Two mysteries remained. Who was the lady with the quick fingers? And where did the $7,500 diamond ring come from? There may well have been an unnoticed progression up to it as well, leading one journalist to wonder if it all started at Woolworth's.

DICKENS, CHARLES See HANSARD'S GUIDE TO REFRESHING SLEEP.

DILLINGER'S WOODEN GUN ESCAPE *hoaxing the law*

One of the most enduring hoaxes in criminal history, embraced eagerly by most writers, is that public enemy John Dillinger used a wooden gun he had whittled in his cell to make a spectacular escape from prison in Crown Point, Indiana. More than anything else, this supposed exploit made Dillinger the most celebrated and storied criminal of the 1930s. Actually, as John Toland relates in *The Dillinger Days*, Dillinger carried out the plot the old-fashioned way—with a real gun—and while releasing his hostage captives, he playfully told them his gun had been made of wood.

According to the hoax version, Dillinger used a knife to whittle a wooden gun out of the top of a washboard, colored it with shoe polish and used it to escape. The non-hoax version was that Dillinger's lawyer, an infamous character named Louis Piquett, met with a prominent Indiana judge on the grounds of the Century of Progress exposition in Chicago and turned over an envelope containing several thousand dollars. In turn the judge said he would arrange to have a gun smuggled into the jail. (In the 1930s most successful prison breaks were not accom-

Public enemy John Dillinger hammed it up after his celebrated escape from an Indiana jail, supposedly with a wooden gun he carved in his cell. Here he poses with a gun carved after his escape.

plished through cunningly crafted plots, but by simple bribery.)

Using this real gun, Dillinger locked up several guards and broke into the warden's office where he seized two machine guns. Giving one of the weapons to a fellow prisoner, Dillinger snatched the car of a lady sheriff, Mrs. Lillian Holly, and the pair escaped with two hostages whom they later released unharmed.

The newspapers latched on to the supposed wooden gun escape with journalistic gusto that captured the public's fancy. Meanwhile, a secret investigation conducted by the Hargrave Secret Service of Chicago, on the orders of Indiana Governor Paul McNutt, uncovered the true story concerning the gun. However, the governor and his attorney general, Philip Lutz Jr., kept the facts secret because, properly, they did not want Dillinger to know that certain informants whom he might trust again in the future had betrayed him to private detectives. By the time Dillinger was shot dead by the FBI, the judge had also died and the findings remained secret.

While still on the loose Dillinger had written to his sister, saying his gun had been a wooden one, and he even had his picture taken holding a whittled wooden gun. However, Dillinger was playing along with the secret plot and covering up the real facts about the smuggled gun. His posing in such a fashion also greatly satisfied his own ego.

Ironically Dillinger's fakery inspired two of his criminal confederates, Harry Pierpont and Charles Makley, to try a similar, real-life hoax in an attempted breakout from the death house of the Ohio State Prison a few months after Dillinger's death. They carved pistols out of soap and managed to overpower one guard. They got as far as smashing through a door leading from the death house when other guards opened fire on them. Makley was killed and Pierpont wounded, but he recovered well enough to die in the electric chair a month later.

DIP OF DEATH   *daredevil hoax*
Known as the Dip of Death in American circuses and Auto-Bolide (auto meteor) in France where it was invented, this car stunt was probably the most thrilling spectacle in the United States around the turn of the 20th century. The leading practitioner of the Dip of Death was Mademoiselle Octavie LaTour, who left audiences boggle-eyed. The exhibit required a framework as high as a three-story building and was divided in two sections, separated by a gap of about 10 feet. Mlle. LaTour climbed into a car on a small platform at the top of a tower on one section. Strapped into the car, she would soar down a runway and shoot the gap to the second section, a wooden receiving track.

Perhaps the suspense is best described in the Barnum & Bailey press kit description of the "death-defying ride":

As the car descends the incline it gathers velocity. You are dimly conscious that its speed is so terrific

as to be beyond comparison with anything you have ever seen. An express train is seemingly slow beside it. You think of a pistol shot; a speeding arrow; a meteor. It is all three in one. Before you can realize it, the car has descended the incline, turned upside down and still inverted, has shot into space. Twenty feet away, across a veritable chasm of death, is a moon-shaped incline.

Yes, the car struck the incline and it was upright every time. There was good reason for this, since the car was always under strict control; the crowds were watching a deception. The rubber-tired wheels never so much as touched the runway in the descent, although they were spinning. There were small wheels in the axles that were fixed to the tracks under the incline, guaranteeing that the car could not be swerved off the runway until it reached the bottom and was thrown in the air in a gasp-producing back somersault and landed snugly on the second runway. This runway was three times the width of the first runway. Its angle and distance were so calculated that the car wheels landed at the same spot every time, with a shock to Mlle. LaTour that was no worse than the smoothest aircraft landing today.

The Dip of Death was nowhere near as dangerous as it appeared. Mlle. LaTour admitted as much in a 1905 interview with the *New York World*:

At present, I am courting each day in La Tourbillon De La Mort, the supposed limit of human daring. But this act of plunging down the steep incline in an automobile that turns a back somersault in midair and lands on a runway is not really the limit of human daring. It is only the most perilous act that human imagination has so far devised for human daring. But it is the limit for only a moment. Hundreds of inventors are hard at work trying to perfect a machine that will make a double turn. . . . For hairbreadth as the escape must seem, the probability of accident must be really small. No one wants to see people die. The game is one of mettle, not of death. So get your minds fermenting; give your imagination free play; and invent the real limit of human daring. Show us how to fly to the moon; direct the way to Mars; point the signboards down the roads of human daring. And I for one will go.

There was much tension when her act was performed, even to those who knew trickery was involved. Circus showman James A. Bailey himself was too petrified to watch the action and, says circus historian Dexter Fellows, "hid himself in his private office and waited until the success or failure of the act could be reported to him."

DIRTY TRICKS   *political sabotaging*
The byword "dirty tricks" is associated with Richard Nixon during the Watergate scandal following the

1972 presidential campaign, although Nixon undoubtedly saw himself as more the victim of the technique than the original practitioner. In 1962, while attempting a political comeback by running for governor of California against incumbent Democrat Pat Brown, Nixon was beset by questions about a secret loan of $205,000 made by billionaire Howard Hughes to Nixon's restauranteur brother Donald, who was on the edge of insolvency. It was an issue that drove Nixon to distraction, and one that he was unable to answer satisfactorily. Although Governor Brown never raised the issue, Nixon regarded it as a potent, embarrassing and nagging problem. Certainly, some Brown supporters made use of the issue, but the most nerve-racking to Nixon was Dick Tuck, the Democratic political prankster.

While campaigning in San Francisco's Chinatown, Nixon at last felt he was enjoying a rest from the issue as he met a line of smiling residents holding up signs bearing a message in Chinese characters. Nixon thought he had found a haven among some supporters and shook hands with the people, until Chinese friends informed him the message on the signs read: "WHAT ABOUT THAT HUGHES LOAN?" A frustrated Nixon grabbed several of the placards and ripped them to pieces.

Later, at a Chinatown luncheon rally (which Nixon attended) guests opened their Chinese fortune cookies and found the same query on the messages.

In 1972 Nixon had not forgotten Tuck's "dirty tricks" and ordered Bob Haldeman to find their own hoaxer "with a Dick Tuck capability."

What Nixon-Haldeman came up with was not a relatively benign hoaxer like Tuck, but one Donald Segretti, who did real dirty tricks in his forged letters that accused Nixon foes of homosexuality and fathering bastard children. Whereas Tuck had produced belly laughs, Segretti's illegal tactics earned him a prison sentence. It was said that all this merely confirmed in Nixon's mind that there were two different standards in politics, one for his enemies and a harsher one for himself.

DISTRIBUTORSHIP FRAUDS *selling business dreams*

Distributorships can be legitimate and often profitable forms of business enterprise. This is true of fast food franchises and new car distributorships offered by national organizations to individuals willing to invest a substantial sum of money for the right to operate such a business. Unfortunately, there are other devious promoters who use the cover of legitimate businesses to advertise fraudulent opportunities that are nothing more than pyramid schemes. Some are called "multilevel marketing plans" in which the customer must sell the product or service and also recruit others in his area to do the same.

Take, for example, a cosmetics distributorship in which the distributor has to sell five other distributorships to break even on his investment. That means those five would have to sell no less than 25 distributorships and they in turn 125. Here is how the distributorship or multilevel marketing plan would progress numerically:

5
25
125
625
3,125
15,625
78,125
390,625
1,952,125

At this point the pyramid is already at the stage at which half the population would have to be in the cosmetic distributorship business. Who would be left to do the buying? (Running the pyramid scale only three more rounds would just about hit the population level of the United States; an additional two rounds would exceed the population of the entire world. Next stop, distributorships on Mars?)

The only one who profits is the original distributorship marketer. He has taken several thousand dollars from the early investors and has moved on. See also PYRAMID SCHEMES.

DOG RACE DOPING *greatest betting coup*

The most remarkable betting coup in dog racing history occurred in December 1945 at the White City Stadium in London. Just before the last race of the day, five of six dogs in the contest were fed some doped fish by a fixer. The five slowed down in the running to let the sixth dog, going off at odds of 11 to 2, win by a wide margin. Usually, doped dogs behave in a peculiar way during a race, which is a tipoff to the track stewards. In this case, however, the dogs had been given a very precise measure of the dope—Chloretone—and it was just enough to make the animals run slower without causing them to exhibit any signs of doping.

As a result, officials suspected nothing, and the race results were declared official. The fixers raked in an estimated $200,000. It was not until several hours later that the plot was discovered; but by that time the mutuel money was gone.

DOLLAR STORE *early swindle technique*

In the great migrations to the West, wagon-train settlers faced far less danger of being scalped by Indians than by shrewd con men. The most important of these characters was Ben Marks, in that he pioneered what became a mainstay con game for the next 100 years. In 1857, Marks, a jolly sort of red-whiskered man with the look of a cherub, opened the first "Dollar Store" in America in Cheyenne, Wyoming. The establishment was a great lure for pioneers, since it was stocked with a great number of wares, all selling for $1. But Marks had no interest in that business whatsoever, his preoccupation being in suckering male customers into crooked games of chance.

A pioneer who wandered into Ben's store to replace a broken ax handle usually ended up spending all of his money on the games played there. Among these were three-card monte, shell games and wheel games of various sorts. The shills kept right on winning, but the pioneer continually lost. But Ben was not the sort to let a victim go off completely empty-handed. The man had come in for an ax handle, so Ben gave him one for free and wished him good fortune henceforth.

Ben Marks' Dollar Store was developed by other confidence men into the bigger and better and even more dishonest concept of the Big Store—the fake gambling club, phony brokerage or horse parlor (as in the movie *The Sting*)—which netted thousands or tens of thousands of dollars per scam compared with Ben's hundreds. But Ben Marks fathered it all.

Before the advent of the Big Store, cheaper dollar stores sprung up all over the country. One in Chicago actually turned into one of America's most fabled department stores. Its founder had launched it as a dollar store scam specializing in monte games, but soon discovered he could make a fortune selling cheap goods at a handsome profit, perhaps proving that if you give a con man enough money, he can turn honest.

DONATION OF CONSTANTINE *spurious claim of papal authority*

For centuries the See of Rome laid claim to almost limitless temporal powers based on the so-called Donation of Constantine, or *Constitutum Constantini*. It was the most famous document in the medieval collection "Forged Decretals of Isidore" and was a blatant monkish forgery. The Donation indicated that Constantine the Great, the first Christian emperor of Rome, granted to Pope Sylvester I (314–355) and all his successors spiritual supremacy over all other patriarchates on matters of faith and worship and, more ambiguously, full temporal power over Rome and the entire Western Empire. Constantine made this gift supposedly in gratitude to the pope for miraculously curing his leprosy and converting him to Christianity.

Although the Donation was alleged to have been written in the fourth century, the Roman Church did not press its claims under it until the ninth century, when it was embroiled in controversy with the Eastern Orthodox Church. Thereafter and throughout the Middle Ages many popes used the Donation to claim temporal powers.

It was not until the 15th century that scholars rejected the Donation as a complete fraud. Lorenzo Valla (c. 1407–1457) demonstrated by historical chronology and the use of language in various time spans that the document could not have been written during the rule of Constantine. A glaring error was that the emperor had allegedly granted the Roman Church religious authority over his new capital of New Rome (later Constantinople and now Istanbul) at least a decade before New Rome was even founded. Papalists continued to dispute the findings of Valla and other scholars, but the religious and temporal oppositionists embraced the debunking. In England, Thomas Cromwell had Valla's text published in 1536 as part of his propaganda campaign against Rome on behalf of the desires of King Henry VIII.

The dispute continued for centuries, but by the 18th century Voltaire could denounce the Donation as "that boldest and most magnificent forgery" and meet little contradiction. Today the Donation of Constantine is universally acknowledged as a forgery written in the 700s by monks whose identities remain unknown.

DOSSENA'S GENUINE FAKES *superior art forgeries*

In 1928 the art world was thrown into shock when a little known Italian sculptor, Alceo Dossena, filed a lawsuit against an art dealer named Alfredo Fasoli, charging him with swindling Dossena. It developed that since 1918 Dossena had been turning out reproductions of numerous pieces of Renaissance sculpture and delivering them to the dealer for $200 apiece. The dealer told Dossena he was disposing of them as what they were—copies; but the Dossena works were so good they were readily sold as originals for much higher sums, a fact not told to Dossena. In 1928 the sculptor learned the truth by happenstance and sued for $66,000 in "back wages."

Dossena had still underestimated his own worth. During the suit it was determined that his imitations had been sold for fabulous sums to a number of museums in Europe, as well as to the Cleveland Museum of Art, New York's Metropolitan Museum of Art and also a great number of private collectors, including Helen Clay Frick and William Randolph Hearst.

The resultant publicity made Dossena's reputation. However, five years later, in 1933, when a public auction of his work was held in Manhattan's Art Galleries, collectors wanted to make sure they were not subjected to a further hoax. The Italian government therefore issued with each purchase an official document guaranteeing the item was a genuine fake.

DOUBLE COUNT *shortchanging scam*
Double counting is one of the oldest methods of shortchanging practiced by dishonest cashiers. Its virtue from the cheater's point of view is that if detected it readily appears to be an honest mistake or, more importantly, allows a customer to think he has come out ahead.

Say, for example, a customer makes a 75-cent purchase and pays with a $10 bill. The clerk counts the purchase first, announcing, "Seventy-five and twenty-five is one dollar . . ." Here the cashier will pause a brief instant since the scam works best if the customer picks up the quarter. Then the count continues, ". . . two, three, four, five, six, seven, eight, nine and ten—and seventy-five and twenty-five. Thank you."

The count is quite fast and seems logical; most customers do not notice that the "ten—and seventy-five and twenty-five" is all one count and that they have paid twice for their purchase, first and last. If, however, a customer objects, the cashier makes a quick correction with a shake of the head. Most often, though, if the customer does notice anything it is that he has gotten two quarters instead of one. Since it appears that there has been a quarter error in his favor, he is frequently most concerned with leaving as quickly as possible. In other cases the customer feels the cashier has erred in his favor and returns the last quarter, leaving with the warm glow of an honest man.

DOUBLE-TRAYS *gambling con*
Crooked gamblers frequently get conned out of their money in plots to cheat private gambling clubs or casinos. In actuality, the house is in on the con, which often involves "double-trays"—dice that have two 3s on them. Such dice guarantee that the shooter will win most of the time, but not every game. The mark or victim is convinced the operation will work because the dice man is in on the fix and will deliberately fail to look at the mirror built into the craps table, which will often reveal the double 3s.

The scam is pulled a couple times for tiny stakes and works so that the mark becomes hungry and now wants the big killing. He puts up a huge amount of money and is supplied with double-tray dice—but ones that are also loaded, so they will automatically turn up a losing number. Usually the mark will take the scam as nothing more than a woefully unlucky break. In one of the legends of the con world a mark was taken for $50,000 in such a scam, immediately

hurried home, obtained a mortgage on his home and returned, determined to make up his losses and still turn a profit. The con men took him again and then dismissed him, saying he was too unlucky a partner for them. The mark himself went off, convinced he was a jinx.

DRAKE BRASS PLATE *forged relic*
Sir Francis Drake, on his three-year circumnavigation voyage, landed on the California coast in 1579. He ordered that a brass plate be set up claiming the territory in the name of Queen Elizabeth and calling it New Albion. Over time the Drake brass plate disappeared, until finally, some three and a half centuries later, it was said to have been found near San Francisco. Many authorities considered the plate and its inscription to be authentic, although some had doubts.

A replica of the plate was presented to Queen Elizabeth II who in turn had it displayed in Buckland Abbey, Drake's Devonshire property, which had been turned into a museum. The scientific community continued to have doubts about the authenticity of the plates, and in 1977 a new method was used to analyze the composition of the brass. The work, done at the Lawrence Berkeley Institute of the University of California and the Research Laboratory for Archaeology at Oxford determined that the plate was of late 19th or perhaps even early 20th-century make.

DRAKE INHERITANCE SWINDLES *centuries-long con*
Francis Drake, the great English navigator and marauder against Spanish territories in the New World, died at sea in 1596. Immediately, tales spread of a huge fortune he had left. This great wealth was supposedly to go to his son. In reality Drake had no fortune and no son, but within months of his death British swindlers were selling "shares" in the Drake "inheritance." This went on for 30 years, despite the government's warning that there was no fortune and that, in any case, no claims were valid under English common law after 30 years.

That did nothing to stop the con men over the next hundreds of years. First the swindlers zeroed in on people named Drake, informing them they were related to the great freebooter. Once the claim was settled, they would share in the enormous fortune. Of course, there were legal costs. The suckers had to pay them, being told the case would be settled shortly. Soon the swindlers took in victims who weren't named Drake at all, but who could cut themselves in for a piece of the action by helping out with the legal fees.

By 1835, the Drake swindle had spread to the United States, and in 1919 one operator, Mrs. Sudie B. Whiteaker, made the most significant hit when she took an Iowa farm family named Hartzell for several thousand dollars. One of the sons, Oscar, often described as a typical lumbering "hayseed," thought about the family investment for a while and decided they had been conned along with many of their farm neighbors. Hartzell had no trouble going to Des Moines and tracking down Whiteaker and her partners. Hartzell took back his mother's share for himself, but wasn't that concerned about getting back his neighbors' swindled money. Instead, Hartzell wanted to join the scheme, having decided he could mastermind the Drake swindle better than it had ever been done before. From that time onward Oscar Hartzell trimmed 70,000 Americans for at least $2 million. When postal authorities finally sent him off to Leavenworth, it was over the screaming protests of 70,000 suckers who still believed their magnificent fortunes were just around the corner.

Hartzell had formed the Sir Francis Drake Association, and he even dug up one Ernest Drake as the sole heir to the inheritance because he was the descendant of the bastard son of Drake and Queen Elizabeth I. Hartzell's pitch was so spellbinding he once held a public meeting in Quincy, Illinois, and signed up virtually every man and woman in the town.

Although the money was pouring in, Oscar shifted gears in his ploy. He now declared the midwestern Drake he'd dug up was a fraud. The real heir was residing in England, and Hartzell had to go to London to be with him and pressure the British government, which was illegally trying to hang on to the inheritance. Hartzell warned that any Drake investor who talked too much about what he was doing or objected would be cut out of his share of the money. Every investor actually had to sign a pledge of secrecy, which meant instant "disinheritance" if violated.

In London Oscar required $2,500 to be sent each week for "legal expenses." Since there were no expenses, London came to view Oscar as a wild-spending Texas millionaire. Back in the United States, postal inspectors readily determined the Drake matter was a swindle, but could not convince any of the suckers to admit knowing anything about it. Some got so far as to say they were involved in a "business deal abroad," but would then whisper, "I can't talk about that, even to a government man."

Meanwhile, the master kept sending back news of promising developments. He had finally uncovered the actual birth certificate of the illegitimate heir. Now the British government offered to settle, but Hartzell was not impressed with its puny offer since he had proved that the estate had grown to a worth of $400 *billion.* That meant the Drake suckers' original worth of at least 50 to 1 on their investments were hopelessly low and would amount to a thousand times more.

Hartzell continued to make his pitch. An erudite article on economics in a weekly magazine was offered to the American faithful as proof that the disposal of the estate was just a matter of weeks away. This was done despite the fact that the article writer did not mention the Drake estate and in fact knew nothing about it. When there was a slight fluctuation in the British pound, this became evidence that the financial gnomes were acknowledging that the currency was being adjusted so that Britain could make its gigantic payoff.

When the Depression hit in 1929, Oscar reported back that it had been caused by the fact that Britain would sink to near bankruptcy with the settlement. Then President Herbert Hoover was blocking the settlement because of his devotion to England. Then the king of England had agreed in direct talks with Oscar to sign the agreement. But then the Church of England had intervened with the king. When Franklin Roosevelt became president, his every Hyde Park weekend or fishing trip was really a sojourn to meet with England's rulers and lay down an ultimatum that the Drake inheritance had to be paid. In Iowa, a minister (a Drake victim himself) explained from the pulpit that only fear of scandal was keeping England from acknowledging its debt.

During all of this time the suckers were hit for more and more donations for expenses; Oscar's $2,500 per week kept flowing in. Not that Oscar didn't have a few woes in the Mother Country. A crystal ball reader tried to blackmail him after he'd gotten drunk and talked too much about the swindle. Miss St. John Montague trimmed him for over $50,000, but that was a drop in the bucket for what he was raking in.

Oscar had a potentially more serious problem when an English girl was about to become the mother of his child without the usual formalities. The girl's very irate father of the non-bride confronted Oscar in his plush quarters and for a while Oscar's very survival was at risk. But the father was duly placated when Oscar gave him the grand opportunity to invest £552 in the Drake estate. With their future thus secure, father, daughter and illegitimate tot-to-be gladly retired from the scene.

Finally, the U.S. postal authorities got evidence of mail fraud against some 30 of Hartzell's American agents. Some confessed and informed on Oscar, who claimed he had never used the U.S. mail himself; but the agents' testimony was sufficient to indict Oscar.

In the weeks before his trial, some $350,000 in donations came in to the inheritance operation. Oscar ordered his suckers to lobby local, state and national authorities to free him. They did and kept right at their assigned chores after Hartzell was convicted and got 10 years. Several of Hartzell's boys kept on operating, and suckers were assured the estate was about to be settled and all the postal inspectors and government lawyers would be fired and jailed instead of Oscar. Then word went out that Hartzell was not in prison but under the protection of the government against gunmen of the "interests," who were in a panic because they knew the jig was up.

Oscar Hartzell lost his mind in Leavenworth in 1935. He continuously raved about what he was going to do to those who had jailed him when he got out. Apparently, the end of his good life had affected his mind, and he started suffering delusions of grandeur. He was transferred to a mental institution, where he died in 1943.

The Drake inheritance scheme died with Oscar, but other heir swindles continue to this day.

DRIVEWAY SCAMS *leading home-repair gyp*

One of the most common home-repair gyps is the so-called "driveway scam," which seems to be an offer that cannot be refused. A truck stops before a house, and the driver tells the homeowner that he and his helper have just finished doing a seal-coating job in the neighborhood and that they have some leftover material. "I can give it back to the boss and make nothing on it," the driver says, "or I do a special job for you at two-thirds off."

Many homeowners accept the deal and get a "sealant" treatment that looks wonderful but is really nothing more than used engine oil that never dries. The goo washes away with the first rain. The same pitch is made for rewaterproofing a roof or fixing cracked foundations.

THE DROP *shortchanging gyp*

"The drop" is a shortchanging technique used by crooked cashiers in a wide variety of businesses. It works especially well in saloons where the victims very obligingly are not the most alert. A man pays for a drink with a $20 or $50 bill; the crooked bartender makes sure he hands back a lot of loose silver, putting the coins and the paper money down on the bar after very deliberately counting the bills in front of the drinker. As the customer is picking up the change—or often leaving it on the bar for future drinks—the bartender will count the bills once again, straightening them by tapping them on the bar and handing them over in a neat pile. The customer, now perhaps a bit tipsy, has seen the paper money counted and recounted and is certain the

amount is accurate. He will either leave the pile on the bar or tuck it into a pocket without giving it another thought.

Actually, the drinker has been robbed before his very eyes. While the customer was retrieving his coin change and watching the ritual stacking of the bills, he does not notice that when the bartender tapped the bills on their edges, he let the back bill—the one farthest from the customer—slip off and drop behind the bar into a stack of bottles. The bartender will pick up the bill later. If the drinker notices that he has been shorted, the bill can miraculously be found and returned to him.

DROP SCAM *street hustle*

A well-worn but still viable con game, the drop scam is practiced in a variety of ways, the most common of which involves the "dropper" dropping a wallet full of counterfeit money at the feet of a likely sucker and pretending to find it. The dropper is elated at his find but is mournful of the fact that he is in a hurry and won't have time to return it to the owner. He tells the victim, "It looks like four or five hundred bucks here. The guy who lost it ought to give at least a couple of hundred as a reward just to get it back plus all his credit cards and ID. Tell you what, mac, give me fifty bucks and you can take over returning the dough and getting most of the reward money."

As is common in virtually all con games, the appeal here is to the victim's likely larcenous streak, since he obviously can keep all the money. Kid Dropper (Nathan Kaplan), one of the most infamous New York criminals in the 1920s, earned his sobriquet from his proficiency at working the scam in his youth. In his first efforts Kid Dropper, as well as other novice practitioners in the field, had to learn the first rule of the scam, which is not to hand over the wallet before getting the payoff. Otherwise the victim might simply fish the payoff out of the "lost" wallet.

It is not uncommon for the average big-city police department to handle 50 or so complaints a year, almost all unsuccessfully, involving the drop; it is estimated that many times that figure go unreported.

DUPRE, GEORGE *teller of tall spy tales*

It was hardly surprising in 1953 when a book reviewer for the *New York Herald Tribune* said of master spy George DuPre (1906–): "Compared to DuPre all other spies whom we have read about were amateurs."

There was no disputing that statement. DuPre's account had appeared in the *Reader's Digest* and was printed in book form, under the authorship of noted reporter and writer Quentin Reynolds, as *The Man Who Wouldn't Talk*. It told of "quiet, religious" Canadian DuPre being recruited by British Intelligence during World War II to train for a bizarre mission. He was schooled for nine months on how to behave like "the village half-wit" and was then dropped behind German lines to pose as a harmless, moronic French garage mechanic. DuPre helped smuggle Allied flyers out of German-occupied territory until he was finally picked up by the Gestapo and tortured. He was given a sulfuric-acid enema, had boiling water poured into his clamped-open mouth, had his finger squashed in a vise, was subjected to several savage beatings and so on. Through all of this DuPre maintained his half-wit guise, mumbling "I don't know" until the Gestapo turned him loose.

DuPre's story had been around in western Canada for several years, as he had spoken at church and club gatherings since the end of the war. When the *Digest* heard about him, it brought him to New York, where he impressed both the editors and Quentin Reynolds, who was recruited to write the book, which was sold in advance to Random House.

Everything about DuPre reeked of honesty. He had scars on his chin, no teeth, a broken nose and a speech impediment—all caused, he said, by the Nazi tortures. Everyone in western Canada, business people, religious figures and government and military officials sang DuPre's praises. DuPre lived in Reynolds' home for about a week as they worked together. Then Reynolds went to Calgary to check his facts carefully with people who knew DuPre. Reynolds dined together with DuPre and the mayor, witnessed DuPre's close ties with high government officials and went to a Royal Canadian Air Force officers' party in DuPre's honor. "Everyone was delighted," he said later, "that at last DuPre was to get recognition outside of Canada."

Reynolds submitted his manuscript to British Intelligence for confirmation only to be informed that the tight-lipped service would not even look at it because of its policy never to confirm or deny an individual had ever been in its employ. Since DuPre's story had gone unchallenged for more than a half-dozen years, Reynolds had no doubt of DuPre's honesty. *Digest* editor DeWitt Wallace said, "If there

ever was a man who inspired confidence and seemed deeply religious, it was he." When Reynolds insisted on splitting the book royalties with DuPre, the Canadian at first refused and then assigned all income to the Boy Scouts of Canada.

The roof fell in within days of the book and *Digest* publication, when a R.C.A.F. officer walked into the offices of the *Calgary Herald* with a photo of himself and DuPre taken in Victoria, British Columbia, in 1942 when DuPre was supposed to be in France. The *Herald* sent reporter Douglas Collins, an ex-Intelligence man himself, to talk to DuPre and he soon tripped him up by getting him to say he knew Intelligence figures and training camps that Collins had made up. DuPre finally confessed his entire story was a falsehood; he had spent the war in the R.C.A.F. in England and Canada and had never even been near British Intelligence.

He said he had started out in 1946 just telling a little lie, but when everyone got so interested the lie "grew." As his embellishments increased, so did the impact of the story on his listeners. "The story eventually got bigger than I was. I was only a means of telling it. I honestly felt I had a message—that no man can survive without faith in God, and that with faith a man can endure anything. I thought this story of tremendous self-sacrifice as a means of leading youth—and grownups, too—to new insight into what man can be capable of. The story may not have been true, but the message is the truest thing in the world."

Author Reynolds described himself as "duped" by the "greatest hoax ever perpetrated" and said, "Trust George DuPre? I'd have bet my life on that man!"

Reader's Digest published a three-page retraction of its story of "The Man Who Wouldn't Talk" under the title of "The Story of an Extraordinary Literary Hoax."

President Bennett Cerf of Random House was a bit more commercial-minded about the episode. While he announced that any of the purchasers of the book could have their money back, he also suggested to bookstores all over the country that they move the book from the "nonfiction" shelf to the "fiction" section where it clearly belonged.

E

EDWARDS HEIRS SWINDLE _long-running fraud_

With the exception of the Baker Estate swindle (see entry), the Edwards heir swindle was probably the longest-running, major inheritance con perpetrated in America. In fact, it was a sort of family business passed over the decades from father to son to keep on cheating the gullible. The grand deception began in the 1880s with Dr. Herbert H. Edwards, who maintained with considerable fervor that he was a descendant of Robert Edwards, the alleged owner of 65 acres of Manhattan Island in 1770—right in the middle of which was erected the Woolworth Building. It was obvious that this bit of real estate had become one of the most valuable in the world.

Dr. Edwards set up the Edwards Heirs Association, which his son continued after his death, to regain the property that, he said, was lost through legal flimflammery. Thousands of people named Edwards were permitted to join after they passed a genealogical investigation, which indicated they were entitled to a share of the inheritance. The genealogical determination was made by a carpenter friend of Dr. Edwards, one Milo Pressel, who somehow never seemed to turn anyone down. A sample of Pressel's work was that in one case he discovered evidence of the marriage of Blount J. Hassell to Frances Kirk on November 1, 1885. No matter that this was 11 years before the groom was born and 13 years before the bride was born.

Members of the Edwards Heirs Association paid $26 a year as dues so that the organization would protect their rights. One Tennessee man paid for himself as well as 47 others. Of course, the members were certain they would receive at least 1,000 times their investment when a final settlement was made. Edwards and his son always indicated this was imminent.

Warm relationships formed among the society of millionaires-to-be, climaxed each year by a great fete. Members from all parts of the country showed up by the hundreds, sometimes thousands, to feast in celebration of the coming good fortune. The suckers even had their own "alma mater," of which the first two verses and chorus went:

> We have rallied here in blissful state
> Our jubilee to celebrate.
> When Fortune kindly on us smiled,
> The Edwards Heirs now reconciled.
>
> Our president deserves our praise,
> For strenuous work through dreary days,
> In consummating our affairs
> And rounding up the Edwards heirs.
>
> _Chorus_
> We're Robert Edwards' legal heirs,
> And cheerfully we take our shares.
> Then let us shout with joy and glee
> And celebrate the jubilee.

Finally, after several decades of successfully gouging victims and their descendants, the great swindle was crushed by the postal authorities. The members of the association never got any of the promised rewards, but at least they had fond memories of their annual hangovers and their uproarious celebrations.

EGG SEX DETERMINATOR _chicken testing con_

It is the real chicken-egg dollars-and-cents dilemma on the farm. Does that egg that's going to be sold and eaten have the promise of being a hen or a much-prized cockerel? Traveling farmland hustlers claim to have the answer with their "egg sex determinator," which they have hawked to farmers for decades. It's a sort of weighted metal device that hangs from twine. All a farmer has to do is hold it over an egg, and if it tilts in any direction but one, it will be a hen. Otherwise it's a cockerel. The incubation period for a chicken is 21 days, and by that time the egg sex hustler is three weeks gone.

EGRESS   *P. T. Barnum's most tantalyzing humbug*

Of all the famed humbugs foisted on Americans by the fabulous showman P. T. Barnum, the "Egress" was in a sense the most tantalyzing, and perhaps gauged the tolerance of the public for being conned. Certainly many of Barnum's great hoaxes—the Cardiff Giant; the Feejee Mermaid; Joice Heth, Washington's "161-year-old Nurse" (see entries)—were more infamous. But none was more blatant than the "Egress."

This phenomenon was featured at Barnum's American Museum in New York City. The establishment was constantly clogged by gawking crowds viewing Barnum's outrageous and often preposterous exhibits, and the showman's chief concern was how to keep the audience moving quickly so that waiting ticket buyers could be admitted. He came up with the solution one St. Patrick's Day in the 1840s, when long lines of Irish customers jammed the museum. In desperation Barnum ordered a carpenter to cut a new door over which he had a sign painted, reading: "THIS WAY TO THE EGRESS." Other signs were placed leading to the door.

Eager patrons spewed forth to see what fabulous offering this "Egress" was—perhaps a freakish human, a bizarre animal, or something even more horrifying. As they went through the door they found themselves out in a back alley, the door locked behind them.

If patrons were so cunningly "egressed," few seemed to take the misadventure with ill temper. It was an example of what Barnum biographer Arthur Saxon said of the showman: "Barnum realized that in the interest of a good laugh—even one directed at their own folly—people loved nothing so much as a grand hoax, a dazzling bluff, a glorious humbug. And they would pay handsomely to get it."

It was said that many of the "egressed" hurried back around to the admission line to return to Barnum's house of hoaxes. Some took particular delight in stationing themselves near the egress to watch other gullible patrons head for involuntary ejection. This may be considered proof perhaps of a variation of a theme credited to Barnum, that there's a con artist born every minute.

EIFFEL TOWER SALE   *monumental swindle*

Compared to the bogus sale of the Eiffel Tower, sales of the Brooklyn Bridge must sink to the level of a dime-store operation. True, the Brooklyn Bridge was sold hundreds of times, but frequently at very low prices to gullible "greenhorns." The sale of the Eiffel Tower—for the patently ridiculous reason of having it torn down—was a fraud pulled on shrewd and well-heeled businessmen.

The sale was made by "Count" Victor Lustig, a man many regard as the premier confidence man of the 20th century. Born in 1890 in Hostinne, in what became Czechoslovakia, Victor Lustig was a con man who worked both sides of the Atlantic, having been forced to flee France around 1920 after a number of shady deals. He engaged in the same practice in the United States until 1925, when he read in a newspaper that the Eiffel Tower was in need of repairs. Built for the Paris Exposition of 1889, it was once the tallest manmade structure in the world. From the start it was (and still remains) a tremendous tourist attraction and to this day is in need of repairs.

Lustig had a brainstorm and went scurrying back to Paris. He had some very impressive looking French government writing paper made up and sent out confidential letters to six leading scrap metal dealers, summoning them to a secret meeting in a luxury hotel. Lustig, calling himself "Deputy Director-General of the Ministry of Mail and Telegraphs," informed the dealers that the government had determined that repairs on the Eiffel Tower would be too costly and that it would have to be torn down and sold for scrap instead. But he added the government was fearful of the public reaction, so the plans would have to be kept secret until the demolition work actually commenced. Later, he predicted, once the public saw how much taxpayer money was saved, the people would change their minds.

The scrap dealers were enthusiastic, since this was a multimillion-dollar deal. Later, as the meeting broke up, Lustig whispered to one dealer that the government would favor his bid since his firm was "the most qualified." Lustig added that it was so hard to work for the government since the pay was so low and his expense so much higher. The dealer understood a bribe solicitation when he heard one and, as it was a common way of doing business at the time, nodded. Within an hour after he left, the dealer was back with a thick bundle of money, somewhat in excess of $100,000.

As soon as Lustig had the money, he hopped on a train to Vienna, figuring to lie low until the scandal broke and then blew over. Day after day he read the French papers and found no report of the swindle. He realized that the scrap dealer had either been too frightened or too ashamed to hold himself up to public ridicule by going to the authorities. If that were so, Lustig reasoned, the dealer most certainly had not gone to his competitors either.

Lustig returned to the French capital, contacted a second scrap dealer and pulled the same caper again. This time he got exactly $100,000 and again went into hiding; but this time the outraged victim went to the police. Lustig's gold-laying goose was dead, he realized, and he headed back to America where he pulled an endless string of other imaginative swindles.

See also LUSTIG, "COUNT" VICTOR.

ELECTRIC CHAIR IMMUNITY *false imperial claim*

Learning in the late 1890s that electrocution had become the newest method of capital punishment, Emperor Menelek II of Ethiopia (1844–1913) immediately ordered three electric chairs imported from the United States. The emperor was most chagrined to learn upon their arrival that the chairs required electricity, an advance that had not yet been introduced in Ethiopia. To make the best of a bad situation, Menelek used one of the chairs as his royal throne. His aides soon realized the public relations value of the emperor sitting in the white man's "hot seat," and spread the claim among his subjects that the great Menelek was immune to the white man's killing ways.

ELEVATOR DROP *pickpocketing scam*

A few years ago New York City's Office of the Comptroller issued a warning about a scam becoming common in high-rise elevators.

A man and woman enter the elevator with the victim and appear not to know each other. The woman strikes up a conversation with the victim and shortly thereafter drops her purse, causing several dollar bills to scatter on the floor. Even without a request for help, the victim bends down to pick up the loose bills. As he does so, the male partner removes the wallet from the victim's pocket or purse. The act is timed to finish just as the thief's stop a few floors above the lobby is reached. Thus, he is gone before the victim notices his loss.

ELIZABETH I "HAG" COIN *fake that fooled Horace Walpole*

In 1742 Horace Walpole purchased a coin in the sale of the Earl of Oxford's collection. The coin showed Queen Elizabeth I as a hag and, according to Walpole, it was "a fragment of one of her last broad pieces, representing her horridly old and deformed: An entire coin with this image is not known: It is universally supposed that the die was broken by her command, and that some workman of the mint cut this morsel, which contains barely the face . . . it has never been engraved."

How much of all this was "universally supposed" can only be speculated since nothing about the sup-

posed coin seems to be known before Walpole expounded on it, and the entire thesis appears to have originated with him. After Walpole's declarations, forgers went to work producing a complete coin utilizing the hag design, and it enjoyed some popularity among collectors.

The true origin of the original hag fragment was never discovered, although it was apparently circulated by some of Elizabeth's many opponents—perhaps Catholic, extreme Protestant, republican or aristocrat. Experts in due course were able to demonstrate it was nothing more than a doctoring of a genuine coin of the realm, a sovereign piece that had been rudely gouged to give the queen a haglike appearance. Apparently as such recut coins were found, they were quietly removed from circulation.

EMMA SILVER MINE BUBBLE *infamous stock scam*

From the early 1870s until the turn of the century, mining activity in Utah was the exact opposite of that in other western states and territories. While there was a craze for finding gold and silver and other valuable ores throughout the country, Utah was treated as a land of pestilence and unworthy of investment, despite the presence of huge ore deposits. The reason: Utahans were not to be trusted.

Actually, this was a bad rap even though virtually all earlier investors in Utah's mining activities lost their shirts in the largest American mining con ever perpetrated. In fairness, it should be noted that Utahans themselves were far more sinned against than sinning, having also been taken in the infamous Emma Silver Mine Bubble. Investors, Utahans and other Americans and a great many more in England, lost millions in the Emma mine fraud.

It all started in 1868 when two prospectors hit what appeared to be a huge deposit in Little Cottonwood Canyon near Alta. Lacking capital to exploit their supposed find the pair was forced to cut in James E. Lyon, a New York mining speculator, who moved in to take effective control. Lyon in turn found it necessary to yield a large portion of the operation to San Francisco mining interests, and they in turn brought in Trevor W. Park of Vermont and Gen. H. Henry Baxter of New York. Lyon made a rather unwise move by introducing Sen. William M. Stewart of Nevada to oversee his interests.

A number of illustrious names were also added to the roster, including Professor Benjamin Silliman Jr. of Yale, who was given $25,000 for preparing a glowing report on the mine's ore deposits. By then the combine had decided to sell stock in the mine not only in the United States, but in England as well. They created a board of directors of the English operation, including three members of the British Parliament, the U.S. minister to the Court of St. James, and a former president of the New York Central Railroad, among others. Hawking the stock was assigned to Baron Albert Grant, a London financier noted for his brilliant flair for promotion, if rather limited ethical standards.

In England alone the floating of stock in Emma Mining brought in £600,000 of which £170,000 went to Grant for his labors. All of the American operators came out extremely well save for original investor Lyon. His supposed protector, Senator Stewart, maneuvered him out of the firm, paying him only 50 cents on the dollar for what he had been promised.

For a time English investors thought they were doing quite well, and the stock in Emma rose from £20 to £50 a share. Then a rival firm, Illinois Tunnel Company, burst the Emma Mine bubble by declaring the Emma claim had not been recorded correctly and that the English company was actually mining silver to meet its initial dividends on the stock it had sold. By 1872 the directors admitted that—despite the earlier glowing estimates—the available ore had run out.

In the United States a congressional investigation proved a massive fraud had been perpetrated. Then the most startling disclosure was made. It turned out that the head of Illinois Tunnel was none other than shrewd New Englander Trevor Park, himself perhaps the biggest profiteer on Emma's board. All kinds of litigation followed, and in the end everyone who had made money in the deal kept their boodle and the shareholders were left with almost nothing. In 1877 Park offered shareholders a piddling $150,000 for their holdings, something less than a nickel on the dollar. The shareholders could do nothing but accept. Ironically, Park was able to keep Emma going and managed to take out a bit over $150,000 in profits from subsequent operations to make up his "losses" to the shareholders.

When the dust settled, investors and speculators of all stripes simply refused to consider any other mining deals in Utah for close to a generation. In England the Emma fraud was cited with droll British understatement as an example of "Yankee ingenuity."

EMPLOYMENT GYPS See GULF WAR SCAMS.

END-OF-THE-WORLD EGG *Doomsday con*
While most doomsday prophecies have been based on the forecasters' religious beliefs, the most bald-faced claim of all was perpetrated by . . . a chicken egg. In the autumn of 1806 in a tavern in Leeds, England, Mary Bateman's hen started laying eggs inscribed with the words "Christ Is Coming." To the religious-minded this meant only one thing—the fast approach of Armageddon. Large prayer meetings were held in the surrounding area.

Meanwhile, back at the tavern Mary Bateman was being quite specific, telling gathering hordes that God had revealed to her that her hen would lay 14 similarly inscribed eggs and then the Earth would be consumed in flames. While she was speaking, the hen laid another egg bearing the same frightful message.

But Mary had some good news: There was some hope of salvation, but it would cost everyone a penny to hear it. Everyone in the crowd paid willingly. The pitch: God had decided to allow all those bearing a piece of a certain type of paper sealed with the inscription "J.C." to enter into heaven immediately after the 14th egg was laid. The price of the heavenly ticket was a shilling. All paid who could afford it.

With each additional egg, hundreds and then thousands flocked to the tavern to get "sealed." Then a doctor who had heard about the strange doings in Leeds showed up. He inspected the hen and the eggs and discovered the eggs were inscribed with corrosive ink. He imparted his discovery to the authorities who raided the tavern on the day the 14th egg was to be laid. They caught Mary just as she was jamming an inscribed egg back into a very angry hen.

Mary was arrested but soon released. Oddly, most people were not too upset about having been conned, being delirious that Doomsday was being postponed indefinitely. Mary Bateman went back to making prophecies, but does not appear to have prospered at it. Apparently for that reason she switched to performing illegal abortions, for which she was convicted and hanged.

ENVELOPE SWITCH *laying the flue*
The "envelope switch" is used in various con games in which money is stuffed into an envelope and then, when the sucker is unaware, that envelope is switched for another one, which contains only cut paper.

A more sophisticated version is "laying the flue," in which several bets are placed on a sporting contest in a bar. A single genuine $500 bill is put in the envelope, in exchange for the loose bills, and is then sealed. To make sure there is no envelope switch, several of the bettors—including the sucker or suckers—sign their names on the envelope. The envelope is then offered to the bartender to hold, but most often the bartender will reject it, since it could affect the establishment's license. If that happens, the envelope is returned and stuffed in the sucker's pocket for him to hold. If the game comes out the way the con men bet, they simply retrieve the envelope. If they are losing, they head ostensibly for the men's room "to cut our throats."

They keep on going, since they have the $500 bill anyway. It had been slipped out of the envelope early on through a slit in the side or bottom of the edge of the envelope.

EQUITY FUNDING CORP. FRAUD *billion-dollar computer scam*

There are those experts who say the monumental Equity Funding Corporation fraud of the 1960s and 1970s represents the wave of the future in corporate grand theft. Involved was something like $2 billion, but the swindle was so great that no one has ever figured out where all the money went or even how much money was lost. Chances are it will never be known. It still remains the greatest known computer fraud.

In 1964 Equity Funding was a small company that started growing into a big one. Several companies were growing in the late 1960s, so that didn't seem so unusual. When there was a big business slow-down in the early 1970s, Equity Funding still kept growing and thus won accolades on Wall Street as being a brilliant company loaded with brilliant young executives who accounted for the firm's impressive success.

What many of these brilliant young executives had learned to do was lie to a computer. They told the computer the firm had sold 64,000 more insurance policies than it actually had. Being a simple-minded if complicated computer, the machine believed them. The more life insurance the company claimed it sold, the more money its computer said it had. The more money the computer vouched for, the more money Equity Funding could borrow and the more stock it could sell.

Technically, a company like Equity Funding should have been checked from time to time by experts not connected with it. But it is no easy matter to doublecheck a giant computer. As a result, the monumental con went on for nine years. Thousands of people who put money into Equity Funding lost everything.

What was truly frightening about the mess was that it had not been uncovered by any fail-safe auditing procedures. At least 40 top executives were in on the grand hoax, and many more within Equity smelled something rotten. Some started talking, but no one believed them. Equity Funding was too good to be nothing more than a scam. Finally, a stock expert named Ray Dirks heard the stories and started looking into the matter. It hadn't really been a part of his job, but once he started investigating, he quickly uncovered the fraud. Within weeks there was an exodus of executives from the firm. Many were later convicted of fraud. Were it not for stock detective

Dirks, the fraud could have gone on for years—and might still be going on today.

Some business experts insist that such a major fraud could not occur again, that there are now ways to check on what a company claims it is doing. But then again, no one believed the Equity Funding scandal could happen in the first place.

See also COMPUTER SCAMS.

ERANSO, CATALINA DE *male impersonator*

Spanish-born Catalina de Eranso was schooled as a nun, but upon suffering sexual abuse in the institution, she escaped her Dominican novitiate and took up an existence as a man. Taking the name of Alonso Diaz Ramierez de Guzman, she joined the Spanish army and for several years acquitted herself bravely in combat in Chile and Peru. She was able to keep her true identity from her superior officers, as well as her own brother, with whom she came in frequent contact.

De Eranso was exposed in 1624 only when she was wounded. She returned to Spain where she was regarded as a heroine of the nation. Pope Urban VIII granted her a special dispensation allowing her to continue to dress in male attire.

ESTES, BILLIE SOL *con man*

Back in the early 1960s people looked upon Texan Billie Sol Estes (1925–   ) as a genuine boy wonder of business. Estes, a strong supporter of Lyndon Johnson, appeared to have everything: He was a good family man, a regular churchgoer and very rich while still in his 30s. No one thought of him as a swindler. Estes had no trouble at all convincing farmers to invest in liquid fertilizer tanks. The only trouble was that the tanks didn't exist. And there was no fertilizer either. When Estes' scheme was finally exposed, his $150 million business collapsed. None of the investors' money was ever recovered.

Estes was sentenced to 15 years in prison and was released in 1971 after serving six. Under the terms of his parole, Estes was barred from any more promotional schemes; but he did not take the stipulation seriously. Almost immediately he was back to his old tricks, this time conning investors by borrowing money and using oil field cleaning equipment as collateral. The equipment didn't exist.

Typical of Estes' victims was an Abilene used car dealer named J.H. Burkett, who loaned the con man his life savings of $50,000. Burkett described having met Estes in 1975: "I met him in church, in Bible study in Abilene, and he struck me as a very nice guy. He seemed very humble, very earnest, remorseful. I was very impressed by him, and I still am, but in a different way. The man is the world's best salesman. Just go and meet him, and you'll find out. He'll sell you something."

In 1979 Estes got two five-year terms for his latest capers. Before sentencing Estes told the judge: "I love this country. I'd rather be in prison here than free anywhere else in the world." He insisted that whether or not he went to jail, he would pay the money he owed, including some $10 million in back taxes. He claimed he had more than a million friends and could raise $10 from each of them. There were some observers who said he very possibly could.

When he went to prison, Estes said that upon his release he would help solve the 1961 murder of a man named Henry Marshall. Marshall's bullet-ridden body had been found in June 1961 on a remote part of his Texas ranch. At the time the death was ruled a suicide, something many people never accepted. When released, Estes told a grand jury that Clifton Carter, an aide to Lyndon Johnson, ordered Marshall, a U.S. Department of Agriculture official, to approve 138 cotton deals as a favor repaying Estes for his campaign contribution to Johnson. According to Estes, Marshall told Estes' lawyers in January 1961 he thought the scheme was fraudulent. Estes claimed he, Johnson, Carter and Malcolm Wallace—a Johnson friend who had once been convicted of killing a man—met in Johnson's Washington home to discuss the threat Marshall represented. The fear, Estes testified, was that Marshall would tattle to Attorney General Robert Kennedy. Thus, Estes said, Johnson ordered Marshall killed. Estes said Wallace had poisoned the USDA official with carbon monoxide and then shot him with his own gun.

Nobody bought the tale, neither Johnson's friends nor foes. Conveniently, all of the conspirators in the alleged murder plot—except Estes—were dead.

Estes made his revelations while promoting his daughter's biography of him. It was entitled *Billie Sol: King of the Wheeler-Dealers.* No one objected to the title.

EULENSPIEGEL, TILL *14th-century German hoaxer*

While he is by no means the first grand hoaxer in history, Till Eulenspiegel, a 14th-century German from the village of Brunswick, became noted as that country's most renowned prankster. His mischievous pranks and wild jests are so numerous that many apocryphal hoaxes have been attributed to him.

The magnificent Eulenspiegel is credited with originating that long-standing German hoax known as the Blindmen's Dinner. Accosted by 12 blind men begging for alms, he told them: "Go to the inn; eat, drink and be merry, my men; and here are 20 florins to pay the bill."

The blind men thanked him effusively, each assuming another member of the party had received

the money. They ate and drank heartily and when the proprietor presented the check, each called on the one who had gotten the florins to pay. No one had.

This hoax is the ancestor of the American joker who announces, "When I drink, everyone drinks. Bartender serve everybody." The magnanimous soul then beats a hasty retreat by declaring, "When I pay, everybody pays."

A collection of Eulenspiegel's hoaxes or depredations was printed in 1515 and was translated into many languages. Till Eulenspiegel is also the picaresque hero of Charles de Cosque's 1867 novel *Ulenspiegel* and is featured in several operas as well as Richard Strauss' 1895 symphonic poem, *Till Eulenspiegel's Merry Pranks.*

EYE BET *small betting con*

One of the oldest betting scams around involves a hustler in a bar who bets fellow drinkers that he can bite his own eye. Invariably, a victim will fall for the ploy and the wager is made, whereupon the hustler plops a glass eye out of its socket, bites it and returns it to its proper place. The hustler collects his money and then announces he'll bet he can bite his other eye as well. Most victims, having been taken once, generally refuse to take the wager—at first. However, the more they reflect on the situation, they realize the hustler cannot do the same thing with the other eye since he obviously had to be totally blind. Most victims therefore bet again—and lose again—as the hustler blithely takes his false teeth out of his mouth and clamps them on his good eye.

One leading practitioner of this delightful scam is an old reprobate in Las Vegas who haunts the bars and wins enough bets to keep him active at the gaming tables for hours every night. Recently a reporter asked a leading gambling executive in Las Vegas if he didn't think it would be proper to rein in the old hustler who, after all, was constantly skimming the tourists. The gambling man, reflecting the town's special ethics and appreciation for a cunning scam, was adamantly opposed. "Why should we?" he demanded. "He cheats 'em fair and square."

EYE IN THE SKY SCAM *gambling gyp*

It is a little-known fact that virtually all gambling casinos in the United States have peepholes in the ceiling and men with binoculars watching the play. The casinos insist the spies are there not to cheat but to watch out for cheaters, more often crooked employees than the customers themselves. Without such protection, many casinos claim that crooked employees working with outside confederates would put them out of business. But the technique—called "eye in the sky"—has long been used in gambling scams as well, especially by organized crime.

Mafia leader Vito Genovese was especially addicted to eye-in-the-sky scams. In one operation he and his lieutenant, Mike Miranda, took a gullible businessman for $160,000, getting signals from a spy in the room above as to what cards the victim had in his hand. The information was transmitted via a small radio receiver worn under the clothing of one of the mobsters.

The same tactic was used in 1947 at Bugsy Siegel's newly opened Flamingo—the first lavish casino built in Las Vegas—shortly before mobster Siegel was murdered. The hustlers lured fabled gambler Nick "the Greek" Dandolos into a poolside gin rummy game. Both the Greek and his opponent wore only bathing suits but the opponent had a receiver tucked under his trunks. A telescope was set up in a room overlooking the pool and was used to spy on the Greek's cards. Nick never suspected the scam, and because the chairs were riveted to the floor, he was never out of the telescope's probing eye. The Greek was trimmed for a half-million dollars. Later, when the details of the scam became known, Ian Fleming appropriated the incident for use in his James Bond novel *Goldfinger*.

Similarly, the late Johnny Roselli, the mob's long-time overseer of its interests in Las Vegas and Hollywood, was convicted in 1968 of a similar dodge at the Beverly Hills Friars Club. Comedians Phil Silvers and Zeppo Marx and singer Tony Martin were among those taken in an operation that netted $400,000. Roselli had even smuggled an electronics engineer onto the premises to set up the intricate spy system.

F

FAKE MURDER FAKES *deadly insurance fraud*

A particularly deadly scam that insurance companies constantly guard against is what may be called "fake murder fakes." Swindler-murderers have attempted many such capers in every country in the world and undoubtedly have succeeded on numerous occasions. The theory behind the scam is to kill off someone after he or she has taken out a large insurance policy to the plotters' benefit. Of course, few victims see any reason to cooperate in a plot that requires their actual murder. The plotters solve this dilemma by concocting a scheme in which the victim becomes a willing partner after being assured a substitute corpse will be used. The insurance policy is purchased with the victim's eager participation and then the plot is put into operation. But there is one catch: Substituting another corpse is no easy matter. The obvious solution: Use the real thing.

Perhaps the classic example of this involves a beautiful but dumb 21-year-old Chicago model named Marie Defenbach (1879–1900) who was inveigled into such a conspiracy by one of the plotters, who pretended to be in love with her, and a murderous doctor, August M. Unger. Marie was to take out $70,000 in various life insurance policies, naming her lover and another conspirator as beneficiaries. Dr. Unger assured Marie he would personally handle her "demise" in a most careful manner. He would give her a special medicine of his own concoction that would induce a deathlike sleep. Later, the doctor told her, she would be revived in the back room of the funeral home and spirited away while an unclaimed body of another female would be cremated in her stead. For her cooperation in the plot, the conspirators thought it eminently fair that Marie should get half the loot.

Marie swallowed the story, never realizing to her the men could save themselves a lot of effort and add $35,000 to their profit by simply feeding her some real poison. This was precisely what occurred on the night of August 25, 1900, with poor Marie dying in terrible agony after 15 minutes of suffering. Dr. Unger signed the death certificate, and the body was cremated forthwith. The conspirators claimed all the insurance money but eventually were caught by private investigators hired by the girl's uncle to find out what had happened to her. Ironically, they could not be convicted of murder because there was no body left to be examined. However, one of the trio turned state's evidence and Dr. Unger and one accomplice, Frank Brown, were sentenced to five years in prison for fraud.

FALLON, WILLIAM J. *courtroom trickster*

According to many legal authorities William J. Fallon (1886–1927), labeled *The Great Mouthpiece* by his biographer Gene Fowler, was one of the most resourceful defense attorneys in America. He was also one of the most dishonest, not averse to using bribery and theft to win cases. But Fallon was perhaps most in his element as a courtroom trickster, relying on hoax lines of reasoning to discredit prosecution witnesses in the eyes of the jury.

Typical of Fallon's tactics was his defense of a Russian accused of arson. The case against him looked solid. The defendant had been convicted twice of setting fire to stores he owned in attempts to collect on his insurance. Fallon realized his best—indeed his only—hope was to discredit the prosecution's witnesses. The prosecution presented a fireman who had entered the burning structure and had smelled kerosene on a number of wet rags. Fallon countered that the rags had contained water and demanded that the fireman be given a test to see if he could tell the difference between water and kerosene. The fireman was perfectly willing to oblige.

Fallon produced five bottles numbered 1, 2, 3, 4 and 5 and asked the fireman to sniff each bottle and testify if it contained water or gasoline. Sniffing bottle number 1, the fireman declared it to be kerosene. In turn, he sniffed each of the remaining bottles and announced the same conclusion.

Fallon picked up bottle number 5 and took a sip of it. Addressing the jury, he said: "The contents of this bottle does not taste like kerosene to me. This bottle—this bottle that the gentleman on the witness stand would have you believe contains kerosene— doesn't contain kerosene at all. It contains water. When you get into the jury room, I wish you would all help yourself to a taste of its contents. If what you taste in the slightest resembles kerosene, I think it is your duty to convict my client. If what you taste is water, then it is your duty to acquit my client."

The defendant was promptly found not guilty, since the liquid was pure water. Fallon simply had the fireman inhale deeply from the first four bottles, all of which contained kerosene. Thus when he sniffed the water, the fumes from the previous bottles were still in his nostrils.

FALSE ARREST SCAMS See CAR RESALE SWINDLE; LAUNDERED HANDKERCHIEF SCAM.

FALSE DMITRYS See PRETENDER CZARS.

FAMINE FRAUD *cheating aid programs*
In May 1991, 46-year-old Martyn Merritt, an American shipping company executive, was convicted of conspiracy after admitting sending hundreds of tons of cheap milk powder used for animal feed to African famine victims. Merritt's company, AMG Services, had won a $936,000 contract to provide low-fat powdered milk to the Sudan as part of a U.S. foreign-aid program. Instead, it supplied animal feed that was "not fit for human consumption" and contained "scorched particles and appearance quite below that normally found in Grade A skim powder." Merritt also admitted that he supplied false documents saying the milk powder had come from Sri Lanka, since there had been a requirement that it be bought from a third world nation. Actually, the powder came from a Netherlands supplier. The animal feed was never distributed because officials discovered the plot and confiscated the delivery in a Sudanese port.

At Merritt's sentencing, prosecutors noted that sentencing guidelines called for a prison term of 24 to 30 months in such a case, which included a guilty plea. However, federal Judge John S. Martin Jr. sentenced Merritt to five years and fined him nearly $2 million, the maximum possible under the law.

FANNING *butcher shop weight gyp*
While the standard description of shortweighing butchers is that they have a "big thumb," that is, make it a practice of putting their thumb on the scales while weighing meat, such gyp artists use more sophisticated methods. One of the most common is fanning. Even air conditioned butcher shops and supermarkets have a need to keep the actual meat counter still cooler and frequently add an overhead fan or two to the area.

A sure mark of a chiseling store is the location of these fans or, more precisely, where the butcher's meat scales are in relation to them. When the fans are going full force, the breeze will play on the scale tray and tote up close to an ounce of weighted air, enough to increase the price of a pound of meat by almost 7%.

Besides fanning, butcher shops and other stores may engage in "tacking," inserting several tacks through a strip of adhesive and sticking it under the weighing pan. This adds up to a fast two ounces. Theoretically, the sharp-eyed customer should be able to spot a scale that starts out a few ounces over the zero—if, that is, the dishonest merchant gives the customer the chance. Of course, the storekeeper doesn't dare conceal the scale from view; that's against the law and would arouse instant suspicion. Instead, he piles a display of "bargains" in front of the scale so that the customer at the counter cannot stand directly before it. That way the shopper can read the scale only at an angle; because of the inevitable distortion he cannot expect to see the needle directly on the zero.

FASTED TWO YEARS MINUS 721 DAYS *non-eating impostor*
A most tragic fasting hoax occurred in the 1870s when a young teenage girl named Sarah Jacobs gained fame in Wales for her alleged ability to fast. She was exhibited by her parents with the claim that she had lived over a two-year stretch without a single bit of food passing her lips. Authorities decided to test the young imposter by placing her under the surveillance of a professional nurse. The girl died of starvation in nine days. Sarah's mother and father were convicted and sent to prison for fraud. (According to *The Guinness Book of Records*, the longest period a person has gone without food and water is 18 days, accomplished by Andreas Mihavecz of Bregenz, Austria, in 1979.)

FEEJEE MERMAID *Barnum's fabulous find*
Of all the hoaxes perpetrated by that master showman, P. T. Barnum, the one that catapulted both him and his American Museum into national prominence was the Feejee Mermaid. Barnum obtained the so-called mermaid in 1842 and used a massive mailing to the New York press from various locations reporting the incredible discovery of a mermaid in the Feejee [sic] Islands and that it was then being preserved in China. By the time Barnum announced he

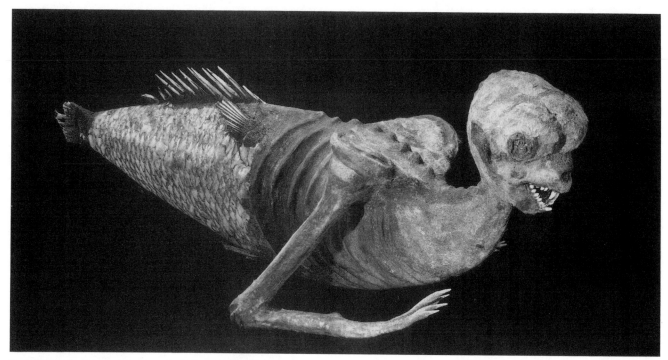

In 1842 P. T. Barnum astounded New Yorkers with his Feejee Mermaid, which was actually a combination of the upper portion of a monkey with the lower half of a fish.

would have the Feejee Mermaid on display in his American Museum in New York, the public was more than prepared to pay almost any price, including Barnum's then hefty 25-cents for admission.

What they saw, however, was a dried, ugly specimen that has some fish and some humanlike characteristics. In later years, Barnum admitted the Feejee Mermaid was a hoax, having been constructed by combining the upper portion of a monkey with the lower half of a fish.

FELLER, PROFESSOR JOHN QUENTIN *museum insider-thief*

Most thefts from museums in recent years have been "insider crimes," the work of trusted staff members or scholars who are frequently afforded special privileges. One typical scholar scam artist is John Quentin Feller, a widely published expert on Chinese export ceramics and a professor of history at the University of Scranton, a man who found a most ingenious method of upward mobility within his field.

On January 10, 1991, Professor Feller was examining a beautifully crafted Chinese serving platter at the Winterthur Museum near Wilmington, Delaware. The dish had once belonged to George Washington and later to Robert E. Lee. The professor did not return the platter to the locked case, but instead hid it in a drawer of a sideboard in the museum and announced the dish was missing. The professor insisted to the Delaware State Police that he did not steal the platter, but it soon became apparent that

his denials wouldn't wash. Feller then started spewing forth the details of his bizarre 18-year career of theft in which time he heisted well over 100 precious objects from eight museums in the United States and England. It was soon apparent that Professor Feller was one of the greatest art thieves of the 20th century.

Feller started stealing in 1972 when he discovered some 30,000 pieces of porcelain gathering dust in the Wadsworth Atheneum in Hartford, Connecticut. He later recalled he had been chagrined that these "van Goghs of the porcelain field" were left dusty and ignored, and he made off with 18 of the most impressive items by smuggling them out from time to time in his camera case or under his shirt.

Feller donated them to the Peabody Museum of Salem, Massachusetts, which put them on display. The Peabody was so grateful for these and later donations that it put Feller on its board. Feller was now on his way to a most prestiguous career, and he began to publish a distinguished series of five books and 34 scholarly articles, most about antique ceramics and glass.

Everything turned to shambles that day at the Winterthur Museum. Professor Feller pleaded guilty to the theft of eight objects worth $133,000, the statute of limitations having long ago expired on most of his other thefts. In a subsequent sentencing memorandum Feller's lawyer argued that the professor had a diminished capacity to tell right from wrong. Feller himself said he could not exclude the possibility of demonic possession. The prosecution on the other hand insisted Feller had stolen, lent and sometimes sold (a dish to the State Department for $4,500) artworks simply to "advance his career and standing in the academic and art community." The court leaned to the prosecution view of a professional advancement scam and sentenced Feller to an 18-month prison term.

FERRIS, DANNY See JAILHOUSE SHOPPING NETWORK.

FERTILITY FRAUDS *preying on the childless*
In recent years there has been a rash of "sperm scandals" in fertility clinics around the country. Most have been attributed as much to incompetence as to deliberate fraud in the form of mixing up sperm samples, including by race. Most recently, officials have started to bring cases alleging deliberate fraud in some fertility clinics. A typical case, in a Virginia suburb of Washington, D.C., involved a clinic operator Dr. Cecil B. Jacobson, charged in 1991 with telling women whose husbands were unable to father children that he had an "extensive, carefully regulated donor program" involving physical, mental and social characteristics. However, authorities alleged that the doctor himself was the only donor, and that he produced the sperm in the privacy of his office bathroom shortly before the patient arrived at the clinic.

In addition, the doctor charged was using special drug treatments (at a fee of $5,000) to cause some patients with fertility problems to test positive for pregnancy, when they actually were not. Later, the doctor was said to have deflated his patients' high hopes with the pronouncement that they had suffered a miscarriage and now needed more expensive tests and treatment. According to Richard Cullen, the U.S. attorney for Eastern Virginia, "These people came to this man at one of the most trusting and vulnerable points in their lives and this indictment charges that he cruelly abused and violated that trust."

The doctor was charged as having referred to himself as "the babymaker" and boasting "God doesn't give you babies—I do." Convicted in 1992, Jacobson faced a possible sentence of up to 280 years in prison and up to $500,000 in fines.

FEY, DIETRICH See MIRACLE OF LÜBECK.

FIREPLACE FIXERS *home repair gyp*
They show up claiming to be fire inspectors or "fireplace experts" assigned by the community to check on safety conditions. Most homeowners assure them there is nothing wrong with their fireplace, but the expert says he'll check just to be sure. He pokes around the fireplace, using a flashlight to search for cracks. He grunts and puts a lighted match to the cracks he finds. There is a flash of flame.

He informs the homeowner that it is not safe at all. There could be an explosion and/or fire any time. Or the inhabitants of the house could be asphyxiated in their sleep. Repairs are urgent. "We're consultants and we can do the work immediately." Few homeowners dare disagree, convinced by that ominous blue flame. Frequently, the work is done on the spot for immediate payment or a time-payment contract can be worked out.

Most owners breathe much easier once the important safety work has been taken care of. Few ever learn how the so-called fireplace experts used sleight-of-hand with lighter fluid to produce the spurt of fire. Some even had a little "squirter" attached to their flashlight.

FISH-POND CARNIVAL SCAM
There is a saying in carnival circles that the one game in which the sucker always loses is the one that guarantees that every player must win. Typical is the fish-pond game in which about 100 wooden fish float in a stream of water flowing down a narrow channel past the counter. The player has a hidden slide with a number written on it. Every number is a winner and displayed on the side of the booth are the numbers of big-prize winners: 9, for instance, might be worth a record player; 16, a coffee maker; 18, a Walkman; 66, a gigantic stuffed animal; 89, an electric shaver; and 98, a portable color TV. Other numbers quite obviously pay off in lower prizes or in carnival lingo "slum"—whistles, tie clips, dice, ashtrays, etc., all costing about five cents wholesale.

These near-worthless prizes are the only ones gullible customers are permitted to win. Not that the carnival operator has any problem should authorities make an inspection of the game. The big-winning numbers—9, 16, 18, 66, 89 and 98—are all in the pond, ready for hooking. The key to the scam becomes obvious when a close study is made of these numbers. If turned upside down, they become the losing numbers 6, 91, 81, 99, 68, and 86. The operator makes losers out of winners simply by holding the slide the way that costs him less.

FLOPPERS AND DIVERS *faked car accident specialists*
The elite among car insurance swindlers are "floppers" and "divers" who give vivid performances as supposed victims of automobile accidents. A flopper can be quite acrobatic, moving in front of a car coming around a corner and faking being hit by it. This appears quite frightening but for an expert it is not a difficult maneuver. The flopper stands in the street and starts across just as he sees a car make its turn.

The car is moving relatively slowly at the time and the flopper simply bounces off the front fender and flips backward to the ground. As a crowd gathers, the flopper groans and some blood comes from his ear. (Just before beginning his act, the flopper bites his lips and dabs some blood in his ear.) A prize flopper is a person who has an old skull fracture. No matter how old the fracture, it will always show up on an X ray. In due course, it's time to collect.

"Divers" do a much more impressive performance than even the most adept flopper. The diver prefers to work at night, since witnesses are far less likely to spot his act as a phony. As a car approaches, the diver moves into the street and while crouching slams his hand against the car door as hard as he can. The bang quickly attracts passersby who are actually sure they have seen more than really happened.

At times the driver is in on the scam but usually the floppers and divers pick on innocent motorists so that insurance investigators cannot prove any collusion. Sometimes freelance floppers work near parking lots of roadside cafes, and fake being hit by patrons driving away. Since such motorists will often test positive for alcohol, the flopper has a sure-fire case. Sometimes, instead of waiting for an insurance settlement, the driver is shaken down on the spot and pays rather than face arrest for hitting a pedestrian while driving intoxicated.

Usually, however, it is better for the flopper or diver to go through the lawsuit process and take a settlement from the insurance company. While the floppers and divers are the "elite" of the racket, they are seldom well paid. Usually they work for a "manager" who arranges to get a shady lawyer and doctor to handle deals with the insurance companies. One such manager admitted after he was caught that he swindled his own floppers and divers, giving them only a paltry few hundred dollars per caper and insisting he had to make huge payoffs to the lawyers, doctors and dishonest insurance adjustors. For every $100 his floppers and divers got, he netted $2,000 or $3,000.

FLORIDA LAND BOOM *America's greatest real estate swindle*

The great Florida land boom of the 1920s remains the greatest real estate swindle in U.S. history. At the height of its frenzy in 1925–1926 it was estimated that more than $7 billion worth of real estate changed hands, the major portion of which property sadly happened to be underwater. Whole communities in "America's tropical paradise" sold out while still on the drawing boards, and were never built.

The key word common to all the swindles was "proposed." Whatever it was, once it was proposed it sold. Why not have the Grand Canal of Venice,

complete with Rialtos, lavish landings and electronically driven gondolas? This was Florida and any magic was possible. However, the "proposed" blue-watered Grand Canal never got beyond being an ugly, muddy stream. Still, the proposals came forth. Kenneth Roberts tells of a group of hustlers who hired a painter to do a sign reading: "A MILLION-DOLLAR HOTEL WILL BE ERECTED HERE." This was a surefire way of peddling surrounding lots for supporting businesses. The only trouble was the fledgling capitalists could not come up with the $18 to pay for the sign, so the painter sold it to another group of capitalists to use in their proposed deal.

Charley Ort, one of the most brilliant hustlers of the boom, arrived broke in Miami and promptly took options on a city dump. He covered the refuse, ashes, broken bottles, tin cans and furniture pieces with blazing tropical flowers and unloaded this enchanted oasis for millions. He headed for his Key Largo City, where he would earn the swindler sobriquet the "King of the Keys."

Not that Ort was not rooked himself. A shrewd realtor unloaded a tract on Key Largo without mentioning that it had been a quarry and was gutted with deep holes. Ort surveyed his atrocious buy and suddenly danced a jig of joy, crying, "Sunken Gardens! Sunken Gardens!" He blithely doubled the prices on the deepest lots and palmed them off to suckers and investors.

The hustlers who peddled Wyldewood Park, near Fort Lauderdale, had little in the way of natural features to boost their subdivision. But there was one large tree, a banyan, which had branches rooted to the ground and thus resembled a mini-forest. The hustlers erected a huge sign that said "$2,000,000 Tree," the claim being that one banyan-crazy Northerner had once offered $2 million for the tree if it were moved to his home up North. The suckers snapped up the extra-large homesites just to have a banyan tree of their own.

The suckers swallowed almost everything, even when rational voices were raised in opposition. Humorist Will Rogers weighed in with an imaginary world capital to be built in Florida. "All of these here lots," he propounded, tongue very much in cheek, "are by our Proposed Ocean."

Perhaps the grandiose dream of all was El Camino Real, or "the King's Highway," which was at least partly built by two grand real estate swindlers, Addison and Wilson Mizner. It was to be the broadest highway in the world, with 20 traffic lanes—219 feet wide in all—allegedly leading to the Mizner principality of Boca Raton. The highway would have indirect illumination with concealed curb lights instead of lamposts. And El Camino Real was waterscaped as well as landscaped; down the middle was that celebrated Grand Canal of Venice. Unfortunately, El Camino Real ran only a half-mile before petering down to a mere two lanes and disappearing as a lost trail in the sand. But of course on proposed blueprints and maps El Camino Real would run past a series of magnificent, if nonexistent, cities. In real life, the highway simply died in swamps and brambles.

And while investors awaited the completion of El Camino Real, they bid up the prices of corner lots in Boca Raton to dizzying levels. Operating on the greater fool theory, Wilson Mizner himself offered Lytle Hull, the well-known society figure, $50,000 for a choice Boca Raton lot, certain that he could get double the price on a resale. Hull was insulted by the offer and refused to talk to Wilson for some time thereafter. Hull held on to the lot through the entire boom, not selling for $50,000 or $100,000. After the bubble burst, he got only $200.

The great boom had victimized upper-middle- and higher-income people. After that it took some decades before land prices picked up and the swindlers came back as well, now to zero in on lower-income folks and retirees seeking to find the rewards of Ponce de Leon country. Many were victimized by these new-breed "swamp swindlers."

See also FLORIDA'S PIRATE GOLD CONS; SWAMP SWINDLERS.

FLORIDA'S PIRATE GOLD CONS

Are there pirate gold treasure troves still to be unearthed? Quite possibly, but the real money to be made in pirate gold comes not in finding it but rather in talking about it. Tales of pirate gold especially abound in Florida, most tracing their origins to the Florida swindlers who promoted the fraudulent land boom of the 1920s.

Besides buying a retirement and vacation paradise homesite, buyers were assured they could very well end up finding a few odd millions of pirate treasure on their property. Two of the grandest hustlers of the state's land boom, Addison and Wilson Mizner, blatantly claimed that Captain Edward Teach (better known as Blackbeard) had headquartered around their Boca Raton development and littered the sands with buried treasure (always having the chest buried with a dead pirate).

Later on, Wilson Mizner and the celebrated publicist-hoaxer Harry Reichenbach buried some doubloons and some phony Blackbeard relics in Boca Raton inlet, and had them disinterred with much public excitement. Nobody noticed there were never any confirming skeletons. Other land promoters planted stories, if not buried treasure, to promote their subdivisions. A Portuguese fisherman gave a boost to Miami real estate by claiming he'd hauled

up an iron chest weighing 200 pounds, but his fishing line had broken and he hadn't been able to latch on to the chest ever since. And over at Grassy Key a large trove of ancient Mexican money was allegedly found.

Public relations men roped in Captain Kidd, Sir Henry Morgan, Black Caesar, the Laffite boys, Gasparilla and Sir Francis Drake to hype sales. The greatest center of pirate gold yarns was Key Largo. One press agent alone successfully sunk 17 Spanish galleons jammed with gold, jewels and coins off Key Largo with a single inspired sentence on his magic typewriter.

The Key Largo City subdivisions being peddled by the audacious Charley Ort—one of the boom's grandest scam artists—excited the public the most about finds of pirate gold all over the property. Ort got the best PR men he could find—Broadway author J. P. McEvoy and novelist Ben Hecht. This sterling pair immediately managed to have two ancient crocks filled with doubloons turn up in the Key Largo sands, found by a fisherman worthy named Captain Chester, who had to be led by his nose to what he truly believed was an honest find. Hecht wired accounts of the Chester find to hundreds of newspapers. Pulitzer Prize-winner Herbert Bayard Swope of the *New York World* wired Hecht that he intended to come down to report on the fabulous finds, but first insisted that Hecht personally guarantee that the tale was not a hoax. Hecht most ethically pretended he never got the telegram.

Meanwhile scores, then hundreds of treasure hunters descended on Key Largo to dig and dive for treasure. Some with the true fever even bought homesites so they could hunt for the treasures well into their golden years. The real pirate fever lasted right up to the end of the high point of the land boom in 1926. By then most of the treasure hunters gave up and headed home. The prize victim of all—Captain Chester—kept right at it with his 13 grandchildren for a long time. The lucky ones were treasure hunters who had departed. Those who bought homesites did not get either gold or homes.

FLUE See ENVELOPE SWITCH.

FLY BET

The so-called Fly Bet has been worked over the years by many cheats, among them such diverse characters as Arnold "the Brain" Rothstein, gangster Bugsy Siegel, gambler Nick the Greek and multimillionaire John W. "Bet-a-Million" Gates. The last mentioned was probably the most successful at it since he had a reputation, not really deserved, for making wild bets with seemingly no advantage to himself. Once,

Gates was having lunch with wealthy playboy John Drake, son of a former governor of Iowa who had founded Drake University. Bet-a-Million dunked a piece of bread in his coffee and put it on a saucer.

"You do the same," Bet-a-Million challenged, "and whoever attracts the most flies to his piece of bread wins. How about a thousand dollars a fly?"

Drake fell for the bet and lost $11,000. Over the years Gates worked the bet regularly and never lost at it. None of his victims ever figured out that Bet-a-Million had the flies on his side. They also never noticed that Gates didn't try to finish his coffee. How could he, since he had filled it with six spoons of sugar?

FLYPAPER REPORTS *army hoax*

It happened during World War II when Hugh Troy (1906–1964), the noted illustrator and perhaps the number-one American practical joker of the century, was doing officer's training in a Southern camp where he was frustrated by the amount of paperwork he faced. As a form of protest he invented a special "flypaper report," which he sent in to the Pentagon each day to account for the number of flies trapped on supposedly coded flypaper ribbons hanging in the company mess hall.

Day after day the reports went to Washington until the inevitable occurred. Someone in the Pentagon started wondering where the rest of the flypaper reports were. Could it be that some officers were not fulfilling their task?

One day Troy was approached by two officers from other units who said they were "catching hell" for not sending in some flypaper reports. "Do you know what this is all about?"

"Certainly," Troy announced. "I send mine in every day."

The other officers protested they had never been supplied with any such forms, so Troy offered them a mimeographed blank he had been using in order to copy it and religiously file their own reports thereafter. They did and it is to be presumed that the Pentagon raised hell with other Army posts that had also been derelict about their flypaper reports.

How standard the procedure became is not known, the Pentagon archives never yielding such military secrets.

FOOTBALL HOAXES

Back in the 1920s the Providence Steamroller won the 1928 championship of the fledgling National Football League. A star performer of that team was a brilliant lineman named Perry Jackson—but he was not Perry Jackson. In 1927 the Steamroller had invited the real Perry Jackson, a college star in Okla-

homa, to try out. Jackson, however, was badly ill and sent his friend Arnold Schockley to pretend to be him. The masquerade worked; Schockley made the team as Perry Jackson. When the real Perry Jackson regained his health, he tried out for the Steamroller as Arnold Schockley. He was cut from the squad.

If the unreal Perry Jackson enjoyed an illustrious career, it was nothing compared with that of the redoubtable Johnny Chung, the half-Chinese "Celestial Comet" who in 1941 led New Jersey's Plainfield Teachers to victory after victory, renewing his amazing strength at halftime by wolfing down wild rice. With Chung in the lineup, the little-known Plainfield Teachers were fast becoming a small-college powerhouse, their victories duly reported in such newspapers as the *New York Herald Tribune* and the *New York Times*.

There was a good reason the school was so little known until that time. It didn't exist. Neither did the Celestial Comet. The hoax was concocted by a group of Wall Street brokers who telephoned in mythical scores of the Teachers' seven straight wins and deluged the papers with press releases of the never-ending heroics of Johnny Chung. The pranksters' grand plan was to take their creation through an undefeated season so that they would get an invitation to the first annual—and fictitious—Blackboard Bowl.

Unfortunately, a traitor tipped off *Time* magazine, and it prepared an expose of the Celestial Comet. The chief culprit, stockbroker Morris Newburger of Newburger, Loeb & Company (one Morris Newburger played right tackle for the Teachers), rushed to the magazine's office to plead desperately that the team be allowed to complete its undefeated season. As an inducement he even offered *Time* the scores of the remaining games in advance.

Time waited not. Determined to have the last word, the pranksters sought to outflank the newsweekly by firing off one final press release: Johnny Chung and a number of other players had flunked their exams and lost their playing eligibility. Plainfield Teachers had to cancel the rest of its season. Not even the most trusting of newspaper sports desks could swallow that one, and the *Trib* dispatched sportswriter Caswell Adams to New Jersey, where he found the real city of Plainfield and its real Chamber of Commerce ignorant of any learning institution called Plainfield Teachers. Adams checked telephone lines and found his way back to Newburger's office (Plainfield Teachers maintained a one-way telephone that made outgoing calls but received none), and the real father of the unreal Johnny Chung was unmasked at the very moment *Time* hit the newstands with its scoop to an astonished and amused public.

The *Trib* took the hoax with good grace and joined in the general laughter, but the *Times* maintained an icy silence.

FOOT RACE CON *oldtime swindle*

The foot race con, now obsolete but living on in other forms, was one of the favorite ploys of con men in the 19th century. At the time, foot race contests were illegal because they were used in confidence games. One con man posed as the personal secretary of a millionaire who enjoyed betting heavily on such contests. The secretary would approach the victim with a plan to doublecross his boss by fixing the race and then share the profits with the mark who had to put up the bulk of the money. The racer, who was fixed to win the race, would collapse during the running and a phony doctor would pronounce him dead. The mark would lose his bet because of this supposed "act of God."

Eventually the foot race con became so well known that it was abandoned by swindlers who moved on to such newer scams as "fixed" horse races, phony stock deals and so on.

FOREIGN CURRENCY SPECULATION SWINDLES
high-tech scams

Although the foreign currency speculation swindle sounds like something new, it is based on a very old concept. Here is how a Florida scam artist worked it recently:

At the outset, the investment gypster approached a relatively small number of well-heeled persons in the community and offered them the chance to invest, at a guaranteed high return, in a computer-generated program of arbitrage in foreign currency fluctuations. To the potential victims it looked like a very high-tech approach used by extremely knowledgeable and wealthy investment banks and individuals to speculate and have the ability to get in and out of large positions at a fraction of a moment's notice.

No sooner than the gypster had hooked some victims, he approached a new group of investors with the same pitch. Then he used a portion of their investments to start paying dividends to the earlier clients. Quite naturally, as word spread on how well the gypster was doing at making money in this complicated field, still more investors sought to get in on the good deal. The gypster, with even more money, recycled some of it into the fictitious profits payments. Like a pebble tossed into the water, the word spread farther, and this in turn brought in an ever-widening circle of eager investors. The money poured

in, but 90% of the money went right down the drain, as the gypster pulled up stakes and left town.

In the final analysis the entire operation was nothing more than a chain letter or Ponzi scheme that couldn't last—except for the gypster himself who was very computer-generated when it was time to run.

FOREIGN JOB SCAMS *phony information offers*

Thousands of men and women interested in good paying jobs overseas—in construction work, various white-collar professions, and even in soldier-of-fortune-type activities—have fallen for a variety of foreign employment scams. They send $5 or $10 in answer to advertisements in newspapers and magazines offering what are alleged to be lists of companies seeking employees for their foreign operations—office clerks, electricians, carpenters, draftsmen, plumbers, welders and laborers—at huge salaries "tax-free" and frequently with "guaranteed contract renewals."

Postal inspectors who have checked on thousands of those receiving and using such lists found no one successful in obtaining any position. In most cases the firms weren't even looking for help and did not grant permission for their names to be used in any list or bulletin. The fact is most companies who need skilled foreign help have their own careful methods of recruitment. One Texas scam artist grossed many tens of thousands running his ads in 300 daily newspapers before postal inspectors nailed him. All of his information came from free government bulletins and public news sources.

Of course, at a few dollars a pop such scam artists need a huge volume to make their operations pay off. Other operators shoot for bigger game, claiming they are agencies hiring for overseas firms, paying exotic salaries and, in the case of "action-minded" veterans, semi-mysterious jobs that will provide uniforms, rations, PX-type shopping privileges and weapons. These applicants are hit for various charges. (Sample pitch: "Due to numerous insincere applications, and to cover the cost of visas, a fee is required.") Applicants are usually ripped off for fees from $200 to $400 and then informed they are on the "short list" and will get their assignments in about six weeks. That usually is the last the applicants hear of the foreign job. Later letters of inquiry either produce no response (or at best some gibberish) that "the files have been moved to Bangkok" and that there will be a short delay.

Soldier of Fortune magazine has been particularly incensed about such foreign employment scams in the past and has published many exposes of such cons. The magazine has warned of con men who make hit-and-run appearances in various cities, do interviews and make off with $350 deposits supposedly "to insure that a hired person would show up for his flight and stay on the job for a certain amount of time. After that it would be refunded."

Some operators rent suites from a real estate firm for a few weeks and deliberately leave the realty company's name on the door, thus inferring that it is merely a sort of "cover." There are maps all over the walls to indicate the outfit's supposed global interests. Applicants calling for appointments are answered with no more than a mysterious "Overseas." Applicants are probed on their background; whatever it may be, those are the very qualifications needed. A veteran with two years of duty in Vietnam was offered a position involving security work in diving operations in the Gulf of Tonkin.

In these types of deals, investigative reporter George V. Chiles found, "The con men involved were creative. One of them showed an ability to read a potential victim at once and fabricate a contract to order."

And the gouge goes on, especially in times of economic decline in the United States, when thoughts of foreign employment become the new panacea. The scam artists have thousands of fictitious jobs for woebegone applicants; some are so thoroughly conned they actually quit their jobs for a new, adventurous, glamorous and profitable career in foreign lands, only to discover later that they have been following a mirage.

FOSSIL WILLY *spurious artifacts maker*
The 19th century has been called the "Age of Fossils" because of its increased interest in science, notably evolution and geology. Unfortunately, this spurred on scientific forgeries of all types. One Briton alone—Edward Simpson (1815–?)—can be credited with starting more false trails for historical investigation than anyone else. Simpson became known by a number of nicknames, including Fossil Willy, Flint Jack and Old Antiquarian.

Born in Yorkshire, Simpson went to work as a teenager for a historian, first, and then a geologist and soon developed a keen interest in the past himself. He became skilled at collecting fossils and earned a decent living selling them to dealers. In 1843 an unscrupulous dealer gave Simpson a flint arrowhead and asked him to make a copy. Simpson's copy proved impossible to distinguish from the real thing, and a remarkable non-scientific career was launched.

From fake arrowheads Simpson went on to set up a kiln so that he could produce "ancient urns." These sold extremely well, and Simpson decided he could go into mass production of just about any "genuine" relic from the past. His one-man production turned out pottery, armor, old teatrays, Roman milestones, seals, hammers and ancient inscribed stones. Everything moved well, even though, aside from the arrowheads, practically nothing really resembled the real thing. Simpson simply didn't know better; but then again, in the mid-19th century, neither did his clients. Fossil Willy became the most important supplier of artifacts in Yorkshire.

Then his greedy dealer-partner started shipping his work off to London dealers who accepted the artifacts as genuine. Even the British Museum acquired a number of his arrowheads.

The main problem that developed was Simpson's enormous output. He was producing so much that there just didn't seem to be enough excavations to explain the flow of material. Finally, a London dealer, Tennant of the Strand—who had accepted much of Simpson's material—quizzed him on his sources. Simpson, rather loose-lipped when under the influence of alcohol (which he usually was), said more than he should have. Determined to set the record straight, Tennant hauled Simpson before a meeting of geologists in January 1862. Simpson readily produced perfect historical arrowheads on the spot.

In a sense Simpson had gained great fame in scientific circles, but his wholesale cottage industry was shattered. He drank more, stole money and goods for yet more drink, and in 1867 was imprisoned for a short time for theft. In October 1867 a profile of Simpson and his forgeries appeared in the *Reliquary Quarterly Architectural Journal and Review*. Oddly, an appeal for money for Simpson was included in the publication. Says one biographer of Fossil Willy: "Simpson vanished soon afterwards, taking with him a unique skill that has not been seen since." That was undoubtedly a triumph for science.

FOX SISTERS *founders of modern spiritualism*
What today is considered modern spiritualism—the belief that there is life after death and that some individuals called mediums can communicate with those who have "crossed over"—was born in 1848 as the result of a prank by two teenage girls in upstate New York. Fifteen-year-old Margaret Fox discovered she could crack a big toe so that it sounded like a hard rap on wood. One night Margaret and her younger sister Kate decided to keep that "talent" a secret and have some fun with their parents. Pretending alarm, they summoned their parents to their bedside and told them they'd heard strange rappings. With their parents watching, Kate snapped her fingers three times and as though in response there were three sharp knocks, seemingly from the wall next to their bed.

Father John Tobin Fox, an upright Methodist, had no fear of ghosts, which was why he had rented the small farmhouse near Rochester, New York, even

Margaret Fox (left) had the talented big toe, which she and her sister Kate (center) promoted into a grand hoax of communications with the afterworld.

though there was much talk of the place being haunted by the ghost of a peddler who had been murdered there many years before. Now even John Fox was perplexed by the uncanny sounds.

Neighbors were summoned to witness the strange rappings, and all agreed the noises had to be "spirit rappings" from the departed. An alphabetical code was worked out, which the spirits quickly learned, and soon they were rapping out messages to the Fox family. Even John Fox admitted that his two daughters—the spirits would only respond in their presence—had "supernatural powers."

Within a few months the Fox sisters were known throughout the United States, and millions firmly believed in their abilities, which proved beyond doubt that there was an afterlife. The sisters gave a series of public demonstrations, and among those in attendance were James Fenimore Cooper, first lady Mrs. Franklin Pierce and William Cullen Bryant. Wisconsin Governor N. P. Tallmadge was ecstatic after carrying on a communication with the ghosts of Benjamin Franklin and John C. Calhoun. Horace Greeley jumped on the Fox sisters' bandwagon by declaring in an editorial: "We believe . . . that these singular sounds and seeming manifestations are not

produced by Mrs. Fox and her daughters nor by any human connected with them."

The Fox sisters carried through their hoax for 40 years, establishing themselves in New York City to conduct professional seances at $100 and up per client. During the Civil War the Foxes really cleaned up on thousands of grieving parents seeking contact with their sons and husbands killed in combat.

The ruse continued until 1888 when the two sisters, now in their 50s and chronic alcoholics, had had enough of spiritualism, especially as criticism from scientists and clergymen grew. Finally, Margaret decided to confess. At an audience of believers and nonbelievers at the New York Academy of Music she declared, "Spiritualism is an absolute falsehood from beginning to end." Then Margaret told how she and Kate had concocted their hoax to tease their parents, and especially their mother who was a very superstitious and gullible person.

As the clincher to her confession, Margaret hopped on a table without her shoes and proceeded to perform a concert by cracking her "talking toe."

The next day the *New York Herald* headlined the confession: "HER BIG TOE DID IT ALL."

"FREE LAND" SWINDLE *Yellow Kid Weil con*

The key ingredient to vacation or retirement plot swindles is selling worthless land to victims sight unseen, on the theory that a thousand words are better than one clear picture. Easily the most successful swindle of this sort involved not selling the land to victims but actually giving it to them free, no strings attached. It was an offer few gullible victims could refuse.

The "Free Land" swindle early in this century was concocted by a colorful rogue named "Colonel" Jim Porter, an ex-Mississippi riverboat gambler, and his young protege, who would become the notorious Yellow Kid Weil, the most successful con man in U.S. history.

The gimmick in the plot was that the good colonel had a cousin who was a county recorder up in Michigan. The area was loaded with thousands of acres of undesirable or submarginal land. Porter and Weil bought up hundreds of acres of the land at $1 an acre and subdivided it into one-half- and one-third-acre plots. Then, setting up a sales office in Chicago, they showed off the usual artist's concept of a clubhouse, marina and other enticing features that would be offered to buyers. However, they announced nothing was ready yet for sale.

Porter played the part of an eccentric millionaire while Weil unsuccessfully sought to curb his excesses. The good colonel went around town giving away hundreds of lots to people. In a single evening Porter might visit several dives and a brothel or two and give away as many as 40 lots to madams, prostitutes, bartenders and waiters. Weil would be beside himself at such mindless extravagance and beg the recipients not to say anything to others or they too would want a free lot. Weil himself offered freebies to newspaper reporters and Chicago police detectives, whose good graces he wished to enjoy. Weil informed the ecstatic recipients they should immediately write and have the transaction recorded at the county seat. Then he would race off, allegedly to keep the colonel out of charity's way.

There was nothing more for the swindlers to do. Once their pitch was complete, all they had to do was wait for the money to roll in. The proud landowners would do as they were told and happily send the recording fee of $30 (which had begun at $2). This fee constituted the swindle. Of this amount $15 went to Porter's cousin and the rest to Porter and Weil. The two swindlers raked in $16,000 in profits, no tiny sum at the turn of the century, in a scam that was perfectly legal since all they had done was give away land of no value and not taken a penny from any of the recipients. In fact, many victims did not learn for many years that they had been given a bill of goods.

FROG-FARMING CONS *home industry dud*
The promises of the promoters are impressive. There is a small fortune to be made in frog farming. For several hundred dollars or more, they'll set anyone up in a sure-fire home industry enterprise. Will the consumer succeed at it? Probably not, unless one happens to have a nice swamp in one's backyard.

But even in a swamp it is not likely to work. Small-scale culture requires a rigidly controlled frog climate. In addition, frogs are not cooperative. They eat prodigiously and as parents couldn't care less about their offspring. Additionally, the United States is not France, and there is only a small market for frogs legs.

FROLICS CLUB HOAX MURDER *underworld frame-up*
While Chicago's Capone Mob in the 1920s and 1930s was noted for settling underworld territorial disputes with hot lead, they were ready to consider other means when offered by one of the organization's most cunning members, Jake "Greasy Thumb" Guzik. One of the outfit's most prosperous "clubs" was the infamous Four Deuces, the four-story pride and joy of Al Capone, on South Wabash Avenue. The first floor was a bar, the second and third gambling joints and the fourth one of the mob's prize bordellos.

The Four Deuces was so successful that it invited imitation, especially from the nearby Frolics Cafe and Club. The Frolics offered all the inducements of the Four Deuces and at lower prices. The Capones considered using firepower to get rid of the competitor, but since the area was rife with violence and murders as it was (the Four Deuces could be counted on to produce a corpse or two every few weeks) such violence might cause undesired legal repercussions.

Greasy Thumb thus came up with one of his brainstorms. The boys waited until there was a minor shoot-out in the Four Deuces, and then Guzik announced what was to be done with the troublesome corpse. He ordered the boys to lug it over to the Frolics, break into the basement and stuff the corpse into the furnace. Then, in his finest outraged-citizen tone, Greasy Thumb telephoned police headquarters and complained that the Frolics was "running an illegal crematorium—and without an undertaker's license." Several police cars descended on the Frolics and found the remains of the body. The law padlocked the premises and proceeded to rip apart the Frolics in a search for more corpses. The police did not find any more or solve the murder of the one in the furnace, but the Frolics never did reopen.

FUNERAL CHASERS *victimizing the bereaved*
Shortly after the death of a relative, someone delivers to the bereaved a leather-bound Bible that the deceased allegedly ordered. Or the grieving relatives get a bill in the mail for an expensive item on which they allegedly must make the remaining payments. These are the tactics employed by "funeral chasers" who use the obituary notices to prey on bereaved families.

Another typical scam is trying to collect on an alleged loan made to the dead man. Here is a sample letter sent by one funeral chaser:

> Dear George,
> How are you, old man? Well, I just got back to town today and as I promised, I'm dropping you a line so we can get together soon. Ran into Tom Newberry in Rochester the other day and he told me to pass along his regards. . . . Oh, say, old buddy, I hate to bring it up, but I hope you can return that $275 I loaned you a few months ago at the _____ Lodge. You remember what I was telling you about the missus, about not knowing if it was serious or not. Well, it looks pretty bad now, and I'm pressed with bills, so I hope you can come through for me. But you know, that isn't the only reason I want to get together with you again. As you said, we just don't see enough of each other and we are getting older.

Again, this is also a fraud, and while one might wonder why such a dear friend had not tried to call the dead man by telephone rather than communicate by letter, few grieving relatives do not send a check immediately. The wiser course is not to be conned by funeral chasers. One is not responsible for anyone else's purchases or debts. If there is a legitimate claim, the law sets up methods for the estate to settle it.

See also PORTRAIT SCAM.

FUR-BEARING TROUT   *the abominable snowman of the waterways*

Trout with fur? There is a logic to it since the waters of Canada are so deep and icy. That's probably why this fishy canard has endured since the 17th century, when a Scotsman wrote home about the abundance of "furried animals and fish" he found in Canada. The record indicates that when asked to send home a sample, he apparently obliged. How he faked that is no longer a matter of record, but later fakes are readily discernible since the fur-bearing trout just won't die.

Into the 20th century there are still dealers who offer such wares for sale. In the early 1970s one proud owner of this bewhiskered breed of fish proudly submitted one of his prize holdings to the Royal Scottish Museum. The museum recognized it for what it was, a brown trout with white rabbit fur carefully attached to it. Not being interested in such a hoax, the museum declined to retain the submission. But stories of the furry trout circulated, and public interest soared to such intensity that the museum was obliged to recreate the "find." Thus a fake of a fake became a museum exhibit.

In 1990 this fur-bearing trout became one of the most viewed entries offered at a British Museum exhibition called "Fake? The Art of Deception."

FURGUSON, ARTHUR   *actor turned confidence man*

Not much is known about an enterprising Scottish actor, Arthur Furguson, who turned con man extraordinaire. He was hardly an overly accomplished performer, but on the Manchester stage he once played the role of an American who was tricked by a swindler. Considering that his career was less than promising, he began to give serious thought to the possibility that what worked in art might well work in life—if American tourists could be as stupid as in the play.

It must be admitted there was some merit to the concept, and Furguson, as a sober-appearing, middle-aged gentleman of impeccable demeanor, was just the character to carry off such cons.

In about 1920 Furguson started his incredible act on the stage of real-life London, confiding to gullible Americans that he was carrying out a secret assignment for His Majesty's government to sell off valuable pieces of London real estate to help lift the costly burden of war loans from America. If he judged his victim as not being quite so credulous, he explained that the real estate itself was not for sale but rather the "leaseholds." Thus Americans, including many free-spenders visiting Europe for the first time, viewed the purchase of Nelson's Column in Trafalgar Square as a steal at a shade over $30,000, Big Ben was marked down to a trifling $5,000 and Furguson secured $10,000 as a down payment on Buckingham Palace. All of this from folks who would have howled in laughter at greenhorns in America who thought they were buying the Brooklyn Bridge.

By 1925 enough howls of protest had reached the American Embassy to the Court of St. James, that Furguson felt it wise to head for safer climes. He came to America at a time when swindlers were selling everything that was or was not nailed down, from the Brooklyn Bridge to the information booth at New York's Grand Central Station (oddly, the latter at a higher price than the former), mostly to greenhorns and "suckers just off the farm."

By his demeanor Furguson realized he was ill-suited to con such victims, so he picked out his own brand of suckers: British and that nation's colonial visitors. In Washington, D.C., he disposed of the White House leasehold for $10,000 of the first year's rent, while reserving thereafter a smaller portion of alleged future rent from his purchaser as soon as the money was paid.

Perhaps Furguson's master coup was peddling the Statue of Liberty to a gullible Australian for a paltry $100,000 advance payment. It seemed the New York Harbor was about to be improved, and Lady Liberty would have to go. She was worth much more than the asking price and indeed it seemed likely to Furguson that any purchaser would make a mint selling scrap of her metal as souvenirs as well. The sucker was most impressed at soon taking possession of the grand statue and beamed with delight when he had a snapshot taken of himself with Furguson in view next to the statue. Trouble developed when immediately after that Furguson put pressure on the buyer to quickly complete negotiations. The Australian finally got suspicious and showed the photograph to police who identified Furguson as a swindler. Furguson served five years for sundry cons and on his release in 1930 headed for California. There was a report that he worked for a time as a salesman—a fitting profession—but the silver-tongued Scot completely vanished. It is not inconceivable that he went on to make the sale of a lifetime.

G

GALLIENUS' REVENGE   *Roman punishment hoax*

In the gruesome history of the Roman arena, Emperor Gallienus (reigned 253–268) hardly stands among the more benign rulers; but in one case at least he rendered justice by a bloodcurdling hoax rather than by the more common bloodletting. The emperor learned from his wife, Salonina, that she had been cheated by a jewel dealer who had sold her imitation gems. Determined to punish the dishonest jeweler in a manner befitting his crime, Gallienus ordered the culprit to be sent to the arena, with the royal couple and a full audience in attendance.

Roman Emperor Gallienus utilized a bloodcurdling event in the arena to impose truth in advertising on a dishonest jeweler.

The jeweler, half-dead with fright, was dumped into the empty arena with the sounds of lions to be heard from behind a closed door. For the longest time the emperor did nothing, letting the tension mount for the jeweler and the spectators. Finally the door swung open—and out pranced a tiny chicken. The emperor then signaled a herald to proclaim the royal message: "He practiced deceit, and has had it practiced on him."

The jeweler, tottering still in fear, was sent home, perhaps certain that he had suffered a punishment worse than death.

GARFIELD ENGRAVING SCAM

After President James A. Garfield was assassinated in 1881, there was an outpouring of sentiment for the chief executive, certainly greater than any expressed during his lifetime. As a result, the public responded with enthusiasm to a blatant scam advertisement, which soon appeared in more than 200 newspapers from coast to coast. The grieving public was given the opportunity to obtain an apparently rare portrait of the now martyred president. The ad stated:

> I have secured the authorized steel engravings of the late President Garfield, executed by the United States Government, approved by the President of the United States, by Congress and by every member of the President's family as the most faithful of all portraits of the President. It was executed by the Government's most expert steel engravers, and I will send a copy from the original plate, in full colors approved by the Government, postpaid, for one dollar each.

The thousands who sent in a dollar received exactly what was promised by the mail-order con artist—the engraving of President Garfield—on a 5¢ postage stamp.

The Garfield portrait swindle gave birth to a host of imitators. Other swindlers went back to Abraham Lincoln and offered an engraving "done from a photograph by Mathew Brady." And the racket continues to this day involving other notables and subjects appearing on commemorative stamps. Some clip artists even seek to keep their overhead down by sending out canceled stamps rather than unused ones.

GERMAN UNIFICATION SCAMS

During the great rush to German unification in 1991, East Germans—for decades used to an over-regulated society—became prize victims of what some publications referred to as "the dark side of capitalism." Businesses from western Germany descended on their new compatriots in droves, dispatching door-to-door hustlers, sending out misleading junk mail, and so on. Confused East Germans, used to a market with limited product selection but with fixed prices and virtually all services administered by the state, fell for gimmicks that hadn't worked for decades in the West. In Leipzig an elderly woman living alone signed up for a magazine subscription without reading the fine print and found she was obligated to take several additional magazines and pay more than $20 a month. Gullible consumers received notification they'd won a sweepstake prize entitling them to a stereo system and accompanying that good news was an invitation to buy any item from an enclosed catalog of household goods. They got the goods they paid for, but somehow the stereo prize never came.

Insurance scams in particular abounded. Rather than offer basic life insurance policies many agents—set up in makeshift offices in train and subway stations—guided East Germans into policies that combined insurance with savings. But during the life of the policy the money is inaccessible and the client cannot cancel the contract without losing most or all of the money he has already paid.

Because unemployment was certain to rise, scam operators brought out all the standard pitches used elsewhere to victimize the most desperate persons. Sorely in need of income, many unemployed responded to advertisements that promised quick money doing odd jobs, such as addressing envelopes at home, raising chinchillas in their backyards and other typical scams that have cheated the unemployed worldwide.

GEYSERS ON COMMAND *enduring Yellowstone Park hoax*

Yellowstone Park rangers have long abandoned hope that some day there will be no cynical sightseers who

To this day many visitors to Yellowstone Park remain conned by tales that park rangers are engaged in a monumental fraud, turning on and off geysers by means of an underground steam system.

believe that the rangers themselves are involved in a colossal fraud. For decades now there have been people who are not at all convinced that the park's geysers are true wonders of nature and not a man-made con operation. They firmly believe that geyser displays are activated by an artificial underground steam system and are used to increase attendance at Yellowstone.

How this bizarre theory got started is not known. One version has it that it was started by a couple of college boys working summer jobs in the park during the 1920s. They came to dislike a particular ranger who regularly guided tourists to the famous geysers and lectured on the wonders of the unique forces of nature. They decided to sabotage the ranger's lectures by a devilish performance to convince his audience that he was an actor in a grandiose hoax.

Salvaging a steering wheel and post from a junked car, they positioned themselves on a slope where the ranger could not see them but the sightseers could. The pranksters zeroed in on a certain geyser that spouted with clocklike precision and waited until the geyser gave its first rumble—a few preliminary puffs of steam. At that moment, one of the boys yelled, "Let 'er go!" and the other made a show of turning the steering wheel vigorously; the geyser shot 150 feet into the air. Undoubtedly, the lecturing ranger must have been rather perplexed when his audience

Lords of the English manors had a vested interest in promoting the idea of ghosts—especially in the wine cellar—to ward off uninvited tipplers, as depicted in this celebrated watercolor by Thomas Rowlandson.

seemed rather unenthused by the dramatic display of the eruption.

The story may be apocryphal, in so far as a fully acted out performance, but there is no doubt that many park temps returned home to tell family and friends that they took part in operating the geyser controls at Yellowstone. Other park employees have told similar whoppers while elbow bending at a bar. As a result, the story of Yellowstone's manmade geysers has never quite died, and there are those cynics who simply smile at the gullibility of the average park sightseer who accepts such nonsensical displays as nature at work. The belief endures that it is simply an attempt by the government, or at least the Parks Department, to promote interest in the national parks.

GHOST HOAXES

The belief in ghosts and haunted houses is an undying one, which traces back to the 1500s, the so-called ghost century in England. Ironically, they were very necessary hoaxes for those terrible times. The army of ghosts that appeared in the 16th century was a result of the many bloody attempts to prosecute innumerable clergymen, on both the Catholic and Protestant sides.

Obliged to disappear, many clergymen took refuge in the homes of friends or sympathizers, who for their own protection, as well as that of the hunted man, would design a secret room in the attic and a stairway leading to it within the walls. The clergymen were obliged not to move around and certainly not light a candle until well after midnight, when presumably no neighbors or passersby were likely to see them. Of course, this was much easier ordered than carried out; inevitably a figure would at times be observed moving about in the wee hours of the

morning. Additionally, the clergymen were heard shuffling about the hidden stairs by other members and servants of the household. The explanation of ghosts and haunted houses became the only logical way to continue the coverup, and the concept of ghosts became embedded in British culture. Thus the United Kingdom to this day undoubtedly remains the most ghostly inhabited area on Earth.

See also FOX SISTERS; POLTERGEIST HOAXES.

GIANT GRASSHOPPERS OF BUTTS ORCHARD
monster hoax
Like many newspaper hoaxes, the so-called Giant Grasshoppers of Butts Orchard was swallowed by many newspaper readers despite a printed disclaimer. The story appeared on September 9, 1937, on the front page of the *Tomah* (Wisconsin) *Monitor-Herald*, headlined: GIANT GRASSHOPPERS INVADE BUTTS ORCHARD EAST OF CITY.

The paper even had an explanation of the origin of the giant insects. They had eaten some special plant food that farmer A. L. Butts had sowed on his apple orchard. The result: grasshoppers who quickly grew to an astonishing length of three feet. The creatures were now so heavy they snapped off tree limbs as they hopped around the orchard. The *Monitor-Herald* sported photographs of the mutant insects being hunted by men with shotguns, including a snapshot of Farmer Butts holding up a prize kill.

Many people in the community reacted with extreme nervousness as a result of the story, even though it ended with a paragraph that stated: "If there are those who doubt our story it will not be a new experience, inasmuch as most newspaper writers are thought to be the darndest liars in the world." Such disclaimers seldom get much attention since they are usually buried in the "jump" of the story, in this case the continuation on page 4. In most "panic-type" stories many readers become too upset to complete a full reading of the account. Later, Farmer Butts and *Monitor-Herald* publisher B. J. Fuller confessed the full details of their elaborate hoax.

GIFT FAMILY   *transatlantic con*
An enduring con game that has enjoyed considerable success on both sides of the Atlantic is the so-called gift family racket. As near as can be determined, it first appeared in England when two con women assured victims they enjoyed certain mystic powers that allowed them, through a "divine source," to invest funds not in this world but in the next—at 300% interest. All the victims had to do was turn over their total savings and they would get it back quadrupled. To ensure the success of the scam, the women paid out a few interest payments, which of

course caused a victim's relatives and friends to rush forward eagerly with their savings as well. Since Great Britain in the early 20th century had witnessed a number of "investment" schemes that had robbed the poor and uneducated of their small savings, the gift family racket seemed the answer. After all, this was the Almighty making the payouts, and if one couldn't trust God whom could one trust?

Of course, in time the payouts of interest ceased, and the devout investors were advised to keep the faith during a heavenly test of that faith. Before the original scam was broken up the two women made the equivalent of a half-million dollars out of the divine con.

In time the gift family racket took a hiatus in England and other parts of Europe and hied across the ocean to the United States where it turned up in a number of localities. One of the biggest operations of the sort occurred in the Boston area in the 1920s, and since then it has appeared sporadically both in America and Europe.

GOAT GLAND SEX REJUVENATION   *potency quack scam*

Few areas of quackery have had a longer or more insane history than that of sex rejuvenation. All sorts of diets, aphrodisiacs, spells and potions have been used, but there probably has never been quite a crackpot scheme offered to compare with the efforts of "Goat Gland" Brinkley of Kansas in the early half of the 20th century. "Doctor"—title courtesy of a Midwest diploma mill—John R. Brinkley (1885–1942) would provide male patients the transplanted glands or testicles of a billy goat for a mere $750. And, for the very affluent who were feeling their age, Brinkley offered the equipment of a very young goat for a trifling $1,500. Following this bit of surgery, his patients were to be suddenly blessed with a return of their youthful powers.

Apparently Brinkley got his grandiose idea from working in the slaughterhouse of Swift & Co., the meat-packing firm, and a two-month stint in the Army (four weeks of which were spent under psychiatric observation). Although there is no evidence indicating that transplanted animal glands have any effect, it must be admitted that some of the thousands of men he treated actually did take on some renewed stud qualities—through the well-known benefits of the so-called placebo effect. In the process, Goat Gland Brinkley became a millionaire.

Brinkley was not given to the soft sell. His advertising read: "Just let me get your goat and you'll be a Mr. Ram-What-Am with every lamb." For every observer he had chuckling over his preposterous claims, he had an equal number of enthusiastic supporters.

"Goat Gland" Brinkley became a millionaire with his quack surgery for reviving male sexual prowess. As his ads thundered: "Just let me get your goat and you'll be a Mr. Ram-What-Am with every lamb."

The Maharaja Thakou of Morvi rushed all the way from India for the transplant. E. Haldeman-Julius, the publisher of the Little Blue Books, was conned by Goat Gland Brinkley as well, and for years he ran the sex quack's advertisements free. He also did enthusiastic profiles on him in a periodical devoted mainly to debunking American life. By the time Haldeman-Julius figured out Brinkley was a con artist and issued an apology to the public for his own errors, Brinkley had long since hit the quack's pot of gold.

Despite the American Medical Association's designation of him as a "giant in quackery," Brinkley continued to meet with fame and fortune. By the mid-1920s he sported a fleet of Cadillacs, a yacht, a plane and his own radio station. In 1930 his popularity was so great in Kansas that he was able to mount a vigorous campaign for the governorship as an independent. The Democratic and Republican candidates garnered 217,000 and 216,000 votes, respectively, Brinkley received 183,000 write-ins because he couldn't get on the ballot.

Brinkley tried again in the next election and lost to Alf Landon who got 278,000 votes to Democrat Woodring's 272,000 and Goat Gland's 244,000. Brinkley also garnered thousands of votes in adjacent counties of Oklahoma, where he wasn't even running.

In the meantime, the AMA waged war on Brinkley until he was finally forced to close his Kansas operation. The government also stripped him of his radio station license. Brinkley moved south of the border to Mexico, where he set up a powerful radio station and a new clinic. He pretended to perform prostate operations and sold a "medicine" that was found to consist of blue dye and a bit of hydrochloric acid. As troubles developed with Mexican authorities, Brinkley set up a new hospital in Little Rock, Arkansas; he flitted between there and his Mexican operations. In 1942 Mexico had had quite enough of Brinkley and tore down his transmitter. Some say this was the cause of his fatal heart attack shortly thereafter at the age of 56.

GOLD BRICK SWINDLES

The gold brick swindle is one that has at least nine lives, coming in a variety of plots to appeal to every type of victim. During one period the bricks were sold to people eager to protect their fortunes when it was illegal to hoard gold. Others were told the gold bricks were stolen and thus available at cut rates. In any event, the victim is induced to buy what is presumed to be gold brick ingots but is really gold-coated lead or brass.

The origin of the basic swindle is unknown, but most probably dates to the California gold rush days in the 1850s. Wyatt Earp, never quite the honest lawman legend claimed, and Mysterious Dave Mather worked the racket in Mobetie, Texas, conning gullible cowboys into thinking that the gold bars were part of a stolen Mexican stagecoach shipment. Earp as a lawman in Kansas had observed how well the racket worked there and found it a more profitable pursuit that lawmanning.

An Illinois-born swindler, Reed Waddell, brought the gold brick swindle to New York and hoodwinked some of the brightest and supposedly sharpest men in the business world. Waddell's scheme had some of the qualities of a "big store" operation, including a phony assayer's office. And his bricks came with all the trimmings, including triple gold-plating and marked with identification of the United States Assayer's Office. The assay would show the brick was pure gold and worth a fortune, but sometimes the victim still hesitated. Waddell would grow impatient and pull a slug from the brick and tell the victim to take it to a jeweler of his own choice. "I don't appreciate having my character impugned like this," he would angrily say.

Of course, Waddell had previously taken the precaution of sinking a slug of pure gold into the center of the brick. The act invariably worked when the victim returned with a glowing estimate made by an independent expert. Another gold brick gang worked the Chicago World's Fair in 1893 and readily made a profit of over $100,000 in just five months.

Probably the greatest gold brick coup occurred in the 1930s when a Texas widow gave her full confidence to two crooks because one of them posed as a minister and wore clerical garb. According to the crooks, gold ingots had been buried about a century earlier in various spots of what was now the woman's vast ranch. Happily, there were ancient maps that could be bought in Mexico from an old man who didn't realize their worth. The widow felt the crooks were honest, but they could be misguided, so she gave them just enough money to buy one map as a sort of trial run. The pair returned with the map and promptly used it to locate some gold bricks. Her appetite duly enhanced, the widow advanced more map-purchase funds. In three years she gave the two operators some $300,000, which seemed to be quite a bargain as they had dug up what appeared to be some $4 million in gold. During that time the men succeeded in keeping the woman from learning the truth by warning her that she would get into trouble if she allowed anyone to even examine the bricks since, at the time, the hoarding of bricks was illegal. In fact, they pointed out, if the government found out about them it could seize them without compensation.

The con artists' grievous error was living in a manner a bit too extravagant, especially when one of them was a man of the cloth. By 1935 government agents had the pair under surveillance and investigated their seemingly ceaseless flow of funds. The swindle was uncovered, and the pair brought to trial and convicted.

Most big-city bunco squads still deal with several such cases a year. With the possession of gold now legal, some gold brick vultures continue the swindle sans the brick. They invest their clients' money in gold bars and charge hefty storage fees as well—for bars that are pure lead.

See also WADDELL, REED.

GOLD BULLION FRAUDS *making millions vanish*

Gold bullion frauds come in various packages, the most common of which is simply to take investors' money, keep it and then charge them storage fees for gold that isn't even there.

In the 1980s one baldfaced swindle was pulled by two brothers who had a fancy Florida office building with their own company name on it and an investment pitch that seemed quite logical: "Instead of buying gold outright and holding it for appreciation, make a small down payment that the firm could use to secure financing that would permit much larger quantities of gold to be bought and held for the investor's account." Thus when the gold prices went up, which was "sure to happen," investors would make huge leveraged profits.

This unscrupulous company even had vaults where investors could view wall-to-wall stacks of glittering bullion. By the time law enforcement officials became suspicious and investigated, the only things left were the cardboard bars that had been painted gold and fashioned to look like bullion. The investors' millions were never recovered.

GOLD EXTRACTION SWINDLE *mining gold from the ocean*

Many frauds are based on the so-called commercial value of ocean water. Perhaps the greatest of these involved an alleged gold accumulator device that could extract gold flakes from the ocean. The scheme was dreamed up by a longtime English con man named Charles E. Fisher, who appeared in 1897 in the town of Lubec in the Passamaquoddy Bay region of Maine. Fisher's pitch was that the eddies of Passamaquoddy Bay offered just about the best locale anywhere in the world for extracting "gold present in minute amounts in all sea water."

Before launching his fraud, Fisher needed a man of prestige to give his operation credibility. Being a sound judge of poor character, Fisher soon found his man in the person of Prescott Ford Jernegan, a Connecticut Baptist minister and family man. He pitched his idea to Jernegan who may have bought it at first, but soon recognized it to be an outright scam; ultimately, he decided it was a very promising one. Jernegan not only joined in the scheme but also soon became the driving force behind the swindle, which took supposedly hardheaded New Englanders for thousands of dollars.

Demonstrations were made of the gold accumulator, which was painted with mercury and Fisher's mystery compound, and lowered into the water. When the device was raised some 24 hours later it was crusted with thin flakes of gold. The pair of swindlers found Yankee investors a hard sell; a group of businessmen insisted on standing guard all through the night at the experiment site to make sure no one tampered with or salted the equipment. But these potential investors did not know that Fisher was a seasoned deep-sea diver and would swim to the accumulator during the night and fasten the gold flakes to it.

Once the swindlers had convinced the businessmen that they had a genuine operation, the Electrolytic Marine Salts Company was founded and shares sold at $1 a share. The initial offering was for 350,000 shares; by the time some $25,000 in gold had been supposedly retrieved, the shares were being bid up as high as $50. In gratitude, the board of directors voted a bonus of $200,000 to be paid to both Jernegan and Fisher for making them all rich.

By this time Fisher decided it was time to cut bait, apparently without informing Jernegan. He quietly sold off his stock, added the proceeds to his $200,000 and announced he was off to Boston "for supplies." When he didn't return, the gold accumulator didn't extract any more gold from the bay.

It didn't take long for the Reverend Jernegan to figure out he was left holding the bag. He also announced he was off for Boston "to find Fisher."

Jernegan and his family, which had also disappeared, turned up more than a year later living in luxury in the south of France. When this information got back to Electrolytic Marine Salts, the directors petitioned the French government to arrest Jernegan and deport him to the United States. The French seized the minister but eventually freed him. There was no question that Jernegan had obtained his $200,000 legally from the directors, and there was no law requiring that he return it. The French also wondered what crime Jernegan had committed, since he had only operated a gold-mining operation that had run dry.

Eventually Jernegan came back on his own and even returned the bulk of his bonus money, which hardly made a dent in stockholder losses. Jernegan continued to live the good life in the Philippines and Hawaii, on the sale of his stockholdings. When he died in 1942, a rumor started that Fisher had been living in the South Seas as a rich American, that he had had an affair with a tribal chief's wife and had been executed along with her according to tribal law. It made for an exotic story and, if not true, probably somewhat pacified the still-living investors in the gold extraction swindle.

GOLD MINE DIRT *updated high-tech con*

It's the 1990s switch on gold mining scams, with a supposed high-tech tie-in. A California company offered to sell consumers tons of dirt from an abandoned gold mine in Nevada for a mere $16,000. According to the scam outfit, a new technology made it possible to extract gold ore that miners of the Comstock Lode in 1876 had ignored because it was too difficult to mine back then.

Charged with investigating the deal, postal inspector Kacy McClelland checked the historical records and found that the mine had never produced any gold at all. When laboratory tests were performed on a full ton of the sample dirt, not a single speck of gold turned up. The reason for this was that the Comstock Lode was a silver strike, not a gold strike.

The company's president was arrested in March 1991 and charged with mail and securities fraud. And investors were stuck with tons of plain old Nevada dirt.

GORDON-GORDON, LORD *international swindler*

The true identity of one of the most audacious international swindlers of all time, "Lord Gordon-Gordon," was never definitely ascertained, although it is generally said that he was the bastard of a English clergyman's son and the family maid. The only thing that is established is that he brought such 19th-century leading lights and financial institutions as Horace Greeley, the Northern Pacific Railroad, Colonel Thomas A. Scott and a number of supposedly sharp-minded financial manipulators (including Jay Gould, perhaps the most notorious of the "robber barons") to their knees. In the process of his grand swindle—often referred to with much public approbation as "the taking of Jay Gould to the cleaners"—the bogus nobleman precipitated an "invasion" of Canada and a near shooting war with that country's large neighbor to the south.

In 1868, using the equally bogus name of Lord Glencairn, he swindled Marshall & Son, a society jeweler, of £25,000 and departed Britain with his ill-gotten jewels. He surfaced in Minneapolis, where he deposited $40,000, the remnant of his jewelry caper, in a local bank in the name of Lord Gordon-Gordon. He identified himself through intermediaries as the heir of the great Earl of Gordon, cousin of the Campbells, collateral relative of Lord Byron and glorious descendant of Lochinvar and the ancient kings of the Highlanders. Then he let officials of the Northern Pacific know he was looking for some large tracts of lands on which to settle his overpopulated Scottish tenants. He allowed he would need at least a half-million acres, a prospect that had the railroadmen salivating, since the railroad was badly in need of capital.

Officials of the Northern Pacific fell all over themselves to please the supposed nobleman, wining and dining him and taking him on hunting expeditions. He was also presented with "trinkets," which in one case alone amounted to some $40,000. After three months of the royal treatment Lord Gordon-Gordon picked out all the acreage he wanted to buy and left for New York, supposedly to arrange the transfer of his funds from Scotland for the huge purchase. With him he carried letters of introduction from Colonel John S. Loomis (the line's land commissioner) to Jay Gould (then fighting for control of the Erie Railroad) and publisher Horace Greeley (an associate of Gould and a major stockholder in the Erie).

Gordon-Gordon promised to help Gould retain his hold on the Erie, but he offered stiff terms. The bogus lord claimed to have proxies from several Europeans with stock in the railroad and, along with his own holdings, he could provide Gould with the margin of victory. Gordon-Gordon said he wanted a reform of management with a large say for himself

and in exchange he would leave Gould in charge. Gordon-Gordon had another important stipulation, one that the notorious Gould immediately appreciated. In supposed gratitude Gould presented Gordon-Gordon with $1 million in negotiable securities and cash in what was called "a pooling of interests." In other words, a bribe.

Immediately thereafter, large chunks of Erie stock came on the market. Gould finally figured out that Gordon-Gordon was selling the stock he had gotten in the bribe. Realizing that he had been swindled, Gould sued the Scotsman. The slippery Gordon-Gordon then joined with the forces seeking to depose Gould in the Erie. Brought to trial in March 1873, Gordon-Gordon made an imposing figure as he reeled off names of important European personages he was supposedly representing in the Erie deal. Before these references could be checked out, Gordon-Gordon decamped on the second day of the trial and fled to Canada with the bulk of his loot.

Turning on the charm, Gordon-Gordon, still posing as a personage of high blood, convinced Canadian authories that Gould and the Minnesota railroaders were smearing him because he declined to invest in their lands. He proposed instead to buy his needed acreage in Manitoba, sums that would bring great prosperity to Canada.

Frustrated in their inability to force Canada to return Gordon-Gordon, his foes mounted a kidnap plot, almost certainly ordered by Gould and the Northern Pacific. They succeeded in crossing the border and seizing Gordon-Gordon, but were apprehended at the border by the Northwest Mounted Police and Canadians determined not to see their savior snatched away. The kidnappers, including two future governors of Minnesota and three future congressmen, were jailed and refused bail.

The affair grew into an international incident, with the governor of Minnesota ordering the state militia to full readiness and demanding the return of the kidnappers. Minnesotans by the thousands volunteered for a military invasion of Canada; finally, however, negotiations between Canada and the United States let the raiders go free on bail. Gordon-Gordon remained safe in Canada, since under existing treaties such minor peccadillos as embezzlement and larceny were not considered major enough crimes to warrant extradiction.

Lord Gordon-Gordon might have been able to carry off a new major con on Canadians had the news of the entire incident not received big play in the European press. The jewelry firm of Marshall & Son noted a similarity between Lord Gordon-Gordon and the long missing "Lord Glencairn." A member of the firm was sent to Canada to make an identification and readily identified Gordon-Gordon as the con man.

Gordon-Gordon described it all as part of the continuing smear against him by U.S. forces, but he lost an extradiction battle and was ordered to return to Great Britain.

He threw a lavish farewell party, sent his guests home with expensive presents, retired to bed and shot himself dead in 1873.

GRAND CENTRAL STATION INFORMATION BOOTH SWINDLE *sold for $100,000*

Incredible as it may seem, the Grand Central Station information booth in New York City was once sold for $100,000—double the amount swindler George C. Parker received in a single scam for the Brooklyn Bridge. The feat, pulled by two unidentified con men, proves the swindlers' credo that it isn't what you sell but how well you sell it that counts.

The victims of the amazing coup were two brothers and well-to-do Italian fruit dealers named Tony and Nick Fortunato who operated a thriving store in midtown. One day in 1929 a stranger dressed in a conservative business suit entered their place of business and presented his card:

T. Remington Grenfell
Vice President
GRAND CENTRAL
HOLDING CORPORATION

Mr. Grenfell informed the fruit dealers that the Grand Central had made an intensive search and they had been selected as the persons who would be offered the rights to the information booth. He said the Grand Central had wearied of travelers besieging the big circular booth in the center of the station with unnecessary queries. Henceforth, they would have the ticket sellers take care of all questions, which meant the information booth was now cleared for business purposes. The railroad had decided that a fruit stand was the most logical.

"What's the rent?" Tony Fortunato asked.

Mr. Grenfell answered matter-of-factly, "Two thousand a week, with the first year's rent in advance."

It was a great deal of money for that day, but the Fortunatos were not turned off by the price. They had the money, having worked hard for the 25 years they'd been in America; without more than glancing at each other both knew the rental could be justified. No place in the city had the traffic of Grand Central, and besides the usual fruit sales, travelers would undoubtedly be buying expensive gift baskets. Still, the brothers wanted time to think about it.

"Impossible," Mr. Grenfell replied. He mentioned the name of a nearby competitor of the Fortunatos and said he was to get second option if the brothers refused. Seeing a grand opportunity slipping away,

the two fruit dealers agreed. They followed Mr. Grenfell into a building connected with Grand Central and then to a door on a suite of offices that read:

Wilson A. Blodgett
President
GRAND CENTRAL
HOLDING CORPORATION

They were led past a busy blonde secretary into Mr. Blodgett's office, and Blodgett buzzed his secretary to hold all calls for two minutes. Clearly he was a very busy man and this was not a major matter for him. When the fruit dealers again asked for some time to decide, Mr. Blodgett seemed to deduce that they could not manage the price and imperiously dismissed them. Only Mr. Grenfell's intervention assuring his superior that the Fortunatos were serious businessmen caused Mr. Blodgett to relent. The brothers anxiously agreed they would close the deal the following morning with a certified check for $100,000.

The deal was completed the next morning, and the brothers got papers permitting them to take over the information booth at precisely 9 A.M. on, appropriately enough, April Fool's Day.

The two fruit dealers showed up well before the appointed time with a gang of carpenters who would have to redo the information booth into a plush fruit stand. Eager to get started, the Fortunatos had the carpenters stack up lumber outside the booth and start measuring it. The clerks in the booth were mystified, having no information as to what was going on. At precisely 9 o'clock, Tony Fortunato approached the booth and demanded that the clerks vacate. He and his brother and the carpenters all began shouting indignantly as the clerks held their posts. Railroad guards were summoned to clear away the carpenters who were blocking travelers from getting to the information booth.

A melee ensued until finally the brothers were escorted to the administrative offices of the New York Central Railroad, where they brandished their written contract. They were told there was no such thing as the Grand Central Holding Corporation.

The Fortunatos insisted on leading the officials to the offices of the firm. What they found was an empty suite. Railroad officials tried to explain to the fruit dealers they had been swindled, but the brothers remained convinced that a brutal American corporation was trying to cheat two foreigners out of $100,000 and then lease the information booth to someone else. They insisted they had the rights to the booth. Finally, they were physically ejected from the terminal.

The brothers appealed to leaders of New York's Italian community who went to the police. The police had extensive files on con men but they were unable to ever identify T. Remington Grenfell or Wilson A. Blodgett, who had made the perfect crime. There remained many in the Italian community who never stopped believing that a rich corporation had taken advantage of two naive Italians. For many years Tony and Nick Fortunato would come to Grand Central Station and shake their fists and hurl insults at the hapless information clerks. In time native New Yorkers made it a practice of taking visitors to Grand Central Station in the hope of catching the Fortunatos in their act, which became one of the sights of Manhattan.

GREAT BOTTLE JOKE *performing the most impossible act in the world*

In an exclusive London club in 1749, a number of high-born Englishmen got into a discussion on the outer limits of human gullibility, with the duke of Montague insisting there was nothing the public would not swallow. The earl of Chesterfield said the most impossible thing he could think of was the claim that a man could jump inside a quart wine bottle. Montague promptly wagered the British public would fall for even as preposterous claim as that.

Anonymously renting the New Theatre in the Haymarket, Montague advertised that a man would perform this astounding trick the following Monday. By curtain time all seats and standing room were sold at double the usual price; the surrounding streets were jammed with hundreds of people who had to be turned away.

Alas, the curtain did not rise on time. The audience sat in patient anticipation, but after an hour they started turning restless and finally concluded they had been gulled. A riot ensued and the patrons proceeded to smash every seat in the house and rip decorations and wall coverings to pieces. Large sections of debris were dragged into the street and burned.

Montague won his bet that he could fill the theater with his outrageous fraud, but the cost of repairs he was forced to make came to considerably more.

GREAT DIAMOND HOAX *monumental swindle*

Two "desert rat" prospectors named Philip Arnold and John Slack had worked the California goldfields long and hard in the 1860s and after several years finally developed a small claim that they were able to sell for $50,000. They took their windfall back east and for a time kept their booty in a safe on Arnold's Kentucky farm. The boys lamented the fact that it was no longer easy to find gold. In fact, they noted that worldwide the big strikes were being made in diamonds. Unfortunately, America just didn't have any diamonds.

In 1871, after being absent from California for a couple of years, the pair turned up at the Bank of California in San Francisco with a leather pouch for safekeeping in the vault. They were required to state the pouch's contents and spilled them out, a glittering collection of uncut diamonds. The boys had nothing to say about where they'd gotten the diamonds. As soon as they left, the teller charged into the office of the bank's president, William C. Ralston, who was a former miner himself.

Ralston went looking for the pair, found them in a saloon and made them a proposition. It was quite obvious, he said, that the boys had located a diamond field and that they would need help in mining it. Ralston said he could form a syndicate to do the work. Slack and Arnold were interested, but they certainly were not going to reveal the location of their find without a lot of cash in hand.

Ralston was a bit too cautious for that, and he insisted that first the diamonds would have to be evaluated. The stones were sent to a leading jeweler in the city for evaluation and found to be genuine. Still, Ralston and several associates whom he'd brought into the deal wanted more assurance, and the stones were shipped to New York City to be evaluated by Tiffany's. That noted jewelry firm reported back that the San Francisco jeweler had, if anything, undervalued the stones, which were worth at least $1.5 million!

This meant that Ralston and his partners now faced the task of wheedling the diamond find from the grizzled prospectors. Without telling Slack and Arnold of the results of the Tiffany evaluation, the pair was offered $300,000 apiece for the location of the diamond find. Clearly Ralston and company were out to swindle the prospectors, since after paying them off they would still have $900,000 for the diamonds in hand. But Arnold and Slack were delighted, allowing that was more money than they'd ever seen in their lives.

Of course, before the deal was to be closed the prospectors would have to lead a member of the syndicate to the field. The pair agreed to lead one person—a mining expert named John Janin—provided he was blindfolded the entire time. Slack and Arnold insisted they'd reveal the location of the field only after they got paid.

The trio traveled for 36 hours by train and then two days by pack mule with the mining expert blindfolded. At the final destination Janin became so excited by what he saw he danced a jig. The area was infested with diamonds. They glittered between rocks, lay just below the surface of the ground and even in ant hills.

When they got back to San Francisco, Janin refused to make his report until he was given an opportunity to buy into the mining syndicate.

Ralston's company paid off the two prospectors who, after leading an expedition back to the field, headed back east. Naturally, the report of the strike spread and Ralston's group moved quickly to mine the diamonds before other diamond hunters found the area. To divert the other hunters, Ralston and his associates sent out phony mining groups in diverse directions. Meanwhile, the syndicate set about establishing a diamond-cutting industry in San Francisco, something that did not exist in diamond-ignorant America.

Then the whole bubble burst. A leading geologist, Clarence King, and two others set out to survey the field. They determined that it had been "salted" and not too professionally. The trio found that some of the diamonds even showed lapidary marks.

The *San Francisco Evening Bulletin* broke the story:

THE DIAMOND CHIMERA
It Dissolved Like the Baseless
Fabric of a Dream
The most Dazzling Fraud of the Age

Arnold and Slack were checked up on. It turned out that they had previously appeared in Amsterdam with some $25,000 they had used to buy a huge amount of flawed uncut diamonds. They had salted the diamond field with these diamonds and swindled the businessmen who had tried to swindle them.

Reputations and careers were ruined. In New York Charles Lewis Tiffany was forced to acknowledge that his experts—while the best there were in America—knew nothing about uncut diamonds and had no idea how much of a raw stone had to be cut away to fashion a jewel. Many California tycoons lost out in their investments, and Ralston's bank collapsed.

Most of the diamond syndicate sharpies were too ashamed to ever go after the two missing prospectors. However, one did hire private detectives who located Arnold living in his home in Elizabethtown, Kentucky, quite content with his $300,000 take. The local courts did not look kindly on efforts to extradite Arnold to California, reflecting community attitudes that admired the swindlers for the way they had defrauded the sharpies. Finally, in return for having all charges dropped against him, Arnold gave back $150,000, leaving himself plenty for the good life and even to form a bank of his own. For many years nothing was known about John Slack, who had informed saloon buddies that he was leaving California with the intention of drinking up his $300,000 or dying in the attempt. Years later, he surfaced in White Oaks, New Mexico, running a thriving coffin-making business, perhaps an appropriate finale for a man who had found and buried America's one and only diamond mine.

GREAT SALAD OIL SWINDLE   *false-bottom con*

What the press was to dub "the Great Salad Oil Swindle" of the 1960s was 15 years in the planning

The "Great Humbug," P. T. Barnum, outdid himself in giving people nothing for something with his "Great Unknown" exhibit.

by its mastermind, Anthony "Tino" De Angelis. The key was the accumulation of a number of oil tanks, many of which were false-bottomed. In 1963 De Angelis announced he had loads of tanks full of vegetable salad oil, which he had stored with various storage firms. Using his receipts for these tanks, he secured loans that brought in $219 million. Some of the tanks were empty, others filled with water and yet others with only oil above the false bottoms.

De Angelis bribed warehouse workers and storage company officials as part of his colossal scam. He was also not above forging additional receipts (since those oil tanks themselves were rather expensive). Exposed in 1963, De Angelis was sentenced in 1965 to 20 years in prison. The $1 million or so De Angelis skimmed off for himself was never found.

Upon his release from prison in 1972, De Angelis announced he was going to write his memoirs and start a public campaign against swindlers like himself.

GREAT UNKNOWN, THE   *Barnum's infectious con*

Of all of P. T. Barnum's outrageous hoaxes, the "Great Unknown" best illustrated how well the Great Humbug understood his audiences. The showman could not only con them but also make them like it. With much fanfare and on numerous showings Barnum offered his "Great Unknown" on a railroad siding. Customers lined up in single file and paid for a quick look at the "Unknown."

What was this great mystery of the universe? Nothing but an empty freight car—and a fervent printed request not to reveal this marvelous secret to later customers! Virtually all the victims complied with the request, perhaps because in a way, as Barnum grasped, they achieved a certain absolution, graduating from the ranks of the hoaxed to that of the hoaxers. And what if an occasional tight-lipped soul was asked what he had witnessed and answered with a curt "Nothing." Who would believe that?

GREAT WALL OF CHINA *demolition hoax*

It has long been a custom of newspaper "pool reporters" to get together and concoct a story that will demonstrate their worth to their editors. Usually this is done by having the journalists report the same basic event so that each lends credibility to the other. No such faked story had more unintentional international ramifications than one made up by four Denver newsmen in 1898. It was a scoop that the Great Wall of China was going to be destroyed.

Over beers reporters Jack Tournay, Al Stevens, John Lewis and Hal Wiltshire from Denver's four newspapers (the *Times, Republican, Post* and *Rocky Mountain News*) concocted a report that four American engineers had stopped off in Denver on their way to China at the request of that country's rulers to develop plans for demolishing the Great Wall of China as a gesture of goodwill and to welcome foreign trade. The *Times* headline read: "GREAT CHINESE WALL DOOMED! PEKING SEEKS WORLD TRADE!"

As stunning as the story was, it was soon relatively forgotten by Denver's press and public; but, unfortunately, the report was picked up elsewhere. The Sunday supplement of a large Eastern newspaper offered a doublespread account complete with illustrations, coupled with the key significance of the Chinese government's historic plan and what turned out to be additional bogus quotes from a Chinese mandarin visiting in New York who confirmed the story.

Inevitably, the story spread to Europe and Asia and finally to China itself, where seething revolutionaries were campaigning at the time to drive out all hated foreigners. Despite repudiation of the story by the government, the great Boxer Rebellion was ignited. A missionary to China later recalled: "The story was published with shouting headlines and violent editorial comment. Denials did no good. The Boxers, already incensed, believed the yarn and now there was no stopping them. It was the last straw and hell broke loose to the horror of the world. All this from a sensational but untrue story."

Although the origin of the report traced back to Denver, the early belief was that the reporters had been hoaxed by four strangers who told them a phony tale. The reporters had covered their tracks well. When they first developed their scheme they had even gone to the Windsor Hotel (at the time Denver's best) and talked the night clerk into cooperat-

A faked Denver newspaper story about the demolition of the Great Wall of China is credited with triggering the Boxer Rebellion.

ing and making up an overnight registration in four bogus names. The night clerk would then tell any inquirers that the four men—who had identified themselves as engineers—had indeed talked to the reporters and had left very early the following morning for California.

After turning in their stories, the reporters celebrated their journalistic coup over more beers and swore to each other never to tell the real facts while any of the others were alive. Thus it was many years later before Hal Wilshire, the last survivor, revealed the secret of a fake news story that made a real story and history.

GREEN, JONATHAN F. *sham reformer*

To some, Jonathan Green, who became famous in the mid-1800s United States as "the Reformed Gambler," was a knight in shining armor; to others he was nothing more than a smooth-talking charlatan. If the truth lay somewhere between, it certainly tilted more to the latter side than the former. It was amazing how many prominent and hard-headed citizens, including newspaper publisher Horace Greeley, swallowed his claims. In fact, Greeley, as a leader of the New York Association for the Suppression of Gambling, hired Green—a self-confessed crooked gambler and passer of "queer" or counterfeit money—as chief undercover agent for the group.

In 1847 Green, labeling himself a reformed gambler, published a startling book called *The Secret Band of Brothers* which offered up a grand conspiracy. The Secret Band, Green said, was formed in the 1830s and run almost in the same way that informers in the 20th century described the workings of the American Mafia. They had initiation rituals, codes and orders that had to be obeyed without question. The hierarchy of the organization included grand masters, vice-grand masters and the equivalent of a boss of bosses called the worthy grand. The group, said Green, was "pledged to gambling, thievery and villainy of all kinds," and members "wandered from place to place, preying on the community in the character of barkeepers, pickpockets, thieves, gamblers, horse players, and sometimes murderers." Orders from the top were supposedly written in secret ink and left at message drops in caves and hollow trees. "We will not wonder," Green wrote, "when we learn that there are men of wealth and influence in almost every town, who are sworn to aid and befriend these villains. They are sometimes lawyers and jurors, and even judges."

Existence of the Secret Band of Brothers was never proved or disproved, but later historians noted that Green's Secret Band was strikingly similar to situations described in a book published in Europe, *The Secret Societies of All Ages and Countries* by C. W. Heckethorn. Be that as it may, Green moved on to a more detailed exposure of gambling and cheating as practiced from time immemorial. Many of his exposures had some merit, but all had been published long before in other newspapers, magazines and books. Still, when Green published *Gambling Unmasked*, it became a best-seller of the day, much promoted by anti-gambling crusaders, who bought up several editions to spread their gospel.

It must be said that Green did give them their money's worth, embellishing fact with the most remarkable fiction. Green hit the lecture trail and stunned audiences by claiming that every deck of playing cards manufactured in America was coded by the Secret Band so that professional gamblers could readily decipher them to rob the amateur and the trusting, honest citizen. Green would have a volunteer in the audience—a local citizen of impeccable character—go forth to purchase a pack of cards. Green would lay them on the table before him, face down. Then he picked up a card and held it toward his audience and left them astounded as he proceeded to identify card after card. The most astonished—and outraged—group of all were professional gamblers who bridled at Green's false claims but were unable to disprove them. All they could do was charge that the volunteers were secretly in Green's pay and had simply provided previously marked decks. It was only in later years that the gamblers learned to their chagrin that he had fixed the lecture table with a concealed "shiner," or mirror; as he lifted a card he caught a flash of it and could identify it while apparently seeing only the back of the card.

Green left the anti-gambling movement in the 1850s, apparently after Greeley and others lost faith in him. Green's books, several on gambling specifically, continued to sell briskly even though the antigambling crusade—minus his flamboyant nonsense—lost much of its steam. Green must have been quite amused, having proved that while it is possible to reap handsome returns from a life of dishonesty, it was equally possible and much less risky to win rewards with a dishonest exposure of dishonesty.

GREEN, LESTER *nonexistent inventor and genius*

Almost as well-known as the infamous Winstead Liar, Lester Green was the redoubtable nonexistent genius of Prospect, Connecticut, who gulled the credulous elements of the press time and again. Lester was the creation of C. Louis Mortison of the *Waterbury Republican and American* who, from the 1930s to the 1950s, assured his readers and those elements of the press that could be conned by almost any outrageous story that Mr. Green was among the greatest and most inventive yankees of them all.

For example there was the time Lester's chimney caught fire. He rushed up to the roof and heaved sand down it. Meanwhile Mrs. Green in her panic mistook washing soda for salt and fired the stove with it. The heat fused the two materials and filled the stovepipe and chimney solidly with glass. This whopper brought some prominent chemical engineers to Prospect in a vain effort to locate Lester and inspect the chimney filled with glass.

Newsweek magazine, in its February 9, 1935, issue, fell for a Lester Green whopper, unsuspectingly printing the following as fact:

> Logic: Lester Green of Prospect, Conn., put two setting hens on his automobile motor cold nights. "A setting hen's temperature is 102," Green explained, "and consequently two hens is 204. With that heat the engine is sure to start the first time it kicks over."

Similarly, *American Magazine* printed in its "It Takes All Kinds" column the following:

> Lester Green, a farmer of Prospect, Conn., has trained his hound dog to run away from foxes, not after them, thus developing what he claims is a successful new system of fox hunting. It works like this: Hound finds fox, legs it for home; fox chases dog; then as both round the corner of the barn, Farmer Green blazes away.

This stirring tale seemed so all-American for its ingenuity that the *Kansas City Times* reprinted it on its editorial page.

Then there was the time Lester found a way to assure a winter supply of fresh apples. He simply sprayed his trees with glue to keep the fruit from dropping off in autumn. Then he also could have a fresh apple by just washing off the glue. Inevitably, several glue manufacturers made inquiries to find out what kind of glue he had used. One Boston concern even sent a representative to Prospect to try to make a deal with Lester.

Then there was the matter of Lester's fur-coated chickens. While cutting ice on a meadow one February, Lester found a setting of hen's eggs on the ice. He cut out a block and put them in a pan on his furnace to thaw. A few days later Lester found eight Leghorn chicks in the pan, covered with what resembled fur instead of feathers. Naturally this brought offers from farmers to buy a pair of these fur-coated chickens. Green-Mortison got off the hook on that one by explaining the poor chicks had all sweltered to death when the weather turned warm.

Only the fact that Lester Green never lived prevented him from becoming one of the greatest con men ever, one who could clearly fool the experts in many fields.

GREEN GOODS SWINDLE *counterfeit money con game*

A recent retiree named William A. was, like most senior citizens in his Southern retirement community, on a very tight budget, with costs always increasing faster than his fixed income. Thus he was impressed when he met a well-to-do oldster who spent money like water at the local community center. He told the man he wished he had been so well fixed after a lifetime of working. It was then that the stranger told him a dark secret. He hadn't been that well off, but recently had found a way to *triple* his money. He was dealing with a passer of counterfeit money. While William was shocked at first, he gradually became interested.

In due course William accompanied his friend on a bogus money-buying expedition. He was permitted to watch the transaction only from a distance, the passer of the counterfeits understandably not wishing anyone to witness his activities. His friend returned with a large envelope stuffed with fresh-looking $20 bills. To William's untrained eye they looked perfect. On the way back to the community, they paused long enough to change five of the bills in various outlets, making purchases of under $1 with each $20.

A few days later William's cash-laden friend informed him his supplier wanted to move $25,000. Did William want some of it? William wanted all of it, but the friend insisted he needed some for himself. So William withdrew $5,500 from his bank and his acquaintance put up $2,800 of his own money.

They hastened to a new rendezvous with the counterfeiter and William's friend took the money. They entered a luncheonette while William waited outside. William waited and waited. It took him a long time to realize something was wrong. Finally, he entered the luncheonette to discover there was another exit around the corner. Frantically, William asked about his friend. No one even remembered seeing him. William collapsed to the floor, weeping. He had lost three-quarters of his meager savings. He never saw his supposed friend again.

William A. had been victimized by a modern version of the "green goods swindle' " in which the sucker thinks he is buying well-executed counterfeit money, only to find out later that what he gets is nothing more than a bundle of worthless paper. In William's case the flimflam worked without his receiving even the fake bundle. Of course, the key to the con was that the supposedly fake money he was shown in the swindle was newly-minted legitimate currency.

The green goods swindle first appeared in America in 1869 although it had been practiced in Europe long before that, being called the "sawdust game" in Great Britain. Shown genuine bills, which were described as counterfeits, a mark would be offered them at extremely attractive rates. Just before the completion of the sale, the money package would be switched for one containing nothing more than cut-up green paper.

Within a decade several groups of green goods swindlers operated in the United States, screening potential victims in a scientific manner. Sucker lists were assembled of persons who would logically become involved in such a crooked scheme. Favorite victims were those who had answered ads for marked cards or bought large numbers of lottery tickets. Caught in this net were many small-town bankers and businessmen. Remarkably, the approach to them might even be made by mail. One brochure heavily used in 1882 read:

Dear Sir:

I will confide to you through this circular a secret by which you can make a speedy fortune. I have on hand a large amount of counterfeit notes of the following denominations: $1, $2, $5, $10 and $20. I guarantee every note to be perfect, as it is examined carefully by me as soon as finished, and if not strictly perfect is immediately destroyed. Of course it would be perfectly foolish to send out poor work, and it would not only get my customers into trouble, but would break up my business and ruin me. So for personal safety, I am compelled to issue nothing that will not compare with the genuine. I furnish you with my goods at the following low price, which will be found as reasonable as the nature of my business will allow:

For $ 1,200 in my goods (assorted) I charge $100
For $ 2,500 in my goods (assorted) I charge   200
For $ 5,000 in my goods (assorted) I charge   350
For $10,000 in my goods (assorted) I charge   600

Faced with the prospect of making a killing, very few of the carefully screened potential victims notified the authorities. And in the rare cases when the swindlers were seized in the act of closing a deal, they were released when their wares turned out to be genuine currency. One fast-talking swindler convinced a New England police chief that he represented a bank executive who was planning to offer an important position to a local banker but first wished to test his honesty.

A list of successful swindlers in the green goods game reads like a Who's Who in criminality, including Reed Waddell (see entry), George Post, Tom O'Brien, Pete Conlish, Yellow Kid Weil (see entry) and Fred Buckminster (see entry). Mafia gangsters in New Orleans ran a very successful operation for a number of years and even Mafia "godfather" Carlo Gambino supposedly worked it from the 1950s to 1970s. Police bunco squads receive a small number of complaints about the racket every year, but it is an established fact that no more than 1% to 10% of the victims ever come forward.

GREETING CARD CHARITY CONS   *seasonal scams*
They come at the right time of the year, the holiday season when many people are in a "giving" mood. They are unordered greeting cards mailed in the name of charity. Your purchases, you are informed, will help the needy poor. The schemers might even cite a few case histories. In one known case the disabled beneficiaries were relatives of the greeting card schemer. Unfortunately, a number of studies by various Better Business Bureaus revealed that an average of 88% of all collections stayed with the card operator. The balance went to a local charity as a token contribution—but only if the charity con artist was in a giving mood himself.

GUARANTEE PRORATING   *meaningless refund offer*
On New York's Fifth Avenue it is not unusual for street hawkers to offer "guarantees" on their wares—watches and such. All the customer has to do—indicates the meaningless bit of paper enclosed with the watch—is to return it to the retailer within 12 months for any necessary repairs absolutely free. Since many such street hawkers are from Nigeria, that may take some doing.

Unfortunately, guarantees are frequently meaningless, unless one is dealing with a legitimate retailer or manufacturer. There was a time when many articles of clothing, such as cheaper men's pants, carried such labels as "FULLY GUARANTEED FOR THE LIFE OF THE GARMENT."

A very common guarantee scam, currently favored by certain less-than-scrupulous carpet companies, involves generally a guarantee prorating. Let us say carpeting is bought at a reasonable enough price of $3.99 a square yard, and customers are informed the carpeting is "guaranteed to last three years." Thus if the carpeting suffers from fading, wrinkling, shrinkage or unraveling during that period, the customer is entitled to a cash refund. However, the sales contract makes clear—in small print—that all the carpet company will do is prorate the purchase so that if a claim is made during the last month of the guarantee, all the refund will amount to is about 11 cents a yard. And frequently the buyer will have to go to court to get even that rather then accept 11-cents-a-yard-off on another carpet—with the same wonderful guarantee.

GULF WAR SCAMS   *con games revisited*
The 1991 Gulf War was a period of double uncertainty for the American people, who were worried about both the military outcome and the country's economic outlook. Typically, these are periods that produce a bull market for fraud. The war effort per se brought forth a burst of patriotism that translated into opportunities for gouging the public. In Connecticut, hucksters used phone pitches to get the public to donate money to buy water filters for troops growing thirsty and sick in the Saudi Arabian desert. For a mere $10 contribution, the swindlers declared, soldiers would be sent a $49.95 water purifier. The tens poured in; the water purifiers, for $49.95 or any lesser price, did not go out.

As soon as Iraq invaded Kuwait, telephone con artists emerged all around the United States luring people into investing in bogus domestic oil and gas wells with the promise that domestic energy supplies were "guaranteed" to soar in value. In California, William McDonald, chief of enforcement with the California Department of Corporations, coordinated a raid on 32 telephone sales firms, or boiler rooms, in Los Angeles, Salt Lake City and Dallas. Among the 3,500 victims of the pitches was a certified public accountant who lost $75,000 to a company that promised a 35% annual return on investments in Texas panhandle oil wells. The wells were never even drilled.

Also surfacing were the standard employment gyps concerning overseas jobs. In New Jersey, officials were deluged with a wave of complaints about newspaper ads that appeared in local newspapers. Most of the advertisers had no connection whatsoever with any construction firms, but charged applicants $19.95 to $29.95 for the telephone numbers of government offices that offered free information on employment in the Middle East.

Another company extracted no money from applicants, but worked a gimmick intended to give them a profit down the road. The firm took 4,000 applications for jobs in Kuwait, supposedly paying up to $57.50 an hour. Patricia A. Royer, director of the New Jersey's Division of Consumer Affairs said, "The prospects of lucrative employment rebuilding Kuwait seemed like a dream come true for many tradespeople suffering from the regional downturn in the construction trade. It was the talk of union halls. People took days off to apply and made plans to quit their jobs."

The guess was that the company planned to use the names of applicants, electricians, plumbers and carpenters, to set up an employment service that would approach construction companies with an offer of lists of workers. (Some employment agencies servicing all fields sometimes use the deception about jobs that aren't there just to build their own list.) Another theory was that the names would be used in all sorts of future sucker lists.

Still, these Gulf War job hunters were more fortunate than several dozen applicants some time ago who were summoned to a hotel suite in Baltimore, Maryland, for interviews and were informed they were accepted for high-paying jobs. The "company representative" said they would have to pass physicals and were told to disrobe and wait in the next room for the doctors. Everyone was told to turn over their wallets and other valuables, which were placed in envelopes in exchange for receipts. The applicants waited and waited and waited—but no doctors came. Finally someone peered into the interview room and saw no one there. The "interviewers" and the applicants' valuables were gone. No quick pursuit was possible as the applicants' trousers were gone as well.

GYPSY MONEY CURSES *bunco operation*

A favorite gypsy gambit is convincing the gullible that their misfortunes are due to the fact that their money is "cursed." For a fee the gypsy buncos will remove the curse from the money—by actually removing the money from the victim. The racket, far more sophisticated than might be imagined, begins with a careful weeding out process. The victim is told

his or her fortune to test the victim's gullibility. If the victim takes the fortune-telling as a "lark," he is simply dismissed after a single session. On the other hand, if the victim appears impressionable and is clearly a person with some means, the full force of the con is loosed. The gypsy fortune teller, card reader, palmist or tea leaf reader says the full power of prayer must be utilized to solve his problems. Often a candle must be burned during this prayer session, and the size and price of the candle is determined by how long the prayers must be continued.

Unfortunately, the prayers by themselves prove not to be sufficient; but they do reveal the real source of the victim's difficulties. To confirm this mystical intelligence the victim is told to bring a raw egg on the next visit. When the egg is handed to the gypsy it is broken and, by sleight of hand, a black mass is revealed in the egg. The black mass, the victim is informed, is bad luck that evil spirits have transferred from the victim to everything with which he comes in contact.

Now it is back to the prayer sessions and at last the gypsy determines why the evil spirits infest the victim's body. The money he possesses is cursed and until his possessions are "purged" the evil spirits will not depart. This is a delicate moment in the scam, since there is a real danger that even a gullible victim might become suspicious. The gypsy informs the victim that she, the fortune teller, does not dare touch the victim's money thereafter, as she might become cursed herself. Still, she orders the victim to return with a large sum of money, preferably in big bills.

The stripping of the money from the victim is accomplished in various ways. One of the oldest methods is for the money to be placed in a very large handkerchief which is sewn shut. The handkerchief is then to be buried in a graveyard, flushed down a toilet or thrown into the river or ocean. In New York a popular gambit is tossing the handkerchief from the Staten Island Ferry. Of course, somewhere along the way a different handkerchief stuffed with cut paper is substituted for the one containing the money. A more sophisticated ploy favored now is to insist that the victim hold the money at all time. No handkerchief or container is used and, after many incantations, the victim is ordered to throw the money down a toilet and then flush it away himself. In this con the toilet's plumbing has been fixed so that the money is trapped in the pipes and can be retrieved later.

HABEAS CORPUS TRICK *false vote count*

In 1679 the English House of Lords was considering adopting the principle of habeas corpus, a guarantee that no one was to be imprisoned without a specific charge and a legal trial. However, prospects for passage were poor as sentiment in that conservative body seemed to be leaning slightly against the proposal.

In fact, were it not for an incredible bit of mischief on the part of one of the vote talliers, what has proved to be one of the most important bulwarks of personal liberty would not have won in the balloting. This nameless counter playfully decided that a "yea" vote of one peer deserved to be tallied as 10 votes because of his huge girth. The prank went undetected and no recount was demanded. Great Britain's Act of Habeas Corpus became law, later to be included in the U.S. Constitution as well.

HADFIELD, JOHN *impostor*

Born in the 18th century, John Hadfield (d. 1803) suffered the misfortune of being born 100 years too early. He was a compulsive impostor, a trait that might have stood him in good stead in the present day when impostors—even those who steal in the process—receive slap-on-the-wrist penalties and are sometimes even celebrated.

A member of a prosperous English family, Hadfield became bored with his training in the wool trade and immigrated to America in the 1770s, where he married the niece of the marquis of Granby. He deserted her and settled in London where as a bachelor-about-town he ran up huge debts and forged drafts against individuals who he knew would not have him prosecuted. When, finally, he realized he was deep in a financial hole, he got the duke of Rutland (related to his wife's family) to pay off the bills for the sake of the family honor.

In 1784 Hadfield turned to posing as a relative of the viceroy of Dublin and worked a number of swin-

dles. The duke of Rutland once more paid his way off the hook. Hadfield went back to forging and swindling until he was arrested in Scarborough; this time he got no more aid and was sent to prison for eight years.

Even behind bars Hadfield continued his impersonations, identifying himself as an ill-fortuned aristocrat who composed poetry and attacked the authorities. He attracted a Mrs. Nation, a rich widow, who was taken by his charms and paid off his debts.

When Hadfield was released in 1800, he and Mrs. Nation were wed. But within two years he was on the run again for having engaged in an imposture-swindle.

Hadfield returned to London and, fearful of being recognized, decided on an extended tour of Ireland and Scotland. It was then that he met Mary Robinson, "The Beauty of Buttermore," who had earned the admiration and praise of Coleridge and De Quincy. The Robinson family was not about to let their 25-year-old beauty marry just anyone; they were determined to make a prosperous match. This was no problem at all for Hadfield. Was he not the extremely wealthy Colonel Alexander Hope? The Robinsons were thrilled, unaware that Hadfield, in another imposture, was engaged to an Irish heiress.

The marriage of Hadfield and Mary Robinson in October 1802 was a gala event, probably more than Hadfield had expected, especially as he had appropriated the identity of a living person. Unfortunately, a local judge knew the real Colonel Hope, and Hadfield was exposed as an impostor.

Hadfield was on the run three days after the wedding. Mary was heartbroken, all the more so when she found Hadfield had left behind some letters from the long-deserted Mrs. Nation.

A reward was posted for Hope-Hadfield, and he was caught and brought to trial at Carlisle in December 1802. Hadfield's full history was then revealed. In actuality, the defendant was being tried only for defrauding the post office and forging two bills of exchange. Normally he would probably not have been executed for his financial impostures. But there was the matter of his having treated his latest bride so shabbily. It was also revealed Mary Robinson had become pregnant before the wedding. All this proved too much for British sensibilities, and impostor John Hadfield went to the gallows in 1803.

HALDEMAN-JULIUS, EMANUEL *book title hoaxes*

While the changing of book titles is a legitimate function of a book publisher, it is generally expected that the altered title be logical and accurate. One of America's most successful publishers, Emanuel Haldeman-Julius (1889–1951), who pioneered the line of "Little Blue Books"—cheap reprints of the classics—never felt so constrained. He referred to himself as the "Book Doctor" for his ability to increase sales enormously by retitling. Thus Theophile Gautier's novel *Golden Fleece* went from an annual sale in the United States of 600 copies to 50,000 when retitled *The Quest for a Blonde Mistress*.

Similarly, Victor Hugo's play *Le Roi s'amuse*, or *The King Amuses Himself*, was gathering dust until Haldeman-Julius came up with *The Lustful King Enjoys Himself*. The how-to trend attracted the Book Doctor's attention as well, and Thomas De Quincey's *Essay on Conversation* turned into a bestseller as *How To Improve Your Conversation*.

Whenever a critic complained that Haldeman-Julius was misleading and actually cheating the reader, the publisher dismissed the criticism by pointing out that his tactics brought great literature to the masses.

HALE, WILLIAM K.   See INDIAN SWINDLES.

HALLIBURTON, RICHARD *controversial adventurer*

There are many who believe the claims of Richard Halliburton (1900–1939), the noted adventurer-traveler; but many also doubt that he actually followed the itinerary of his *The Royal Road to Romance* and later travelogues. Memphis, Tennessee-born Halliburton spent most of his adult life exploring the world. Halliburton's literary career was based on his logging the details of his own adventures. *The Royal Road* was on the best-seller lists for three years from 1925 to 1928 and was translated into some 15 languages.

On his later journeys, Halliburton often followed the routes taken by famous figures of fact and fiction, such as Ulysses' route through the Mediterranean. He matched Lord Byron by swimming the Hellespont; he swam the Panama Canal; he ran the course from Marathon to Athens; and he climbed mountains such as the Matterhorn, Fuji-san and Mount Olympus.

Much doubt was raised about some of his adventures, especially in his first work, which established his reputation. The sad light of reality dimmed some of his claims, one of the most famous being his triumphant swim in the pool of the Taj Mahal. That feat lost much of its heroic flavor when other visitors discovered the basin of dark liquid was barely three feet deep.

In 1939 Halliburton and his 75-foot junk disappeared in a typhoon as he sought to sail from Hong Kong to San Francisco.

HAMPTON, DAVID *impersonator*

Few scam artists have seen their capers immortalized on the Broadway stage, but one such individual is David Hampton (1964–   ). Hampton was arrested in 1983 after posing as the son of actor Sidney Poitier and talking a number of prominent New Yorkers, such as Osborn Elliot, dean of the Columbia Journalism School, into giving him money and letting him stay at their homes. All of Hampton's victims knew he was good for the money, since he had a famous father. Of course, Poitier did not make good on the money, as he didn't even know Hampton, who later described himself as a struggling actor. Hampton, with a history of arrests for fraud and criminal impersonation, ended up doing 21 months in prison for this scam.

In 1991 playwright John Guare made Hampton's Poitier-son scam the subject of a Broadway hit play, *Six Degrees of Separation*. In May of that year playwright Guare obtained a court order of protection against Hampton after the latter allegedly made death threats against him. The following November, Hampton was charged with impersonation of a police officer and sexual abuse. Hampton had walked into a mid-Manhattan police station with a man who said Hampton had grabbed his genitals and threatened him. The man told police Hampton had seized his privates, identified himself as a police officer and threatened to "blow [his] head off" in a taxi cab. Hampton was handcuffed and taken for arraignment.

According to police, Hampton listed his address as 820 Fifth Avenue, a luxury co-op apartment building overlooking Central Park. However, employees and residents at the building told newsmen that Hampton had never resided at the building but "has repeatedly pretended to live there and brazenly called for and received mail sent there in his name." There are those who regard Hampton as a truly remarkable actor—in real life.

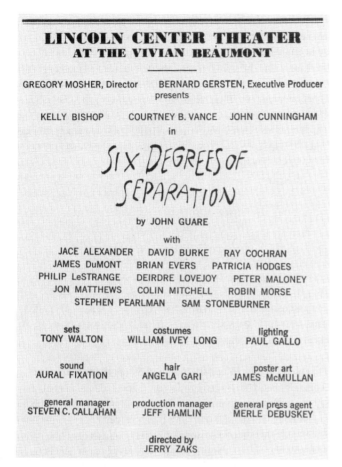

**LINCOLN CENTER THEATER
AT THE VIVIAN BEAUMONT**

GREGORY MOSHER, Director   BERNARD GERSTEN, Executive Producer
presents

KELLY BISHOP   COURTNEY B. VANCE   JOHN CUNNINGHAM
in

*SIX DEGREES OF
SEPARATION*

by JOHN GUARE

with

JACE ALEXANDER   DAVID BURKE   RAY COCHRAN
JAMES DuMONT   BRIAN EVERS   PATRICIA HODGES
PHILIP LeSTRANGE   DEIRDRE LOVEJOY   PETER MALONEY
JON MATTHEWS   COLIN MITCHELL   ROBIN MORSE
STEPHEN PEARLMAN   SAM STONEBURNER

| sets | costumes | lighting |
| TONY WALTON | WILLIAM IVEY LONG | PAUL GALLO |

| sound | hair | poster art |
| AURAL FIXATION | ANGELA GARI | JAMES McMULLAN |

| general manager | production manager | general press agent |
| STEVEN C. CALLAHAN | JEFF HAMLIN | MERLE DEBUSKEY |

directed by
JERRY ZAKS

The playbill for the hit Broadway play *Six Degrees of Separation,* which was inspired by the hoaxing career of David Hampton.

HANAU, MARTHE   *French swindler*

The daughter of a French industrialist, Marthe Hanau (1890–1935) launched a series of pyramid holding companies in the 1920s that bilked investors out of an estimated $4 million. Her depredations also had near-disastrous ripple effects on the nation's economy. Her gimmick was taking options on good real estate and issuing stock against them. Some of her own companies bought this stock and sold it to the public. Her companies gained much favorable publicity from the financial pages of *La Gazette du Franc et des Nations,* which Hanau owned. She enhanced the newspaper itself by inducing prominent leaders of the government to contribute to it, including premiers Poincare and Briand. Hanau went on to launch her own financial news service, which sent out reams of wire copy puffing her companies.

Partners in her operation included her ex-husband, Lazare Bloch, and a Mademoiselle Joseph, who split with her in 1928 and informed the authorities about her bogus bond sales. Because of her well-placed friends Hanau was able to fight off investigation for some time. Finally, despite fears that her

arrest might well cripple the nation's economy, Hanau, Bloch and a number of others were arrested. Hanau's remarkable defense was that she herself did not know what was going on in her own companies.

Held in prison for 15 months, punctuated by a couple of hunger strikes and an escape from a hospital, she was finally tried in 1931 and found guilty. Her punishment proved extremely light—two years and a minor fine. Angry mobs reacted by storming some government ministries and beating up state workers; they complained bitterly that the French Republic could not protect the rights of small investors.

Hanau was freed in December 1931, but she was jailed again the following April when her paper *Forces* printed documents stolen from the desk of the minister of finance. On July 19, 1935, Hanau was found dead in her cell, having taken an overdose of sleeping pills. On the previous day she had told her lawyer: "I shall always be mistress of my fate."

HANSARD'S GUIDE TO REFRESHING SLEEP

Novelist Charles Dickens was somewhat obsessive about masking woodwork he did not like in his home at Gad's Hill. Fittingly, he chose to do so with books. However, Dickens believed it unworthy to use authentic works for such a mundane purpose and therefore designed make-believe books to achieve that end. One non-work Dickens utilized was *Hansard's Guide to Refreshing Sleep,* which did an excellent cover-up job since it ran 19 volumes in length. Presumably, no one ever wondered how such a limited subject required 19 volumes. Another invented book was *Modern Warfare* by General Tom Thumb.

HARTZELL, OSCAR   See DRAKE INHERITANCE SWINDLES.

HEIGHT-STRETCHING CONS   *quack devices*

Height-stretching cons are one of the medical quack's favorite gambits. A leading staple is a sort of harness sold under various names that will supposedly increase a person's height. At recent count it costs 75 cents to produce and is sold for 12 to 20 times that amount. When postal inspectors tracked down a leading promoter of the device they found him to stand only 5 feet 1 inch himself. He blandly informed the investigators that he just never had the time to use the contraption since all of his time was taken filling orders for it.

The "pandiculator" is another growth gadget, which much resembles an old Chinese torture instrument. It isn't quite as bad since the victim at least controls the extent of his own pain. Not only will the pandiculator make one taller, according to the quacks, it will also allegedly cure virtually every ailment known to humanity. All the user-victim has to do is lay on his back, ankles and head strapped securely, and crank a wheel that tightens the straps and stretches the body. The hustlers recommended that people subject themselves to the contraption's ravages once every half hour. It was last sold at a bargain price of just $45.

HEIR-HUNTING RACKET   *false inheritance scams*

Often all it takes to be a missing heir is a common enough name, such as Smith, Jones, Johnson, Williams, Black, White, Brown, Green and many more. If you have such a name or hundreds of others, you or a member of your family may at some point become the target of the heir hunting racket. A letter will arrive informing you that a person of the same name, let us say Williams, has died in some distant locality across the country. Since this Williams person appears to have lived in your locality in the past, there is some possibility he or she is a distant relation. Since the deceased left no will and no known heirs, the firm feels you might wish to check further to determine if you may be in some way a relative. "If you wish us to represent you in obtaining the relevant preliminary probate court papers which might reveal you are a true heir, we will do so for a charge of $15 to cover the costs." The letter also indicates—truthfully—that the estate is quite large, anywhere from $100,000 to three-quarters of a million.

It does seem to be worth gambling $15 to protect your legal right. That's all it costs—at first. In virtually all states when people die without a will or known blood relatives, their estate is assigned to some sort of public administrator who has the duty of trying to locate possible heirs. This administrator files estate documents in probate whereupon hosts of heir hunters descend on the records. The scam artists among them simply busy themselves digging out people with the same name and send out sucker letters fishing for $15 fees. As one probate official notes, "People have much more chance spending that $15 on some state lottery in the hopes of striking it rich. Fifteen dollars in response to a letter like this is money down the drain."

And there may be far more money down that gobbling drain for those who send the $15. Within a few weeks the photostats of the records arrive, along with an urgent message from the so-called heir hunters. Their own research indicates a Williams in your very town seems to be a legitimate heir. Now, if you wish to file an actual claim, the firm says it would be happy to do so. The fee ranges from $200 to $300.

Some victims don't bite for this second gouge; but those who do will be ripe for yet another, even more

hefty con. "In our opinion," the next letter says, "you are a lawful heir and we have filed your claim. Now it is necessary to develop the actual proof." That effort, say the heir hustlers, means tracing through old family history records as well as other files in all parts of the country. This will be expensive, the heir hustlers say, but their information now suggests that there are no more than two other legitimate heirs so that "your share will be one-third" of $300,000, $500,000 or higher.

This time the fee can be as much as $2,500. As time goes by, however, the inheritance-hungry victims hear no more about their good fortune. Letters of inquiry to the heir hustlers' mail drop come back stamped "MOVED—NO FORWARDING ADDRESS." The heir hustlers are still around, using another name and bringing temporary joy to a new batch of victims. The sad fact is that no heirs are ever found for a number of estates. Thus the state and the heir hustlers are the only ones to benefit in many of these cases.

HETH, JOICE   *Washington's 161-year-old nurse*

Some consider Joice Heth (d. 1836) P. T. Barnum's most audacious humbug. The great showman-hoaxer presented Joice, a wizened black woman, as the 161-year-old nurse of General George Washington. Historians theorize that it was the adulation of Washington that made so many hoaxes about the "Father of His Country" possible. The general thirst for information about Washington allowed Heth to gain public acceptance.

The press recorded everything she said and did, and everything Barnum reported about her. He said he had bought her for $1,000 along with a document, which declared that Washington's father, Augustine Washington, had obtained her as a slave for "thirty-three pounds lawful money of Virginia." She was, Barnum ballyhooed, "the first person who put clothes on the unconscious infant who in after days led our heroic fathers on to glory, to victory and freedom." Barnum gave his assurance that Joice was born on Madagascar off the coast of Africa in 1674. Though she now weighed only 46 pounds and was toothless, she was still robust and certainly voluble. When a reporter for the *New York Evening Star* found her smoking a pipe, he asked how long she had smoked. She replied, "One hundred and twenty years."

Newspapers could not resist complimenting such candor since, as one pointed out, most women are "unwilling to tell their age."

Thousands flocked to Barnum's exhibit of Joice Heth, weeping as she related memories of little Georgie. She also told first-hand anecdotes about the

Revolutionary War. When the crowds in New York finally thinned out, Barnum took to the road, exhibiting this "living national treasure" in Providence and then Boston's Concert Hall.

As Joice's novelty started to wane, Barnum came up with another gimmick to spike up interest. It came in the form of an anonymous letter to Boston newspapers declaring, "Joice Heth is not a human being. What purports to be a remarkably old woman is simply a curiously constructed automaton, made up of whalebone, india rubber, and numberless springs ingeniously put together, made to move at the slight touch of the operator. . . ."

The result was great public outrage and charges of fraud. As letter-writer Barnum had anticipated, this also renewed long lines of paying customers. With considerable flair Barnum demonstrated that Joice was indeed a living, breathing female.

Less than two years later, in February 1836, Joice Heth died. Barnum had rashly promised Dr. David Rogers, a renowned surgeon, that he could perform an autopsy when the sad event came to pass. Barnum attended the autopsy, as did Richard Adams Locke, a writer for the *New York Sun*. The following day, the *Sun* carried a report by Locke, which read: "DISSECTION OF JOICE HETH—PREVIOUS HUMBUG EXPOSED." Offering a detailed account of the autopsy, it reported Dr. Roger's conclusions that Joice Heth had been no more than 75 or 80 years old.

Criticism once more descended on Barnum, but again he wriggled off the hook by having his assistant, Levi Lyman, supply the "true facts" to James Gordon Bennett's *New York Herald*. The journal immediately broke a brand-new exclusive, announcing; "ANOTHER HOAX! *Joice Heth is not dead*." The story, apparently written by Bennett himself, began: "Annexed is the long rigmarole of the dissection of Joice Heth, extracted from yesterday's *Sun*, which is nothing more than a complete hoax from beginning to end."

According to the *Herald*, the Negro woman on whom the postmortem had been performed was one "Aunt Nelly" of Harlem. Joice Heth was actually still being exhibited in Connecticut.

In time Bennett learned he had been duped by Lyman-Barnum, and he later upbraided Lyman for the hoax. To make amends, Lyman now offered Bennett yet another true story of Joice Heth. In September the *Herald* published a six-part series entitled "The Joice Heth Hoax."

The gist of the story was that Barnum had found an old Negro woman on a plantation in Kentucky, coached her with Washington tales and had all her teeth pulled. He then put her on display in Louisville as being 110 years old, and by the time they hit

FOR ONE DAY ONLY!!!
JOICE HETH,

Now on her return to the SOUTH, where she must arrive before cold weather, will, (at the urgent requests of many ladies and gentlemen) be seen at

CONCERT HALL
FOR ONE DAY ONLY.

This is positively the LAST OPPORTUNITY, which can ever be afforded to the citizens of New England, of seeing this most wonderful woman.

JOICE HETH is unquestionably the most astonishing and interesting curiosity in the World! She was the slave of Augustine Washington, (the father of Gen. Washington,) and was the first person who put clothes on the unconscious infant who in after days led our heroic fathers on to glory, to victory and freedom. To use her own language when speaking of the illustrious Father of his country, "she raised him." JOICE HETH was born in the Island of Madagascar, on the Coast of Africa, in the year 1674 and has consequently now arrived at the astonishing

Age of 161 Years!

She weighs but *forty-six pounds*, and yet is very cheerful and interesting. She retains her faculties in an unparalleled degree, converses freely, sings numerous hymns, relates many interesting anecdotes of *the boy* Washington, the red coats, &c. and often laughs heartily at her own remarks, or those of the spectators. Her health is perfectly good, and her appearance very neat. She was baptized in the Potomac river and received into the Baptist Church 116 years ago, and takes great pleasure in conversing with Ministers and religious persons. The appearance of this marvellous relic of antiquity strikes the beholder with amazement, and convinces him that his eyes are resting on the oldest specimen of mortality they ever before beheld. Original, authentic and indisputable documents prove however astonishing the fact may appear, JOICE HETH is in every respect the person she is represented.

The most eminent physicians and intelligent men in Cincinnati, Philadelphia, New-York, Boston and many other places have examined this *living skeleton* and the documents accompanying her, and all *invariably* pronounce her to be as represented 161 *years of age*! Indeed it is impossible for any person, however incredulous, to visit her without astonishment and the most perfect satisfaction that she is as old as represented.

☞ A female is in continual attendance, and will give every attention to the ladies who visit this relic of by gone ages.

She was visited at Niblo's Garden New York, by *ten thousand persons* in two weeks.——Hours of exhibition from 9 A. M to 1 P. M. and from 3 to 6 and from 7 to 9 P. M.—Admittance 25 cents—Children 12½ cents.

☞ For further particulars, see newspapers of the day. ☞ Over

Advertisement for Joice Heth, allegedly the 161-year-old nurse of George Washington.

Cincinnati she was 121 years, then 141 in Pittsburgh and 161 in Philadelphia.

Poor Bennett had been conned again. The account, as Barnum later stated in his autobiography, was all invention (but Barnum insisted it had all been Lyman's work).

The simple truth was that Barnum had bought Joice Heth from a Tennessee showman who had simply been exhibiting her as an aged human being, not seeing her great potential. All the hoaxes swirling around Joice Heth served to make Barnum himself—still only in his mid-20s—the most famous exhibitor of the era. As John Culhane states in *The American Circus*, "The Age of Showmanship had begun."

HEWITT, MARVIN   *academic impostor*

Probably the most active impostor in American academia, Marvin Hewitt (1922–   ), was a high school dropout who readily passed himself off as a Ph.D. in physics and had little trouble earning the respect and admiration of his "peers." In about a decade of deception Hewitt lurched from one teaching position to another under his own name and a number of others, some made up and some impersonations of learned scholars.

To his Philadelphia high school teachers, Hewitt probably looked like a lost cause. No one grasped his potential or tried to move him to a higher level of mental activity. He seemed nothing more than a bored youth who would not amount to anything. Seventeen-year-old Hewitt left school but in his own way reentered the learning process. In the public library he discovered a treasury of thought on mathematics, and he absorbed it all. In the process he became so adept at the specialization that he also gained mastery of physics.

Hewitt's ambition lay in teaching, but the credentials of a high school dropout did not quite fill the bill. Thus Hewitt forged certificates that made him a graduate of Temple University; with this required background he readily obtained a post at a military school teaching arithmetic, history and geography. However, this was mere eighth-grade stuff, and Hewitt decided to move on, posing as an aerodynamicist and finding employment in an aircraft factory. Hewitt used the name of a real person but worried constantly that his imposture would be discovered. Finally, the pressure caused him to resign.

Fear continued to mix with Hewitt's yearning to fulfill his academic ambitions. Using the transcript of Julius Ashkin, a physics Ph.D. from Columbia University, Hewitt taught briefly at a number of schools— the Philadelphia College of Pharmacy and Science, Bemidji (Minnesota) State Teachers' College and at St. Louis University. His tenures were always short, as the fear of detection forced him to move on.

Hewitt turned up next at the University of Utah, where Ashkin finally confronted him and asked him to quit his imposture. Ashkin was not unimpressed by Hewitt's brilliance and offered to aid him. The university's president offered him a job as a research assistant with the opportunity for Hewitt to earn his own credentials. Or, the president said, he would support his efforts to enter another institution of learning. However, the depressed Hewitt felt defeated and returned to his native Philadelphia.

Later Hewitt was granted interviews by world-famous astronomer Harlow Shapley and the renowned physicist J. Robert Oppenheimer, and he was offered a place at the Institute of Advanced Studies at Princeton. Getting cold feet once more, Hewitt turned down the offer.

He next taught at Arkansas under his own name but again with fake credentials. Under an alias he then moved to the New York State Maritime College. Next he went to the University of New Hampshire as Kenneth Yates, Ph.D. This imposture was discovered in 1954 and publicly revealed. He was dismissed not for being unqualified, but for misrepresentation. In point of fact, many felt Hewitt was eminently qualified for every position he'd held. For a time Hewitt received acknowledgements for his scholarship, and he was offered jobs and there were inquiries about his publications from the U.S. Atomic Energy Commission, Britain's Admiralty Office and the California Institute of Technology. Hewitt subsequently faded from sight.

Many thought Hewitt's personal position was not the important facet of the affair. There was talk of reforming the school system, which had so badly botched Hewitt's formal education and the need to tighten the academic credentials system. Nothing much came of that or of plans for the utilization of our best and brightest like Hewitt, who should have achieved his proper position among scholars long ago without the need for any deception.

HILL, MRS. SUSANNA MILDRED   See LONELY HEARTS QUEEN.

HILLEY, AUDREY MARIE   See BLACK WIDOW OF MARLOW.

HITLER'S DIARIES   *massive hoax*

> Since my written notes from earlier years have partially disappeared, these books shall always be kept at the party archive at my disposal.
> They remain my property.
>
> Munich in September 1932
>   —Adolf Hitler

For a short time in April 1983 the world was astounded by the above words and the existence of what seemed to be 62 diaries written by Adolf Hitler. In fact, a number of historians and handwriting experts declared the diaries to be authentic, and some of the world's top newspapers and magazines fell over one another to offer huge sums of money to publish the supposedly magnificent historical find. People were so eager to accept that the finds were genuine, that distinguished experts lent their support to the documents, which were later judged by observers to be both grotesque and superficial. Among these leading lights was Oxford historian Hugh Trevor-Roper, who granted the documents a hasty okay despite a huge series of misspellings, wrong dates and other gaffes.

The Hitler diaries were no more than a massive hoax, the main victim being the West German magazine *Stern*. That such a prominent and reputable publication could be so gulled proved less a tribute to the hoaxers than to the blind greed of *Stern* itself, which sought to make a fortune in marketing the world rights.

The forger of the diaries, later described as a "scoundrel difficult to dislike," was one Konrad Fischer who also used the name of Konrad Kujau. Through the 1970s Kujau trimmed the suckers of postwar Germany with all sorts of phony memorabilia. One of Kujau's patsies was a wealthy Stuttgart collector to whom he peddled the "complete, original, two-volume manuscript of *Mein Kampf*." He indicated he was hot on the trail of an unknown third volume. Next there were a number of poems young Adolf supposedly penned; and then Kujau was getting close to unearthing an original opera by Hitler, which Adolf had called "Wieland der Schmied" ("Wieland the Blacksmith"). Kujau did a lively business peddling such items to true believers, and then thought up his grandest coup of all, the 62 volumes of diaries.

The diaries would be a godsend to Hitler lovers, since they contained no reference to such matters as gas chambers or death camps. Instead they inferred the Führer was a jolly good fellow or, as one analyst later said, "Beneath the ranting, tyrannical, uncompromising, ferocious, murderous exterior of Hitler, we learn, beats the loving heart of a kindly, gentle, and not-very-bright utterer of platitudes."

The projects soon came to the attention of Gerd Heidemann, a *Stern* reporter with an affection for old SS officers. He sold *Stern* a bill of goods with a statement that the diaries, the third volume of *Mein Kampf* and the opera would be worth millions.

It cannot be said that Kujau and Heidemann did not make a delightful team. Heidemann gave Kujau a uniform that had belonged to number-two Nazi Hermann Goering, and Kujau in return presented the reporter with a rare oil painting by Hitler. Both items were, of course, fakes.

Despite the gullibility of *Stern* and other publications, the deception collapsed in May 1983 when the West German government announced that chemical tests proved the diaries to be forgeries. The diaries were subjected to the tests now routinely applied to questioned documents—analysis of the composition and dating of type, ink and paper, in addition to the intricate techniques of handwriting comparisons. It turned out that some of the paper used was not available before 1955, ten years after Hitler's death. The bindings for the diary notebooks contained synthetic substances not around until after World War II and the typewritten labels on two diary volumes —one dated 1934 and the other 1943—were "either written at the same time or were produced by a machine that was never used between those years."

In short *Stern* had been swindled out of at least $3 million (with probably more to come). Other publications such as the *Sunday Times of London* sought

the return of $200,000, the first payment of $400,000 it had agreed to pay for its rights to the diaries.

The publisher of *Stern* announced that Heidemann, a 30-year employee, had been "summarily fired." The magazine said he had "fallen into the hands of a swindler and possibly enriched himself."

After disappearing from view for a brief period, Heidemann finally revealed Kujau to have been his source of the forgeries. He insisted it had not been his fault that the publication had not tested the diaries carefully before releasing them. "I am no Hitler researcher," he said, a monumental understatement.

Eventually both Heidemann and Kujau were convicted on fraud charges. Heidemann was sentenced to 56 months in prison and Kujau 54 months. The sentences were regarded as quite lenient; the judge largely accepted the thesis offered by Kujau's defense, which claimed that Kujau was an accessory in a much larger fraud perpetrated by *Stern* and its owner, Gruner & Jahr & Co. The judge accused the firms of buying and publishing the diaries without trying very hard to verify their authenticity.

Upon completing his term, Kujau has since been reported to have been supporting himself "forging forgeries of his forgeries." His current output bears the certification: "Guaranteed Fake."

HITLER'S SILLY DANCE *propaganda film fakery*
It is a dance or jig still seen in film studies of World War II. The scene: the train car memorial to the Great War, at Compiègne, France, where the French were forced to surrender to Nazi Germany in June 1940. Adolf Hitler emerges from the train and proceeds to dance a comic little dance.

It is propaganda film fakery. What Hitler had done was take what film editor Laurence Stallings of Movietone News later described as "a small leap of astonishment at himself" on the signing of the surrender terms. What followed was a "looping" of the film by Allied propagandists. They took Hitler's miniature hop and ran it over several times. (This is not much different than the current television commercial technique that permits dogs and cats and other animals to do similar little dances of joy over their vittles or whatever.)

Overall, the silly and even cutesy dance had the effect the propaganda technicians wished for: It made Hitler look to the world like, according to Stallings, "the sissiest, most ludicrous conqueror that ever lived."

HOCKNEY FORGERY *contemporary fake*
There is a danger to art forgers who imitate the work of living artists: that the artist himself will label the work a fake. One such incident occurred in 1981 involving a fake work of David Hockney (b. 1937), the

English painter of realistic, witty and clearly illuminated compositions. His pencil, pen-and-ink and crayon work of a "Colourful head-dress with colourful nose" was executed in 1963 and sold in 1980 for £4,000. A forgery of the same work turned up on the market the next year in New York City. The enraged Hockney located the copy and scribbled on the work by the unknown forger: "This is not my work, 24th March, 1981. D.H."

HOLLYWOOD CAREER HOAXES

It has been said that few places on Earth are as well stocked with impostors as Hollywood. Tinseltown thrives on publicity stunts, aimed at promoting movies or turning nonentities into stars; but Hollywood executives themselves are often victimized by inventive and most outrageous scams. To paraphrase a wise adage, he who lives by the hype, perishes by the hype. Money can be extracted from even the most hard-nosed film executives.

When filmdom's first Ben-Hur, Francis X. Bushman, was being considered for a movie career in the 1920s, his agent brought him to Metro's New York offices from Chicago, where Bushman was making a top of $250 a week. The agent, the legendary Harry Reichenbach, determined to get him much more than that in Hollywood gold. As the pair debarked at Grand Central Station, Reichenbach had his coat pockets stuffed with 2,000 pennies. As they marched up 42nd Street to the Metro offices, the agent dropped handfuls of pennies in their wake. At first children followed the pair to pick up the coins, then everybody became curious and joined the strange parade. By the time the marchers reached the Metro offices, the streets were a sea of people and the police were unable to disperse them.

Metro executives looking down at the mob scene could only assume the public knew and thought more highly of Bushman than they had. Reichenbach had no trouble negotiating a starting salary of $1,000 a week. As Reichenbach later recalled; "Metro wouldn't think of letting him out of the offices before he signed the contract. The fact was not a soul in the entire mob knew Bushman from Adam then. But they had a natural flair for pennies."

In the golden age of moviemaking, the 1930s, movie moguls could be held in awe of talent. And despite the frequent and typical statements by the brothers Warner that "writers are schmucks with typewriters," the fact was studio bigshots were awed by writers who could so much as put one word after another with some logic. Playwright and screenwriter Charles MacArthur once determined to prove that even a person with no writing ability at all could extract a tidy fortune from these supposed business geniuses. For this role he chose an Englishman named Basil, working for an oil company for $65 a week, whom he met on the tennis courts. MacArthur's campaign was to ensconce his protege—"who couldn't even write a check"—in a $2,000-a-week screenwriting position.

MacArthur showed up at studio story conferences with Basil in tow. In time producers eyed the newcomer curiously and finally asked MacArthur who he was.

"The next Noel Coward," MacArthur informed them earnestly. "Just out here for a rest and not interested in working for pictures. Wouldn't make a move on a story line unless I asked his advice."

Inevitably the studio head wanted to know if Basil would join the studio. MacArthur insisted there was absolutely no chance of that. Inevitably, Basil was lured to a private meeting behind MacArthur's back and offered a screenwriting job. Despite MacArthur's coaching that he hold out for $2,000 a week, Basil's resistance crumbled and he accepted $1,500.

Basil held the job for an entire year, without so much as committing a single word to paper. Whenever given a story idea to work on, he followed MacArthur's coaching and after a few weeks sent it back untouched, sniffing it just wasn't his kind of story. Finally, the studio sent Basil off to frigid Canada to develop a picture idea about the Hudson's Bay Company.

Upon his return MacArthur was already set with a strategy to put that idea in the deep freeze, but by then disaster struck. Basil, it seemed, felt insecure with his newly-found income and had never quit his job with the oil company. This was not a problem until it developed there were too many deductions made for Social Security, and the government informed the studio not to deduct so much from Basil's salary.

HOME, DANIEL D. *greatest of the spiritualist fakers*

The greatest of American spiritualists, Daniel D. Home (1833–1886), was one of the first to take to the "rapping" rage that established modern spiritualism when first performed by the Fox Sisters (see entry). In 1850, two years after the Foxes first performed their "Rochester rappings," 17-year-old Daniel left the home of his aunt with whom he lived in Waterford, Connecticut, to become a medium and cash in on the craze in spirit communication that was sweeping the world. It was a matter of personal choice; had he opted to run away and join the circus he would undoubtedly have become a celebrated magician.

Within four years young Daniel was established as America's best spiritualist, and then he set off to swindle new worlds in Europe. He was quickly accepted by high society, which of course had the financial wherewithal to be impressed with such foolishness. For the next 17 years Home conducted seances by the thousands, many by invitation to noble houses and royal courts. Among those for whom he performed were such noble "sitters" as Napoleon III and his empress of France, King Maximilian of Bavaria, Queen Sophia of the Netherlands, the king and queen of Württemberg, the crown prince of Prussia, the duchess of Hamilton, and Czar Alexander II of Russia, who perhaps above all became a dear, if gullible, friend.

One of Home's most celebrated performances occurred at the French court of Napoleon III. Knowing for certain that the empress would seek communication with her dead father, Home smuggled in a rubber replica of the dead man's right hand. When the empress touched it in the dark, she knew she "recognized it at once" since the third finger was missing.

The dummy hand was one of Home's staples. While Home sat at the seance table, he was not part of the hand-holding circle, but his hands appeared to always be in sight in the dim light on the table. Actually, he most certainly used a dummy hand made of some flesh-colored leather. Meanwhile, his real hand, concealed in a black glove, was free to do its dirty work. While sitting at the table he could make distant chairs leap and glide about. For this he used the "patent pocket fishing rod," a collapsible device of telescoping steel sections that when folded was no bigger than a lead pencil. Painted dull black, it was indistinguishable from the dark surroundings. Besides moving furniture, it could whirl glowing hands over the heads of the sitters. A hinged steel bar could be used to raise the seance table itself by means of leverage.

One of Home's most electrifying tricks—which convinced many that he truly had supernatural powers—was having his chair rise up and carry him around the room over the heads of his guests.

It must be said that although Home was involved in one messy court trial (he had conned a gullible old widow out of £40,000), he had never been caught in any deception. But then again, seance sitters by definition are hardly the most inquiring of souls. The salient fact is that every single one of Home's supposed exercises in psychic powers and other tricks have been duplicated by magicians using wires, pulleys and magic gadgets of all kinds available to Home. During his lifetime Home remained the most heralded medium of them all, and by 1871 he was able to retire an incredibly wealthy man. After that he refused to perform any more, fortunate indeed since this at last was the period when the exposure of me-

diums began in earnest. Even after he died in France in 1886, Home remained regarded by true believers as the most reputable medium in the annals of spiritualism.

HOME EQUITY SCAMS *hidden repair traps*

In October 1991 the *New York Times* reported the newest home repair scam, which involved a sophisticated technique called home equity theft. A study indicated that at least 100,000 people in 20 states had had their homes literally stripped of all value. The swindlers concentrate on the elderly, minority members and those with little access to conventional credit because of poor credit histories.

Often the loans taken out for the repairs are secured by the homes of the customers without them being aware of it; in other instances, they are aware they are borrowing money, but are unaware of the costs or the consequences of defaulting, which in many cases result in loss of the house.

One 35-year-old married Alabama factory worker with three children was approached by a home improvement contractor who offered to renovate his home. The factory worker signed what he thought was a $4,000 loan application, but actually it was a legal instrument that put up his home as security on a $9,000 mortgage at 18% interest and $1,000 in advance fees. The contractor kept $7,700 of the loan and gave the homeowner $300. After making 18 months of bloated payments with no repair work done, the factory worker sought legal assistance.

Millions of homeowners have equity loans or second mortgages. Most such loans are as equitable as those found in first mortgage activities, but in fraud cases victims have been charged 18% to 40% interest and "origination fees" that amount to 20% to 30% of the value of the loan. In a new wrinkle some of these gouges are also made for such diverse objectives as carpeting, satellite dishes and even cancer treatment.

In the case of the Alabama factory worker, his was one of five families awarded $45 million by a jury that found fraud on the part of the mortgage company, a Dallas firm owned by a Finnish bank. However, the bank has appealed, and it is believed that many years lie ahead before any settlement will be achieved.

In many states established financial institutions have settled equity fraud lawsuits, but for every case seen by lawyers it has been estimated 100 deals go unchallenged because the homeowners are too embarrassed or distraught or do not realize their legal recourse.

The home equity swindles have also severely hurt many major institutions, including the Federal National Mortgage Association, known as Fannie Mae, as well as insurance companies, pension funds and mutual funds. In one case involving $600 million in fraudulent second-mortgage securities—sold to such institutions by the Freedland Mortgage Company of Richmond—Fannie Mae's share amounted to $25 million. The institutional investors were informed that the mortgages had a default rate of 5% when in fact it was 30%. In September 1991 company president Eric Freedlander was sentenced to nine years in prison. First Jersey Savings and Loan, which lost millions on Freedlander investments, later went belly up itself.

The standard operating procedure by the equity thieves is high-tech, high-pressure selling. In California, the victim search is now computerized with teams in cars cruising south-central and east Los Angeles. Target houses are those that look rundown but valuable, and a car phone call is made to the office. There computers check county records and credit agencies. The choice targets are those in which a spouse is dead and the owner seriously ill, or the children gone. Then comes a knock on the door. As for the collection process later, it is dogged. As an assistant U.S. attorney says, "Lenders call 15 times a day; we're talking old people absolutely panicked."

In Boston an elderly black man was put hundreds of thousands of dollars in debt for a few thousand dollars in repairs by crooks who used forged loan documents and other techniques. Given the lack of legal controls in a climate of deregulation, equity loan thieves appear to be here to stay.

HOOK, THEODORE See BERNERS STREET HOAX.

HOOP AND BLOCK CARNIVAL GYP

Of all the games one encounters on the carnival midway, Hoop and Block traditionally offers the most valuable prizes. There are no slum (junk prizes) payoffs here; instead there are watches, TV sets, stereos, etc. Win anything and you have a fortune on your $1 investment. All you have to do to win is toss a hoop over a prize and encircle the small wooden block it's displayed on. The catch is that there is a metal rod projecting from the center of each block so that ringing a hoop is much more difficult than it looks. But, of course, the operator is constantly tossing hoops that ring a prize with relative ease. It's all a matter of positioning. If a player's hoop is to clear the rod, it has to drop straight down from above; but the player's toss comes in at an angle, making it nearly impossible to avoid hitting the rod. The operator, by contrast, is inside the counter and simply drops the hoops straight down so that a goodly percentage avoid the rod. It looks so easy that many players buy

three more hoops and continue up to 30. No matter how many times they try, the sad result remains the same.

HOPKINS, MATTHEW, WITCH FINDER GENERAL
murderous charlatan

Among all the witch hunters who plagued Europe during the witch mania of the 16th and 17th centuries, Matthew Hopkins (?–1647) stands out as one of the worst of the breed. True, he did not "expose and cause the death of the most persons. Jacob Sprenger of Germany had at least 500 victims; Cumanus in Italy burned 41 poor women in one province alone; Bodinus, Delric and Boguet in France had incalculable totals, and another inquisitor, Remigius, took great credit for himself for having convicted and burned 900 witches over 15 years." Hopkins' total number was perhaps 230 (including a few Anglican clergymen) over about three years. It may be assumed he would have taken first place, if he had enjoyed a longer run.

Not much is known of Hopkins before 1644, except that apparently he practiced as a lawyer. In March 1644, he made his first discovery of witches, six of whom, he said, were accused of trying to kill him. He was so successful forcing confessions out of them that he won instant fame among a credulous society and immediately thereafter he became a "Witch Finder Generall." He went about Essex, Suffolk, Norfolk and Huntington getting villagers and townspeople to hire him and his two assistants (for a substantial fee) to root out witches in the community. The Witch Finder General demanded advance pay of 20 shillings per visit whether he turned up witches or not. For those he found he received an added fee of 20 shillings a head if the witches were executed.

Hopkins used any number of deadly hoaxes to find witches. He spotted devil's marks on people, identifying and pricking any bodily excrescence that was thought to be an extra pap for suckling imps—devilish helpers of witches ranging in size from insects to large animals. Hopkins was also a devotee of "swimming" witches, whereby the suspect was bound hand and feet crosswise, the thumb of the left hand tied to the toe of the right foot and the thumb of the right hand to the toe of the left foot. The suspect was then wrapped in a large sheet or blanket and laid upon her back in a pond or river. If the accused sank to the bottom, she was innocent (but dead), and if she floated she was a witch and thus doomed. Odds were that almost anyone cast upon the water in such fashion would sink; but the witch finders—especially Hopkins—proved very adept in laying the victim down carefully so that she almost always floated.

A contemporary depiction of Matthew Hopkins, the notorious "Witch Finder General." The illustration shows a few of the 230 "witches" condemned after confessing to being aided by imps such as dogs, cats, rabbits, moths, wasps and even four flies so numbered.

Another method Hopkins used was tying suspects to a chair and setting them in the middle of a room. It was assumed that during a 24-hour period one or more of the witch's imps would appear to suck the witch's blood. A hole was made in the door or window to let the imps in the shape of a moth, wasp, fly or other insect enter. Hopkins ordered the watchers to kill all such insects, but if any managed to escape, they were imps and proved the guilt of the accused. In one case an old woman subjected to torture after such a test admitted to Hopkins that four flies in the room were named "Ilemazar," "Eyewackett," "Peck-in-the-crown" and "Grizel-Greedigut." Hopkins sent her to the stake. In his first year of operation, Witch Finder General Hopkins burned 60 witches, providing him with a handsome living and giving him an awesome reputation. He traveled in a luxurious carriage and always insisted on being put up in the best inn in the community, with the townsfolk also picking up that tab. Hopkins became so rapacious that in time he earned the enmity of persons both high and low. Finally, the Reverend Mr. Caul, a clergyman in Houghton, published a pamphlet attacking Hopkins and his methods. Hop-

kins angrily wrote the functionaries of Houghton that he intended to visit their town and demanded first a guarantee of payment for his services. The letter was ignored and while Hopkins menacingly wondered if the community was infested with "sticklers for witchcraft," he decided to go elsewhere.

Hopkins' failure to take vengeance on Houghton may have started his downfall; but in any event more and more magistrates refused his services and common people finally took note that not even the most virtuous and innocent were immune to his accusations. Then, in August 1647, the Witch Finder General's foes found a way to turn his own deadly hoax back on him. He was accused of being a wizard. The story spread that through sorcery Hopkins had cheated the devil out of a memorandum-book, in which he, Satan, had entered the names of all the witches in England. Now Hopkins' accusers declared, "Thus you find out witches not by God's aid, but by the devil's."

Hopkins desperately denied the charge, but he was seized by a mob and it was decided to put him to his own test of swimming. Properly bound, he was set upon the water with the same care he always used. Hopkins floated. Despite some accounts, there is no judicial entry of his subsequent trial and execution; most historians concluded he did not enjoy the luxury of a trial. The mob became so charged when Hopkins floated that he apparently was lynched on the spot.

HOUSE OF ALL NATIONS *great brothel scam*

It need hardly come as a surprise that the field of prostitution suffers from scam operations. The House of All Nations is a prime example of one such house of ill repute. Upon its inception in Chicago at about the turn of the 20th century, it became known worldwide for offering courtesans from more countries than any other brothel in history. The house, located on Armour Avenue, was regarded as a must stop for out-of-town sports.

Allegedly, a customer's desire for a woman from any nation at all could be fulfilled, which meant that ladies who could affect the proper accents were much in demand by management. The house constantly sought to recruit talent from among the pupils of foreign language schools. Convincing verbal gobbledegook proved most satisfactory to clients who required uncommon dialects from places such as Africa and obscure sections of Tibet.

Inmates from warmer oriental climes were most popular and added a bit of "exotic charm." In the winter months, these women were clad in long underwear because it was said they could not take the cold climate of the Windy City.

Just as the women themselves were mostly fakes as to their nationalities, the same flimflammery extended to the matter of fees. Charges were kept at a reasonable $5, the explanation being that the women were willing to be rewarded by the standard prices in their native lands. However, because some sports might consider $5 too much, the brothel also had a separate $2 entrance. The ladies of the house, unknown to the $5 clients, worked both entrances, eager to dispense the same charms at either price.

The House of All Nations was closed down just prior to the start of World War I in a major vice crackdown. An added factor in some quarters was that such a troop of "foreign" women would constitute a security risk in wartime.

HOUSTON, TEMPLE L. *courtroom trickster*

Temple L. Houston (1860–1905), the son of Texas patriot Sam Houston, was a lawyer with a reputation for producing "courtroom magic" with deceptive methods, forcing many judges to go along with him despite full realization that he was engaging in lowdown trickery.

In one instance Houston was defending a client who had killed a skilled gunfighter by the expedient of shooting first instead of engaging in a "fair fight." Houston argued that the victim was simply too fast on the draw so that his client was forced to seek an unfair advantage. As demonstration of how much speed the gunfighter possessed, Houston suddenly whipped out a pair of Colt .45s and started shooting at the judge and jury, all of whom scattered for cover.

When things settled down Houston explained his guns had been loaded with blanks. While the lawyer had engaged in a most dramatic display, it did not sway the jury, which proceeded to find the defendant guilty. However, Houston expected as much. Now he appealed for a reversal, pointing out that when he had started the fracas, the jurors had dived for cover amongst the courtroom audience. Therefore, the jury could hardly be considered sequestered. Houston won the argument on appeal and, even though he himself had caused the turmoil, the defendant eventually went free.

HUGHES, BRIAN G. *champion prankster*

By most accounts New Yorker Brian G. Hughes (1849–1924), a wealthy paper-box manufacturer and founder of the Dollar Savings Bank, spent more time and money on perpetrating hoaxes than any other person in U.S. history. Humorist H. Allen Smith stated, "Hughes' skullduggery occupied more of his time than business matters."

In a typical hoax he would visit a fashionable cocktail lounge, have a drink or two and leave his expensive umbrella hanging on the bar. He'd retire around the corner to await the inevitable. Soon someone would emerge from the establishment, open the stolen umbrella and discharge a rain of posters and banners proclaiming: "This umbrella stolen from Brian G. Hughes."

Hughes, a round little man with a ruddy face and a walrus mustache, is also credited with the hoax of walking out of Tiffany's and spilling a bagful of imitation jewels all over the sidewalk amid the noonday throng. Another time he drove the management of the Metropolitan Museum of Art into a frantic search of the premises by leaving a set of burglar tools and some empty portrait frames by the main entrance.

Once Hughes was having his mustache trimmed in a barber shop when a boy walked in with a handsome alley cat, offering it for sale for the price of a drink. Hughes gave him a dime and took the cat, which some time later turned up entered in the city's annual cat show. He fooled some of the world's top cat judges by claiming the cat was the "last of the Dublin Brindle breed." The cat bore the name of Nicodemus, by Broomstick out of Dustpan by Sweeper, and actually garnered a first prize. Hughes brought the cat back the following year to compete again, but made the mistake of whispering his secret to the wrong party and the jig was up.

Despite the wide publicizing of the cat hoax, the horse show at Madison Square Garden almost fell for another of Hughes' animal impostors, this time a nag he had bought for a trifling $11.50. The horse's name was Orphan Puldeca by Metropolitan out of Electricity, and the judges in the early rounds were much impressed by the way the horse responded to the rider's instructions when she rang a tiny bell. Unfortunately, Hughes once more imparted his dark secret to a loose-lipped individual, and the judges finally got it: Metropolitan out of Electricity was the Metropolitan Street Railway Company, which was run by electricity. Orphan Puldeca often pulled a car! In its labors, the horse reacted to trolley bells as a signal to pull the car.

The Hughes hoax that fooled the most people was his great South American Reetsa Expedition. Hughes informed the press that he was financing an expedition to bring back the first reetsa to be seen on this side of the equator. For over a year New York's gullible newspapers carried the latest information of the great hunt, details provided by Hughes himself. Finally came the wonderful announcement: A reetsa had been captured!

Thousands gathered at the pier when the ship with the exotic reetsa docked. Hughes went on board to personally lead the animal marvel down the gangway himself. At first Hughes tried to get the beast to descend backwards, but the reetsa resisted and so had to be turned around. Down the gangplank came what was nothing more than a very ordinary steer.

Now try spelling ''reetsa'' backward.

THE HUMBERT MILLIONS *fabulous French fraud*

In 1878 a young peasant girl named Thérèse d'Aurignac went to Paris, ensconced herself in a smart hotel and began one of the most colossal frauds in history by announcing to the press that she had been left $20 million by a grateful American millionaire, Robert H. Crawford. Thérèse said she had nursed Crawford through a very serious illness some years before and that he had promised not to forget her. Crawford left Thérèse his entire fortune, consisting of stocks and bonds, and it was soon to be dispatched from the United States. Not surprisingly, Thérèse was deluged with offers of credit and bank loans (at steep interest rates of course) to tide her over until her fortune arrived. Thérèse gratefully accepted.

Then Thérèse had two nephews of her alleged late benefactor, Robert and Henry Crawford, appear on the scene with the announcement that there was a later will that gave them half the estate and Thérèse the other half. Through French attorneys the Crawford cousins sought to seal the fortune. In the meantime, the money arrived, in a special container kept in Thérèse's safe, with the funds to remain frozen until the matter of the two wills was adjudicated. An angry Thérèse declared she would fight to keep the entire fortune. Thérèse's creditors were hardly concerned, since even at $10 million as the girl's inheritance, they were very well protected.

The cousins lost their suit but promptly appealed. Meanwhile, Thérèse created a new sensation by marrying Frederic Humbert, the son of the minister of justice. Since Humbert himself was heir to a large fortune, Madame Humbert's credit rating rose accordingly.

The cousins lost their appeal, but they kept on appealing and appealing. Sometimes Thérèse would go to court against them only to keep the cousins from annoying her. Oddly, the Crawford cousins were seldom seen after conferring with their lawyers. They rejected any interviews with the press, their attorneys reporting the cousins were uneasy about the hostility exhibited toward them by the French populace.

The years passed and the estate remained unsettled, but this did not stop bankers in France and in other European countries, including even the supposedly hard-headed Swiss, from showering Thérèse and her husband with loans. With the passage of 24 years, it was estimated that the Crawford millions, still sealed in Thérèse's vault, had grown through interest to probably $50 million. The Humberts lived according to their anticipated station, buying large estates, luxurious yachts, works of art and valuable gems.

In the meantime, the Crawford cousins disappeared from the scene, but they bestowed instructions on their attorneys to continue the case. The attorneys complied, since the Crawfords sent them their fees from afar. In actuality, the Crawfords were Thérèse's brothers, and the money to cover their legal costs was secretly paid by Madame Humbert herself.

In the late 1880s a French court ruled that in view of the failure of the Crawfords to appear for a hearing, Mme. Humbert could go ahead and open the safe and start spending her $20 million plus. Thérèse said she was doing nothing of the sort. She insisted she had an agreement with the Crawfords that if the vault was opened without the Crawfords in attendance, she would forfeit her fortune. Court or no court, she was not about to jeopardize her wealth. With the ardent approval of public opinion, she made that stand stick.

The bankers kept their vaults wide open for Thérèse until 1902. Several bankers who had advanced money to Mme. Humbert had come upon hard times, economically pinched by the huge amounts they had advanced Thérèse and her husband; thus they had tightened up on credit to other clients. Finally one creditor asked a question that had never been raised in 24 years. Who in America knew of millionaire Crawford and his nephews?

It turned out nobody ever had. The Crawfords' background had never been checked on. Now, it turned out, all addresses and references given in the United States were bogus.

That was enough for a French court to order the safe be opened. When officials did so, they found two packets of securities. The contents of one packet contained genuine securities, which, alas, came to a mere 5,000 francs. The other packet contained nothing but yellowed French newspapers. There was also an empty jewel case, a brass button, a copper coin and a number of worthless deeds.

Two days before the safe was opened, Mme. Humbert had said she was feeling rather fragile and that she was off for a rest in the country. Now all the authorities had to do was figure out was which country. Eventually Thérèse was tracked down in Spain. With her were her husband and her two brothers, Emile and Romain, a.k.a. the Crawford cousins.

For the second time in her life Mme. Humbert came to Paris as a heroine. The French press swooned over her magnificent hoax, a sentiment echoed by such international journals as *The Nation* and *The Spectator*.

One journal said shortly before Thérèse's trial: "Let us hope this gifted woman may be spared the rigors of long and obscure exile from her beloved Paris." Picture postcards of the female impostor became enormous sellers. The only ones not impressed were Thérèse's creditors. Most were outraged and many faced economic ruin. One banker, however, became a sort of national hero by taking his losses in good graces, saying, "Oh, I'll be paid back somehow, one of these days. And, if not, well, I shall have had the privilege of serving a truly gifted woman." On the other hand, a banker in Lille, who had lost $1.4 million, solved his financial fiasco by committing suicide.

Despite the huge sums involved in the fraud, Thérèse Humbert got off with a mere five-year sentence. Her husband and brothers got only three years.

Thérèse came out of prison singing the favorite tune of the exposed confidence operator. The courts had done her wrong, she said, and the Crawfords would appear in due course and clear her. Then she vanished from Paris, leaving some to say she went elsewhere in Europe and others to say she went to America.

I

ICE WORM COCKTAILS *vile saloon fake drink*

It is still possible today to find Alaskan picture post-cards showing gold-hunting miners pulling ice worms from a glacier or posing in barrooms with wriggly creatures swimming in their booze. The latter were the so-called ice worm cocktails invented during the Alaskan gold rush of 1898.

It may well be that more journalistic hoaxes were perpetrated in Alaska and the Yukon during this period than anywhere in North America. Since storms frequently cut off communications with the outside world, local papers were put under considerable strain to come up with news. One of the masters of the craft was E. J. "Stroller" White, who was with the the *Klondike Nugget* until he created his own *Stroller's Weekly*, which lasted 35 years.

It was with the *Nugget* that Stroller reported such wonders of the weather as the appearance of blue snow (with an appropriate bow to Mark Twain) and of the appearance in adjacent glaciers of "ice worms," which came to the surface "to bask in the unusual frigidity in such numbers that their chirping was seriously interfering with the slumbers of Dawson's inhabitants."

As Stroller fondly recollected, virtually all the town citizens believed the report, and to capitalize on the publicity every saloon in town began offering "Ice Worm Cocktails." As the father of this grotesque creature, Stroller was under considerable obligation to try the beverage, and watched with considerable distaste as the bartender hacked a squirming worm from a cake of ice. White managed to gulp down the drink, which he found not unpalatable at all. Then the bartender whispered the plot of a hoax within a hoax to the newspaperman: "Say, Stroller, we couldn't get any of the real thing, so we faked 'em by poking spaghetti through gimlet holes and letting it swell. But don't tell any of the boys the difference."

INDIAN ROPE TRICK *hoax claims*

The Indian rope trick is the most amazing conjuring feat of all—if it really ever happened. A small boy climbs a rope before an open-air audience and simply vanishes in thin air! Of course, this illusion has been performed often on an indoor stage and is readily accomplished by conjurers employing any number of theatrical tricks, such as mirrors, special light effects and light-absorbing material for the boy's clothing. The "rope" rising is in itself no major test for magicians, since it really consists of jointed bamboo rods.

However, no non-Indian conjurer—and no Indian conjurer for that matter—has ever pulled this off in the open air, as the trick is often described. In 1875 the viceroy of India, Lord Northbrook, offered £1,000 for anyone who could demonstrate the Indian rope trick out of doors. The offer was given wide publicity throughout the subcontinent, but no one came forward to seek the reward.

INDIAN SWINDLES *victimizing Native Americans*

Fleecing Native Americans became a major sport of con men in the early part of the 20th century, with many of the swindles fostered by the obvious bias against Indians in white courts. Any claim by a white against an Indian would almost certainly be held valid by the courts. William K. Hale became known as the King of the Osage Hills in the 1920s, as he accumulated great wealth by fraud against Indians. He got into the practice almost by happenstance after an Indian with whom he had just concluded a business deal died. Hale sued the dead Indian's estate, claiming he hadn't been paid in the deal (although he had).

The courts ruled in Hale's favor, even though he did not produce documentary evidence but only the statements of white cronies. Hale eventually could be counted on to file a claim whenever an Oklahoma Indian died. Later on, Hale found that Indians simply weren't dying fast enough, and he got into murdering Indians after insuring them through various fronts.

More common frauds against Indians were committed by whites who suddenly developed a supposed concern for Indian welfare. Typical of these was a notorious con man named Odie Moore who told Indians that, since in the last century the whites had broken treaties with them, they could readily win redress from the U.S. Congress.

In 1930 Moore sold that bill of goods to the Choctaw Indians of Neshoba County, Mississippi, promising that great rewards were due them because of the breaking of the Dancing Rabbit Treaty of 1839. He assured them they would most certainly get $1,000 for themselves and each of their deceased relatives through a readily obtainable enabling act by Congress. To finance the lobbying necessary the Choctaws were asked to contribute a mere $5 per person. Since there had been wide intermarriage between whites and Choctaws over the decades, thousands of white suckers came up with their contributions as well. Moore's fanciful association even had a slogan, promising "$1,000 for every dollar." A number of young whites eagerly sought out girls with traces of Choctaw blood in them to hop aboard the gravy train.

Moore's victims gave contributions over and over again, as Moore assured them the bill enriching them was just about to be passed. And even long after Moore had died in 1945 many of his victims remained firm in their belief that their promised windfall would soon be in the mail.

INSTALLMENT PAYMENT CONS *scams against stores*

A racket that smaller stores—not up on the latest con wrinkles—frequently fall for is the installment payment con. In one case in Florida a flimflam artist bought $900 worth of merchandise and agreed to pay it off in six installments of $150 each. On the first due date he paid $150 with a $500 check. The store first checked with the man's bank to make sure the check was good. Once the bank did so, the store stamped the customer's payment book and gave him $350 in cash. The next month the man paid $150 with a $400 check and got $250 in change.

But the next month he didn't make his payment, nor the month after. When several reminders got no response, the store threatened to repossess the merchandise. The next morning the sharpie, acting very indignant, entered the credit manager's office and blustered: "Look here! Unless you stop annoying me with your nasty letters, I'm going to see my attorney about filing suit against you!"

The creditor manager was stunned at the deadbeat's gall. "Well, if you want to stop your troubles, just pay your bill. Otherwise, we'll turn the matter over to *our* attorney."

Now the sharpie showed his hand. "I just dare you. For your information, I've paid my bill in full. Here's the canceled checks to prove it—one for $500 and one for $400."

The store could do nothing but swallow its losses, having no receipts for the cash given in change on the checks.

INSULL, SAMUEL *false Midas*

In the world of stock manipulation only one American stood in league with the amazing Ivar Kreuger (see entry), the swindling Swedish Match King. He was Samuel Insull (1860–1938), who constructed a multibillion-dollar Midwest utility empire, one of the financial marvels of the 1920s. He did it by adding several minuses together and coming up with a gigantic plus in the form of troubled small electric companies that somehow became a united, well-running combination. It seemed to be impossible to quarrel with his success, and he seemed to deserve the adulation of the nation's press as the financial wizard of the age. The height of success for a banker was to have the fabulous Samuel Insull borrow funds from him. Even at the very depths of the Depression in 1931, Insull's electrical empire reported the second most profitable year in its history. Investors threw money at Insull, thinking they were making the shrewdest investments of their lives. The money, almost a billion dollars in an era when a billion really was a billion, actually disappeared into a financial black hole.

Insull's rise to financial success began when he dropped out of school at 14 in his native London and went to work as an office boy for the equivalent of $1.25 a week. Later he became a clerk for Thomas A. Edison's London agent. The agent was so impressed with the hard-working youth that he recommended to Edison that he was worthy of being brought to the United States. Edison brought him in as his secretary in 1881 when Insull was 21.

Over the next two decades Insull moved steadily upward, organizing a number of Edison companies and 1902 becoming president of Chicago Edison. In 1907 he handled the merger of all the electric companies into Commonwealth Edison. Finally Insull decided to apply his business acumen for his own benefit completely; he struck out on his own, forming small, often poorly run and marginally profitable utilities into one operation.

By the 1920s he was among the most wealthy men in America, with a personal worth of at least $100 million. Moneymen viewed investment in his stock as the sure road to riches. Insull's wizardry was based on the flimflammery of having one of his electric companies sell properties to another of his companies at a nice profit over the original cost. Rather than take on a white elephant, the second utility in turn would sell other properties to still other of his utilities, a neat chain-letter process. Thus well into the Depression, while other utilities foundered left and right, Insull's Middle West Utilities group thrived. Of course, it got so tough for Insull that phony sales between his companies were not enough to keep him afloat, and he cut the depreciation allowances for his utilities and eliminated some of them entirely.

To the world Insull looked like the man with the Midas touch; but in the end that was his downfall. Desperate Wall Street operators, themselves backed to the wall, looked to salvage their own careers by latching on to some strong holdings like Middle West. They made takeover bids, which Insull had to fight off, since if anyone took over his holdings they would discover he'd done it all with mirrors. As a result, Insull had to drain his own treasury of $60 million to keep his dark secret. The bubble burst in June 1932, and the swindler's fanciful empire fell apart, causing investors to lose at least $750 million.

The still-arrogant 72-year-old scam artist fled to Paris, where he still enjoyed an annual pension of $21,000 on his holdings of a few of his utilities that did not collapse. He fought off extradition attempts for a time, and when it looked like France was about to return him, Insull scurried to Greece. The Greek government let him remain a year, but under pressure from the U.S. government he was ordered to leave the country. To avoid capture Insull leased a tramp steamer and drifted the Mediterranean. When he stopped at Istanbul for supplies, he was seized by the Turks and shipped back home for trial.

Ironically, the government could not prove embezzlement and mail fraud charges against Insull because the various laws on financial finagling had many gray areas. Insull was finally released and immediately took off for Paris again. One afternoon in 1938 he dropped dead on a street corner. The 78-year-old swindler was not completely broke, having assets of $1,000—and debts of $14 million.

INSURANCE FRAUDS *fake claims*

It is difficult to estimate how much money insurance companies lose in fraudulent claims made by policy holders and fake victims of accidents. It is not at all unusual that whenever a bus accident occurs, claims of injury are made by more people than could have been accommodated in the conveyance. But overall, the main reason the figure is unnameable is the fact that insurance companies tend to be close-mouthed on the subject, fearing that any publicizing of the extent of the fraud would only encourage others to join in the pastime.

It is known that one insurance scam operation in Birmingham, Alabama, netted several million dollars over seven years. It is common for such insurance rings to obtain duplicates of legitimate X rays from doctors and then use them to bolster phony claims of industrial, auto and personal injuries. An operation in Missouri involved lawyers, doctors, osteopaths, nurses, insurance agents, farmers, businessmen and a county sheriff. In all, 66 persons were eventually convicted and sentenced, including the head of the operation, a rogue insurance agent.

Claimants had their wrists broken with crank handles and fingers smashed with hammers. Crooked osteopaths compounded the injuries by manipulating the bones of the hand and giving injections to cause infections. In some cases things were overdone so that amputations proved necessary. Happily from the fraudsters' viewpoint this served to increase the amount of the payoff from the insurance firms. Obviously, the men, women and children who posed as victims were poor and of limited intelligence. The supply of volunteer victims soars in periods of poor economic conditions.

Other claimants are highly skilled, especially those who conspire in faked car accidents, including drivers with racing car or demolition derby experience and "floppers" and "divers," who are adept at taking falls in front of oncoming cars. Sometimes both the victim and the driver are in collusion, but very often the motorist is an innocent participant, the fraudsters preferring these because they can survive rigorous investigation.

Scam artists come up with some truly bizarre plots. One involved the father of identical twins. One of the twins was completely normal but the other severely retarded. The retarded child was, however, too valuable to be institutionalized. The father would take the normal child into a store and, when nobody was looking, knock something heavy off a shelf and have the child start screaming as though he'd suffered a terrible blow to the head. Later, the father would file suit against the store, charging brain damage to a perfectly healthy child. As proof, he presented the retarded twin. No insurance company was about to let such a horrible case go to a jury and so made a quick and hefty settlement. The scam was exposed only when an investigator made a routine check at the family's home while the parents were away and saw the normal child playing in the yard.

Cases of "dead men" turning up alive are not unusual in insurance files. Some couples about to divorce use the dying method to produce a form of "alimony" money. The husband might leave a note that he was going to end it all and leave his clothes on a pier or along a desolate beach. No body would ever be found, presumably having been washed out to sea. The grieving widow might have to wait seven years to get the insurance money, but that seems acceptable in some cases when a marriage is all washed up anyway.

One of the most famous disappearance frauds of this sort was perpetrated in the 1930s by John H. Smith, who had once run for governor of Iowa. Smith had allegedly burned to death in an auto accident, but actually had used an embalmed body in the car. The plot was finally revealed by Mrs. Smith who admitted it was an attempt to collect on a $60,000 life insurance policy: "Under our plan, I was to collect the insurance or accept it when the insurance company paid it to me, and then meet John when he got in communication with me, which might be from one to two years."

The plan went awry only because Mr. Smith developed a roving eye, committing bigamy during his disappearance. When Mrs. Smith discovered her husband had married an 18-year-old blonde from Kansas, she lost all interest in the insurance money and went to the law.

See also FLOPPERS AND DIVERS.

INTERNATIONAL FUR TRADING *competitive trickery*
About the end of the Stalin era (and under Stalinist adherents) a shrewd trading con occurred between the Soviet Union and Canada. Soviet Russia had sable, the most expensive fur-bearing animal in the world. Canada had mink, which is nearly as precious. In a sudden burst of economic cooperation it was suggested in high-level negotiations that the Russians send four sable to Canadian fur-breeders and, in exchange, receive four mink for Soviet furriers.

The swap was made with the appropriate toasts of vodka. Two male and two female mink, the picture of health, went to the Russians and two male and two female sable came to Canada. The sad conclusion to this first attempt at Russo-Canadian cooperation in the postwar era was a disaster. As Louis Beam reported, "This tale of the sable is no fable . . . [as] the Canadians learned that the two girl sable had been desexed prior to shipment."

INVESTOR FORECASTING SWINDLE *the "always right" financial con man*
How can an investor go wrong when he has been dealing with an advisor who has given him accurate forecasts gratis for some time? Here's the recent flimflam pitch made by a supposedly infallible investment forecaster.

All the gypster has is a telephone, a lot of patience and absolutely no knowledge of the financial markets. He calls up a potential client and says, "No, I don't want you to invest a single cent. You should never invest with someone you don't know." What the gypster wants to do is demonstrate the "research skill" of his firm (which may be a boiler room operation or even out of his basement).

He then shares with the potential client the information that such-and-such a commodity—wheat, coffee, corn, pork bellies, soybeans or whatever—will shortly have a large price increase. And, sure enough, the price does indeed soon go up.

The second phone call still does not solicit an investment. Now the gypster wants to advise the client that a certain commodity was about to go down significantly. "As I say, I just want you to take your time and decide if ours is the sort of firm you might sometime in the future want to invest with."

And once again the gypster's forecast proves exactly right.

By the time the potential client gets his third call, he has been converted into a true believer. Not only does the client want to invest but also he wants to jump in in a big way—to make up for the missed opportunities of the first two predictions.

What the customer does not know is that the gypster had started out with a sucker list of 200 persons. On the first call he told 100 of them that the price of a certain commodity would go up and the other 100 that it would go down. After the prediction proved to be the right one, our "infallible forecaster" called that 100-person group and informed 50 that a second commodity would rise in price and 50 that it would fall.

The end result: The gypster now had a list of 50 persons literally dying to invest with him. Clearly, how could they possibly go wrong when this adviser was an absolute genius at commodity investing? As the National Futures Association, a congressionally authorized self-regulatory organization of the futures industry, later noted: "But go wrong they did, the moment they decided to send [him] a half million dollars from their collective savings accounts." In short, the gypster left with their money.

IRELAND, WILLIAM HENRY *Shakespearean forger*
The son of a London engraver and bookseller, William Henry Ireland (1777–1835) was only a teenager when he pulled off the most audacious hoax in literary history, forging documents and plays that he falsely attributed to the Great Bard. The grand hoax was possible because there was very little left in Shakespeare's own hand. Even Shakespeare's sig-

nature was rare. Thus the excitement was pronounced when teenaged Ireland unveiled a number of seemingly ancient leases and other documents said to be in the Bard's handwriting. There was also a love poem to "Anna Hatherrawaye." Ireland produced even more finds from the alleged ancient family holdings of a gentleman who refused to let his identity become known.

It is difficult to determine why Ireland started his extraordinary fraud, perhaps to impress his father, Samuel, perhaps to protest his father's unloving treatment of him, or perhaps for the sheer deviltry of it. Early in 1796 his father published the collection of his son's astounding discoveries under the title *Miscellaneous Papers and Legal Instruments under the Hand and Seal of William Shakespeare*. This was followed by a new version of *King Lear* and a fragment of *Hamlet*.

Once Ireland had embarked on his deception, there was no turning back. The emboldened youth now came up with his greatest "find" of all, two manuscripts of "lost" Shakespeare plays: *Vortigern*, a love story of the Saxon conquest, and *Henry II*, both written completely in the Bard's hand.

Scholars and important personages came to inspect and pay homage to the finds, among them William Pitt, Edmund Burke and the duke of Wales. All were deeply moved, and James Boswell fell to his knees before the fakes and cried: "I now kiss the invaluable relics of our Bard, and thank God I have lived to see them."

Richard Brinsley Sheriden acquired the rights to produce *Vortigern* at the Drury Lane—with half of all profits to go to the Irelands. Only a handful of scholars had doubts about the authenticity of the work and Ireland's other supposed discoveries. Ireland's long-range plans were to write a whole series of newly-found "Shakespearean works."

What finally caused Ireland's downfall was less the doubts expressed by some scholars than the actions of the actors called upon to act in *Vortigern*. The dialogue they were required to speak lacked the fire, the grace, the genius of authentic Shakespearean works. Some of the performers, not bound by an ironclad contract, withdrew from the play. That was a terrible blow but nothing compared to the deeds of those who had to remain. *Vortigern* opened and closed on April 2, 1796, fittingly only a day after All Fools Day. It was truly a case of tragedy turning to farce as the actors mocked their own lines, at times delivering bellows in falsetto. Soon the audience was hissing, and Ireland fled the theater before the final curtain.

Before the year was out William Ireland confessed his fraud in a book entitled *An Authentic Account of the Shakespearean Manuscripts*. Of his own shattered

glory, young Ireland wrote: "Had the play of *Vortigern* succeeded with the public, and the manuscripts been acknowledged as genuine, it was my intention to have completed a series of plays from the reign of William the Conqueror to that of Queen Elizabeth; that is to say, I should have planned a drama on every reign the subject of which had not been treated by Shakespeare."

Many persons found it hard to believe that a 19-year-old youth could have perpetrated such superb forgeries without help. The older Samuel Ireland remained for them a perpetrator rather than a dupe and went to his grave in 1800 still proclaiming his own innocence.

In 1805 the younger Ireland wrote another more detailed book, *Confessions of William Henry Ireland*. He lived another 30 years and, under a number of pseudonyms, produced a number of lightly regarded verses and novels. Perhaps his best work was a catalogue of William Shakespeare's works, from which both *Vortigern* and *Henry II* were missing.

IRVING, CLIFFORD *Howard Hughes autobiography hoaxer*

In 1977, the editors of the *Book of Lists* asked Clifford Irving (1930–) to make his selection of the "10 Best Forgers of All Time." Irving, the author of the most publicized literary hoax of the 20th century, complied—by including himself! In 1971 Irving conned McGraw-Hill Book Co. out of $765,000 by convincing the firm that billionaire recluse Howard Hughes had authorized him to do Hughes' "autobiography." *Life* magazine was also conned in the deal, paying $250,000 to publish excerpts along with 20 pages of handwritten letters by Hughes. The letters were submitted to a number of handwriting experts, or "questioned document examiners" as they prefer to be called. All found the letters and contracts Hughes supposedly signed to be absolutely authentic, an amazing accomplishment for an amateur forger who had not even seen an original of Hughes' handwriting. As one investigative reporter later put it, "His most lasting accomplishment may well be that he set back the science of handwriting verification by a hundred years."

Together with Richard Suskind, a friend and children's book author, Irving composed an engrossing 1,200-page book, which veteran newsmen—who had covered the enigmatic Hughes for many years—found startlingly accurate and authentic. The scheme was so daring and outrageous it was widely accepted even after Hughes said in a telephone call from his hideaway in the Bahamas that he had never met with Irving and that the work was "totally fantastic fiction." McGraw-Hill and Time-Life executives did not take the denial seriously, feeling that Hughes had

When *Time* magazine featured Clifford Irving on its cover as the "CON MAN OF THE YEAR," it used a portrait of Elmyr De Hory, himself a noted art forger and subject of an Irving biography.

commissioned the book and was now trying to renege because of fear that his disclosures might cause problems for his own company.

Irving's grand hoax collapsed for two reasons: the work of investigative reporter James Phelan and revelations made by a Swiss bank. Phelan acted in an advisory capacity for Time-Life to determine the genuineness of the Irving manuscript. Eventually Phelan discovered Irving had appropriated huge chunks of information from an unpublished manuscript worked up by Phelan himself earlier. Phelan had been commissioned by a former Hughes executive, Noah Dietrich, to ghost a book on his experiences with Hughes. By the time Phelan finished his manuscript, he and Dietrich had a literary falling out, and Phelan filed away his copy while Dietrich kept a copy. When Phelan, as a Hughes expert, was called in to investigate Irving, he was forced to labor under a crushing restraint. McGraw-Hill refused to let him see the Irving manuscript because it had agreed to what it thought was a Hughes stipulation that no one be allowed to see the manuscript before it was printed. However, brief anecdotes came to his attention, and he realized that his manuscript was the main source of Irving's material. (Dietrich's copy had fallen into the hands of a literary agent who had secretly passed it on to Irving.) Then a Swiss bank broke its vow of secrecy and revealed that a $650,000 check from the book publisher to Hughes had been cashed in one Swiss bank by "H. R. Hughes" and deposited in another under the name "Helga R. Hughes"—actually Irving's wife.

In March 1972 Irving pleaded guilty to federal conspiracy charges and was sentenced to $2\frac{1}{2}$ years in prison and to make "full restitution." What McGraw-Hill got back was $450,000, all that Irving maintained was left.

Irving served his 17-month sentence. When he got out, he went back to writing—this time what he said was the true story of his hoax. Irving seemed to function as a good reporter in writing the book, *What Really Happened*. Not wishing to speculate on facts, Irving even checked with the government and postal inspectors on how their investigation on him had developed. In the book Irving even quoted Phelan, declaring that Phelan said Irving had written "a very great book on Hughes" and that Phelan was sympathetic with him because he "was knifed by some of the great corporations of this country, because he's shown them the truth."

Phelan's response to that appears in Phelan's own book, *Scandals, Scamps and Scoundrels:* "Those quotes came out of Irving's head, not my mouth."

J

JACKASS NOTES   *doctored dollars*

During the presidential administrations of Ulysses S. Grant and Rutherford B. Hayes, several U.S. legal tender notes of 1869, 1875, 1878 and 1880 were eagerly sought by members of the public as "jackass notes." Their engravings had been doctored by some dedicated Democrat to poke fun at the Republican administrations. The fronts of these bills sported the engraving of an eagle, but when turned upside down, the eagle turned into the head of a donkey, the symbol of the Democratic Party. The prankster who performed this work of art was clearly a Democrat working in the engraving department, but the culprit was never apprehended. Collectors eagerly paid more for a jackass note than for the usual uninteresting greenback.

JACKSON, PERRY   See FOOTBALL HOAXES.

JACKSON, "STONEWALL"   See SPRING, ROBERT.

JAILHOUSE SHOPPING NETWORK   *convict's credit card con*

While credit card fraud is easily a billion-dollar business, some frauds are in a manner of speaking more fraudulent than others. That is perhaps the only way to describe the scam that became known as the "nationwide jailhouse shopping network" in the early 1990s. It was worked in Miami's Dade County jail, since there was a legal requirement that inmates were to be provided with access to telephones. The scam was thought up by Danny Ferris, a shrewd con man convicted of murder who, for more than four years, made local calls and 1-800 calls free of charge.

What Ferris did was simply order all sorts of merchandise over the telephone and steal an estimated $2 million in that fashion. It turned out that Ferris' accomplices on the outside provided him with hundreds of credit card numbers (retrieved from hotel dumpsters and the like), and the convict in turn used the numbers to order from catalogs by telephone. He arranged to have the goods delivered overnight to his accomplices who then sold the goods and split the profits with Ferris. Ferris ordered incredible numbers of video camcorders, Rolex watches, champagne, gourmet gift baskets, gold and silver coins and raked in a fortune.

Later he admitted to interviewers, "I split right half with everybody. I mean, I never took more than half. I got robbed a lot, but, again, you kind of take it on the chin. You know what I mean? It was like you said, 'Heck, it was all free.' "

When at last Ferris was exposed, jail officials found they could not legally deprive him of his phone rights. They did, however, raid his cell and confiscate hundreds of credit card numbers.

That failed to put Ferris out of business, as he managed to salvage a single number and use that to order a newspaper ad and a telephone answering service. He ran the ad in *USA Today* offering, "Cosmetics package, $89.95 value for only $19.95. All major credit cards accepted. Please call Regina Donovan Cosmetics." Danny supplied a 1-800 number but never sold any cosmetics. He got what he really was after—a brand new batch of credit card numbers.

Eventually Danny Ferris was sentenced to five years for credit card fraud on top of his earlier life term for murder. He was transferred to a tougher Florida state prison, where more stringent controls were placed on telephone calls. Meanwhile, back at Dade County jail it was discovered that other inmates were pulling Danny's routine, one operating in Danny's departed personal cell. Finally, after the CBS television program "60 Minutes" featured the case, Dade County jail officials removed the in-cell telephones, requiring prisoners to make their calls in open corridors and the like, in hopes this would put a serious crimp in their operation. And Danny's fame continued; a book on his bizarre scam was in the works.

JERSEY DEVIL *monster hoax*

The Jersey Devil is perhaps the most enduring monster hoax in American history, having allegedly been spotted by colonists in the Pine Barrens of New Jersey in about 1650. Today it is still earnestly believed to be real by many rural folk in New Jersey and eastern Pennsylvania. According to the original legend, it all started when a mother put a curse on her seventh child who was born shortly thereafter. According to the mother's wish, the baby turned out to be a devil and confirmed that fact by flying up the chimney and away, not an unusual feat in an era when belief in witchcraft was prevalent.

The first, but hardly the last, sighting of the Jersey Devil in the 20th century occurred in January 1906. It happened after one Norman Jeffries, a publicist for Brandenburgh's Museum in Philadelphia and highly suspect by the city newspapers for a number of faked stunts he had pulled, came across an old tome that related the story of the original Devil. Because the Philadelphia newspapers would have found any story emanating from Jeffries odoriferous, he headed into southern Jersey and planted a story in a small-town paper. It read:

> The "Jersey Devil" which has not been seen in these parts for nearly a hundred years has again put in its appearance. Mrs. J. H. Hopkins, wife of a worthy farmer of our county, ·distinctly saw the creature near the barn on Saturday last and afterwards examined its tracks in the snow.

Other stories turned up in other small papers and were soon picked up by the Philadelphia press and then by the Associated Press. Thereafter, following any sighting the press descended on the scene and duly reported the measurements of footprints in the snow and quoted prominent persons on seeing the monster. Women were reported to have gone into hysterics on lonely roads at having viewed the Devil. One report read:

> Reputable citizens described in detail his horrific form, the great wings, the frenzied countenances, half human and half animal, the long tail, the eleven feet, the deadly vapors which were exhaled in a mixture of fire and smoke. The fiend was ubiquitous. He was seen all over the southern part of the state. He was seen in the rural parts of Pennsylvania, Delaware and Maryland, all on the same night.

The same beast was reportedly seen in California on the same night it was seen in New Jersey. This proved no problem for the thoroughly conned press.

Aviation pioneer Samuel P. Langley was interviewed, and said that, considering the wing spread as reported, he allowed the beast could easily make it from coast to coast in one night, given the time differential.

Then the Devil was caught in Hunting Park, New Jersey. A group of self-proclaimed farmers said they had nabbed it and chained it to a tree. By the merest of coincidences photographers were almost instantly on the scene.

Once the Jersey Devil was captured, publicist Jeffries stepped out of the mists and announced he had arranged to have the bizarre creature exhibited at the Arch Street Museum. Attendance was enormous so that all anyone could get was a brief look at the Devil as a curtain was drawn open and the creature leaped forward at the cage bars, trying to attack the crowd. The curtain was closed and a fresh audience then ushered in.

Actually, the so-called Devil was a kangaroo painted with green stripes, with bronze wings attached to a harness made of rabbit skin. As for the Devil's attacks on viewers, these were inspired by a poke with a stick by a small boy concealed behind the cage. The cage itself was decorated with a large number of previously gnawed bones.

After a long run the Jersey Devil disappeared. For the next quarter of a century there were many more sightings. Publicist Jeffries finally confessed the hoax in 1929 and insisted he was behind all the later reports, a dubious claim since monster sightings inevitably take on a life of their own. Nevertheless, Jeffries enjoyed considerable income on the writing and lecture circuit about his numerous hoaxes, with the Jersey Devil always the centerpiece.

JESSE JAMES IMPOSTORS *parade of fakers*

It was one of the most famous murders in Wild West history. The notorious Jesse James (1847–1882), living in St. Joseph, Missouri, in 1882 under the name of Howard, climbed up on a chair to straighten a picture and was shot dead by a turncoat gang member named Bob Ford for the reward money. That act of treachery further established the outlaw's reputation as a cult hero and battler against "the interests" in the public's mind. It was inevitable that tales would spread that Jesse hadn't been killed at all, and almost from the time he was laid in his grave, one impostor after another appeared claiming to be the real Jesse James.

One after another they were proved to be lying and they disappeared. Still, sensationalist publishing entrepreneurs continued to make small fortunes reporting the real Jesse James turning up again. That barbershop staple, the *National Police Gazette*, could in its twilight in the 1960s get another gasp of life

Because the death photo of outlaw Jesse James did not show a missing fingertip—his left hand being covered—impostors continued to step forward for the next seven decades.

with yet another exclusive Jesse story (along with its other goldmine—"HITLER IS STILL ALIVE!").

The most famous Jesse of the post-World War II era, a time that really started pushing the longevity of the famed outlaw to the limit, was J. Frank Dalton, then living in Lawton, Oklahoma. Emerging in 1948 to claim he was Jesse James in the flesh, Dalton cited his age as the appropriate 101. He had been turned up through a tip to Rudy Turilli, an authority on Jesse James. The Turilli-Dalton claim was that Bob Ford had not killed Jesse, but another member of the gang, Charlie Bigelow. Bigelow was said to have looked like Jesse, having frequently passed himself off as the famous outlaw. He was due for death in any event, being suspected of having turned informer. According to Turilli, those involved in the hoax were James' mother and wife, the Ford brothers and even Gov. Thomas Crittenden, who allegedly was a longtime friend of the James family.

In 1966 Turilli published a booklet, in cooperation with the Jesse James Museum of Stanton, Missouri, entitled *I Knew Jesse James*, describing his locating

Dalton. Then he said he rounded up two surviving James cronies, 108-year-old James R. Davis, a former U.S. marshal, and 111-year-old John Trammell, the gang's longtime black cook. Both were convinced that Dalton was Jesse.

National reporters descended on Dalton. After a three-day stint columnist Robert Ruark came away absolutely convinced Dalton was the real thing.

Less taken were real western experts, such as Homer Croy, one of the more reliable Jesse James biographers. Croy came on Dalton early, before the old man had time to school himself on all the details of Jesse's life, which might be brought up by non-believers. Under questioning by Croy, Dalton identified Red Fox as the name of a scout for Quantrill, a part Indian. Red Fox was Jesse's racehorse.

The real catch, however, was the fact that Dalton's left-hand middle finger was intact. The established fact was that Jesse had accidentally blown off part of that finger cleaning his pistol during the Civil War, when he rode with Bloody Bill Anderson. Turilli challenged anyone to produce a photo of Jesse showing a missing fingertip. It was a safe challenge, since there were few photographs taken of Jesse. However, testimony at the coroner's inquest made reference to the missing fingertip. Several witnesses testified they recognized the dead man as James (thus greatly enlarging the suspects in a hoax), including Sheriff James H. Timberlake of Clay County, who knew what Jesse looked like. Timberlake, who had last seen the outlaw in 1870, said he recognized Jesse's face. And he declared, "He had the second joint of his third finger shot off, by which I also recognize him." Other witnesses beside Timberlake made the same point about the missing part of the finger.

J. Frank Dalton died on August 16, 1951, just short of what would have been Jesse James' 104th birthday.

JOB REPORT *employment opportunity scams*

The "jobs available" scam works anytime, but especially during tough economic times when layoffs are occurring. Job hunters are desperate and are attracted to advertisements that indicate there are great employment opportunities wherever. It might be Seattle, Denver, Las Vegas, Orlando or Cincinnati—wherever the scam artist happens to hang his hat at the moment.

Americans are footloose and historically ready to go where the jobs are, and the ad indicates the scam's job report or index has listings of hundreds of jobs paying $20,000, $30,000, $50,000 and even more. The report seems like a good buy for a mere $5 or so. Desperate job hunters send off the money and in return get listings of hundreds of jobs—nothing more than the classified job ad section from a local news-

One of the most enduring hoaxes concerning a U.S. president was the rather bizarre claim that President John Quincy Adams once had to hold still for a "nude press conference" with woman journalist Anne Newport Royall.

paper. Of course, any such job information is totally out of date for any out-of-towner and for a do-it-yourself job survey of some other city one could try an out-of-town newsstand or the public library.

JOHN QUINCY ADAMS' NUDE PRESS CONFERENCE
presidential hoax

One of the most enduring historical hoaxes, in keeping with Washington's cherry tree incident and Voltaire's famed quotation, is John Quincy Adams' renowned "nude press conference." No roundup review of presidential press conferences would be complete without the anecdote being cited.

During his White House years (1797–1801), John Quincy Adams was in the habit of rising before dawn, grabbing a towel and slipping out the back door for a dip in the Potomac before having breakfast and assuming his official duties. The story is told that one day Adams had skinny-dipped and, as he stepped onto the river bank, he found himself face

to face with Anne Newport Royall, the crusading editor of *Paul Pry,* sitting on his underwear. Adams retreated to a modest depth of water and demanded that Miss Royall leave; but she insisted on getting answers to some current political questions. Adams did not want to respond, but evidently he had no choice. It is this incident that gave rise to his so-called nude press conference.

The tale has been repeated ever since in many feature articles and books, the most recent of the latter apparently in 1975. However, as Cedric Larson, Mrs. Royall's biographer, stated in *Quill* magazine in 1939, the incident appears to have had no basis in fact, save for the fact that the President did take dips in the Potomac and Mrs. Royall was a journalist. She did not even begin publishing *Paul Pry* until almost three years after Adams had left office. It may well be that the story was invented by persons who were seeking to illustrate Mrs. Royall's reputation for being an obnoxious "common scold"—a charge on which she was tried and convicted in later years.

JONAH AND THE WHALE HOAX   *newspaper fake*
One of the grandest newspaper fakes of all was done by Canadian journalist Charles Langdon Clarke of the *Toronto Mail and Empire,* who was given to whiling away the time between assignments by inventing news items supposedly culled from biblical stories in the *Babylon Gazette,* the *Jerusalem Times* and other fictitious publications. Once, while attending a lecture by a leading evangelist at the World's Fundamentalist Conference in Toronto, Clarke concocted a yarn about the discovery of what appeared to be the fossil of the whale that had swallowed Jonah.

The report, which electrified fundamentalists, said that the find was made by two scientists, Dr. Schmierkase and Dr. Butterbrod, who found a whale with a muscle that worked a trapdoor, which gave access to its stomach. The following day evangelists from the lectern ecstatically cited the story as confirmation of the biblical story of Jonah's having been swallowed by a big fish.

If this proved astonishing to Clarke, he was even more nonplussed when a rival newspaper seriously reported the evangelist's speech. The hoax was then exposed by the *Mail and Empire* in a story by Clarke, which translated the scientists' names as Dr. Cheese and Dr. Butter Bread.

KAMMERER, PAUL *biological hoaxer or hoax victim?*

In the early part of the 20th century, Austrian biologist Paul Kammerer (1880–1926) was exalted by many of his scientific peers as the "modern Darwin." He had made experiments that appeared to prove the most important biological thesis/breakthrough of the era: Acquired traits can be inherited. Kammerer experimented with salamanders and other amphibians, and starting in 1904 published technical papers and books claiming that he had caused the offspring of the viviparous alpine salamander to take on certain characteristics of the spotted oviparous lowland salamander and vice versa. In more tests he said he had caused the male midwife toad—which lacked the pigmented thumb pads found on other toads—to inherit like pads.

This thesis of acquired traits was not popular or supported by science and thus produced considerable criticism; but his experiments seemingly proved his claims true. In 1926, faced with growing demands to make his evidence available, he finally agreed, and a committee of investigators journeyed to Kammerer's Vienna laboratory to sift his findings. Later, the British scientific journal *Nature* published the committee's findings, including the conclusion that nuptial pads did not exist on a toad as Kammerer claimed, but rather the supposed pads were merely areas where India ink had been injected into the creature's forelimbs. Later, when the toad was immersed in water, the ink dissolved and the spots vanished. Similarly, India ink colorings had been used on the salamanders.

As outrage swept the scientific community, Kammerer kept insisting he had not used the ink. Shortly before the exposure of the hoax, Kammerer had accepted a professorial post at the University of Moscow. The communists had always approved of Kammerer's conclusions, since his theories were more in line with the Red dogma that humans as well could be changed by modifications in the environment.

Now facing condemnation, the humiliated Kammerer wrote a farewell letter to the Communist Academy in Moscow:

> Who besides myself was interested in perpetuating such falsifications of the test specimen can only dimly be surmised. There is no doubt, however, that thereby almost my whole life work has become dubious. Consequently, although I didn't participate in this fraud, I feel I am not entitled any more to accept your nomination. Moreover, I find it impossible to survive my life work's destruction. I hope to find tomorrow sufficient courage and fortitude to end my wretched life.

The next day, September 23, 1926, Kammerer fired a bullet into his brain.

There are some who agree the hoax was not Dr. Kammerer's doing; but many more point out how long he had evaded revealing his experiments. From the scientific view, aside from the personal tragedy involved, it was important that the hoax was exposed or it might have confounded scientific thought for decades longer.

KANGAROO MONSTER WHO TERRORIZED TENNESSEE

In January 1934 news accounts out of the Tennessee hills reported the depredations of a giant kangaroo, which was killing ducks, geese and dogs. Big-city newspapers unquestioningly picked up the stories and in Tennessee shotgun-armed farmer posses took to the fields to try to stop the monster. The New York City police wired they were ready to supply firepower reinforcements that might be needed. Finally, Horace Minnis, a stringer in South Pittsburg, Tennessee, for the *Chattanooga Times*—apparently concerned with the way the story had escalated—admitted he had concocted the fake reports, and the great kangaroo terror ended.

KEATING, CHARLES H., JR. *savings and loan figure*

Throughout the entire savings and loan scandal, which hit American finance in the late 1980s, Charles H. Keating Jr. (1923–   ) stands as the most blatant participant. Keating's case—estimated to cost U.S. taxpayers eventually some $2.6 billion—played havoc with the reputation of the U.S. Senate in the case of the so-called Keating Five. It stands as the prime instance of unfettered S&L officials living high on the hog and playing fast and loose with the depositors' and investors' money.

The Keating story is best told in the form of a chronology:

February 1984—American Continental Corp., formed by Keating, buys the Lincoln Savings and Loan of California for $51 million.

March 1986—The Federal Home Loan Bank in San Francisco starts an examination of Lincoln's rapid growth and hectic investment activities.

Mid-1986—San Francisco bank examiners urge Washington officials to come down hard on Lincoln for questionable accounting and loan procedures.

November 1986—Five U.S. senators—Alan Cranston of California, John Glenn of Ohio, Donald W. Riegle of Michigan and Dennis DeConcini (all Democrats) and Republican John McCain of Arizona—meet with San Francisco examiners on behalf of Keating, who has made large political contributions to them.

May 1987—Examiners recommend that Lincoln be seized for operating in an unsound manner and dissipating its assets. Nothing happens.

April 13, 1989—American Continental files for bankruptcy protection, making its junk bonds worthless.

April 14, 1989—The government now takes control of Lincoln and puts the bailout at an eventual cost of $2.6 billion, the most expensive in history.

September 1990—A California grand jury charges Keating and three others with securities fraud, saying they had deceived investors into buying junk bonds without telling them the risk. Many Lincoln investors thought they were buying government-insured bonds.

February 1991—After a three-and-a-half month investigation the Senate Ethics Committee renders a "verdict" in the case of the Keating Five. It declares there was "substantial credible evidence" of misconduct by Senator Cranston (leading to a severe rebuke from the Senate in November). Riegle and DeConcini are described as giving the appearance of impropriety, but no further action is taken against them. Glenn and McCain are criticized less severely.

December 4, 1991—After a four-month court case, Keating is convicted of securities fraud. He faces a possible penalty of 10 years in prison and a $250,000 fine. However, the Keating case is expected to remain in the courts for years as the convicted felon faces federal prosecution and a great many civil lawsuits.

The S&L scandal has provoked a tightening of regulations against such institutions, which took their investments far afield. It is also expected to play an important role in the political campaigns of future years.

KEATING, TOM *art forger*

The leading British art forger of the post-World War II period was Tom Keating (1917–1984). From youth Keating was driven toward a career in art, as an artist or at least an art teacher. Meeting with less than resounding success, Keating gravitated into the more shadowy edges of "restoration" work and finally into outright forgery. Over a 20-year period he produced more than 2,000 fakes, specializing largely in the work of Stuart Palmer.

He fell from grace in 1976 when the art specialist for the *London Times* exposed him. Keating made a detailed confession at a press conference, insisting—as have so many art forgers—that his acts were a form of protest against the exploitation of artists by dealers. He also pointed out that he often gave away his forgeries, but it was also obvious he enjoyed the monetary fruits of his less-than-creative labors.

Formally charged in 1977, Keating was never brought to trial because of his failing health. He did, however, give a series of television performances illustrating the techniques of the great painters. Keating and his forgeries enjoyed a growing popularity, and following his death in 1984 a sale of his work brought in £274,000—seven times more than the auctioneers had estimated. Keating had gone full circle—from aspiring artist to forger to acceptable artist. The art public paid no mind to the majority of art experts, who now sniffed that his forgeries really weren't very good.

KEELY, JOHN E. W. *swindler*

One of the hoariest gasoline swindlers is the filling station man who earnestly assures a sucker that he can make his car run on water provided he drops a couple of secret-ingredient capsules into the tank to convert the water into gasoline. He then ends up letting the sucker twist his arm and sells him a supply of the pills. That con will work only on the uninformed. John E. W. Keely (1827–1898) pulled the same water-to-fuel con (sans pills); but unlike the service station pitchman he managed to fool some of the most sophisticated money men in the United States. More amazingly, he kept up his colossal con for a quarter-century.

In 1874 ex-carnival pitchman John Keely, a Philadelphian with an open, earnest expression, convinced four leading financiers—Charles B. Franklin, an official of the Cunard steamship line; John J. Cisco, a leading banker; Henry S. Sergeant, president of the Ingersoll Rock Drill Co.; and Charles B. Collier, an attorney—that he could convert a quart of water into sufficient fuel to run a 30-car train 75 miles in 75 minutes. Over the following 24 years he staged demonstration after demonstration in his workshop that apparently confirmed his claim that he was going to revolutionize the entire field of energy. Keely's four prize suckers helped him to form the Keely Motor Company, and time after time advanced him huge sums of money to further his research. Keely Motor stock was traded on exchanges both in the United States and Europe, enabling Keely to extract funds from a wider pool of people.

One of Keely's favorite victims was a wealthy widow, Clara Jessup Moore, who plowed in a half-million dollars and also wrote an adoring book entitled *Keely and His Discoveries.* With suckers like Mrs. Moore, Keely could actually sniff away John Jacob Astor who was panting to invest $2 million.

Unlike the business world, the scientific community was not taken in by Keely's claims. *Scientific American,* for example, characterized it as ridiculous, but this did nothing to cool the ardor of thousands of investors. And the financiers dismissed the scientific opposition as trivial. After all, what did scientists know about the practical world and the science of making money? It became an article of faith for Keely's followers to believe in him, much as they would a religious messiah.

The basic Keely operation involved what he called "a vibratory generator with a hydro-pneumatic-pulsating vacue machine." As Keely put it:

> With these three agents alone [air, water, and machine] unaided by any and every compound, heat, electricity and galvanic action, I have produced in an unappreciable time by a simple manipulation of the machine, a vaporic substance at one expulsion of a volume of ten gallons having an elastic energy of 10,000 pounds to the square inch. . . . It has a vapor of so fine an order it will penetrate metal. . . . It is lighter than hydrogen and more powerful than steam or any explosives known. . . . I once drove an engine 800 revolutions a minute of forty horse power with less than a thimbleful of water and kept it running fifteen days with the same water.

Occasionally, some key backer would lose heart with Keely as he worked on what he called commercial uses for his great find; but for every sucker that fell to the wayside a dozen more were eager to fill the breech. Keely was able to keep up his grand deception right up to the day of his death in 1898. Then

professors from the University of Pennsylvania dismantled his house and found Keely's mysterious force was plain compressed air. On February 4, 1899 *Scientific American* described the discovery, under the kitchen floor of the house, of "a steel sphere forty inches in diameter, weighing 6,625 pounds." This was "an ideal storage reservoir for air . . . at great pressure."

The compressed air traveled upward to a second-floor workshop, where Keely held his demonstrations, through steel and brass tubes nine inches in diameter with a three-inch bore, strong enough to withstand the great pressure. There was a 16-inch space between the ceiling on the first floor and the floor of the workshop "well calculated to hide the necessary tubes for conveying the compressed air to the different motors with which Keely produced his results." It was a setting in which "for a quarter of a century the prince of humbugs played his part." Concealed in the walls and floor of the workshop were spring valves that could be operated by foot or elbow to "run" a motor whenever Keely wished.

How had Keely come up with this incredible design? Obviously the ex-carnival man had run fun and mystery house contraptions in his youth. The same blast of air that could send a lady's skirt flying could also extract money from the wallets of gullible financiers.

KELLY, SHANGHAI *America's worst crimp*

In the history of crimping (the kidnapping of sailors) in America, no man had a more feared name than Shanghai Kelly (1835–?), a stubby, red-bearded Irishman who became the most prodigious shanghaier on San Francisco's Barbary Coast. During the 1870s Kelly provided no fewer than 10,000 unwilling seamen for sailing vessels. While Shanghai Kelly was thoroughly committed to the use of drink and drugs to collect his stock, he often relied on ingenious ruses.

Once Kelly faced the awesome task of coming up with no less than 90 sailors for three vessels sailing on the same day. Kelly was extremely understocked at the moment, so he announced a "sex excursion" to be held to celebrate his birthday, renting an old paddle-wheel steamer for the occasion on which he installed a few dozen "ladies of the docks" and several bartenders. Customers were promised three days of fun, including all the drinks and feminine attention they could handle. Naturally, Kelly charged a hefty admission for his love-boat excursion, but customers literally had to be fought off.

Kelly kept close count of the passengers and as soon as they hit the 90 mark, he ordered the gangplank up and the steamer paddled away. Barrels of beer and whiskey were opened and Kelly graciously accepted the first drink in his honor. All of the drinks were heavily doped and within a brief time the celebrating customers were out stone cold.

Kelly's paddle-steamer pulled up to the three ships in succession. He turned over the contracted number of bodies, collected his fee and ordered his craft back to shore, having collected twice—once for a sex excursion that never was and once for providing men with a long sea voyage they never wanted.

See also SHANGHAIING SCAMS.

KEY GAME See MURPHY GAME.

KILLER HAWK OF CHICAGO *newspaper hoax*

In January 1927 the city of Chicago was terrorized by a killer hawk, which was first observed preying on pigeons around the Art Institute and the downtown elevated platforms. The first observer of this predator was a reporter for the *Chicago Journal;* in fact, this reporter was the only person who ever claimed to see the vicious hawk. Despite this the flying beast became front-page news in all of the Chicago papers. The killer hawk was a true menace. Were small dogs on a leash safe from attack? For that matter were babes safe in their carriages?

Following the lead of the *Journal,* the *Chicago Tribune* featured front-page political cartoons by John McCutcheon, front-page stories for five consecutive days, an impassioned editorial, hosts of letters to the editor and a question to be asked by the paper's inquiring reporter. The *Tribune* produced a picture of the hawk holding a dead pigeon in its claws while perched atop the Art Institute. It was a fake, something apparent to even superficial examination by professionals. So were other photos appearing in rival newspapers.

Nevertheless, the public hysteria mounted. Walter J. Greenbaum, an investment banker, offered a reward for the hawk's capture or death. The Boy Scouts joined in the hunt to protect the city. The Lincoln Park Gun Club assigned a group of shooters to stalk the feathered public enemy and hopefully not blast away any innocent bystanders.

One week after the first appearance of the killer hawk, the *Journal* announced the start of a new serial entitled, "The Pigeon and the Hawk." Instantly all the other Chicago papers stopped running stories on the killer hawk, realizing they had been hoaxed into giving huge advance publicity to a competitor's promotion.

KING TUT'S GOLDEN TYPEWRITER *archaeological hoax*

One of the most outrageous but successful claims ever made in a newspaper story was that of King Tut's celebrated "golden typewriter." Shortly after the opening of the untouched tomb of the Egyptian Pharaoh Tutankhamen in 1922, Charles Langdon Clarke of the *Toronto Mail and Empire* wrote a serious article about the priceless treasures found there. The most amazing of these, said Clarke, was a remarkable golden typewriter. Clarke waxed enthusiastic about this incredible—and impossible—instrument, never answering the question how one could print hieroglyphics with typewriter keys and how could a typewriter be constructed large enough to hold all the symbols.

Desperate to follow up on this exciting archaeological find, a rival editor assigned a reporter to interview noted Egyptologist Dr. C. T. Currelly, curator of the Royal Ontario Museum. Realizing such an expert would question the claims, Clarke decided it was time to admit his hoax.

KNIFE SHARPENER CON *updated swindle*

It was a common con back in Colonial days: The knife sharpener who traveled door to door and, instead of sharpening them, made a fast getaway with the cutlery when no one was unwatching. The crime continued throughout the 20th century, and in one case a BBB spokesman reported that when the sharpener failed to return, "residents a short distance away report a man of the same description attempting to sell knives and scissors at bargain prices."

Today the knife sharpener con also seeks to clean the teeth of electric can openers and the like. Still another pitch is to offer a free sample cleaning of one piece of silverware "with our magical cleaning compound." The scam artist takes the piece out to his van and actually does a masterful job, so good that many homemakers actually let him take the rest of their precious silverware for the same treatment. "It'll take an hour and a half," he says cheerily and even more merrily disappears at the first opportunity.

The next stop: Probably not a mere block away but perhaps a mile or so, at a flea market where the gypster's loot is passed to a confederate and offered at such attractive prices the loot is snapped up in a matter of minutes.

KNITTING MACHINE RACKET *homework scheme fraud*

Of all the so-called work-at-home frauds, the knitting machine racket is among the most heartless, since it usually gouges more from the victims than other such frauds. One knitting machine firm is known to have sold the machines under 10 different names. Most of the machines are made in Germany and imported for less than $50. They are resold to homeworkers in the United States—often elderly widows or others confined to their home—for upwards of $500, plus finance charges.

Buyers are informed that the hefty cost of the machine is trivial compared to what they will make selling knit garments back to the company. Of course, with the caveat that the company has to find the work acceptable. As a convincer, machine buyers are sometimes given six different garments to make as samples; all are found acceptable and the firm pays $10 each for them (actually out of the first of three monthly payments due on the machine). The spiel goes that as soon as the knitting machine is paid for the homeworker will be deluged with work. A "trickle" would be a more apt description. And, mysteriously, the work done is now found unacceptable.

KORETZ, LEO   *Ponzi for the super-rich*

Leo Louis Koretz (1881–1925), a successful Chicago stockbroker, was a contemporary of Charles Ponzi, the man who gave his name to the art of swindling. After Ponzi was exposed, Leo Koretz operated in precisely the same way; but no one could discern any of the Ponzi in him. With a cherub's face and heartwarming gullibility, Koretz's victims playfully referred to him as "Our Ponzi" because of the enormous profits he was apparently giving them. Even his family got the full Koretz treatment: His elderly mother pushed $50,000 on him; his brother $140,000; and his hard-working secretary $3,000.

But Koretz's main target was the elite of the Chicago business world. The full extent of his fraud was never determined because a number of businessmen were known to have suffered their losses in silence, fearing that knowledge of their having been swindled would ruin their reputations as supposedly shrewd businessmen.

Koretz's original scam was rooted in stock of the Bayano Timber Syndicate of Panama, which had supposedly garnered a fortune in mahogany from its vast land holdings. To really get the suckers panting, Bayano Timber suddenly struck oil, the biggest find ever in Latin America!

Koretz started promoting stock in Bayano in 1917. In no time at all the company was paying stockholders a quarterly dividend of 5% on their investments. The only trouble was there was no Bayano Timber Syndicate. The swamp land it allegedly owned actually belonged to the Panamanian government, which couldn't interest anyone in taking it off its hands, as its only abundant resource was mosquitos.

But stockholders couldn't argue with the huge dividends they were getting and the projected payments of up to 1,000% when oil production got on line. Of course, Koretz was going to have to pay the dividends out of the stockholders' own money, the same pyramid scheme that eventually brought down Ponzi. However, Koretz was far smarter than Ponzi

and, appealing to his suckers' greed, convinced most of them to invest their dividends in additional stock—pieces of paper worth no more than the originals.

Even as Ponzi himself was being exposed, the Koretz stockholders started calling him "Lovable Lou" and "Our Ponzi." They saw him as a financial genius in the mold of John D. Rockefeller. Once 500 of his leading suckers held a fete to honor Koretz at Chicago's plush Congress Hotel. Seated beside him was Arthur Brisbane, William Randolph Hearst's top editorial man and Koretz's number-one chump. At the height of the festivities, newspaper boys invaded the hall with an extra edition announcing, "Leo Koretz' Oil Swindle." For a moment there was shocked silence. Then Brisbane roared with laughter. It was all his joke. He had dummied up phony newspapers for the joyous occasion. Brisbane hugged Koretz, crying, "Mr. Koretz is a great and honorable financier!" Everyone was now close to tears with laughter. The real tears were to follow in less than a year.

In 1922 a large party of joyous stockholders felt it was time to make a personal visit to their money in Panama. Koretz stalled them for many months, but in November 1923 they sailed from New York. Leo Koretz knew it was time to fold his tent. Taking $5 million in loot, Koretz disappeared into Canada where, for the previous three years, he had carefully cultivated a new identity as one Lou Keyte. If not for his physical condition, his masquerade might have succeeded. Unfortunately, Koretz suffered from diabetes and had to take insulin to treat it. That drug at the time was both rare and expensive, and a prescription trail led investigators to him in Halifax. In the ensuing investigation, Koretz was in no position to deny the charges against him. He insisted he had gypped his mother, brother and secretary only because he could think of no way of dissuading them without arousing suspicion.

Koretz drew a 10-year sentence but told one of his lawyers, "I won't survive more than a month in prison." He was right. He got a lady friend to bring him a five-pound box of chocolates. He ate the whole box on January 9, 1925, and keeled over dead, certainly one of the most bizarre prison suicides in history.

Even after they buried Leo Koretz, many of his gullible victims were neither satisfied nor convinced. One of them said, "I know for a fact that he was seen in Toronto just the other week. He must have bribed someone to escape. You know how tricky he was. Maybe he managed to escape and had another body replaced for his own. I still maintain that the real Leo Koretz is still alive."

Many of Koretz's suckers continued to believe that. It did them no good. Koretz never sent back their money.

KREISLER, FRITZ *musical forger*

From about 1901 on, Austrian-American violinist Fritz Kreisler (1875–1962) was perhaps the most popular violinist in the United States. He gained considerable fame early in his career by playing, for the first time, certain "little masterpieces" of the violin, which he found "in libraries and monasteries while visiting Rome, Florence, Venice, and Paris"—the works of masters such as Antonio Vivaldi and lesser known lights such as Pugnani, Francoeur, Porpora, Louis Couperin and Padre Martini. The critics found them most edifying and some called them "worthy of Bach," although occasionally Kreisler's performances were faulted. Said one German critic: "We heard Fritz Kreisler again last night. He played beautifully, but naturally his temperament lacks the strength and maturity to reach the heights of the Pugnani music."

Critics and audiences disagreed. Kreisler was a genius and had found for the world some great musical treasures. In point of fact, Kreisler had not "found" these treasures; he was a musical forger. Everything he had supposedly resurrected from dusty collections was actually of his own composition! He had done so because the concert violinist's repertory for unaccompanied pieces was far too small; as a young performer he could not expect to get a great pianist to accompany him and, being poor, he could hardly afford to hire an orchestra for important concerto works.

If there simply were not enough works for a fledgling to play, Kreisler decided to create those that would show off his talents. But he could hardly list himself as the composer as well, since that would present a case of the work of a beginning composer being played by a beginning violinist. It went unnoticed that many of the musical styles Kreisler attributed to composers were completely at odds with those of the master's era.

Kreisler felt many critics should have known better. He later said:

> Once I wrote a few special pieces for a Viennese recital. I called them "Posthumous Waltzes" by "Joseph Lanner." The following day Leopold Schmidt, the critic of the *Berliner Tageblatt*, accused me of tactlessness. He raved about the Lanner waltzes. They were worthy of Schubert, he said. How dare I bracket my little salon piece, "Caprice Viennois" with such gems?
>
> I wrote to Dr. Schmidt. I said I was pained, but I felt compelled for once, to say that he was "not devoid of tactlessness" himself. I was terribly sorry, but if the Lanner pieces were "worthy of Schubert," then I was Schubert, because I had written them! The letter was reprinted everywhere.

The letter was circulated in Berlin, but still did not create the full stir anyone—including Kreisler—might

By 1915 Fritz Kreisler had become the best-selling recording violinist in America, his fame rooted in playing "newly-discovered musical masterpieces"—which he had forged.

have expected. As Kreisler recalled, "Now don't you suppose critics and musicians who saw the letter would have said to themselves: 'If this is so, then the same thing must be true of the Francoeur, Couperin, Vivaldi pieces.'"

None did, and no one ever asked him directly if he had composed those pieces himself until 1935, when Olin Downes, the music critic for the *New York Times* who was serving as lecturer and commentator for a program at the Brooklyn Academy of Music honoring Kreisler on his 60th birthday, cabled Kreisler in Vienna and asked the question. Not wishing to lie, Kreisler cabled back "I composed them myself," and gave his reasons. The story appeared in the *Times*, and an earthquake hit the musical world. Some accused Kreisler of playing the cheat while others gave him credit for having pulled off a grand musical hoax. In London Ernest Newman mounted a heavy attack in the *Sunday Times;* The *Musical Times* even accused Kreisler of using the names of these composers to increase sales and subsequent royalties.

For his part Kreisler was unruffled, saying he relied on the sportsmanship of the musical public. The great violinist was right and suffered no loss of popularity. Perhaps the best analysis of the affair was offered by the *Philadelphia Record:*

In the first place, no one would have wanted to hear the pieces if they had been ascribed to the then unknown Kreisler. In the second place, no one would have bought them. In the third place, rival players would not have put them on their own programs if they had known who the composer really was. . . . We like to think of a composer as a man high above sordid earthly cares and of a virtuoso as one who has no thought for anything but his music. The glimpse here given of the maneuvering and strategy sometimes demanded by the divine art will comfort realtors, morticians and bond salesmen. Business is, as the saying goes, business.

KREUGER, IVAR *the Swedish Match King*

Almost certainly the biggest thief of all time was Ivar Kreuger, the Swedish Match King. A mechanical engineer from Kalmar, Sweden, Kreuger built the greatest financial empire of the 1920s, theoretically on matches supplying 75% of the world's needs from factories in 34 countries. But more importantly he controlled scores of other important businesses—banks, film companies, newspapers, mines, telephone companies, railways and entire forests.

Kreuger's dream was to produce every single match struck anywhere on earth—at monopolistic prices—and to gain exclusive rights on match production in various countries. He loaned enormous sums of money to more than a dozen countries, including Spain, France, Poland, Greece, Hungary and Yugoslavia. He had holding companies built on holding companies, and no one else in his organization had any overall grasp of his operations. Whenever Kreuger had a need for a few tens of millions, he simply issued a glowing financial report on one of his companies, extolling its holdings in some of his other companies, including nonexistent ones. Investors, including many leading banks, competed to buy Kreuger securities. Many nations begged him for loans, so that he became known as the financial savior of many nations. With these nations' indebtedness to him, he was able to raise ever more bank and investor credits and begin his monumental scam cycle all over again. International banks and political leaders came hat in hand to Kreuger's 125-room offices in Stockholm, which became known as the Match Palace.

Like other great swindlers, Kreuger knew how to use outrageous acts to get people to not only trust him but also to become totally awed. Once a leading banker was sitting before Kreuger's desk when the telephone rang and Kreuger spoke with Benito Mussolini of Italy. The Match King took no nonsense from

Il Duce and warned him he'd better get Italy's finances in proper order. The banker left Kreuger most impressed and told his associates of the incident, inflating the Kreuger legend ever more. After Kreuger's death, it was discovered that he had a hidden button under his desk, which rang his telephone whenever he wished. Kreuger did his Mussolini routine—and those with other political figures who were also not on the line—dozens of times.

Any thought that Kreuger might be even slightly less than forthright was always instantly out of the question. When an English executive suggested that Kreuger have his books audited, the Match King replied, "Do you think I'm a crook?" That was enough to put the matter to rest.

It was not the intelligence of others that brought about the great hoaxer's downfall but, rather, the market collapse of 1929, which dried up Kreuger's cash flow. Now Kreuger forged scores of securities and bonds—even misspelling the names of finance ministers on the agreements—in an effort to get more credit. Unfortunately, his creditors were looking to sell the Match King's obligations. Kreuger was in no position to buy them up himself to cover his tracks.

In his Paris home on March 12, 1932, at the age of 52 the fabulous financier shot himself just below the heart. King Gustaf of Sweden hurried back to Stockholm from his vacation retreat on the French Riviera and ordered the nation's flags lowered to half-staff in mourning. Within weeks the mourning shifted to Kreuger's countless victims. Bankers found their institutions ruined. It took years to straighten out the Match King's bizarre, nonexistent financial empire. It was found that from 1917 to 1932 he had skimmed off well over a half-billion dollars for his personal use. His personal spending money averaged $180,000 a week. He maintained five homes in as many cities and three country estates. The auditing firm of Price Waterhouse wrote 57 reports about "the delicate varies of Kreuger's global manipulations over a decade and a half." About half of the losses to Kreuger's financial fantasies came from the United States.

Not surprisingly, since everything else about Ivar Kreuger was a hoax, the story started that even his suicide was a fake. Rather than having died in Paris, the rumor went, he had successfully fled to the island of Sumatra. French officials denied the wild rumors, but they persisted for years. Even the Match King's tobacconist declared he had received a large order from Sumatra for Kreuger's special custom-made Havana cigars and, he said, only Kreuger himself could have known how to place the order.

L

LADY IN BLACK *Valentino's eternal mourner*
It started two years after the death of Rudolph Valentino (the "Great Lover" of the screen, on August 23, 1926), when the "Lady in Black" came to kneel at the side of the screen idol's burial crypt in Hollywood Cemetery. Attired in mourning, the unknown woman left a tear and a red rose at the spot and departed without a word to anyone.

By what some might consider the sheerest of good fortune, the scene had been captured on film by an enterprising filmmaker, Russell Birdwell (later to become one of Hollywood's legendary publicists), who just happened to be shooting a one-reeler entitled *The Other Side of Hollywood.* The narrator of the film was later able to inform movie audiences that the same "Lady in Black" arrived at dawn each year on August 23 and disappeared into the morning mist just as she had arrived. Actually, Birdwell had hired an unknown girl to pose at the gravesite especially for his film.

No one was more surprised than Birdwell when the Lady in Black reappeared year after year to perpetuate the myth. And it was not the same Lady in Black each time; sometimes there was even more than one. In 1938 the tradition was so firm that newspapers staked out reporters and photographers before dawn in hope of interviewing the mysterious lady. They hit the jackpot that year as three worthy mourners turned up. One was plump and passed by. The second was scrawny and also moved on. Number three proved to be a newspaper's dream; she was blonde, attractive and came by chauffeured automobile. She happily deigned to be interviewed, declaring she had met Valentino when he was a waiter in a New York restaurant. It had been a memorable encounter, since the screen-idol-to-be spilled soup down her neck.

After this, Birdwell confessed all; but some time later Hollywood gossip columnist Hedda Hopper decided to chime in with her own exclusive version of the origin of the hoax. It had been concocted, she said, by a recently retired florist whose thriving business was in close proximity to the cemetery. He had started the annual practice to encourage others to follow suit and buy flowers for Valentino's grave. The Lady in Black still shows up from time to time, somehow withstanding the passage of the years.

LADY WONDER *mind-reading horse*
Lady Wonder was a brilliant horse, over the years a great tourist attraction and civic treasure in Richmond, Virginia. She was a smart old mare who could answer almost every question, operating a specially constructed horse-typewriter and spelling out words or giving out numbered answers by lowering her nose on keys spread out on hinges. When Lady Wonder was a three-year-old filly, she got the seal of approval from Dr. J. B. Rhine of Duke University, the renowned expert on extrasensory perception (ESP), who tested her and concluded in the authoritative *Journal of Abnormal and Social Psychology:* "Lady Wonder seemed responsive to telepathy and possesses a degree of psychic power." Dr. Rhine never changed his mind on that, but later said that after the age of four Lady Wonder lost her telepathic powers and that her owner, Mrs. Claudia Fonda, had taken to signaling her.

Other scientists and experts felt that Dr. Rhine had been conned from the beginning, having simply ignored in his testing the likelihood that Mrs. Fonda was using standard signaling methods common in all "talking horse" and "talking dog" acts. What impressed Dr. Rhine was the fact that whenever Mrs. Fonda herself did not know the correct answer, Lady

When Hollywood's Great Lover, Rudolph Valentino, died in 1926, thousands of women in black grieved over his emaciated corpse. The tradition continued at his graveside for years thereafter through a press agent's hoax.

Wonder still came up with it. To Rhine the only possible answer was telepathy between the questioner and the horse. Rhine would follow Fonda's standard procedure of writing down on a pad the answer, in words or number, without the horse's owner seeing it. What Dr. Rhine overlooked was the fact that, as Martin Gardner noted in *Fads and Fallacies in the Name of Science*, "There are some fifty different ways a clever medium or mentalist can secretly obtain information that has been written down."

Mrs. Fonda's routine remained the same for 30 years. Visitors paid their fee and were handed a long pencil and pad and told to write down their answers to three questions. Whether or not Mrs. Fonda saw the answers had no effect. Lady Wonder answered them, just as the young filly had answered Dr. Rhine in 1927.

It turned out Mrs. Fonda was using a very ordinary method long employed by magicians. This was demonstrated in 1956 when professional magician

Milbourne Christopher visited Lady Wonder without informing Mrs. Fonda of his profession. Christopher wrote the number 3 on the pad but moved the pencil in such a way as to indicate he had written the number 8. Lady Wonder answered 8, a clear indication that Mrs. Fonda was "pencil reading"—a simple enough art in the magic field.

Nevertheless, Lady Wonder maintained her true believers among the public and much of the media, all of whom refused to believe she was any sort of a "phony pony." Leslie Lieber, a magazine writer who had spotted Fonda's signaling technique as "a little whip with a piece of string dangling down over the horse's head," still offered a charitable view of Lady Wonder. "She was the world's first—and probably last—horse stenographer. She took dictation from Fonda."

Lady Wonder was laid down with a fatal attack on March 19, 1957, while spelling out E-I-S-E-N-H-O-W-E-R on her typewriter. Lady Wonder is buried in the exclusive Pet Memorial Cemetery in Henrico County, Virginia.

LANCASHIRE WITCHES   *deadly blackmail scheme*

During the first 80 years of the 17th century, the number of persons executed for witchcraft in England averaged 500 a year and about 40,000 in all. Few persecutions could match the horror of the case of the "Lancashire witches," a phrase that in later years was used to compliment the county ladies' bewitching beauty. The origin of the term was far more menacing and centered around a vicious boy named Robinson.

In about 1634 the Robinson boy, the son of a woodcutter residing at the border of Pendle Forest in Lancashire, began talking about witches in the area, especially one elderly woman, Mother Dickenson. The boy's talk came to the attention of the local magistracy, and the boy was brought in for interrogation. At the time, the witch mania in England was at its height, and was probably more on the minds of the common folk than the impending conflict between royalist and republican forces.

Young Robinson told a straightforward story in an open and apparently honest manner, and the magistrates and the public had little doubt that he spoke the truth. The boy told of being in the woods one day and attempting to play with two greyhounds. One of them transformed into a little boy and the other into a woman—Mother Dickenson. The old woman, he swore, offered him money to sell his soul to the devil but young Robinson refused. The old woman then waved a bridle over the other little boy's head and transformed him into a horse. She mounted the horse, seized young Robinson and rode off with him through forest, field, bog and river until reaching a barn. She took him inside where there were seven more witches present. They engaged in obscene rituals, including eating the flesh of dead men taken from the old church of Berwick. By the time the supper was ready several other witches showed up to join in the feast.

When the boy finished his testimony, authorities took him from church to church so that he could identify the hags who had been at the barn. Robinson pointed out some 20 in all, and they were thrown into prison. Of these, eight, including Mother Dickenson, were tried, convicted and burned at the stake.

Some years later, Robinson admitted to perjury, that he had been suborned by his father and other relatives and persons to make the false charges. The elder Robinson had extracted huge sums from a number of people whom he threatened to have his son expose. Still, as Charles Mackay points out in *Extraordinary Popular Delusions and the Madness of Crowds,* "Among the wretches who concocted this notable story, not one was ever brought to justice for his perjury."

LAND FRAUDS   *great treasury raid*

Many observers regard the Western land frauds of the late 19th and early 20th centuries to have been the greatest raid on the public purse in American history. About 40 million acres of treasured public lands were set up as forest reserves, and the General Land Office was charged with protecting these grand treasures. Instead, almost immediately land office agents began peddling rich acreages to private speculators who in turn resold the properties to lumber companies for a huge profit.

By the time Theodore Roosevelt came to office, the land looters had gained so much influence over key congressional figures that they succeeded in legally stripping the Department of Justice of the investigative power to uncover these frauds. Finally, Interior Secretary Ethan A. Hitchcock launched his own department's investigation into the manipulations of many individuals in the General Land Office, including that agency's own detectives. Heading up the investigation team was William J. Burns, at the time the star agent of the Secret Service. In 34 cases that went to trial, 33 ended in convictions, among them cases against Senator John H. Mitchell and Representative John N. Williamson, both of Oregon. Senator Mitchell's case was under appeal to a higher court when he died in 1905. In a rare instance of senatorial behavior, that body refused to follow custom and adjourn its session or send a delegation to Mitchell's funeral.

In time some of the prosecution was found to have been politically tainted and corrupt. Burns was attacked on a number of grounds, including the fact that witnesses had been intimidated into providing perjured testimony. In 1911 Attorney General George W. Wickersham reported to President William Howard Taft that Burns had stage-managed the selection of jurors. Although similar charges were later made against Burns in other cases (especially those involving labor and unions), there is general acceptance among historians that most of those charged in the land frauds were guilty.

LASSETER'S GOLD   *treasure hoax*

One hoax that truly stretched credulity was perpetrated in Sydney, Australia, in 1931 by a treasure hunter named Harry Lasseter who fired up a number of promoters with a tale of having discovered, as a lone prospector, a solid gold reef in the barren back country some 30 years earlier. Lasseter said that the elements had defeated him as he tried to get back to civilization with some of the ore packed on two mules. He had lost the pack animals and barely survived himself.

From Lasseter's description, the promoters estimated the gold was worth at least $5 billion. None of them had the slightest suspicion that Lasseter suffered from one of three possible ailments common to down-and-out prospectors: He was lying to get a job or stake; he was dreaming; or he was unbalanced.

The promoters agreed to outfit a major expedition with Lasseter in charge to find the great gold reef. After many months of wandering through the back country, the promoters decided that Lasseter was fantasizing (which Lasseter partially admitted) and ordered the expedition back home. Lasseter insisted on going on prospecting alone. His body was found later; he had died of thirst.

Because Lasseter's story was such a patent hoax, the Australian government gave it considerable publicity to discourage others from going off in search of "Lasseter's Gold." Despite this, 10 additional expeditions were launched by gullible promoters. In every case the expeditions met with grief, became lost or faced varied disasters. Overall, it cost the Australian government more than $2 million to find and rescue the survivors.

THE LAST GIRAFFE *circus con*

One of the big attractions of the old-time American circus was the display of "exotic" or "rare" animals—although sometimes they were not very rare at all. It is easy to find old circus posters offering the preposterous to a gullible public. An example is an 1895 Ringling Bros. poster that offered:

> THE LAST GIRAFFE
> Secured at the cost of a Fortune as a SPECIAL FEATURE . . . The one and only GIRAFFE known to exist in the entire world/To be seen at each exhibition of Ringling Bros.' Tremendous Triple Managerie. The sole and lonely survivor of a once numerous family/The last of his kind/Brought direct from Samona Land, Africa. He cost a fortune, but now is beyond all price for there is no other in the whole world. WHEN HE IS GONE, THE GIRAFFE WILL BE EXTINCT. Human eyes will never behold another. This is your last chance to see THE LAST SPECIMEN. See him now! You may never have another opportunity.

Many did believe it was their last opportunity. They didn't realize that they could visit any of a score of American cities that had giraffes in their zoos. How could Ringling Bros. get away with such a whopper? According to Robert Parkingson, research center director of the Circus World Museum in Baraboo, Wisconsin, Ringling Bros. simply did not use the poster in cities sporting giraffe-stocked zoos.

And what if a wary ticket buyer in some Kansas hamlet announced he'd seen a giraffe in the Chicago zoo not too long ago? "Died a spell back," the ticket seller said. "Sad, sad, sad."

LAUDER, WILLIAM *literary forger*

One of the most shameful literary hoaxers in English history, Scottish Latin scholar William Lauder (d. 1771) bore such a hatred for John Milton that he concocted an incredible deception that enmeshed and conned even the venerable Dr. Samuel Johnson, no Milton enthusiast himself. Lauder, an exponent of the poet Arthur Johnston, became enraged by Alexander Pope's criticism of Johnston's works as compared to those of Milton. At the time, Lauder was seeking to get the schools to adopt his edition of Johnston's works.

Determined to destroy Milton, Lauder published *An Essay on Milton's Use of an Imitation of the Moderns in His Paradise Lost* in 1750. Lauder cited a number of works by Latin poets and literary authorities to demonstrate Milton was a plagiarist. He also interpolated eight lines in a Latin translation of *Paradise Lost* by Hogg so that they were the same as lines written by a Dutch divine.

Dr. Johnson was taken by Lauder's thesis, relishing the idea of the demise of Milton's reputation. Johnson clearly encouraged Lauder, and it is assumed that he wrote the preface to Lauder's anti-Milton diatribe. The only problem with Lauder's literary bombshell was that it was itself entirely bogus. His Latin poets, his literary authorities and his Dutch divine were all fictitious. No one seriously believed that Dr. Johnson was anything but gullible in his faith in Lauder, fired by his own latent hostility to Milton. When Dr. John Douglas disproved Lauder's claims, the angry Dr. Johnson is alleged to have written the confession that Lauder then signed. This was not Lauder's last confession. Still on an anti-Milton binge, he tried to absolve Charles I of plagiarism when the Puritan Milton demonstrated the king had lifted lines from Sir Philip Sidney's *Arcadia* to use as his own in *Eikon Basilke*. Lauder was also not above lifting from poets of the past. In one instance he credited Virgil to Ramsay, a Scotch poet, merely "to improve Ramsay."

Bloodied in the literary wars Lauder finally departed England for Barbados, from where he issued a number of summations and evaluations of his own career, with often one claim contradicting another. He opened a grammar school which failed, and later bought an African slavewoman who helped him in a huckster's shop he operated. Lauder died in severe pecuniary distress in 1771.

LAUNDERED HANDKERCHIEF SCAM   *false arrest swindle*

In an effort to halt the depredations of shoplifters in the 1980s, many department stores tightened their security methods by apprehending shoplifters even before they left the premises. In some states many laws were made specifically for this purpose. Unfortunately, this still leaves the stores vulnerable to what has come to be called the "laundered linen handkerchief scam" by bogus shoplifters.

The origin of the name goes back to a shrewd little lady who bought a fancy linen handkerchief in an expensive Fifth Avenue store in New York and then returned a couple of weeks later. By acting properly suspicious she got herself taken into custody for stealing a handkerchief.

No, no, no, she told the police who were summoned, she had bought the handkerchief two weeks ago. No, as she told the store security man, she didn't have the receipt any more. It never occurred to her to keep it, she said. The store management people smirked.

The little lady was just about to be taken for booking when she remembered something. Why, she had had the lovely linen handkerchief laundered, naturally by an expensive laundry that left no visible numbers. But under an ultraviolet ray there were the code figures just as big as life. The little old lady proved she had been falsely accused, and the store saw the wisdom of apologizing, along with a settlement amounting to a few thousand dollars.

Naturally, this false arrest scam is not restricted to linen handkerchiefs and is worked in endless varieties by scam artists.

LAWYER . . . THIEF   *scams against clients*

Not long ago a crooked Otsego County, New York, lawyer tacked a non-existent heiress onto a client's will. He then sought to build up a paper trail for her by dressing in drag and checking into a Little Falls motel under her name. At a later probate hearing the judge got wise when a clerk from the motel described the previously unknown woman as being 6 feet tall, weighing 200 pounds and being "a Bea Arthur look-alike."

The lawyer was only one of a long list of New York lawyers who have ripped off their clients in recent years. There was Robert B. Anderson, a former U.S. secretary of the Treasury, who stole a widow's retirement money. There was also Jack B. Siolerwiz, whose 86 victims cost the state's Lawyers Fund for Client Protection the sum of $3 million.

Almost every state has some sort of fund established to protect clients of lawyers who have been convicted of robbing their funds. In the early 1990s

it is clear that lawyer scams against clients have skyrocketed. The North Dakota fund, faced with a boom in claims, went bankrupt. In 1990, payouts by the Florida Client Security Fund quadrupled over the rate in previous years, and the fund had to reduce the size of all repayments so that all claimants would get at least some money. New York, which had a $100,000 cap, had to cut it to $50,000.

The causes of the rise in lawyer scams are at least three-fold: (1) hard economic times; (2) drug and alcohol abuse; and (3) perhaps most important, the ease with which cheating attorneys can get away with it.

A New York lawyer, Sergio Taub, was unmasked in 1991 only after he had been murdered in an unrelated love triangle plot. When authorities sifted through his estate, they found about $200,000 missing from his clients' trust accounts, with most of those funds going for down payments of about $3,000 each on a number of homes in Queens.

When North Dakota's fund went belly up, there were six unpaid claims, all against lawyers who were satisfying their cocaine cravings.

A New York lawyer, Steven Winston, declared: "I can tell you as an addict, all that matters is your drugs. You don't think about your wife or kids, so the last thing you think about is your career or clients." The New York fund paid a Winston client $12,500, which Winston later repaid. He then became general counsel for Daytop Village Inc., where he had undergone drug treatment himself.

Actually, very few lawyers steal, or at least are caught at it. Of 45,000 lawyers in New Jersey, only one half of 1% of attorneys are ever involved—or at least caught. And of all 126 claims of theft in 1991, 36 lawyers were responsible.

Still, the fact remains few persons can break the law quite like a lawyer. There is the New York career of Jerome Louis Spiegelman, who secretly settled dozens of personal injury cases and simply pocketed the money, leaving the clients out in the cold. Because of this case, the law since 1988 has required insurance companies to notify clients whenever they send a settlement check to their lawyers. The trustees of clients security funds are pushing for more changes, such as regulations that would require banks to report when checks bounced against attorney trust or escrow accounts. Without that, a fast-moving crook can shift funds from another trust account and continue to cover his tracks.

LEAD-HEADED FOWL   *poultry weighing scam*

The lead-headed fowl scam is said to go back centuries and is used in every continent. It turns up constantly in localities with weights and measure price-supervision systems.

Bird carcasses in poultry stores doing business the old-fashioned way—frequently the case in various ethnic stores—are hung by their feet with a sackcloth covering the head to absorb blood drainage.

The con in this caper, extra weights (frequently more than eight ounces) are concealed by the sackcloth. After weighing the bird, the butcher chops off the head and charges his inflated price without leaving any evidence. A smart weights and measures inspector will enter such a poultry establishment and pick each bird off its hook, hold it by the feet and let it dangle. The bird's head, if lead-weighted, will drop like an anchor. Nonsqueamish consumers can do it on their own.

LEIBL-BLUM PAINTINGS *substitution scam*
It cannot be presumed that outright forgery of a leading painter's work is the only tack used by crooked dealers and their ilk. A case in point is the work of Hans Blum (1858–1942). In 1880 Blum, never to achieve anything near top ranking among painters, executed a portrait of a Bavarian military man. In 1924 the painting was auctioned off in Munich for less than 1,000 German marks. Five years later the same picture, described as that of a Bavarian officer and then on loan from a prestigious collection, appeared in a place of honor at the Leibl Exhibition in Berlin. Hans Blum's signature had been erased at sometime between 1924 and 1929 and that of Wilhelm Leibl (1844–1900) substituted. In the course of later legal action it was determined the transformation had occurred in the hands of art dealers in Rome and that the portrait had been subsequently bought as a genuine Leibl by a German diplomat for 110,000 marks.

The deception might have gone unnoticed (since the Blum work resembled the technique of Leibl) except for the fact, almost certainly not known to the forgers, that Hans Blum was still alive, although considerably advanced in years. Blum religiously read the newspaper art pages and was astonished to see that an alleged portrait of a Bavarian officer was part of the exhibition. Blum immediately recognized that his work was not Leibl's and that the "Bavarian officer" was actually a military assistant at the gun foundry at Ingoldstadt named Stadelmann.

Summing up the outrageous scam, art historian Fritz Mendax noted in *Art Fakes & Forgeries*, "He had, however, not received one hundred and ten thousand marks for it, since he was merely Hans Blum and not Wilhelm Leibl, whose technique, at his happiest moments, Blum's work so closely resembled."

It cannot be said that Blum's works ever commanded the value of a Leibl; this is perhaps a perverse acknowledgment that the signature forgers had done the right and proper thing—at least from their perspective.

LENIN-FOR-SALE *media fake*
One of the most preposterous hoaxes ever to fool much of the American media occurred in November 1991 during the momentous breakup of the Soviet Union. *Forbes* magazine faxed a press release to news organizations with a sensational report from its quarterly supplement *F.Y.I.*, declaring that the embalmed remains of the first Soviet leader, Vladimir Lenin, were to be removed from the mausoleum in Moscow's Red Square and auctioned off to the highest bidder.

Presumably, some very wealthy individual might put up enough money to buy the dead dictator's body—which was lying in "a sealed, climate-controlled glass casket—and put it in his living room. Talk about impressing one's friends!

Did this all sound improbable? Not to a number of leading media institutions that fell for it, including *USA Today*, the Associated Press, Public Broadcasting's "Nightly Business Report," several radio stations and ABC's "World News Tonight." Anchorman Peter Jennings reported the *Forbes* exclusive on the news show, adding that the Russians expected the price tag to be very steep. "They won't consider anything less than $15 million," Jennings said in full innocence.

According to *Forbes*, the deadline for bids was December 13; it also listed the Moscow address of Interior Minister Gennady Barannikov as the clearing house for all offers. The following day Barannikov issued a terse denial, carried by the official TASS news agency, labeling the *Forbes-USA Today*-ABC story "sheer nonsense . . . a brazen lie" and threatening to sue.

The following evening's telecast carried Jennings' apology for the hoax, saying, "We said it was an extraordinary story. More to the point, it wasn't true. We were gullible, and we assure you that the next report . . . is no joke." Jennings added that ABC believed *Forbes*, which was regarded "until now, as a responsible news organization."

Behind the hoax was Christopher Buckley, editor of *F.Y.I.*, described as "the playful son of William F." Buckley then acknowledged the story was a fake, saying, "So many extraordinary things have happened in the Soviet Union that we thought it would be fun to test the limits of credulity." He explained, "We kind of thought of it as a 'modest proposal,' in the Swiftian sense." (Eighteenth-century Irish satirist Jonathan Swift had once suggested that the British eat babies to reduce the population and avert food shortages.)

One of history's "baddest raps" was the charge that Marie Antoinette said, "Let them eat cake," in reference to the poor of France who had no bread.

Clearly the *F.Y.I.* story wanted to test how trusting news people could be. The answer was very trusting indeed.

LET THEM EAT CAKE *false Marie Antoinette quotation*

It is the most famous quotation attributed to the rather trivial and mindless queen of France, Marie Antoinette, and has been cited as the "mindset" that produced the French Revolution. Told that the people of France were suffering from a lack of bread, Marie Antoinette replied, "Let them eat brioche." The term "brioche" was later refined to "cake."

Actually, the "let them eat cake" incident pre-dates Marie Antoinette. Jean-Jacques Rousseau notes the incident in his *Confessions* and attributes it to an unnamed *"grande princesse."* It is difficult to date the composition of the *Confessions*, but this particular part of it is commonly believed to have been written in 1766. At the time Marie Antoinette was a mere child of 11, and four years away from even coming to France. And reading Rousseau in context it is clear that he had heard of the saying in about 1740, 15 years before Marie Antoinette was even born.

Writing in 1843, Alphonse Kerr reveals that a 1760 book credits the remark to a "Duchess of Tuscany."

Kerr concluded that the saying was "put in circulation" not *by* Marie Antoinette but *about* her. He attributed it to unknown enemies, of which the queen had many, among revolutionaries, republicans and even the aristocracy. Commenting on the attribution to Marie Antoinette, an unknown commentator allowed "if she did not say it, it would be entirely in keeping that she should have."

LEVINE, DENNIS *Wall Street inside trader*

It was the "singing" of Dennis Levine (1953–) that broke open the 1986 Ivan Boesky scandal involving insider trading, which symbolized to many the boundless avarice existing on Wall Street. The Securities and Exchange Commission discovered that Boesky, a millionaire hard-ball stock trader and arbitrager, had agreed to pay Levine a total of $2.4 million for his illegal tips. But Levine was also an illegal stock trader in his own right.

Over a period of five years Levine traded in at least 54 stocks and stashed away $12.6 million in profits through illegal trading on inside information. At the time he was unmasked, Levine was a hotshot managing director of the investment banking firm of Drexel Burnham Lambert. He conducted his own trading through a secret bank account in the Bahamas.

Using his Wall Street position, Levine profited from information about various companies' dealings before that information reached the public. The extent of Levine's ease in making illegal profits was typified by his 1985 activities in Nabisco stock. With inside information he had obtained, Levine made two phone calls on the stock and walked away with almost $3 million in illicit profits. Later Levine would tell the CBS news show "60 Minutes": "It was this incredible feeling of invulnerability. . . . That was the insanity of it all. It wasn't that hard. . . . You get bolder and bolder and bolder, and it gets easier, and you make more money and more money, and it feeds upon itself. And looking back, looking back I realize that I was sick, that it became an addiction, that I lived for the high of making those trades, of doing the next deal, making the bigger deal."

After he was caught, Levine pleaded guilty to securities fraud, perjury and tax evasion, and cut a deal for himself by exposing Boesky and his own circle of financial wheeler-dealers. Levine gave up $11.6 million in illegal profits and did 15 months in the federal penitentiary in Lewisburg, Pennsylvania. He was released in 1988 and thereafter claimed to have turned his life around, lecturing college students around the country about what he'd learned from his past mistakes and operating his own financial consulting firm.

Some have questioned how much Levine has changed. Since that time Levine was involved in a number of dubious "up-front" deals, bringing together struggling business people needing financing and supposed financial institutions willing to make money available in exchange for an up-front commission. For his part Levine also received thousands of dollars in fees. The only trouble was, no monies were ever advanced and some Levine clients said they were out almost $200,000. One Levine client said he had been told by Levine that a person named Jim Massaro could help out on the deal. The client said Levine described Massaro as a friend he'd done business with during his days at Drexel. Levine actually met him at Lewisburg where they had been jailmates.

Levine insisted he had exercised the required "due diligence" in all cases and that it was not accurate for him to be described as the consummate con man. He insisted, "I have never conned anybody in my life. . . . People are entitled to their own opinions, but it's not true. I have to live with myself. I don't think I've done anything wrong." See also entries for Boesky, Ivan; Up-front Fee Scams.

LEVY, JAY *parapsychology research hoaxer*

There are many true believers in parapsychology, extrasensory perception (ESP) and psychokinesis (PK). But there is probably no firmer believer than Dr. Jay Levy (1947–). When his test results didn't conform with his theories, he altered the facts to suit his goals.

In the early 1970s Levy had a bright future in parapsychology, having been appointed at the age of 26 as director of Dr. J. B. Rhine's famed Institute for Parapsychology in Durham, North Carolina. Indeed, Levy was regarded as heir apparent to the aging Rhine.

Levy blazed new trails in his research, attributing ESP powers not only to such standard subjects as rats, but to *unborn* chicks as well. His 1974 scholarly article "Possible PK by Chicken Embryo" in *The Journal of Parapsychology* burst upon the field like a bombshell. Levy announced he had put fertilized eggs in an incubator, which was turned on and off at regular intervals by a randomizing device. His astounding data indicated that while the laws of probability required that the heat in the incubator was to be on precisely half the time, the computerized records revealed that the heat was on 52% of the time. This meant, Levy concluded, that the chicken embryos were "mentally" ordering the incubator to remain on and warm them! To further test this thesis, Levy said he switched to hard-boiled eggs and the results were exactly 50–50, proving that the cooked eggs had no force of will as did the embryos.

Then Levy switched to rats and first taught the rats to self-stimulate their brain's pleasure center by bar pressing. A computer was used to stimulate the pleasure zones at random intervals. Again this stimulation should have worked out to exactly 50% of the time. However, the rats got the stimulation time up to 54%, which again appeared to indicate psychokinetic ability. In other tests with gerbils and hamsters, Levy came up with data demonstrating that these little creatures used PK to avoid unpleasant shocks.

Levy seemed to really be on to something in his continuing experiments, but alas, there was fowl play afoot. A number of assistants noticed Levy tinkering with the apparatus from time to time and began to suspect he was fudging his tests. They set up a duplicate set of instruments and planted a hidden observer. Levy was caught red-handed interfering with the automatic equipment so that it registered "hits"—data that confirmed PK effects. The hidden equipment came in with precise 50–50 scores. It turned out that the gerbils, hamsters, rats and chicks-to-be were just hard-boiled eggs as well.

Confronted with these discoveries by Dr. Rhine, Levy admitted to having falsified the data. He was egged on, it seemed, by a desire to keep interest in this line of research. He resigned and vanished from the ESP scene.

LIEN SHARKS *traps for home owners*

Many homeowners fail to comprehend how liable they may be when they hire a contractor to do additional work on their houses. If the main contractor fails to pay his subcontractors for their work, they can file a lien against the homeowner. Therefore, a homeowner should make some written agreement with the main contractor declaring the latter responsible for all liens filed for the work done. Additionally, a homeowner should not pay the contractor until he receives copies of receipted bills from the subcontractors.

When this isn't done, the homeowner becomes the victim if the subcontractors file such liens and he is suddenly forced to deal with a "lien shark." This character buys up the liens from the subcontractors eager to get some money. The lien shark files a document that describes the lien with the proper authorities, which gives him "the color of ownership." To clear title to the property, particularly urgent if the work was done to enhance the house's selling price, the homeowner has to buy a quit-claim deed from the shark—at a price much higher than the shark paid for the liens.

LI HUNG CHANG MEMOIRS *literary hoax*

To this day it is not too difficult to obtain a copy of *Memoirs of Li Hung Chang*—the great Chinese statesman—in a great many college and public libraries, even though it is a completely bogus work. Few literary hoaxes were ever as successful in hoodwinking experts as this work, which actually was composed by William F. Mannix.

An incorrigible American journalistic hoaxer, Mannix served time in a Honolulu prison in 1912 for forging a check of his employer, the *Honolulu Advertiser*. The territory's Governor Frear, a friend of Mannix, sent him a typewriter so that he could keep busy. At his request, friends brought him a number of historical works on China. Mannix used these to paraphrase his bogus Li memoirs, chapters of which were printed before book publication in the *London Observer* and the *New York Sun*.

The publisher of the fake work, Houghton Mifflin, did not check too thoroughly into Mannix's background, which included many journalistic hoaxes. Instead the publisher relied on the enthusiastic approval of the manuscript by a number of China experts, including John W. Foster, secretary of state under Benjamin Harrison, who had taken part with Li Hung Chang in an 1897 peace conference. However, after publication a number of American and Chinese historians began turning up obvious discrepancies in the so-called memoirs. This fact was widely publicized, and in 1923 Houghton Mifflin brought out a new edition with an introduction by Ralph D. Paine that outlined the hoax in full detail. Despite this,. the 1913 edition continued to be the better seller. As late as 1948 a leading encyclopedia still listed the volume as one of two recommended to readers seeking further facts on the life of Li Hung Chang.

LITTLE BLUE BOOKS See HALDEMAN-JULIUS, EMANUEL.

LITTLE JOKER *19th-century safecracking scam*
The "Little Joker" was the most ingenious method of safecracking in the latter half of the 19th century. This is so not only because it opened bank safes with incredible ease, but also because it sent authorities on wild goose chases looking for bank employees engaged in an inside job.

The device was utilized by the two greatest bank thieves of the era—George Leslie and George Bliss— who carried out or masterminded about 80% of all bank burglaries in the United States from the 1860s to the 1880s. Both claimed to have invented the Little Joker and there is no way to disprove this, since both kept the device secret for years, even from their own confederates.

Operating alone, Leslie would break into a bank, force the knob of the safe off and insert the Little Joker, a steel-wire contraption that could be fitted inside the combination knob. The safe would be used by bank employees for a few weeks, and the wires would put grooves under the dial every time the combination was worked. Then Leslie would break in once again for the real job and remove the device. The grooves would reveal all the numbers of the combination and, by trial and error, Leslie would get them in the correct sequence. The safe would be opened and thoroughly cleaned out by Leslie's mob, and the safecracking expert would relock the safe.

The next morning startled bank officials would find an empty safe. The police, seeing no signs of forced entry, focused more on possible dishonest bank employees rather than the robbery being the work of outside criminals. To make sure matters stayed that way, the boys frequently sent anonymous tips to the police reporting this employee was a heavy gambler, another was keeping a mistress and yet another had serious financial problems—all likely motives for a bank thief.

It was well over a decade before authorities and safe makers figured out how the safes were being opened. Experts thus designed new knobs that could not be used in the scam. Leslie and Bliss subsequently engaged in a bitter feud as to which of them had invented the Little Joker.

LOAN CHURNING *deceptive loan practice*
Frequently offered by credit card and loan finance companies is a "skip-a-month" payment, which appears very attractive to a cash-short borrower. Often this practice—in some forms called "loan churning"—can be a very bad idea for a borrower but a great deal for the lender, especially if the debt has run only for a short time.

Essentially, the deception involves a rewriting of the loan. It should be remembered that interest payments in the early part of the loan are far greater than in the later life of the loan, when more of the amount loaned is being deducted. Let us say only three payments have been made. The financial firm agrees to churn the loan, simply pushing back the termination date three months. This lets the finance company restack the amount of interest it will make at the beginning of the new agreement and in effect make more interest.

While this is bad enough, it can be argued that it is an agreement the borrower desires. In truth, however, he can't quite figure out that it will cost him more. Unfortunately, the same borrower may again find himself in the same mind and have his loan churned one or more times, again inflating his interest costs.

Often there is another kicker he fails to recognize. Many loans have an extra charge for life insurance tacked on. Sometimes lenders are forbidden from requiring this additional option, but it is frequently forced on borrowers. Many of these insurance "riders" also call for a 60-day waiting period before becoming effective. This may not always be the case, but the borrower should watch out for such a clause if he is getting a loan churned. Let's say he renews his original loan after two months. He has paid for insurance during that period without having any real coverage. Then his loan is renewed as is his insurance coverage—*but with a new 60-day waiting period.* Some borrowers have their loans churned so often they are gouged for months and months of insurance payments during which they have no coverage. Thus, in addition to being hit for more interest charges, they are also in large measure paying a lot for nothing as well.

LOAN FACILITATORS *credit scam artists*

They advertise in newspapers and magazines and assure prospective victims with credit problems that they can find financial institutions that will lend them money at reasonable rates. These "loan facilitators" explain that they screen applicants for banks and other lenders and they obtain loans on their assurances.

"Don't worry," they tell a typical victim who has been turned down all over town for a mortgage or loan, "your recent record is good and we'll find an institution that will deal with you." The victim-to-be fills out a simple application and is then informed the loan will be processed once he pays the "standard facilitation fee"—usually about $250. Once that money is handed over, the victim is told it will take three or four weeks to process his loan.

Frequently that is the last heard from the facilitator, who has always been the one to communicate with the victim, by letter or by telephone, rather than the other way around. When the victim has gotten or heard nothing of his $250 after three or four weeks, he sometimes gets a letter of apology for the delay and is informed it will take a few more weeks for the matter to be arranged. That is certainly the last message.

When the victim writes the facilitator, he gets no response. Phone calls do not work, since the phones listed on the gyp's letterhead are always off the hook, or recorded messages get no response. If a victim travels to the address listed as the firm's offices, he usually finds no more than a mail drop, with the mail in turn forwarded to another mail drop, then another and another.

A new wrinkle used by these facilitator con men is to zero in on the credit-worthy victim as well. Their ads state, "Shop around and get the best rate you can—AND WE'LL BEAT IT!" One Georgia man, an insurance agent, could do no better locally than 11% for a large personal loan and was very pleased when informed the facilitator firm could get him a loan at 8%. That promise cost the victim $249—but no interest charges at all, since no loan ever materialized.

LOCH NESS MONSTER *less-than-meets-the-eye sightings*

In April 1933 a motorist driving on a newly opened road along the shores of Loch Ness, Scotland, saw a strange object at some distance away in the water. The motorist later described the object as being some 30 feet long with a snake-like head at the end of a long neck, with two humps on its back and two "flippers" at mid-body. This was followed by a rash of other observers who swore they too had seen the "monster." It was the beginning of the modern sightings of the Loch Ness Monster.

The British press jumped on the story, and the *Daily Mail* sent an expedition to locate the monster. The newspaper's monster hunters claimed to have turned up some odd footprints along the shores of the loch, but no real evidence of the existence of any sort of prehistoric monster. Nevertheless, the *Daily Mail* and other British newspapers declared the monster to be genuine. The British Museum, on the other hand, labeled plaster casts of the supposed monster's spoor to have been made by a dried hippopotamus foot, quite possibly from a Victorian umbrella stand common in the front hall of some better homes.

Still, the "sightings" of "Nessie"—as the press labeled the monster—have continued regularly since then, and a large, devoted group of Loch Nessians have consistently spread their gospel. In fact, they had a law passed that made it illegal for anyone to molest Nessie.

In 1975 two leading Loch Nessians, Robert Rines and Sir Peter Scott, offered three allegedly genuine photographs of the monster to *Nature*, the leading British science journal. They even bestowed a very scientific sounding name on the monster, *Nessiteras Rhombopteryx*, which in Greek means "diamond-finned Ness monster."

According to Scott, a naturalist, the pictures were "genuine photographs of what looks like an animal." Others at the press conference thought it more resembled "a dead swan lying on its side." Others said it appeared more like "a sunken Viking ship."

When Rines and Scott were asked why in all these years no remains of Loch Ness monsters had ever turned up, they opined that Nessies might be cannibals who ate their dead. Another suggestion was that the monsters swallowed a bellyful of small stones when sensing death and thus sank to the bottom of the loch to expire peacefully.

Then Nicholas Fairbairn, a member of the Scottish Parliament, formed an anagram of the letters of Nessiteras Rhombopteryx to spell out: "Monster hoax by

Sir Peter S." As to that naturalist Scott had no comment.

LONELY HEARTS QUEEN   *phantom bride scam*

During the 1940s Susanna Mildred Hill won the dubious accolade of "Queen of the Lonely Hearts." A 200-pound woman in her 60s and the mother of 10 children, Mrs. Hill operated out of her home in Washington, D.C., applying for membership in a number of matrimonial and lonely hearts clubs. Using names such as Miss Mildred Hill, Miss Beatrice Hill, Miss Daisy Hill, Miss Alice Moody, Miss Evelyn Moody and Miss Edna Jane Waugh, she gave her age as being from 18 to 23 years, and said she was the holder of an excellent job with substantial savings as well as great expectations of an inheritance. This very desirable young female was looking to marry the "right one."

Not surprisingly, the responses poured in and Mrs. Hill in turn shipped off a picture of her prettiest daughter as being the phony miss of the ad. The lady swindler never responded to any suitor living less than 500 miles from Washington, to try to eliminate any who might decide to make a quick visit. Whenever a suitor seemed determined to come, he was dissuaded due to an illness or sudden death in the family. Still, some suitors slipped through the safety net; when they showed up at the Hill home, the bulky lady simply posed as a housekeeper, the mother of "Mildred" and other characters.

Through the mail Mrs. Hill proceeded to trim the would-be suitors with the sad tale that her current funds had been used up due to an illness of "dear Mom." She wondered if the boys, under the circumstances, could help out. Most did, and they also took the hint when the young lady of their affection expressed an interest in certain types of jewelry, clothing, etc. When a suitor became impatient at the lack of progress toward even meeting the girl, on whom he'd showered so much material forms of affection or who didn't appear when sent money for her transportation, Mrs. Hill wrote back (as the mother) that her daughter had eloped with some worthless salesman. If, however, Mrs. Hill gauged the gullible suitor as still likely to stand for another touch, she would make a trip to him, explaining that she herself needed more medical care but that she really wanted her daughter to be happy and not waste her life taking care of her poor old mother. If the suitor would advance Mrs. Hill funds for her medical treatment, she would see to it that her daughter would cut free her apron strings and be ready for marriage.

Mrs. Hill was on just such a trek in 1945, calling on a number of suitors between Washington and Chicago, when she was nabbed by U.S. postal inspectors. In her possession was thousands of dollars in checks and money orders from several victims.

Appearing in court to face charges of bilking at least 100 known victims, Mrs. Hill continued to play her sick role, pleading guilty from a stretcher. A hardhearted, most unromantic judge sentenced her to up to five years' imprisonment.

LOREN AND LORENE   *birth and death hoax*

Perhaps the most bizarre-ever murder case started in Indiana in 1922, when 69-year-old Frank McNally of Hammond became beside himself with joy when his 23-year-old wife, Hazel, announced that she was pregnant. Shortly thereafter, Hazel—assisted at home by a woman friend residing with the couple—gave birth to twins. The babies, named Loren and Lorene, were so weak and susceptible to germs that the doting Hazel refused to allow her husband to see them. Frank had to be satisfied that he was a father by standing outside the bedroom door and listening to the babies cry.

This odd arrangement continued for a year, until Hazel tearfully told her husband that the babies had gotten much worse and had to be rushed to Chicago for emergency treatment. When Hazel returned a week later she was alone, explaining that the twins had died and been buried in Chicago. Suspicious that his wife had murdered the children, Frank went to the police. As Hazel could produce no death certificates, she was tried for murder.

In a startling trial Hazel was acquitted when her lawyer proved that she was physically incapable of having a baby and had simply made up the whole story to stop her husband's ceaseless nagging for a baby. As further evidence, Hazel's lawyer unwrapped a box and brought forth "Loren and Lorene"—two large crying dolls.

LOSING HORSE WINS   *unfixable race*

Because of the dangers of fixed horse races, western rodeos and fairs at times stage a contest in which the last horse to finish, rather than the first, is the winner. The race is then regarded as unfixable, since jockeys do not ride their own mounts, but are assigned a different one at post time. As a result, each jockey rides as fast as he can, as he would in a regular race, so that he will keep ahead of his own horse and thus make that animal a contender to win—by losing.

LOST MINES   *treasure hoaxes*

Many of the most enduring hoaxes of the American West are stories of "lost mines," which treasure hunters to this day still try to find. While there might be a germ of truth in some of the tales, it must be noted that the real fortune in lost mine ventures belongs to those selling the "secrets" and "maps" to them. One of the legendary operators in the field was a notorious mountaineer, rustler, thief and swindler named Thomas L. "Pegleg" Smith. In *Loafing Along Death Valley Trails*, William Caruthers notes:

> Smith may be said to be the inventor of the Lost Mine, as a means of getting quick money. The credulous are still looking for mines that existed only in Pegleg's fine imagination. . . . [He] saw in man's lust for gold, ways to get it easier than the pick and shovel method. . . . When his money ran out he always had a piece of high-grade gold quartz to lure investment in his phantom mine.

Born in Kentucky sometime between 1797 and 1801, Smith headed west as a fur trapper in his teens. Since it was easier to steal furs than to trap animals, Smith soon practiced that method to victimize both white trappers and Indians. He got his pegleg when one Indian shot him just below the right knee. An expert horseman despite his wooden leg, Pegleg became a horse rustler. When a market developed for Indian children, he kidnapped them for resale to slave-owning Mexicans.

With the discovery of gold in California, Pegleg developed his lost mine swindle, situating them in places such as the Santa Rosa or Chocolate Mountains or the Borego Badlands. The locales changed but Pegleg's spiel was the same: He had found rich samples of gold-bearing black quartz before he was forced to flee for his life from murderous Indians. The gullible always swallowed Pegleg's story. Some staked him on a private expedition on the promise of one-half the profits on his return, while others eagerly snapped up maps he offered pinpointing the alleged location of the gold.

Once Pegleg was hospitalized in San Diego suffering from dehydration and malnutrition after a hectic flight from Fort Yuma (presumably from some bilked gold seekers). He rambled on about finding gold near some twin peaks that reminded him of maiden's breasts [the Great Tetons]. His story seemed to have credibility, since gold-bearing ore worth about $1,500 was found in his pockets. Of course, Pegleg always carried such props with him. On his release from the hospital he did a land-office business selling maps to the gold locale, explaining he was too weak to make the trek himself. Among his victims were a number of hospital personnel.

Old Pegleg checked out of this life at the San Francisco City Hospital on October 25, 1866. In the century and a quarter since, innumerable fortune hunters have continued to search for the Lost Pegleg Mine or, more correctly, "mines"—a lasting tribute to the old reprobate's snake-oil charm.

LOTTERY CON GAMES

With a majority of the states in the country now sponsoring lotteries, the field has become a lush one for confidence operators. The most common ploy involves a man or woman who claims to be an illegal immigrant. If he tries to cash the lottery ticket and is required to show I.D., he'd be subject to deportation. The supposedly illegal immigrant then offers to split the payoff with the mark if he will cash the ticket instead. The usual procedure is for the victim to check the ticket against the results posted in any lottery outlet and then go to the main office and collect. Frequently the gypster can coax half-payment out of the victim in advance, since once the ticket is handed over, the victim can turn around and simply insist it was his ticket all along. If the victim balks at paying half (the usual pitch is for a $1,000 prize) or simply doesn't have that much cash, the gypster offers to hold something of value belonging to the victim, a watch or wedding ring.

Whatever happens, the swindler is long gone by the time the victim leaves the lottery office. Which may not be all that soon. The victim may have a lot of explaining to do on why he tried to cash a counterfeit ticket.

LOTTERY SIDEWALK SALES *fake contests*

First prize is this spanking new car right on display at the curb. Lesser prizes are color televisions, VCRs and the like. Tickets are only a dollar apiece. Isn't it worth $1 for a chance in a drawing like that—or why not buy five or more? After all, it's for a worthy cause—a church, a hospital, the needy and the poor, handicapped children, disabled veterans. And one doesn't even have to be present for the drawing. Winners can be notified by mail.

What are the chances of buying an honest lottery ticket? According to an estimate once made by the U.S. Postal Inspection Service for a profile of the agency: about one in 10.

LOTTERY TICKET SWINDLES

It was estimated in 1959 that 90% of the lottery tickets sold in the United States were clever counterfeits of foreign lotteries smuggled into this country, as well as domestic phonies of drawings allegedly held for the benefit of the poor, handicapped children, hospitals, churches and disabled veterans. As John N. Makris noted in *The Silent Investigators*, a history of the U.S. Postal Inspection Service, "No drawings are held and no big cash prizes are paid. In some instances small 'come-on' payments are made to bait more suckers."

Today the incidence of dishonest lotteries in the country has decreased if for no other reason than that a majority of the states now operate their own lotteries. (This of course is not an absolute guarantee of honesty. In the mid-1980s the Pennsylvania lottery was blatantly fixed right on television by false numbering of the balls!)

The recent experiment in permitting state lotteries is not the first of its kind in America. From 1776 until 1820 some 70 lotteries were authorized by the U.S. Congress for public works. Inevitably the cheaters moved in until the New York lottery swindle of 1918 led to federal outlawing of lotteries. It turned out the lottery operators had arranged for certain numbers to win in return for kickbacks from the pre-arranged winners.

While the lottery was supposedly held for the benefit of the unfortunate, the vast bulk of the revenues went to fortunate insiders. The lottery scam was exposed by Charles Baldwin, editor of the *New York Republican Chronicle* and the first of the city's great journalistic muckrakers. He wrote:

> It is a fact that in this city there is SWINDLING in the management. A certain gentleman in town received intimation that a number named would be drawn on Friday last and it was drawn that day! This number was insured high in several different places. A similar thing had happened once before in this same lottery; and on examination of the managers' files the number appeared soiled as if it had been in the pocket several days.

Several of the lottery operators promptly sued Baldwin for libel, and a select committee was appointed to investigate the newspaperman's charge. The finding was that one of the complainants, John H. Sickles, was a secret supplier of the lottery forms and saw to it that certain politicians got the winning numbers in advance. By thus paying off political figures, Sickles and his confederates were able to ensure that the lottery would enjoy governmental approval and support. Baldwin was found innocent and the New York lottery, and eventually others around the country, were banned.

After the Civil War some lotteries started up in individual states. The biggest of these was the Louisiana Lottery, which operated legally at times and clandestinely at others and sold tickets throughout the nation. The lottery was smart enough to have its drawings supervised by commissioners who enjoyed universal confidence, such as former Confederate Generals P. G. T. Beauregard and Jubal A. Early, each of whom earned $30,000 a year for about two days' non-arduous labor each month. Critics of the lottery considered the generals (and, after their deaths, General W. L. "Old Tige" Cabell of Texas) to be nothing more than respectable fronts. Finally, in 1895 Congress made it illegal for publications carrying advertisements of the lottery to cross state lines. The lottery changed its name to the Honduras National Lottery and tried to operate clandestinely, but it folded by 1907.

In other countries, lotteries and scams have long been bedfellows, with scandals at times extending even to the heads of state. King Louis XIV of France spoke of himself as the "Sun King" and proclaimed "I am the state," so it probably seemed quite reasonable to him that he should be the chief beneficiary of any French lottery. Once the free-spending and hence cash-short monarch "won" a 100,000-franc grand prize, and his queen and the dauphin came up with lesser prizes in the same event, an incalculable mathematical possibility. The result was a national uproar. Finally bowing to the public outrage, Louis "graciously" announced he was returning the money and was authorizing a new drawing. Had he not done so, there are those observers who say that the French Revolution might have come a century sooner.

LOWBALL HOME REPAIRS *shady contractor con*

When getting bids for some home repair work, owners frequently receive a wide range of estimates. If it is a scam bid, going for the lowest one may not be that wise. Let us say Mr. Jones jumps at a price that is invitingly low. After the contract is signed, he is hit for all kinds of extras at extra cost. He objects, but is told by the contractor to look at his written agreement. He does and it says that all extras needed to fully complete the job must be paid for by the homeowner. In the end, the homeowner is required to pay more than 50% over the original estimate. This is a trade gimmick called "lowballing," practiced by shady contractors.

LUCAS, VRAIN *forger*

The dream of any efficient con man is to latch on to a single victim and keep milking him for money for years without end. That was what an obscure French clerk named Vrain Lucas (1818–?) succeeded in doing. His victim was Michael Chastes, eminent French mathematician who, while he did know numbers, proved to be completely at sea in the matter of history and autographs, his lifelong avocation.

In the end the audacious Lucas managed to seduce the entire country so that there would be a time when Parisians would mill in the streets, shouting "Vive la France," and denouncing as a traitor anyone who doubted that this little forger's historical documents were genuine. Just as Lucas had struck a patriotic nerve in his prize victim so too did he affect the citizenry.

The son of a laborer, Lucas came to Paris as a young man seeking to become a librarian. Lacking a school certificate, he found such hopes dashed. Next he sought employment with a bookseller, but he had not learned Latin in his village school, and that was considered a necessity at the time in French bookstores. Lucas finally landed work with one Monsieur Letellier who dealt in family trees, patents of nobility and the like. There Lucas learned that to enjoy a steady income from such genealogical endeavors it was prudent to always satisfy the client. If the true record were murky, a few invented facts would make everything clear.

While still engaged in this kind of work, Lucas met the wealthy M. Chastes in 1861. Lucas could soon retire from all such efforts but one, as he sold the gullible and wealthy Chastes one historical phony after another for handsome sums.

Chastes clearly hungered to be a discoverer of patriotic lore, and Lucas supplied whatever he desired. There was a letter from Alexander the Great to Aristotle in which the Macedonian praised the inhabitants of ancient Gaul; there was a letter from the risen Lazarus to St. Peter; Mary Magdalene corresponded with the king of the Burgundians; and a Gallic doctor named Castor sent a communication to Jesus Christ.

Chastes squirreled away these great historical treasures but, in due course, others were made public and he became a hero of France. He had letters from Blaise Pascal to Isaac Newton, dated 1654, that indicated that the former had anticipated the latter's discoveries in gravitation and the fundamental laws of physics.

In due course that would prove to be a sad revelation, since finally someone noted that at the time Newton would have been but 11 years old. Why would Pascal have imparted the secrets of gravitation to a mere boy who, until then, had not exhibited the slightest scientific bent? There were other lapses. An alleged Pascal letter of 1652 mentioned a cup of coffee, but coffee had not appeared in France until 1669, when it was presented as a gift by the Turkish ambassador.

As these little problems developed, Professor Chastes started to entertain a smidgen of doubt; Lucas haughtily informed his victim that he would refund his money upon return of all the letters. But Lucas was in no position to make refunds. He had taken to high living, maintained expensive lodgings and kept a properly expensive mistress. However, Professor Chastes was absolutely terrified at the thought of surrendering his treasured letters and clung to blind faith in his supplier, worrying that Lucas might unfaithfully find another buyer. Thus he became interested in buying more letters.

Chastes continued to offer his treasures to the French Academy. They were labeled forgeries, and the gullible professor finally had to identify his source.

In February 1869 more ancient letters became public. Besides those of Alexander the Great and Mary Magdalene and Lazarus, there were five epistles from Alcibiades to Pericles, four by Aristotle, even two from Attila the Hun to a chief of the Franks.

Now the derisive laughter reached a crescendo, since incredibly all were written in medieval *French*. But then what could Lucas do, since he wrote neither Latin nor Greek. Even more amazingly, some of the ancient letter writers used paper containing a fleur-de-lis watermark. Lucas' lawyer made the only defense he could under the circumstances. It was, he told the court, all Professor Chastes' fault; he had displayed reprehensible credulity, which was most unforgivable in a scholar, and thus must be held responsible for Lucas' decade of frauds. Lucas himself told the court he had committed no crime, and if there were a few spurious items in the thousands of letters he had uncovered, that was merely unfortunate. What he had done, he said, was raise the reputation of France in the eyes of the entire world. He was a true patriot, and the crowds in the streets seemed to concur.

Nevertheless, Lucas was found guilty and sentenced to two years imprisonment—a light sentence that reflected the influence of public opinion. After serving his sentence, Lucas soon was in trouble again, arrested and convicted of selling a bogus family tree to an elderly priest. After that Lucas disappeared from sight.

LUKAS, THE BABOON-BOY *human raised by baboons*

Throughout the late 1930s and early 1940s Lukas, the South African baboon-boy, held audiences enthralled as he explained in rough Afrikaans how he had lived for years among the simians. His story was deemed so authentic that it was featured in "The 'Baboon Boy' of South Africa" by Dr. John P. Foley Jr. in the *American Journal of Pyschology* and in other writings by Professor R. M. Zingg of the University of Denver, including a popular account in the *American Weekly*.

Lukas's tale included his account of how, like other baboons, he developed a sweet-tooth for cactus. In one demonstration he managed to devour no less than 89 cacti at one sitting, an accomplishment that seemed to learned scientists to corroborate all his claims.

Lukas's imposture was exposed when it was learned that he had been a forced resident in Burghersdorp jail and never lived with baboons. His discoverer was a policeman who had known him then.

In a follow-up article in the *Journal of Psychology* the credulous scientists honorably recanted their pronouncements. But the Lukas hoax hardly ended, as Professor Zingg apparently neglected to inform the *American Weekly* of his revised opinion, and the article was printed again on his authority. In later years the baboon boy continued to cavort in the popular press.

As for Lukas himself, as Bergen Evans noted in *The Natural History of Nonsense*, he "but he alone, was placed in an institution for the feeble-minded."

LUSITANIA MEDAL HOAX *propaganda ploy*

On May 7, 1915, the British liner *Lusitania* was sunk off the Irish coast by a German submarine. Of the 1,195 lives lost, 128 were U.S. citizens. Within a few months the so-called Lusitania medal appeared and was sold by the thousands in Britain and the United States. The medal, erroneously dated "5 May, 1915," was accompanied by a label that read:

> An exact replica of the medal which was designed in Germany and distributed to commemorate the sinking of the "Lusitania."
>
> This indicates the true feeling the Warlords endeavour to stimulate and is proof postive that such crimes are not merely regarded favourably, but given every encouragement in the land of Kultur.

To many people even the mistaken date on the medal was damning against the German government, indicating that the Germans had made plans to commemorate the sinking in advance. Many in Germany saw the use of the medal as a hoax perpetrated by British Intelligence specifically to turn sentiment in the United States against Germany; but the fact was that the medal was indeed produced inside Germany. However, as Britain's *Imperial War Museum Review* has pointed out, the German government had nothing to do with it. It was a fake produced by the "satirical medallist" Karl Goetz, and the German government had immediately suppressed the medal when it learned of its existence.

Even Goetz could not be accused of glorying in the bloodletting that resulted from the sinking. His motive had been to justify the sinking on the grounds that the ship had been carrying arms (which it was) and that the German government had urged in advertisements in U.S. newspapers that Americans not take passage on British ships. The German government immediately grasped that the fake medal would cause it to suffer an enormous propaganda defeat in the United States, which proved to be the case. The sinking of the *Lusitania* did contribute mightily to the rise of American sentiment in favor of entering World War I on the side of the Allies; and Goetz' hoax medal clearly did much to fuel that sentiment.

LUSTIG, COUNT VICTOR *remarkable con man*

He made hundreds of thousands with his "money-making machine." He sold the Eiffel Tower twice.

He victimized underworld characters such as Al Capone, Legs Diamond and Big Bill Dwyer. He once said, "I can't understand honest men. They lead desperate lives, full of boredom." He was "Count" Victor Lustig, not a count but a no-account; he was probably the most successful confidence man in America, equal if not superior to Yellow Kid Weil (see entry).

Lustig was born in 1890 in what later became Czechoslovakia; fluent in several languages, he was a confirmed con man by the age of 20. He pulled a number of frauds in several countries before and during World War I; he was caught several times and served short prison terms. By just after the war, police in several European countries were after him, and Lustig decided to immigrate to the United States.

It was at this time that he became the leading practitioner of the so-called money-making machine. He told suckers he had invented a process that permitted him to feed plain paper into a machine and turn it into currency so perfect that no one could tell it from the real thing. There was good reason for this, since the "counterfeit" that spewed out of the contraption *was* real money. The success of the outrageous swindle was in its telling. Lustig sold the machine over and over again to such diverse characters as businessmen, bankers, gangsters, madams and even small-town lawmen.

There was no con big or small that Lustig would not pull. He was a master at "tishing a lady" (see entry). A devotee of brothels, Lustig was a lavish spender, at least in a manner of speaking. Upon bidding farewell to a harlot, he would flash a $50 bill, fold it and tuck it into her stocking. Lustig would tell her not to take it out before morning or it would turn to tissue paper. Needless to say, the prostitute would take it out early and find that it *had* turned to tissue paper (which it was all along).

One of the Count's prize brothel victims was Billie Scheible, a renowned madam who ran a string of very plush houses in Pittsburgh and New York. Lustig trimmed her for $10,000 for a money-making machine (see entry) and departed. Billie got one $100 bill but no more. Finally realizing she'd been robbed, she sent some of her strong-arm boys after him. They caught up with him in Philadelphia, where he was working a scam with worthless securities. Lustig refunded Billie's $10,000 and then sold her $15,000 in the watered stock.

Lustig was a major operator in the "stolen" security racket, dumping stock for 10 cents on the dollar by telling buyers that they could hold it for several years and then cash it safely. Nick Arnstein, Big Bill Dwyer and Legs Diamond were among the underworld characters he suckered. Diamond actually bought some of the phony stock for his own and his family's golden years. Oddly, these gangsters did not go after Lustig when they found out he had swindled them, realizing that if it got out how he'd played them for chumps, they would become laughing stocks.

Lustig also took the very homicidal Al Capone for $5,000, without the ganglord even realizing he'd been conned. Lustig asked Capone for $50,000, promising to double it in 60 days in a crooked deal he was working. (Con men could not operate in Chicago without Capone's approval.) Capone handed over the money with a grim warning that he reacted fatally to welchers and swindlers. Lustig simply banked the money and did nothing with it. At the end of 60 days he came back to Capone downcast, saying the deal had collapsed. Capone was about to explode when Lustig handed back the $50,000, keeping up his string of apologies. Capone was not prepared for a con man playing square with him, and he said, "If the deal fell through, you must be down on your luck." He peeled off five $1,000 bills from his roll and gave them to Lustig. "I take care of guys who play square with me." Lustig had figured Capone would do so and then allow him to operate freely in Chicago.

In 1925 Lustig returned to Europe and twice sold the Eiffel Tower (see entry). He returned to America the following year to continue all of his regular scams. Until 1935 Lustig had never been arrested in the United States, but that year he got involved in a major counterfeiting operation and was nailed.

The day before he was to go on trial in New York, Lustig escaped from the Federal House of Detention by climbing out a lavatory window with nine bed sheets tied together. On the way down, he saw lunch-hour pedestrians watching him, so he began going through the motions of cleaning the windows. Floor by floor, he scrubbed every pane he passed until he got to the street and fled. Some minutes later a bewildered pedestrian approached the guard window at the jail door and asked, "Do you know your window cleaner has run away?"

The Count's escape made news coast to coast and loosed a major manhunt. Billie Scheible knew nothing except that she too was looking for him. The police questioned Arthur "Dapper Don" Collins, who was known to have been associating with Lustig before his arrest. Collins, one of the country's leading con men himself, knew nothing. Lustig, it seemed, had also trimmed him for several thousand dollars and then disappeared.

Finally, Lustig was nabbed in Pittsburgh. He got 15 years for the counterfeiting charge and five more for his jail escape. He died in prison in 1947.

M

MACPHERSON, JAMES *literary forger*

No literary forger ever achieved such acclaim as Scotsman James Macpherson (1736–1796). He was declared by Goethe to be the equal of Homer; Napoleon ranked him above Homer. In 1760, the 24-year-old Macpherson, fresh from his own book of poems, *The Highlander*—which created no literary excitement at all—announced that he had translated parts of a grand epic from scattered Gaelic manuscripts, which he published as *Fragments of ancient poetry collected in the Highlands and translated from the Gaelic or Erse languages by James Macpherson.*

These were the works, Macpherson said, of Ossian, in Gaelic (Irish and Scottish) legend, the third-century poet-son of the warrior Finn MacCumhail. Previously some poems allegedly by the real (or leg-

Left: An illustration from the great Ossian epics. Right: James Macpherson. Goethe called him the equal of Homer, but the works were found to be forgeries.

endary) Ossian had appeared in *The Book of Lismore* compiled by James Macgregor in 1512. Macpherson's apparent find was far more impressive and created a literary furor in Scotland, England, France and Germany. For the Scots the Ossian find revealed a glorious page from their heroic medieval past.

In 1762 Macpherson followed with *Fingal, an Ancient Epic Poem in Six Books . . . Composed by Ossian, the Son of Fingal, Translated from the Gaelic Language.* This was followed in 1763 with yet another alleged Ossian epic, *Temora*. These two works Macpherson published as *The Works of Ossian* in 1765.

Macpherson had been financed in his research by donations and fund-raising conducted by poet John Home and Hugh Blair, the rhetorician and eloquent Presbyterian minister of Edinburgh, neither of whom could read Gaelic.

Ossian's works were translated into Italian, Spanish, French, Polish and, most especially, German, where eight different editions appeared. Goethe was so completely entranced by the "Homer of the North" that the great writer had his hero *Werther* declare, "Ossian is nearer my heart than Homer. What a sublime and noble world he has revealed to me!" The fictional Werther finds his own suffering made bearable by reading Ossian. Goethe's famous treatise, *Ossian and the Poetry of Ancient Races*, remains the standard work on the subject. The German philosopher and critic Johann Gottfried Herder declared after absorbing Ossian, "To judge by their recently discovered poems and songs, there has never been a race possessed of such powerful and at the same time tender emotions, who, individually, were so heroic, and at the same time, so supremely human—as the ancient Scots."

Others, like Lord Kames in Scotland and Diderot in France, were overwhelmed by the works. But controversy arose, especially as there were no other writings from the Gaelic until the 10th century. English poet Thomas Gray admired the work but with great doubts. Scottish philosopher David Hume viewed the manuscript with skepticism.

The main counterthrust came from Dr. Samuel Johnson, who traveled to the Hebrides in 1773 to investigate the legends and their sources. He declared in 1775 in *A Journey to the Western Islands of Scotland:* "I believe they never existed in any other form but that which we have seen. The editor, or author, never could show the original, nor can it be shown by any other."

Macpherson expressed outrage at Johnson, writing that only the latter's age prevented him from the challenge of a duel or a good thrashing. To this Johnson replied, "I hope I shall never be deterred from detecting what I think a cheat, by the meanness of a ruffian. . . . I thought your book an im-

posture; I think it is an imposture still. For this opinion I have given my reasons to the publick, which I dare you to refute. Your rage I defy. Your abilities, since your Homer, are not so formidable, and what I hear of your morals inclines me to pay regard, not to what you shall say, but to what you shall prove."

That was the rub. Macpherson never produced the originals on which he had based his translations, despite declarations to do so. Others supported Johnson in his charges, among them Horace Walpole, who had previously brought down Thomas Chatterton (see entry).

Even after Macpherson died in 1796 no originals appeared, although some so-called originals turned up in the early 1800s; these were poems copied in the hand of Macpherson. It was clear from these that Macpherson had appropriated some of their ideas, plots, names and phrases, but his two "Ossian" epics were his own work.

Many scholars refuse to allow the fact of Macpherson's forgeries to obscure his genuine contributions to Gaelic studies. Will and Ariel Durant magnanimously declare in *The Story of Civilization:* "The deception was not so complete or so heinous as Johnson supposed; let us call it poetic license on too grand a scale."

MAELZEL, JOHANN NEPOMUK See CHESS-PLAYING AUTOMATON.

MAHARAJA OF MANCHESTER *governmental hoax*
In 1832 Edmund Roberts, a U.S. government agent, arrived in Cochin China (Vietnam) to arrange a commercial treaty. However, Roberts' request to see the emperor was denied by lower-rank officials, since his letter of introduction did not show his name followed by a number of titles to indicate his importance. Roberts withdrew and rewrote the document, this time identifying himself as the holder of a number of illustrious titles, all drawn from his native state of New Hampshire. While this magnificent forgery no longer exists, it is believed that he made such typical claims for himself as the exalted position of "Maharaja of Manchester." Likewise he was "Lord of Lake Winnepesaukee" and "Sultan of Sullivan County."

Now the much-titled Roberts was deemed worthy of a royal audience, and he was able to complete his assignment.

MAIL-ORDER LAB TEST SCAMS *fake screenings*
The growth of mail-order laboratory tests has produced a large number of frauds in supposedly regular screenings for such medical difficulties as cancer,

high cholesterol and AIDS. The tests are either never done or are performed only the first time, with fake results sent out thereafter. The clients are thus locked into expensive long-term arrangements that are difficult to break. Medical authorities strongly recommend that patients see their personal physicians to arrange for all tests and treatments if they are really needed.

MALSKAT, LOTHAR See MIRACLE OF LÜBECK.

MALTLESS MALTED   *million-dollar penny-ante gyp*

It might seem picayune, but the "maltless malted" is undoubtedly a multi-million-dollar racket in this country. As a newspaperman once wrote, "If Willie Sutton [the bank robber who hit banks because "that's where the money is"] had any brains he would have opened an ice cream store and put more money into banks than he ever took out with a gun."

While there may be a bit of hyperbole in that statement, the average person should try to estimate the malteds he and his family drink in the course of a year, and tote up a nickel for each of them. Virtually everywhere in the country, the price of a malted is five or ten cents over that of a milk shake, the difference in price being the charge for the spoonful of malt that is added.

In New York City, where millions and millions of malted milks are sold each year, one of the nation's leading malt manufacturers once estimated that malt is used in only one-third of the "malteds" sold. Of course, one always "sees" the malt being put into one's shake, or at least one sees the soda jerk snap the automatic dispenser so that a portion of malt plops into the mixing container; but it is possible that the dispenser is jammed with cardboard so that little or no malt comes out. Or perhaps the malteds are bought in a store with no dispenser; there one sees the counterman spoon it into the mixing containers—unless the "loaded spoon" treatment is being employed. A spoon of malt is moistened and quickly hardens so that the cheater can dish out what looks like a heaping spoonful of malt without using up even a penny's worth of supply.

Consider what five cents on 50 million maltless malteds mounts up to in New York alone. That's at least $2.5 million a year; many insist that is an under-estimate. For many years after World War II one Times Square gyp sold an estimated 1,500 maltless malteds a day during the summer months, which added up to an illicit profit of $500 per week. Today a reasonably sized fountain with a good lunch and dinner business can easily net the crooked owner anywhere from $5,000 to $10,000 a year—just on malteds that aren't.

MAN-EATING TREES   *biological hoax*

To date science has failed to turn up any carnivorous plants that have managed to devour anything larger than insects, despite claims that mice, rats, lizards and birds have been so consumed. This has not dampened hoax tales of trees that eat people. In some tales the tree that allegedly does so is referred to as "the Devil Tree."

One of the most famous, or infamous, accounts was offered by one Dr. Carle Liche in a Hearst Sunday supplement, the *American Weekly*, on September 26, 1920. The good doctor earnestly reported having seen a young maiden consumed by a floral people-eater in Madagascar in 1878. The victim, despite the locale of the story, was suitably portrayed in the accompanying art work as a lissome, naked blonde with bobbed, marcelled hair. She was, Dr. Liche asserted, a member of the cruel tribe of "Mkodos," about which little was known. Dr. Liche's man-eating tree was perhaps as rare as its victim, being a sort of "gigantic vegetable octopus."

Not wishing to limit the scientific knowledge of its devoted readers, the publication served up yet another version of a man-eating tree on January 4, 1925. This tale was offered by a Mississippian, Mr. W. C. Bryant, who had a near-fatal encounter with the vegetative gourmet, and presented Mr. Bryant cavorting in a sort of "forbidden zone" or a taboo mesa on the Philippine island of Mindanao. One of these devil trees reached for him, leaves writhing and making a great hissing sound. Had it not been for the quick action of a local guide—who of course knew the menace of these floral carnivores—Mr. Bryant would have been digested by the plant. The guide knocked Bryant down and out of reach of the greedy, outstretched branches and pulled him to safety so that he could in due course carry the magnificent tale back to the offices of the *Weekly*.

Even the devoted readers of the *Weekly* found the story a bit hard to swallow, especially as the illustrations of the account showed skulls all around the tree and an entire human skeleton, impaled and bleached, gripped in its sated branches. Mr. Bryant was accorded space to answer such criticisms and said the drawing had not been meticulously accurate. As he remembered, there were not really that many skulls around, since a large number might have triggered a warning signal to him. He said it seemed much more like a friendly tree, offering a welcome haven from the noon-day sun.

That seemed to have been the last time the *Weekly* thought it prudent to devote space to the devil trees, but so good a tale could not be allowed to simply fade away. As late as 1947 the tale of the nude young blonde, helpless and doomed, was resurrected in the

December issue of *Pageant* magazine. The magazine proclaimed: "Man-Eating Trees? Could Be!"

MANHATTAN ISLAND SWINDLE

We are taught in school that Peter Minuit bought Manhattan Island from the Indians in 1626 for a piddling $24 worth of beads, needles and trinkets. In truth the deal was a downright swindle, although it is seldom noted these days who really swindled whom. As head of the New Netherlands colony, Minuit bought Manhattan from the Canarsee Indians and figured he had made a good deal. The Canarsees figured they had made a better one, since they didn't own Manhattan and actually lived in what is now Brooklyn. The ones who should have been paid were the Weckquaesgeeks. That tribe quite understandably took offense at being cut out of the transaction and warred against the Dutch for many years. Finally, to secure peace, the Dutch bought the island a second time.

The Indians of the New York area must be regarded as premier con men of early America. The Raritan Indians, for instance, managed to peddle Staten Island to the whites no less than six times, about the same time.

MAN MEDICINE *quack sex treatment*

Probably no "sex rejuvenator" enjoyed a greater success for its promoter than "Man Medicine." Early in the 20th century Edward Hayes, the con man-promoter of Man Medicine, raked in a large fortune with his pitch that users of his product would enjoy "once more with gusto, the joyful satisfaction, the pulse and throb of physical pleasure, the keen sense of man sensation."

Many of Hayes' patient-victims really thought they were experiencing new stirrings; and well they should have since Hayes' concoction was nothing more than a laxative. Of course, if one holds that regularity is beneficial to all human endeavors, Hayes could claim some worthiness to his "miracle" treatment. However, the federal government took a different view and charged the sex promoter with fraud. Hayes was convicted in April 1914 and fined $5,000. Man Medicine was removed from the market, and Hayes agreed to promote no other sex treatments. But by then he had become a millionaire. And while he kept his pledge on sex products, Hayes blithely moved on to so-called cures for obesity.

MANN ACT SCAMS *victimizing both men and women*

The White Slave Traffic Act of 1910, popularly known as the Mann Act after its sponsor, Representative James Robert Mann of Illinois, outlawed the transport of women across state lines for immoral pur-

poses. The law was used successfully to prosecute a number of minor criminals over the years, but it was never as effective as hoped. Organized crime's activities were hardly crippled by the law; in recent years, the decline of prostitution as an organized crime activity—the result of changing sexual mores rather than effective law enforcement—has relegated the Mann Act to relative unimportance. Indeed, some critics have insisted the law was more effective as a valuable blackmail tool for scheming prostitutes and con women.

Oddly, the most enterprising use of the Mann Act was made by a man, leading confidence operator Robert Arthur Tourbillon (alias Dapper Don Collins) who targeted women as victims and assembled a gang of criminals for that endeavor. An attractive rogue and meticulous dresser, Collins would attract and seduce women only to have their love sessions interrupted by confederates posing as law officers. The phony officers accused Collins of being a Mann Act violator or perhaps a procurer for white slavers. Ostensibly to protect the good name of his female companion, upper-class and often married, he would seek to bribe the bogus officers with all his cash, only to be visibly shaken when they insisted they had to have more. The panicky woman, facing disgrace if the case became public knowledge, eagerly offered up her own money, furs and jewelry.

Collins even maintained a yacht for such blackmail scams and trapped society women on love-boat cruises by having the craft boarded by law enforcement "agents." One of Collins' victims, a Connecticut society matron, was shaken down aboard ship to the tune of $7,000 in cash and diamonds. Collins was so fearful that the shakedown might have missed something of value that he had his accomplices take the victim's luggage with them to search through at leisure.

On occasion the unforeseen did develop in Collins' shakedown operations. He once took a Maryland matron to Atlantic City and was then supposed to usher her on to Washington for the payoff finale. Instead, he became so entranced with the lady that he remained with her for a week of bliss in the ocean resort and went on to Washington alone, where he had to pay off his four confederates $350 apiece for the setup, which had been likely to net $10,000. A week of true love had done Dapper Don wrong.

MANNIX, WILLIAM F. See LI HUNG CHANG MEMOIRS.

MAN WHO BROKE THE BANK AT MONTE CARLO *casino hoaxer*

One of the most baldfaced swindles involving alleged winning at casino gambling was pulled near the end of the 19th century at Monte Carlo by a puckish, bearded and balding little Cockney named Charles Wells (1841–1926). Most undeservedly, Wells has been immortalized in song as "The Man Who Broke the Bank at Monte Carlo." In truth, Wells did no such thing, and in the end, inevitably, the bank broke him.

With a long record as a confidence man, Wells was fresh out of an English prison when he appeared at the fabled Monte Carlo casino in July 1891. He boasted a $2,000 stake, probably from some recent scam he'd pulled.

No one ever figured out the method to his betting, but Wells proceeded to wipe out a table of the casino a dozen times in 11 hours. (It should be understood that wiping out a table is hardly akin to breaking the casino. Indeed, few gambling tables are stocked with an inordinate amount of chips, since once action begins the payoffs to winners are usually more than covered by the rake-ins from losers.) Time after time the table's chips had to be replenished. Wells returned the next day and won again. In fact, over a three-day period it was estimated he won the equivalent of $200,000.

Gamblers studied his play as did the house, but they were unable to find any rhyme to his betting other than the fact that he seemed to concentrate on low numbers.

A few months later Wells was back again, and he won yet another $200,000.

Charles Wells' exploit turned out to be a godsend to the Monte Carlo casino, as amateur gamblers from all over the world hurried to Monaco to repeat Wells' winning skein. And in music halls in England and elsewhere he was celebrated in rollicking song.

In 1892 Wells was back yet again, sporting a yacht with a gorgeous lady friend in tow. This time around Wells was not using his own money but rather that of eager English backers who staked him. Evidently it did not occur to these starry-eyed investors that if Wells could break the casino there would be no reason for him to share his certain winnings.

For a while Wells won again, and then suddenly all went sour. He lost repeatedly and had to wait until his backers in England wired him more funds. He lost again. It is questionable whether or not the casino got all of the losses. It seems likely Wells had the prudence to skim off some of his backers' funds in the process.

When Wells left Monaco this time, he was without the yacht (rented) and lady friend (likewise). Charles Wells retired from roulette gambling and went back to his smaller confidence games. He ended up doing time in prison for a number of his capers.

It was only in 1922 that 81-year-old Wells finally confessed his monumental Monte Carlo hoax. He had been there several times before his great win, but

had attracted no attention since he'd always lost. In 1891 he had a magnificent run of luck—something many consistent gamblers enjoy once in a great while. What he hadn't had at the time was any sort of gambling system. He just bet indiscriminately and won, much to his own astonishment. When he returned to England, he was swamped with offers from others to back him; he reasoned he had nothing to lose but their money. Upon his return to Monte Carlo Wells even made a heroic effort to win, using for the first time a gambling system. That was when the good fortune ended.

MARATHON DANCE DEATH HOAXES

It was a craze that began in 1923 and continued unabated during the Great Depression. The dance marathons drew desperate young (and not so young) people to compete for prize money by seeing what couple could last the longest on the dance floor. Some allegedly dropped dead on the ballroom floor, others committed suicide or were obligingly (and fictionally) shot by partners to end their misery. The idea of dance marathons as killing events started in 1923 when a story was given out that one Homer Morehouse of North Tonawanda, New York, had dropped dead after dancing 87 hours. Although the story was later exposed as a hoax, Mark Sullivan had been conned by it and related the anecdote in volume two of *Our Times.*

Clearly, the "killer dance marathon" was pure hype invented by the promoters of such contests, obligingly aided by public authorities who viewed the events as dangerous and sought to stop them—thus providing yet more marvelous publicity. The promoters decreed that the marathoners had to be checked out by a physician daily. One doctor so engaged said with a straight face, "They'll be all right if they escape insanity. This music may get them, but otherwise they should last."

Based on a statistical study of fatalities, it appears that opera singers on stage are far more in mortal danger than dance marathoners. Despite this, the concept of marathon-dancing deaths remains etched in our folklore.

MARCY, LOUIS *the anarchist forger*

The term "Marcy fake" is today a byword in the art world. Louis Marcy was a brilliant faker of medieval and Renaissance jewelry, caskets and reliquaries. He duped knowledgeable collectors and museums with a huge output of bogus art. And while he was doing this, Marcy (real name, Luigi Parmeggiani) was a virulent anarchist and editor who published a journal devoted in large measure to sneering attacks on capitalist art collectors, dealers and art forgers.

Born in 1860 in Reggio Emilia, northern Italy, Marcy was apprenticed in 1872 to a printer and later to a jeweler. He moved to Paris when he was 20. It is not known when precisely he sold his first forgeries; but by 1894, now living in London, he was obviously deeply involved in the illicit trade, and he started selling expensive medieval fakes to the Victoria and Albert Museum and the British Museum.

He continued undetected during his London tenure until 1903 when he once more relocated in Paris. In June he was arrested as an anarchist. Police who raided the house where Marcy was found discovered it jammed with "antiquities" estimated to be worth millions of francs and concluded that Marcy was either an art thief or an international fence.

The only charge that stuck against Marcy was the anarchist one, and he served five months in prison. On his release Marcy remained in Paris, where he edited and wrote an art journal in which he vented his spleen against capitalist art collectors and the like. At the same time he continued to secretly flood the field with bogus art.

Marcy's true role was not revealed until 1922 when Otto von Falke in *Belvedere* exposed his ingenious forgeries. None of this appears to have totally stunted Marcy's activities. In the meantime, he had returned to Reggio Emilia to live out his last years. In 1932, despite his notoriety, he succeeded in unloading his collection of "antiquities" to the municipality. They may still be viewed there today, although now correctly attributed.

Despite Marcy's roguish behavior, the art world still remains in awe of his fakes. A publication of the British Museum speaks glowingly of "the skilled craftsmanship of his material, and the inspired eclecticism of his designs." And, needless to say, forces on the left saw in Marcy's magnificent hoaxes a political statement of protest, or perhaps vengeance.

MARK *victim of a swindle*

The term "mark" enters a scam dictionary as a term describing a "pigeon" or victim of any sort of ripoff operation. It originated in the early days of carnivals in America, when the victim was cheated of his money at a crooked concession. The swindler would find some way to pat the victim on his back as he left the concession counter and in the process leave a chalk mark there. As the marked man wandered past a number of other concessions, the chalk on his back indicated to other grifters that he was someone who could be taken—hence a "mark."

Similarly, the chalk mark indicated to pickpockets who held exclusive rights to work the carnival that he was a man who still had money. The chalk mark also pointed out where he was carrying it. A chalk mark low on the back indicated the man's money

was in the back pocket directly below. A mark high on the shoulder would indicate his cash was in the hip pocket on that side, and so on.

See also BALLOON BUSTERS.

MARKS, BEN See DOLLAR STORE.

MARRIAGE SHAKEDOWNS *New York registrar racket*

In bygone days the holding of municipal jobs in New York City was regarded by many as a license to steal from the public. No one was more appreciative of and determined to benefit from the opportunity than James J. McCormick, registrar of marriages during the 1930s. His salary was a not-unsubstantial $8,500 a year; but McCormick regarded this as a mere pittance and found a simple and direct scam for boosting it.

At the time the standard fee for a license was $2. Whenever McCormick was paid the fee, he threw open a drawer in his desk—revealing a large sum of high-denomination notes—and asked the groom: "How about it?"

If the bridegroom demurred to come across with a more substantial payment, McCormick would shout, "Cheapskate!"

Few couples could weather such an outburst, and they paid the gratuity. In six years on the job registrar McCormick garnered $385,000, which he squirreled away in 34 bank accounts. When his blatant scheme was squashed, he was fined $15,000 and sent to prison for four months. Stricter controls were then enforced to forbid the payment of gratuities to city employees carrying out Cupid's work.

MASTERSON, BAT See CELEBRITY SCAMS.

MAXWELL, ROBERT *grand scale fraudster*

In life, Robert Maxwell (1923–1991), the flamboyant Czech-born British publisher, was regarded by many as a brilliant ringmaster who fought his way up from poverty and personal tragedy to build a financial empire that made him one of the business world's most feared operators. In the 1980s Maxwell sought to be viewed as the savior of downtrodden newspapers such as Britain's Mirror Group Newspapers and New York's *Daily News.*

After his mysterious death on November 5, 1991, it became apparent that Maxwell was more the scourge of the companies he controlled.

While the 1980s can be regarded as the decade of the super swindler—producing such financial sleaze artists as Michael Milken, Ivan Boesky (see entry), Charles Keating (see entry), and the like—Robert Maxwell stood in a class by himself. While it will probably take years into the 21st century to unravel the full extent of his depredations, it is now clear that Maxwell and perhaps a few others siphoned off at least $1.63 billion from pension funds and the two flagship companies of his publishing empire, Mirror Group and Maxwell Communication Corp. The total losses to the pension funds and other creditors will at some point escalate by many billions of dollars more.

Maxwell died at sea, having either fallen, been pushed or jumped from his luxury yacht, *Lady Ghislaine*. Was he murdered to silence him? Had he died accidentally? Or had he finally realized the jig was up and taken his own life? Of the three alternatives, the last seems the more likely since, according to investigators, he faced certain exposure in a matter of days.

Perhaps most amazing is that Maxwell had gotten away with it for so long, considering that 20 years earlier Great Britain's Board of Trade found that he was not "in our opinion a person who could be relied on to exercise proper stewardship of a publicly quoted company." Nevertheless, Maxwell continued to thrive, proving that nothing succeeds like excessive success. Even while picking up the nickname of "The Bouncing Czech," Maxwell blithely went from one megadeal to the next, using looted assets to keep afloat the heavily indebted private companies at the heart of his empire. In the firestorm after Maxwell's death, even the most austere elements of the British press descended to colorful and livid terms to denounce him, calling him a "fraudster on a grand scale." Whittam Smith, editor of *The Independent*, declared, "He was a crook. Shareholders other than his family were lambs to be fleeced; pensions were fair game." Peter Jenkins wrote in a column in the same publication: "Ask anyone with knowledge of financial matters the secret of his success, and they would explain how he could make money move from bank to bank, company to company, faster than the eye could see. Some called this wizardry business, but most knew in their hearts that Maxwell was simply not kosher, no friend of widows and orphans."

Within a month of Maxwell's death, his financial empire had crumbled in bankruptcies. Perhaps Maxwell knew the house of cards was rushing headlong to collapse. In a television interview shortly before his death, Maxwell said in response to a question that in the hereafter he couldn't say if he would meet his "maker . . . or the baker."

At least Maxwell left a few somewhat laughing—and others stone-cold broke.

MAYFIELD, IDA *hoax socialite*

She was the belle of New York in the 1860s, and in the 1870s she was the wife of newspaper publisher and congressman Benjamin Wood. As the former Ida

Mayfield she had previously been the belle of New Orleans, the vivacious daughter of Judge Thomas Henry Mayfield of Louisiana. In New York it was inconceivable to hold a ball of social import without the presence of the beautiful wife of the publisher of the *New York Daily News*. The Prince of Wales (later King Edward VII) found her a most charming dance partner, and the glorious Mrs. Wood could count Samuel J. Tilden and President Grover Cleveland among her personal friends.

Ben Wood died in 1900. While his widow continued to be a star of society, she appeared to be losing interest in that world. In 1907 the Widow Wood withdrew all of her money from the Morton Trust Company—close to $1 million—stuffed it into a large brown shopping bag and stepped into obscurity. She was not seen again for 24 years, when she turned up living in New York's Herald Square Hotel in squalor befitting a Dickens novel. She was now 93, and her living quarters were carpeted with yellowed newspapers, hundreds of letters and old pictures. There were hundreds of half-century-old ball programs from New Orleans and New York and portraits inscribed by famous personalities. Newspapers and cardboard boxes were stacked ceiling-high and all about lay valuable jewelry of all sorts, gifts from her doting millionaire husband. There was a crackerbox that contained a diamond-and-emerald necklace.

When the police, summoned by reports of her living in squalor, opened the cardboard boxes they found approximately a half-million dollars worth of negotiable securities. Mrs. Wood also wore a canvas pouch tied to her body that was found to be holding 50 $10,000 bills.

The media had a field day reporting on the society belle turned recluse. The courts declared Mrs. Wood incompetent and assigned legal counsel to watch over her interests, a situation that amused her to no end. She claimed she had done right well for herself, holding her cash and avoiding the Panic of 1907 and the bank depredations and failures of the 1929 crash.

The following year Mrs. Wood died and, as the saying went, Louisiana Mayfields came out of the woodwork to share in her estate. Naturally a full search was required concerning Ida's family roots. Only then was it discovered that there never was an Ida Mayfield. The late Mrs. Wood was really one Ellen Walsh (1838–1932). Her father was an immigrant Irish peddler who had resided in Malden, Massachusetts, and died in California in 1864.

Ida Mayfield was born of Ellen's ambition to crash New Orleans' high society. Not even Ben Wood suspected the truth when he married her and, in fact, remained so ignorant until his death. Ellen had done an excellent job of claiming the Mayfield name. She applied the name to her mother, brother Michael and sister Mary, the latter two becoming Henry Benjamin Mayfield and Mary E. Mayfield. Ellen Walsh even changed the name on her father's tombstone, to Thomas H. Mayfield. When her mother died in 1883, she had her buried as "Ann Mary Crawford, widow of Thomas Henry Mayfield."

Ellen Walsh's long-ago deception shattered the inheritance hopes of scores of Louisiana Mayfields. When the Wood estate was finally settled, 10 Walsh descendants each received $84,490.92, from an ancestor who had covered up her own roots.

McCARTNEY, PAUL See PAUL IS DEAD!

McCORMICK, JAMES J. See MARRIAGE SHAKEDOWNS.

McGLUE, LUKE *baddest man in the West*

He was evil incarnate, the baddest man the Wild West ever produced. True, many of his crimes were minor ones, petty thefts and sometimes practical jokes that netted the most minor of sums, but the nefarious Luke McGlue was plainly the most active thief around. Considering that his bailiwick from 1877 to 1887 was Dodge City—"the wickedest little city in America"—it is obvious that Luke McGlue was a one-man crime wave.

If a tourist had his luggage stolen, it was the work of Luke McGlue. If a hotel room was looted, it was that damned Luke McGlue. If a man's trousers disappeared while he visited a harlot in a crib, she (or lawman Wyatt Earp) would tell him, with a straight face, that it was a dirty deed by rotten Luke McGlue. McGlue, it seemed, specialized in robbing greenhorns or playing practical jokes on them.

However, no one had ever seen McGlue. Luke McGlue himself was a hoax, invented by the denizens of Dodge City to explain away the petty thefts to which visiting dudes were subjected. Deputy Marshal Earp, who extracted considerable tribute from the red-light establishments and low saloons, found Luke McGlue a handy character. He would earnestly inform McGlue's victims that he was on the lookout for McGlue and would deal with him in the hard manner of the West when he finally ran him to ground.

Alas, Luke McGlue never did get caught.

McGREGOR, GREGOR See POYAIS LAND FRAUD.

MEANS, GASTON BULLOCK *flimflam detective and swindler*

J. Edgar Hoover had two great hates during his long tenure as head of the FBI: Robert Kennedy and Gaston B. Means (1880–1938). In the latter case Hoover was justified. Means was the most artful dodger ever to appear on the Washington scene, and Hoover rightfully viewed him as a man who gave law enforcement a bad name. Incredibly Means, a rogue of unrivaled effrontery, was considered as a likely head for what was later called the Federal Bureau of Investigation. Despite his many depredations, he was called "the greatest natural detective ever known" by William J. Burns. Others, more accurate than the head of the Burns Detective Agency, would have changed the operative word to swindler, con man, hoaxer, spy, influence peddler, fixer, blackmailer and quite possibly murderer. In fact, Means was all of the above.

As impossible as it sounds, Means did more to tar the reputation of the Harding administration than even the Ohio Gang (see entry) and Teapot Dome (see entry). Means had the ability to turn almost any tragedy to his own profit. He garnered far more money out of the Lindbergh baby snatch than Bruno Hauptmann, the actual kidnapper.

After an early, undistinguished career in North Carolina as a towel salesman, cotton speculator and occasional lawyer, Means landed a job with the Burns Detective Agency in 1910. Means consistently whispered about "secret informants" and other phony claims, which indicated to Burns that he had an investigative genius in his employ. Burns was sorely disappointed when Means left the agency in 1915 for bigger and better things.

He became the personal overseer of madcap heiress Maude B. King. Means caught the woman's attention by concocting a fake robbery of her and her friends on a Chicago street and just "happening" to come along in time to rout the robber. Having been hired on the spot to be her protector, Means was soon managing her financial affairs, truly a case of the fox guarding the hen house. Within two years Means had milked the King holdings of an estimated $150,000. In time even a madcap like Maude King started noticing things; but she did not live long enough to do anything about it. Means squired the lady off on a hunting trip in North Carolina in 1917 and, somehow, she ended up shot to death. Means was tried for murder but was acquitted, convincing the jury that the woman had killed herself.

Means found that stealing Mrs. King's money was not a full-time occupation. Shortly after the start of World War I he signed on as a secret agent for both the British and the Germans. He provided the Germans with information for disrupting British shipping; at the same time he supplied counterintelligence to the British warning them about such capers. Shortly before the U.S. entry into the conflict, Means severed his connections with German Intelligence, not for patriotic reasons but for the very practical reason that he found it difficult to collect his pay. Thus Means moved on to activities on behalf of U.S. Army Intelligence.

When Warren Harding took office in 1921, Burns (now head of the Bureau of Investigation) recruited his old employee to work there, much to the distress of another rising star, J. Edgar Hoover.

Means soon turned the common practice of bribe taking into a fine art. Besides his devotion to the graft system, Means also made his services available to Mrs. Harding, secretly undertaking investigations into the president's love affairs. Means' activities became so notorious that for a time he was removed from his job; but he was instantly reinstated as an "informant" at William Burns' behest. Means functioned quite well until he was indicted for having swindled a number of bootleggers by telling them he was collecting graft for Secretary of the Treasury Andrew Mellon. Means got off; after all, one had to believe a "master detective" over a bunch of untrustworthy bootleggers. Later, during a Senate committee investigation, Means told how he had acted as a go-between in the payment of $50,000 to an associate of Attorney General Harry Daugherty to stop a $6 million government suit against an aircraft manufacturer.

By this time Means was actively trying to blackmail the Hardings for $50,000, claiming he had proof that the president had fathered a child by Nan Britton, an undistinguished young poetess from Ohio. When Harding inconveniently died, Means coauthored a book with Nan Britton entitled *The President's Daughter*. Means' luck ran out, and he was sent to prison for bribery scams. Released in 1930, Means continued his literary career with *The Strange Death of President Harding*, a scandalous best-seller in which he intimated that Mrs. Harding had poisoned the president.

Perhaps the most outrageous of Means' many cons occurred during the investigation of the Lindbergh baby kidnapping. He swindled Mrs. Evalyn Walsh McLean out of $104,000 by claiming he would be able to recover the baby through his underworld contacts. When the baby was found dead, Means did not return the money to Mrs. McLean, telling her one bizarre tale after another and finally insisting he had returned the money to an associate of hers. This was a provable lie and Means was brought to trial in 1935 for conspiracy to commit larceny. Means testified in his own defense and told the court one cock-and-bull story after another. When Means stepped down from the witness stand, he moved beside J. Edgar Hoover (who attended the trial) and said, "Well, Hoover, what did you think of that?"

"Every bit of it was a pack of lies," Hoover retorted.

Means blinked, then smiled and said, "Well, you've got to admit that it made a whale of a good story."

The story was not quite good enough. Means was sentenced to 15 years. Three years later Means suffered a massive heart attack, and Hoover dispatched agents to his prison bedside in hopes of discovering the whereabouts of Mrs. McLean's money. Means put on a broad smile and died.

MECKLENBURG DECLARATION OF INDEPENDENCE
false historical claim

Did Thomas Jefferson engage in plagarism when he wrote the Declaration of Independence? If we believe the "Mecklenburg Declaration of Independence," which was supposedly dated May 20, 1775, Jefferson's inspired work becomes a shocking "political lift." The so-called Mecklenburg Declaration—which is engrafted on the great seal of North Carolina—announced that the inhabitants of Mecklenburg county were "free and independent people." This and other thoughts contained in that Declaration were ones that Jefferson did not espouse until more than a year later.

There is no doubt that the committee of safety for the county did adopt 20 resolutions announcing that the British king and Parliament were "wholly suspended" and that the "resolves" were to be kept in force until modified by the provincial congress or until Parliament repealed obnoxious acts opposed by the colonies. The resolves were sent to the delegates for North Carolina at the Second Continental Congress, but were never presented.

Claims of a Mecklenburg Declaration of Independence are mired in fraud and forgery. The actual text of the so-called declaration was published April 30, 1819, in the *Raleigh Register* and was followed by a strong denial of authenticity by Thomas Jefferson. The *Register*'s list of the resolutions had been written from memory in 1800 by John M. Alexander, the recording clerk of the convention. Many others came forward to say they were in attendance when the declaration was adopted.

The matter lay in dispute for almost a century. In 1905 *Collier's* magazine published the claim and came up with an original source, a facsimile of the front page of the *Cape-Fear Mercury* for Friday, June 3, 1775, announcing the declaration and its resolutions.

In 1906, however, Dr. Worthington Chauncey Ford, chief of the Division of Manuscripts of the Library of Congress and A. S. Salley Jr., secretary of the Historical Commission of South Carolina, offered proof that the *Mercury*'s account was spurious and itself a forgery. Among other things, June 3, 1775, was not a Friday; the numbering of the edition was inaccurate; and the type did not match known copies of the

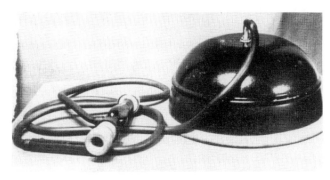

"Hair growth" contraptions remain a leading medical fraud, such as this one, which supposedly generated hair-producing infrared or ultraviolet rays.

Mercury. Besides that, the *Mercury* had ceased publication prior to June 1775.

Nevertheless, the date of the supposed Declaration was declared a state holiday by the North Carolina legislature.

MEDICAL QUACKERY *phony cure-alls*

Every year Americans spend tens of billions of dollars on quack medical products and services that not only do not cure them but also frequently cause great harm. Why do we patronize quacks and look for quick cures for ailments? We do so for the same reason that people did it in ancient times: We want to believe in miracles. And we want shortcuts. We like to have devices that get us to lose weight while we are resting or even asleep. And hundreds of health and exercise fakers have all sorts of aids to provide this impossible result. And if we have cancer, we want our hopes raised and the treatment without pain— so why not go to those quacks who play records and tell us that the musical vibrations will make cancer dance away.

If we have arthritis we can try any of the following quack-hawked treatments: (1) sitting in an abandoned uranium mine; (2) gulping down Dr. Fenby's Formula X; (3) swilling a dose of "Chuei-Fong-Tou-Geu-Wan"; (4) wearing a Vryllium tube on your lapel; (5) burying ourselves up to the neck in horse manure.

With these and other zany treatments, arthritis quacks trim credulous victims for over $2 billion a year. But no matter what they propose, they will come up with nothing in a way of a cure for arthritis. There is none.

Quacks do more than rob people of money. They are in the business of stealing their health away. They take lives. When quacks hook the seriously and often desperately ill, such as cancer victims, on a phony cure, they are keeping them from seeking real medical help, and the illness progresses, sometimes past the treatable stage.

People in pain tend to believe what they want to hear, that some new and exotic discovery can cure our most troublesome medical problems. We can eat all we want and still lose weight, or we can buy an electric rolling pin that melts away fat. We can grow taller or develop a bigger bustline. Baldness, aging, arthritis, rheumatism, impotence and cancer are easily cured.

Quacks offer a smorgasbord of miracle devices or treatment cure-alls, which can simultaneously handle a half-dozen or more ailments. A plug-in vibrating cushion takes care of both arthritis and varicose veins. There's the "radon ball," which attaches to a water faucet and makes drinking water a cure for cancer, dandruff and sometimes even cataracts (but no guarantee on this one, as the operators say it does not work for everyone). If one's body tissues are ravaged by any of several diseases, there's a treatment offered by a "painless doctor" who uses a steel ball, which is allegedly charged with 150 million volts of electricity and works like an atom smasher to clean out problem body spots. But perhaps it is more modern than the cancer quack who rubs ointment on a patient's lesions, the same stuff used in the last century on horses.

Certainly one of the grandest miracle devices of all was the "Zerret Applicator," which consisted of two celluloid cylinders joined together. The quacks behind this masterpiece declared it would expand the hydrogen atoms present in the human body and cure every known disease. It was a real bargain at a mere $50, until analysis of the device showed that it was filled with cotton saturated with ordinary tap water.

Most quack products are easy for the discerning to spot, such as the magic pills that allegedly keep you young forever. But the old-style snake-oil salesmen are quick to pounce on current thinking. Some of their products are vaguely based on some medical report that you may have heard about in the news.

The Food and Drug Administration offers an "it-sounds-too-good-to-be-true" test to detect the common phrasing in ads for quack products:

- A quick and painless cure
- A "special," "secret," "ancient" or "foreign" formula, available only through the mail and only from one supplier
- Testimonials or case histories from satisfied users as the only proof that the product works
- A single product effective for a wide variety of ailments
- A scientific "breakthrough" or "miracle cure" that has been held back or overlooked by the medical community

Before patients buy into a suspect or unusual product or treatment, they should find out more about it. Checks should be made with a doctor, pharmacist or other health professional; the Better Business Bureau; the local consumer office; the state attorney general's office; the Federal Trade Commission; the nearest office of the Food and Drug Administration; and the postmaster or the Postal Inspection Service.

See also ARTHRITIS CURE CONS; CANCER CURE CONS; HEIGHT-STRETCHING CONS; OZONE QUACKS; SAFETY MILK; SEAWATER SWINDLES; SEX REJUVENATOR AIDS; URANIUM QUACKERY; WEIGHT AND FITNESS CONS.

MENCKEN'S BATHTUB HOAX *immortal fakery*

Probably no journalistic hoax of the 20th century has had its spurious facts more totally accepted by the greatest number of people than Henry L. Mencken's article on America's original bathtub. Writing in the *New York Evening Mail* on December 28, 1917—the supposed 75th anniversary of the event—Mencken (1880–1956) informed his readers that the nation's first bathtub had been "purchased by Adam Thompson and installed in Cincinnati in 1842."

Mencken's story was accepted at face value because the satirist had long mastered the secret of the journalistic hoax: the use of convincing detail. According to Mencken, Thompson—a wealthy grain and cotton trader—considered he was doing a great good and promoting the public health only to be shocked at the hostility provoked by his act. The medical world denounced the bathtub as a menace to health. The *Western Medical Repository* was quoted by Mencken as warning that the bathtub "softens the moral fibre of the Republic." Boston passed an ordinance prohibiting its use except with the advice of a doctor. The Philadelphia City Council tried to pass a law forbidding its use in winter, a move that lost by a mere two votes. Virginia levied a $30 tax on bathtub installations. Providence, Rhode Island, Wilmington, Delaware and Hartford, Connecticut, put extra charges on the use of water in such wicked contraptions.

Despite these oppositions, Mencken related, Millard Fillmore had the first White House bathtub installed and took the first presidential bath. This act of political courage (Fillmore was never accused of making many of them) finally made it apparent that the bathtub could not be relegated to oblivion, and the great American institution of the Saturday night bath gained momentum.

Mencken's history of the bathtub was accepted as fact for many years, even after Mencken himself stated that the story was a "tissue of absurdities, all of them deliberate and obvious." In 1926 Mencken said of his celebrated hoax, "My motive was simply to have some

harmless fun in war days. It never occurred to me that it would be taken seriously."

Nevertheless, it was taken so seriously that noted reference books and serious magazines and journals unhesitatingly and faithfully repeated Mencken's nonsense. A Harvard professor used the Mencken "facts" to advance his thesis on rats and lice. In the 1950s John Hersey reported that President Harry Truman "seemed reluctant to let go of his belief" that Millard Fillmore introduced the first bathtub in the White House in 1850. Truman could be counted on to report the absurd story in lecture tours he gave distinguished visitors to the White House. And, in 1990, a New York television news program noted the 140th anniversary of the Fillmore bathtub.

MENELEK II, EMPEROR OF ETHIOPIA See ELECTRIC CHAIR IMMUNITY.

MEN FROM MARS PANIC *Orson Welles' radio scare*

- In Pittsburgh, Pennsylvania, a man came home to find his wife about to take poison. "I'd rather die this way than like that!" she screamed.
- In Hillside, New Jersey, a frantic man dashed into the police station and begged for a gas mask as protection against "the terrible people spraying liquid gas all over the Jersey Meadows."
- In New York City the Dixie Bus Terminal in Manhattan was jammed with people who wanted to board a bus heading anywhere—away from impending doom.
- In Indianapolis a woman rushed into a crowded church, shouting hysterically, "New York is destroyed—it's the end of the world! You might as well go home to die. I just heard it on the radio!"
- In San Francisco, volunteers poured into the local army headquarters, ready to take up combat with the awful menace.
- In Birmingham, Alabama, people flocked to the churches in prayer.
- On the campus of a southeastern college, girls in sorority houses and dormatories weeped in each other's arms, separating themselves only to take turns at making long distance calls to their parents to say goodbye for what they thought would be the last time.

Such were some of the panicked results of the famous "Men from Mars" broadcast of Orson Welles' Mercury Theater, a dramatization of H. G. Wells' *War of the Worlds,* aired appropriately enough the night before Halloween, 1938. No radio broadcast ever produced as much panic in America as this program, which ironically was almost not aired.

Most of Orson Welles' (1915–1985) radio colleagues argued against doing the story, calling it "too fantastic" and "just not believable." They didn't feel anyone would listen, since the drama series was garnering small ratings as it was; the week before the Crossley ratings were 3.6 of the listening audience compared to 34.7 for Edgar Bergen-Charlie McCarthy.

Despite the dissents, genius Welles pushed for airing Howard Koch's adaptation of the 1898 science fiction masterpiece about a Martian attack on the Earth, with updating radio bulletins from the scene, which was switched in the radio program from England to New Jersey.

The show went on, and Welles carefully explained the premise at the beginning of the program. Apparently, a lot of listeners paid no attention, were swept up with the hysteria of the moment or tuned in late. Particularly adding to the panic was that the Bergen show went into the doldrums at 8:12 P.M. when a not-too-popular singer went on. An estimated 13% of the Charlie McCarthy fans started twirling their dials. They stopped twirling when they hit CBS and listened to the scariest news bulletins they'd ever heard:

"Flash! Meteor reported landing near Grover's Mill, New Jersey. . . . Fifteen hundred killed. . . . No, it's not a meteor—it's a flying metallic cylinder. . . . Poison gas is sweeping over New Jersey. . . . The invaders are flying over the nation, raining bombs. . . . The Martians are using death rays."

The hysteria was in full force before the hour-long broadcast was half over. The bravest of the listeners seized shotguns and rifles and stood ready to do battle. But, for the most part, there was panic. Hospitals were jammed with people in shock; some even suffered heart attacks.

Those listeners who stayed tuned in for the second half-hour of the broadcast—who were not many compared to those who'd heard quite enough—listened to a faithful adaptation of the rest of Wells' original story. Humanity survived, as the invading Martians—never before exposed to microorganisms—all collapsed and died.

At 9:01 when the show was off the air, CBS was deluged with phone calls. Police swarmed into the studio and shunted the entire cast—plus producers, directors and technicians—into a safe studio where they were kept much of the night in protective custody while authorities tried to calm enraged citizens and measure the extent of the disaster. By early morning they were released with no charges brought against them.

Much of the hysteria had subsided by the following day, leaving in its wake a nation of irate and

Orson Welles' 1938 dramatization of H. G. Wells' *War of the Worlds* caused the greatest panic in radio history.

embarrassed listeners. One angry midwestern mayor—his streets having been choked with mobs—threatened to come to New York to personally punch Orson Welles in the nose. Welles prudently went into semi-seclusion.

Later, the Columbia Broadcasting System issued a public apology. The Federal Communications Commission held some hearings, called the broadcast "regrettable" and passed some regulations.

Overall, newspaper and other commentators referred to the "incredible stupidity" and "gullibility" of the American public. Columnist Dorothy Thompson wrote, "Nothing about the broadcast was in the least credible . . . Mr. Orson Welles and his theater have made a greater contribution to an understanding of Hitlerism, Mussoliniism, Stalinism, anti-Semitism and all other terrorisms of our times than all the words about them that have been written by reasonable men.''

Ironically, the least-fooled members of the listening public were children. Many youngsters recognized the voice of Welles as one they frequently had heard in the role of ''The Shadow.'' To some observers it appeared that innocence was the most basic element of intelligence.

A great many suits were filed, but all were thrown out by the courts since there had been frequent announcements during the broadcast that it was a piece of fiction. Welles and his show did not suffer as a result. Within a few weeks Campbell Soups signed up and sponsored the Mercury Theater of the Air at a most lavish figure.

A more grim footnote was offered the following year in Quito, Ecuador, when a similar broadcast caused more deadly panic as listeners fled into the streets. When they found out it had been fiction, enraged residents burned down the radio station and a newspaper plant. Before order was restored, 21 people had been killed, including six of the show's participants.

MERMEN AND MERMAIDS *fake creations*

While tales of mermaids go back hundreds of years and art studies of such fabulous marine creatures, half-woman and half-fish, have appeared as sideshow exhibits since the 17th century, it was the ''merman'' who more often appeared as a three-dimensional curiosity in Western drawing rooms. The mermen appear to have been more a creation of Asian cultures; many of these audacious fakes originated in Japan. The mermen consisted of the dried parts of monkeys to which fish tails were attached on wooden cores. They were frequently given to Westerners as gifts. Thus the British Museum sports one donated by HRH Princess Arthur of Connaught, which was allegedly caught in Japan in the 1700s. It was given to Prince Arthur by a Japanese man named Seijiro Arisuye.

MEXICAN CHILDREN MASSACRE STORY *Hearst newspaper hoax*

Well before World War I and just before World War II U.S. newspaper publisher William Randolph Hearst consistently sought American intervention in Mexico. To this end Hearst filled his publications with all sorts of conspiracy and massacre horror stories about the savage conditions in that country.

Perhaps Hearst's most notorious effort was a report on December 22, 1913, published in his *New York American*, which told of a great number of children being driven into the water and shot by authorities. Published with the account was a photograph of a number of Mexican children with hands upraised, supposedly taken just as they were about to be shot.

The shocking report was believed until the English tourist who had taken the picture indignantly came forward to explain the children had been swimming peacefully and had raised their hands at the tourist's request so that he could get a better shot of them.

In fact, the photograph had not been taken in Mexico at all, but in British Honduras.

M.I.A. RACKETS *false prisoner of war reports*

The missing-in-action (M.I.A.) racket can be viewed as one of the most cynical and manipulative scams to come out of America's ill-fated Vietnam War. As the *New York Times* editorialized: ''Exploitation of the M.I.A. families' lingering hopes supports a cruel industry in the U.S. and Southeast Asia. Asians seeking money or favorable immigration treatment offer faked photos, dogtags and letters. American groups use such 'evidence' as the basis for publicity and fund appeals.''

A standard pitch works as follows: ''As you know, we are very close to bringing out a live P.O.W. But the monsoon season in Southeast Asia has just begun. Within the next twelve days, I must raise a minimum of $27,630.''

According to investigators, the racket has become so rewarding that Cambodians in the United States specialize in collecting M.I.A. background information from American families. This information is faxed to swindlers in Southeast Asia who recycle the data into M.I.A. documents and reports.

As of late 1991 the Pentagon listed 2,273 U.S. servicemen as missing in action in the conflict, and investigators have been inundated with 1,483 reports of their existence. Most reports were false or described Westerners who were not even military personnel. At that time only 103 cases were unresolved.

In 1991 there was a major flurry of activity because a photograph from a Southeast Asia source showed three men in a wooded setting holding a cryptic sign. The photo was supposedly of three American fliers long given up for dead, and they were identified by anxious relatives as the three fliers. But government investigators came up with persuasive doubts about the photo's authenticity. There were several aspects of the photo suggesting fakery: the scale, the awkward placement of the faces and a highly suspect sign allegedly dating the scene. The photo was accompanied by so-called biographical data sheets and letters in English that could be regarded only as amateurish fabrications.

While at the time the photo still was not proved to be 100% invalid, the hoax thesis was far more likely. Government investigators were sent to Cambodia to trace the origins of the photo and quickly discovered that the source of the picture had turned over three others that actually had been copied from a Soviet magazine. These photos, supposedly showing missing Americans, had been found in a January 1990 issue of the Soviet magazine *Sovyetskiy Soyuz*, meaning "Soviet Union." All the photos were of Russians.

Nevertheless, because of the photo flap the Pentagon decided to increase the number of people investigating reports of missing Vietnam War servicemen.

More cynical observers felt the Pentagon had been boxed into a corner because of a standing political hoax perpetrated by the U.S. government. Under what has become known as the "clean war syndrome," it was charged by some experts the military can never meet family requirements that the bodies of *all* dead servicemen should be produced. Consequently, the next of kin feel they have the right not to abandon hope that their relatives are still alive and being held "captive." The reality of modern warfare, certainly true in every American conflict since the Civil War, is that "missing in action" is often an euphemism for combatants who were "vaporized" so that there are no bodies to be found. Some see the failure to be explicit about this fact as a cruel hoax.

At least in part this lack of candor has been seen by some critics as setting the ground for continuing M.I.A. frauds. In December 1992 Senator John F. Kerry, chairman of the Select Committee on P.O.W.–M.I.A. affairs, condemned as "fraudulent" and "grotesque" some lucrative strategies used by fundraisers to exploit the hopes of families of missing or allegedly imprisoned Americans. At hearings one direct-mail specialist testified that of $1.9 million he had raised, his fees of almost 18% of all expenditures and production costs used up all but $200,000.

A typical direct-mail appeal sent out by another firm made an emotional appeal that purported to have been written on the deck of a ship in the China Sea. The letter said, "Just today, I heard one more heart-rending account of an American serviceman being held captive by Communists in Vietnam."

Senator John McCain, Republican of Arizona, who was a prisoner of war in Vietnam, said, "Sadly, the publicity attending this issue has been a powerful attraction for far too many scoundrels. They have preyed on the anguish of families, and helped to turn an issue which should unite all Americans into an issue that often divides us."

MICHELANGELO *art forger*

As many of the biographers of Michelangelo (1475–1564) have noted, the great master himself started off his career as an art forger. As an apprentice at the studio of Domenico Ghirlandajo, young Michelangelo copied the drawing of a head that was given to him. His facsimile was so well drawn that Michelangelo could not resist keeping the original and turning over the copy.

Michelangelo would have gotten away with this dishonest caper had he not suffered a loose tongue and boasted about it to a friend. In time the owner of the original heard of it and hurried to Ghirlandajo's studio to determine the truth. It turned out that neither the owner nor others present at the studio were able to tell the difference between the two drawings; Michelangelo had given his work the appearance of age by exposing it to smoke. "As a result of this" skillful forgery and numerous others, says Condivi, Michelangelo's contemporary biographer, "he gained a great reputation."

Some biographers insist that Michelangelo was driven more by disgust at the critics' incessant praise of all things classical and acted more out of protest; but in the process he most certainly turned many a dishonest ducat. At the instigation of Lorenzo de' Medici, Michelangelo palmed off a marble Sleeping Cupid on Raffaello Riario, Cardinal di San Giorgio, as a genuine antique. To protect himself from legal retribution, Michelangelo carved his initials under one of the statue's wings. Through de' Medici the Cupid was passed on to an unscrupulous art dealer named Baldassare in Rome who paid 30 ducats for the bogus work. It turned out that the cardinal was gouged for 200 ducats for it. Through informers the cardinal grew suspicious that he had been conned, and finally demanded that his money be refunded. In the process, Michelangelo learned he himself had been shorted 170 ducats.

Even though Baldassare refused to return the statue to Michelangelo, he also refused to up his payment above the original fee, insisting that it was handsome enough pay for a young artist. Apparently this experience did much to convince Michelangelo that there more fame and fortune awaited him doing his own original masterpieces.

MILES, LOUISA See RENTED FLAT SCAMS.

Left: Lorenzo de' Medici, who instigated the young Michelangelo into forgery. Right: The marble *Sleeping Cupid* **Michelangelo sold to Cardinal di San Giorgio as a genuine antique.**

MILK BOTTLE CARNIVAL SCAM

"Milk Bottle Toss" is probably the most enduring scam on the crooked carnival circuit. It is offered not only at carnivals, but also at fairs, amusement parks, seaside resorts, etc. It also cannot be beaten—unless the operator wants that to happen to a player or two as a way to induce others to play. Quite often the successful pitcher is a "shill" or worker at other concessions.

The object of the game is not merely to knock the wooden bottles down, but to completely send them off their pedestals. They are set up in pyramid form of three on the bottom, two above and one over that. Unfortunately, not even a professional pitcher such as Dwight Gooden or Nolan Ryan would stand much chance of success. A bottle that is lead-weighted on the bottom will be knocked over, but will seldom tumble off the pedestal.

Somehow, however, the operator is able to lob baseballs at the bottles and properly tumble them. This demonstration is all part of the pitch, and is easy to do, since only three of the bottles are lead-weighted. When the operator wants to demonstrate how easily he or a shill can do it, he simply stacks the lead-weighted bottles on the upper two layers of the pyramid. With one hit they go flying off the ped-

estal. When the victim goes, the lead-weighted bottles are set on the bottom layer and usually need three direct hits to be dislodged.

MILLER, WILLIAM F. "520%" *swindler*

When the notorious con man Charles Ponzi (see entry) was at last exposed for his rob-Peter-to-pay-Paul swindle in the 1920s, one journalist was given to speculate on a man who "wherever he is he is probably the world's most angry man. He knows Ponzi to be a thief—but twice over, for not only did he steal from his victims but he stole [this man's] technique. And there is no wrath to compare with that of a criminal 'genius' whose ideas have been purloined."

The writer was referring to one William F. Miller (1874–?) who, in 1898, was a 24-year-old Brooklyn, New York, bookkeeper; he became one of the most remarkable swindlers this country ever produced. Charles Ponzi had appropriated William "520%" Miller's modus operandi. This hardly means that Miller invented the robbing-Peter-to-pay-Paul scheme; but he carried it out in a way never before witnessed in America. By 1899, in a dazzling display of flamboyant activities, Miller suckered investors out of at least $1 million and possibly $2 million in an era when a million dollars was really a million and an excellent seven-course restaurant meal went for less than a dollar.

Miller had slaved away as an insignificant bookkeeper since his high school days. He tried in vain to achieve a fortune by playing the stock market for small amounts, so small and yet so large for Miller that he had to borrow sums—in the mere hundreds—from friends. But Miller had a fine reputation, since he always repaid his debts. That was one lesson Miller had learned of Wall Street's machinations. One can develop a fine credit rating by borrowing small and repaying the debt simply by borrowing slightly more elsewhere.

One day a sign appeared in his home window:

WM. F. MILLER
Investments
The way to wealth is as plain as
the road to market—B. Franklin

While Ben Franklin was noted for his words of wisdom in his *Poor Richard's Almanack,* he was not known for any endorsement of a Peter-to-Paul concept.

When Miller showed up at the adult Bible class that he taught at the local church, everyone had seen the sign and inquired about it. He explained to the people that he had learned the secrets of Wall Street. He commented, "It's not fair that the Morgans and the Goulds and the Vanderbilts are making so many millions when us little people are making so little—and I've decided to do something about it."

A few interested souls inquired what return they could expect on their investments. Miller said they could get 10%. "Ten percent," one of the flock noted with enthusiasm, "that's four-five times what the banks pay."

"You don't understand," Miller responded. "I don't mean ten percent a year. I mean ten percent a week."

"That's 520 percent a year!" one parishioner exclaimed.

Miller modestly allowed that it was, which was enough to make many of the members of the Bible class invest right on the spot. Miller held up his hand. "I'll accept no investments on the Sabbath."

On Monday evening, when Miller returned from a dull day at the office, he found a line of investors waiting outside his home. Many were eager but had only tiny sums, as little as $10. Miller nodded approvingly. "Caution is the byword in high finance," he said. "Always test the water before diving in."

Sure enough, after one week every investor got back 10% on his original investment; more correctly, the operating word should have been "of" rather than "on." The same thing happened seven days later and

continued for several weeks. Once the interest payments came spewing forth, the faithful began adding to their investments and plowing back their interest as well. Others, not in on the ground floor, eagerly threw money at Miller.

Soon the young bookkeeper's fame spread far beyond his Brooklyn neighborhood. He was no bookkeeper anymore; he was the financial wizard of the age. In 11 incredible months Miller garnered a fortune. The exact amount is unknown, since his records were a true bookkeeper's nightmare, coded in many strange ways. He suddenly lived a very lavish life and, by some accounts, had salted away $480,000—or was it twice or three times as much? No one could be sure, but it is known that in one month alone in 1899 his profits amounted to $430,000.

As the money poured in, the strain on Miller also increased, and he himself became ripe for a con. It was said that a notorious fixer named T. Edward Schlesinger was the first to figure out Miller's scheme and approached him with a way to keep the law off his neck. Miller was very interested and eagerly turned over about $240,000 for protection. Schlesinger immediately took a fast boat for Europe and finished out his years in pleasure spots such as Baden Baden and the French Riviera.

That sad experience did not temper Miller's judgment, and he soon fell victim again, this time to a slick but unethical lawyer named Robert Ammon. Miller explained to the lawyer that the time was fast approaching when he could no longer make the interest payments. Ammon immediately wanted to know how much was still in the till. Miller clearly understated $240,000 to the lawyer. Ammon thought it best that Miller leave the country. He also suggested he turn over the $240,000 to him "because if you are caught and have the money in your possession, it would be proof of your guilt."

Miller skipped to Canada after getting Ammon's pledge to send money to him whenever he needed it. Ammon never sent a dime. Miller was eventually apprehended and sent to prison for 10 years, a sentence many of his victims found intolerably low. Miller actually did less time than that. The authorities had long wanted to nail Ammon, and Miller gladly told them what they wanted to know. Ammon screamed that Miller had given him nowhere near $240,000, but he was sent to prison in 1907, the year Miller was freed.

Miller returned to Brooklyn and got another job as a bookkeeper. He often mumbled something about planning to open a grocery store. Then, like the half-million to a million dollars still missing from his fabulous swindle, Miller packed up and disappeared. Even some of Miller's most gullible suckers thought there might have been some kind of connection there.

MILLET-COROT ART FAKES   *mass-production forgeries*

In 1935 authorities uncovered art forgeries carried out on a mass-production basis by Jean Charles Millet and a confederate, Paul Cazeau (or Cazot). Millet was the grandson of Jean François Millet of the Barbizon School. Grandson Millet commissioned Cazeau to forge the name of the great painter on many works, which Millet then sold for huge sums. The swindle was first discovered by the London police. They notified their Paris colleagues, who finally tracked down Cazeau in his studio at Maison-Lafitte. He was occupied at the time on a bogus painting when the gendarmes poured into his studio.

Both young Millet and his forger were convicted. Millet, who had lived at the artists' colony at Barbizon like his grandfather, had become a millionaire through the forgeries. He admitted that every Millet painting at the Barbizon Museum was a forgery.

"You can sell anything to Americans and Englishmen," the grandson pleaded in his own defense. "They know nothing about art. Even their experts know nothing. All you have to do is ask a fabulous price."

For his part, Cazeau did much more than fake Millets, having been well into forging the works of landscape and figure painter Jean Baptiste Camille Corot. While he most certainly could not claim to have been the sole producer of Corot fakes, it is a fact that today there are far more phony Corots than originals. Of Corots, Dr. George de Cornell, director of the Fine Arts Guild of America, said, "out of 3,000 Corots 8,000 are in the United States and England—only Corot never painted 3,000 pictures." It is believed the genuine Corots probably total no more than 700.

MINA, LINO AMALIA ESPOS Y   *impostor turned murderer*

Few impostors inveigled their way into Philadelphia society as thoroughly as Lino Amalia Mina (1809–1832). The young Mina appeared in the city proclaiming himself the son of the Spanish governor of California and said he had been stranded without funds until the arrival of a clipper rounding the Cape. Social figures were much impressed and pleased to have such an important personage in their midst, and vied for offering him honor and shelter. Dr. and Mrs. William Chapman were considered to have scored a major social coup when young Mina accepted their proffered hospitality. Mrs. Lucretia Chapman was a very socially minded woman and was not above bragging of her victory over many other matrons of the city.

Within the Chapman household Mina seemed to establish himself as a sort of master; the servants felt he was simply used to his exercise of rank. They soon saw him kissing Mrs. Chapman many times, and the 41-year-old matron clearly showed no objections. If Dr. Chapman was aware of such goings-on, he exhibited no outward acknowledgment of the situation and, indeed, was always most solicitous of his important guest.

Unfortunately, Mina's status was not sustainable for the long term, since there was no clipper coming from California, a fact that his host and the rest of society would note in time. But for the present Mina was much sought-after for social engagements, all of which he fulfilled with considerable grace. Mina did engage in some dubious practices as well, such as patronizing a Philadelphia pharmacy and purchasing a large amount of arsenic for "stuffing birds." A few days later, Dr. Chapman suddenly became ill and died. If that development put Mina's presence in the household in a peculiar position, the situation was resolved two weeks after the funeral when Mina and the widow Chapman traveled to New York and were married. Upon the couple's return to Philadelphia, events took a Hitchcockian turn when valuables and jewelry in the mansion started to disappear. Mina started vacating certain bank assets, and thought nothing of posing as Dr. Chapman to complete certain financial dealings that put the deceased's estate in a more liquid form.

Such matters reached the attention of authorities, and an inquiry was made into Dr. Chapman's death. It was found that he had consumed a huge amount of arsenic. Both Mina and Lucretia were indicted for murder. The lady wept at the trial and insisted she knew nothing about what had transpired; she had been totally taken in by Mina, whose bogus identity had by then been established. A male jury accepted her story and acquitted her, while finding Mina guilty.

Philadelphia society turned out for Mina's hanging, not only because of the sensational nature of the case, but also, perhaps, because of the way the impostor had bamboozled the highest and the proudest.

MIND-READING HOAXES

There is nothing telepathic about the abilities of stage mind readers who astound audiences by answering revealing secrets about members of the audience. The various acts, practiced for centuries, rely on any of an estimated 200 signal systems that pass the information to the mind reader.

By far the most complete and effective system was developed by Mr. and Mrs. Julius Zancig around 1900 on the American vaudeville circuit. The Zancigs had an intricate code of about 500 innocent phrases and apparently normal gestures with which Zancig, standing in the aisle, could convey information to his wife on the stage. One of their favorite tricks was revealing the telephone number or address of a person in the audience as shown on a personal card or note. Zancig would pass on a telephone number to his wife as quickly as anyone could dial a telephone.

MINKOW, BARRY *wonder kid of finance*

Barry Minkow (1966–   ) has the distinction of being perhaps the youngest hustler who ever conned Wall Street. In 1982, when he was 16, Minkow started his own rug-cleaning business in his parents' garage in Reseda, California. He called it ZZZZ Best. He was a marvelous entrepreneur who convinced Wall Street that he had built a tiny company into a financial giant. In retrospect, Barry's record might have been a little more impressive if his business had actually made a dime.

Daniel Akst, his biographer, said, "There was always a quality about Barry that suggested he held an MBA from the Dada School of Business."

His business methods to get capital had no restraints. He staged burglaries to collect insurance. He borrowed $2,000 from his grandmother and then stole her pearls for good measure. In 1984 he forged $13,000 worth of money orders from a liquor store.

ZZZZ Best prospered by such methods. By 1985 Barry hit on a lush source of income, opening up a merchant's account at a local bank, thus allowing him to take credit card payments. Whenever he needed money, he added bogus charges to customers' credit card accounts and got cash from the bank. If a customer noticed and complained, Barry ranted about forgeries by crooked employees, made refunds and then simply took from other accounts.

Since Barry wanted to eventually float stock in his company, he set up another firm called Interstate Appraisal Services. This company was headed up by a weirdo friend who collected guns and had a special fondness for Hitler and SS jewelry. Interstate's only activities were confirming ZZZZ Best's job contracts, which allegedly included large orders from insurance companies to repair fire-and-water damage in large buildings.

The phony revenues convinced banks and investors to put money into ZZZZ Best. Actually Barry's scheme was now little more than the classic Ponzi ploy. Those who got in early reaped wonderful returns, which were of course provided by the investments of those who hopped on the bandwagon a bit later.

As late as 1986 nobody had actually seen a site where any of ZZZZ Best's work had taken place. Barry blandly explained that such information was confidential. Finally, an auditor for Ernst & Whitney insisted he'd have to see a site. Barry and his aides thus leased office space and put up signs indicating that ZZZZ Best was doing work on the premises. The actual work was handled by an outside contrac-

tor who was paid a big bonus to do the work. The act was successful.

Barry enjoyed a massive success. He was favored by lavish newspaper stories, indulged on the Oprah Winfrey show and just about ready to make a smash entrance on Wall Street. He lived in high style with all the trappings of a successful young millionaire and then some. Fostering an apparent smoldering hatred for his parents, he put them on the ZZZZ Best payroll just so he could have the pleasure of threatening to dismiss them. Always a believer in the fix, he coached a girls' softball team and passed out up to $100 a piece to spectators to cheer for his team.

Barry negotiated with the securities firm of Rooney, Pace (a company that would go defunct) to take his company public, so that he could start trimming thousands of small investors who saw him as epitomizing the American Dream. In December 1986 ZZZZ Best stock made its debut on Wall Street, and Barry got a hero's welcome. By the following March the shares were worth $64 million; a month later $100 million. At its peak ZZZZ Best commanded a stock market valuation of $200 million—with no actual value. Eventually its assets would be auctioned off for $64,000.

Oddly, it was Barry's credit card frauds, not the nonexistent fire-and-water job revenues, that were exposed. Biographer Akst, a former reporter for the *Los Angeles Times* and the *Wall Street Journal*, had originally been conned by Minkow and wrote a flattering article in 1985, which helped establish the myth of Barry's acumen. On May 22, 1987, he uncovered the credit card skulduggery with the following story headline: "Behind 'Whiz Kid' Is a Trail of False Credit-Card Billings." The next day ZZZZ Best stock fell 28% and continued plummeting straight down to nowhere. In December 1988 Barry Minkow was convicted of 57 counts of fraud and sentenced to 25 years in prison. *Barron's,* the financial weekly, stated: "ZZZZ Best had earned a chapter in the long history of financial scams written by the 'Eighties.'"

MIRACLE OF LÜBECK *forged Gothic frescoes*

It was a glorious miracle coming out of World War II. The Marienkirche (St. Mary's Church) in Lübeck had been destroyed by bombings in 1942. Amazingly, the ruined walls revealed the remains of Gothic frescoes. It had been decided that an artist named Lothar Malskat and a restorer named Dietrich Fey would restore the work in the church. Malskat and Fey completed their task in 1951 when the church was reopened for worship.

The sight was one of magnificent inspiration, with 36 figures of saints all 10 feet high and positioned 60 feet up the nave. The figures of the choir were Romanesque, dating from 1275 while those in the nave were Gothic dating from 1337. Worshippers and sightseers flocked to see "the miracle of Lübeck." The public was unaware that a contentious relationship had developed between Malskat and Fey, with the artist Malskat being irritated by the fact that most of the income had gone to Fey. They continued working on their renovations for another year without Malskat receiving financial satisfaction. It was then that he made a stunning announcement. The true miracle at Lübeck was not the brilliant frescoes, but rather that they had not been unmasked as frauds.

Malskat had painted all the frescoes, using numerous historical figures such as Ghengis Khan and Rasputin as models. He also utilized a great many modern German starlets, one of whom served as the model for the Virgin Mary.

The two renovators were brought to trial in mid-1954, and experts testified that a detailed inspection of the frescoes and choir work made it obvious they all were fakes. As for the original frescoes uncovered by the crumbling walls in 1942, none had survived the several subsequent winters before the restoration work began.

It was also found that Malskat and Fey had marketed some 600 pictures supposedly done by great masters. Malskat, capable of painting in no less than 70 different styles, had faked van Gogh, Cezanne, Degas, Renoir, Grosz, Matisse, Pissarro, Rembrandt, Gauguin, Utrillo, Lautrec and dozens of other painters. Fey had sold a majority of the works to art dealers, most of whom were gullible but others astute and equally greedy.

In January 1955 Malskat and Fey were found guilty of their Lübeck deception, and both were sent to prison; Malskat served 18 months, while Fey did 20. Both were officially banned from doing any church restoration work for three years.

MISSING LINK   *P. T. Barnum's version*

With the publication of Charles Darwin's *Origin of Species* in 1859 the American public's interest in the theory of evolution became enormous, and there was much speculation about the "missing link" between man and ape. This proved no problem at all for that audacious showman, P. T. Barnum, who immediately trotted out his version of the exotic species. Barnum dubbed his specimen "Zip, the What-is-it?"

"Zip, the What-is-it?" was actually a black man who proved as intelligent as the old black woman Joice Heth (see entry), whom Barnum had foisted on the public as "Washington's 161-year-old nurse." Joice Heth was glib and entranced people with her witty dialogue. Zip—one William Henry Jackson (d. 1926)—was just as witty and sharp but had to carry off his acts with grunts, groans and wheezes. Jackson fit his role, since he had the ill luck to have been born with a bizarre deformed skull shaped as a cone and only about two inches in diameter at the crown.

Barnum presented Zip as the missing link and advertised him as having been caught by accident by hunters in Africa searching for gorillas. Zip put on a magnificent show for the humans, who considered themselves of a higher mental order than him. Given cigars and coins, Zip ate or swallowed them whole and grunted for more. Remarkably, he had the ability to understand human talk, although he could not converse. Asked where he would go when he died, Zip pointed skyward. And where would a creature companion named South Sea Island Joe go on his demise? Zip pointed straight down. It was comforting to many that the concept of heaven and hell was not alien to this lower species.

Zip was exhibited at Barnum's American Museum until it was destroyed by fire. Thereafter he went with the Barnum circus and its successors, often leading a band and thus demonstrating how music soothed the savage beast. Actually, Zip was an uncommon man, one who enjoyed reading history and the classics; it was said that he greatly resented the impostor's role he had to play.

In 1924 Zip took part in an extravaganza to commemorate the demolition of the second Madison Square Garden in New York with a special tribute to P. T. Barnum and his most famous attractions. Actors were used to impersonate Jenny Lind, Tom Thumb and Barnum, but Zip appeared as himself. Zip continued in harness until 1926 when he died during the circus's New York engagement. He had been in show business for 84 years and was somewhere in his 90s. Shortly before dying, Zip told his sister, "Well, we fooled 'em a long time."

The "missing link" was buried in Bound Brook, New Jersey, where he had been born.

MISSISSIPPI AND SOUTH SEA BUBBLES

The Mississippi and South Sea "Bubbles" were but flip sides of the other, each selling New World dreams, the first in France and the second in England.

The idea for the Mississippi Bubble was conceived by a Scottish financial wizard named John Law, who founded the Banque Royale in Paris in 1716 to attempt to repay the enormous debts incurred by the wars of Louis XIV. Law then combined the bank with the Mississippi Company, which held title to huge tracts of land in North America, and convinced the French government to back his scheme. With the assistance of the French regent, Law soon had all of France in a frenzy, as the people—hearing about the

John Law concocted the Mississippi Company, which left French investors destitute when the bubble burst.

Company, which likewise took over a major part of England's national debt in exchange for a government-approved monopoly of trading with South America and the Pacific Islands.

But neither bubble could last long. When it finally started dawning on speculators that stories about the fabulous assets of the New World were nothing more than fables, they rushed to sell out. Overnight in 1720 the stock in the Mississippi company tumbled from a high 1,800 French livres to 400. It was even worse in England when the South Sea Company's stock collapsed from about £1,000 a share to £124.

Investors by the thousands in both countries were bankrupted. As Professor John Kenneth Galbraith of Harvard wrote in *The Age of Uncertainty*, "Parisians got what pleasure they could from a song that recommended that the paper be put to the most vulgar possible use."

With the popping of the South Sea Bubble, "bubble cards" appeared in Great Britain, chiding the gullible investors in the South Sea Company.

amazing riches of the new lands—snatched up Mississippi Company stock. Notes issued by the Banque Róyale were also snapped up by a public that believed the securities were backed by huge gold and silver sources in Louisiana. Frenchmen invested their entire savings in the glorious company that was to yield such fabulous riches. The national currency was inflated by Law, who as a national hero was put in charge of the nation's finances. It must be said that a few lucky investors, those who got in early and got out early, made as much as 36 times their investment.

Meanwhile, across the Channel, other promoters saw the "miracles" Law was pulling. They started their own bubble by selling shares in the South Sea

France itself tottered on the brink of ruin, while Law, disguised as a beggar, escaped certain lynching by fleeing the country. He died in abject poverty in Venice nine years later.

In England, after the South Sea Bubble burst, an investigation by the House of Commons revealed that at least three ministers had taken bribes and speculated in the stock. John Aislabie, the chancellor of the Exchequer, was expelled from the House and clapped in prison.

MODEL PHOTO BOOK SCAM *vanity con*

Various model photo books are printed constantly, but perhaps the most rewarding for the con men are books containing pictures of children. The books, parents are promised, will be supplied to movie and TV booking agencies and advertising agencies who are forever on the lookout for beautiful tots for models or even acting roles. The con artists even list scores of agencies, networks, movie studios and the like, which will be supplied copies. The sales pitch indicates that the tots are right on the edge of great financial success. The books often carry a price tag of $50, but this is reduced to $30 or $35 for families of tots featured. Naturally the doting family can be counted on to buy several copies for grandparents and other relatives.

These are the sales the con men aim for. But what about the copies sent to all the agencies? They have simply been dumped on these agencies, who in turn dump them in the trash as quickly as they come in.

MODERN WARFARE See HANSARD'S GUIDE TO REFRESHING SLEEP.

MONA LISA FAKES

The *Mona Lisa* by Leonardo da Vinci has been described as the portrait of the most-looked-at woman who ever lived. As such it has been the most lucrative of targets for art forgers, although the greatest crimes in this connection remain unsolved. Incredibly, one swindler managed to sell six copies of the famed portrait to a half-dozen gullible American art collectors in 1911–1912. All firmly believed they had the authentic painting.

In 1908 an international art swindler came to the United States and, using a variety of aliases, gained the confidence of a number of millionaire art collectors. Knowing the minds and morals of compulsive collectors, he had little trouble concluding secret deals with six of them, separately, to sell the Mona Lisa— if he could contrive to steal it from the Louvre Museum in Paris. He then commissioned a talented art forger to do six imitations of the painting and had them stored in New York.

Then, in 1911, the genuine *Mona Lisa* was stolen by Vincenzo Peruggia, an Italian who worked at the Louvre. He cut the precious painting from its gilt frame and smuggled it out of the museum under his coat. He got it to his apartment and hid it in the false bottom of a trunk, where it remained for two years. To this day crime experts are uncertain if Peruggia's act was part of the art swindler's plan or whether it happened most fortuitously while the swindler's plot was still afoot. In any event, the heralded robbery set the stage for the millionaires to be plucked for $2 million.

In the meantime, Peruggia took his treasure to Italy where he tried to sell the *Mona Lisa* for about $95,000. He was apprehended by Italian police who returned the 300-year-old masterpiece to France without a scratch. Brought to trial in Florence, Peruggia insisted his was a crime of patriotism; his only motive was to return the masterpiece to the land of its creator. Peruggia drew a relatively light sentence of one year and 15 days.

The art swindler himself was never caught, and in fact his grand scam was repeated a quarter of a century later when five more American millionaires were likewise conned out of an average of $300,000 apiece for imitations. They too believed they had gotten the original, while a copy had been smuggled into the Louvre to replace the genuine article. While there is no proof, many authorities have little doubt there are many other collectors who continue to secretly gloat that they have the real *Mona Lisa*.

MONEY-MAKING MACHINE *classic swindle*

On the face of it the "money-making machine" seems to be a scam that only a dolt could fall for. But the fact exists that many hard-headed business people have been victimized by the swindle, as well as less-educated people or recent immigrants awed and uncertain about the American Way. More highly informed people have become susceptible to the scam because of an awareness of the advances made in high-tech photocopying techniques; to the sophisticated, the very unsophisticated money machine swindle becomes thoroughly believable.

The success of the swindle is in its telling. The victim must be made to believe that the contraption can duplicate currency so exactly that not even an expert can spot it. The machine is even set to make one alteration in the bill it spews forth, the serial number. A special "scrambler" device slowly alters all the digits, but this is said to be a tedious process and as a result a bill can be reproduced once every six hours. This amounts to $80 a day in $20 bills (the recommended denomination) or $200 a day in $50 bills.

The con man demonstrates the machine by putting a plain piece of white paper on a tray inside the machine and closing it up. Then he places a genuine bill in another compartment of the machine. The con man and the potential victim stay with the machine the entire six hours so that it appears evident that the crook has not resorted to any deception. At the end of the waiting period the con man takes out the genuine bill and then opens the compartment that held the plain paper. In its place is a perfect bill, a seeming reproduction.

The victim is advised to take the bill to a nearby bank and change it. He finds that the teller accepts it without any problem. Sometimes a businessman-victim is told to take it directly to a bank officer and say he got it from a customer and was fearful it was counterfeit. The bank official will examine the bill and pronounce it genuine, sometimes adding with a laugh, "We'll take all of these you can get."

Now the victim is fired up about the machine, wanting to buy it. At first the con man appears loathe to sell it, but then he admits he is working on a new machine that will turn out bills in three hours. Under the circumstances he might be willing to sell, provided he got a good offer. Some victims have paid five-figure sums for the machine, and others have agreed to lease it for $50 a day plus a deposit for the machine. A California motel owner bought a machine on these terms for $3,000 down.

As soon as the deal is closed and the victim pays for the machine, the con man sets up the machine with a $20 bill and tells him to open it in six hours and then insert another blank paper. As a result, the swindler has a 12-hour head start before the victim discovers the machine doesn't work.

The secret to the money machine is the tray in which the plain paper is placed. As the operator closes the compartment holding the tray, he presses a pin that drops a false top, which holds a real bill that he previously planted. When the tray is opened, the real bill is what is retrieved, while the plain paper is concealed from view.

Money-making machines were common both in the United States and Great Britain in the 19th century and continued to be big business in the first half of the 20th century. One operator in America, the fabled "Count" Victor Lustig (see entry), is reputed to have made a million dollars from the device in the 1920s and 1930s before he was sent to prison.

Today police bunco experts estimate that the money machine scam is worked hundreds of times a year in this country. Among the victims are bankers, store owners, stockbrokers and other professionals, but it is generally assumed that most of these do not come forward to admit they were cheated and had conspired to counterfeit money.

One con man most unforgiving of money machine swindle victims was the notorious Yellow Kid Weil (see entry) who said of them: "He even admits that he had planned to counterfeit the currency of the United States. But in the eyes of the law, he is another victim of a con game. In my opinion, he should be made a party to a conspiracy to obtain money illegally. He should go on trial alongside the con man and be subject to the same punishment. The same should be true of anybody else who enters into a con man's scheme to get money dishonestly."

Of course, that was just the Yellow Kid's way of trying to silence his victims.

MONK, MARIA *anti-Catholic hoaxer*

In the 1830s no person in America did more to fuel Catholic-Protestant ill feelings than an incorrigible tart named Maria Monk (1817–1849). Her lies became a rallying point for American Protestants against what were considered to be the evils of popery and fanned the emotions that were later exploited by the Know-Nothings.

In January 1836 Maria arrived in New York with a Canadian clergyman, the Reverend W. K. Hoyt, who announced Maria had been nothing less than a sex-slave victim in the famous Hotel Dieu nunnery in Montreal. Actually, as Maria was later to state, she had met Hoyt upon making a street solicitation of the man of the cloth.

The pair sported what they claimed was the first draft of Maria's memoirs of her years as a novice and nun at the Hotel Dieu. When *The Awful Disclosures of Maria Monk* appeared it was to make some startling charges, including the claim that the cellar of the nunnery was strewn with the bones of nuns who had resisted the advances of amorous priests. She said the nunnery was invaded nightly by priests coming through subterranean passages from a nearby monastery. When Maria arrived in New York, she also had in tow a babe who she claimed had been a love child born of these sexual escapades. Canadian authorities later determined that the father of Maria's baby was a Montreal policeman.

Maria and Hoyt found a fertile field for their charges in the Society for the Diffusion of Christian Knowledge headed by Dr. W. C. Brownlee. Brownlee was the pastor of the Collegiate Dutch Reformed Church and author of a best-selling anti-Catholic work, *Popery*. Brownlee saw to it that the Monk epic was published and that Maria herself had safe refuge under his roof. This proved rather upsetting to the Reverend Mr. Hoyt who now considered Maria a "damned jilting jade."

One can readily see Hoyt's displeasure at losing control of Maria Monk, since in almost no time at all her book sold 20,000 copies, an immense figure for the day. The Monk book offered plenty of torrid reading for anti-papists. It should have, since in final manuscript form the lies of Monk and Hoyt were further larded by one Theodore Dwight, a virulent anti-Catholic. Dwight, a master of languages, greatly embellished the charges of Catholic misdeeds by borrowing heavily from Italian, French and German works on both convents and torture. Maria was so taken by Dwight's contributions that she offered to elope with him in gratitude.

Maria's anti-Catholic readers were equally impressed by accounts of one nun's punishment for some minor infraction by being stretched out on a mattress

> with her face upwards, and then bound with cords so that she could not move. In an instant, another bed [mattress] was thrown upon her. One of the priests, named Bonin, sprang like a fury first upon it with all his force. He was speedily followed by the nuns until there were as many on the bed as could find room, and all did what they could do, not only to smother, but to bruise her. Some stood and jumped upon the poor girl with the feet: and others, in different ways, seemed to seek how they might beat the breath out of her body. After the lapse of fifteen or twenty minutes, Father Bonin and the nuns ceased to trample on her and stepped from the bed. They then began to laugh.

Maria's gasping readers no doubt agreed with her that "speedy death can be no great calamity to those who lead the lives of nuns." And they were equally impressed by her offer to visit the Hotel Dieu "with some impartial ladies and gentlemen, that they may compare my account with the interior parts of the building, and if they do not find my description true, then discard me as an impostor."

Had that challenge been taken up at once, the Maria Monk hoax would have ended quickly since the girl had never been in the Hotel in her life. Not that doubts didn't develop among her supporters. They were shaken when her mother in Montreal denounced her as a wastrel and said she'd never entered a nunnery. And Maria's mother added that in 1835 the Reverend Mr. Hoyt had offered her $500 to say that her daughter had been at the Hotel Dieu. Perhaps the man most shaken by all this was Dr. Brownlee. He may have been upset at the holes in Maria's story and the exposure of the contributions of "scribe" Dwight; but what really seems to have shattered him was the fact that Maria had in the meantime decamped with John J. L. Slocum, his young clergyman protege.

In 1836, Slocum, allegedly looking out for Maria's interests, filed suit against the publishers of the book for Maria's share of the royalties, all of which had been appropriated by the Society for the Diffusion of Christian Knowledge. In the subsequent trial it was decided that Maria was not entitled to anything, since her story had been a hoax.

This did not stop Slocum and Maria. In August 1837 Maria turned up at the home of one Dr. Sleigh, a Philadelphia clergyman, claiming she had been held captive by lecherous priests in a nearby convent. She said she had managed to get away by promising to marry one of the priests. Soon *Further Disclosures of Maria Monk* hit the book stalls. There were still enough people who wanted to believe Maria's diatribes, and the sequel did rather well. When the money started coming in, Slocum convinced Maria to give him the funds and sign over to him the rights to both publications. He would go to London, he said, to arrange for their foreign publication. Slocum did indeed do as he said, but that was the last Maria Monk heard of him.

Maria's life now was in decline. No one appeared to be interested in any more disclosures from her. Her looks gone by, Maria ended up on the Bowery pilfering for her livelihood. In early 1849 she went to jail for picking a man's pocket. Later that year she died at the age of 32. Her true identity was not realized for some time thereafter. The same oblivion did not befall *The Awful Disclosures of Maria Monk*; it is still being sold and is believed by many, with total sales estimated to be considerably more than 300,000 copies.

MOON HOAX *sightings of lunar life*

The astonishing "moon hoax," easily the greatest scientific fake in New York journalistic history, began with an announcement in Benjamin H. Day's *New York Sun* of August 21, 1835: "CELESTIAL DISCOVERIES. . . . We have just learned that Sir John Herschel has made discoveries of the most wonderful description by means of an immense telescope of an entirely new principle. Details are forthcoming." The announcement proved to be a grand understatement.

From August 25 through August 31, a series of daily installments were published, allegedly reprinted from the *Edinburgh Journal of Science*—a high-sounding publication, which incidentally did not exist. The series, running under the title "Great Astronomical Discoveries, Lately Made by Sir John Herschel, L.L.D., F.R.S. &c. at the Cape of Good Hope" astounded newspaper readers.

Herschel's telescope, an awesome contraption standing on 150-foot-high pillars and using a method of artificial light "transfusion," could magnify an object 42,000 times. Through this marvelously powerful telescope he discovered "wonderous secrets which had been hid from the eyes of all men that had lived since the birth of time." Some of the awesome sights: moon forests, an amethyst crystal almost 10 feet high—and life. There were goat-like animals with one horn, and something like a beaver that knew how to make fire.

And there were *people!* Sir John allegedly wrote of their first sighting:

> While gazing up these heights in a perspective of about half a mile we perceived three flocks of large winged creatures, wholly unlike any kind of bird, descend in a slow, even motion from the cliffs and alight on the plain. We changed to lens Hz, which brought them to apparent proximity of 80 yards. They were like human beings, for their wings had now disappeared, and their attitudes in walking was both erect and dignified. . . . The moon creatures average four feet in height; were covered, except on the face, with short and glossy copper-colored hair . . . their gesticulation, more particularly the varied actions of the hands and arms, appeared impassioned and emphatic.

Sir John said that as the scientists watched, "The three groups spread their wings and were lost in the dark confines of the woods before we had time to recover from our paralysing astonishment. We scientifically denominated them *Vespertilio Homo,* or man-bats. . . . They are doubtless innocent and happy creatures, notwithstanding some of their amusements would but ill comport with our terrestrial notions of decorum."

At this point the rival New York newspapers were forced to admit the *Sun* had scored the scoop of the century and blithely proceeded to pirate the reports, pretending to have access to the *Journal of Science* as well. But the *Sun's* circulation soared to 19,360, 2,000 more than even the *London Times*.

In the concluding article of the series, Sir John was quoted on the moon folk: "We had no opportunity to see them actually at work. So far as we could judge, they spend their happy hours in collecting fruits in the woods, eating through the skies, bathing and loitering about upon the summits of precipices."

If the public was impressed, scientists were not at all sure they could dismiss the reports. A committee from Yale hurried to New York to view the original articles, but the members were shunted between editorial offices and the print shop until the haggard scientists returned to New Haven. Meanwhile, men of God were very much impressed; one clergyman talked of finding a way to get the Gospel up to the moon folk. A theater did a land-office business exhibiting a huge canvas of moon scenes.

It was weeks before the hoax was exposed. A *Sun* reporter, Richard Adams Locke, ran into a colleague

This illustration was the most audacious element in the utterly absurd 1835 newspaper hoax of life on the moon. The caption in the *New York Sun* read: "Lunar animals and other objects, discovered by Sir John Herschel in his Observatory at the Cape of Good Hope and copied from sketches in the Edinburgh Journal of Science. For description, see pamphlet published at the Sun Office."

from the highly respectable *Journal of Commerce* in a taproom and was informed the *Journal* planned to put out the full reports in pamphlet form. Locke, a 35-year-old graduate of Cambridge, had come to New York after several publishing failures in his native England. Now, however, he was flying high, having seen his salary rise from $12 to $18 a week during the series. Locke was chagrined when informed of the *Journal's* plans and blurted out: "Don't go out on a limb. I wrote the whole thing myself."

The newsman raced back to his office and soon news accounts appeared saying the moon reports were a gigantic hoax. Nevertheless, publisher Day was able to brazen it out for some time since his rivals had themselves presented the reports as authentic. As a result the *Sun* continued to maintain its worldwide circulation lead.

And what about the great Sir John Herschel, all the while much occupied in charting the Southern skies with a telescope of his own construction in Cape Town and unaware of the furor going on in his name? When the articles finally reached him, he read them with considerable amusement and declared, as one account put it, "he could never hope to live up to the fame thus gratuitously heaped upon him."

MOORE, ANN   *the fasting woman of Tutbury*

It has been observed that the English have always been entranced with non-eaters and fasters who, as one old account put it, "ate not, slept not and voyded not." The problem that arises in evaluating such accounts is the lack of scientific investigation methods.

That discrepancy was avoided in 1813 in a study of Ann Moore, "the fasting woman of Tutbury."

Ann gave up eating, she said, simply because she couldn't stand it. Thus she stopped and noted no ill effects. On July 17, 1807, according to her and her family's account, she ate some black currants and then "gradually diminished her liquids" over the following months; subsequently she consumed nothing else.

Ann became the subject of a number of pamphlets. Many people speculated that she was able to live on air. But there were those who thought that Ann might be cheating. To clear up the matter a number of neighboring folk decided in September 1808 to keep watch on Mrs. Moore in nonstop four-hour watches over 16 consecutive days. At the end of that time Ann was in better health than when she started; she had demonstrated to the committee that she was not a fraud.

Although there were still some doubters, Ann took in a tidy fortune over the next few years. Then, in 1812, Dr. Alexander Henderson, physician to the Westminster General Dispensary, published a denunciation of Mrs. Moore. The non-eating lady's supporters quickly announced an agreement to a second and more scientific observation of their heroine. Ann herself did not appear enthused by the situation, but could do nothing but submit to the learned committee's investigation, which included Sir Oswald Mosely, the Reverend Leigh Richmond, a Dr. Fox and his son. The committee began its study on April 20, 1813, with a period of a month set for the test and one of the committee always in attendance in her room.

The committee decided to place the bed, with Mrs. Moore aboard, on a weighing machine; it soon developed she was losing weight steadily. Within nine days her life was ebbing away, and the learned men warned she would be bringing about her own death if she did not take food. Frightened, Ann Moore took nourishment and then confessed she had always taken sustenance during the years of her professed fasting. She revealed how she had deceived the first set of watchers in 1808. She had been fed by her daughter despite the presence of observers in the room. The girl had soaked towels in milk and broth and wrung the liquid into her mother's mouth while ostensibly washing her face. The daughter also kissed her mother frequently and passed food to her from her own mouth in the process.

MOORE, LESTER *phantom Boot Hill occupant*

It is recorded in every collection of graveyard epitaphs and humor. In fact, the well-kept grave and plank marker itself can still be seen in the Boot Hill Cemetery in Tombstone, Arizona. It reads:

Despite the charming doggerel, there is much reason to believe that no one lies buried in "Lester Moore's" grave.

HERE
LIES
LESTER MOORE
FOUR SLUGS
FROM A .44
NO LES
NO MORE

Alas, that is all we know about poor Lester. Who was he? Who killed him and when? How old was Lester? There are no answers to any of these questions.

There is one theory that a Wells Fargo guard plugged Lester, but historians have found no confirmation of such a tale in either official or other written record.

And what do Western historians think about Lester? One would be hard pressed to find any who take Lester very seriously. In *Wild and Wooly: An Encyclopedia of the Old West*, historian Denis McLoughlin opines that Lester Moore neither lived nor died, stating: "The aroma of the prankster emanates from this plot of ground, no date of death accompanies the verse, and had the latter originated during Tombstone's lead-swapping period, *'four* balls *from a .44'* would have been apt for the time.''

The matter could be resolved. Lester could be dug up, and the slug holes in him counted—if the body is even there. This could, however, put a fine tourist site in harm's way.

MOORE, ODIE   See INDIAN SWINDLES.

MORENO, ANTHONY   *greatest welfare cheat*
While welfare swindling is hardly an uncommon profession, there is little doubt that the greatest welfare cheat of all time was Anthony Moreno, a gypsy who bamboozled the French Social Security system out of millions of dollars in a nine-year career of audacious fraud. From 1960 to 1968 he deluged the Marseilles Social Security office with forged birth certificates and school registration forms and claims for benefits for 197 fictitious families and 3,000 children. By the time he decamped to his native Spain in mid-1968 he had become a gypsy folk-hero nicknamed *El Chorro,* or the Fountain, because of the limitless flow of funds he garnered—an estimated $6,440,000.

He was last reported living in luxury and free of extradition worries under Spanish law.

MORSE, CHARLES W.   *confidence man*
By any standards, Charles W. Morse (c. 1860–1942) was one of the most successful confidence operators ever to ''stick a mark.'' In fact, he stuck thousands for millions of dollars, using more than 100 different swindles. What was all the more remarkable was that he was convicted of a crime only once—when he was about 50 years old—and then managed to escape punishment through another con.

Convicted in 1910, he was sentenced to 15 years for working a complicated swindle on the Bank of North America. Two years later, government doctors discovered Morse was dying of Bright's disease; in an act of mercy President William Howard Taft granted the emaciated swindler a full presidential pardon. Then, to the astonishment of doctors, Morse lived happily ever after for another 30 years. The medical men learned to their chagrin that the resourceful con man had faked the deadly disease by drinking over a period of time a concoction composed mainly of different soaps.

MORTAR MICE MENACE   *home repair scam*
Nothing terrifies homeowners more than a report that termites are taking over their house. As a result, many homeowners overpay for termite treatments that do

little or no good. But the home repair swindler needs more than these little bugs to con homeowners with fears that their house is about to crumble down upon them at any moment. Thus they create nonexistent ''mortar mice.'' These awful little critters can do awesome damage to foundations and chimneys, to a point that they can crash into a heap of rubble and powder.

Before going ahead with any pest extermination service, one should contact a county agricultural agent who can identify which kind of pests, if any, are likely to be hiding in your woodwork and wallboard. They can also recommend efficient and *economical* ways to get rid of them.

MOTHER OF MANKIND HOAX
For several decades in the late 19th and early 20th century, thousands of Muslims trekked to a cemetery near Jedda, Arabia, to seek the advice of the ''Mother of Mankind.'' At the Tomb of Eve they deposited a coin in a slot and could ask Eve questions through a speaking tube. No one appears to have questioned why the Mother of Mankind needed a resting place that ran 500 feet long and 40 feet wide or how the language barrier was overcome.

By the time exasperated authorities ordered the mausoleum torn down in 1927, the woman who answered the questions from the underground chamber (which had a secret exit in the rear) retired with a fortune.

MOUSE GAME CARNIVAL GYP
Easily one of the most popular games on any carnival, county or street fair midway, the ''mouse game'' attracts bettors because it seemingly can't be fixed. A large revolving wheel is divided into sections, usually numbered from 1 to 60, with a small hole in each numbered section. The wheel man places a small mouse in the center of the horizontal wheel, covering him with a tin cup or can. The wheel is spun vigorously, and the wheelman removes the covering to liberate the mouse, who dizzyingly looks for a point of safety. The mouse finally ducks for one of the 60 holes. Any person—there can be more than one—who has bet on that number wins a substantial prize. In what must be considered a remarkable performance, the mouse never causes the game to take a big loss; it is as if he is a partner in the game.

Like most other carnival games, the mouse game produces easy profits when played honestly, but shady operators cannot resist tilting the odds much more in their favor. There is a mechanical gadget under the wheel that closes every other hole. The operator surveys the betting counter, and if he sees big money bet on odd numbers, he'll close these; if there is more bet on even numbers, he does the opposite. (Additionally, some layouts permit even-money betting on odd or even.)

Upon his release the mouse staggers toward a number, and if he finds the slot blocked, he simply reels onward toward another slot. This hardly arouses suspicion by the players. After all, what can you expect from a dizzy mouse?

MOXIE NERVE FOOD *snake oil remedy turned soft drink*

It started out as "Moxie Nerve Food" in 1884 in Lowell, Massachusetts, the brainchild of Dr. Augustin Thompson. Moxie was good for a lot of ailments but especially for "paralysis, softening of the brain, and mental imbecility." The good doctor named it after a certain Lieutenant Moxie who, while he had not been an officer in the U.S. Army, had been a West Point classmate of Thompson's. (It was irrelevant that Thompson had never gone to West Point himself.)

The intrepid Moxie had spent several years, said Thompson, exploring the mountains of South America near the Equator, or the Straits of Magellan, and somewhere in this vast expanse he had come across a mysterious food plant looking something like turnips or sugar cane. Learning of the plant's miraculous properties, the peerless lieutenant headed north, getting as far as Lower California where he died, leaving it to Thompson to acquire the trademark for Moxie.

In due course, Moxie lost its reputation as a medical cure. But by that time hardy New Englanders had developed quite a taste for it, and it became a favorite soft drink, which is all its real contents amounted to.

One might say that the outrageous Dr. Thompson certainly did, in fact, have a lot of moxie.

MOZART FORGERIES See NICOTRA, TOBIAS.

MULTIPLE BIRTH HOAXES *religious and secular prejudices*

For centuries folklore, fired by religious fervor, has produced an enormous number of multiple-birth hoaxes. The basis of these tales was the deep-rooted belief, without the slightest scientific foundation, that multiple births at best are signs of the immorality of the mother and at worst the work of the devil. Twins, such as the mythical Romulus and Remus, were believed to inevitably doom one or the other. Even today, there is the commonly held belief that twins are somehow less intelligent than other people—again with no scientific support—although it must be added that few twins other than Auguste and Jean Felix Piccard (of stratospheric flight and sea-diving fame) have achieved much renown.

The clergy and exponents of witchcraft have attributed fanciful multiple-births to foes. Religious leader Ann Hutchinson so offended the Puritan clergy with her emphasis of grace as opposed to the covenant of works that she was banished as a heretic in 1637 from Massachusetts Bay. She was accused of bringing forth "thirty monstrous births at once," declared the Reverend Samuel Clarke, one monster for each of her "monstrous heresies."

Certainly the most immoral mother of all, according to this thesis of wickedness, was Countess Margaret of Henneberg, Holland. Having offended the church, the countess was said to have refused alms to a poor widow with two babes in arm, and she finally drew down the wrath of God. On the Friday before Palm Sunday, 1276, the countess gave birth to 365 children "in bigness of all like newbred mice." Of these 182 were male and a like number female, with the leftover being a hermaphrodite. They were baptized in two basins by the Suffragan Bishop of Utrecht, who named all the males John and the females Elizabeth. The hermaphrodite's name is unknown. Happily (from the religious point of view) all of the children and their wicked mother died right after the baptism. For centuries thereafter no attack on the credibility of the tale was possible, since after all the two basins were still on display in the church at Loosduinen.

MUMMY FAKES *fresh corpse cure-alls*

The preserved corpses of ancient Egyptians—mummies—have through the centuries been used in quack cure-alls. By the 1100s "powdered mummy" was used in medicines for a whole range of ailments, but the supply had dried up by the late 1500s when the exporting of mummies became illegal. The result was a black market in which swindlers substituted the muscles from fresh corpses, packed them in asphalt and then pickled them for three or four months.

Medical science was thus presumably saved. Many Renaissance artists joined in the powdered mummy craze, adding the substance to their paint pigments in hope that the ancient embalming resins would keep their paintings from cracking. As late as the 1970s "powdered mummy" was sold in a New York pharmacy at a price of $40 an ounce.

MURPHY GAME *sex swindle*

As nearly as can be determined the Murphy Game—a blatant sex swindle—originated in the mid-19th century and was named after an engaging character named Murphy whose face and mannerisms inspired trust in the eyes of "good time Charlies."

In the purest form of the scam—which is still practiced today—the con man-"pimp" describes the delights of a young lady whom he "manages." Guiding the eager customer to the supposed sex rendezvous in an apartment house, the con man says he will have to collect the lady's fee so that she can't be arrested later for accepting money for services rendered. The victim hands over the fee and hurries up to a nonexistent apartment. By the time the victim gets back to the street, the Murphy man is long gone. One particularly profitable operation of this kind involved a blonde who was stationed in a cocktail lounge as a lure and whiled away her time until she was signaled by five confederates that they had each lined up a victim. Then she would leave and each sucker was led off in a different direction for their expensive nondates.

A switch on the Murphy Game is the so-called Key Game as practiced by bar girls in more notorious clubs who are forbidden to leave with customers for "dates." This racket started in San Francisco shortly after the 1906 earthquake, at a low dive named the Seattle Saloon and Dance Hall. The girls told would-be romeos that their boyfriends would be picking them up after work so that an assignation was impossible at that time. Instead, the girls would give the men the key to their place and say they would join them in about an hour. Of course, the girls had to be sure the men showed up and that if they did they would not steal the girls' belongings before they arrived. Thus a considerable sum of money would change hands. The customer would write down the girl's address, which, of course, was false. Some women at the Seattle sold as many as a dozen keys a night, and the practice spread to other dives on the Barbary Coast. As a result on any night, long after the dance halls closed, shadowy figures would be seen staggering through the streets, key in hand, trying to find a door the key would open. In time slumming parties were organized among San Franciscans who would proudly go down to the Barbary Coast to watch the travails of the "key men." Finally, however, the police had to stamp out the racket because of hundreds of complaints from householders harassed by drunks trying to unlock their doors.

These straight Murphy games continue, but the con artists have learned to switch the emphasis from sex to "stolen property," etc., instead, a racket generally called the $75 Sony Trinitron Swindle (see entry) today.

MUSHROOM RAISING CONS *home growing duds*

The eternal promise is made by hustlers peddling mushroom-growing schemes and equipment. "YOU CAN TURN YOUR CELLAR INTO A GOLD MINE," says one high-powered advertisement. Home-work promoters assure customers that mushroom spawns will set them up in a true, money-making, backyard or cellar business. Actually, mushrooms are very difficult to grow for the average person. Special shelters are required with very exact control of light, humidity and temperature. The right mushroom spawn is a very expensive item, and even if the spawn is brought to maturity, the little home grower will have to contend with the potent competition of mass-culture professionals. The gyp mushroom promoter sells cheaper spawns—the kind that are more expensive in the long run since they produce little or nothing.

MUSICA, PHILIP *impostor and swindler*

Had one Philip Musica ever been approached by *Who's Who in America* it would have made a most unusual entry, starting off somewhat as follows:

> MUSICA, Philip, importer, stool pigeon, swindler, forger, rumrunner, smuggler, bootlegger, gunrunner, hijacker, briber; b. Naples 1877; s. Antonio and Marie. . . .

Needless to say, the publishers of *Who's Who* would have rejected the entry. On the other hand, they had no difficulty at all accepting the following:

> COSTER, Frank Donald, corpn. official; b. Washington, D.C., May 12, 1884; s. Frank Donald and Marie (Girard) C.; Ph.D., U. of Heidelberg, 1909, M.D., 1911; m. Carol Jenkins Schiefflin, of Jamaica, L.I., N.Y., May 1, 1921. Practicing physician, N.Y. City, 1912–1914; pres. Girard & Co., Inc. (succession to Girard Chem. Co.), 1914–26; pres. McKesson & Robbins, drug mfrs., since 1926; also pres. McKesson & Robbins, Ltd.; dir. Bridgeport City Trust Co., Fairfield (Conn.) Trust Co. Methodist. Clubs: New York Yacht, Bankers, Lotos, Advertising (New York); University, Black Rock Yacht (Bridgeport); Brooklawn Country. Home: Fairfield, Conn. Office: McKesson & Robbins, Inc., Bridgeport, Conn.

Sadly, in the interests of truth, *Who's Who* would have been better advised to have rejected the Coster biography and accepted the Musica one. The Coster biography was a complete fiction, from the name on. In fact, Frank Donald Coster really was Philip Musica!

Philip Musica was born in Naples, Italy, in 1877 and came to America with his family six years later. By the time he was in his early 20s, Philip was the most Americanized of all the Musica children and the active head of the family. He kept informing Papa Antonio that this new country was nothing like the old, with entirely different ethical standards. In 1898 at Philip's behest he and his father set up an import company dealing in Italian foodstuffs. The firm was very profitable, especially since Philip forged bills of lading and invoices so as to greatly reduce the 50% import tax.

Philip also set up his father and a number of brothers and sisters in other dishonest schemes. Soon the family prospered so much that they occupied a mansion in the fashionable Bay Ridge section of Brooklyn, complete with landscaped grounds, horses, stables and a carriage house.

In 1909 Philip's house of cards suffered a setback when several customhouse weighers confessed they had taken bribes from Musica and *pere,* and the young Musica went to prison for 5½ months, shouldering all the blame personally.

When Musica got out of prison, he started a new enterprise making wigs from human hair imported from Italy. He secured large bank loans on shipments and bilked some 22 banks out of somewhere between $600,000 and $1 million through phony invoices. When boxes containing the supposedly highly desirable long hair were opened, investigators found tissue paper and short hair, worth a mere $1 a box and known in the field as "trash."

The entire Musica family fled but was captured in New Orleans after boarding a ship bound for Honduras. One of Musica's sisters tried to throw overboard the $18,000 she had hidden in her girdle. Philip Musica himself was carrying $80,000 in cash and a quarter of a million dollars in money certificates. Brought back to New York, Musica took all the blame personally and was lodged in the Tombs Prison. He was kept in New York because he convinced authorities it would be easier for him to effect restitution to the banks if he was in the city. There Musica gained favor with prosecutors by becoming a jail stoolpigeon, spying on other prisoners and aiding in their convictions. In 1918 grateful officials secured a suspended sentence for the swindler.

That was the last heard of Philip Musica. The man who turned up next was one "William Johnson" who was an "investigator" for the district attorney's office. Johnson's investigative career ended when he was indicted for perjury after testifying falsely in a murder case. William Johnson vanished.

By now Prohibition lay on the land, and one Frank Costa secured a permit to obtain 5,000 gallons of pure alcohol each month for his Adelphi Pharmaceutical Manufacturing Corporation to use in the production of hair tonics. Instead, the alcohol ended up as illegal booze. Eventually authorities got wise to Adelphi's racket and moved in. A number of officials were caught, but Frank Costa vanished.

In 1923 Costa became F. Donald Coster and was the president of Girard and Co., holder of yet another alcohol license. By this time Papa Musica was dead and Philip Musica-Coster was the head of the family. He gave his mother and sisters the family

name of Girard—all except one sister who "disgraced" Philip by eloping with a gardener. Girard and Co. also gained three new officials, "George Vernard," "George Dietrich" and "Robert Dietrich"—actually Musica's three brothers, Arthur, George and Robert. Through a companion company called W. W. Smith, Girard and Co. bootlegged millions of dollars worth of liquor.

Coster, more precisely "Dr. Coster," became a business tycoon and socialite. Graying and distinguished-looking, he was now an American-born Methodist and not an Italian Catholic. In 1926 he became a leading Wall Street figure with the acquisition of the 93-year-old drug firm of McKesson and Robbins. Obtaining loans to do so proved no problem because Girard and Co. was so highly profitable, although it was not known its revenues actually came from bootlegging.

Coster built McKesson and Robbins into a powerhouse firm with a string of additional acquisitions. The company looked extremely solid, but it was actually a hollow shell. McKesson was kept afloat with fake deals, inventories that were never checked by auditors, forged invoices, coupons and orders. More stocks were held in warehouses that did not exist. Even following the 1929 market crash, which destroyed many apparently solid firms, McKesson continued to thrive. Coster simply created a huge amount of nonexistent assets.

Coster kept his juggling act going until 1937, when the McKesson board, eager to shore up the company's cash, suggested that $2 million in drugs be sold. Coster could hardly do that since the drugs did not exist. It developed that was also true of some $21 million worth of drugs in five Canadian warehouses. In fact, the warehouses weren't there. Coster stalled as long as he could, but in December 1938 all trading in the firm's stock was halted by the New York Stock Exchange. Each of McKesson's 82 vice presidents shuddered, none more than George Vernard and George and Robert Dietrich. Coster himself remained calm as story after story appeared in the press about him. Inevitably, authorities started to check up on the past of F. Donald Coster.

On December 14, Coster was fingerprinted in his lavish home. Within 24 hours newspapers revealed the story of Coster, alias Philip Musica. On December 16 government agents arrived at the mansion to arrest Coster. He stepped into the bathroom and shot himself to death.

The master swindler left two notes. One was to his wife, asking her forgiveness. The other, eight pages long, attempted to justify his dealings.

According to Musica, McKesson would have collapsed several times in the early 1930s had he not doctored the paper profits. He claimed all the alleged "lost" millions were nothing more than "fictional profits to save the company . . . what is missing is the alleged profits plus expenses and blackmail money paid to maintain it."

He concluded, "As God is my judge, I am the victim of Wall Street plunder and blackmail in a struggle for honest existence. Merciful God bring the truth to light! F. D. Coster."

The brothers Musica all got off with mild three-year sentences, possibly because some of Coster's claims were accurate. True, he had milked $10 million for his own use, but the rest of the "loot" probably never existed. In fact, the conventional opinion on Wall Street was that without Coster's underhanded dealings McKesson and Robbins would probably have been destroyed and the stockholders wiped out. Instead, the firm weathered the storm, and the stockholders never suspected they were broke. In the final analysis the stockholders had been both robbed and saved.

N

NAIL-HAMMERING CARNIVAL SCAM

The Nail-Hammering Game, a carnival scam that victimizes macho types, seems totally honest. The object is to hammer a nail into a two-by-four with a single blow of a hammer. The operator has no trouble at all accomplishing the feat. He will pull several nails from a carpenter's apron he's wearing and start them into the wood, which is mounted on two wooden horses. He then proceeds to bang each of them into the wood with a single blow.

Now the "mark," or victim, tries it but botches the job. In a shady carnival this becomes a big betting game, with the operator luring the mark to play more by boosting odds on bets to 2 to 1 and then 3 to 1. Since the victim is sometimes permitted to strike the nail successfully, he cannot escape the lure of better odds. For all it matters, the operator could offer 50 to 1 and still be worry-free. The gimmick is the nail and the apron the operator is wearing. There is a secret inside pocket in the apron, which contains some extra-hard nails that will penetrate the wood with one solid blow. However, the main part of the apron contains soft nails, which bend easily. Since all the nails appear to come out of the same pocket, the mark is assured everything is on the level. At times, to allay suspicion, the operator lets the player pick the nail he wants from a bunch in his hand; of course these are all soft losers.

NATIONAL STUDENT MARKETING CORPORATION

In the 1960s a recent college graduate named Cortes Randell blossomed forth as the wunderkind of Wall Street by founding the National Student Marketing Corporation. It was an outrageous fraud that victimized such prominent institutional investors as Morgan Guaranty, Bankers Trust, and the Cornell and Harvard endowment funds.

Randell, whose thesis a few years earlier had been "How to Start a Small Business," organized the company, he said, to corner the student market in items such as employment guides, posters and coffee mugs.

Cortes took N.S.M. public in 1968 at $6 a share and then launched a series of acquisitions. That same year the stock had rocketed to $82. Randell toured the country boosting his firm and claimed it would triple earnings every year. Wall Street knew a hot stock when it saw one, and individual investors and institutions snapped up shares. The 1969 N.S.M. annual report confirmed Randell's enthusiastic prediction, and the company's earnings tripled to about $3.5 million. Randell himself reflected N.S.M.'s good fortune. He bought a $600,000 mansion on the Potomac, a Lear jet and a 55-foot yacht.

Randell's profits were real, based on the rise of the stock, but N.S.M.'s profits were unreal, being based in part on $2.8 million in "unbilled receivables"—which turned out to be money that was never received because it was never demanded. Then there was $3 million from subsidiaries that the firm just hadn't acquired. It was creative accounting carried to the ultimate. When the fall came, N.S.M. stock, which had reached $140 a share, tumbled to $3.50.

Randell pleaded guilty to four counts of stock fraud. He served eight months in Allenwood Federal Prison and paid a $40,000 fine. Some prominent institutions were harder hit, including White & Case—a leading New York law firm—and N.S.M.'s accountants (Peat, Marwick, Mitchell & Co.), who spent a decade in legal battles and had to pay millions of dollars to shareholders.

As for N.S.M. genius Randell, he ended up playing a role in yet another financial fraud—during his prison stay, no less. Along with a deputy assistant secretary of labor, Randell sold unregistered securities and obtained loans with false financial statements. Randell drew a seven-year prison term for this second scheme.

NICOTRA, TOBIA *Mozart forgeries*

The forging of faked autographs of Wolfgang Mozart became a mass-production industry in the 1920s and early 1930s thanks to an international swindler named Tobia Nicotra. Among the victims of Nicotra's frauds were Walter Toscanini (son of the great orchestra conductor Arturo Toscanini) and the august Library of Congress.

To pull off his mass frauds Nicotra traveled to the United States claiming to be the celebrated Richard Drigo, the former orchestra conductor for Czar Nicholas II of Russia. (Drigo had actually died several years earlier.) Nicotra claimed to be an avid collector of Mozart memorabilia and sold his faked wares to gullible music lovers. In one sale he took Walter Toscanini for 2,700 lire (then worth $521) for what he said was a Mozart signature. Nicotra also peddled phony Handel and Wagner autographs in the form of signatures, letters and other documents. In 1928 the cunning Italian took the Library of Congress for several supposedly unpublished Mozart autographs and manuscripts, which Mozart experts had examined and agreed were genuine. It took the library several years to learn the Mozart manuscripts were phony.

What Nicotra had going for his frauds was an unending supply of old papers, which he had actually appropriated from the Milan Library by ripping the flyleaves from old books or stealing empty pages from manuscripts. To these sheets he added "autographs" of leading musicians. He composed a great number of documents and letters supposedly written by these musicians, particularly Mozart. Because his forgeries had been accepted by the Library of Congress and other prestigious purchasers, Nicotra had little trouble dumping off huge volumes of bogus works on general music lovers so that it is impossible to determine his total take.

Nicotra was finally arrested in 1934 and tried in Italy for his depredations. He was fined and sentenced to two years in prison. His conviction apparently came at a fortuitous moment since, according to the police evidence presented at the trial, Nicotra was preparing a new raft of false autographs for the U.S. and European markets, including George Washington, the Marquis de Lafayette, Thaddeus Kosciusko, Abraham Lincoln, Warren Harding, Christopher Columbus, Lorenzo the Magnificent, Leonardo da Vinci and Michelangelo.

NIGHT OF THE SICILIAN VESPERS *Mafia myth*

Probably the most blatant hoax about organized crime is the so-called Night of the Sicilian Vespers in which, according to a former U.S. attorney general, "Forty members of La Cosa Nostra died by gunfire" on September 10, 1931. The plot was allegedly hatched by younger elements of the Mafia and their allies, principally by Lucky Luciano, Frank Costello, Meyer Lansky and Bugsy Siegel, to wrest control from the old-timer "Mustache Petes" who stood in the way of the development of true organized crime.

Serious crime historians have tended to regard the so-called purge as a flight of imagination, although it remains an article of faith for many popular writers. *The Valachi Papers* by Peter Maas states it was "an intricate, painstakingly executed mass execution. . . . On the day Maranzano died, some forty Cosa Nostra leaders allied with him were slain across the country, practically all of them Italian-born old-timers eliminated by a younger generation making its bid for power."

In real life it would be remarkable to set up 40 or more elderly men, on average in their 70s, without some being in a sickbed, if not a hospital, at the wrong time.

Of course, it is entirely different in Mario Puzo's classic book (and subsequent film adaptation) *The Godfather.* There it is relatively easy to set up any number of killings at a precise moment, since, after all, the victims have had the luxury of reading the script.

900-NUMBER TRAVEL SCAMS

The postcard sounds wonderful. Congratulations, it says, you have just won complimentary hotel lodgings to almost any exotic place in the world. In order to take advantage of your good fortune all you have to do is call a certain 900 number for details. When the would-be travelers call, they discover that "all" they have to pay for is the transportation at full coach fare. Worse than that, it takes time for the setup to be explained—and the meter is running. Victims end up paying as much as $30 in phone charges to the 900 number, and all they get in return is a brochure or a travel voucher. A spokesman for the American Society of Travel Agents warns, "The whole game is to avoid delivering anything."

The society warns the public to watch out for the following gimmicks: when the travel operator won't give the caller the hotel confirmation number or the name of the hotel; and when the caller is asked to pay up front and allow 60 to 90 days for processing (during which time the operator can close the business and disappear).

The spokesman adds, "Unfortunately, during recessionary times, the public is more vulnerable to travel scams." The advent of 900 numbers has made it simple for scam artists to reach large numbers of people—and have the telephone company collect their profits for them.

NININGER SWINDLE *town-site fraud*

Today prospective buyers of homes and vacation retreats are at least somewhat schooled in watching for misrepresentations. In the mid-19th century buyers were much more easily taken. One of the most audacious frauds of the 1850s was the so-called Nininger swindle in what was then Minnesota Territory.

Glowing prospectuses depicted the growing city of Nininger, depicted on large and beautifully engraved maps printed by one Ingenuous Doemly. In time Nininger would house some 10,000 inhabitants. It already sported an impressive courthouse, five different churches and was jammed with stores and warehouses to service the surrounding area. The levee was always crowded with freight brought in by packets. Here, in God's Country, was America's future.

Buyers were told to ignore the land agents' claims. One had only to read the *Nininger Daily Bugle*. Unlike all the phony attributes of Nininger, at least the *Daily Bugle* was real; it was loaded with endless ads—hardware stores, millinery shops, dry goods stores, groceries, shoe stores, blacksmith shops, all obvious and wonderful moneymakers. Every issue sported a news story on yet another new store opening, complete with the opening day's receipts. It was all a very impressive fiction. The *Daily Bugle* came out only weekly or biweekly or triweekly, depending on how many copies the selling agents needed.

As a contemporary account put it: "Every name and every business was fictitious, coined in the fertile brain of this chief of all promoters. It was enough to deceive the very elect—and it did. When the Eastern man read that there were six or eight lots, lying just west of Smith & Jones' drygoods store on West Prairie Street, that could be had at a thousand dollars per lot if taken quickly, and they were well worth twice that money on account of the advantageous situation, they were snapped up as a toad snaps flies on a summer day."

The Nininger prices were very high for that day. Land that hadn't obtained even a title was priced for as much as $10,000 per acre. "If the editor or the proprietor had been found in Nininger in the following spring when the dupes began to appear, one or two of the jack oaks with which the city lots were plentifully clothed would have borne a larger fruit than acorns. Even the printer who set the type was forced to flee for his life."

See also ROLLING STONE COLONY.

NORTH OPHIR CLAIM *salting swindle*
One of the most blatant attempts to "salt" an area (that is, to make it appear to be rich in gold, silver or other mineral ore) occurred in the 1860s at the North Ophir silver claim in the fabled Comstock field of Nevada. When great nuggets of silver turned up there, the stock in the claim produced a fortune for the promoters, if not the investors.

What the swindlers had done was chop up silver dollars into small pieces, pound the pieces into lumps, blacken the lumps and salt them throughout the claim area. The grand hoax collapsed when an alleged nugget turned up with "ted States of" still legible.

NUNS OF LOUDUN *mass hysteria hoax*
While some have held that the events surrounding the "possessed nuns of Loudun" represented one of the greatest examples of mass hysteria, many historians see the tale more in terms of a deadly politico-religious hoax perpetrated by France's Cardinal Richelieu.

The victim of this bizarre hoax was Father Urbain Grandier who became parish priest of St. Pierre du Marche in 1617. Grandier turned out to be a master of debauchery and for many years seduced married women, his own penitents, and sisters at the local Ursuline convent at Loudun. He came to grief when he got Philippa Trincant, the daughter of the local public prosecutor, pregnant. The father had the errant priest brought up on charges of immorality before the bishop of Poitiers. The bishop already had reason to hate the errant priest, who had written satirical broadsides against Richelieu, the bishop's mentor.

Grandier was suspended from his priestly duties but restored after a year. Richelieu remained determined to bring about the priest's complete downfall; through other enemies of Grandier, he used money to induce a spurned lover of the priest, Jeanne des Anges (mother superior of the Ursuline convent), to charge she had been possessed by a demon following the priest's commands.

Many of her sisters became so possessed as well. At unpredictable times they would suddenly writhe on the ground, expose themselves, howl obscenities and go into bizarre contortions.

Grandier was brought before a religious court on a charge of witchcraft. Dozens of supposedly possessed nuns appeared and accused Grandier, who was cast into prison. Yet even with Father Grandier in a cell, Loudun's Ursuline sisters continued their thrashing exhibitions, and the town became a magnet for hordes of the morbidly curious. In 1634 Father Grandier was declared guilty of "the crime of magic, *maleficia*, and of causing demonical possession of several Ursuline nuns . . . as well as of other, secular women." He was sentenced to torture and interrogation and was burned at the stake on August 1, 1634.

Even with the priest's death the nuns continued to be subjected to fits of possession. After some years passed, Cardinal Richelieu's interest in the affair flagged, and he cut off paying for the nuns' performances. Miraculously, they were then "cured."

OHIO GANG   *the Harding administration's grand frauds*

When it comes to governmental fraud probably no era in American history can match that of the depredations by the Harding administration grafters popularly known as the Ohio Gang. This group of political cronies from Ohio put Warren G. Harding in politics and eventually the White House, clearly with theft on its mind. In 29 months of unparalleled corruption they made off with an estimated $300 million or more in an era of a mighty dollar. Teapot Dome (see entry) was one of their great frauds, but hardly the major one.

Heading up the Ohio Gang was President Harding's attorney general, Harry M. Daugherty, who had masterminded Harding's political career from the turn of the century until the moment of final triumph at his inauguration as president in 1921. Daugherty and his henchmen soon made it clear they had a price tag on everything they controlled. Up for sale were public lands, oil reserves, judgeships, lucrative Prohibition-agent positions and more. Bribes and payoffs were made at the "House on 16th Street." The "Little Green House on H Street" featured poker games, bathtub gin and women to convince the dubious to join the graft setup.

Historians more or less agree that Daugherty and his chief henchman, Jess Smith, had a hand in every single payment of graft, and that certainly the president himself knew much and suspected more. "My God," he told journalist William Allen White, "this is a hell of a job. I have no trouble with my enemies. I can take care of them all right. But my damn friends, White, they're the ones that keep me walking the floor nights."

Harding hardly spent any time at all walking the floors, being more involved in his personal peccadilloes. He sat in long poker sessions with the boys.

Clearly the president was incapable of controlling Daugherty and was as fearful of him as he was of Mrs. Harding. Daugherty knew of Harding's illegitimate child, and he had also advanced Harding $100,000, which he dropped in the stock market. As the stocks dipped, Daugherty's hold on Harding tightened.

The Ohio Gang's plundering became so immense that scandals had to break despite Daugherty's position as the nation's No. 1 lawman. The roof caved in even before Harding died in office in 1923. At the Veterans Bureau frauds were estimated to be running as high as $200 million. In due course Colonel Charles R. Forbes went to prison for extracting kickbacks from contractors in the construction of veterans hospitals. Bagman Jess Smith committed suicide, with speculation filling the press that he killed himself because of enormous pangs of conscience, all the way to he had been murdered to keep him from talking. The secretary of the interior, Albert B. Fall, did prison time for his part in giving away the government oil reserves at Teapot Dome. Daugherty himself wriggled out of a bribery conviction in a complicated case involving the alien property custodian.

Historians say the Ohio Gang could not have functioned if Harding had been a strong president; William Allen White dubbed him "He-harlot" because of the ease with which he could be used. Harding's father gave perhaps the best comment on this characteristic when he said, "If you were a girl, Warren, you'd be in the family way all the time. You can't say no." But, on the other hand, if Harding had ever shown any evidence of backbone he never would have promoted his career. As Senator Frank Brandegee of Connecticut said at the time of his nomination, Harding was "no world-beater but he is the best of the second-raters."

Harding, the second-rater, had spawned a first-rate scam machine.

OLMEDO STATUE *economical fake*

In the town of Guayaquil, Ecuador, there is a statue honoring the poet Jose Olmedo (1780–1847). However, the statue is not of Olmedo but rather a second-hand one of Lord Byron. The town bought this imitation after officials determined it would have been too expensive to commission a statue of Olmedo himself.

OMAR KHAYYAM'S QUATRAINS *suspect verses*

Today there are those observers who wonder if there really was an Omar Khayyam, the Persian poet, astronomer and mathematician of *Rubaiyat* fame. There are other scholars who insist that whatever his other accomplishments, he did not write poetry. They base this on the fact that no reference to his poetry can be found in contemporary sources and that the first quatrains under his name appeared some two centuries after his death.

"Khayyam" means "tent maker," and if there was an Omar Khayyam when and where he was born and died is a matter of dispute. Some have placed his death as occurring in 1122, 1123 or 1131 at an age variously ranging from about 50 to 83; but there is some question as to whether he was the same one who wrote a treatise in Arabic on algebra.

If the poet Omar Khayyam remained unheralded in his own time and land, it was much later before his work reached the Western world. In 1859 Edward Fitzgerald published a poetical translation of his poems in *The Rubaiyat of Omar Khayyam*. Fitzgerald never pretended that his work was anything but a free translation of Omar's quatrains (verse complete in four rhymed lines, although Omar's third line usually does not rhyme) arranged in a continuous elegy.

Little notice was taken of Fitzgerald's work until the early 1890s when it suddenly took Britain and America by storm. The *Rubaiyat* was frankly hedonistic in tone, touched with a melancholy that hit a common vein in Eastern and Western pessimism. Many of Omar's phrases have become imbedded in Western culture, such as "A Jug of Wine, a Loaf of Bread—and Thou," "The moving finger writes," "Take the Cash, and let the Credit go" and "The Flower that once has blown forever dies."

While Omar's quatrains have been translated into almost every major language and have personified the Western concept of Persian poetry, most of the verses are highly suspect. It would seem that a poetical cottage industry has been at work serving up Omar Khayyam quatrains. In 1971 Ali Dashti in *In Search of Omar Khayyam* concluded that of 1,000 quatrains attributed to Omar, 898 could be readily labeled unauthentic.

ORTON, ARTHUR See TICHBORNE CLAIMANT.

OSSIAN See MACPHERSON, JAMES.

OTTO, KING OF BAVARIA See THE PEASANT SHOOTER.

OVER-ISSUE CON GAME

In the last third of the 19th century, counterfeiting was a big business, and so were related confidence games that duped the dishonest and the unwary. One particular scam that developed then and occasionally appears today is the so-called Over-Issue Game. Dupes are told that a friend of the con man works for the mint in Washington and that he has secretly run off an over-issue for a million dollars in genuine currency. Since the printing is "real" money and could not possibly be spotted as phony, it commands a high value in illegal circles. Ordinary counterfeit in the 1880s and 1890s sold at a discount of 10 cents or 12 cents to the dollar, but the real thing—this over-issue—could be had for a full 50 cents to the dollar.

Once a dupe was convinced, he was talked into making what was to be a trial run of $5,000 to buy $10,000 in the over-issue money. The transaction was generally made in a pool hall-saloon in a disreputable section of town, and the victim was shown a bundle of $10,000 in what was clearly genuine currency. The currency was wrapped in newspapers, and the victim handed over his $5,000 in payment. Just when the transaction was made, a police officer—bogus or a real one involved in the scam—entered the pool hall-saloon and seized the con man, uncovering the $5,000 just given to him by the victim and demanding to know where it came from. While this was going on, confederates of the con man shoved the newspaper-wrapped bundle containing the $10,000 behind a curtain.

As soon as the officer and the con man left the premises (allegedly heading for the police station for more questioning), the victim was handed the newspaper-wrapped bundle and told to disappear quickly in case the law returned. What he was given was a dummy package of blank paper wrapped in the same issue and pages of the newspaper used on the other package. By the time the victim discovered the switch, the con men had all vanished.

Today the racket is still worked, with the switch accomplished in a number of ways. Amazingly, there are still people ready to believe that the government is without fail-safe methods for preventing an overrun of currency during the printing process.

JESSE OWENS OUTRUNS A RACEHORSE *hoax exhibitions*

One of the most preposterous claims made in sports is that a man can outrun a racehorse. This was seemingly accomplished by Jesse Owens, the noted black Olympic runner, who took unfair advantage of the horse in a 100-yard sprint. As Owens himself later stated, he and the promoters of the event deliberately sought out a high-spirited thoroughbred, a type more likely to rear than an average plug horse.

Owens and the horse were lined up together but the starter would be positioned right next to the horse. When the starter fired his gun, the horse inevitably reared. As Owens put it: "I would be off with a tremendous break and by the time he came down I was 50 yards down the track, and at that point even though he would be covering 21 feet for every 7 I covered, it was too late; I would win."

OZONE QUACKS *health scam*

Worried about the depletion of the ozone layer? Well, one can be assured that medical con men have been even more concerned about it for years—at least to the extent of making a buck out of the dilemma. An individual can solve his or her own anxieties by consulting a "pneumotherapist." This quack has a very hush-hush device imported from Europe, the secret of its operation known only to a certain few. It's so valuable that he won't consider selling it, but he will lease it out for about $150 per quarter year.

This mystery contraption seemingly manufactures ozone right in front of your face by sending "high-voltage current through the air." Now you have your own protection from the loss of the ozone layer. Even if everyone else develops skin cancer at a high rate and the planet starts withering away, you will remain an island with your own personal protection.

PALISADE, NEVADA See TOUGHEST TOWN WEST OF CHICAGO.

PARIS EXPOSITION DISAPPEARANCE *enduring hoax report*

One of the most enduring newspaper hoax stories is that of an English mother and daughter who, returning from India, stopped off in Paris for the 1889 Exposition for the opening of the Eiffel Tower. They checked into a fashionable little hotel, and the mother suddenly became ill. The hotel physician was summoned and sent the daughter to his suburban home for a special medicine he needed for the treatment. The daughter made the panicked trip out and back in about two hours but found not only her mother gone, but their room, number 333, completely repapered and refurnished. Furthermore the hotel denied she and her mother had been staying there, and their names did not appear in the hotel register. The physician insisted he had not seen the young woman before and that he had not treated her mother. The daughter went to the police and was not believed.

The nightmare continues and, in some versions, the daughter went mad, having been unable to convince the French or British authorities that she had not suffered a hallucination. Finally, the unfortunate girl died in an asylum. The upshot of the story was that the mother had contracted bubonic plague on the voyage from Asia and when the hotel learned of the ailment, it covered up her even being there, since the establishment would have been ruined if the facts leaked out. French authorities aided in the obliteration of the facts out of fear that the Exposition would be similarly ruined.

The story has been repeated in varying forms in different locales over the decades. It was the basis of a news story in the *London Daily Mail* in 1911 and resurfaced in 1937. A book about missing persons published in 1978 repeats the tale as true. Fictioneers eagerly embraced the plot, and a variation of it appears in Mrs. Belloc-Lowndes' novel, *The End of Her Honeymoon*, as well as in Lawrence Rising's *She Who Was Helena Cass*. In his classic movie, *The Lady Vanishes*, Alfred Hitchcock simply transferred the basic elements of the story to international intrigue aboard a train.

Author and literary critic Alexander Woollcott studied the genealogy of the hoax and traced it as far back as 1898, when reporter Karl Harriman wrote the original story in the *Detroit Free Press*. Years later Harriman informed Woollcott he could no longer recall if he had obtained the story from an earlier source or simply made it up out of whole cloth.

PARKER, GEORGE C. *Brooklyn Bridge impresario*

No man ever made more money out of selling the Brooklyn Bridge than an amazing swindler named George C. Parker (1861–1937). Almost from the time of its completion in 1883, Parker, in his early 20s, started selling the Brooklyn Bridge to the most gullible of sightseers who came to gawk at the engineering marvel. Parker found the scam so easy that he went into it as a full-time business.

He became the chief dealer of some of Gotham's best-known and beloved landmarks, regularly selling the Metropolitan Museum of Art, the first Madison Square Garden, Grant's Tomb and the Statue of Liberty for whatever the sucker market would bear, from $50 to $50,000. But the Brooklyn Bridge was his special pride, and by his own later confession he sold it at an average of twice a week.

At times Parker simply walked up to a "greenhorn" on the bridge and said he was the structure's owner and offered him a job operating a toll gate he planned to set up for both vehicular and pedestrian traffic. He said he was going to charge a penny for passage across the bridge and was surprised when his potential victim assured him he could get more. Parker seemed dubious, and finally the sucker, exasperated, said he'd buy the bridge himself. Sold!

Parker usually operated with the use of "ropers" who hunted up gullible but wealthy buyers and conned them into paying important money for the bridge. They were overwhelmed by Parker's sincere manner and convincing appearance as he produced impressive forged deeds and documents. When a victim couldn't meet Parker's asking price, the suave swindler was very understanding and accepted a down payment as a binder and collected the rest in installments. Victims would come to Parker with a payment and rush off to get more funds, impatient for the day when they would own the bridge and the toll money would come rolling in. Several times Parker's victims had to be rousted from the bridge by police when they tried to erect toll barriers.

In 1928 Parker, then 67, was finally convicted in a swindle. As he had previously served three short prison terms, he was given a mandatory sentence for life as a fourth offender. He died in Sing Sing in 1937. It cannot be said that the nine, last prison years were unhappy ones for Parker. He was, because of his incredible career in con, held in high esteem by other inmates as one of crime's true elite.

PARKHURST, CHARLIE *impersonator*
He was one of the bravest and toughest six-in-hand stagecoach drivers in the Old West, the one man folks felt safe with as he negotiated his Concord over the rugged trails of California's Sierra Nevada. Nobody knew much about Charlie Parkhurst (?–1879) until he turned up in Gold Rush territory in about 1850. He told folks he had been an orphan back in New England, had run away and worked for a time in Worcester, Massachusetts, as a stableboy. It was here, he said, that he learned his craft driving a team of horses at breakneck speed.

In 1851 Charlie took a job holding the "ribbons" for the California Stage Company. He was not a man to be pushed around; at about five feet seven with broad shoulders, he could chew tobacco, drink, gamble and battle with the best of them. And he was a near legend at driving a stage. Once he whipped a team across a tottering bridge just before it went down. Another time road agents tried to stick up his stage. Charlie plugged the leader and outran the rest of the gang, bringing his passengers and a valuable cargo home unscathed. Over the years Charlie had one fetish that set him apart from other men; he shaved every day, causing observers to op-

ine that Charlie had himself a fair lady somewhere along his run.

Shortly after the Civil War, Charlie Parkhurst retired and lived out his years in a small cabin in Santa Cruz County. On December 31, 1879, friends found him dead. A doctor was summoned to determine the cause of death. It was cancer, but the medical man made a more startling discovery. Charlie was a woman; in fact, at one time in her life she had been a mother, whether during her California years or earlier could not be ascertained.

Nobody quite knew what to do with the stage driver with the strange secret; but everyone agreed the only proper thing to do was bury her under the only name by which she had been known—Charlie Parkhurst.

PARNELLISM AND CRIME *political smear campaign*
In April 1887 the august *London Times* began publishing a damaging series of articles entitled "Parnellism and Crime," attacking the Irish leader and member of Parliament Charles Stewart Parnell, a campaign now regarded as the most daring political hoax in British history. Highlighting the series was the publication of a letter attributed to Parnell expressing extreme pleasure at the 1882 Phoenix Park Murders in which Lord Frederick Charles Cavendish (the newly named goodwill emissary to Ireland) and a lesser official were assassinated in Dublin. Additional letters were published confirming Parnell's supposed approval of the killings. The expose caused a furor in the House of Commons as well as great expressions of outrage from vast segments of the English public.

Parnell denounced the letters as forgeries, but the *Times* stood by its stories, and the Irish leader became more isolated in Parliament, his denials producing only vicious derision. Counseled by his supporters, Parnell did not start legal action. In 1888 a former member of Parliament, F. H. O'Donnell, likewise implicated by the accounts, sued the *Times* for damages. O'Donnell lost his suit, and in the course of the trial a number of other alleged Parnell letters—even more damaging than those already published—surfaced.

Now Parnell demanded that a select committee be appointed to ascertain the authenticity of the letters. Although members of Parliament continued to torment Parnell, they finally agreed to appoint a commission of judges to carry out a sweeping investigation. In court Parnell's supporters were able to trace the forgeries to their source, one Richard Pigott, who had sold the letters to the *Times* for a large sum. Under biting cross-examination by Sir Charles Russell, Pigott was required to write certain passages that appeared in the letters. He committed the

The Pigott letters—forgeries concocted to smear Charles Stewart Parnell, the great Irish leader and member of Parliament—isolated Parnell politically until they were at last proved false.

same spelling errors that appeared in the texts. Recalled to the stand the following day, Pigott failed to appear, having taken flight from the country. However, he had made a signed confession to Parnell's supporters, which was introduced in court and cleared Parnell. Pigott had composed and sold the letters with only one motive: money. Eight days later Pigott committed suicide in a Madrid hotel as he was about to be apprehended by Spanish police.

Parnell received several thousand pounds in an out-of-court settlement with the *Times,* and the newspaper was required to pay 250,000 pounds in costs for the investigation.

PASTE-UP MONEY   *doctored dollars*

Not long ago, during the evening rush hour at New York's Grand Central Station, a businessman rushing for his train was stopped by a distressed woman with a baby in her arms. Holding a $20 bill, she said, "Please, mister, I'm not begging. Could you change this for me? Even two tens would be good. The man

at the milk and ice cream stand is not allowed to change a $20 bill."

Although he was in a big hurry, the commuter could not turn away from a young mother in distress. He dug into his wallet for a ten and a couple of fives, exchanged them for her twenty and charged off for his train, feeling rather good when he made it and satisfied he had managed to do a small good deed. It was after he got off at his destination in Rye and stopped in a liquor store for a bottle of bourbon that the businessman found out he had been taken. He used the $20 bill to pay for the bottle only to have the clerk hand it back to him. It turned out the "distressed mother" had simply clipped a corner from four different $20 bills and pasted them over the 2s on a $2 bill. Pressed with a warm iron, the patches become barely noticeable, especially to someone in a hurry.

This particular bunco game, which is currently enjoying a revival, netted the female passer a quick $18 profit since the four mutilated $20 bills she had used each lacked only one corner and as such suffered no loss of value and were easily disposable. Previously, $1 and $10 bills were used in this scam, but grifters have found the $2 bill makes a better switch since the "TW . . ." makes it look like a $20 to a rushed victim. As a matter of fact, it was discovered that this particular female passer had palmed off two other bogus twenties at different entrances to the station within minutes of her first victim.

The paste-up money racket may explain why some banks have reported many more requests for $2 bills.

PAUL IS DEAD!   *Beatles death hoax that grew*

Those cunning Beatles! They'd pulled off the greatest death cover-up ever. In November 1966 Paul McCartney died in an automobile accident near London. He was buried, and the clever Beatles secretly brought in a substitute—a youth in his 20s who looked amazingly like Paul, was also a left-handed master of the bass guitar and kept right on being a successful song writer, to say nothing of his being an accomplished singer and pianist.

Before this nonsensical bit of Beatlemania ran its wild course, Beatles fans ran down every zany confirming rumor, many of which were said to be contained in the group's records. Some people bought albums only to look for clues, and sales skyrocketed.

Who started the hoax that escalated into a craze that swept the world? As is the case with many rumors, this is not conclusively known. It was later variously traced to a thesis by an Ohio Wesleyan University student, a satirical but straight-faced story in the October 14, 1969, issue of the University of Michigan *Daily.* It was also linked to a Detroit disk jockey who repeated loads of the nonsense over radio station WKNR. Then again, it may be that the first fans of the zany tale were listeners of Roby Young of New York's WABC, who unreeled reams of evidence that Paul Present was not Paul Past. When Young was dumped by the station, the torch was picked up by night-yapper Alex Bennett of WMCA. Bennett even sojourned to England to uncover ever more "confirming" facts. Thus one may make a selection from columns A,B,C,D or E—and undoubtedly more so. In any event, the "Paul Is Dead!" legend was born.

Mourners gathered outside the McCartney home in London. In the States, aficionados alternately wept and laughed, still clinging to the hope that the rumors were false. The song "Strawberry Fields" revealed a wealth of secrets when played backward and forward and at various speeds. Naturally everyone had to run out to buy the record and decide if John said "I buried Paul" at the end. (Lennon later claimed he said "cranberry sauce.") Then there was the cover of the *Abbey Road* lp. Was it not strange that McCartney was out of step, barefoot and holding a cigarette in the wrong hand?

It completely spooked Beatles fans. They spiraled down every Beatles record ever cut, then speeded them up from 33 to 45 rpm, to 78 and then slowed them to 16. They even taped the records and reversed the tapes. That produced all sorts of clues. When certain moans were reversed, some thought they could hear John Lennon declare, "Paul is dead. Miss him. Miss him. Miss him."

Others reversed Lennon's "Revolution No. 9" and said they came up with the horrifying sounds of a traffic accident. There seemed to be a collision, crackling flames and a voice crying, "Get me out, get me out!" It was apparently the death of Paul McCartney. When the piece was taped stereophonically and then reversed, one of the four tracks came up allegedly with the words "He hit a pole! We better get him to a surgeon [scream] . . . My wings are broken and so is my hair. I'm not in the mood for words [Gurgling, battle sounds]. Find the night watchman. A fine natural imbalance. Must have got it in the shoulder blades."

Perhaps the most revealing and disturbing of all was the "O.P.D." patch Paul wore in the *Sgt. Pepper* photo. Frightened fans were sure it meant "officially pronounced dead" in British police jargon.

As the mania raged, a cynical view developed that the Beatles were rather slow debunking the rumors. Was Paul dead? He himself finally announced, "If I were dead, I'd be the last to know."

The circus continued at a fever pitch for about five months. Then Beatles fans had to cope with an even more dreadful disaster. Paul McCartney announced he was quitting the Beatles.

For the fans this was no hoax—and a fate worse than death.

THE PEASANT SHOOTER   *hoaxing a mad king*
Few monarchs in history can be said to have been quite as mad as Otto, king of Bavaria (r. 1886–1913), who had to be kept confined in the royal household and out of contact with his subjects in order to keep him from shooting them. Believing that spirits inhabited various pieces of furniture, Otto would open a drawer where such a spirit resided and carry on long conversations with it. The most important royal prerogative in Otto's twisted view was a requirement that he shoot one peasant each morning. Thus after breakfast one of his guards brought him a rifle loaded with blanks while another guard, disguised as a peasant, hid in the bushes on the royal grounds.

Otto waited at his customary vantage point in a window until the "peasant" stepped out of the bushes and walked insolently across the lawn. Upon hearing the king's shot, the man would "drop dead." The mad monarch watched with satisfaction until his apparent deadly handiwork was carted off and then turned back to his other nonexistent royal duties.

PEDIGREED DOG SCAM   *enduring swindle*
A con game with a long and dishonorable past and still practiced today, the pedigreed dog swindle is the granddaddy of some of the greatest con games, including boiler room sales of worthless gold mines or oil stocks.

The early-19th-century con men who developed the pedigreed dog scam often hit on bartenders. The bartender would be approached by a stranger with a dog (usually a mongrel terrier) and be informed the mutt was actually a rare breed. The customer would produce some impressive-looking papers to back up his claim that the dog was a champion. Then he would say he was in town for a meeting with some bankers, adding, "I can't very well take him to the meeting, and I'll gladly give you ten dollars to watch him for a few hours."

The bartender was happy to oblige, and the customer would leave with another reminder of how valuable the canine was. Shortly thereafter, another stranger entered the drink emporium and would express keen interest in the animal, saying he would like to buy it for his family. The bartender would say the dog was not for sale, but the man would keep pressing, offering $100. The bartender would refuse the offer even as the price was increased. Finally, the second stranger would say, "Look, I won't bamboozle you. I know dog flesh and that dog is worth good money. I'll give you $500 for it."

By now the bartender was in pain at having to turn down such an offer, and he would explain the dog was not his. "Look," the second stranger said, "I'm from out of town. If you can work out a deal for me for the dog for $500, I'll pay you a $100 bonus. I have to catch a train, but I can stop back in three hours to see if we have a deal."

A short time after the second stranger left, the dog's owner returned, looking glum. He ordered a drink, and the bartender would ask what was wrong. The man shook his head and said, "My deal fell through and I was really counting on the money. I don't know what I'll do now."

Trying to sound matter of fact, the bartender said he thought he might be able to help out. He had, he said, taken a liking to the dog and would be willing to take him off the man's hands for, say, $100. The dog owner wouldn't hear of it, saying the dog was too valuable. The bartender would work his offer up to $300 and then $400, and finally the customer gave in, but he added, "It's a deal because I really need money right now, but I reserve the right to come back next month and buy the dog back for $500."

The bartender readily agreed to that; after all, he could always say the dog had run off. The bartender would take the money from the register and buy the mutt. Now, with the original owner gone, the bartender simply had to wait for the prospective buyer to call back and make himself a quick $200 profit. Of course, the second stranger never returned and, needless to say, his partner, the original owner, never came back to claim his "valuable" canine either.

Con men have used this swindle as a short con whenever they needed to raise some cash quickly. The scam itself evolved into bigger cons with profits of 100-fold or more. The victim was no longer a bartender but a greedy businessman or banker or real estate man, and the property no longer a mutt but a gold mine, an oil well, stocks or some property that was allegedly drawing a high bid the so-called seller was not aware of. Whatever the property, it was some dog.

PENNIES MADE OF GOLD *speculation hoax*
In 1906 a rumor started in Virginia and the two Carolinas that the U.S. mint had accidentally mixed gold with the copper in 1902 one-cent pieces. As a result speculators began buying up 1902 pennies, and within a week the price had risen to 12 cents apiece. The federal government stepped in at that time to squash the rumor before the craze spread throughout the country. The penny market bubble burst.

Despite an intensive investigation, it was never determined who had started the hoax; undoubtedly someone had made a pretty penny out of it.

PERKINS, DR. ELISHA *America's first medical quack*
While Dr. Elisha Perkins (1740–1799) was clearly not the first medical faker to operate in the New World,

he is generally given the sobriquet of "America's First Quack," as he was the first to patent his so-called treatment and attracted a considerable following. In 1796 he patented a device he called a "Tractor," which consisted of two three-inch-long rods—one composed of an alloy of copper, zinc and gold; the other, of silver, platinum and iron. It was the claim of this Plainfield, Connecticut, charlatan that human ailments could literally be yanked from the body by the correct combination of metals acting in magnetic concert. All that had to be done was to pull downward over the sickly portion of the body and the disease, presto, was pulled free.

Among Perkins' notable customers were George Washington, who had his entire family on the Tractor, and Chief Justice Oliver Ellsworth. In 1796 Perkins and his son Benjamin published a book filled with hundreds of enthusiastic testimonials from intelligent citizens, including doctors, scholars, ministers and members of Congress. Of course, today the medical world appreciates the power of suggestion in dealing with psychosomatic ailments, but the Tractor was a complete "cure-all." While Elisha pushed the Tractor on this side of the Atlantic, son Benjamin took it over to Europe where he peddled the device with considerable success, although some authoritative voices were raised against the so-called treatment. When other doctors secretly substituted a wooden tractor for the real thing, there was no difference in the treatment results.

Oliver Wendell Holmes, the first dean of the Harvard Medical School, later stated he was certain that Benjamin was no fool and realized full well that the Tractor was sheer humbuggery. Some said that old Elisha actually was a true believer in his invention, and cite as proof the fact that he ventured off to New York City in 1799 to treat people during a deadly yellow fever epidemic. On the other hand, Elisha could hardly have failed to offer his sure cure-all device. Perkins arrived in the beleaguered city and announced he would soon put things right. His cure rate turned out to be zero, a major tragedy considering that Perkins himself perished of yellow fever a few weeks later.

This did not stop Benjamin from continuing to hawk his father's treatment back in this country. The younger Perkins lived to retire a very rich man in New York City. There is nothing on the record to indicate that Benjamin ever used the Perkins' Patented Metallic Tractor on himself.

PETERS, FREDERICK EMERSON *king of rubber*
Dubbed "the King of Rubber," Frederick Emerson Peters (1885–1959) was perhaps the most prolific passer of bad checks in U.S. history, a considerable accomplishment since many crime experts rank check

passers as the cream of con men because they must convince a victim to part with cash with no real "build-up."

Starting his criminal career at 17, Peters used hundreds of different names to cash thousands of worthless checks over a 57-year career (minus jail time). One of his standard ploys was to pose as the relative of well-known figures, especially Theodore Roosevelt, whose appearance he was able to match. Engaging a merchant in conversation, he would casually mention his bogus identity and then use a check made out for a somewhat larger sum to make a purchase. Few shopkeepers could resist getting a check from such a celebrity and some would not even cash it, preferring to keep the check as a keepsake. Others who did and were burned still framed the check and proudly recollected the time they "got took by Teddy Roosevelt's kid."

"Teddy Roosevelt's kid," among other phantom celebrities, crisscrossed the country dozens of times on check-passing tours. Peters later recollected having passed 30 worthless checks in a small Indiana town whose name he no longer remembered. Still, Peters was caught a number of times and served several prison terms. He did not allow such "sabbaticals" to go to waste. He helped establish several prison libraries and used his time to read up on biographies so that he could later pose as relatives of yet more prominent persons. Asked why he continued to write bad checks after a number of convictions, Peters shrugged and blamed his behavior on the gullibility of his victims. He insisted it would take the "rock-like willpower of the Sphinx to resist such temptation."

Peters was on checkpassing duty in New Haven, Connecticut, at the age of 74 when he suffered a fatal stroke on the job. He was given a pauper's funeral, although it was observed at the time that with some advanced warning he would have given the undertaker a handsome check.

PETERS, SAMUEL ANDREW   *the lying Episcopalian parson*

One would be hard put to find in the America of the 1700s a more compulsive liar or teller of tall tales than the Reverend Samuel Peters (1735–1826), a rector of Hebron, Connecticut. He was once tarred and feathered, not, as one might think, in retribution for his many whoppers, but for his Tory sympathies during the American Revolution. After this experience Peters fled back to England and proceeded to compose his peculiar histories of the developing new nation. It is tempting to describe his writings as a form of vengeance on a land that had treated him so vilely, but Peters was clearly a liar from his earliest days in public life. The Reverend Peters gained his reputa-

tion by extracting potent but patently nonsensical meanings from biblical events to flesh out his sermons.

Having fled the country, Peters had the leisure to take quill in hand and compose in his *General History of Connecticut* and many other works absurd chronicles of America. Yet to this day it is possible to find texts that repeat some of the parson's fanciful tales, especially concerning preposterous laws supposedly imposed on colonists by Puritan lawmakers. Serious scholars today have found absolutely no contemporary records of such bizarre laws as those that banned parents from kissing their children on the Sabbath, or the making of mince pies or playing any musical instruments save the trumpet, drum and Jew's harp.

In the field of natural disasters Peters outdid himself, reporting the "Great Caterpillar Invasion" along the Connecticut River, an event worthy of repetition in undiscerning, believe-it-or-not style tomes today. This awesome army sported insects, two inches long and with red throats, so numerous that they formed a phalanx three miles wide and two miles long and devoured every patch of green for 100 miles. Even more fearsome, if just as fanciful, were giant bullfrogs who rampaged through Windham in 1758 and laid waste to the entire town.

How did Peters get away with such fantasies? His technique has been used by many of the more convincing writers of the absurd ever since. He mixed real events with his improbable tales so that if A was true and readily proved, then it followed that B was also true. As a result, turn-of-the-century readers in their uncritical bent came to accept Peters' fantastic histories, some achieving best-seller status. By 1805 Peters was able to return to America and live out the last 21 years of his life in comfortable fame on the royalties of his many hoaxes. Like many other hoaxers the Reverend Peters was lucky enough to expire before his detractors came on the scene. It was only after his death that serious historians delved into the details in his works and found an abundance of the sort of falsehoods called "facticide." In time Peters became known in learned circles as that "lying Episcopalian parson."

See also BLUE LAW HOAXES.

PETER-TO-PAUL   *pyramid swindle technique*

Many confidence games are based on the principal of paying many victims a very handsome profit. This is not an unreasonably honest deed, as long as other, potential victims see these results and fight to make similar investments. The introduction in America of the tactic of robbing Peter to pay Paul is generally attributed to an engaging turn-of-the-century swindler named William F. "520%" Miller (see entry), although Miller always insisted he'd learned of the concept on Wall Street. Not only able to keep his con going by taking Peter's money to pay Paul, he was even able to rob Paul to pay Peter, because many original investors eagerly plowed their profits back into the scheme, thus extending the life of the bubble.

PHILADELPHIA ALARM *military hoax*

One of the earliest efforts in America to stampede the population into a military posture was a deliberate hoax that occurred in colonial Pennsylvania in 1706. The ruse, later known as the Philadelphia Alarm, was fathered by John Evans, the colonial governor, who was an ardent advocate of a strong militia but was frustrated by the pacific beliefs of the Quakers. Apparently Evans was seeking to prove that the Quakers were not nearly as nonviolent as they claimed and that therefore the provincial assembly should pass a militia law.

On the day of the annual Philadelphia fair in 1706, Evans rode his horse into the crowd, frantically waving his sword and calling the people to arms against the French and Indians who, he shouted, were marching on the city. The report was enough to scatter the fairgoers, many of whom headed for their homes; but only Evans' tiny militia and a few non-Quakers took up defensive positions for two days along the waterfront to repulse the mythical attack.

In *The History of Pennsylvania* Thomas F. Gordon later wrote:

> This experiment on the principles of the Quakers was wholly unsuccessful; the greater part attending their religious meeting, as was their custom on that day of the week, persisted in their religious exercises amid the general tumult instead of flying to arms as the governor had anticipated. Four members only repaired with weapons to the rendezvous.

Evans reaped more than a failure to "expose" the Quakers with his hoax; he also earned the enmity of the fair's businessmen, since panicky non-Quaker fairgoers took flight without settling their bills, which was customary at the end of the day.

PHONY CRIPS *begging frauds*

They sit in wheelchairs or on the ground and give the impression of having a leg missing. Commonly known as "phony crips," these con artists simply tape their legs right under themselves. With a little yoga training, a phony crip doesn't even have to use tape. Others, practicing a more simple type of deception, encase their perfectly sound legs in form-fitting shells, which appear to be artificial legs. Some professionals, willing to sacrifice comfort for their art, wear steel braces that distort the position of their bodies or heads. The brace may be a mite uncomfortable, but

the boys earn more than enough to afford a good rubdown in an athletic club every night if they should need one. One "legless" pannie, who added a "broken neck" collar to his paraphernalia, admitted to police that the extra touch had actually tripled his take.

More than other scam artists, phony crips seem to need public appreciation. Thus one who frequents the side of fabled Tiffany's, the jewelry firm, will suddenly jump up, stretch his previously hidden leg and announce to passersby: "You try sitting there eight or ten hours a day and see what hard work this is." Then he bounces away into the crowds.

See also BEGGING SCAMS.

PICKPOCKETING TECHNIQUES

Where can one find a pickpocket? It's elementary; look for a public place with a sign warning "BEWARE OF PICKPOCKETS." Pickpockets hang around such signs because they know many people will automatically touch their money or wallet when they see such a warning.

It is often said that the art of pickpocketing is in a state of decline, since modern "dips" cannot compare with their counterparts of three or four decades ago. However, some very talented crooks are active, men and women with an uncanny and unerring "grift sense," which enables them to anticipate what the victim will do next. For example, the thief may rest his forearm against the back of his victim's shoulders in a crowd to keep him from getting too close. He then uses his free hand to lightly fan the back pocket or another pocket to locate the exact position of the wallet. If the victim gets suspicious, his muscles along the spine will tighten and the crook feels the reaction through his forearm.

The pickpocket also watches for a reddening of the skin below and behind the ears. By the time the victim goes for his pocket, the crook's hand is no longer there and the wallet is safe—for a brief time. Talented pickpockets immediately repeat the process, for even if the victim is still nervous or suspicious, he will generally be too embarrassed to grab for his wallet a second time, since it would be obvious he suspected the man behind him of being a thief.

PIGOTT FORGERIES See PARNELLISM AND CRIME.

PILGRIMAGE CONS *preying on the pious*

The great pilgrimages from Europe to the Holy Land came into vogue in the 8th, 9th and 10th centuries. Most of the pilgrims were very pious, but among their ranks was an impious group who today would be labeled charlatans and confidence men.

The pilgrims found rapture in drinking the clear waters of the Jordan or being baptized in the same stream where John had baptized the Savior. They wandered in awe and pleasure on the outskirts of the Temple, on the Mount of Olives and on terrible Calvary. Before leaving, these pilgrims sought precious relics. They eagerly brought back buckets of mould from the hill of the Crucifixion and flagons of water from the Jordan. At home they were offered huge prices for them, and soon many had the idea of replenishing their wares from a local stream or mound of dirt in the forest. These false relics decorated many churches and monasteries.

More audacious swindlers offered even more apocryphal relics, as Charles Mackay wrote in his brilliant 19th-century work, *Extraordinary Popular Delusions and the Madness of Crowds:*

> the wood of the true cross, the tears of the Virgin Mary, the hems of her garments, the toe-nails and hair of the Apostles—even the tents that Paul helped to manufacture—were exhibited for sale by the knavish in Palestine, and brought back to Europe "with woundrous cost and care." A grove of a hundred oaks would not have furnished all the wood sold in little morsels as remnants of the true cross; and the tears of Mary, if collected together, would have filled a cistern.

PILTDOWN MAN   *infamous fossil forgery*

In 1912 English attorney and amateur antiquarian Charles Dawson (1864–1916) dug up some bones, which became known as "Piltdown Man," from a gravel pit near Piltdown Common in East Sussex, England. Experts from the British Museum were thrilled by the find and labeled it the "missing link" between man and ape. It was heralded as a confirmation of the Darwinian theory, and they willingly bestowed the name of *Eoanthropus dawsonii* (Dawson's Dawn Man) upon it. It would take more than a generation for the scientific world to agree that it was nothing but a "most elaborate and carefully prepared hoax."

What were found were pieces of a skull and jaw. The skull appeared quite human but the jawbone fragments more ape-like. The face was not present, so a great deal of interpretation was necessary, and a few scientists wondered whether the jaw and skull bones even belonged together. Nevertheless, most eminent scientists agreed this was the most important find since Charles Darwin advanced his theory of evolution.

Still, Dawson's Piltdown Man confused anthropologists. If he was genuine it meant man—"The Earliest Englishman"—had lived on Earth for half a million years. This did not seem to match the evolutionary tree that had been based on previous discoveries.

As the years passed, Piltdown's authenticity came under repeated questioning. But there seemed no way

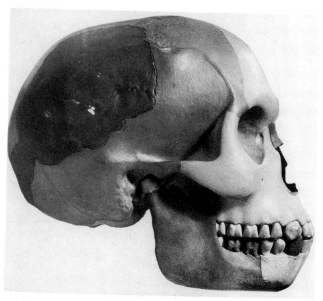

Although the supposed skull of "Piltdown Man" was regarded as the missing link for a generation and seemingly fleshed out evolutionary thought, the scientific world eventually agreed it was a "most elaborate and carefully prepared hoax."

to prove fraud until the late 1940s when English geologist Kenneth P. Oakley of the British Museum devised a new way of determining if ancient bones were of the same age. By 1949, Oakley had announced there was doubt about the Piltdown bones; four years later he devised newer and more sophisticated radioactive fluorine tests, which determined that the skull was 50,000 years old and the jaw much younger. They could not be from the same individual unless, as one scientific wit put it, "The man died but his jaw lingered on for a few thousand years."

The explanation was that in 1911 someone, presumably Dawson, had planted a human cranium in the gravel excavation along with the doctored-up jaw from an orang-utan. As Richard Milner states in *The Encyclopedia of Evolution*, "The orang teeth had been filed to make them look more human, and the jaw was deliberately broken at the hinge, to obscure correct identification. All the fragments had been stained brown with potassium bichromate, which made them appear equally old."

In his book, *Piltdown Forgery*, Dr. J. S. Weiner of Oxford offers evidence that Dawson was known to stain bones and otherwise forge ancient finds.

Dawson died in 1916, much honored, and safe from scientific debunking by almost four decades. He was known as the "wizard of Sussex," and a monument there commemorates his famous find.

Most experts consider Dawson the guilty party. Harvard's Stephen Jay Gould believes Dawson started the deception as a prank and then gained the aid of his sometime-assistant, Pierre Teilhard de Chardin, then a young seminarian. A more novel theory was advanced by Professor John Winslow, who finds the villain to have been Sir Arthur Conan Doyle, the creator of Sherlock Holmes. The incriminating evidence: Doyle lived just a short distance from the Piltdown gravel site. Motive: Doyle was a fanatic spiritualist and believed in an afterlife and might have sought revenge on the many scientists who ridiculed his beliefs.

In 1987 Professor Charles Blinderman in *The Piltdown Inquest* runs through a roster of about 10 of the "usual suspects." Then he came up with a fictional "missing link" of his own: The Piltdown hoax was the work of Doyle's Professor Moriarty, the ubiquitous Victorian villain. It was all Moriarty's effort to discredit the creator of his nemesis, Sherlock Holmes.

What remains certain about Piltdown Man is that there was skullduggery afoot.

POCKETBOOK DROP *enduring con game*

It is usually called the "pocketbook drop," the "pigeon drop" or the "envelope drop," but whatever the name or the particular pattern that follows, the final result is the same. The greedy victim is relieved of his or her money while dreaming of making a most elusive financial killing. Recently, New York City's Comptroller's Office identified the caper as one of the eight most common street con games perpetrated in the city. It works this way:

Con man A finds a wallet, purse, attache case, envelope or even a paper bag apparently filled with money. The unsuspecting victim is set up to witness the discovery. Just then con man B appears and insists he too is entitled to a share as much as the other two. If the victim had, up until then not thought he was entitled to share in the find, he does now. A dispute breaks out as to whether they should simply divide the money on the spot or first check to see if it is stolen.

Con man A says his boss is a very smart person and has close ties to the police and can check. They adjourn to a pay phone and a call is placed to the "boss." He calls back 30 minutes later with the inside word that it was probably dropped by some big gambler, a numbers runner or a tax evader and that the three of them should share it. Now one of the con men raises doubts that the others will be able to keep the secret; if not, all three could be in trouble. Again the "boss" is consulted, and he offers to hold the money until all three can produce a substantial sum of money to demonstrate they are responsible citizens and will in good faith keep the secret. Con man B, apparently fearful of being cut out of the deal puts up his share of cash right on the spot. Con man A and the victim have to head for their banks to get

their share of the money. When the victim returns and hands over his share, it proves to be the last he will ever see of the two con men.

While the plot appears almost juvenile, it must be remembered that the victims are usually older persons and the acting very high-powered. When the two con men bicker, the victim becomes terrified that if he fails to abide by whatever ground rules are established he will be dealt out of his share. The reliability of the "boss"—sometimes alleged to be a police detective—with the act carried out a block away from the station houses—is the convincer. The amount of money allegedly found is always so great that the victim is forced to want to believe. In an infamous instance in New York City, two sisters in their sixties leapt to their deaths in a joint suicide pact after realizing they had been swindled out of their life savings of $17,000 in a variation of this swindle.

POLTERGEIST HOAXES *age-old deceptions*

Poltergeist activity is defined as "recurrent spontaneous psychokinesis" and is used to describe otherwise unexplained noises, the smashing of dishes, the movement of objects and other allegedly bizarre household happenings. Houses where these events occur are "haunted." Is this true? Many poltergeist activity reports turn out to be fraudulent, or the activity can be explained by natural causes or even mass hallucination. Other reports may be classified as unexplained—which is not necessarily the same as "authentic."

The origin of "poltergeist" is from the German, meaning "noisy spirit"; the term dates back at least to the Reformation period, when people generally still believed in ghosts, devils, imps (devil aides in the form of insects, etc.), wolf men, and witches who fly on broomsticks and transform themselves at will from human forms to cats, dogs, horses and other animals.

It may be said that the real study of poltergeists did not begin until the second half of the 17th century, but such researches were governed by the superstitions and limits of scientific knowledge of the time. More complete studies developed by the mid-1800s.

Even before this latter period it had become quite common for poltergeist hoaxes to be exposed. One of the most famous English examples was that of the "Stockwell Ghost" of 1772. An elderly lady, Mrs. Golding, lived alone with her servant, Anne Robinson, in Stockwell, near Vauxhall, England. The pair was harried by weird ghostly antics: Cups and saucers crashed to the floor from their shelves (one of the easiest poltergeist tricks to pull off); other crock-

The most complete study of poltergeists occurred in Victorian England with proof of fraud readily obtained.

ery flew down the chimney and pots and pans soared out windows or down stairs; and hams, cheeses and loaves of bread tumbled to the floor with no apparent explanation other than the devil did it.

Poor Mrs. Golding became so rattled that she invited neighbors to stay with her to save her from the strange event that had invaded her previously tranquil home. The neighbors did no good other than themselves becoming witnesses to similar bizarre happenings. As chairs and tables went on the move around them, the neighbors decided it was quite possible the house itself might crash down on them. Ultimately they deserted Mrs. Golding and her servant.

Finally, Mrs. Golding fled her home, taking Anne Robinson with her to the house of a neighbor. Incredibly, the tumult went right along with them, and now the neighbor's glass and crockery met with constant disaster. In self-defense the neighbor ordered the refugees to depart, and they went back to the Golding home.

Further disturbances followed there once more. It must be observed that Mrs. Golding was not addle-brained. She began to see a human cause for all her woes: She dismissed the servant girl, and the weird happenings all ceased.

A long time later Anne Robinson confessed the entire matter to the Reverend Mr. Brayfield, and eventually an explanation to the mystery was published. Her reason, says one account, was that she "was anxious to have a clear house, to carry on an intrigue with her lover, and resorted to this trick to effect her purpose."

She simply arranged china on the shelves in such a way that pieces could fall at the slightest motion. For other articles she attached horse hairs, which she could jerk on from an adjoining room, where no one could see her, and thus be so far away she attracted no suspicion of causing the tumult. "She was exceedingly dexterous at this sort of work," says one later study, "and would have proved a formidable rival to many a juggler by profession."

A dozen years before the appearance of the so-called Stockwell Ghost, there was the much celebrated Cock Lane Ghost in London. This too was demonstrated to be a fraud. Involved was the homeowner and his wife, his young daughter, a servant girl, as well as the Reverend Mr. Moor and his friend, a prominent businessman. Not all of the deceptions were ever explained, but knockings on the wall were attributed to the homeowner's wife, and the mysterious scratchings were assigned to the little girl.

At the trial of the hoaxers, the man of the cloth and the businessman were reprimanded and ordered to make financial payments; the homeowner was made to stand three times in the pillory and was given two years in prison and his wife one year; the servant girl got six months. Even a printer who had been hired to publish the story for their profit was fined £50, a legal precedent that might play hob with publishing practices today.

Two servant girls in 1838 in Scotland produced similar havoc, including the tumbling of bricks from the chimney of a farmhouse after they secretly loosened them earlier. In 1958 parapsychologists found some bizarre elements in happenings in the Seaford, New York, home of a couple with two young teenage children. The investigators attributed many of the strange events of crashing objects to the 12-year-old son, but found others "credible," i.e., unexplainable to them. The investigators did have to note that the entire family refused to submit to lie detector tests.

To this day many poltergeists turn out to be patent frauds, while others remain not disproved. But the question remains on how competent these investigators are.

See also GHOST HOAXES.

PONIATOWSKI GEMS *bizarre imitation plot*
One of the strangest motives for flimflammery in history involved the renowned Poniatowski gems. The gems belonged to Prince Stanislas Poniatowski (1754–1833), the nucleus having been inherited from his uncle, King Stanislas Augustus of Poland, who died in 1798. The king had been a noted collector and had been supplied gems from his Italian and French agents. The collection comprised ancient, Renaissance and modern gems.

Even before the king's death Prince Poniatowski was himself an almost uncontrollable collector of antiquities. Determined to eventually possess the greatest collection of any Pole, the prince settled in Rome in 1791 to devote himself entirely to collecting. Over a period of 35 years Prince Poniatowski achieved his ambition of being the greatest of all Polish collectors. He guarded his hoard with determined zeal, letting no more than a few of the gems be seen at any one time.

By 1831 when the prince published his collection, it totaled over 2,600 gems. What struck some experts was the number of gems attributed to ancient engravers—no less than 1,737. The French scholar R. Rochette noted: "The collection . . . is full of works

by Pyrgoteles, Polyclites, Apollonides, Dioscurides, in greater numbers than there were in antiquity itself." And E. Tölken, the Berlin curator of gems, was puzzled by the closeness in style of gems signed by Greek and Roman engravers, over a span of more than 400 years.

The perplexity was not solved until a full-scale scandal broke in 1839, six years after the prince's death. Almost half of the Poniatowski gems were purchased by an avid collector, Colonel John Tyrrell. Seeking to publish his new collection, Tyrrell engaged antiquarian Nathaniel Ogle to write an introduction for it. However, Ogle declared the gems to be contemporary works, produced in the late 18th and early 19th centuries. Not surprisingly, Tyrrell was greatly angered and this led to one of the art world's most furious feuds.

The Ogle view proved accurate as it was demonstrated that Prince Poniatowski, determined to have the grandest collection of all, had achieved his purpose by ordering the gems made by certain Italian engravers to illustrate episodes from Greek literature and mythology. The prince then had other engravers add false signatures. In his zeal as a collector the prince had all but invented an entire antiquity of his own.

PONZI, CHARLES *swindler*
Charles Ponzi (1883–1949) became for a time such a successful swindler that his name has entered the English language: Any scheme in which the original investors are paid off with money supplied by a succeeding army of suckers is now known as a Ponzi scheme.

Ponzi came to America from Italy in the late 19th century and had been a fruit peddler, a dishwasher, a waiter, a forger and an alien smuggler. Despite these undistinguished and/or notorious activities in his past, Ponzi was to become the most-beloved Italian in America, especially to those who got in early on his fantastic scheme and actually made money. Once, when hauled before a government inquiry to explain his money-making operations, he was cheered by worshiping crowds before the State House in Boston. A voice called out: "You're the greatest Italian of them all!"

"No, No," Ponzi responded with appropriate modesty. "Columbus and Marconi. Columbus discovered America. Marconi discovered the wireless."

"Yes, but you discovered money," replied his supporter.

Ponzi had discovered that he could purchase international postal-union reply coupons at depressed prices in some foreign countries and sell them in the United States at a tidy profit of up to 50%. In his first private transaction he bought up $1,250 worth of coupons and redeemed them at a profit of $750. It was a beautiful get-rich-slow caper, but strictly small-time and quite boring to Ponzi.

Ponzi then came up with a way to increase his profits dramatically by simply telling people he needed a lot of capital to make a lot of money. For using their funds, he offered investors a 50% profit in three months and later cut the time period to 45 days. It was an offer not many people could refuse. The money started rolling into Ponzi's Boston office. He shortly began to open offices in surrounding states.

Once Ponzi actually started paying out the interest, the real deluge began. At least 40,000 people virtually threw money at him. How much can only be guessed, but the figure was far in excess of $10 million. In one remarkable day in 1920, Ponzi garnered $2 million out of the country's newest gamblers, the little folk who squeezed money out of small bank accounts, mattresses, piggy banks and cookie jars. There were days when Ponzi's office looked like a hurricane had hit. Incoming money littered the place, stuffed in closets, desk drawers and overflowing in wastebaskets.

The more that Ponzi took in, the more he paid out, which of course simply brought in yet more money. All Ponzi was doing was following the technique used a couple of decades earlier by William "520%" Miller (see entry), but Ponzi did it with much more flair. With his seemingly endless supply of cash Ponzi bought up huge tracts of land and property in Boston. He gained a controlling interest in the Hanover Trust Company and also bought J. P. Poole, a brokerage firm where he had worked as a messenger for three years. He promptly fired his old boss. In his personal wardrobe he had 200 suits, 100 pairs of shoes, 48 Malacca canes with gold handles, 24 diamond stickpins and so on. On the street people cheered him; he was Boston's grandest hero.

But in 1920 the *Boston Post* dug up Ponzi's past record and revealed he had spent time in prison in Canada for check forgery and in Atlanta for smuggling aliens. That was enough to cause some of Ponzi's enthusiastic investors to hold up; as soon as that happened, Ponzi's cash-voracious scheme fell apart. His books showed a deficit of $5 million to $10 million, but the records were chaotic and the shortfall was probably much more. No one ever knew for sure.

Ponzi was sentenced to five years in federal prison. During this time he sent out reams of Christmas cards to thousands of victims promising he would recoup their money once he got free. When he was released in three and a half years, he was convicted for larceny under Massachusetts state law. While on appeal, Ponzi took off for Florida, where he tried selling swamp land. A Florida court found him guilty, but

Charles Ponzi was hailed as "the greatest Italian of them all" by his gulled investors for having "discovered money."

Ponzi fled to Texas. When caught he was shipped back to Massachusetts to serve his seven- to nine-year sentence.

Upon completion of that term Ponzi was extradicted to Italy. Here the Ponzi dossier is hazy, but there seems to be considerable evidence that he conned his way into the confidence of Benito Mussolini and gave the Italian dictator the benefit of his financial advice. It did not prove to be a profitable experience for the Italian regime, and Ponzi is said to have skipped the country just before Mussolini was to have him shot. Just before the outbreak of World War II, Ponzi surfaced in Brazil, where he worked for a time for an Italian airline, but the firm went out of business during the conflict. After that Ponzi proved unsuccessful at running a hot dog stand and then eked out a living teaching English and French. His last few years were ones of true deprivation. Partially blind and paralyzed, he ended up in the charity ward of a Rio de Janeiro hospital. He died there in January 1949.

See also PYRAMID SCHEMES.

PORNOGRAPHIC ESCAPE RUSE

A prison escape that in its time amused all of Europe (except Germany) and is still fondly recalled by French Intelligence occurred on December 29, 1911, at the military fortress in Glatz, Germany. French Intelligence agent Captain Charles Lux, imprisoned there six months before, had immediately started plotting an escape. He discovered that he could escape by unlocking three doors, which would take him down to the second floor—one below his—where he could drop outside the walls from an unused cell, if he could saw through its window bars. He also found a way to pass secret messages to the outside by writing invisibly on the inside of envelopes. Lux wrote his brother to mail him a forged passport, some coin money, several saws and material for a rope. Meanwhile Lux, an expert on locks, made keys to open the three doors.

The first package to arrive included a dozen towels (the rope-to-be) and a passport concealed inside a book diary. The gift parcel easily survived the warden's inspection. However, the remainder of the items—several small saws and 24 gold coins—was far more difficult because of its weight. Lux's brother concealed them inside the covers of a novel, making the book very heavy. Nevertheless, the warden passed the novel along with no more than a cursory glance. The official was much more concerned about two other books in the package, both of which he immediately confiscated with disparaging observations about the "decadent French." The two books were filled with obscene illustrations.

PORTRAIT SCAM *rooking the bereaved*

Shortly after a wealthy man dies, a large carton is delivered to his home. The family opens it and finds a striking oil painting of the deceased. It has an eerie impact on the family, since it appears that the dead man had apparently posed for the portrait shortly before he passed away. And it certainly is something to remember the person by, much better than a mere photograph. There is no bill enclosed, merely a return label, listing a name followed by the word "Portraits."

The next day a bill, anywhere from $1,000 to $3,000, comes. The family feels it *is* a lot of money, but it is also a haunting painting. Of course, the deceased never posed for any such portrait; the painting had been done from a recent photograph, from a picture published with an obituary in the local newspaper or from a business trade journal.

Some artist con men make a nice living from such a scam. They don't collect on every painting, but on more than enough to earn themselves a handsome income. Generally speaking, they can avoid legal prosecution as long as they make no false claims about the portraits. However, one particularly successful con artist did go to prison after engaging in such a lucrative practice for years. He had painted brown eyes on a blue-eyed man, proving that the deceased had not sat for him.

This deception is merely a high-priced version of scams police bunco squads and postal inspectors refer to as the work of "Funeral Chasers."

See also FUNERAL CHASERS.

POSTAL IMPOSTORS *mail beggars*

We have never been without fraud by mail, especially solicitations for money by swindlers with a sad tale to tell. Nowhere did fraud by mail thrive as an organized cottage industry as much as in 19th-century England. It was Charles Dickens who led the battle against these charlatans, dubbing them "postal impostors" in a series of articles he wrote for the *Morning Chronicle* in 1836. He related his own personal experiences with letter-writing swindlers and their special delivery techniques:

> He has besieged my door at all hours of the day and night; he has fought my servant; he has lain in ambush for me, going out and coming in; he has followed me out of town into the country; he has written to me from immense distances, when I have been out of England. He has fallen sick; he has died and been buried; he has come to life again, and again departed from the transitory scene; he has been his own son, his own mother, his own baby, his idiot mother, his uncle, his aunt, his aged grandfather. He has wanted a great-coat to go to India in; a pound to set him up in life forever; a pair of boots to take him to the coast of China; a hat to get him a permanent situation under Government. He has frequently been just seven and six pence short of independence; he has had such openings at Liverpool—posts of great trust and confidence in merchants' houses which nothing but seven and six pence was waiting to him to secure—that I wonder he is not mayor of that flourishing town at the present moment.

In the period of Dickens' travail it was estimated there were no less than 250 professional letter charlatans in England, mostly in London, some earning as much as an estimated 1,000 pounds per year, a rather fabulous income for the 1830s. According to the authorities, many of these highly talented specialists needed clerks to run their businesses at top efficiency. Their identities were far from secret, and they were noted for owning expensive carriages and fast horses, useful when they felt the need to recuperate from writer's cramp.

One of the most infamous specialists of the era was one Blind Williams who, in his prime, netted at least £600 to £800 annually from his letter writing—after the expense of his top aide, Joseph Underwood, at £80, and another aide at £50. Blind made many appeals by telling potential donors he was on the verge of going blind.

Typical of the Williams-Underwood operation (Underwood married Williams' "widowed mistress") is this sample letter dated July 1, 1833, to the earl of Stamford, highlighting Williams' talents, which seemingly could have qualified him as one of the more noted potboiler novelists of the day, if not quite up to the masterly Dickens. It is written in a girlish script, at which Williams and his aides were most adept, and tells of a young girl whom a scoundrel of a gentleman had seduced from her "happy and tender home." Williams wrote:

My Lord—It is with shame, indescribable shame, I presume to address your Lordship with these lines; but from having a knowledge of your Lordship's person from my infancy, and through the report of your Lordship's sympathising and benevolent character, I am about entrusting a most unfortunate affair to your Lordship's honor and secrecy. I am really ashamed to detail my misfortunes, my Lord, but I must; I must acquaint your Lordship. I know of no other person so likely to render me some assistance in the hour of need, and to save me from perdition and a premature grave, as your Lordship, whose humanity does honor to the feelings of a susceptible heart . . . .

As Ralph Hancock and Henry Chafetz note in *The Compleat Swindler*, ". . . such letters, though written more than a hundred years ago, are not much out of date. They are just longer than the ones we get today and are perhaps written in prettier English."

POYAIS LAND FRAUD *peddling Panama's Mosquito Coast*

One of the most outrageous land swindles in history was the work of a colorful military adventurer named Gregor McGregor (1786–1845), scion of an ancient and noble Scottish family. Bred for the military life, McGregor served in the British army and then went to Venezuela in 1811 to fight for South America's great Liberator, Simon Bolivar.

With the early success of the revolution, he moved on to fight in the U.S. conflict with Spain in 1817 (over the colony of Florida). He then rejoined Bolivar in renewed fighting against colonial Spain. He married Bolivar's daughter and in 1820 headed up a mercenary expedition against Portobello, a Spanish settlement on the Mosquito Coast (or Caribbean shore) of the Isthmus of Panama.

The area was a nominal British protectorate, but because of the unhealthy nature of the land had remained basically uncolonized. McGregor befriended the only inhabitants of the unsettled area, the Poyais Indians.

Returning to England as Gregor I ("the Prince of Poyais"), McGregor started up a commercial enterprise to peddle the Mosquito Coast (which stretches from Panama to present-day Honduras) as an unspoiled paradise. The natives, he reported, were friendly, and the rising cities brimming with culture. There were also many natural beauties, lush forests and fertile land tracts. With an impressive and colorful entourage Gregor I toured the British Isles, touting the investment and settlement values of the Poyais Nation. William John Richardson, a McGregor accomplice who had fought alongside the adventurer in his many campaigns, was received at court as the Poyais ambassador. McGregor himself was knighted by King George IV who sought to ensure that his subjects would be ruled by a British titleholder.

Potential settlers eagerly bought holdings in exotic Panama, a land about which little had been known, save for the glorious information offered by McGregor's land offices in London and Edinburgh. The titled McGregor had little trouble getting the prestigious banking firm of Sir John Perring & Co. to extend a £200,000 loan and shares were floated.

The first settlers landed in 1822, and it took a long time for information of what they found to filter back to Britain. They did not discover any fabulous cities or thriving land tracts, but, rather, impoverished natives living in pathetic huts. And they found mosquitoes. Of the first seven ships to bring settlers to the Poyais Nation, all returned full of embittered passengers.

As for McGregor, he had decamped for Paris, where his ardent sales force launched his fraudulent campaign among the French. He also conned financial interests there into granting him a loan totaling £300,000, posting as security the "gold-mines of Paulaze."

In 1827 McGregor showed up once again in London, assuming that the passage of time had dulled memory of his financial transgressions. It hadn't and he was arrested; but he managed to get some of his still-deluded backers to post bail for him, arguing their original investments were about to bear fruit. Mc-

Gregor immediately jumped bail and recrossed the Channel. Unfortunately, the French had come to realize how he had skinned them, and he was imprisoned there.

After serving a term in a French prison, he retired to the provinces to lead a quiet existence for a time. McGregor made another attempt at reviving interest in his Poyais settlements, but by then he had run out of gullible investors. In 1839 McGregor petitioned Venezuela for citizenship, which was granted to him as an honored campaigner of the revolution. McGregor returned to the scene of his more gallant enterprises and lived out his six remaining years on a comfortable general's pension.

PRETENDER CZARS *impostor trio*

Pretenders to a throne are hardly unique; but in Russia around the turn of the 17th century, there were three impostors who pretended to be Czar Dmitry Ivanovitch, the son of Ivan the Terrible. And carrying their impostures to the logical limits in this period known in history as the "Time of Troubles," impostors numbers 2 and 3 likewise claimed to be impostor number 1.

The real Dmitry died mysteriously at the age of nine in 1591, during the reign of his older brother, Fyodor I. Because he had died of stab wounds, an official inquiry was ordered under the leadership of Prince Vasily Shuysky. The inquiry concluded that the young Dmitry had suffered an epileptic fit and in the process stabbed himself to death. Dmitry's mother did not accept the findings and insisted the child had been murdered. She was forced to take the veil, and her relatives were all banished from Moscow.

In 1598 Czar Fyodor I died and was succeeded by his brother-in-law, Boris Godunov. Two years later a pretender appeared, announcing he was the real Dmitry and insisting he had not died at all in 1591. There is considerable evidence that this so-called Dmitry was really a monk named Grigory Bogdanovich Otrepvev, but there is also evidence indicating this youth actually believed himself to be the legitimate heir to the throne. He took up residence in Moscow in 1601–1602 and held court as "Prince Dmitry."

Faced with official reprisal, this Dmitry fled to Lithuania, where he was embraced by Lithuanian and Polish nobles and the Jesuits. By 1604 this false Dmitry had raised a substantial army and swept into Russia. Although defeated in several battles, the pretender nevertheless continued to gain supporters throughout southern Russia, and more importantly he gained the support of Prince Vasily Shuysky, who announced early in 1605 that Dmitry had not died in

1591. Meanwhile, Czar Boris died in April of that year, and immediately large segments of the governmental armies shifted their support to Dmitry. Shuysky and his supporters made sure there would be no dispute on the succession by murdering Boris' infant son and heir, Fyodor II.

The Russian nobles pledged loyalty to the false Dmitry, who was crowned czar in Moscow. The alliance did not last. Dmitry antagonized the Russian elite by catering to Polish influence and marrying Marina Mniszek, a member of a noble Polish family. Dmitry's wife and her Jesuit supporters influenced the czar to join in a projected Christian alliance aimed at ejecting the Turks from Europe. With the growing disaffection for Dmitry, Shuysky once more changed his position. He said Dmitry was an impostor after all.

Dmitry banished Shuysky from Moscow, but the latter rallied other nobles to his cause. In May 1606 they fought their way into the Kremlin and, after a fierce fight in which Dmitry killed a number of his foes, the pretender czar was slain.

Dmitry's corpse was hauled to a public place and left for a time with a ribald mask over his face and a flute placed in his mouth. Then the corpse was burned and his ashes shot from a cannon in the direction of Poland as a warning against further resurrections. Shuysky mounted the throne as Czar Vasily IV.

The vicious treatment of the dead Dmitry did not have the desired effect. In the superstitous Russian countryside the belief spread that Dmitry had not died, and in August 1607 a second false Dmitry appeared. Although he claimed to be the first, he looked nothing like the "original." Nonetheless, the second Dmitry rallied the same coalition of cossacks, Poles, Lithuanians and other rebels who had supported his predecessor. The second Dmitry held court in the north at Tushino, and with Marina Mniszek's acknowledgment of the pretender as her husband, the second Dmitry became as powerful as Vasily was in Moscow.

Desperate for aid, Vasily made an alliance with Sweden, and the second false Dmitry was forced out of his stronghold. However, the tie with Sweden angered Poland, which went to war against Vasily. Soon a Polish army was moving on Moscow as was another force under a reinvigorated second Dmitry. In July 1610 Vasily's position became untenable, and he was driven from power and forced to take monastic vows. However, in December of that year, the second Dmitry himself failed to reach Moscow, having been mortally wounded by one of his own followers.

History has been unable to determine if that attack was accidental or willful, but in any event the predictable happened again. Within a few months a third false Dmitry appeared, claiming to be the same Dmitry. By March 1612 Dmitry had penetrated as far as the outskirts of Moscow, and appeared unstoppable. Then in May he was betrayed, captured, brought to Moscow and executed. Russia had now run out of fake Dmitrys.

PRICKERS *witch-hunting con men*

During the 17th century (especially in England and Scotland) "prickers" (or "common prickers" as they were called) roamed the countryside as witch hunters, capitalizing on the ludicrous belief that witches could not feel the prick of a pin, when it was jabbed in a mark the devil had put on their bodies. These common prickers worked on commission, being paid for every witch they exposed who was consigned first to the rack (to gain a confession) and then inevitably to the flames.

A typical case was the trial of Janet Peaston in 1647, when the magistrates of Dalkeith in Scotland stated, as related in Pitcairn's *Records of Justiciary:*

> . . . caused John Kincaid of Tranent, the common pricker, to exercise his craft on her. He found two marks of the devil's making; for she could not feel the pin when it was put into either of the said marks, nor did the marks bleed when the pin was taken out again. When she was asked where she thought the pins were put in her, she pointed to a part of her body distant from the real place. They were pins of three inches in length.

As a result, Janet Peaston was burned at the stake.

Another woman in Scotland was executed on the most flimsy claims of one John Bain, a common pricker, who was apparently most determined at his trade or at least in the collection of fees. Bain swore that as he passed the woman's door, he heard her talking to the devil. The poor woman's only defense was that she foolishly often talked to herself; this fact was confirmed by several neighbors, but perhaps without much fervor since too much expressed sympathy for a witch might also incriminate them as practitioners of witchcraft. Thus Bain's evidence was received by the court, including his statement that no one ever talked to himself who was not a witch. Bain found supposed devil's marks on the woman and after demonstrating she did not feel his pricks she was "convict and brynt."

The English and Scottish parliaments had long fortified the claims of the common prickers and armed these charlatans with a measure of authority, consequently forcing magistrates and ministers to accept their evidence. But the chief villain in the common pricker frauds has been named as James VI of Scotland (who became James I of England after the death of Queen Elizabeth). In 1597 James published his famous treatise *Demonologie,* in which His Majesty urged witch hunters to engage in "finding of their mark, and trying the insensibilies thereof."

The frightful reign of the common prickers thus had almost free reign for the better part of a century before authorities finally worked up enough nerve to seek curbing them. In the 1660s James Walsh, a common pricker, was publicly whipped through the streets of Edinburgh for falsely accusing a woman of witchcraft. Thereafter, judges refused to accept their evidence, simply because their claims had become so numerous the dishonest ones were considered nuisances.

In 1678 the privy council of Scotland, on hearing the complaint of a woman who had been indecently exposed by one of them, stated the opinion that "common prickers were common cheats." This did not mean the end of pricking in either Scotland or England, for as late as 1711 one Jane Wenham, better known as the Witch of Walkerne, was convicted of witchcraft on evidence of pricking. Lord Chief Justice Powell was reluctantly forced to pass the death sentence, but he finally obtained a royal pardon for the woman, who was set free. It was not until 1736 that King James' penal statutes in both England and Scotland were repealed. Witches could be subjected to the pillory or imprisonment only for their "crimes."

By about this time pricking, with a few notable exceptions, had fallen into disrepute on the European continent as well.

See also HOPKINS, MATTHEW, WITCHFINDER GENERAL.

PROHIBITION REPEAL HOAX

Most newspaper hoaxes are intended either for the writer's personal amusement or the paper's desire to gain a scoop over the competition. In one famous journalistic incident, however, the motive was to prevent the *competition* from inevitably gaining a scoop.

In 1933 Don Howard, news editor of the *Salt Lake City Telegram,* was in a quandary. At the time 35 states had voted for repeal of the 18th Amendment (Prohibition), and it was clear that Utah would be the 36th. Delegates to the state repeal convention assembled, but they had decided to put off a vote for some four hours to allow for an extensive nationwide radio hook-up so that, according to Howard, Utah politicians could "make a lot of long-winded speeches they imagined would be good publicity for the state."

That might be fine for the politicians and perhaps even Utah, but it was bad for the *Telegram,* which would not have any news to report until the following day, while competing papers would have it in their editions much earlier. "It was a case of my paper going to press without the repeal story unless something was done," the editor said.

Thus Howard decided to take control of the voting schedule by inventing a news report from Maine. He passed along the story to the Utah delegates that the delegates to the Maine repeal convention were altering their own schedule to cheat Utah out of its 36th position, the one that would put repeal over the top. The fake news electrified the Utah delegates, and plans to hold off the vote until an evening session were scrapped, radio coverage or not. They hurriedly made do with whatever radio coverage could be made available on short notice, and politicians—in one of the more rare instances in political history—reduced their speeches to brief comments. The Prohibition era ended in time for the *Telegram* to hit the newsstands first and, needless to say, sell out.

PROTECTION CON   *Mafia scam*

It is well known that the Mafia and other elements of organized crime operate protection shakedown rackets in which a person on the fringe of the law or an honest businessman is forced to pay money to prevent anything "bad" from happening. However, the Mafia is seldom satisfied with just this shakedown. After years of taking money from a victim, the mobsters themselves secretly set up a threat against the victim, perhaps in the form of a competitor threatening to take over a bookmaker's operation. The protection victim suddenly calls upon his "protectors" to deliver.

The mobsters survey the situation and declare this is a major deal and that the victim will have to pay a hefty one-time additional charge to make the threat go away. The victim desperately pays for a service he does not really receive.

Jack Dragna, the late crime boss of Los Angeles, was big on such protection cons. In one case, however, the victim was so worked up about the threat to him that even after the fake muscling-in ploy was canceled he insisted that the supposed villain in the setup be murdered. When Dragna finally determined the victim would never cool off, he simply had him killed. True protection, by Mafia standards, means protection only for the mobsters' own.

PROTOCOLS OF ZION   *anti-Semitic hate forgery*

Few lies have had the staying power shown by the so-called *Protocols of the Learned Elders of Zion,* which first appeared in Russia in 1905, purporting to outline secret Jewish plans for achieving world power by undermining Christian morality, health and family life. This goal was to be accomplished in part by

securing a monopoly of international finance (and oddly at the same time tearing down this financial monopoly by fomenting communist revolutions and so on).

The *Protocols of Zion* was translated by anti-Semites in many countries and into most major languages of the world. From its introduction to the onset of World War II it is believed to have achieved the highest total circulation of any modern literary work up to that time.

The protocols had been forged by General Pyotr Rachkovsky, head of the Russian secret police in Paris, and an aide, Matthew Golowinsky. It was first promoted in Russia by the religious mystic Sergei Nilus who publicized it as an appendix to his 1905 book *The Great in the Little.* In it Nilus insisted that the 25,000-word work was a translation of the French text of a speech delivered some years earlier to a secret conclave of 300 prominent Jews. In a later edition, Nilus identified the speaker as Theodor Herzl, the founder of modern Zionism, and said the meeting had been in Basel, Switzerland, in 1897 at the time of the founding congress of the World Zionist Organization.

Nilus announced that the elders' plan was to "corrupt the young generation by subversive education, dominate people through their vices, destroy family life, undermine respect for religion, encourage luxury, amuse people to prevent them from thinking, poison the spirit by destructive theories, weaken human bodies by inoculation with microbes, foment international hatred and prepare for universal bankruptcy and concentration of gold in the hands of the Jews."

While the Russian government used the protocols for a rationale to justify pogroms against Jews, even Czar Nicholas II—a hater of his Jewish subjects—banned the work for a time as a fraud. After the Russian Revolution, the foes of the Bolsheviks distributed the protocols throughout the country in an effort to characterize Russia's woes and the Bolsheviks as a Jewish plot. One hundred thousand Jews were slaughtered in the pogroms of 1918–1920 that followed.

In America the most prominent believer in the protocols was industrialist Henry Ford, who printed them in his newspaper *The Dearborn Independent* in 1920, and then in book form as *The International Jew.* According to one observer, Ford's efforts represented "one of the most important anti-Semitic campaigns ever attempted in the United States." It was only when Ford was sued in 1927 by Aaron Shapiro, a Jewish lawyer, that the falsity of the protocols were clearly demonstrated to him, and Ford finally retracted his charges with a public apology to the Jewish community.

Next to promote the protocols in the U.S. was Father Charles E. Coughlin, the fascist-minded, anti-Semitic priest who published the text frequently in the 1930s in his *Social Justice*. Coughlin even resurrected Ford as a supporter of the protocols, quoting him in *Social Justice* as feeling "they fit in with what is going on," even though they might in themselves be false. Coughlin similarly stressed the "factuality" of the protocols.

Of course, in the 1930s the greatest exploitation of the protocols was by Nazi Germany to justify the oppression of the Jews. Like Coughlin, the Nazis felt no compulsion about using a document demonstrated to be an outright forgery in 1921. Philip Graves, a correspondent of the *London Times*, revealed that the so-called protocols were nothing more than an almost word-for-word, extravagant phrase-for-phrase plagiarism of a pamphlet *Dialogue in Hell Between Machiavelli and Montesquieu* written in 1865 by Maurice Joly. Joly made no reference to the Jews at all and was instead making a satirical attack on Napoleon III and discussed how a democratic state could be subverted. Joly was imprisoned and fined for his insult to the Second Empire.

The protocols' forgers had simply substituted the Jewish element for the Napoleonic in the *Dialogue*. Mystic Nilus further embellished the work by adding an extra chapter, "In the Jewish Cemetery of Prague," which he blatantly lifted from an 1868 novel, *Biarritz*, by Hermann Josedsche.

Despite endless exposes of the so-called protocols, they continued to be promoted over the years. Many Arabic editions appeared from the 1960s onward, especially in Lebanon and Kuwait, with thousands of copies printed in French and Spanish for distribution in Asia and Latin America. The protocols were endorsed by late Egyptian President Gamal Abdel Nasser. In Saudi Arabia copies were customarily given to foreign visitors by King Faisal before his assassination in 1975. The same gift giving was true of Libyan dictator Muammer el-Qaddafi. The biggest promoter in non-northern Africa was Idi Amin of Uganda. Most recently, the forged works have been heavily distributed in Italy, Argentina and Brazil among other countries.

PSALMANAZAR, GEORGE   *the Formosan cannibal*

In early 1704 George Psalmanazar appeared in London and launched one of the most impressive hoaxes of all time. Introduced by a military chaplain, the Reverend William Innes, to the bishop of London as a converted heathen from Formosa (a place that Psalamanazar had never seen, as had not any Englishman), Psalmanazar was to be lionized by British society. Before the year was out, he had published *An Historical and Geographical Description of Formosa* that presented incredible, bizarre and mind-boggling details about his alleged country's strange language, manners, religion, customs, history and geography. Psalmanazar, it seemed, was a member of a princely Formosan family who had some six years earlier made his way to Japan and then the outer world, living for a time in France, where he was educated and persecuted by Jesuits. In time he was completely converted to the Christian faith. He could converse in six languages, including ancient Greek and Latin. His handsome appearance, erudition and wit absolutely charmed English society.

His conversion did not cure him of all his Formosan past, it seemed, and he was particularly addicted to eating raw meat. Psalmanazar held social and scientific societies spellbound and offered brilliantly glib answers for any questions made about his more wild declarations.

In view of the fact that he was Oriental, people asked, why was his skin so fair? Psalmanazar smiled and explained that he, like most members of the upper classes, passed most of his life in "cool shades or apartments underground." Only the lower classes toiled in the hot sun and had their skins tanned yellow.

In truth, it would later be learned that Psalmanazar was French. He had been educated by Franciscans and then Jesuits until he left his cloistered life at 16. He first pretended to be a Japanese prince, until he met up with the roguish Reverend Innes, whereupon the pair decided to convert him into a true unknown, a Formosan.

Psalmanazar continued to inform audiences of Formosan culture and strict laws. One statute read: "Whosoever shall strike the King, Intendant, or Governor shall be hanged by his feet till he dies, having four dogs fastened to his body to tear it to pieces." And since the English were utterly taken by accounts of cannibalism, Psalmanazar made his own devotion to the practice a centerpiece of his lectures. He also explained that if a Formosan husband wearied of his wife, he had only to accuse her of adultery, and he then was entitled to cut off her head and eat her.

"Barbarous!" exclaimed one shocked noble woman.

Yes, Psalmanazar agreed, it most certainly was if the husband had made the accusation falsely, but as for eating human flesh, he said, "I think it no sin to eat human flesh, but I must own that it is a little unmannerly."

Soon after the publication of Psalmanazar's first book, the bishop of London sent the bizarre foreigner to Oxford where he was to study and also lecture on Formosan history. The Anglican Church also commissioned him to translate the Old and New Testaments into Formosan.

Despite his unmasking as a hoaxer, George Psalmanazar was championed by Dr. Samuel Johnson (pictured)—otherwise caustic in his denunciation of literary fakers—as "the best man I ever knew."

At Oxford he attended lectures with a pet snake wrapped around his neck, an old Formosan custom for keeping cool. He also left candles burning through the night in the windows of his quarters to create the impression of being a most ardent scholar.

In time the scientific questions mounted, and Psalmanazar issued a new edition of his original work dealing with 25 serious objections to his many tales. These answers satisfied most of the public, and his reputation remained intact. In 1707 a Jesuit priest named Father Fountenay who had served 18 years in China declared Psalmanazar to be a fraud and challenged him to a debate. It was an offer the good father should never have extended. With savage wit and rhetoric, Psalmanazar drove the truth-telling Jesuit father from the rostrum.

Nevertheless, questions continued to be raised. Sir Isaac Newton charged parts of Psalmanazar's book had been lifted from obscure foreign texts on Formosa and Japan that were 40 years old. Psalmanazar did not choose to respond to the venerable scientist, but Reverend Innes saw the handwriting on the wall. The pair had made fortunes out of the masquerade, and the military chaplain had indulged himself in lavish quarters ever brimming with wine and women. Now he saw the wisdom of wrangling an appointment as chaplain-general of British troops in Portu-gal. The bogus young Formosan was left to face his critics on his own.

It was skeptical Dr. Edmund Halley, the astronomer of comet fame, who finally broke down Psalmanazar. Halley asked how long the sun shone down the chimney of the Formosan underground homes on average days in different seasons. Psalmanazar's answers were wildly inaccurate mathematically. Halley asked more questions about other astronomical phenomena, and Psalmanazar did not supply correct answers.

In the end Psalmanazar admitted his hoax and faded away into the English countryside. Not without writing talent, Psalmanazar finally wrangled some translation work from printers for substandard pay. Eventually he returned to London, where he did some ghostwriting work and produced a fine, annotated edition of the *Book of Psalms*. He had few friends in his later years, but among them was Dr. Samuel Johnson with whom he had long alehouse discussions on literature and religion. Johnson defended his friendship for the old-time hoaxer by saying "his piety, penitence and virtue exceeded almost what we read as wonderful even in the lives of the saints."

Psalmanazar secretly spent some 25 years writing his own memoirs, which were a complete confession of his grandiose hoax, but told nothing of his true identity. He died on May 3, 1763, his age estimated between 80 and 85. After reading Psalmanazar's memoirs, Dr. Johnson called him "the best man I ever knew."

PYRAMID SCHEMES *confidence game*

Pyramid rackets have been around in various forms for many centuries and today swindle Americans out of millions of dollars annually. Some pyramid schemes make no attempt to hide their identity, coming in the form of dollar bills in chain letters. Others, in the form of distributorships and franchises, are so well concealed that most victims do not even realize that they are in a pyramid game. Only in theory can a pyramid scheme continue indefinitely. Actually all pyramid bubbles have to collapse as the numbers grow outlandishly.

One of the most bizarre pyramid financial schemes swept California in the 1970s and left in its wake a trail of broken families and wrecked friendships. In the scheme each well-to-do player paid an entry fee of $1,000. The player was then required to bring in two new players, each of whom also contributed $1,000 apiece. Half of each $1,000 went to the top of the pyramid, while the remaining $500 from each newer player went to the player who recruited them. Thus, the first player got his money back and then waited to move up another rung on the pyramid. Meanwhile, each of the second two players recruited two more players so that they could recover their original $1,000 investment. The way the pyramid was to work, the initial player moved up from the 16th rung, to the eighth run, to the fourth run, to the second rung and finally to the first rung. At the first rung the player would have received a total of $16,000.

Of course, it appeared simple enough for each player in a rung to recruit two new players, but some very grim mathematics soon took over. Actually, each player on the 16th rung was creating two new pyramids and this progression of twos kept getting bigger and bigger. Since there were 16 players on the bottom rung, it took 32 players to get them to go up to the next rung. Then each of these 32 had to recruit a total of 64. The 64 had to find 128. The 128 had to find 256. By that time the first set of 16 players reached the top of their pyramids, which meant that the next set of players on the 16th rung re-quired 512 recruits, and the next group had to find 1,024.

By June 1980 the California pyramid collapsed. Even that state ran short of gullible folks needed to join. There were howls of pain and charges of thievery.

A spokesman for California's attorney general's office stated that a number of operators had been arrested as they attempted to start new pyramids in New York, Florida and Canada. It should be understood that sophisticated victims are often part of a pyramid. They tend to know that a pyramid scheme has to collapse, and they are always informed they are getting in at the start "so there's no way you can lose." Of course, they are told this no matter how long the pyramid has been going. The way the original promoters work is to start up a dozen or more pyramids at once.

See also DISTRIBUTORSHIP FRAUDS.

QUIZ SHOW HOAXES

The 1950s were the golden age of television quiz shows, when big-money winners became national celebrities and such shows built enormous audiences. The crash came in 1959 when many highly acclaimed winners were exposed as frauds, having been fed hints and answers by the shows' producers. Perhaps the most shocking fraud was Charles

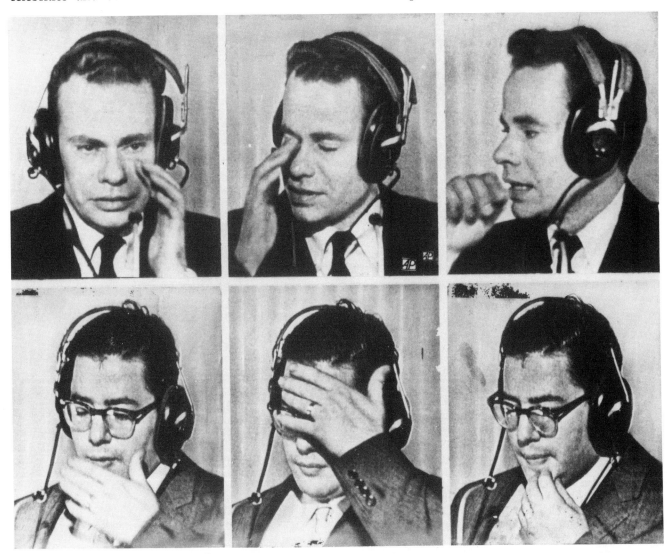

Van Doren, a 33-year-old Ph.D. and a member of one of the country's leading intellectual families.

A $5,500-a-year instructor at Columbia University, Van Doren won $129,000 on NBC's "Twenty-One" after having been supplied with a trumped-up script in advance. The producers had convinced Van Doren to take part in the intellectual charade because it would be a boon "to the intellectual life, to teachers, and to education in general." After his exposure Van Doren said, "In fact, I think I have done a disservice to all of them."

As a result of his new fame and seeming ability, Van Doren was given a $50,000-a-year post with the network. When the scandal was revealed he lost that post as well as his teaching position at the university.

In its investigation, the Manhattan district attorney's office called 150 persons to testify before a grand jury. Of these, District Attorney Frank Hogan declared that about 100 had lied. Over the next three years 18 contestants who had won from $500 to $220,500 on the now-off-the-air quiz shows pleaded guilty to perjury and were given suspended sentences, although they could have been sentenced to three years and fined. Nothing was done to the corporate sponsors, who according to the shows' producers, decided if a contestant was allowed to win or be bumped from the show.

An amusing sidelight was revealed by television insiders who said some so-called panel shows were not above fixing answers some of the time to heighten the "socko entertainment level." It was said some major celebrities refused to appear on such shows unless guaranteed they "wouldn't be in a position to look stupid by giving wrong answers." Even with the right answers some plans went awry. Insiders tell of a retired boxing champion who was informed in advance that sometime during the show a correct answer would be "poison ivy." The champ was so excited at the prospect of showing off his intelligence that he shouted "poison ivory" in response to every question. That was embarrassing enough, but when at last the poison ivy question was asked, the champ, having been squelched too often, simply sat there sullenly and said nothing.

◄ In the great quiz show scandals of the 1950s, two leading players were Charles Van Doren (top), a Ph.D. and member of one of the nation's most esteemed intellectual families, and Herbert Stempel (below). As tension and the prize money built, Van Doren was schooled on how to look perplexed under pressure until inspiration hit, while Stempel, as he later admitted, got detailed "acting instructions" on how to take a dive.

R

THE RABBIT WOMAN *giving birth to bunnies*

In Godalming, England in late April 1726—more than 200 years before the giant rabbit Harvey made his bow on the Broadway stage—Mary Toft, a mother of three and wife of a journeyman clothier, babbled a strange tale to neighboring women. She had been weeding a field when she was criminally assaulted by a huge rabbit. Normally, a woman telling such a whopper would have been considered daft, but neighbors knew Mrs. Toft as a healthy, cheerful woman, not at all given to wild flights of fancy. Additionally, the attack had taken place on St. George's Day, a day on which occult forces were believed to be especially powerful.

In subsequent days Mary stopped her babbling and behaved normally. Some five months later she became very ill, and her husband Joshua hurried off to summon Mr. John Howard, a surgeon, from nearby Guildford. Dr. Howard examined the patient's abdomen and felt what he took to be life within. He visited his patient weekly thereafter and about a month later published a report that Mrs. Toft had given birth . . . to five bunnies!

It was a story that electrified the entire nation. (Alexander Pope would write Carlyle inquiring what faith he had in "the miracle at Guildford.") And Mrs. Toft told her physician she felt more rumblings within herself. Sure enough, Dr. Howard, who was a physician of high repute and had been delivering babies for some 30 years, shortly announced the birth of seven more rabbits!

The national excitement rose to a feverish pitch. Even George I took notice of the sensational occurrences. Skeptical doctors insisted the whole affair was a fraud and demanded an examination of the rabbit mother. By royal order two experts arrived on the scene. They were Nathaniel St. Andre, anatomist to the king and surgeon at Westminster Hospital, and

the Honorable Mr. Molyneux, secretary to the Prince of Wales. Both had spoken with disdain of the reports and were not to be readily deceived. They arrived just in time to witness the birth of two more little bunnies.

The next expert to appear was the Honorable Cyriacus Ahlers, surgeon to His Majesty's German Household. He came to Guildford on a mission to brand Mary Toft a fake, but he was present for the birth of yet another bunnie. Ahlers was a man transformed, departing with a promise to secure a pension from the king for amazing Mary.

By now the tale of Mary Toft's rape by a giant rabbit had spread throughout Europe, and King George ordered a final determination to be made by Sir Richard Manningham, F.R.S. Manningham brought along two surgeons as assistants and then packed Mary Toft off to a hospital in London. Manningham sat up with Mary the first night and noted that her belly was leaping but nothing occurred. He ordered that Mary be kept under constant surveillance by doctors and nurses so that it was impossible for any rabbits to be smuggled into her. The result: no more bunnies.

Manningham issued a report denouncing Mary as a phony. The initial reaction was much sympathy for Mrs. Toft—until it was announced that she was arrested and had made a full confession. A monster bunnie did not have its way with Mary Toft. Her husband had slipped her a bunny or two whenever no one was looking, and she hid them in her bedding, transferring them to the proper orifice as needed to confound the supposedly brilliant doctors. Later the artist Hogarth would engrave a satirical print entitled "The Wise Men of Godalming in Consultation."

Not long after Mary Toft's unmasking, a magician obtained a silk hat from a member of his audience and drew out a rabbit. Actually he used a variation of Mary's technique, drawing the rabbit from a secret pouch in his cape. Thus Mary Toft—whatever her other accomplishments and failures—at least became the "mother" of the rabbit trick.

A collection of works on the Mary Toft case can be found in the U.S. Army Medical Library in Washington, D.C. Among the recommended works on the subject are *British Medical Journal*, 1896, 2:209; *Gentleman's Magazine*, May 1842; *Sketches of Deception and Credulity, An Exact Diary*, Sir R. Manningham; *A short Narrative of an Extraordinary Delivery of Rabbits*, Nathaniel St. Andre.

RACE HORSE FIXER   See BARRIE PADDY.

RAMIREZ NO-SQUAWK CUT-OUTS   *cheating bootleggers*

Overall, counterfeiting may well be the least rewarding criminal activity, since at least 95% of all counterfeiters in the United States are caught and convicted. Perhaps that was why two very mediocre counterfeiters, Mexican brothers named Ramirez, decided in the 1920s that their wares would do much better if restricted to a very specialized clientele: bootleggers. For a time their operation—later to be dubbed by admiring law officials and journalists as the "Ramirez No-Squawk Cut-Outs"—was foolproof. Considering the poor quality of their $100 bills, it had to be perfect.

Bootleg liquor was always delivered for cash on the spot, which meant suppliers were paid off at sea outside the three-mile limit. With the boat pitching, the night moonless, the Ramirez bills were readily accepted. Later, of course, the bootleggers would discover they had been swindled, but they could hardly complain to the law, and by that time the Ramirez boys had moved to a new port of call.

Eventually the liquor suppliers hired bank tellers for a weekend's cruise at sea to check all of the payoff money. As a result, the Ramirez boys were put out of business by the bootleggers long before authorities had a chance to catch up with them.

RANDELL, CORTES   See NATIONAL STUDENT MARKETING CORPORATION.

REALTORS AS SCAM VICTIMS   *con men customers*

Realtors have long been a prime target for confidence men, since such agents can be counted on to aggressively cater to a prospective client. A legend in con men circles is the swindler fresh out of prison with just $25 in his pocket who was determined to have his first good meal without paying for it. He wandered into a real estate office and put on a big act about buying some large property. The agent was not about to let him get away and took him to a plush restaurant and wined and dined him. The con man told the salesman he was very impressed with him and they would continue their discussions. The con man lit up the expensive cigar the realtor had given him and wandered on his way.

Had the con man had the time he undoubtedly could have swindled the agent. He might perhaps have used the horse tip approach. The conservatively dressed swindler introduces himself to the realtor and says he is looking for a nice home for his elderly parents. He plans to live with them, but as an avid horseman he needs a home with several acres. Price, he tells the near-drooling agent, is not very important. The client gets the lavish treatment and a tour of restaurants while he is shown several expensive properties. After about three days the buyer selects the property he likes and presents the realtor with a large out-of-state check. The realtor is glowing, since he will earn several thousand dollars in commission.

Then, as they celebrate over another nice meal, the buyer reveals he is a racehorse owner. He tells the realtor he knows of a "sure thing" running the next day across the country at Santa Anita. The buyer tells the realtor he is placing a long-distance bet on the horse and asks the realtor if he would like to get in on the action. "I'm placing $10,000 myself. Would you like a few thousand?"

The realtor never had made a bet of that size in his life but does not wish to offend his customer. Besides, he was making so much on the real estate deal. Thus he agrees to put up $2,000 himself on a horse appropriately named No Trouble. The con man takes the money and says, "What do you say I come back tomorrow evening and sign those papers you have? And we can have a celebration on the horse as well."

It doesn't matter if the horse wins or loses, as the swindler never comes back. For his three days he has been lavishly entertained and picked up $2,000 in the bargain. Not bad at all for a non-real estate deal.

As con men say, they love sticking real estate people because they find so many worthy of being trimmed. There is the oft-told tale of Eddie Mines and Johnny on the Spot who took a St. Louis realtor for all he had. Mines, one of the greatest ropers ever, approached a realtor with a story that he was traveling with the black-sheep family member of a very dear friend. The man had just inherited a half-million dollars and was rapidly running through it, gambling and otherwise. In fact, right then he feared his errant charge (played by Johnny on the Spot) had $200,000 in a moneybelt. Mines said he wanted the broker's assistance in tying up the young man's funds in property he could not dissipate.

The realtor was much impressed and then became startlingly cooperative. "I have a big farm away up in the country," he confided. "Let's bump the kid off and split the two hundred thousand. We can bury him on the farm and no one will ever know what happened to him."

Mines managed to keep a straight face and said he'd think about it. Instead, Eddie and Johnny on the Spot became so incensed at the realtor's ethics that they swindled him at an unmerciful rate.

The standard gyp worked on a realtor is to make an offer of about $100,000 if he can get a certain piece of lakeside property for the con man. The real estate man knows it is worth no more than $35,000, and he hunts up the owner of the site and offers him $40,000 for it. The property owner, one of the con men, will not part with the property for less than $65,000. The real estate man is irate but agrees to the price since he has a fish on the line who will pay $100,000. The realtor buys the property and waits for his potential customer to come back. Of course, he never does. He and his con man partner have split the $35,000 in profit they have made on the property they'd purchased earlier for $30,000.

REAVIS, JAMES ADDISON *baron of Arizona and swindler*

One evening in 1881 a tall stranger rode into the territory of Arizona and, with a great deal of ceremony, demanded the best rooms in a Phoenix hotel. The next morning the stranger and his companions set about to shock the wits out of the citizens of the town. They emerged from the hotel bearing armfuls of placards and busied themselves nailing them all over town. Written in Spanish and English, the placards gave notice that everyone who claimed to own land, houses or property must get in touch with James Addison Reavis (?–1908) forthwith. The signs said that Reavis was the rightful owner to a 75-mile-deep stretch of land that ran from Phoenix 200 miles east to Silver City.

Naturally the notices were read with surprise, disbelief and horror. There was an immediate hue and cry for Reavis' head and later, when tempers had cooled, for an explanation of what it was all about. The explanation was forthcoming, and they learned that J. Addison Reavis had "irrefutable claims" to the ownership of every inch of land in a 15,000-square-mile area, the right of way to the Southern Pacific Railroad and possession of all the gold and silver mines in the area. Since they were on his land, he could put up a strong claim to every last house, store and ranch building.

The people who had accepted land from the government and developed it with sweat, hard work and privation were completely staggered. From that moment, there wasn't an owner of a single parcel of land, house, store or stable who knew whether he was going to be evicted the next moment or, if he wanted to sell out, what the value of his land really was. A great pall of unrest and confusion settled over the entire area.

For well over a decade Reavis' claims were accepted as legitimate, and he pointed out to railroad executives, mine operators and big ranchers that they were trespassing on his property. However, Reavis was ready to discuss rents with all "trespassers," large and small. The rental for the Southern Pacific's right-of-way was put at $50,000 a year.

The full story of Reavis' monumental fraud was never established, since he never confessed or revealed its origins or intricacies. However, it is known that he served in the Confederate Army during the Civil War and showed a knack for forging his commanding officers' signatures. After the war he was employed for a time as a streetcar conductor in St. Louis, where he used his writing talents to forge a fake real estate document that netted him a large sum of money. He headed west before he was apprehended.

Settling in Santa Fe, Reavis obtained a job as a clerk in the records division of a special governmental commission handling claims on property annexed by the United States following the Mexican War. Under a treaty settlement, the United States was to honor all legitimate claims of Spaniards and Mexicans and return to them the title to their lands. With this in mind Reavis laid the groundwork for his stupendous fraud. He studied the pure Spanish used in ancient documents and eventually forged one that indicated he was the undisputed heir of a grant given by the Spanish crown in 1758 to Miguel Silva de Peralta de la Cordoba, a nobleman known for his military exploits in the New World. Additionally, Reavis presented himself as the husband of the last of the mythical Peraltas, a young woman he had found working as a serving girl on a California ranch. The girl became convinced that she was indeed a long-lost Peralta.

Government experts and outsiders brought in to study Reavis' forged documents were completely fooled. They checked his papers against historical records, which Reavis had also doctored over a five-year period, in Mexico City and on trips to Madrid and Seville. As a result, no challenge was made to Reavis' claims until 1894, by which time Reavis had taken in some $10 millions in rent from hundreds of companies and thousands of families.

Then two small errors were unearthed. Reavis had used old inks and paper that appeared to be old, but a suspicious printer discovered that the watermark on the paper had not been designed until 1878. Besides that, incumbent to Reavis' tale was the long-ago birth of a pair of Peralta twins near San Bernardino, California. Their births were listed in the birth register at the Mission of San Salvador. It is not known how Reavis did it, but he had removed an entire page from the register and forged a new one that listed the twins in place of the names of two other babies. Unfortunately, and unknown to Reavis, the births were also recorded each day in another volume, which was kept hidden. This second volume turned out to name two other babies rather than the mythical Peralta twins.

Reavis was indicted in 1895 and convicted in federal court, despite a lavish defense he mounted with his immense wealth. He went to prison for six years, during which time his wife divorced him and vanished with their children. When Reavis was released a broken old man in 1901, he returned to Arizona. He lived there until his death in 1908, a vagrant who spent most of his time in the Phoenix library, pouring over old newspaper accounts of his glory days.

RECEIPT RACKET   *free testing sales gimmick*
One of the oldest scams utilized by unscrupulous salesmen is the "free testing period"—with nothing to pay and nothing to sign but a receipt for the merchandise. The hawkers peddle almost anything from encyclopedias (a particular favorite) to vacuum cleaners to television sets to vibrating chairs for the elderly. A hawker will say he is so certain that the customer will want to buy the merchandise that he's willing to risk him having it for no charge for up to two weeks so that it can be fully tested. Naturally, he must protect himself by, as a mere formality, having the customer at least sign a receipt for the merchandise.

There are various standard receipt forms, but it takes only a minor change or two in the wording to make it into a legally enforceable written contract. One thing to watch out for is any indication of the price of the item on the receipt. There is no need for this if the paper is not a sales contract. Once a customer signs an agreement and holds the item for the time allowed, he cannot get out of paying for the item—unless intent to defraud can be proven. Any oral assurances are meaningless whenever there is a written agreement, and the salesman always makes sure that there are no witnesses to any of his verbal statements.

RED ARMY OFFICER CORPS PLOT   *Nazi hoax*
One of the deadliest hoaxes in military-political history was perpetrated by the Nazis before World War II to get ever-suspicious Soviet dictator Joseph Stalin to decimate his own general staff. The plot proved an incredible success, and military experts agree that the lack of competent generals caused much of the early losses suffered by the Soviet Union to the German invaders and, said Winston Churchill, almost led to total Russian defeat.

In 1937 the Nazi secret service used voluminous forged evidence to convince Stalin that Marshal Mikhail Tukhachevsky and a number of other generals were in league with elements of the German general staff to overthrow him. This grand deception was the brainchild of Reinhard Heydrich, Heinrich Himmler's cunning and conscienceless second in command. Heydrich presided over the collection and forging of a vast number of documents that were turned over to Stalin via the Soviet secret police.

Stalin swallowed the bait, and within two weeks the marshal and other Red Army officers were arrested and brought to trial on June 4, 1937. All were found guilty in a trial that lasted until 9 p.m. the same day and was accompanied by the usual purge-trial confessions of the accused. Four hours later the defendants died before a firing squad.

The hoax succeeded beyond Heydrich's wildest expectation, as Stalin extended the purges until about half the Red Army's officer corps was destroyed, including three of five marshals, 13 of 15 army commanders, 30 of 58 corps commanders, 110 of 195 divisional commanders and 211 of 406 regimental commanders.

However, it must be added that the Nazis themselves were hoaxed in the affair, albeit to a lesser extent. When the doctored evidence was first offered to Stalin, the Russian dictator inquired what price the Nazis put on the information. According to Walter Schellenberg, chief of the German secret service, Heydrich and Hitler were unprepared for such a situation, but decided for appearance's sake to demand payment of three million gold ruble certificates, a price Stalin found acceptable.

The Nazis later used some of the payoff money for the infiltration of German spies into the U.S.S.R., but the Soviet secret police had recorded all of the serial numbers so that the enemy agents were quickly apprehended and executed.

RED DYE MURDERS   *Mafia hoax killings*
Worked in recent years by Mafia figures, "red dye murders" are non-killings used as convincers against extortion victims and the like to force acceptance of the criminals' demands. The tactic is often used against recalcitrant bookmakers to extract protection money, generally taking the stubborn one along on a "one-way ride" with another supposed victim. A sit-down meeting is held in a car, and both victims are pressured to pay. The phony victim resists, becomes violent and is gunned down. The fake victim has actually been fitted with small explosive caps that discharge blood—red dye. The man is declared dead and, with the real victim in attendance, the body is

taken into the woods and a hole is dug. As the victim is about to be tossed in, the extortion victim is led back to the car and asked if he wishes the same treatment. Not surprisingly, he agrees to meet the money demands.

Once in a great while the extortion victim is overly terrorized and goes to the police and relates what has happened. He leads the officers to the fresh burial site, which is opened, but no body is found. The police are unable to determine if the body has been moved or whether it has been a red dye affair.

It is said that red dye murders have declined in recent years because some gangsters have become leery of staged killing. In a deadly hoax within a hoax some mobsters have been told they are taking part in a red dye affair but are then shot with very real bullets.

RED LETTER SCARE   See ZINOVIEV LETTER.

REDLIGHTING   *circus grift*
One of the most notorious grifts of dishonest traveling circus managements in America was the practice known as "redlighting." It would be performed on creditors, complaining patrons or even some circus workers themselves. In the case of circus workers, this was done to avoid paying salaries.

The key to the scam was to take the victim aboard the circus train and at the appropriate moment toss him off the moving train. The practice was dubbed redlighting because, as John Culhane described in *The American Circus*, "as you look up from the ground, broken and bleeding, you can see the red light of the caboose disappearing down the track."

In a notorious incident in 1931 several workers for the Robbins Bros. Circus were cheated out of their pay and handed only $1. Those who protested were redlighted. Several of the workmen were badly injured, and one died of his injuries at the Mobile, Alabama, City Hospital. The owner of the circus was indicted for responsibility in the death, but the case never came to trial.

See also CIRCUS GRIFTING.

REFERRAL CONS   *salesman's hustle*
It doesn't matter what the salesman is trying to sell—a food freezer plan, silverware, a water softener, a mower/composter/shredder combo, etc.—the referral pitch is the same. His company is allegedly looking for people to publicize the product. Now all the customer (most often a housewife) has to do is show the $600 item to friends and "you'll get $100 off every new customer you bring to us. Just come up with six and your own cost drops to zero. Not only that, but if the customers you bring in refer us to customers

on their own, they get the standard commission and you get a $25 override on those buyers as well. You can become rich with this purchase!"

With contract in hand the salesman says, "Just sign and you could be on your way to a financially secure future."

If the customer reads the contract carefully, he or she will find it says nothing about any commission but concerns only the purchase of the product.

In fact the salesman has no expectation that the customer will ever bring in another customer; all he is looking for is this sale. In any event, promises on referrals mean nothing. Only the written contract is enforceable in court. This doesn't mean a salesman won't give a bonus for bringing in another customer, and six bonuses if there are six customers. And 36 more bonuses if these referrals bring in other referrals. But why stop there? Some salesmen say their customers have gone through 10 rounds in all. If a customer doesn't know his math, he might believe that one—even though that means 60 *million* buyers. But why stop there? Only a couple of more rounds, and the total is up over two *billion* buyers—or half the population of the globe.

Go back down to six or seven rounds and the customer would be a millionaire—and the salesman a billionaire. In reality, however, referral schemes are pipedreams. Not that it isn't a lucrative con for the salesman. He's made a juicy sale on an overpriced item. It has to be overpriced to cover those nonexistent commissions that never get paid out.

REIS, ARTURO ALVES   *forger*
A mild-mannered Portuguese with grandiose ideas, Arturo Alves Reis (1896–1955) became the ultimate forger in the 1920s. Reis took control of a country's economy without even dirtying his hands; he had legitimate experts do it for him instead.

Reis' first attempts to achieve great success proved disastrous. A civil servant in Angola, he started his own mining company in the Portuguese colony and then embezzled shareholders' money. He went to prison and there had the luxury of developing his life's work.

Reis' concept was that there is nothing in the world quite as valuable as money for the purpose of making money. He realized that countries such as Germany and Portugal were printing money far in excess of their own gold reserves. Whenever Portugal needed more money it simply turned to the Bank of Portugal and ordered it to print more currency. Reis wondered why he couldn't simply place a print order for himself.

Reis had certain contacts who he felt would see the wisdom of his scheme, including: Karel Marang van Ysselveere, a Dutch financier; Jose Bandeira, the brother of Portugal's minister at The Hague; and Gustav Adolph Hennies, a German adventurer with heavy experience in counterfeiting. The quartet put their heads together and eventually headed for the London firm of Waterlow & Sons, which printed banknotes for the Bank of Portugal. The conspirators presented the printing firm forged documentation for the issuance of $10 million worth of 500 and 1,000 escudo notes, all allegedly for distribution in Angola. The documentation indicated the money was to be handed over to Reis personally, as his mining syndicate was backing the currency issue in exchange for mining concessions.

It all seemed as above board as most governmental transactions of the period, and Waterlow & Sons complied. With the money Reis promptly set up his own private bank in Portugal, and then proceeded to enact the key element of his daring plot. With his forged legitimate money he started buying up stock in the Bank of Portugal itself. Eventually, he figured to become its major stockholder and finally achieve full control. Since only the Bank of Portugal could ever prove Reis' original deception with Waterlow & Sons, he would thus be in the position of being the only one who could investigate himself.

Reis knew that once he reached that stage, he could print all the banknotes he wished and, in effect, own the entire country of Portugal. Certainly Arturo Alves Reis was fast becoming the most celebrated financial wizard in Portugal and Angola, and he and his accomplices lived it up in grand style. Unfortunately, he was tripped up by a duplication of serial numbers on the notes. The printing firm was limited as to the serial numbers it was allowed to use, and Reis' total had gone over the limit. Under the circumstances Waterlow & Son used old numbers over again, since the firm had been assured by the plotters that the notes would be surcharged "Angola" when shipped to the colony. Once Reis used them in Portugal proper, the duplication was eventually noted.

Threatened with arrest and the rapid departure of his accomplices, Reis tried to bluff his way out of the mess, claiming that the real plot had been committed by the Bank of Portugal itself; for years it had been overprinting currency and was now trying to shift the blame on him. The charges and countercharges kept Reis from going to trial for four years, but in 1930 he was convicted and sent to prison for 30 years. Waterlow & Son fared worse, with the British courts allowing the Bank of Portugal's claims against the firm and forcing the company to make restitution. Reis was released from prison in May 1945, having served 15 years. He died a pauper in a rundown Lisbon basement in 1955 and was buried in an unmarked grave.

REMUS, GEORGE *courtroom hoaxer*

No defendant in a murder trial ever pulled off a more preposterous coup to win his freedom than George Remus (1874–1952), a celebrated Cincinnati lawyer-bootlegger, who had murdered his wife, Imogene, in October 1927. Earlier Remus had been sentenced to federal prison for bootlegging and came out convinced that his wife and her lover were plotting to steal his fortune and illicit business. Thus Remus shot his wife, a crime that certainly seemed cut-and-dried to produce a conviction.

Although he was disbarred, Remus won the right from the trial judge to conduct his own defense in part—a rather amazing situation since Remus' main plea was that he was not guilty on the basis of his own insanity. The trial itself was remarkable, since much of the prosecution's case was a parade of alienists testifying that Remus was totally sane while the defendant countered with his own uninhibited behavior and with witnesses who said he was both dangerous and insane.

Remus' performance made a shambles of the prosecution's case, handled by Charles Taft, a son of William Howard Taft (the former president of the United States and then chief justice of the Supreme Court). The jury took only 19 minutes to find Remus innocent "on the sole ground of insanity." One juror said, "If we could have acquitted him clean, we surely would have done so. We decided that the man had been persecuted long enough."

While Remus was jubilant at the verdict, his joy was short-lived as the state now sought a lunacy hearing for him and was determined to put him behind bars for life in an asylum for the criminally insane.

Remus argued his case anew before the Ohio Court of Appeals. There he proved to the satisfaction of the three-judge panel that he was perfectly sane and was set free.

RENTED FLAT SCAMS *swindling merchants*

Perpetrators of "rented flat scams" tend to masquerade as members of upper-income groups. Two of the earlier practitioners of the swindle were a notorious Russian woman named Sophie Bluffstein, nicknamed "the Golden Hand," and an English confidence woman named Louisa Miles.

Bluffstein operated in the late 19th century and traveled the capitals of Europe, staying in the best hotels and posing as a woman of quality. As such, she would order gems sent to her suite for perusal and evaluation. Doting jewelers obliged, since this was the standard custom when dealing with nobility and wealth. When they would finally call on the lady to conclude the transaction, they would find she and their gems had flown. Bluffstein was finally apprehended in her native country while pulling such a swindle and was shipped off to Siberia.

Miles was far more successful, driving Scotland Yard wild for 20 years in the early 1900s with one con game after another. In one rented flat caper she breezed into a Bond Street diamond establishment and announced herself as Miss Constance Browne, secretary to Lady Campbell of a most impressive address. It seemed her ladyship had a niece who was about to be married, and she had decided to give a wedding gift of some diamonds to be set in jewelry. Would the merchant be so kind as to have a trusted employee bring over a "dozen or so" of the firm's finest diamonds so that Lady Campbell might make a selection?

At the house, her ladyship's "secretary," the bogus Miss Browne, took the diamonds from the jeweler's representative and instructed him to wait while "Milady makes her choice forthwith."

After waiting a prolonged period of time, the jeweler panicked and tried the door through which the woman and the diamonds had vanished. It was bolted, as were other doors. In fact, the jeweler was trapped; even the front door he'd entered was now locked. Only after some delay did he break a window and cry for help. By that time Miss Browne had disappeared for good, and Louisa Miles was far away with the loot. It was subsequently revealed that the house had been rented for a month, during which time Miles sought out the most cooperative jewelry merchant.

Today the rented flat swindle thrives, especially with con artists who sublet luxury apartments for a brief period and make purchases with stolen credit cards or even using the apartment owner's own credit card numbers, identification of which is accomplished with little difficulty.

REVERE, PAUL   *engraving forgeries*

There is a saying in the art field that it is most difficult to find an "original original Revere engraving." Paul Revere (1735–1818) was a practicing Boston dentist who later won fame for his midnight ride as immortalized by Longfellow. In 1783 Revere gave up his dental practice to become a silverware maker, winning fame for a number of his engravings. His most popular work, "the Boston Massacre of 1770," however is clouded by charges of pilferage. The scene was actually first rendered by colonial artist Henry Pelham, who labeled his engraving "An Original Print . . . taken on the Spot." Before the Pelham work made it to market, Revere copied the print, signed his version and took away Pelham's sales.

An angry Pelham wrote a letter accusing Revere of taking "undue advantage" and declared Revere had engaged in "one of the most dishonourable Actions you could well be guilty of."

Others also found reason to consider Revere's actions as "dishonourable." Revere "lifted" a large number of British political cartoons and sold them under his own signature. In a 1772 book Revere rendered what he said was a portrait of Indian fighter Benjamin Church. It turned out, despite Revere's denials, to be a portrait of English poet Charles Churchill done by an unknown artist. The similarity was another striking instance of an unoriginal Revere "original."

RICHEBOURG, M.   *impersonator*

Probably the most dangerous impersonation during the French Revolution was carried out by a 21-year-old Frenchman, M. Richebourg (1768–1858), who faced certain execution time after time if caught in his bizarre disguise—that of an infant in swaddling clothes. Richebourg was able to carry off his deception because of his height, reportedly 1 foot 11 inches.

When the French Revolution exploded in 1789, Richebourg was in the employ of the duchess of Orleans, the mother of the future King Louis Philippe. Orleans was isolated from the royalist forces in the capital and desperately needed to get information in and out of Paris. Because of his size, Richebourg volunteered to play the espionage role and, wearing infant's clothes and cuddled by an Orleans maid acting as a nurse, the tiny Richebourg passed through the revolutionary guards manning the gates of Paris. Exposure would have meant prompt execution for Richebourg, but numerous times the midget and his "nurse" were able to secretly deliver vital military dispatches.

With the triumph of the Revolution, Richebourg remained in Paris while the ever-grateful Orleans family sent him a secret pension of 3,000 francs a year. With the accession of Louis Philippe in 1830, the pension continued openly. Richebourg, one of the most daring and tiniest spies in history, died in 1858 at the age of 90.

RING-A-PEG CARNIVAL SCAM

Ring-a-Peg is a carnival game that you play until you win—but you never win. For 50 cents or $1 a player gets as many rings as he needs to encircle an upright wooden peg on an elevated three-by-four platform a few feet behind the counter. The prizes are determined by the number on the bottom of the peg. There are usually 156 pegs, and in areas where cash payouts are permitted, a player can win cash or merchandise valued at $5 to $50 if he rings the right peg.

However, almost everyone ends up getting "slum" prizes, like whistles, tie clips or ashtrays—all worth five cents or ten cents wholesale. Of course, most players think those are just the breaks; it's worth the risk since you always "win."

In the carnival trade Ring-a-Peg is considered one of the best and easiest games to "gaff" or fix. All the operator has to do is mark the pegs bearing the big prizes in such a way so he can recognize them and always know where they are. When a valuable peg is ringed, the operator simply blocks the player's view as he removes the ring and lifts up the next peg for a lesser prize. The pegs are arranged so close together that this sleight-of-hand is impossible to spot.

THE RIP *shortchanging sleight-of-hand*
In case you've ever wondered why carnival ticket booths are built high, it goes back to the days when shortchanging customers was not only in vogue but also a vital part of carnival activity. Whenever a customer gave a $10 bill for tickets amounting to less than a dollar, the ticket seller would lean over, peer down at the customer and count out his change in $1 bills. He would do the count slowly, complete the process and then repeat it. As he handed over the money, he would shift hands and with that peal off one of the bills. Having seen the count paid twice, the customer would not recount the money but quickly stuff it in his pocket so he could enter the exhibit, especially if it happened to be a girlie show.

The "rip" remains with us, more often than not being practiced today in check-cashing establishments. Again the cashier counts the money twice before sticking it through the window. Not operating from a high carnival booth, the gypster has to be quite adept at what he's doing. Just before he hands out the money, he holds the neatly stacked bills in his left hand so they stick out above the thumb and fingers. Handing them over, he switches the money to his right hand; as he does so, the cashier's left thumb holds back the top bill, usually one of several tens that he has counted out. Invariably the customer's eyes follow the change of hands, keeping up with the money. The money in the right hand now covers the left. The cashier's left thumb crumples the bill into the left palm. Meanwhile, as the cashier passes out the money, he turns the pile of money over so that the tens are now at the bottom of the pile. Having seen the money counted twice, the customer usually tucks the money away without counting it himself.

THE ROCKS *fake diamond swindle*
"The Rocks" is a con game in which a victim is shown what are purported to be "stolen" diamonds and is invited to accompany the possessor to a jeweler of the victim's choice to have them evaluated. The jeweler makes an estimate and perhaps even a bid. Under those circumstances the victim is willing to buy the stones; but in the process, the diamonds are switched for look-alike paste versions.

If the jeweler evaluated the stones as worth $30,000, the gyp artist offers to sell them to the sucker for $15,000 because he says he is afraid they are still "hot." The victim can have them, he says, if he promises to hold them for at least a year until the heat is off.

ROCK-WEIGHING SWINDLE *short con game*
A con man turned honest, John Philip Quinn was one of the first to explain that the basic philosophy of most crooked scams was to appeal to the dishonesty of the victim. His theory was that, though you can cheat an honest man, it is far easier to concentrate on the many dishonest ones.

During the latter half of the 19th century Quinn perfected the rock-weighing swindle. In his autobiography, *Fools of Fortune* (1892), Quinn explains how the swindle worked in a typical outing in Hot Springs, Arkansas:

. . . where I had been playing poker—of course on the principles of the "skin" gamblers—in connection with a partner. We had succeeded in fleecing a sucker out of a considerable sum of money. He was moody over the loss of his cash, and we believed that he was disposed to be slightly suspicious. In order to disabuse his mind of any such idea, my partner accompanied him down the street, consoling with him as to his losses. My accomplice suggested to him that he might possibly get even with me by venturing a wager on some subject. "That man, Quinn," he said, "is ready to bet on anything; he would even bet on spitting at a mark or the weight of a stone," pointing to a rock which lay in the street. As though struck by a sudden inspiration, he suggested, "Suppose we weigh that rock and bet on a certainty. That is the only chance which we will ever have to get our money back." The greenhorn assented, and the weight of the stone was carefully and accurately ascertained. The next morning, having been fully posted by my confederate, I walked down the street and met my partner and the dupe in company. After cordially greeting them, I asked if either of them wished to bet upon any chance whatever. After some badinage, the sucker offered to bet as to the weight of the stone which he and my partner had caused to be carefully weighed the day previous. Of course I assented and the bet was made. Very much to our surprise the prospective victim had only $87 in his pocket, but this he cheerfully staked. The stone was weighed and my guess proved to be the exact weight of the rock. The reason was, that between the moment when my partner suggested the scheme to the dupe and the time the stone was weight, we had chipped off a section whose weight we knew exactly. The sucker submitted to the loss of his $87.

While the take in this case was what Quinn considered "small potatoes," it could at times be far larger, especially if the hometown dupe saw fit to inform his friends of his impending coup. They would join in the plot and put up additional money, as would Quinn's secret partner. Quinn would win the big bet and quickly decamp. Meanwhile, the victims would be left in a stunned rage. Quinn's partner would act just as enraged, perhaps accusing the first dupe of acting in league with the departed stranger. Before leaving town, Quinn's partner would depart, leaving the dupe for a considerable time thereafter with the reputation in the town as a man not to be trusted.

RODRIGUEZ, AGUSTIN   See SALOMÉ, MARIA.

ROLLING STONE COLONY   *19th-century town-site fraud*

One of the most prevalent rackets in the 19th century was the Western town-site fraud, in which land sharks swindled gullible Easterners with phony investment prospectuses. One of the worst and most tragic of these swindles was the Rolling Stone Colony in Minnesota Territory in 1852.

Suckered into buying supposedly valuable lands in the colony, some 400 buyers, mostly from New York, arrived in the spring of 1852, expecting to find a thriving metropolis with lecture hall, library, hotel, a greenhouse, a large warehouse and a fine dock. The steamboat officers told the investors they never heard of such a place. The colonists nevertheless produced maps supplied by one William Haddock, and from these the steamboat men pinpointed the location some three miles above Wabasha Prairie, on Sioux Indian land.

Put ashore, the colonists found absolutely nothing and were forced to build sod houses or burrow shelters in the river bank. Sickness ravaged the colony, and many died throughout the summer and autumn. With the coming of winter, the death rate soared, and finally the survivors abandoned the area.

See also NININGER SWINDLE.

ROPER   *victim-hunting con man*

BUSINESS OPPORTUNITY: Seeking a dependable, honest business person with $50,000 for investment at 100 percent-plus return. References·exchanged.

Is this advertisement in the business opportunity section of a newspaper legitimate? It could be, but it could also be a swindler's come-on by use of a "roper."

The roper is a man or woman who is vital to most confidence scams. He performs the task of lining up likely suckers for the scheme; when he does so, he turns them over to the "insideman" to be trimmed in a franchise deal, stock swindle, fixed horse race caper, oil deal, or whatever is being run. It's the roper who convinces the victim or mark that the insideman is a true genius or man with special power or information that makes the deal a sure thing. After the introduction, the roper is required to keep the victim tied up. He stays with the victim while all either go for the victim's funds or await their arrival by wire. Sometimes the roper pretends to be drunk and talks loosely, which upsets the insideman and the mark. In such cases the insideman urges the mark to watch the roper carefully; this actually makes the roper's job a breeze as he continues to watch the man who thinks he's watching him. Sometimes the mark becomes so exasperated or is just so greedy that he proposes to the insideman and others involved that they cut out the roper; he can handle more of the financial support himself.

In days when most long-distance travel was by train, ropers did much of their "fishing" there, picking out well-heeled suckers. Today there is some recruiting done on planes, but ropers prefer a longer time frame for judging a potential mark. More recruiting now takes place on cruise ships or at resorts, casino hotels and the like. Besides placing dummy business opportunity ads, ropers also themselves answer bone fide advertisements by other persons seeking to sell established businesses, farms, real estate and the like.

Ropers insist they are always under severe strain, listening to a mark's constant chatter (never interrupting a sucker is a roper's vital credo) and also coming up with a story about themselves and maintaining it against a slight slip in a detail that might alert the mark. The entire nurturing period may run as long as a week or a month, and then he still might lose the sucker who backs out of the deal. Because of this investment of time ropers try to keep several marks in reserve at various stages of development so that a substitute can be brought in as required.

The importance of the roper to the swindle is indicated by the fact that he gets 45% of the net out of any successful score. Some ropers work in pairs so each cut is half of the above. While there is a well-developed sense of honor among con men, it is a fact that many ropers can be gypped by their confederates, since it is the insidemen who control the funds and can skim the profits. The roper's only chance for cheating involves "padding the nut" or falsifying his expenses, which seldom amounts to much.·

While ropers are experts at their labors, they are seldom able to compete with the charms of the best insidemen who can take them in hand and with silver-tongue eloquence assure them they are not being shortchanged. Some ropers continue to work with top swindlers even though they know that they themselves may be conned. This was the case with Yellow Kid Weil, who conned not only the mark but the roper as well in the right situation. There were cases in which some ropers finally had to call on Weil in his home and renegotiate the split at the point of a gun.

See also TEAR-OFF RATS.

ROSARY GAME   *short con swindle*

The "rosary game," or "hot seat," is a short con game played in Europe by con artists who prey on rich Roman Catholic tourists from America. They populate the deluxe hotels, usually in teams of three, although only two are involved in the actual trimming of the victim.

One of the con men—the roper (see entry)—picks out a rich-looking tourist who he ascertains is a Roman Catholic. The con artist then identifies himself as a fellow Catholic and says he is on his way to Rome after a sojourn in the present locale, which can be Paris, Zurich, Munich, etc. While they are having a drink in the lobby, the roper suddenly pops off the couch and picks up a rosary lying on the floor. It is a most handsome and obviously expensive item. The roper and the mark, or victim, are admiring the rosary when a man appears, frantically looking about. The roper asks the man what he is looking for, and the man replies a rosary. The man, a partner of the roper, describes the rosary and says it is extremely valuable. The roper looks at the mark, who nods, and they turn over the rosary to the roper's partner.

The partner, who identifies himself as a wealthy Irish-American businessman from Boston, says the rosary belongs to his aged mother and that he intended to take it to Rome to have it blessed by the pope. He is also, he says, making a donation of $25,000 to the church. Unfortunately, he has gotten an urgent message from his business and must hurry to Berlin to close a big business deal. He will not be able to get to Rome.

A man in priestly garb passes the group, and he stops to greet the roper, whom he addresses by name. The phony priest says it is so nice to see the roper and that he will surely meet him in Rome since they are also registered in the same hotel there.

After the bogus priest makes his farewells, the bogus businessman looks thoughtfully at his two newfound friends. He suggests they join him in his room for a drink as he has a proposition to make them.

"Look here," he tells them as they settle down comfortably, "I can't tell you how lucky I am to have run across two honest men like you. I can't go to Rome to get the rosary blessed. If you two would take it, I'll give you the name of a monsignor with whom I have an appointment. You can make the donation, and he'll arrange the blessing of the rosary. After you get it done, you can send the rosary to my hotel in Berlin by Federal Express. I would be most grateful."

The bogus businessman takes a box out of a dresser drawer and reveals what looks like at least $25,000 in hundred-dollar bills. He looks at the two hopefully. The roper says it would be no imposition on him, as he is going to Rome himself. More often than not, the mark is also planning to visit Rome; if not, the businessman then suggests the roper go on his own. The roper demurs. "No, that's too much responsibility for me on my own. Besides, how do you really know you can trust me with all that money? I might agree if my friend would come along."

The bogus businessman turns back to the mark. "Please, won't you reconsider. Whatever way this gentleman is going to Rome I'll alter his flight plans so that you can go together, and I'll gladly pay for your hotel in Rome and your return flight to this city or wherever you're bound next."

The mark is interested, but the roper keeps insisting it is not right that the businessman trust two relative strangers with so much money. The businessman keeps dismissing the objection, but the roper presses the point. The roper proposes that he and the mark put up some money as a gesture of good faith. The pair agree that each will put up $7,500. The roper puts up his money easily, and the mark uses his credit cards to get cash advances and match the roper. By this stage the mark is extremely flattered at the prospect of making such a meaningful trip to Rome; the camaraderie grows among the trio.

The businessman has the pair add their funds to his money box. Then to show how much he trusts them, he insists they take the box and walk around the block and come back. After they return, the businessman and the mark make the same jaunt. The third leg of this blind demonstration of faith involves the businessman and the roper going off with the money hoard.

The mark waits and waits and waits.

ROSS, MRS. HANNAH   *baby-producing spiritualist*

One of the most infamous spiritualists of the 19th century was Mrs. Hannah Ross, a Bostonian who took the city by the bay by storm in the 1880s. Grief-stricken parents who had lost their babies flocked to Ross because she could apparently cause a long-deceased baby to materialize in the flesh. Not only were dumbfounded members of her audience permitted to see their long-departed child, but they were offered the opportunity to touch and kiss the baby.

Ross would position herself in a cabinet in a darkened room, pull the curtain and call the baby back from the beyond. On cue, the baby's image would appear at the front of the cabinet. Ross would allow the awestruck parents to come forward and kiss the baby, most were overjoyed to find the baby had the warm skin of a living person.

The Ross scam was finally exposed in 1887 by reporters from a Boston newspaper and the police. The woman faker had painted a baby's face on her breast and then poked it through a slit in the cabinet curtain. Ross decamped the Boston area just in time to avoid bodily harm from outraged victims descending on her seance studio.

ROULETTE WHEEL SCAMS   *fixing fixed wheels*
One of the most legendary of all gambling scams is the fixed roulette wheel. At any given time the operator can press a button and fix a wheel so that it never lands on any heavily bet number. Today this is certainly not done in legal casinos in the United States or Europe. It isn't necessary, since the casinos make an enormous profit on just the difference between true odds and the amount they pay off. In addition, Nevada has what is called the "pickup," in which government agents come into a casino, pick out a table, confiscate all the gaming equipment and then subject it to meticulous inspection at the laboratory of the Nevada Control Board. Nevertheless, at mob casinos, which operate illegally in many big cities, the wheel may very well be fixed.

See also BUCKMINSTER, FRED.

ROYALL, ANNE NEWPORT   See JOHN QUINCY ADAMS' NUDE PRESS CONFERENCE.

THE RUBAIYAT OF OMAR KHAYYAM   See OMAR KHAYYAM'S QUATRAINS.

RUBY FAKES   *perfect synthetics*
The scene was a high-stakes private poker game in a Caribbean island casino. One player, supposedly a jeweler, had only several hundred dollars on him and offered to put up a bagful of rubies. He claimed he had picked them up on the island and planned to smuggle them into the United States for his business. The other players knew nothing about rubies and, unsurprisingly, would not accept his valuation of them. The jeweler said he had no choice but to drop out of the game. This upset the other players because the jeweler seemed to be a terrible gambler.

Finally, it was decided to have someone take the rubies down to the casino hotel jeweler for a valuation. The jeweler was very impressed and put the value at "at least $35,000." Based on this estimate, it was decided to let the gambler buy $28,000 worth of chips for the rubies.

As the game proceeded, it turned out to be a happy accommodation, for the jeweler gambler was out

$6,000 within an hour. He was then interrupted by a call from the desk that he had an important fax that demanded an immediate reply. The jeweler said this was urgent business but he would be back in 15 minutes. The call was perfectly timed, leaving the gambler just enough time to hop into a car and get to the airport to catch a flight to the mainland. He was $22,000 ahead, since the rubies—despite the jeweler's appraisal—were fakes.

Synthetic rubies were first marketed 75 years ago, and today after much improvements they can often pass for natural gems. In some ways they are even better than the real things because they usually have fewer flaws. They are as hard as the genuine and the color is almost indistinguishable. While most jewelers can accurately appraise most gems, only a few master gem men can spot synthetic rubies. This does not mean jewelers aren't vain enough to try. The casino hotel jeweler did.

In another instance, a West Coast jeweler let a couple have a $15,000 diamond necklace for $25,000 in rubies that he had appraised for them. The deal was that it would take the couple overnight to arrange transfer of the funds to cover the purchase and the woman desperately wanted to wear the necklace to an affair that evening. The jeweler agreed to keep the rubies until the funds arrived the next day. Of course, the rubies were paste.

RUIZ, ROSIE   *marathon hoaxer*
Rosie Ruiz was clearly the strongest finisher in the 1980 Boston Marathon. In fact, she seemingly recorded the third fastest time ever run by a woman. Rosie became the toast of Boston, collecting the adulation of the crowd, her medal and the glory. However, things didn't stay rosy for her. In fact, questions arose from the moment she sat down next to Bill Rodgers, the men's winner. *"Who are you?"* he asked.

It was a good question. Everyone had seen Rosie flashing across the finish, but no had seen her at any of the checkpoints. Then a witness came forth to say she had bolted out of the crowd on Commonwealth Avenue, a bare half mile from the finish line. Rosie's glory started to slip away. Cross-examined on television and challenged to run another course, she took refuge in tears. Out of New York came very disquieting news as well. It turned out that Rosie's previous time in the New York Marathon was also not what it seemed; she'd covered most of the 26-mile course via subway.

The Boston prize was taken away from Rosie and the following week she was expunged from the records. While today almost no one can remember the name of the true winner of the race, Jacqueline Gareau, many can recall Rosie Ruiz, history's fastest marathon half-miler.

S

SAFETY MILK CON *phony arthritis cure*

In recent years there has been a new emphasis to back-to-nature "remedies" to cure arthritis. Among the many valueless items are honey, vinegar, cod-liver oil, blackstrap molasses, alfalfa and orange juice. Recently making a big comeback is "safety milk."

According to the quacks who sell so-called safety milk for as much as three or four times the price of regular milk, it can "relieve" or "cure" arthritis because it achieves an immunity thanks to antibodies produced in cows treated with streptococcus and staphylococcus vaccines. In control group tests safety milk has been shown to have no effect at all on arthritis.

See also ARTHRITIS CURE CONS.

SALOMÉ, MARIA *impostor bullfighter*

From 1900 to 1908 "La Reverte" was one of the most popular matadors in Spain. She was a rare breed indeed—a female matador—one Maria Salomé, born in Jaén, Spain in 1800. Maria made her debut in the bullring in Madrid in 1900; dubbed La Reverte, she became an instantaneous celebrity and was especially admired by the women of Spain.

The Spanish government did not view La Reverte with the same degree of admiration, regarding it both immoral and illegal for women to fight bulls. When it became clear that La Reverte was about to be banned from the bullring, she publicly discarded her wig and falsies and revealed herself to be a man, Agustin Rodriguez.

This obviously stopped the government's actions, and Rodriguez attempted to resume his career. But the Spanish crowds were offended by his fraud, and there was dark talk of lynching him. Rodriguez suffered the fate of never again entering the bullring. He was even forced to leave Madrid; he lived out his days, a broken man/woman, in Majorca.

SALOON SHORTCHANGING GYP See THE DROP.

SALTING *faking mine sites*

The practice of "salting" worthless mining areas was probably the most prevalent form of fraud in the Old West. Mark Twain noted that any salting plot could work because of the irresistible lure of easy treasure on both greenhorns and seasoned treasure hunters. Methods of salting reached the status of a fine art, a common tactic being shooting gold dust into the ground with a shotgun. When a mine was played out a cunning owner would pump several shotgun loads of gold specks all around to prove to a would-be buyer that the vein still was loaded with a fortune.

In time most buyers were on the lookout for salting tricks and would not buy a claim without checking all areas of a site, not merely the area suggested by the owner. This development called for truly creative shotgunning. According to one oft-told tale, some prospectors who were stuck with a miserable claim sought to palm the area off on some Chinese fortune hunters. Clearly the Chinese could not be counted on to only search in spots that might be salted, so the prospectors came up with a clever ruse involving a poisonous snake. They killed the creature just before the potential buyers arrived and, while one prospector led the Chinese about, another tracked them through the brush. The cautious Chinese announced they would probe an area on the far end of the claim. When the search party reached the spot, the hidden prospector was ready and heaved the reptile from cover. The Chinese started to scatter as one of their miner escorts, reacting quickly, turned his shotgun on the apparently live snake and shot it dead. The Chinese were eternally grateful for being saved from the snake and found the incident the work of providence, since there

231

An 1802 print depicts impersonator Sampson with General George Washington at the time of her discharge during the Revolutionary War.

were traces of gold dust right where the snake had expired.

Salting was considered a miner's right, a sort of retirement plan when a claim ran out. As soon as the miners started working a claim, they took to purchasing large portions of certain patent medicines that were spiked with gold salts as a supposed treatment for kidney ailments brought on by excessive drinking. Whatever the health benefits, the miners made sure to spread the liquid results over the full expanse of their claim.

See also CALISTOGA SPRINGS WATER SCAM; THE GREAT DIAMOND HOAX; NORTH OPHIR CLAIM.

SAMPSON, DEBORAH *Revolutionary War impersonator*

In May 1782 young Deborah Sampson (1760–1827) enlisted in the Continental Army as "Robert Shurtleff" in the Revolutionary War. It was her way of winning freedom from her life as a household drudge. Her sailor father had died when she was young, and her mother was forced to farm the children out to relatives or any family that would take them in. Deborah went to a farm family in Middleborough, Massachusetts, where she performed endless household duties. But as her first biographer, Herman Mann, wrote in 1797:

> To a considerable extent, she was a day-dreamer, and a builder of castles in the air. She had a strong desire to see the world, to visit distant regions, to behold

society in new lights and under unusual aspects. . . . She resolved therefore, to put on male attire, and travel; and to this end spun and wove, with her own hands, cloth, which (she says) she employed a tailor to make up as a suit for a gentleman, pretending that it was for a young man, a relative of hers, who was about leaving home for the army. She found these garments became her so well, that even her mother, she visited at Plympton in this costume, did not know her.

Having carried on this ruse Deborah enlisted in the 45th Massachusetts Regiment and soon won respect as a fearless and bold soldier. None of her comrades suspected she was a woman, although they called her "Molly" because she had not yet developed a beard.

Her handsome, clean-cut features made her a favorite with the ladies, and in one case a woman who was particularly smitten with her presented her with a watch, six shirts and 25 Spanish dollars. Deborah felt it was unfair to continue the affair with the woman and wrote her a note breaking off the relationship, signing it "your own sex." The woman kept Deborah's secret.

Private Sampson was wounded twice, once in the leg and once in the shoulder; in the case of the shoulder wound she kept her comrades and a doctor from examining her. In late 1783 she came down with camp fever in Philadelphia, became unconscious and was thought to be dying. Dr. Barnabas Binney examined her and discovered the truth. Deborah herself recollected: "Thrusting his hand into my bosom to ascertain if there was motion at the heart, he was surprised to find an inner vest tightly compressing my breasts, the instant removal of which not only ascertained the fact of life, but disclosed the fact that I was a woman!"

Deborah implored Dr. Binney to keep her secret; he agreed and moved her into his house. But after first his niece and a more insistent woman from Baltimore proposed marriage, the doctor went to Deborah's commander, Major General John Paterson. The general in turn consulted George Washington, who had discharge papers issued on October 23, 1783. It was said later that Washington insisted on giving Deborah a cash gift. General Paterson, a man with a certain sense of humor, asked Deborah to accompany him in a gown when he reviewed her military unit. None of her comrades recognized her.

Returning to New England, Deborah continued to wear her army uniform and took the name of Ephram Sampson. She obtained a farm job and flirted with the country girls. Eventually she shed her male clothes and resumed her life as Deborah Sampson. She married a farmer named Benjamin Gannett and had three children. Her relations with her husband were always stormy, since Gannett had not served in the war and Deborah regard him as a slacker.

In 1802 Deborah went on the lecture circuit, describing the rigors of war. She wore a full military uniform and performed the manual of arms. In 1805 Congress, at the urging of Paul Revere, gave Deborah a pension of $4 a month and a land grant. In 1818 her pension was doubled. She died April 29, 1827, her death attributed to her war wounds.

SAND SWINDLERS *real estate cons*

"Sand swindlers" is a generic term for those real estate hustlers who specialize in selling home sites and "investment opportunities" in inaccessible desert wastelands. True, most of these properties offer tremendous views—if limitless vistas of dry sagebrush is what the buyer has in mind. Of course, the sales brochures offer scenes of "proposed playlands," "proposed gold courses" and "projected lakes." If the property is actually 50 or 60 miles from a lake and an equal distance in the opposite direction to the nearest town, the land is promoted as being "midway between lake and thriving city." Drinking water is described as being easily accessible—provided you get in your car and drive to the nearest town to buy bottled water.

When the great Hoover Dam was under construction in the 1930s, it was predicted that the surrounding land would "bloom" with irrigation. Swindlers took advantage and sold off huge amounts of Nevada and Arizona sand to the gullible. Lots that went for $5,000 can still be had now for $20 an acre—alas with no takers. It is said that two such sand swindlers provided the money that built some of the largest and most glittering gambling casinos in Las Vegas.

See also SWAMP SWINDLERS.

SATURDAY EVENING POST AND BENJAMIN FRANKLIN *false claims*

From its demise as a weekly to its current status as a monthly, the *Saturday Evening Post* has borne on its cover the phrase "Founded A.D. 1728 by Benjamin Franklin." In fact Ben Franklin was never head of the *Saturday Evening Post*, having died 31 years before its first issue. The original founders of the *Post* made no such claims of any tie to Franklin. Furthermore, Franklin never published any magazine that could in any way be connected to the *Post*. It is true that in 1729 (rather than 1728) Franklin took over a struggling newspaper, the *Pennsylvania Gazette*, and turned it into a money maker. The *Gazette* survived Franklin's death and continued publication until 1815. But it never had any connection with the *Post*, ex-

Although the *Saturday Evening Post* claimed for decades that Benjamin Franklin founded the publication, Franklin never heard of it. The *Post* first appeared 31 years after Franklin's death and bore no relationship or ancestry to any of his publications.

cept for the fact that the latter was printed in the same print shop that the *Gazette* had used years earlier.

The Franklin connection was invented in 1899 by the famed editor of the *Post*, George Horace Lorimer. According to some speculation, this was a desperate way to attract readers and advertisers during the yellow-journal news wars. Whatever the reason, the *Post* has lived with the Franklin lie ever since, leading Tom Burnam to mourn in *The Dictionary of Misinformation*, "A magazine so sternly dedicated for so many years to the old-fashioned American virtues should not have been, one cannot help feeling, so cavalier with the truth."

SAWING OFF MANHATTAN ISLAND *grandiose hoax*

In the summer of 1824 a truly monumental undertaking was announced in New York to correct a monumental problem. The island of Manhattan was in deep trouble. There had been too much building at the Battery, the lower end of the island, and now the large buildings were starting to sink the island. (Notice how already it was all downhill from City Hall.) It would only be a matter of time before New York snapped in two and half sunk into the sea. The loss of life and property would be catastrophic.

Only one thing could be done: Saw off the island and turn the long, narrow strip around to keep the heavy end from slipping into the harbor. The severed part would be floated past Ellis Island and Governors Island, turned in mid-bay and then the heavy end reversed and reattached to the remaining part of Manhattan.

Needless to say, such an engineering feat is as impossible today as it was back in 1824. Yet, somehow, many gullible people fell for the hoax. There is even a complete record of the purported sawing off of Manhattan written by Thomas F. DeVoe, a respected member of the New-York Historical Society, in his two-volume work: *The Market Book, Containing a Historical Account of the Public Markets in the Cities of New York, Boston, Philadelphia, and Brooklyn, With a Brief Description of Every Article of Human Food Sold Therein, the Introduction of Cattle in America and Notices of Many Remarkable Specimens, et cetera, et cetera, et cetera.*

The hoax was born in the minds of two outrageous characters, John DeVoe (a retired butcher and Thomas DeVoe's uncle) and another man known only as Lozier. Of the two Lozier had the more fertile mind and always made wild claims at a favorite loafing place of the period, the Centre Market at Grand, Baxter and Centre streets, inhabited mostly by retired butchers and other small businessmen. Lozier, a wealthy retired contractor, had for years convinced the "statesmen" of the Centre Market of his ability to hobnob with the great. Had he not advised President Monroe on issuing his famous doctrine? Apparently he also had advised Mrs. Monroe that she was not required to return social calls, although it was a breech of previous behavior that upset much of society of the day.

The disappearance of Lozier and DeVoe from the usual haunt for several days raised considerable speculation. The pair finally reappeared, but Lozier was not his usual ebullient self, sitting in a corner with his brow furrowed, deep in troubled thought. Only grudgingly did he reveal what was on his mind. He had been in urgent consultations with Mayor Stephen Allen, who had informed him of the mortal danger facing Manhattan.

Lozier said he and Mayor Allen were not in perfect agreement on what had to be done. Both agreed that the island had to be sawed off and turned around; but the mayor was worried that before this could be done it would first be necessary to detach Long Island from its moorings and tow it out of the

way. Later it could be returned to its proper position. Lozier said he was engaged in mathematical studies to determine if this was necessary. A few days later he appeared much relieved, announcing he had convinced the mayor that there was more than enough room in New York Bay to pull off the feat without disturbing Long Island.

Were there any murmurs of dispute in the Centre Market about the truth of this immense undertaking? If there were any doubters they were easily squashed. Was not the Erie Canal nearing completion although once claimed an engineering impossibility? And weren't many skeptical that a simple steam engine could propel a gigantic ship across the ocean as was now happening?

Fully convinced, the Centre Marketeers readily accepted Lozier's claim that Mayor Allen had ordered Lozier and DeVoe to handle the project as private individuals. Thus they avoided the tiresome and long-winded arguments that would result in the legislature—and time was urgent.

The pair started to sign up laborers (mostly new immigrants just off the boat from Ireland and eager for work) and to award contracts for food and equipment. The workers were tested to see how long they could hold their breaths; the most long-winded were to be assigned to the underwater tasks at triple wages. Among the needed equipment were 100-foot long saws with three-foot teeth, 250-foot oars and gigantic anchors to keep the island from being washed out to sea by a storm before the reattaching process could be completed. Carpenters, blacksmiths and contractors adjourned to their shops to produce the equipment. Lozier also commissioned contracts for provisions to feed the work force, estimated at 1,000 strong. He ordered 500 cattle, 500 hogs and 3,000 chickens as a starter, instantly causing a rise in meat prices in the city.

How could such a beehive of activity escape the attention of the more astute New Yorkers? There were a number of explanations. Historian Herbert Asbury has pointed out that aside from a few newspapers of the day, whose coverage of the city's affairs was limited, "the only method of transmitting intelligence was by word of mouth, or by letter, which was even more uncertain. Important happenings in one part of the city did not become generally known for weeks or months, and frequently not at all. And Grand Street then was as far uptown as the farthest reaches of the Bronx are today."

In addition, Lozier exploited ethnic kinships. Virtually all of the butchers victimized by the hoax were of German descent. They sought to guarantee the contracts for themselves by staying tight-lipped and only discussing the matter in their native tongue. The workmen, immigrant Irish, were not told precisely what they were to do, and they religiously kept silent about this great job opportunity.

After several weeks of preparation Lozier and DeVoe issued orders for all involved in the project to assemble at a certain spot to march north, led by a fife and drum corps, to the spot where the groundbreaking would take place. The workmen appeared by the hundreds, as did scores of contractors, butchers and musicians. Hogs squealed, chickens clucked and cattle mooed. The only ones who weren't there were Lozier and DeVoe.

A delegation was sent to Centre Market to locate them. Word was left that Lozier and DeVoe had departed the city on account of their health. As Asbury put it, "At length, for the first time in weeks, if not in years, some of the more intelligent of Lozier's victims began to think, and the more they thought, the less likely it appeared that Manhattan Island would ever be sawed off." Gradually, the shamefaced crowds started to disperse. Some of the more vindictive types considered sawing off Lozier and DeVoe, but they were not to be found, having taken refuge with a friend in the wilds of Brooklyn.

There was talk of having the pair arrested, but that required filing a complaint and the victims admitting how dumb they had been. Several months later, after the furor died down, the pair reappeared at Centre Market; but Lozier was no longer an honored oracle. The statesmen of the Centre Market wanted no more of his grand announcements and schemes.

SCHWANTHALER, LUDWIG VON See CIGAR-FILLED STATUES.

SEA SERPENT OF SILVER LAKE *monster hoax*
In 1855 Perry, New York, located some 50 miles south of Buffalo, was a sleepy little town sorely in need of some way of getting on the map and thereby drawing in business. A dedicated group of citizens headed by A. W. Walker, a local hotel man, decided a spot of terror would do the trick, and they secretly constructed a 60-foot serpent that they covered with waterproof canvas. It was placed offshore in Silver Lake and could be operated from the shore with a bellows-and-ropes contraption.

Soon residents, fishermen and tourists were treated to sudden appearances of what was called the "most horrid and repulsive-looking monster" they had ever seen. Alarmed locals quickly formed a vigilance committee and armed members patrolled the shores of the lake. A tower was built at the north end of the lake to sight the terrible menace.

Unsurprisingly, Perry was now very much on the map as crowds jammed the local hotels (including the Walker House), restaurants and stores to catch a glimpse of the terrible creature. The sea serpent was a gold mine for the town throughout the summer and fall of the year. In 1856 it seemed prudent to Walker and his co-conspirators to cool it, and the monster disappeared. They reckoned that when the monster reappeared a few years hence it would be all the more exciting. A year later the Walker House unfortunately suffered a devastating fire. Firemen at the scene were surprised to find a canvas sea monster in the hotel's attic. A. W. Walker prudently took off to Canada. Today, however, Walker is not regarded a villain; each year a Sea Serpent Festival is held in Perry.

SEASHELL COUNTERFEITS
In the 1700s Dutch merchants brought to Europe from the Southwest Pacific the Precious Wentletrap, a beautifully shaped seashell with unique ladderlike marks. For some European collectors Precious Wentletraps became as prized possessions as rare jewels, and the price of the shells exploded upward so that only the very rich could afford to own them. By the beginning of the 19th century demand for the shells became so great that traders could not keep up with demand, and in China forgers began to turn out fake Precious Wentletraps made from rice-flour paste. Unsuspecting traders could not distinguish the counterfeits from the real thing and neither could European collectors who eagerly gobbled up all offerings. The fraud only become apparent when the buyers washed the shells and were shocked when they melted. As a result, the Precious Wentletrap craze petered out, buyers being too fearful of being taken.

Currently, genuine Precious Wentletraps sell for under $10. A fake version—now most rare—ironically commands a price many times higher.

SEAWATER SWINDLES *quack cure-all smorgasbord*
Concentrated seawater, say those who peddle it, will do away with such varied ailments as diabetes, arthritis, baldness and cancer, among other ailments, while offering our bodily glands "a chemical smorgasbord." Seawater really came into vogue in the 1960s when a physician claimed to have rejuvenated his 97-year-old father with a steady treatment with the stuff. Numerous quacks hopped on the seawater wagon and peddled it to credulous patients, many of whom already had cardiac and rheumatic problems and developed serious complications. Food and Drug Administration Commissioner George Larrick ordered a crackdown on the "nation-wide seawater swindle" and authorities moved into Texas, California, Ohio, Pennsylvania, Michigan and Indiana to seize thousands of bottles of seawater shipped from a Florida laboratory.

Given the supply of seawater, there is little doubt that quacks will continue to peddle this "wonderful health concoction."

$75 SONY TRINITRON SWINDLE *Murphy Game switch*

A straight scam which has largely replaced the old Murphy Game sex swindle (see entry) has now gained in police circles the generic title of the "$75 Sony Trinitron Swindle." In the classic Murphy Game the con man poses as a pimp and leeringly describes the delights offered by a lady he manages. He convinces the victim to pay him outside the hooker's alleged apartment house so that no money is handled by the woman, making her immune from arrest. The victim is then sent up the stairs to a nonexistent apartment.

The Sony Trinitron variation is generally worked in bars, at race tracks and like places. Two hustlers become newcomers to the scene and after a few days one hustler makes a big show of handing over a VCR or some other expensive item to the other for something like 10 cents on the dollar. The pair will be overheard discussing another transaction of like value, and soon other bar customers express interest in getting in on a good thing. It so happens that one of the hustlers has inside contact with a man who has a way to move a lot of Sony Trinitrons at one time by falsely assigning them to another shipment. The important element in the alleged fraud is that all 10 have to be moved at the same time. Naturally, there is no trouble signing up nine suckers when they are told the $600 sets can be had for a total payment of a mere $750, or $75 apiece.

The victims pitch in for a rented van and drive to the warehouse where the valuable shipment will be placed on the loading platform. The con man collects the $750 from the victims, including his accomplice, and enters the warehouse. However, he never returns, having simply gone in, probably asked if there were any jobs available, and when told not, simply walked out another exit, where his confederate was waiting in a car. The victims wait and wait until the dawn comes.

The beauty of the swindle is that, like its parent Murphy Game, few victims ever complain to the police. As a result, there is a dearth of newspaper exposes on the scam. Thus operators can remain in a city for quite a while before finally deciding to move on to safer pastures.

SEX REJUVENATOR AIDS *enduring quack con*

Sex rejuvenator aids, such as salves, pills and liquid concoctions, have been successfully peddled for ages by mail order and in drugstores. Made from low-cost materials, these expensive cures are generally marketed to "restore loss of manhood," but actually have

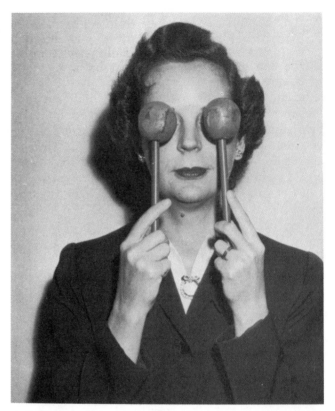

A Postal Service representative demonstrates how a pair of small rubber mallets are to be tapped against a person's eyelids 200 times a day to allegedly improve eyesight. An even more dubious use of the mallets is described in the entry.

no medicinal value whatsoever. Several cures, such as ground-up crocodile tails (surreptitiously brought in from Egypt) border on the absurd.

One commonly sold aid is a small section of dry tree root six or eight inches in length, which has sold for $15.00. An inch of this root is to be soaked in a bottle of liquor for a week, and then drinking the liquor is supposedly a cure for impotency. The only plus for the item is that it does not seem to harm the taste of the liquor.

Because sex rejuvenator con men are fearful of a crackdown by authorities, some now advertise their products as "PLACEBO WONDER PILLS," relying on the fact many people don't know a placebo contains no medication at all.

In the more high-priced category, the "Radiendocrinator," going for $1,000, claimed to get the job done with pure radium, which allegedly charged it. A user was said to experience a renewed sex life with the contraption and also to enjoy such magnificient side effects as a cure for dry scalp, eczema, goiter, diabetes, constipation, fatigue, acidosis, baggy eyes, biliousness, obesity, myxodema, rickets, sciatica, blood pressure (high or low), fallen arches, poor memory and dementia praecox.

The same multiple purpose performed is offered by a very simple device, a set of small rubber hammers. They are to be used to tap the eyelids 200 times a day as a method for improving eyesight so that glasses are not needed. Similarly, it is recommended that the same tapping procedure be done on the male genital organs to boost virility. Adoption of this procedure might well be restrained by reports from those who have followed the routine on the eyelids and ended up with a pair of black eyes.

SHABAKA STONE ancient Egyptian political forgery

Many scholars warn that Egyptian royal inscriptions on documents or stones should not be accorded undue faith as historical testimony. A case in point is the Shabaka Stone, a black basalt slab, said to preserve what has been called the Memphite Theology of Creation.

In early Egyptian thought the creation of the world was regarded to have been the work of the god Atum of Heliopolis. However, in the city of Memphis creation was ascribed to Ptah, the city's patron god. Ptah was credited with the creation of the other gods and thus, indirectly, with the creation of the world.

The Shabaka Stone dates from the 25th Dynasty in the reign of the Nubian pharaoh Shabaka, who ruled from about 716 to 702 B.C. Shabaka ordered the stone to be inscribed from a copy of an ancient worm-eaten document and to be set up in the temple of Ptah at Memphis as permanent testimony to posterity. While the text used some archaic spellings and grammatical usages to "date" the document as a piece of antiquity, many errors in the inscription have led to the universal conclusion that it was concocted in Shabaka's own time.

Apparently the stone was a piece of political propaganda by the pharaoh aimed at buying the support of Memphis. At the time, the Nubian rulers were seeking political control of all of Egypt and had only recently conquered Memphis. By erecting the inscribed stone, Shabaka was offering new prestige for the city's patron god, and was thus seeking the support of the population and especially the very powerful Memphite priesthood.

SHANGHAIING SCAMS

In the 19th century, shady characters who shanghaied sailors for hard-to-fill crewman jobs were known as waterfront "crimps." These individuals were so dishonest they would even swindle the shipmasters whose orders they filled. Crimps could get away with such behavior since few shipmasters returned to a particular port more than once every four or five years.

The crimps were paid by the body and, since most of the kidnapped seamen were either drunk or drugged, it took a discerning captain to note if a corpse or "stiff" (this may be the origin of the term) was slipped in on him at the then going rate of about $100 a man. The presence of a corpse in a batch of 30 or 40 men would generally escape detection until the ship was well out to sea, and even then the captain could not be certain that the man had not just expired of acute alcoholism. The captain's only course was simply to deep-six the victim over the side and continue his voyage.

If a corpse or two was not always available on short notice, the crimps often improvised by mixing a dummy among the sailors they delivered. A seedy suit of clothes was stuffed with straw and properly weighted, and the head was wrapped with mufflers or other heavy cloths. The first crimp to think of this scam was a wizened little character known as Nikko the Laplander, who started operating in San Francisco in the 1860s. It was said that no dummy designed by Nikko was ever discovered in time by any captain, since the Laplander made his dummies sheer works of art. Nikko did not simply try to palm off a straw man but sewed a rat in each of the coat sleeves. Thus, as the dummy lay in a heap among the other live bodies, the efforts of the rats to escape seemingly made the body twitch, and their muffled squeaks resembled the groans of a groggy drunk.

Nikko was so good at his art that he literally cheated himself out of the profession. He became so notorious that captains in almost every seaport in the Pacific warned one another to avoid the cunning Laplander. By the mid-1870s Nikko had become the Barbary Coast's most unwanted crimp and was forced to move on to more mundane criminal pursuits.

But Nikko remained an inspiration to other crimps. In a switch on the Laplander's technique, Joseph "Bunco" Kelly—who controlled the crimp racket in Portland, Oregon—often included a cigar store Indian among his wares.

See also KELLY, SHANGHAI.

SHAPIRA, M. W. religious forger

One of the most persistent religious hoaxers in the mid-19th century was M. W. Shapira, a Polish Jew, who operated an antiquity shop in Jerusalem. Upon any important discovery Shapira could be counted on to offer a forged contribution. Thus, after the discovery of the Moabite Stone at Dibhan in 1868, Shapira promptly came up with some "complimentary" finds, forging and selling Moabite pottery to the Prussian government.

Shapira's greatest plot was his unsuccessful attempt to sell what he claimed to be a ninth century B.C. version of Deuteronomy to the British Museum for a mere million pounds. Shapira credited the "find" to Moses, but it actually consisted of strips of sheepskin cut from the ends of 300-year-old synagogue rolls aged with chemicals. Unfortunately for Shapira, the expert Clermont-Ganneau deciphered the Moabite stone and exposed the fraud. Clermont-Ganneau inspected the Deuteronomy manuscript and determined it was also a forgery. Having exhausted his credibility with his many cons, Shapira committed suicide in Rotterdam in 1884.

SHARE-EXPENSE RIDE SCAMS

The ads appear in local newspapers and are posted on college bulletin boards, offering to share automobile transportation costs on long-distance travel. There are rides from Miami to New York, from New York to San Francisco, from Los Angeles to Chicago. They read:

> Driving West [or East, North or South]. Will take friendly person/persons to share expenses and driving.

The responses go to a mail-box number or a telephone-answering service, and a deal is soon struck with persons interested in making low-cost trips. A ride to California from New York might only be $50 or $60 and less than double that amount for a round-trip.

The driver is certainly the congenial sort as he picks up his fellow travelers at the appointed time, all their luggage stuffed in or/and on top of the car. After they go about 50 miles or so, the driver suggests a rest stop and they all enter the roadside establishment together. The driver excuses himself to tank up while the others finish up. He gets into the car to pull up to the nearby gas tanks but instead speeds off with the victims' passage money. Usually he backtracks to the group's point of origin, where he quickly stores the passenger's suitcases (they'll probably bring a few dollars) as well as their contents (which may bring a lot more). He returns the car he has rented from a car agency under a fictitious ID and driver's license and disappears, most likely to work the same ploy in another city.

SHELL GAME   *age-old swindle*

The shell game was the predecessor of three-card monte (see entry), the most common street swindle in American cities today. Now, because some members of the public have finally figured out that monte is a gyp, the shell game is making a comeback, since there appears no way one can be cheated at it. In fact, the shell game is a far worse gyp. It is rather hard to pick the shell with the pea under it when the elusive pea is under none of them.

According to the late gambling expert John Scarne, the shell game is as old as America itself, with the

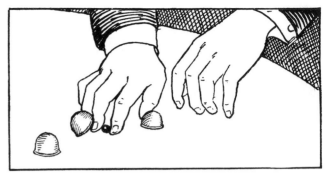

Dating back at least to ancient Egypt, the shell game works on the simple principle that the pea is under none of the shells; it is removed by deft finger manipulation.

first "thimble rigger" (as a skilled operator is called) arriving shortly after the *Mayflower*. While this is undoubtedly true, the game is much older and victims were fleeced at it at least as far back as ancient Egypt. In the second century A.D. Alcipron of Athens gave an excellent description of cups and balls, an early form of the shell game and of course equally dishonest.

In standard present day play, the thimble rigger clearly places a pea under one of three nut shells and starts shifting the shells around rapidly. While the victim concentrates on following the shell under which the pea was placed, he does not notice that the operator lifts that shell ever so gingerly so that the pea is trapped between the back of the shell and the surface. Now it becomes an easy matter for a skilled practitioner to pop the pea out between his thumb and first finger. Then he pulls his hand away, his finger concealing the pea. The victim makes his bet and loses; the operator quickly rakes the other two shells toward him as he turns them over, in the process slipping the pea under one of them. "If you'd picked this shell, you'd have won," he announces.

The basic rule in the shell game is never let the victim win any bets, since he might pick up his winnings and leave. It is far better to make him lose and let him become so desperate that he bets even more to try to recoup. The only persons who ever "win" are "shills," fake bettors in on the con.

The most successful thimble riggers in America were probably two 19th century operators, Canada Bill Jones and Jefferson Randolph "Soapy" Smith. Jones won the deeds to several plantations with the shell game and Smith any number of gold claims in Alaska. An oft-told story is that Smith was only beaten once at the shell game when a well-heeled stranger approached and laid his gun on the table as Soapy went into his shell shuffle. The man put down a considerable sum of money and had Soapy cover it. Then he announced he would not pick the shell with the pea but the two shells that didn't have it. He turned over two shells—no pea. "I reckon there's no need to turn over the last shell," he said, picking up the money. Soapy folded his table and left.

Despite all of the exposés on the shell game over the last 150 years it is, as previously noted, enjoying a considerable rebirth. For instance, one can witness the shell game at lunch time on New York's Wall Street, apparently because financial mavens want to get in on a "sure thing" once in a while.

SHERRILL, AVANNA   *con woman*

Back in 1950 FBI Director J. Edgar Hoover listed the worst female criminals in his reign. They came from the public enemy era of the 1920s and 1930s and most were mass murderers, mothers who trained their broods in crime and molls who masterminded the activities of their men—all dedicated to mayhem. One, however, was a con woman of the era, worthy of inclusion because of the vast and uncaring nature of her depredations. Her name, as best as could be determined, was Avanna Sherrill, unless that too was an alias to go along with the 90 she was known to have used (including Carolyn Ann Ardmore and "Goofy").

In analyzing Avanna's prowess, Hoover did not describe her as a master of the involved confidence scheme, but rather as an expert "instant liar" with the ability of talking to a victim and, by instant invention and improvisation, coming up with a likely story to separate her victim from his money. With earnest abandon Avanna scattered no less than $1.25 million in worthless checks from coast to coast. In her own fashion she was also a master car thief, although she never soiled her dainty hands in the process. She simply posed as a helpless thing and roped in passersby to help her get her car opened and started.

She could turn instant proposals of marriage into some quick money. Once she got a car ride to Colorado with a man who proved so taken with her that he offered to marry her before the end of the trip. Avanna naturally accepted. She gave her beau a phony $1,600 check, which she identified as an insurance payment for flood losses she'd sustained on her home. She took $1,200 in cash and an automobile from her entranced lover and told him to wait for her in a theater lobby. "As far as I know," she said after the FBI caught up with her on another charge, "he is still in the theater."

After doing a short prison stint, Avanna dropped from sight, most likely under alias No. 91.

SHIP'S POOL SWINDLES

On nearly every oceanic liner there is a daily ship's pool involving guesses as to the distance that will be covered each 24 hours. It is widely assumed that because of the generally high caliber of the ship officers, the pool can be regarded as one of the most

unfixable forms of gambling. As a result, there is all sorts of wagering, not only on the exact mileage but also whether that figure will be odd or even. On larger ships, especially in first class, the amounts bet in the pool and in private wagers often reach staggering sums.

At times, however, the fix is in. Alva Johnston, writing in *The New Yorker*, uncovered a case of "transatlantic steward with a private pipeline to the bridge of his ship [who] retired a millionaire merely by selling inside tips on whether an even or odd number of miles would be covered in a given day."

The legendary con man Wilson Mizner, who believed any swindle could be worked whether on dry land or the high seas, was a master of the ship's pool scams. Once he and two confederates zeroed in on a flashy ship's officer who, he decided, could be propositioned to take part in a fix. Mizner and his two companions followed the officer to his cabin and, standing outside, the nervy con man announced in a loud voice the number he had picked in the pool. He added, "You know what I would do to show my gratitude if I won? I'd stick a thousand dollars under the right officer's pillow."

Mizner's estimate was right on the button and he won the huge pool as well as many private bets with several millionaires on odd or even. His confederates also cleaned up. And, of course, $1,000 of the trio's winnings just happened to be tucked under the officer's pillow. One of Mizner's pals won the next pool and his other companion took the third day. After each pool the officer became $1,000 richer.

Several thousands richer, Mizner and Co. turned up outside the officer's cabin yet again on the fourth day and mentioned a figure.

This time they were answered with a growl through the door: "Get out of here, you bastards. I'm four hundred miles off my course now."

SHRUNKEN-HEAD FORGERIES   *souvenir hoaxes*

According to a publication of the British Museum, the demand for Upper Amazonian shrunken heads, or *tsantsas*, by collectors of the ghoulish "has always exceeded the number of genuine examples ever offered for sale, and many of those in both museum and private collections are forgeries."

For the Shuar (or Jivaro) tribesmen, the heads of enemies taken in combat were believed to have great spiritual power, and these real heads were prepared with the most elaborate rituals. In the 19th century the Shuar were kept busy turning out shrunken heads for American and European collectors, and it is believed that corpses were disinterred or the heads of unclaimed bodies in city morgues were acquired by traders and shipped off to South America for shrinking. This was a tedious procedure, however, and new methods of simulation were developed. Shrunken heads today are made of goat skin, or occasionally monkeys. Village industries thrive in a number of American Indian communities in Ecuador in the area surrounding Quito. The goat skin is molded over a clay form and some are quite good, enough certainly to fool most casual buyers and collectors. Experts can generally spot the phonies, which today probably total in excess of 95% of the entire trade in shrunken heads. One obvious mark is the eyebrow hair, since all of the hair on goat skin grows in one direction. The headmakers have to laboriously trim and comb the hair in opposite directions to simulate human eyebrows, not at all an easy task. Nevertheless, the industry thrives, presumably because there's a shrunken-head sucker born every minute.

SIMONIDES, ALCIBIADES CONSTANTINE *manuscript forger*

Few forgers were more ambitious or prolific than Alcibiades Simonides (1818–1890). Yet we do not know too much about him because, although exposed a number of times, he was never caught. Of Albanian-Greek birth, Simonides got into the forging of ancient manuscripts in 1853 when he sold the king of Greece what was purported to be a manuscript written by Homer. The monarch made the purchase only after consulting scholars at the University of Athens. By the time the manuscript was found to be bogus, Simonides had disappeared. Simonides later duped leading experts with many alleged manuscripts from the monastery of Mount Athos, selling a consortium of Turkish scholars some Greek, Egyptian and Assyrian manuscripts for $40,000, then a most significant sum. Once Simonides succeeded in having one of his forgeries accepted and published in a scientific journal.

Simonides frequently changed his name as he moved around Europe and the Middle East. He turned up in Turkey, claiming to have excavated rare manuscripts, which he sold to local pashas. In England he later took the duke of Sutherland for a noble sum for letters supposedly written by Alciabiades to Pericles and from Belisarius to Emperor Justinian. Many of Simonides' false documents were eventually exposed by microscopic examination, but by that time the master forger had always fled. He was once banished from Spain for some of his misdeeds, but throughout his life he could boast that he had never spent so much as a single day in prison for his numerous deceptions.

SIMPSON, EDWARD   See FOSSIL WILLY.

SINGLE-HAND CON   *con game played alone*

Swindlers on the move seek to travel very light, but nevertheless they must have two suitcases stuffed with rags and an attaché case. On a train or plane they will befriend a fellow passenger. They gain his confidence by showing him the contents of the attaché case, which may be what looks like valuable diamonds, but are actually industrial ones worth next to nothing. Now the swindler is ready to work the single-hand con, involving no confederates—only his own sales pitch.

The con man shows a check from a jewelry firm for $10,000 or more. Having thus gained the confidence of the mark, or victim, he explains he must wire home $1,000 as soon as they disembark. He says he will cash the big check in a few minutes at a nearby bank. On this basis the swindler can coax $500 or up to $1,000 from the victim by leaving the check as security with him. The victim is left to guard the phony check, the luggage and the so-called diamonds while the swindler goes off supposedly to wire the funds the victim has advanced him. "Then we'll go to the bank and cash the check and I'll take you to lunch," the swindler says.

The con man does not return.

SKAGWAY TELEGRAPH CON   *gold rush swindle*

During the Alaska gold rush in 1898 the hordes of scam artists who followed the gold hunters to the Klondike invented endless ways of swindling their victims. None were more original than the infamous gambler and con man Jefferson Randolph "Soapy" Smith (see entry). One of his nerviest scams is still remembered fondly in Alaskan folklore as the "Skagway Telegraph."

The town of Skagway was filled with men loaded with ready cash—miners who had struck it rich—and an ever-growing army of new prospectors laden with pokes to finance their search. Soapy Smith took them all in his saloon-gambling hall with its crooked wheels, educated dice cages and marked cards. But if Smith did some dirty deals, he could be said to have offered some truly valuable services for the miners. He set up a telegraph office and charged miners $5 to send a wire anywhere in Canada or the United States. Scores of men sent out telegrams daily, assuring relatives back home that they were well and asking if everything back home was also all right. Within a few hours many got a $5 return collect wire in response with bland messages that indeed all was well. The telegraph office continued its land-office business right up to the day in 1898 that Soapy Smith was lynched by vigilantes for many of his depredations. Ironically, right to the end nobody noticed that Skagway did not have a telegraph line.

SLADE, HENRY   *spiritual faker*

American-born "Doctor" Henry Slade (c. 1840–1905) was one of the earliest practitioners of modern spiritualism, which came into vogue with the Fox Sisters (see entry) in the late 1840s. He was still in his early

20s when he got into the con and continued at it for a decade and a half before deciding to milk Europeans in the mid-1870s. Unfortunately for Slade, he came up against a scientific buzzsaw in the form of such evolutionist luminaries as Charles Darwin, Thomas Henry Huxley and Edwin Ray Lankester. The result was a criminal case in which the "supernatural" was put on trial.

At issue was whether the psychic Slade was actually in touch with the "departed spirits" or just a conjuring con man. Slade was known as the "slate-writing medium," his speciality being posing questions to the spirit of his dead wife, Alcinda, and receiving mysteriously written answers on slate. Since Slade had been patronized by the cream of (well-heeled) English society, the legal matter enjoyed front-page coverage for weeks.

The case had been brought by young Lankester, an evolutionary biologist who had been Huxley's student. Lankester had paid to attend a seance at Slade's establishment in the hope of catching him in trickery. During the course of the seance, the young professor snatched the slate from the medium's hand and found the answer written on it before it had been asked. Lankester hauled Slade into police court as a "common rogue."

The trial produced some amazing contradictions. Appearing on Slade's behalf were a number of public figures, the star of whom was Alfred Russel Wallace, a firm believer in spiritualism and Darwin's co-discoverer of evolution by natural selection. Wallace found Slade to be "as sincere as any investigator in a university department of natural science."

On the other hand, Darwin himself believed all "spirit-mediums" to be mere "clever rogues" who victimized the credulous and bereaved. In fact, Darwin and Huxley had previously sought to expose other fraudulent practitioners. Darwin informed Lankester that he would view it as a "public benefit" if Slade were put out of business, and quietly he contributed funds to the cost of the prosecution.

In his defense Slade insisted he didn't know how the writing appeared on the slate. A well-known stage magician, Neville Maskeleyne, proceeded to demonstrate some tricks with slates to show how such effects might be achieved. The judge finally announced he would have to keep the trial from turning into a circus and in the end ruled he would make his decision "according to the ordinary course of nature." Slade was convicted under an old law against palmists and street fortune-tellers. He was sentenced to three months imprisonment, but the conviction was overturned on a technicality, since Slade was neither a fortune-teller nor a palmist.

Slade left forthwith for the continent and continued his slate-writing seances in Germany, France and Russia. The renowned physicist Zollner and a chief of police were convinced of his powers. It should be noted that physicists can seldom spot spiritualist frauds. Such matters are best left to magicians and conjurers, who think in more deceptive terms.

Slade managed to fool some conjurers as well, but now and then he had to move on when his methods were exposed. He tried to resume his practice in England, but when that proved less than rewarding, he returned to America.

Now Slade's methods became even more exposed. In 1883 a man named J. N. Truesdell managed, through trickery of his own, to get control of Slade's slate during a seance. He wrote on it: "Look out for this fellow; he is up to snuff—Alcinda." Slade became enraged at being caught again.

As he continued to be exposed, Slade, driven to distraction, took more and more to drinking. His reputation and fortunes in sharp decline, Slade ended up in a run-down boarding house. It became the practice among New York newspapers to break in a cub reporter by sending him to interview old Slade and expose his methods once more. Slade was finally committed to a sanitarium in Michigan, where he died in 1905.

SMACK   *matching coin gyp*

Matching coins has been a popular gambling pastime probably since the invention of coin money. It is therefore highly unlikely that the con game called smack was an invention of American swindlers in the late 19th century, as some crime historians claim. But these swindlers may well have brought it to the level of an art form, one that is still worked today in bars, at bus and train stations and now especially at airports.

Con man A joins con man B, who has already befriended a likely sucker. They while away the time matching coins for drinks and soon they are playing for money. The three players each flip a coin at the same time, and if all three flip heads or tails it is no contest. If, on the other hand, two men flip heads and the third man gets tails, he is the winner, since he is the odd person.

Con man A does not have the most pleasing personality, gloating whenever he wins and cursing when he loses. Midway through the game, con man A takes a trip to the men's room. While he is gone, con man B and the soon-to-be victim remonstrate about him and his oafish manners. Con man B comes up with a plan to punish con man A when he returns. He suggests they raise the stakes and that every time he, B, announces he gets heads, the victim should declare he has tails and vice versa. That way A has to lose to one or another of them.

The victim eagerly embraces the plan and it works like a charm. Con man A is losing his shirt, winning only on rare occasions when B gives the sign to the mark that they should let their victim win one for the sake of credibility. What the victim fails to notice—since he is preoccupied counting his potential profits—is that his "partner" is winning most of the time so that not only is con man A giving most of the loot to con man B but so is the true victim.

Finally, con man A loses all his money and leaves. Con man B and the victim adjourn to a corner to split their winnings, but at that moment con man A returns and screams, "Just as I thought! You two creeps have been ripping me off. I'm calling the cops."

Now the victim is in a panic. He truthfully insists that he'd only met con man B a half hour earlier. Con man A is only slightly mollified. Finally he declares, "Well, if that's so, you two separate. I'll stand right here and each of you take off in the opposite directions. Or I'll call the cops—"

While A is distracted looking for a policeman, con man B whispers to the victim that they meet at a certain rendezvous. Ideally, when the scam takes place at an airport, B has previously informed the victim he is traveling on the same flight. This is very reassuring to the victim, who boards his flight fully expecting to meet his supposed partner in larceny. But B never shows. Actually, B has met up with A again to split their profits and then set their sights on a new victim. Airport and train stations are thus favored for this scam, since the crooks know their victim has departed. If it takes place in a bar, the con men are forced to move elsewhere for their next caper.

SMITH, "ANTIQUE" See "ANTIQUE" SMITH.

SMITH, JEFFERSON RANDOLPH "SOAPY" *con man*
Jefferson Randolph "Soapy" Smith (1860–1898) was a con man in the lushest field for its time: the Wild West and later gold-rush Alaska. There were suckers there in droves, easy victims for Soapy's audacious scams. Places such as Creede, Colorado and Skagway, Alaska continue to foster the legends of Soapy Smith. In fact, Soapy is probably the only con man whose gear for skinning suckers was preserved in a museum—Alaska's Pullem Museum.

Soapy picked up his nickname for one of his most infamous scams, in which he would mount a soap box and peddle soap to the hicks, announcing that several of the bars contained a $10 or $20 bill inside the wrapper. Even the most seldom-washed cow puncher would rush to buy the soap, especially after one buyer—one of Smith's shills—waved a $20 bill and shouted that he'd found it under a wrapper.

Soapy was something between the age of 12 and 14 when he ran away from his Georgia home to find his fortune in the West. He was doing back-breaking work as a Texas cattle puncher when he was trimmed

of six-months wages by a shell-game con artist. Smith's reaction was the same as many other great con men: Rather than taking offense, he determined to learn that craft himself. He was a master of the shell game, three-card monte and several other scams when he hooked up with a venerable old con man named V. Bullock-Taylor, who honed Smith's skills to peak. When Bullock-Smith died, Smith took over his master's operations and became the king of the con circuit throughout the West. He opened up a gambling hall in Denver, which became famous for never giving a sucker any kind of break. Recruiting an organization that enabled him to control virtually all of the city's con rackets, he branched into gold-brick swindles and phony mining stock deals. When the great silver strike hit Colorado, Soapy moved his operations to Creede, Colorado, to take advantage of the silver wealth that was pouring into that town. His main competition came from saloon keeper Bob Ford, the man who had murdered Jesse James. Ford himself was conveniently murdered, and suspicions arose that Soapy was behind that killing.

When silver revenues dried up in Creede, Smith and his gang of swindlers headed for the Alaskan gold fields. In Skagway he stripped gold hunters of their pokes even before they could head into the wilderness. Those who came back with wealthy finds were often trimmed in Soapy's gambling saloon, including their dust and the deeds to their claims.

The more idiotic the scam, the more Soapy enjoyed it. Thus he set up a cabin with a sign outside reading "Telegraph Office," and he charged miners $5 to send a telegram to anywhere and another $5 for a response. The miners flocked to take advantage of the service, never realizing there were no telegraph wires out of Skagway.

Soapy also established an "Information Office" to provide newcomers and travelers with whatever intelligence they might need. Smith's men thus learned more from the information seekers than vice-versa, so that somehow Skagway's phantom burglars became clairvoyant in locating sums of money. On an average Skagway night there might be as many as a dozen holdups, mostly perpetrated by Soapy's boys.

A clergyman once sought funds to build a church in town and Soapy proved to be a ready donor, handing over $1,000. That magnanimous act loosened the money belts of many another contributors and the man of the cloth took in a total of $36,000. Unfortunately, the same night all of the contributions were stolen. For his part Soapy considered $36,000 a good return on his $1,000 investment.

Smith followed the pattern that he developed in his Colorado days, taking control of the entire town and naming his own marshal and judges. It became impossible for any miner to prove that he had been gypped in Soapy's games or robbed by Soapy's gang. Finally, in desperation a vigilance committee, called the Committee of 101, was set up and posted notices that no more lawbreaking would be permitted. One of the committee's signs read:

NOTICE
To all gamblers and bunco men:
We have resolved to run you out of town and make Skagway a decent place to live in. Take our advice and get out before action is taken.

The standard procedure in the con game is to get out when the suckers get restless; but Soapy just laughed at such warnings and promptly formed his own Committee of 303 to indicate he had the power and intended to keep it. The vigilance committee quickly lost heart.

In July 1898, however, Soapy's men robbed a miner of $2,500 in gold in a daylight mugging that produced a spontaneous reaction. Led by leaders of the Committee of 101, hundreds of angry miners armed with picks and shotguns stormed into Soapy's saloon. Soapy tried to talk his way out of it with his charm, and for a few minutes seemed to calm the angry mob. Then they looked at each other and shot Soapy to pieces.

Most of the members of Soapy's gang were rounded up and would have been the victims of Alaska's greatest lynching had U.S. infantry troops not arrived and imposed martial law.

When they buried Soapy, it seemed quite fitting that someone tossed three shells and a pea into the grave as the corpse was lowered.

See also SKAGWAY TELEGRAPH CON.

SMITH, THOMAS L. "PEGLEG" See LOST MINES.

SOAP BOX DERBY SCAMS *kids' race scandal*
In 1973 the famed annual All-American Soap Box Derby in Akron, Ohio was hit by scandal. Officials charged it had been loaded with cheaters and that 34 derby cars, including six of the top 10 finishers, had been "doctored up." It was also charged that the list of cheaters included the first-place finisher, 14-year-old Jimmy Gronen of Boulder, Colo., who won the gold championship cup and a college scholarship. Gronen's uncle, engineer Robert Lange, Sr. was accused of spending $22,000 in developing his car for the race. Under the rules of the derby all work on the vehicle had to be done by the competing youngsters themselves and the total cost of the car was not to exceed $75.

After the award had been made, derby officials performed an x-ray examination of the winner's car and discovered a strong electromagnet concealed in the nose. Wires connected the electromagnet to a heavy battery to a switch located behind the driver's head. Whenever the driver's plastic helmet pressed against the switch, the battery triggered the magnet. In the race the cars were to coast down the steep hill utilizing only the force of gravity. However, because of the electromagnet's power the winning car jumped forward slightly faster and thus gained a crucial advantage over the rest of the field.

Another charge alleged against engineer Lange was that he had even sent the car to California to have its aerodynamic body tested there in a wind tunnel.

It turned out that Lange's son had won the previous year's race. When derby officials announced they now wanted to inspect that car as well, it was discovered that the vehicle had mysteriously disappeared. For a time Lange seemed unrepentant about his acts, declaring, "Anyone participating in derby races with eyes and ears open would soon learn, as I did, that . . . the derby rules have been consistently and notoriously violated by some participants without censure or disqualification."

In Colorado, Lange was found guilty of two counts of contributing to the delinquency of a minor, as he had helped his nephew win the Colorado championship, which qualified him for the All-American Derby. Lange acknowledged a "serious mistake in judgment" and agreed to contribute $2,000 to a local boys' club. Still, Lange said he had regarded the cheating to have been "necessary" if his nephew's car was to be competitive at Akron, where so many cars were secretly professionally built in violation of the rules. The disclosures have led to a tightening up of soap box derby rules and supervision.

SOBER SUE *the unlaughable lady*
One of the most successful show business hoaxes on Broadway occurred in 1908 when a woman called "Sober Sue" appeared on the stage at Hammerstein's Victoria Theater during intermission with an offer from the management of $1,000 for any patron who could make her laugh. Nobody succeeded, and the theater then challenged the city's top comedians to get at least a smile from Sober Sue. Many comedians jumped at the challenge, being certain they would succeed and reap considerable publicity for themselves.

One after another they failed and came back repeatedly, desperate to succeed. Not a chuckle escaped Sue's lips, and she became Broadway's hottest attraction. Only then did it start to dawn on the comedians that they had been had, having being conned into doing their high-priced routines for free for weeks. Their chagrin seared to white-hot fury after Sober Sue completed her run and decamped the city. Only then was it discovered that she could neither laugh nor smile because of paralysis of her facial muscles.

SOCIAL SECURITY FAKE CLAIMS

They are Social Security vultures who cheat people of their rightful benefits that the victims don't realize they are entitled to. The more financially precarious a person's condition is, the more likely he or she is raw meat for the Social Security vulture. One female con artist worked the racket by combing small towns searching for people in desperate straits who were ignorant of the Social Security laws.

The con artist happened to find a woman whose husband had died in middle age, leaving her with two young children to care for. "I don't want to raise your hopes but it is possible that you might be entitled to some money from the Social Security," she purred to the unfortunate woman.

The widow, full of hope, gave the woman $15, the standard cost of a "claim search." Two weeks later the con artist woman returned and reported: "We aren't absolutely certain but we believe you are entitled to a pension."

The widow was thrilled, as it seemed the lady was in there pitching for her. On request, the widow turned over the birth certificates for her children and her marriage certificate. She also turned over an additional $3 for notarization forms and $10 to accompany the application. "But don't worry," the lady thief assured her. "In case your claim is refused you get a refund of the $10."

Many weeks passed while the widow hoped for good news. But that is not what she got. The bogus lady inspector returned one day with the papers she had borrowed. She also handed the widow a $10 bill. "I'm so sorry," she said consolingly, "but the ruling went against you. You aren't entitled to any benefits."

The widow took the disappointment philosophically. Sometime later, her meager funds all but exhausted, the widow finally got a job. She did pretty well at it and, in fact, eventually did too well. One morning she received a letter from the Social Security Administration informing her that her benefits were being suspended because her wages had been so high.

The next day she went to the Social Security office in a nearby city to inquire, tartly, just how they could be suspending payments she hadn't been receiving. She was told she most certainly had been getting benefits for the last two years.

It turned out the checks had been going to an address that had been supplied by the con artist who had called on the widow. The woman swindler had used the widow's papers to impersonate her and collect payments the widow was entitled to. If the widow hadn't fouled things up by making too much money, the swindler would have drawn benefits until the widow's children came of age.

In this particular case the woman swindler was caught and given a five-year sentence. Undoubtedly, however, many more unknowledgeable people continue to be victimized in this way.

SOCIAL SECURITY SCAMS   *victimizing pensioners*

It is a sad truth that no one can be more gullible at times than the aging who are forever fearful that their Social Security benefits can be taken away from them. As a result, con men have moved in on Social Security, collecting "fees" from the elderly, the disabled and the harried widows with the promise of helping them keep their benefits.

In Virginia two men visited a widow the day after her survivor's check arrived. They flashed badges with the letters U.S. on them and declared the woman was receiving too much government money. They gruffly explained that, because of inaccurate information her late husband had supplied the agency, his pension rate had been overestimated. They told the woman the overpayments totaled thousands of dollars and that she would have to make complete restitution immediately.

"If you don't," one of the impostors declared, "you'll lose all your benefits until the government withholds the full amount due. And we'll have to turn the matter over to the FBI to see if your husband had attempted a deliberate fraud with your connivance."

The pressure technique worked and the poor widow was scared witless. She handed over money from a recently cashed check, putting it toward "partial payment." She further declared she would mortgage her house to pay off the balance. Only when the "agents" didn't return did the widow confide her troubles to a friend and discover that she had been taken. Had the con men returned to her, they would have made a far bigger killing. However, their one-shot-hit-and-run system was infinitely safer for them. They are usually satisfied with the amount of one check and whatever other cash their victims have on hand. Sometimes they also appropriate jewelry and the like as "security" for the money still supposedly owed.

The fast-talking con men use the overpayment restitution gimmick regularly. One operator, working alone in St. Louis and later in Indianapolis, took dozens of beneficiaries, netting an average of $282 per victim before he was finally caught.

The "doctor gimmick" also works like a charm. Generally, the victims of this particular racket are persons already receiving disability benefits. One day they suddenly get a telephone call informing them that the "Social Security doctor" is coming to see them. The inference is that everything depends on the doctor's verdict as to whether or not the person continues to get his checks. Persons who do not understand how ridiculous it would be for the government to send the doctor around to every pensioner's home are tempted to hand over money to the bogus doctor.

One crook in the Midwest would inform victims they had to pay the full going rate for this medical examination. To turn an extra dollar he would sell the victims medicine for whatever ailed them, thus establishing the "written proof" that they had genuine medical problems. In one case the crook was not satisfied with the cash he was able to squeeze out of a disabled man, and appropriated the man's gold watch as security for some $84 he said was still outstanding.

The government constantly tries to educate pensioners about their benefits and advises them never to pay cash to anyone for services or monies allegedly owed the government. Relatives of Social Security recipients must always keep a watchful eye out for con artists and scams.

SOLOMON, SAMUEL   See BALM OF GILEAD.

SOUTHCOTT, JOANNA   *mother-to-be of the Second Messiah*

In 1792, 22-year-old Joanna Southcott (1750–1814), an English farmer's daughter, began writing rhymed prophecies and announced she had become the bride of Christ and would, in due course, become the mother of the Second Messiah. She developed a following of some 100,000 supporters (known as "Southcottians"), and in 1802 she established herself in London. Southcott made a fortune selling her poorly rhymed prophecies as well as signed certificates that guaranteed the salvation of the buyers.

Meanwhile, some were getting impatient for the coming of the Second Messiah. Finally, Joanna announced it would occur on October 19, 1814. This understandably caused considerable comment, as she would be 64 years old at the time, well beyond the age of motherhood.

As the date neared for the birth, Joanna was examined by 21 doctors and remarkably 17 declared she was indeed pregnant. With the announcement throngs of people congregated on Manchester Street where Joanna lived. During the vigil, many in the crowd collapsed of exhaustion and three died.

The 19th came and went and there was no birth; indeed, Joanna was not pregnant. The bitterly dis-

Joanna Southcott's panacea for the world's ills turned out to be a horde of a lady's nightcap, a horse pistol, a dice box, a puzzle and a novel titled *The Surprises of Love*. But to this day she still has her believers.

appointed crowds slowly dispersed. Within 10 weeks Joanna Southcott died of brain disease.

However, the Southcottian saga was not finished. Joanna left humankind a sealed box of prophecies, which she said would solve a great human crisis when opened a century later in the presence of 24 bishops. (By coincidence this was the date of the start of World War I.) By 1913 demands by the Southcott followers, now organized as the Panacea Society, grew for the sealed box to be opened in 1914. The archbishop of Canterbury refused to do so. Finally, in 1927 under pressure from the Southcottians the bands were broken in the presence of the bishop of Grantham. What was found hardly proved to be a panacea for the world's ills. Among the items removed by the bishop were a lady's nightcap, a horse pistol, a dice box, a few coins, a 1796 lottery ticket, a 1793 calendar of the French court, a puzzle and a novel entitled *The Surprises of Love*.

To this day a dwindling band of Southcottians insists the wrong box was opened. They demand that the right one be discovered and inspected with the required 24 bishops in attendance.

SPANISH INQUISITION TORTURE CHAIRS *a multitude of fakes*

Within the European tourist trade it is acknowledged that no self-respecting castle can hope to lure tourists without an impressively frightening torture chamber. For many, Spanish Inquisition torture chairs are the most impressive accoutrements of a torture chamber. However, most are mere copies of the real thing or at best assembled from a number of separate parts of which but a few are genuine. These torture chairs offer such awesome devices as those used for compressing the head, ripping out the tongue, piercing the ears, crushing the nose and other even more horrible deviltries.

In the 18th century torture tended to be abolished; most torture instruments were destroyed or at the very least disassembled, stored and eventually pilfered or otherwise lost. It was probably the romantic fiction of the first part of the 19th century that led to renewed interest in torture paraphernalia (and into the overstated uses of chastity belts as well). To meet this lurid interest, skilled workmen set about rebuilding the torture chairs for public viewing. For whatever comfort it might be, many of these resurrected versions most likely wouldn't really work.

SPANISH PRISONER SWINDLE *long-standing fraud*

The "Spanish Prisoner Swindle" is more than four centuries old, tracing back to the time of Philip II of Spain and Sir Francis Drake. Today it still works the way it did in the 16th century, with only minor updates. Most common now is a version in which a letter describes an alleged prisoner held captive in Mexico or Cuba. If the setting is Cuba, the prisoner is in a Castro jail. He is a rich man who, before being incarcerated, had managed to smuggle out about $250,000 which is now concealed in the false bottom of a trunk laying unclaimed in a U.S. customs house. Four hundred years ago it was gold coins or jewels. It hardly matters; the con is the same.

In the modern version, the trunk can only be claimed by the writer of the letter, or perhaps his teenage daughter. For a mere pittance, say $5,000 or $10,000, the prisoner would be able to bribe his way out of jail and he and his daughter would then escape from Cuba to claim his fortune.

A variation on that appeal is one in which the letter indicates there is absolutely no way the prisoner can escape; it allegedly cost him a fortune and put him at great risk just to smuggle out this letter. The prisoner says it is not likely he will ever go free, but his daughter can get out of the country with bribe money and claim the money hidden in the trunk.

The recipient is then hit with an offer that seems too good to refuse. If he will send the bribe money to an address in the letter, usually a post office box in Miami, the recipient will get back his money within a month, just as soon as the prisoner or his daughter reaches America. As an added reward he will be cut in for $50,000, $75,000 or $100,000 of the money hidden in the trunk. Needless to say, the money is never sent to anyone forwarding the bribe funds, for there is no prisoner in Cuba and no unclaimed trunk in customs.

These Spanish prisoner letters are sent out wholesale by swindlers. It was once estimated that on any given day 1,000 such letters are received by professional and business people and quite a few respond. Why? For many the lure of reward is important; for others it sparks a desire to play hero and adventurer and act like a pirate or knight. Lately swindlers have found it rewarding to zero in on soldier-of-fortune types who answer phony advertisements for secret enterprises in foreign lands.

There even exists a companion "American Prisoner" swindle. This involves a Latino prisoner in an American prison. This time the prisoner has several millions squirreled away somewhere in South America, the inference being that these are profits from the drug trade. In one case a swindler operated out of New York City, where he kept six typists busy pounding out letters that were sent to wealthy Latin Americans. Since the release of the film *Midnight Express* Turkish prisoners have also been in vogue. Apparently nothing can compare with a conspiracy that is supposed to do good.

The U.S. Postal Service probably sends out as many warnings about the Spanish prisoner racket as for any other swindle. The service's efforts are frequently in vain, and victims continue to be conned.

SPELVIN, GEORGE *world's most prolific actor*

The illustrious actor George Spelvin made his Broadway debut in a minor role in *Brewster's Millions* in 1907. Remarkably, Spelvin is still going strong, forever appearing in literally thousands of playbills, albeit always in minor roles. He can hardly be expected to achieve top billing, since George Spelvin does not, and never did, exist. Spelvin is usually listed as playing a role when one actor is playing two parts. In show business Spelvin has acquired such a reputation of being lucky he is used by some producers to give their offering a better chance.

Spelvin has apparently married and had children, since the names Georgette Spelvin and George Spelvin Jr. have also made it on the boards. When a Russian theater group appeared in New York it listed one Gregor Spelvanovich in the cast. Presumably, the Spelvins would not feel too kindly about an errant member of the clan, one Georgina Spelvin, who has made it big as a porn star.

SPIDER FARM   *journalistic hoax*

Not long after the unification of East and West Germany, a German publication assured East Germans that resourceful entrepreneurs could make money by coming up with good capitalist ideas. One of the more imaginative ones was to start a "spider farm" like several said to exist in France. These elegant spiders would be raised to sell to wine merchants to "cobweb" their wine bottles so they could gain an aged appearance.

Spider farms appear to have been American-born, first originated by Ralph Delahage Paine when he was a young reporter for the *Philadelphia Press* in the 1890s. According to Paine, a Pennsylvania man named Pierre Grantaire was raising spiders for just such purposes. Later Paine moved on to the *New York Herald*, where he reused his old Philadelphia story.

In July 1936 *Mechanics and Handicraft* offered up spider farming as a viable business in a story entitled "Webs for Sale," although it safely transferred its existence to faraway France; thus the future activities in spider farming got its Gallic start. Even the *Atlantic Monthly* fell for a reader's contribution insisting his grandfather had engaged in the activity. In 1940 Curtis D. MacDougall, in a delightful collection of hoaxes, predicted that spider farming was a story "which refuses to die and which, because of its comparative youth, may be just gathering momentum." It was an accurate forecast.

SPINNING-COIN GAME

At a Las Vegas gathering of a number of leading gamblers and gambling experts some years ago, a survey was made to determine the most common gambling gyp of all. Leading the pack was the spinning-coin game. It was estimated that as a dishonest play the game had trimmed Americans of tens—if not hundreds—of millions of dollars.

A hustler asks a mark, or victim, if he would care to bet him which way a coin will fall, heads or tails, if it is spun on a bar, table or army footlocker. To show that it is a fair bet, he permits the mark to do the spinning. The hustler makes the right call every time. The secret to this scam is a nick on one edge. When the coin is spun, the hustler can tell the difference between the edges and bets correctly.

There is another wrinkle in the scam, whereby the hustler has a coin that can be controlled. When the mark does the spinning, the hustler simply needs to watch how he holds the coin. Half the circumference of the coin has been beveled toward the head and the other half to the tail side, so that when the coin is spun with the beveled-head side down it will always come up tails, and vice versa. The mark thinks he is handling a normally worn coin.

Legend has it that during World War II a leading New York City department store tycoon was taken for $15,000 in such a scam between courses at Jack Dempsey's restaurant.

SPIRITUALIST HOAXES   See ROSS, MRS. HANNAH.

SPLIT MASTERPIECES   *cutting up art work*

One of the most outrageous money-making schemes practiced from time to time in the art field is the "splitting" of masterpieces. A great number of the world's famous oil paintings were long ago cut in two and sold as separate pictures by greedy dealers to art collectors who had never seen the entire work. A case in point is *The Finding of Moses at Tiepolo*. The fact that it had suffered from mercenary butchering came to light when the two halves just happened to end up being displayed side by side in a London exhibition.

There are those who view with trepidation so called partial sculpture masterpieces. The Lemnian Athena ended up with her head in Bologna while her body was in Dresden, a tribute to the profit-making theory that the sum of the parts are often worth more than the whole.

SPORTS BETTING 900 LINES   *gambling hustle*

The recent surge of 900 and 976 telephone numbers, whereby a customer can be charged on his phone bill for calls made has opened up a new scam operation in sports betting, especially on professional football games. The con, not fundamentally different from operations done through the mail (but with faster and more assured profits), works by the operator giving the winners for approximately $25—allowing for the point spread—of three area games of most interest to local bettors. The operator guarantees the bettors will make a profit wagering on the games, that is, they will win at least two out of three level bets. If by chance they lose two or three bets, they are provided with a special 800 number they may call the following week and get all the new week's selections for free. First-time callers, lured by newspaper ads, get the same predictions at the full $25 price.

The catch is that there is another 900 service offering forecasts on the same three games with similar, if not exact, terms—but with opposite predictions. Behind this line are the same operators, although due care is taken to use front men who can evade the law.

Thus while one 900 service will be a definite loser, the other will be a guaranteed winner. Should it happen that the same 900 line proves successful twice in a row it will be deluged with eager bettors. Meanwhile, the supposedly incompetent betting line will simply bite the dust and fold; remarkably, a new service will appear a short time later.

SPRING, ROBERT *autograph forger*

In 1858 an Englishman named Robert Spring opened a bookstore in Philadelphia and became perhaps the century's most prolific autograph forger. He offered for sale scores of signatures of figures such as George Washington and Benjamin Franklin on letters, fly-leaves and canceled checks. But his most masterful forgeries were hundreds of letters written by Confederate General Stonewall Jackson to his daughter, Fanny Jackson.

Spring did a land-office business in his Fanny letters, even though Fanny was a purely fictitious character. In addition, Spring did a thriving business in Stonewall Jackson's Bibles. He forged and sold a great number all of which were supposedly the one found on Jackson's body when he was accidentally shot fatally by his own men at Chancellorsville in 1863. Spring was so successful in this trade that Stonewall Jackson Bibles are an industry to this day, many being sold by claimants who say it has been in their family's possession well over a century. Of all these, the Spring versions are regarded as the "best."

SPUR OF AGINCOURT *fake relic*

The legend of the Spur of Agincourt began on October 25, 1415 when a loose spur is said to have dropped from a knight's charger as Henry V led the English to defeat the French at the Battle of Agincourt. The spur lay there for centuries, until a tree root grew around it and lifted it into full view, to be discovered by a souvenir hunter. In due course it was embraced as genuine and placed in the Victoria and Albert Museum's arms-and-armor collection.

By the 1960s some began to doubt the spur's authenticity. Dendrologists went to work on the wood enveloping the spur. They determined that it was almost certainly spruce, a type of wood that does not grow in the Pas de Calais battlegrounds. The scientific verdict: A faker had soaked the root of a spruce to soften it so that when it shrank, it would tighten around the spur.

Doubts about the Agincourt Spur were heightened in 1962 when an auction of a private collection turned up another spur set in a similar tree from a different English battle.

It was concluded that these and other such embellished spurs had been foisted upon collectors and museums in the 1920s by an antique dealer in arms and armor. In that period spurs were rather numerous and hardly garnered hefty prices, so the dealer had come up with a most ingenious ploy to jack up the value of his wares.

SPY INSTRUCTOR HOAX *intelligence double-dealing*

During World War II it was the custom of the German Secret Service to give all agents sent to enemy countries special courses on the way to behave there. Thus, in 1940, one of a long list of agents scheduled to go to England got a final special course from one Herr Linz, who explained how to ingratiate oneself with new friends there. The spy was to pose as a Belgian refugee but give the impression he had been in England for some time. Herr Linz instructed him to open a post office savings account and "accidentally" drop the bankbook before friends, since it would indicate he had been a normal resident for some time.

The spy did so and busied himself setting up a clandestine radio transmitter to send convoy information. He was apprehended before he had even sent his first transmission. Just before the would-be spy was executed he asked how he had been caught. British intelligence revealed to him that Herr Linz, a British double agent, had clued them in to his identity with the dropped bankbook. Linz had successfully used this system to unmask many enemy agents.

STAR ROUTE SCANDALS

One of the greatest frauds and raids on the federal treasury involved the so-called Star Routes, roads built in the West during the 19th century to facilitate the delivery of mail by horseback and wagon. A combination of crooked officials in the U.S. Postal Department, contractors, subcontractors and politicians set up a vast conspiracy. Congress was lobbied for appropriations to construct new and often totally useless roads and to upgrade old ones.

One road that was improved for faster travel had a price tag of $50,000, even though its total use only brought in $761 annually in postal income. Another fraudulent claim, unopposed by postal officials, brought one crooked contractor $90,000. Estimates of the improved value of the roads knew no bounds. It was later determined that the so-called improvement claims stated by contractor John M. Peck would have required the distance that could be traveled in a day actually required a man 40 hours to ride.

A number of probes by congressional investigators, special agents and Pinkerton detectives uncovered frauds on 93 routes and resulted in more than two dozen indictments. However, although the losses to the government were put in the millions of dollars, not a single conviction was obtained.

STAVISKY, SERGE ALEXANDER *archswindler*

No swindler in modern history caused more chaos to a nation than Serge Alexander Stavisky (1886–1934), a Ukrainian-born swindler who precipitated a government crisis in France that ended in the arrest, disappearance, financial ruin, political doom, suicide or death of hundreds of important French citizens.

Stavisky had a long record of business fraud and swindling in Russia dating back to 1908. After one of Stavisky's arrests, his father committed suicide out of shame for his son. Shortly before the outbreak of World War I, Stavisky migrated to France and engaged in a number of economic crimes as well as some drug selling and even armed robbery. He also committed a great number of big-money confidence games, which provided him with valuable information he could use to gain the cooperation of many political and financial figures.

Stavisky paid out millions in bribes, and through those he corrupted, he became the agent for municipal bonds floated by several large French cities, with the bonds making astronomical sums that never reached these cities' treasuries. However, with so many people involved, leaks inevitably developed and Stavisky's grand scheme for milking France collapsed.

Stavisky obtained a fake passport from police officials involved in his schemes, and fled the country. The archswindler paused in the resort town of Chamonix to see if his crooked empire might survive. He was captured there by what much of the press considered a rare group—those police officers not on Stavisky's payroll. A few days later, on January 8, 1934, Stavisky's suicide was announced.

A government crisis ensued, with both the political Left and Right each accusing the other of having been involved in Stavisky's dealings. Twenty defendants were indicted, and many others disappeared or committed suicide. One of the magistrates supposedly investigating the affair, Albert Prince, was actually a Stavisky accomplice and was found dead on the railroad tracks near Dijon. Also exposed was Albert Dalimier, the minister of colonies, who was forced to resign from the cabinet, as did two members of the Chamber of Deputies. Even Madame Arletta Stavisky, the widow of the archswindler, was charged.

The court case proved to be one of exquisite Gallic chaos, and although many were convicted, the French public ended up with no real idea of who had done what. The treasury of France, however, was demonstratively the poorer.

Madame Stavisky was acquitted of all charges in 1936. During her long trial she received many offers, some for engagements on stage, screen and radio and others for marriage. She turned all of them down, save for an eight-week stint in a New York night club.

STEERERS *scouts for gambling victims*

A steerer is a "talent scout" or agent, male or female, who "steers" a victim to a crooked gambling house or game. These days the crooked gambling house is much less prevalent, since there are too many payouts that have to be made—to the steerers, the dealers, the crooked "mechanics" and officials and law enforcement people who provide protection. As a result, most steering is done to crooked games in a private house or hotel room. If the steerer is a female, she might lure a mark or victim to her hotel room. There she would mention a private game where her mark can do better than at a legitimate hotel casino, since there is no house percentage taken out of the pot by the management. Of course, the game is run crookedly to compensate for that.

Gambling gyps prefer to run a poker game with four confederates and three victims, who are in various phases of being taken. That way Victim A, the member of the game for the longest time, might be taken for a considerable amount of money, while B and C lose or win a small amount. In fact, B and C are kept in the game because they see another player losing a lot of money and want some of it. Sometimes one of the crooked players will lose a bundle at a session, but it will go to one of his confederates.

When A is completely milked, it is up to the steerers to provide new blood in the form of Victim D. Meanwhile, the gamblers zero in on B.

See also ROPERS.

STEIN, DAVID *art forger*

French-born David Stein (1935–), a youthful jazz musician in Paris nightspots, did his army service in Algeria in the early 1960s. While there he tried his hand at art, doing some experimental frescoes. When he returned to France he drew a fake Cocteau "just for fun." Suitably impressed himself, he sold it off as the real thing for $100.

By any standard Stein had to be considered an impressive artist when, without any formal art training, he managed over a period of four years to turn out 400 works in crayon, watercolors or gouache, in the style of such masters as Renoir, Cezanne, Van Gogh, Dufy, Modigliani, Picasso, Chagall and others. To add authenticity, he first soaked his paper in cold tea (Lipton's won Stein's approval).

By 1965 Stein invaded New York with his works. In one day he unloaded 40 fake Cocteaus for $100 apiece. He also "sold a Chagall" for $4,000. He even opened his own gallery to facilitate moving his fakes, and in less than two years he made an estimated $1 million.

Late in 1966, an art dealer who was buying some Chagalls demanded certificates of authenticity, which Stein vowed he'd have sent from Paris. Every one of those given to the art dealer were proved to be forgeries. In a sense Stein was tripped up not by his bogus art work but by the paper work that went with them. Stein left town one step ahead of the authorities who found 110 forgeries left in his studio.

With his wife and child, Stein had moved on to San Francisco, where, upon the birth of a new baby, he decided he had to get back into the fake Cocteau art profession. As luck would have it, the New York art dealer who had exposed him happened to be in San Francisco at the time, spotted the drawings and notified the authorities.

Stein was arrested and shipped back to New York, where he was tried on 97 counts of fraud and sentenced to three years in prison. Released in 1970 he was shipped back to France to face other charges that kept him out of circulation until March 1972. After that Stein took up a new career lecturing on art fakes and painting one famous subject in no less than 25 different styles. Many of Stein's fakes remain undetected to this day. Of 400 works, only about 110 had been spotted by the experts by 1990. "I can open an art catalogue anywhere in the world and recognize my stuff," Stein was once quoted.

In 1991 David Stein was interviewed on the CBS television news show "60 Minutes." He was occupied, it seemed, doing a whole series of paintings. One of his chores was painting a large number of works on commission for a controversial Arab financier who was involved in such sundry matters as Iran-Contra and the financial affairs of Ferdinand and Imelda Marcos of the Philippines.

In the television interview Stein revealed that the Arab financier had requested that the artist work with "old materials." When asked why, Stein thought for a moment, as if the question had never occurred to him, and said it was probably because the financier wanted the works to look old. It seemed a reasonable conclusion.

STEPHENS, JOANNA *medical quack*

In the 1730s, one Joanna Stephens took London by storm with her treatment for "Stone"—kidney stones. She tended many rich and powerful personages, and her secret recipes were credited in some cases for allowing some sufferers to enjoy a respite from the ailment. More likely, these were nothing more than periods between attacks.

Nevertheless, there was much interest in 1738 when *Gentleman's Magazine* announced that Stephens was willing to publish her cures for the benefit of all if she were paid £5,000. A public subscription was held and, while some important ministers, bishops and various other notable persons donated funds, it fell short of the goal.

The public was disappointed by this failure and a parliamentary commission was appointed to examine Stephens' recipes. Presumably after considerable testing, the experts announced they were convinced of the "utility, efficiency and resolving power thereof." That was enough to successfully renew the subscription campaign.

Stephens offered three separate cures for kidney stones, each to be tried if the others had no effect. One was the boiling of herbs, honey, soap and swines' cresses. Another was a powder of snails and calcined eggshells. The final recipe was in pill form and was composed of calcined snails, burdock seed, asken keys, wild carrot seed, hips and haws. All of the recipes called for the contents to be burned black, a practice that surely eliminated whatever therapeutic alkaloids had been present. Despite the fact that it became clear that the recipes were all humbug, desperate patients continued to buy the cures. Before he died in 1745, Sir Robert Walpole consumed an estimated 180 pounds of the bogus cures. An autopsy performed after his death revealed three large kidney stones, totally unaffected by the potions.

Joanna Stephens offered no rebuttal to these findings. She had collected her £5,000 and quietly passed from the scene.

STONE SOUP *British beggar's ploy*

Back in the 16th and 17th centuries a favorite beggar's ploy in Britain was to approach a lordly mansion seeking alms, although most masters had informed their household servants to refuse such impositions. When told there was nothing available, the beggar would say, "Sorry for it, but will you let me boil a little water to make some soup of this stone?"

Such a novel request intrigued the servants and they readily furnished a pot, water and a spoon. The beggar popped in the stone and then begged for a bit of salt and pepper for seasoning. This could hardly be denied and, after tasting it, the beggar requested a few fragments of meat and vegetables that might be on hand to improve the taste a bit more. After that the beggar also obtained a few more sauces. When he had it done right, he permitted the servants to taste it; indeed, they found he had made excellent "stone soup."

The masters of the mansions eventually related the tale of stone soup to demonstrate how simpleminded their servants were. Of course, the servants were not the only ones victimized in the process.

STRAUSS, JOHANN See CELEBRITY SCAMS.

STRING GAME *carnival con*

No carnival game better typifies the dishonest promoters' principle of always giving a customer practically nothing for something than the string game. Unlike other carnival scams this one has the virtue, from the operator's viewpoint, of making it impossible to give out a big prize even by accident. The chief appeal of the "string game" to the public is that everyone supposedly wins. The pitchmen lure people in by shouting, "Just pay your buck, folks, and pull a string. Whatever prize goes up, it's yours. You just can't lose."

The pitchman holds a large plastic or leather collar with a number of strings coming out of it and tabs for the strings on the other side of the collar. Players pick a tab and pull, and the appropriate string lifts the attached prize on its pedestal. Admittedly, not all the prizes are gems; there are cheap flashlights, balls, pocket mirrors and the like, all going for 25 cents or less retail. But there are also Walkmans, wristwatches, coffee makers, toasters, even some small TVs, etc. The pitchman demonstrates convincingly that you can win any of these prizes. He pulls at all of the strings at the same time so that every prize behind the counter jumps invitingly.

Now the victim tries his luck, pulling a string coming through the collar. Alas, he draws junk. Most victims are not unhappy; they took a shot and just happened to pick a poor prize. What they don't know is that they can try again and again and again, but never hit anything big. The string game is based on the larcenous concept that players should never win anything valuable. Thus the game is "gaffed," or fixed, so a win can't happen. The gaff is in the collar. All the strings come to the collar all right, but only the cheap ones come out the other side of the collar and have tabs on them. True, everyone does win at the String Game—but especially the operator.

STRINGFELLOW, DOUGLAS R. *fake war hero*

In October 1954, Congressman Douglas R. Stringfellow (1922–) of Utah entered the studios of a Salt Lake television station on cane and leg braces to announce his withdrawal from his campaign for reelection. He talked about his military record in World War II, giving a different version than he had over several years.

Crippled by a land mine in the war, Stringfellow returned to Ogden, Utah and became a radio announcer. He attracted Republican Party attention because of scores of speeches he made to Mormon church gatherings and civic groups. Stringfellow told about his military exploits and with every telling the stories grew taller. He thus went into politics, winning an election to Congress as a Republican.

His favorite war story was his cloak-and-dagger description of his three-week OSS mission behind enemy lines in which he successfully captured a German atomic scientist named Otto Hahn.

According to Stringfellow, every other member of the undercover group was later killed. He himself had been captured and tortured by the Nazis until

he managed to escape, making his way to France, where he was crippled by a land mine. In the early 1950s magazine and syndicated newspapers printed stories about hero Stringfellow, and he was featured on the television program "This Is Your Life."

In 1954 the editors of *Army Times*, an unofficial military journal, began having doubts about Stringfellow and sought confirmation of his lurid tales from the Defense Department. They were met by an odd reticence, which turned out to be fear of offending a congressman. *Army Times* found his story didn't hold water, and the publication demanded that Stringfellow offer proof. It turned out he had not a shred of supporting evidence. The congressman blustered about a libel suit and even called up President Eisenhower to unlock secret files that, he said, could prove his claims. *Army Times* knew there was no way the president could unlock secret files because there were no secret files. His tale about capturing Dr. Hahn was debunked by a letter from the German scientist and by the OSS officer to whom Dr. Hahn had surrendered many months after Private Stringfellow had returned to the United States for treatment for paralyzing wounds.

Stringfellow's allies still tried to get the publication to kill its story. In the words of senior editor Harold Stagg, "Some accused, some warned, some threatened, most reasoned." Stagg was told he would be accused of having Communist sympathies. Nevertheless, *Army Times* went ahead with its story. After being quizzed by Utah's two Republican senators, Arthur Watkins and Wallace F. Bennett, Stringfellow finally confessed.

Stringfellow then went on television to confess that all his claims had been a hoax. "I fell into a trap which was in part laid by my own glib tongue." After his release from a hospital he said that he was asked to speak before various groups. "Somewhere along the line, the thought came in during the introduction that Douglas Stringfellow was a war hero. As the stories grew, I did not correct these erroneous accounts, but rather thrived on the adulation and new found popularity."

He admitted that "consciously or unconsciously I began to embellish the account . . . and wake to find they had taken on an aspect that even I have never expected. . . . I come here tonight to give you the fact. . . . I was never in the OSS. I was never on a behind-the-lines mission. I never captured Otto Hahn or any other German physicist."

He said the fables he had invented weighed heavily on his conscience and he couldn't sleep nights. "I never wanted to do anything personally or politically to bring any disgrace upon the people of Utah. I come before this radio and television audience humble, contrite, and a very repentant individual. I made some grievous mistakes. I am filled with sorrow for those whom I hurt. I wish before my Heavenly Father that I might undo this wrong. . . ."

Republican Party officials accepted his resignation from his political campaign.

STUFFED FLAT *sales con*
It is just about the best way to buy used furniture. Just scan the want ads for private parties who have to sell their practically new furniture cheap. Perhaps there's been a death or illness in the family or perhaps an occupational or retirement move. In any case, you know you're much better off dealing with real people rather than with a furniture store. This is true—if you really are dealing with "real people."

Suppose you go on an average private-party furniture shopping expedition. You answer an ad saying that recently bought furniture is up for sale. At the door you are greeted by a little old lady in black.

She announces, "We were all set to retire, get rid of all our old furniture because my son is in the moving business and said he would move us to South Carolina whenever we wanted to go. Now my husband has died, and I've sold the retirement home we'd paid off, and now I have to sell all this stuff because I'm moving in with my son and daughter-in-law and they barely have room for me, let alone a lot of furniture."

You buy the furniture for about $2,000 or about one-third of what the little old widow said she'd paid just six months previously. Later on you find out the furniture is not very good, and in fact you could have bought the same quality furniture for about the same price—or slightly less—in almost any store.

Of course the little old lady is gone from the apartment. Or is she? If this is a case of the stuffed-flat racket, she is on the telephone to have the local furniture store or wholesaler she works for send over another batch of cheap goods to replace the stuff you just purchased. Soon she gets another response to her ad and her saleslady pitch begins all over again.

There are many stores that do a hefty part of their business out of such stuffed flats, selling everything from furniture to cheaply repaired televisions, stereo units and almost anything else.

SUING INSECTS *legal fee swindle*
From approximately the 1200s to the 1700s, French legal charlatans garnered fortunes by swindling gullible peasants with the assurance that insects that destroyed crops could actually be tried in court for their depredations. Upon being found guilty the insects could be banished from the area by judicial order. Once a plaintiff engaged these con men, the case would be stretched out for a number of years, increasing lawyers' fees, court expenses and all sorts of required actions, forms and documents.

In one classic case in 1445 the inhabitants of St. Julian jointly brought suit against swarms of insects and the case continued for almost a half century. In that time three generations of inhabitants were bled dry in legal fees before the case was finally dropped. There was little else that could be done, since the uncaring insects had steadfastly defied all summonses issued for them to appear in court.

SUMMERLIN, DR. WILLIAM T. *medical research faker*
In the early 1970s a sensational instance of medical research fakery hit the highly esteemed Sloan-Kettering Institute of Cancer Research. Dr. William T. Summerlin, a cancer researcher, gained notoriety for his work there and earlier at Stanford University and the University of Minnesota. He claimed to have performed skin grafts between genetically incompatible black and white strains of mice, thus apparently overcoming the everpresent problem of the immune-system reaction that causes the body to reject transplanted tissues or organs.

Summerlin's research stirred considerable interest among immunologists and surgeons, but other researchers, such as Sir Peter Medawar—a Nobel Prize winner for work on tissue grafts—could not duplicate Summerlin's results. In fact, Summerlin himself could not repeat his claimed results. But in 1974 the 35-year-old researcher seemingly did it again. However, he later admitted that he had faked his experiments by using a felt-tipped pen to darken the skin of some of the mice.

A special committee at Sloan-Kettering labeled Summerlin's conduct "irresponsible" and "incompatible with discharge of his responsibilities in the scientific community" and he was given a terminal leave of absence.

The Summerlin affair produced nationwide speculation about whether more scientists were cheating in recent years or were they just getting caught more often. Many observers held that the percentage of fraud is constant, but since there are more people in the field than ever, the absolute number is growing. Many researchers actually felt some sympathy for Summerlin, who, as *Time* reported, was "caught between the enthusiasm of his superiors and a federal-grant system that tends to award funds for results rather than research." *Time* added: "There is no excuse for any scientist to fake his findings in order to gain more time to prove his theory. But any researcher who has ever submitted a grant application or sweated out a decision as to whether or not his work will be allowed to continue can understand why a colleague might be tempted."

SUN, MONA *stock fund swindler*

One of the most daring stock gyps in decades came to a conclusion in 1991 when a female stockbroker in the New York office of Nikko Securities Company, one of Japan's leading brokerage houses, pleaded guilty to a $120 million scheme to defraud her company and a Swiss investment bank. To some observers it is an indication how little investigation some financial institutions actually make on investments.

The stockbroker, Mona Sun (1933–), blithely set up an entirely fictitious company called the Chinese International Growth Fund in 1987. Capital was allegedly being raised to build a ceramics plant in Japan, but the fund existed merely on paper and had no assets whatsoever. Sun announced herself to clients as "the only officer of Chinese International." To facilitate the swindle, Sun had obtained the signature of Nikko's president, Kiichi Suzuki, on an unrelated document and attached the signature to a number of documents that she used to sell investments in the fund.

The scheme called for $120 million in promissory notes to be sold in 10 installments called tranches. A Lugano, Switzerland investment bank subscribed to the first three tranches for about $36 million. All the monies from the scheme were transferred to a Tokyo bank in Nikko's name on behalf of Chinese International Growth Fund, and Sun authorized herself alone to conduct all transactions. As a result, millions of dollars flowed out of the account. The plan was to sell huge amounts of financial paper throughout the world to a whole range of banks. The phony fund unraveled in the process of negotiations when someone got in touch with Nikko in 1988 concerning Chinese International. That led to questioning of Mona Sun, who confessed. Only about $28 million was recovered from the fund's bank account. When Mona Sun pleaded guilty, she was liable to 30 years imprisonment, fines totaling $1.5 million and was ordered to make restitution to those she had conned.

SWAG HUSTLES *sham stolen goods*

Their trucks turn up at the fringes of street fairs or shopping malls; with their trucks' tailgates down, a couple of nervous individuals sell some expensive items, such as VCRs still in their sealed cartons. One item is opened as a sample. The price is so ludicrously low that people think the goods have to be stolen. The "Swag [meaning stolen goods] Hustle," like most con games, is frankly based on people's willingness to be dishonest themselves as they buy stolen merchandise at bargain prices, no questions asked.

"Hurry up, folks," one of the hustler blares. "We're not hanging around here more than 15 minutes. So pick up your bargain before we're out of here!"

True to their word, the hustlers leave quickly—but not for fear of the police as much as fear of their customers. The swag buyers usually rush right home to inspect their great deals, only to open the carton and find it weighted down with a few bricks and packing material. By the time the angry customer rushes back, the hustlers have long disappeared.

Unlike raw swindles of this type, another form of the swag hustle is the selling of cheap but legitimate merchandise at low prices while inferring the goods are stolen. In some wholesale outlets in New York's lower Manhattan, hustlers openly inquire about goods that will pass as imitation swag and the stores eagerly oblige.

SWAMP SWINDLERS *real estate gyps*

Within the real estate scam profession, the mark of the good con operator is one who can swell land that is several feet under water. Such operators are known affectionately in the trade as "swamp swindlers." The heyday of the swamp swindlers was during the great Florida land boom and bust of the 1920s, where some very moist Florida acreage was unloaded on thousands of suckers.

Since then laws have been put on the books both by state and federal governments that prohibit the sale of underwater homesites. That hasn't stopped the swindlers who continue to peddle jungles, swamps and lake bottoms not technically as homesites but as "investment acreage," a differentiation in terms that spins over the head of the average low- and middle-income American.

Warnings are always made that property should be inspected before it is bought, but this is hardly ever done when the down payment is made so low and the monthly payments are thereafter accompanied by lovely color brochures guaranteed to soothe the average future retiree.

Actual inspection can prove to be a grueling experience. The following testimony was submitted to a U.S. congressional subcommittee in the mid-1960s by a Florida official:

> I spent almost two days, using a slow plane and a four-wheel drive, radio-equipped jeep, to try to locate a certain parcel [for a buyer] in a development called University Highlands, being sold by a corporation named Firstamerica Corp., located approximately ten miles west of Daytona Beach in a dismal swamp.
>
> After two days of some of the roughest riding, we had to give up, as it was impossible to penetrate deep enough into the swamp to a point which we had spotted from the air.

This particular parcel of "land" was foisted on an upper New York state woman who had plans to use it as the perfect spot for a house trailer. As Ralph Hancock and Henry Chafetz comment dryly in *The Compleat Swindler*, "It wasn't even usable as a site for a houseboat."

What the swamp swindlers count upon is that few persons can attempt the actual inspection trip. They pay the extremely low down payment (if any) and make their monthly payments, always meaning "to get down there sometime soon." If and when they finally do, they have been stuck for several years payments, money that's down the drain in more ways than one.

SWIMMING *hoax test for witches*

"Swimming," the centuries-old test to identify witches, is defined as follows by the *Encyclopedia Britannica*: "to fling the accused bound into water, because a witch, having denied his or her baptism, would in turn be repelled by the water so that he or she would float and not sink into it."

This is hardly an accurate description of the technique, for if a person was indeed flung into the water she or he would sink and, whether rescued or not, would be cleared of the charge of being a witch. However, most swimming victims did indeed float and paid with their lives at the stake for this offense.

The technique used in the swimming test for witches was highly recommended by James VI of Scotland (later James I of England) in his 1597 treatise *Demonolgie*. In the test the hands and feet of the suspected person were tied together crosswise, the thumb of the left hand to the toe of the right foot and vice versa. The person was then wrapped up in a large sheet or blanket, and then laid upon his back in a pond or river. They were not flung into the water, but positioned most carefully. Charles Mackay wrote in his 1841 classic *Extraordinary Popular Delusions and the Madness of Crowds*: "If they sank, their friends and relatives had the poor consolation of knowing they were innocent; but there was an end of them: if they floated, which, when laid carefully on the water, was generally the case, there was also an end of them; for they were deemed guilty of witchcraft, and burned accordingly."

Those murderously unscrupulous "witch finders" who earned their living exposing witches had to hone their skills to make sure that the vast majority of their victims floated. A witch finder who had too many victims sink and establish their innocence in the act of drowning could not expect to remain long in the business.

The notorious Matthew Hopkins (see entry), the so-called Witch Finder General, was most successful at getting his victims to float. Ironically, when he was accused of being a witch himself in 1647 and subjected to the swimming test, he too was very artfully set upon the water so that he floated and was sentenced to be hanged.

Although the swimming test would continue for some decades in various countries after Hopkins' demise, the obscene practice came to an end in 1654 when the elector of Brandenburg issued a rescript in the case of a convicted witch that forbade the use of torture and denounced the swimming of witches as "unjust, cruel, and deceitful."

T

TACKING See FANNING.

TALKING TOE TRICKS *spiritualist scam*

The "talking toe" is the name given to a trick that led to the founding of what is considered modern spiritualism. In 1848 15-year-old Margaret Fox of Hydesville, New York discovered she could crack a big toe and made a sound like a sharp rap on wood. She and her sister decided to fool their parents with this physical characteristic until her superstitious parents believed the girls truly possessed "supernatural powers." The fame of the Fox sisters (see entry) grew until they were nationally and internationally famous as great spiritualists—all thanks to some talking toe trickery.

It was decades before the girls, then middle-aged women, finally confessed their fraud. Oddly, the confession was used in an unusually inspired way to make further war on spiritualists by the great evolutionist Thomas Henry Huxley. Learning of the Fox sisters' deception, Huxley, as Richard Milner states in *The Encyclopedia of Evolution,*

> . . . outfoxed them [the spiritualists] at their own tricks. . . . Through long practice, Huxley became adept at loudly snapping his second toes inside his boot. Whenever his sense of humor moved him, he announced that he, too, had the power of summoning the spirits. Then, as if from nowhere, would follow a staccato of mysterious knocking sounds. Psychics were confounded, and true believers astounded.

Huxley also said he wouldn't be caught dead at a seance, in this life or the next, but he made exceptions to this when he trained his talking toe. The joy of garbling a medium's message with extraneous rappings was just too delicious to resist.

TAPEWORM FAKES *quack medicine*

In 19th-century America no remedy scam was more effective in medicine shows than those designed to free the tummies of tapeworms. The medicine show "professor" would case a small town a day ahead of time, seek out an emaciated resident and inform him that he was suffering from the most advanced case of tapeworm infection that the good doctor had ever seen in his extensive professional experience. Out of the goodness of his heart the medicine show entrepreneur pressed on the man a free dosage of his miracle cure, consisting of a bottle of the special nostrum and a capsule that he was to take before going to sleep. In return all the professor asked was that the patient attend the medicine lecture the following evening and bring with him the result of his treatment in a jar.

Since the guinea pig patient was well known in the locality and clearly not in the learned professor's employ, the audience was more than impressed when the much-relieved patient held up the result of the treatment for all to see. It was a three-foot tapeworm. And, announced the professor with considerable fervor, probably eight of ten persons present had an equally vile monster gnawing away at their inner vitals. If they did, he declared, his miracle cure would root out the awesome devil, and if not, the miracle drug would keep the user from getting such a tapeworm. Needless to say, the miracle cure sold quickly to the terrified members of the audience, who in the days following the pitchman's departure imbibed the nostrum with dedicated regularity.

Unlike the first patient, none produced a tapeworm since the capsules sold them were devoid of the delicate rubber worm that had been tightly wrapped inside the first capsule and quickly expelled with the laxative nostrum. The good professor always managed to recover the bogus tapeworm

Alleged Tasaday tribe members ridicule magazines featuring them as naked "stone age primitives."

"for further scientific analysis" and thus had it available for reuse at the next medical point of call.

TASADAY TRIBE   *20th-century stone age cavemen*

It was one of the most heartwarming stories ever, a report in the late 1960s of the discovery of a tribe of cave-dwelling people isolated in the rain forests of the Philippines, living the way they had for thousands of years. They were the Tasaday tribe who became the subjects of a popular book, *The Gentle Tasaday* (1970) by John Nance. The Tasaday were described as living on crabs, tadpoles, wild yams and palm pith. Their technology had never extended beyond crude stone axes and digging sticks, and they made fire the old-fashioned way, with a hand-rolled friction drill. They were a loving and gentle people and their language was devoid of terms such as "weapon," "enemy" and "war."

It was said the Tasaday were first contacted by a local trapper named Defal, who became their first "benefactor" by bringing them metal knives and teaching them to hunt. He then reported their existence to Manuel Elizalde Jr., a government official. Nance wrote: "We saw the Tasaday as a people who were very touching, caring, affectionate . . . [I felt] a whole new perception about who *we* were in that rain forest." A *National Geographic* editor dispatched with a magazine team to visit the Tasaday in their jungle caves wrote: "If our ancestors were like the Tasaday, we came from far better stock than I had believed."

Meanwhile, government official Elizalde supposedly built a wall of protection around the Tasaday to protect the tribe from exploitation by outsiders. Certainly the Tasaday seemed to venerate him, calling him "Momo Dakel de Weta Tasaday," meaning "great man, god of the Tasaday." For 12 years—starting in 1974 when the Tasaday area was declared a tribal reserve—Elizalde kept the cave people surrounded by soldiers. Only the carefully screened could get in to visit the tribe. Some, however, were not screened well enough. A linguist found that the Tasaday had words for "planting," "mortar," "roof on a house" and other terms hardly consistent with a presumably cave-dwelling forest people. An anthropologist observed cooked rice being sneaked into the caves, which led to his ejection from the rain forest.

Area locals then started making remarks that the "cave people" were ordinary peasants who came to market from time to time, fully clothed and smoking cigarettes.

The fall of the Marcos government in 1986 was soon to burst the Tasaday bubble. Swiss journalist Oswald Iten, along with a local writer named Lozano, got into the forest and found the so-called Tasaday families living in traditional frame huts and dressed in shirts and jeans. Worldwide television crews descended on the scene. ABC's "20/20" program interviewed eight of the Tasaday who poked fun at their tribal name and giggled at the nude photos of them printed in the *Geographic* and other publications. They declared the whole thing had been a put-on. They hadn't been born in caves, but in the surrounding area and spoke the traditional language used there. One of them explained, "Elizalde said if we went naked we'd get aid because we'd look poor." Unfortunately, it hadn't worked that way. "We're poorer now than we were before. . . . He lied."

It turned out Elizalde had fled the country even before the fall of the Marcos government. According to media reports, he took with him $35 million of his National Minority Protection Bureau money and "at least 25 tribal maidens."

TAUSEND, FRANZ   *the gold maker of Munich*

In the 1920s one of the most successful con men in Germany was Franz Tausend (c. 1890–1939), who insisted he could make gold from lead with a secret formula he had developed. In 1925 he offered to demonstrate this apparent miracle in Munich. He convinced a number of wealthy burghers to attend several showings and perhaps give him $100,000 to start full production. Tausend's performances proved to be a success, especially after he convinced the great military leader in World War I, General Erich von Ludendorff, to invest in his scheme.

In order to guarantee the authenticity of his formula, Tausend permitted his victims to supply all the equipment and materials he said he needed. Sure enough, after slaving over a bubbling concoction, Tausend managed to extract a tiny piece of gold from the lead he fed into his brew. It was enough to convince the wealthy burghers and the general to come up with $100,000 and Tausend said he could eventually produce 40 pounds of gold a day. Tausend continued to produce minor traces of gold in further experiments, but nothing worthy of his clients' investments, and in 1929 his backers had him jailed for fraud. The investors had some ill feelings toward General Ludendorff as well, since he had sold out his shares at a profit about a year after making his investment, leaving the others to absorb all the losses.

Tausend kept insisting he was not a swindler and was producing gold, and he offered to repeat his experiment at the Bavarian state mint, under the close scrutiny of a dozen officials. He was carefully searched on arrival and all equipment was supplied by the mint. Within two hours, Tausend again produced a small amount of gold. However, the next day on a repeat experiment, Tausend's hoax was discovered. As he was working, Tausend bummed a cigarette from one of his assistants. The cigarette contained some gold dust. When his back was to the officials, Tausend flicked the ashes into the mixture. Unfortunately, on this occasion—unlike the scores of other demonstrations the bogus gold maker had given—a sharp-eyed observer spotted the move. Tausend was sentenced to 44 months imprisonment for his hoax.

After his release, Tausend returned to sundry fraud schemes and was again imprisoned in 1938. He died behind bars the following year.

TEAPOT DOME SCANDAL *looting of government oil reserves*

While Teapot Dome is often cited as the greatest looting of the federal purse, it was only part of a much more widespread net of corruption that marked President Harding's administration of the early 1920s.

In 1922 Secretary of the Interior Albert S. Fall (1861–1944) secretly leased the Elk Hills, California and Teapot Dome, Wyoming oil lands (which were being held by the U.S. government as a reserve in case of war) to Harry B. Sinclair and Edward L. Doheny, two oil millionaires known for their bruising, free-

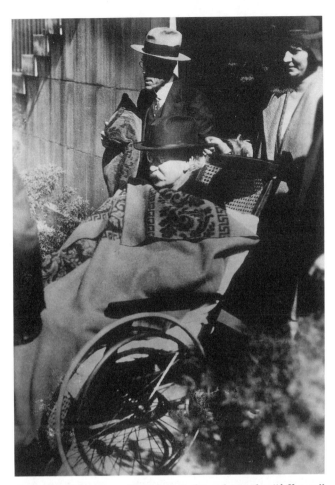

Considered by many historians to have been the "fall guy" for the monumental scams of the Harding administration, Albert Fall was physically broken at the time of his imprisonment and was a penniless invalid the rest of his life.

wheeling business tactics. The two oil men, estimated as likely to net as much as $100 million from the leases, had little trouble showing their gratitude to Fall. Doheny simply passed the secretary a black bag with $100,000. Sinclair arranged a "loan" for Fall for $260,000 in Liberty bonds.

The scheme was exposed when a Wyoming oil man angrily wrote his congressman inquiring how Sinclair had leased Teapot Dome without competitive bidding. This led to a Senate investigation headed by Thomas J. Walsh of Montana that revealed the payoffs made to Fall. At first Fall said he'd gotten the $100,000 as a loan from an eccentric millionaire, Edward B. McLean. However, McLean surprised Fall by denying he had made any such loan. With that cover blown, Fall confessed he'd gotten the money "in a black bag" from Doheny.

For the next several years Fall, Doheny and Sinclair went on trial eight times in various combinations. On the witness stand Doheny told how he and Fall had grown up together; he struck it rich in oil while Fall had nothing but hard luck. "Why shouldn't I lend him $100,000 and tear his name off the note?" he asked. "He was an old friend." Then Doheny called the $100,000 "a mere bagatelle," a remark that fired up the newspapers and shocked the nation. It was felt that the statement, more than anything else, doomed Fall.

While the two oil men were acquitted of the criminal charges against them, Sinclair got nine months for contempt for having a William F. Burns detective follow the jurors during one trial. Fall was convicted of bribery charges and was sentenced to a year in prison and fined $100,000. The financial penalty was dropped when Fall demonstrated he was impoverished. Because he was suffering from tuberculosis, he served his sentence in the New Mexico State Penitentiary, being carried behind bars on a stretcher. An invalid when he was released, Fall needed constant attention by his family until he died, penniless, in El Paso in 1944. Many historians have held that Fall was made the "fall guy" for the scandals of the Harding administration's so-called Ohio Gang, which looted the U.S. Treasury of far larger sums.

See also OHIO GANG.

TEAR-OFF RATS *con men who rip off their confederates*
While there is a certain amount of honesty among thieves in confidence-game circles, not all scam artists can be trusted as partners. Those con men who take advantage of other con men are known as "tear-off rats."

Among con men, the fabled Yellow Kid Weil (see entry) was notorious for "tearing off" his ropers (those who brought victims to him to be swindled) by underestimating the take or by padding the costs for the fix with the authorities and so on. "That Yellow Kid would tear himself off if he could," one of his ropers was once quoted. However, despite his bad reputation, the Yellow Kid never suffered from a lack of willing confederates, since his swindles were so lucrative that his partners still made more than they could on their own. Frequently, to collect anything near their due, con men had to visit Weil in his home and negotiate their differences at gunpoint.

Although con men tend to shy away from violence, the one exception is dealing with a tear-off rat. Many more con men carry bullet and stab wounds from their allies than from their angry victims. John Henry Strosnider actually turned some knife scars on his face—inflicted by a pair of cheated partners named Post and Allen—into a plus by claiming throughout the rest of his capers that he was a Heidelberg graduate and had the "saber-cuts" to show for it.

Con men always loyal to their partners think nothing of tearing off another set of swindlers. In Paris con men have been on guard for decades. An American-based swindler named Australian Harry always beefed about the mistreatment accorded his con mob in the French capital after they had trimmed a sucker out of $84,000 in a phony gambling den. Harry complained that another con man named Tear-off Arthur knew about the play and arranged to have the Paris police raid the "store" and confiscate the loot. According to Harry, Arthur and the gendarmes later divided the $84,000 equally.

See also ROPER.

THE TEAR-UP *alleged return of a mark's losses*
One of the most effective ways for con men to "blow a mark"—get rid of him after swindling him of a huge sum of money—is with the "tear-up." In a typical operation a roper, or steerer, pretending to be a big executive, befriends a businessman in a hotel and invites him to join with the roper's friends in a card game. The game starts out for relatively low stakes and the mark, or victim, is permitted to get ahead. However, the stakes escalate and in a big betting hand the mark is taken for several thousand dollars. He is unable to pay in cash, writes out a check and gives it to one of the other players. At that moment his roper friend reenters the room, having dropped out of the game for a few minutes. He is shocked and outraged that his new friend has lost so much money; he accuses the other players of having no right to escalate the stakes with a relative stranger.

The roper grows more insistent that the mark's money be returned to him. To make his point, he even threatens a couple of the players that he will cancel orders he has just placed with their firms unless they return the mark's losses. With some hard feelings the holder of the check gives it to the roper, who looks at it and rips it up. He then makes a big show of walking into the bathroom and flushing the pieces down the toilet.

The game breaks up shortly thereafter with the grateful mark still a few hundred dollars ahead. He leaves with the roper for whom he now feels an undying kinship. Usually the pair stay together until morning, at which time the mark retires to his hotel room to sleep. Not all of the other players are sleeping; one is aboard a plane to the mark's hometown, where he cashes the mark's check before the latter returns home. Later the victim will be surprised when he discovers his account debited.

The con men operating the swindle readily learn the color of the victim's checks. Having an enormous number of check colors available, they can substitute an imitation for the real thing. The mark is never permitted to handle the refund, which is given to the roper, who flushes the phony check down the toilet.

TEDDY BEAR ORIGIN HOAX *Theodore Roosevelt myth*

In November 1902 President Theodore Roosevelt went on a bear hunt in Mississippi's swamp country. An enthusiastic hunter, Roosevelt was reportedly summoned by servants after hounds treed a young bear. When called upon to kill the bear, Roosevelt refused, indignantly declaring the situation "unsporting" of a gentleman.

A *Washington Star* cartoon drawn by Clifford Berryman depicted the event and the story made headlines from coast to coast. The president's apparent mercy led to an image of a young bear as a sort of national mascot. The original "teddy bear" craze went on to sweep the country.

Lost in the hubbub was the true ending of the story, which was noted in Richard Milner's *The Encyclopedia of Evolution*. While Roosevelt had declined to shoot

The famous 1902 Berryman cartoon that spread the myth that the president refused to shoot a baby bear.

the bear, "out of sight of reporters, however, he instructed one of the servants to do so."

TELEMARKETING FRAUDS-ON-FRAUDS

With the arrival of telemarketing as a sales device, it is inevitable that frauds would also abound. Typically, the caller informs a victim that he or she has won a prize; the end result is that the victim parts with some money and never receives the promised prize.

Innovators of such telemarketing swindles later contact these same victims and pose as representatives of a federal contractor. In this unscrupulous pitch, the con artists claim the bogus company is under contract to something like the "Federal Telemarketing Agency"—a nonexistent entity—and promise that the government is endeavoring to deliver the prizes promised in the previous swindles. The fee for the service is anywhere from $175 to $300.

The technique is elaborate. Victims are told to call an 800 number and leave details about the original swindle. In due course the victims receive an official-looking document informing them that their claims have been found valid and the process for restitution requires the processing fee. In addition to full restitution, participants are also informed they are eligible for special prizes.

If this seems bizarre and unbelievable it must be remembered that all the victims have fallen for a similar pitch the first time around and are now desperate to recover what is rightfully theirs. Officials of the Federal Trade Commission believe such fraud-on-fraud telemarketers have simply bought up the telephone sucker lists from "first-round" swindlers. In 1991 the FTC charged one Long Beach, California firm with falsely representing itself as a federal contractor. An FTC spokesman estimated that several hundred persons had been "recheated" in this particular operation.

TELEVISION QUIZ SHOW HOAXES See QUIZ SHOW HOAXES.

TEN-FOR-ONE SHORTCHANGING SCAM *cheating a cashier*

While the public perception is that most shortchanging rackets involve the cheating of the public by dishonest cashiers, bartenders and the like, retail association spokesmen insist far more prevalent dodges are pulled by customers on employees. That may be arguable but certainly the "ten-for-one" scam is a gold mine for shortchanging cashiers.

The cheater buys something for less than $1 and pays for it with a $10 bill. He gets back a $5 bill, four $1 bills and loose change. Just as he's getting his money, he discovers a loose $1 bill in his pocket.

"Sorry, I looted your bills like that when I have a one," he says. "Give me back the ten for the five and five ones."

As the cashier hands over the $10 bill, the customer has another thought. "You know, I've got too many bills," he says rapidly. "Take it all back and give me a twenty." All this is done quickly, not giving the cashier too much time to think. Sometimes there is an additional distraction from a female confederate of the customer who is next in line. The woman, holding a baby, can get the child crying with a simple pinch or prick with a pin.

The cashier hands over a twenty and rakes up all the loose bills, forgetting entirely that the only $10 on the counter was one that came from the register.

While this may appear obvious as explained it is a very effective con if the cashier is sufficiently distracted.

TERMITE SCAMS   *home repair con*

There are dozens of ways a homeowner can be convinced that his home is infested with termites and may come crashing down at any moment. Very common is for the home repair gypster to carry termites in a jar (or in an infested piece of wood) and deposit them in the house.

In the words of one authority, Maurice Beam (author of *It's a Racket*), the termite scam "is one of the oldest and most respected of all household gyps. Respected, because there are few legal restraints imposed upon it."

Fear of termites is particularly present in homeowners who are seeking to sell their house because in many jurisdictions termite clearance is required in escrow proceedings. Unfortunately, termite "inspections" and "clearances" are not often validated by local government inspectors.

Perhaps more important is the fact that few homeowners really understand the termite "menace" and what can and cannot be done about it. Instead they are subjected to scare talk sales pitches of the dangers to the house, and they are assured that the salesman's services are "exclusive" and the chemicals used are "safe" (implying that all others are "unsafe").

In point of fact termite "control"—no matter what the price—is limited, and the spraying or fumigation done hardly renders effective service to the level of the dollars charged. Any such termite eradication is at best temporary. The most effective termite control is that which is used when a building is being erected.

The danger is not that gnawing termites (which incidentally do not eat wood fibers, but rather the cellulose that binds the fibers together) will cause a building to collapse. In fact, few researchers can find even an instance or two of such an occurrence. What the termite control operators and manufacturers do not tell homeowners is that when wood is destroyed, no spraying will restore the wood; the real termite control is provided by a *carpenter* who replaces the damaged areas.

THIRD-PARTY TELEPHONE CALLS   *bill frauds*

The voice over the phone is very businesslike and efficient. He or she identifies himself as a Federal Communications Commission inspector investigating unauthorized long-distance calls being charged to the consumer. Naturally the telephone customer says he has not made any such calls. The alleged inspector gives a false FCC badge number and says they will check the telephone lines to intercept the calls. As part of the investigation, the customer is told a supervisor will call in a while and place a call on his line; the customer is instructed to accept charges for this call. If the customer complies with the request, he has authorized the billing of a collect or third-party call to his phone—to another state or even another country.

"People think they're helping the government, so they are very ready to accept any charges," an FCC enforcement official says. "But the FCC would never ask someone to accept charges on their phone bill."

This is a simple scam used by third-party callers to make expensive calls for free. The FCC recommends that persons getting any kind of request for billing calls to their account should ask for the caller's name, organization and phone number and then report it to the telephone company and local or federal law-enforcement agencies.

THOMPSON, ALVIN CLARENCE "TITANIC"   *gambler and con artist*

As a big-time gambler, Alvin Clarence "Titanic" Thompson (1892–1974), specialized mostly at cards and golf (for which he had near championship ability). But he was not a man who would or could ever pass up a fixed sure-thing bet.

He often made it a habit of carrying on his person a lead-filled walnut. One day in Hot Springs, Arkansas, Thompson was sitting on a hotel veranda eating walnuts when he struck up a conversation with a local businessman. Titanic wondered if it were possible to throw a walnut over a five-story hotel across the street. The businessman said it was impossible and put up $300 to Thompson's $100 that he couldn't do it. The businessman was goggled-eyed when Titanic hurled the walnut—the lead-filled one—completely over the building.

In another scam, Thompson used a dog he had trained to dive into a local pond and retrieve rocks. He would find suckers unaware of the dog's talent and bet them that he could mark a rock with an "X" and the dog would retrieve that very rock. One fisherman bet his expensive fishing rod on such a wager, and Thompson marked the rock and heaved it into the water. The shocked fisherman handed over his rod when the dog came up with the "X"-marked rock. Of course, Titanic had taken the precaution of littering the pond with scores of other rocks all marked with an "X."

One night in Missouri, Thompson slipped away from his friends and moved a road sign marked "Joplin—20 miles" some five miles closer to town. The next day when he and his companions were driving toward Joplin, they passed the sign and Titanic insisted they were only 15 miles from town. His victims put up and lost $1,000 when, sure enough, the odometer registered only 15 miles from the sign to Joplin.

Titanic acquired his nickname for having been aboard the *Titanic* when it sank in 1912. Thompson and his pals all put in inflated claims for their lost baggage and valuables, but Thompson also had the bright, if ghoulish, idea of obtaining the names of passengers who perished and had other con men put in claims for them as well.

Titanic's greatest hustles took place on the golf course, where, after he first played some disastrous rounds, he bet rich suckers he could beat them. Naturally, with big money riding, Thompson's skills suddenly improved. Afterward, Thompson acted most chagrined at his sudden improvement, and he offered to play another round with the victim double or nothing, saying he would play the game left-handed. The suckers pounced on the offer and sadly lost again.

They didn't have a chance. Titanic was a natural left-hander.

THOMSON'S HEALING SYSTEM   *quack cure*

He was an uneducated New Hampshire farmer, but in the early 1800s Samuel Thomson (1769–1943) almost destroyed the American medical system with a healing process that employed steam baths and herb remedies. In a book he arranged to have written and published, Thomson claimed it was possible for people to self-cure themselves and dispense with medical doctors.

Thomson attracted a legion of followers and made himself a fortune. But then he was arrested and charged with murder after administering an herb called lobelia to a man. Thomson won an acquittal after his lawyer, taking the word of his keen-eyed client, ate the sample of poisonous lobelia that the prosecution had introduced at the trial. The attorney suffered no ill effects and Thomson was freed. Later, it turned out the prosecution had erred by bringing in the wrong plant.

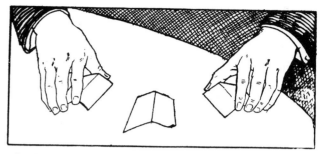

The lure of three-card monte is that it appears to be an easy game to beat because of the apparently stupid play of the shills. The scam artists follow one abiding rule: the sucker is never allowed to win a single bet.

However, the publicity given Thomson and his quack treatment resulted in a loss of faith in his steamery system and it disappeared by the time of his death in 1843. The other side to Thomson's quakery is that when steamery died, it also discredited such medical nonsense as the ancient beliefs in bleeding patients and massive doses of minerals as general cures.

THREE-CARD MONTE   *street con game*

Three-card monte is today America's foremost street con game, being worked regularly in virtually every big city in the United States. It has been a staple since about the time of the War of 1812 and perhaps earlier. In New York City, for example, it is virtually impossible to walk on West 42nd Street and many other cross streets from Fifth Avenue to Eighth Avenue at noontime without encountering at least three or four games in progress. The result is predictable in every game: The sucker never wins.

The rule in three-card monte is to guess which of three face-down cards is a red queen against two black aces. It seems an easy task, as the dealer first shows the position of the queen, does a fast shuffle and places the cards face down. All the victim has to do is pick a card and put his money on it. The victim will study play for a while and is stunned how easy it is to win; amazingly, some bettors lose while others win. Clearly, the victim decides, he is better at the game than the other players. What he doesn't know is that *all* the players (unless they have been milking another victim already) are shills—partners with the dealer to lure in suckers.

When the victim-to-be decides to risk his money, the dealer suddenly becomes very adept at his art. He lays down the cards in such a way that not only does the sucker not spot the queen but firmly believes a wrong card is it.

There are any number of variations of the swindle. The sucker notices that a corner of the queen is slightly bent upward, making the queen indentifiable. Thus he lays heavy bets on the bent card. But the dealer has used his pinkie to straighten out the fold on the queen and bend the corner of one of the aces.

Sometimes the victim still manages to pick the right card and places a $20 bet on it. The dealer immediately insists a minimum of $40 must be bet. When the sucker hesitates, one of the shills puts up the $40 and the dealer announces that $40 is his maximum. If the victim says his bet was first, the shill refuses to share his bet with the victim. Apparently exasperated by the argument, the dealer throws up his hands and yells, "No deal! All bets are off."

He then redeals and the sucker proceeds to make a losing bet. If, however, he still picks the winning card, he is "blown off" by another oft-used ploy. One of the shills yells, "Cops!" and instantly the crowd around the stand—usually just a cardboard box turned on its end—melts away. The dealer is also gone and at times the sucker is left alone with a box with three cards on it, his money still in his hand. There have been cases of the police seizing a hapless victim standing there with the evidence clearly in view. The victim is now faced with the task of convincing the law that he is not the monte operator.

It should be remembered that whenever anyone collects at monte, he can only be a shill, never a player. Monte operators will absolutely never let a victim win so much as a single game, for fear that he will then simply take his profits and walk away. Experience has also taught these gyps that a loser will generally keep betting even more money in the forlorn hope of "getting even." Even a person in the crowd who whispers to others that the game is crooked and identifies the shills to others cannot be trusted. He too is a shill, which will become evident when he proposes to stand behind the dealer. From this angle he can watch the cards and offer to flash the right card to the victim in exchange for half the profits. Once more something will go wrong—guaranteed.

See also SHELL GAME.

TICHBORNE CLAIMANT *impersonator*

Roger Charles Doughty Tichborne was born in 1829, the heir to an ancient English baronetcy. In 1853 Roger went to South America and in 1854 he boarded the sailing ship *Bella* out of Rio de Janeiro, Brazil, bound for Jamaica. The ship went down and nothing more was heard of Roger Tichborne. He was declared officially dead in 1855.

Only Roger's mother believed that Roger was still alive. When Sir James Tichborne died in 1862, Lady Tichborne launched an all-out effort to find her son, placing newspaper ads all around the world. In 1866 Arthur Orton (1834–1898), then working as a butcher in Wagga Wagga, New South Wales, Australia, con-

Arthur Orton, who came forward to claim he was the long-missing noble heir Roger Tichborne, last known to weigh 125 pounds.

tacted Lady Tichborne through a lawyer and declared himself to be her long-missing son.

Lady Tichborne contacted a former black servant of the family, named Bogle, who was now living in Sydney and had known Roger well. Orton, known by the name of Castro, weighed 300 pounds whereas Roger Tichborne had last been known to weigh only 125 pounds. But 14 years had passed and anything was possible. The butcher somehow managed to convince the aging servant that he was indeed Roger Tichborne. Lady Tichborne sent funds for Castro to come to England along with his wife and two children. They all met in Paris and Lady Tichborne was thoroughly convinced she had her long-lost son back. However, the rest of the family was less satisfied, especially since his acceptance meant that he was the rightful heir to all the family fortunes.

Castro-Tichborne wasted no time claiming his estate, and he did convince the Lady Tichborne's solicitor and several tenants that he was the real Roger. Roger's old tutor tried speaking to Castro in French—which he had taught the real Tichborne—but Castro could not grasp the language. Tichborne explained this by saying he had once suffered a severe illness that had affected parts of his memory. Still he did know considerable about family matters, but his foes felt he had gained this information from gossipy letters from Lady Tichborne and their subsequent conversations.

The legal case of the inheritance did not come to trial until 1871, by which time both Lady Tichborne and her solicitor had died. More than 100 persons who had known Roger testified that Castro was the true claimant. However, Castro made a terrible witness on the stand. He didn't know his mother's maiden name. His knowledge of the Tichborne estates was sketchy. He knew nothing about the school Roger had attended. He also lacked Roger's distinguishable tattoo marks. The best he could vaguely remember was that the tattoos had faded or been removed during a period of illness.

Then it was established that Castro was really a man named Arthur Orton, the son of a butcher in Wapping, England and that he was wanted in Australia under that name for horse theft. The jury threw out the claimant's case. The matter did not rest there. In 1873 Orton-Castro was tried for perjury and, after a 188-day trial, he was found guilty and sentenced to 14 years imprisonment.

The claimant stuck to his claims while behind bars and even changed in several ways. He trimmed down to 150 pounds and wrote letters to his friends that surprisingly became better written than his earlier writings. In short, he seemed to be more like the man he claimed to have been all along. His enemies were unimpressed, viewing the transformation as nothing more than the virtues of a prison education.

Arthur Orton was released in 1884, still insisting he was Roger Tichborne. He managed to find some who believed his claims. Orton sold his memoirs to a newspaper, but he died penniless in London in 1898 at the age of 64. His coffin was inscribed: "Sir Roger Charles Doughty Tichborne."

TIP THE TEE *bar bet scam*

The Tip the Tee bar bet is a cunning barroom scam that has endured for decades. It is worked regularly in bars, as well as in some pool halls. Barrooms are preferred because the victims are usually somewhat intoxicated and are even less likely to spot the scam. They are also more likely to be talked into making larger bets.

A golf tee is put on a pool table. Three pool balls are arranged around it, one in front of the tee and two behind it. All of the balls are touching. Victims are then bet that they cannot knock down the tee by shooting a ball that scatters the three balls. The hapless victim feels he can do so merely by slamming the front ball hard enough. However, the laws of physics make his efforts useless. When he shoots the cue ball and it hits the front ball, the impact is diverted entirely to the other two balls and around the golf tee, which remains standing.

When the hustlers have taken their victims for all they are willing to bet, one of them announces he can knock over the tee. Naturally, this produces money bet against the hustler. The hustler's partner arranges the three balls but, unnoticed by the victims, he positions them so the front ball is not quite touching one of the back balls. This is enough to prevent the entire impact from going around the tee. Down goes the tee, and the suckers lose again.

TISHING A LADY *victimizing prostitutes*

Easily one of America's greatest swindlers and an incorrigible rascal, "Count" Victor Lustig (1890–1947) (see entry) invented "tishing a lady," one of the con man's favorite petty swindles. Highly addicted to brothels, the Count always paid well for services rendered. Upon taking his leave, Lustig would flash a $50 bill—high pay indeed in his day—fold it up and make a show of tucking the bill in a harlot's stocking. However, he would actually palm the bill and stuff in a wad of tissue paper.

In his best snake-oil spiel the Count would warn the female that he had given her trick money, and if she removed it before the following day it would turn to tissue paper. The lady would promise to comply with the rules, but as soon as Lustig left, she would remove her reward; alas, it had indeed turned to tissue paper.

Billie Scheible, a madam in the 1920s and 1930s who ran a string of very plush houses in Pittsburgh and New York, was herself tished by the Count. Scheible put it best when she said, "The Count had a way with him."

TNESBA, EVAEL O. W. *hoax veteran*

In 1936, in what was really a protest over the nonpayment of bonuses to veterans of World War I who had not filed for the bonuses 13 years previously as required, Republican members in the Rhode Island state senate introduced a special bill to award Sergeant Evael O. W. Tnesba of the "Twelfth Machine Gun Battalion" the standard late bonus payment of $100. The bill required unanimous consent to get floor consideration in the Democratic-controlled chamber. A Democratic senator seconded the bill and it passed. Later, however, the bill was reconsidered and dropped after someone read machine-gunner Tnesba's full name backward: Absent W. O. Leave.

TOFT, MARY See THE RABBIT WOMAN.

TORNADO ALARMS

Despite constant efforts by officials in many states, various tornado scam rackets abound. Bearing such names as "tornado tamers" etc., they are sold in tornado-prone areas allegedly to ring a bell or set off flashing lights when barometric pressure takes a sudden drop. Fitting right in with the impressive world of high tech, such battery-operated devices supposedly emit a warning signal that tells folks when to rush for cover. Incredibly, a scam operator can blanket the area, sell hundreds of the worthless devices for whatever the traffic will bear and move on quickly.

TORNADO-TAMING PLUTONIUM GENERATOR
weather quack product

Just as there are phony "tornado alarms" (see entry) to con credulous weather-fearing folks, there is also the "plutonium generator," which supposedly carries tornado-taming to its ultimate success. According to weather quacks' mail-order pitch, all you need is this wonder product to stop awesome tornados dead. The generator is also remarkably cheap, sold at the bargain-basement price of $10 for 10 wonderful generators.

The Kansas City Better Business Bureau went to the trouble of testing the product. The bureau determined that it was something like a railroad fusee made of wood fiber, potassium chlorate and a colorant, and it burned with a red flame. The BBB wondered how such a trivial device could affect the "warm inverted layer where it merges with the upper layer" in an approaching tornado. If one could fool Mother Nature so simply, one might suppose the National Weather Service might be a prime customer, because it would use the generator to stop every threatening tornado.

TOUGHEST TOWN WEST OF CHICAGO *massacres by railroad timetable*

In the 1870s big-city newspapers published unending accounts of the newest horrors coming out of Palisade, Nevada. In the process they endowed the town with the journalistic epitaph of "the toughest town west of Chicago."

A typical nightmarish incident would involve train passengers of the Central Pacific debarking for a rest stop in Palisade and stepping right into the middle of a massacre. It started with an explosive shootout between two gunfighters that sent the train passengers diving for cover. The shooting ended when one of the gunslingers bit the dust and the passengers charged back to the train for as rapid a departure as possible. That was wise, since apparently there was no telling what could happen next. The passengers peered out of the train to see some of the townsfolk somberly picking up the corpse and presumably heading for the undertaker's.

But that's not what really happened. When the train chugged from view the folks in town turned instead to the nearest saloon, accompanied by the deadly shootist and his not-quite-dead but very thirsty victim.

Palisade roared with laughter and a trainful of "dudes" had an experience they would remember and most certainly cherish for the rest of their lives. They could say that they had survived Palisade.

Some others had more terrifying remembrances of stepping into the middle of a bank robbery shootout with an even more bloody aftermath. This particular massacre "doubleheader" started when sheriff's deputies converged on a gang of bank robbers and the shooting quickly spread down Palisade's main (and only) street, all the way to the depot. In the midst of this carnage, scores of wild Indians came riding down the street, blazing away with rifles, gunning down men, women and children, including robbers and lawmen alike. The Central Pacific train barely made it out safely, with of course no heads protruding from the windows.

Back in Palisade, Operation Clean-up was begun to clean up the slaughterhouse beef blood that had been used in the "bloodletting." Sometimes the folks of Palisade had to work extremely fast, since they might have to stage five shows a day, depending on the Central Pacific's schedule.

Editorials in eastern newspapers demanded that the local government in Palisade clean up the appalling violence. This was impossible, however, considering that every resident, from toddler to grandfather, was in on the hoax. Even the local Shoshone Indians were in on the joke, as were local army troops who left unheeded editorial calls for military action.

From Palisade's point of view the town needed the "violence." Throughout the early 1870s Palisade was little more than a watering spot on the Humboldt River for the Central Pacific. The town sported some corrals and a loading dock for livestock that could be put aboard freights, but the town grew painfully slowly. Easterners were pouring west, with outlandish ideas of how wild the West was. People were still stunned by reports of Custer's Last Stand. As much as they feared it, they wanted to experience some of the shoot-'em-up deeds of the frontier.

Speculative accounts reveal that it was a conductor on the Central Pacific who first suggested the town make a name for itself—and boost its ridership—by providing visitors with the wild and woolly, if highly improbable, things they had heard and read about. Thus was born what some writers have called "the Palisade Thespian Players." Between trains many of the townspeople kept themselves busy making up thousands of blank cartridges, the most expendable item in Palisade.

The act lasted three whole years, until Palisade had a reputation unmatched in the West. The whole thing had to end with the slow maturing of the West; the U.S. Army could not be expected to go on taking endless abuse for allegedly failing in its duty to secure the frontier. Palisade and its 290 residents settled back to their old ways, living in a town that was so devoid of crime that it had never had a local lawman.

But the old hoax lived on in memory and song. George Russell wrote the song "Massacres at Palisade" to celebrate the town's flirtation with infamous bloodletting. It went in part:

When the train pulled in, the show would begin,
The fightin', the shootin', the robbin', and the dyin'
And the passengers watched from the windows with fear
And the town laughed as the train pulled clear.

And everyone took part, it's true
The cowboys, the Indians, and the cavalry too,
And when the shootin' was done, the battles won,
The town of Palisade just hung up their guns.

TRADE FAIR FAKES *business con*

Depending on one's outlook the shrewd operators who specialize in trade fair fakes are either rather creative business types or absolute incompetents. They qualify for the former category since they do a masterly job of promoting their shows; as for the second they are incompetents because they never get around to putting on any show.

Such was the case of two trade show hustlers who doubtlessly pleased many go-getting businessmen with a most welcome invitation to take part, at virtually no cost, in the "World's Largest International Gift Fair" that was to be held shortly in fabulous Las Vegas. Executives of some 30,000 firms got a glowing mail invitation from a firm called "International Gift Shows, Inc." with offices in London, Los Angeles and Las Vegas.

International Gift was going to stage a truly mammoth exposition with a half million items from 500 American manufacturers as well as from firms in 56 foreign countries. The pitch to the recipients of the invitations read, "We will jet you to Las Vegas and return you to your nearest airport, accommodate you at the new International Hotel for 5 days and 4 nights, along with 4 meals, the dinner show, lounge shows . . . a very enjoyable business trip, all for $199." Few businessmen could resist it. They couldn't get an offer like that even as a gambling casino promotion. And, of course, the trade fair would be a business expense!

In almost no time International Gift took in more than a quarter million dollars. Then they put on the stall. In answer to inquiries as to when the fair would start, International Gift said the exposition had to be temporarily postponed for reasons beyond its control.

By the time postal inspectors got wind of the operation only one of the operators was on hand to be apprehended and sent to prison. The chief plotter, with a long criminal record and a lucrative career promoting bogus trade shows, had vanished.

TRILBY'S TRANCE *publicity hoax*

Hollywood ballyhoo is hardly something new, but by far the greatest practitioner of the art was the late press agent Harry Reichenbach. No scheme of his ever produced a box-office bonanza to match what he did for the film *Trilby* when it opened in New York in 1923. The inspired press agent planted a young actress to sit in the audience and feign a trance after the first showing. When the lights went up, Reichenbach just happened to be nearby and noticed that the young woman was sitting in a strange state. Two physicians were summoned, and they were baffled by the woman's condition, her pulse and respiration gone amok. The doctors spoke to the press and said they had no explanation for what appeared to be a bizarre case of a woman in a trance. The good doctors and newspapers were unaware that Reichenbach had had the woman race around the theater block several times and drop into her seat just as the film was ending.

For days the press published interviews with learned psychologists on the possibility of a person in an audience being hypnotized by a film character such as the movie's Svengali. Needless to say, curious thrill seekers flocked to the theater to determine if Svengali could put them under as well. The movie did enormous box office thereafter all around the country.

TRODMORE RACES *horse-betting coup*

The greatest betting coup in British racing history occurred in August 1898 in England at the Trodmore Races. The fraudsters netted over a quarter million dollars in winning bets on horses that never lived, in races never run, on a track that never was.

At the time it was traditional for small horseracing meetings to be held all around England on bank holidays. The coup started when the editor of *The Sportsman*, a racing newspaper somewhat akin to the *Daily Racing Form* in the United States today, got a press release on the letterhead of the Trodmore Race Club of Trodmore, Cornwall, stating that the inauguration of the Trodmore Races would occur on the August Bank holiday. As horseracing's paper of record, *The Sportsman* obviously would have to cover the Trodmore races, since there would undoubtedly be some betting with bookmakers. No matter how tiny a meet was and even it lasted only one or two days, the English racing fan would be there with some wagers with bookmakers.

The publication's problem of covering Trodmore was solved when a well-dressed gentleman appeared at the editorial offices and announced he was off to Trodmore. He would be happy to wire back the order of finish in each race as well as other pertinent track information for the customary fee. An agreement was struck and *The Sportsman* duly published the entries for the Trodmore races. Just before the first race, London bookmakers got a large amount of action on the Trodmore races, quoting the odds as they appeared in the paper. At the end of the day, *The Sportsman*'s special correspondent wired in the results and the local payoff odds. In some of the races the bookmakers had taken varied action, some on winners and more on various losers; but they had not taken much in the way of real losses. In one race, however, many bookmakers found they had booked very heavy bets on a horse named Reaper, which had paid off at 5 to 1.

One bookmaker who had been hit particularly hard realized afterward that he had never heard of a horse named Reaper and decided to check up on the animal's registry. It turned out there was no horse registered under that name. The chagrined bookmaker also discovered there was no such place as Trodmore. And there was no race track called Trodmore in that nonexistent community or elsewhere.

The swindlers who comprised what later became known as the Trodmore Race Syndicate had simply invented a race track, a racing card and very lucrative results that netted them an estimated quarter of a million dollars. It was a most legendary day at the non-races. Needless to say, *The Sportsman*'s special correspondent, who had forwarded the results to the paper, never returned to pick up the fee for his labors.

TUCK, DICK   See DIRTY TRICKS.

TWEED, WILLIAM MARCY   *Tammany Hall boss*
In the realm of political corruption no organization ever looted the treasury of an American city with the finesse and daring of the Tweed Ring in the post-Civil War period. Headed by William Marcy Tweed (1823–1878), the boss of Tammany, no scam large or small was passed up if it offered an opportunity to loot the New York City treasury. Estimates of the ring's depredations range to as much as $200 million ($12 to $30 million for Tweed himself), an astonishing sum in 19th-century dollars.

Harper's Weekly **found Boss Tweed's greed so insatiable that its cartoonist thought him worthy of a monument at New York's City Hall Park that depicted him wallowing in the public's money.**

Tweed had a scam formula for the amount to be looted—$1 to be stolen for every $2 legitimately spent for city needs. However, the figures were often rather askew. For instance, he once billed the city $10,000 for $75 worth of pencils. Other brazen thefts included $171,000 for $4,000 worth of tables and chairs and charging $1,826,000 for a plastering job on a municipal building that was actually done for under $50,000.

Tweed put members of Tammany in charge of every city department and named his own puppet mayor, A. Oakley Hall, whose only real accomplishment in life was winning the sobriquet of "the elegant one" for his stately attire.

There was nothing the ring did not do, from issuing fraudulent bond issues to the outright selling of franchises and granting acts of tax forgiveness to businesses and individuals that paid the required bribes. In mid-1871, after some six years of colossal thievery, a determined reform movement headed by Samuel J. Tilden brought about the ring's downfall.

It was no easy accomplishment, since Tweed had corrupted virtually the entire court system. Tweed's first trial ended in a hung jury, hardly a surprise since Tammany had bribed several of the panel's members. Determined not to let the same thing happen again, the prosecution took the unprecedented precaution of having every member of the jury watched by a plainclothes detective. Then each plainclothesman was in turn watched by another city detective, who was then watched by a private detective. Each of these watchers were required to supply the prosecutor's office with daily written reports. This 36-man phalanx proved too formidable for Tammany to crack and Boss Tweed was convicted and sentenced to 12 years in prison.

Tweed immediately appealed, but he could not get the sentence vacated as one after another ring judges were purged from the courts. Finally, on appeal Tweed's term was reduced and he was set free in 1875. The state then instituted a new court case to recover the money Tweed had stolen, and he was slapped into jail for safekeeping. In December 1875 Tweed fled the jail and got out of the country, first to Cuba and then to Spain. Ironically, he was arrested in that country after being recognized from a Thomas Nast cartoon. Failing in health, Tweed was returned to prison. He died there in 1878, still not having revealed the whereabouts of all the looted millions.

TWO-HORSE SWINDLE *racing con*

A standard racing coup in the past has been the switching of two horses that greatly resemble each other in every detail except speed. The ploy was to enter the slow horse in a number of races so that the horse quite naturally finished last. Then the fast horse would be entered as the same animal, go off against huge odds and, in a seeming reversal of form, suddenly run a "wake-up" race and win easily.

Such coups happened but never as often as the public imagined. However, the perception was enough to permit con men to come up with a new wrinkle that actually made setting up a fixed race unnecessary. They would simply inform a sucker that they had two such horses when they really had only one. They would even let the sucker witness a secret workout on a private track by the supposedly speedier horse. The nag would run a "dynamite" workout, perhaps even breaking the six-furlong record. Legendary con man Wilson Mizner could get his broken-down animal to do so by the simple expedient of moving the six furlong post.

The sucker would be told the bets would have to be laid off in small amounts with bookmakers all around the country to avoid suspicion. The mark would eagerly turn over his cash to the con men, only to see the horse run his usual rotten race.

Without much effort the con men could convince the victim that the horse had developed some unsuspected ailment just before race time that accounted for his loss, and frequently the sucker could be taken a second time.

Problems at times did arise for the con men. The noted Yellow Kid Weil (see entry) once got hold of a horse that ran too fast for the swindle. Weil was forced to sell off the troublesome animal.

Today the two-horse swindle is much less prevalent, since U.S. tracks have adopted such precautions as lip tattoos and other methods of identification to make horse switching almost impossible. However, foreign horses are not so identified so that one horse may actually be switched for another or in the case of the two-horse swindle the hoax itself worked on the sucker.

U

UNCLAIMED MERCHANDISE SCAM *paying for nothing*

One of the most common mail-order gimmicks is to send unordered merchandise, often C.O.D., to recipients. A bearded variation of this is to notify a victim of some unclaimed merchandise that he can receive for a mere pittance.

In a typical scam, the artist will call himself a representative of something like the Bureau of Unclaimed Merchandise. He will send out letters by the thousands informing the recipients that by remitting a trivial sum of $5.55 they will be shipped "Parcel No. 811," which has been awaiting their claim. Of course, there is no government agency called the Bureau of Unclaimed Merchandise, and there is no parcel to ship.

UNICORN'S HORN FAKES

The first written account of the mythical unicorn, the pure white equine beast with a horn in the middle of its forehead, was offered by the Greek historian and traveler Ctesias in a book about India. He described "certain wild asses which are as large as horses and larger. . . . They have a horn on the forehead which is about a foot and a half long. The dust filed from this horn is administered in a potion as protection against drugs." Thus the unicorn was born, to be discussed by classical authors such as Pliny, Oppian and Aelian, among others. The unicorn became a symbol of virginity and in Christian religion is associated with the Virgin Mary and Christ. In time the mythical unicorn shrunk in size to a small goat-like creature and could presumably be captured by only a virgin.

Hunting the unicorn was frequently a tapestry subject in the Middle Ages and into the Renaissance. The first actual appearance of unicorn horns was in Europe during the ninth century, when owning them became a mark of high distinction in noble circles. Naturally, dealers began to fulfill the demand. In a will executed in 1561 Margaret, the Countess of Bath, left her daughter-in-law Elizabeth Kyton "her unicorn's bone." Queen Elizabeth I kept one unicorn's horn at Windsor and another at St. Denis.

The scam was revealed in 1638 when Ole Wurm, the Danish zoologist and antiquarian, made public a dissertation on the origin of unicorns' horns and proved they came from the tusks of the narwal, a marine mammal. That may have killed the market for the horns, but it did not, at least in some circles, curb the belief in unicorns.

Hunting for the horn of the mythical unicorn was extremely popular from the times of ancient Greece on through the Middle Ages and into the Renaissance. The great physician Ambrose Paré was attacked when he held the view that ground unicorn horn is useless in preventing disease.

UNILLUSTRATED FRAUDS *deceptive ads*

The term "unillustrated fraud" is used by consumer groups, bunco squads and postal inspectors to alert consumers to a simple way to avoid being taken by many of the most outrageous gyps. Mail-order ads frequently offer intriguing names and descriptions for their products when a simple illustration might do best. For instance, what exactly is a "solar clothes dryer"? Victims who sent in $39.99 got exactly what the words implied: clothespins and a clothesline. Here are a few others:

- An "unbreakable coat hangar" for a mere $4—a strong 10-cent nail.
- A "pet baby rattler—non toxic" for only $20—whoever heard of a baby's rattle that bites?
- A "solid-state compact food server" for $40—a fancy name for a stainless steel spoon?

Of course, even a picture can be misleading unless the printed message is read with caution. An ad showing an actual photograph of a complete set of tools in a tool box for $40 might seem like a bargain to purchasers until it turns out the carefully crafted copy only mentions the tool box, which is all consumers get.

UNORDERED MERCHANDISE RACKET

The unordered merchandise racket is an enduring one used by cagey con artists and the like who simply send you a "gift" in the mail—ties, good luck charms, keyrings, etc. No, you didn't order it and don't need it, but you may feel guilty if you don't pay the accompanying bill, especially since an enclosed letter frequently indicates that the money from sales goes "to the handicapped." (In one study by the Better Business Bureau, one company turned over less than 5 percent of the income to handicapped persons.) Many people feel they are obligated to return the merchandise if they do not want it; since it is simpler and easier to send a check, they opt for that way out.

Actually, as the U.S. Postal Inspection Service points out, recipients of unordered merchandise have three options:

1. If the package has not been opened, simply mark it "Return to Sender." The postal service will send it back at no charge to you.
2. If you open the package and don't like what you find, simply throw it away.
3. If you open the package and like what you find, keep it—for free. In this particular instance an unconditional finders-keepers rule applies. By law recipients may keep unsolicited merchandise. Whatever you do, do not pay for the merchan-

dise and don't get conned by further letters, phone calls or even a personal visit

UP-FRONT FEE SCAMS

There is little difference between "loan facilitator scams" (see entry) and "up-front fee scams," in which both swindlers offer to help clients find loan money. Generally loan facilitator scam artists prey on the little man, while up-fronters operate in the headier reaches of business finance. It turns out the victims of this latter group prove no more sophisticated in protecting their financial situation.

Let us say some adventurous business sorts need $20 million or $30 million to get their venture off the ground. They are approached by a financial adviser or company offering to help find them capital. They do so, usually for a fee of at least $20,000. The clients are referred to private lending concerns, which then agree to put up the money provided the client pays an up-front fee of a few hundred thousand dollars more. The financial adviser who first contacted the victim or victims is ecstatic, claiming to have pulled off a bargain deal. The client-victim pays the fees but never gets the capital. In the parlance of the trade, he is simply "stiffed"—taken for whatever capital he has.

In 1991 it was claimed that Dennis Levine (see entry), the bad boy of Wall Street who went to prison for insider trading, had been involved in a number of up-front fee operations as a financial adviser since his release from prison. Further claims revealed that clients were left with nothing but huge losses. For instance, two California builders seeking to put up oceanfront luxury homes dealt with Levine, who took them to Panama and introduced them to two companies that supposedly made megaloans. The results according to the builders: A loss of $150,000. When that deal fell through, Levine put the builders in touch with some Florida lenders and the builders said they proceeded to lose more money. It has been alleged that some of Levine's lender contacts had mob associations. One contact, described to a Levine client as a friend of the trader since before his Wall Street downfall turned out to be one of Levine's fellow convicts in the federal penitentiary.

In a September 1991 airing of Dennis Levine's post-prison "secret life," the CBS news show "60 Minutes" interviewed another client, who said he had paid up-front fees of $20,000 to Levine but pulled out of the subsequent deals for capital loans because he became suspicious about the potential lenders Levine had guided him to. This client said he was still waiting to get his money back from Levine.

Overall, businessmen needing huge capital inflow can be even more desperate than the little man who needs a housing loan. Timers being what they are, businesses are more readily victimized in so-called big business deals.

URANIUM QUACKERY *phony cure cons*

Since World War II medical quacks have made the bogus claim that uranium has magical powers and can literally "pull" all sorts of diseases from the body. Not only have gullible patients paid for the privilege of sitting in abandoned mines to soak up the "cura-tive" powers of this dangerous ore, but they have been hoodwinked into spending $300 each for all kinds of items allegedly filled with radioactive ma-terial—mattresses, mittens, gloves and pads in all sizes. The consumer actually receives fillings of crushed rock with far less radiation than a watch dial emits. Thousands, including renowned and well-ed-ucated public figures, have fallen for these varied uranium ploys.

V

VACATION SCAMS *contest fakes*

The contest offers you a chance at a fabulous vacation just by answering a few very easy questions. You are then entered into a drawing. If you win, you could have a wonderful vacation for two or four in some exotic place. You enter and you win but never end up going anywhere.

Although there are many who are wary of vacation giveaway scams, thousands fall for them each year. Consider an ad that appeared in a weekly with a circulation of 14.5 million and offered some 2,000 prizes to readers from the DeLuxe Vacationer Company. The ad was supposedly placed on behalf of a consortium of leading European travel agencies seeking a profile of American tourists, but was actually the work of two German con artists, Roland H. Graber and Hans Georg Aust.

The questions were simple enough: Did readers prefer to take their vacations in the summer or in the off-season? How many vacation days did they have each year? Was their favorite vacation transportation by sea, air or land? Had they ever visited Europe, did they hope to or did they have no interest in Europe?

First prize was a two-week all-expense paid trip for two to Acapulco and second prize was a similarly enticing trip to Hawaii. The remaining 1,998 prizes were unspecified, but that hardly mattered to those informed they had won either the Mexican or Hawaiian vacation! In all, 57,000 readers responded to the ad, and they all received a printed notification that they had won one of the top prizes. There were some touches designed to add credibility to the award, such as a notation "Tips and beverages not included." There was, however, another minor stipulation that said: "Note: According to regulations, a $25 registration deposit to secure your winning prize is required WITHIN 10 DAYS. This deposit will be FULLY REFUNDED to you on your day of departure." The rationale for this was that the deposit would cover the cancellation fees in case a winner decided to cancel his or her trip.

Apparently this proved a turn-off to thousands of "lucky winners." Others wondered why, if there were only two big winners, the notification had been expensively *printed* rather than sent in the form of a typewritten letter.

Graber and Aust were no doubt disappointed that only 11,000 persons fell for their scam, but at $25 apiece that still came to $275,000. The two scam artists might have gotten away with it save for some of the supposed winners. One woman notified the Hollywood office of the Postal Inspection Service that she had won a trip to Mexico. Inspector Charles J. Lerable thought nothing of it and simply congratulated her. A few minutes later a second woman called to ask what the inspector thought about the validity of a prize of a Hawaiian trip she'd just won. While Lerable also congratulated her, he was considerably less enthused, since it seemed odd that two grand-prize winners should happen to call his particular office. Then there was another call from yet another grand-prize winner, and fraud became very clear. While the postal inspectors launched an investigation, the national headquarters of the Better Business Bureau received 500 inquiries from suspicious winners. Local BBB branches got thousands more.

Eventually, Aust and Graber were convicted on 50 counts of fraud. Graber was given an 18-month suspended sentence and was subjected to immediate deportation. Aust, the brain behind the plot, drew a two-year prison term and was then deported.

VACUUM CLEANER RECALL SCAM

The vacuum cleaner recall scam is worked in almost endless variations. One of the more ingenious meth-

271

ods involves setting up a table at shopping malls (usually on the sidewalk just outside the mall's legal territory) and passing out leaflets offering a free inspection, 48-hour recall and free repair for any vacuum cleaner of a certain prestigious brand. Homemakers who sign up are visited the very next day by a pleasant looking mechanic who inspects the appliance and says, "Yep, bearing's gone." He adds that in another week the vacuum would be ruined. Fortunately, the manufacturer discovered the defect and is attempting to contact all owners to do a free repair.

When the nice young man does not return, the victim is shocked to learn that her vacuum cleaner is only one of hundreds swept up that week and every other week by scam artists. The vacuum cleaner thief has a fence in another city who gives him $20 and more for each appliance, depending on the model. Eventually, the vacuums are funneled back into the market as "rebuilt machines."

VALENTINO DEATH PHOTO *journalistic hoax*

The dubious distinction of the most outlandish and ghoulish fake newspaper photograph ever printed was that of Rudolph Valentino, the screen's "Great Lover," who died August 23, 1926 in a New York hospital. Immediately, the journalistic minds of Bernarr MacFadden's sensationalist tabloid *Evening Graphic* concocted what was to be an incredible photographic coup. The paper sent two photographers to Frank E. Campbell's Funeral Church on Broadway. One was to take pictures and the other to pose in an empty coffin. A headshot of Valentino was superimposed on the "corpse" in the coffin. This was known as the *Graphic's* "composograph" technique.

Within an hour the sensational tabloid hit the streets with a ghastly front-page photograph of the Great Lover "lying in state." Amazingly, it was taken before Valentino's corpse even reached the Campbell parlor. The *Graphic* had to run its presses nonstop throughout the night to keep up with demand for the hoax photo.

See also LADY IN BLACK.

VAMPIRING *sexual blackmail scam*

One of the most loathed scams practiced in America in the 19th century was that of vampiring, a form of extortion that blackmailed men who visited big-city brothels. The practice was much hated by the victims, the brothel keepers and the police as well. The "vampires" were generally young thugs looking for ways to get started in criminal activities. They would follow a man leaving a brothel back to his residence and threaten to stand in front of his home and chant that he'd "just come from a whorehouse, just come from a whorehouse."

If it seemed to be an inventive caper, vampires learned it was not one without its perils. In city after city bordello operators stopped the practice with some serious "head-banging," as the continued activity was particularly bad for business. Additionally, some bordello owners also took offense at the vampires efforts to blackmail some of the housewife-inmates returning to their own neighborhoods, where their secret occupation was not known.

Chicago was the stronghold of the vampires until the 1870s, when the most successful band was crushed after they started harassing patrons of a large bagnio on Biler Avenue. The place was run by one Dan Webster, but unfortunately for the vampires they were unaware that the secret landlord of the building—and most likely Webster's partner—was Superintendent of Police Michael C. Hickey. Suddenly the police swooped down on the vampires and gave them a severe clubbing when they ventured within a block or two of Webster's place. In the process, the police of course also netted some protection revenues from the bordellos.

VAN GOGH'S EAR *museum display hoax*

The late muralist Hugh Troy (1906–1964) was regarded as one of America's greatest practical jokers, a title he did not appreciate, regarding himself as a man dedicated to making life more interesting and exciting for others. Troy had most pronounced opinions about art and the general public's appreciation of the subject. In 1935, when the Museum of Modern Art held the first American showing of Vincent van Gogh's works, Troy was certain the main attraction for most people was the lurid life the artist had led rather than an understanding of his art. He informed friends he would prove that most "art lovers" were more attracted to the fact that van Gogh had cut off his ear than anything else, including his work.

Troy joined the crowds to see the opening of the exhibit. He had molded some chipped beef into what seemed to be a grisly and withered ear and mounted it into a blue velvet shadow box. He had also fashioned an inscription reading:

THIS IS THE EAR WHICH VINCENT VAN GOGH CUT OFF AND SENT TO HIS MISTRESS, A FRENCH PROSTITUTE, DEC. 24, 1888.

Troy slipped the shadow box on a table in a room where the van Gogh paintings were being displayed. He noted with obvious satisfaction that the spectators soon ignored the classic paintings and instead mobbed around the bogus ear, chattering excitedly about the gruesome offering.

VAN MEEGEREN, HANS *art forger*

Clearly, hard-working Dutch artist Hans van Meegeren (1889–1947) was an excellent painter. In fact, he was one of the best of the 20th century, but the art world did not know it. If he had not been labeled a Nazi collaborator, his talents might never have been recognized. Van Meegeren discovered that painting the works of the master Jan Vermeer (1632–1675) was much more lucrative than doing his own. However, not being a mere hack, he did not forge existing works. Instead, he did entirely new Vermeers, even producing the artist's nonexistent "middle period." Van Meegeren's first effort was *Christ at Emmaus*, hailed a masterpiece by the critics and netting the talented forger a quarter of a million dollars.

During the war, van Meegeren painted and sold five more Vermeers, one of which, *Christ and the Adulteress*, was bought by Hermann Goering (the number 2 Nazi) for $256,000. It was this sale, traced to van Meegeren by Dutch authorities at war's end, that led to charges of collaboration with the Nazi enemy for selling "national treasures." Officially the charge was treason, which called for the death penalty; under the circumstances van Meegeren decided to confess his forgeries. At first this brought only derisive laughter from authorities and especially from art critics, who insisted they knew a true masterpiece when they saw one. Still, van Meegeren insisted he had done nothing but sell a "picture" to Goering and charged a huge price for an imitation. He insisted that *Men of Emmaus*, which was in the Boymans Museum in Rotterdam and supposedly found in a Paris linen closet, was also his work. So were four other Vermeers, two Dieter de Hoochs and one Terborch.

To prove how good he was, van Meegeren offered to create another "masterpiece" in his prison cell—Vermeer's previously nonexistent *Jesus in the Temple*. He easily produced the very pigments Vermeer had used, making them from the natural substances the master had used in the 17th century. When he was finished, *Jesus in the Temple* was clearly another Vermeer. That performance, as well as evidence obtained by new X-ray techniques, proved beyond doubt that he had painted all the Vermeers he claimed.

In all, van Meegeren had been paid a total of some $3 million for his forgeries. But he always insisted he had not done it for the money. In interviews before his trial he explained the motivation for his hoaxes:

> For years, I painted and painted. But the museums and art collectors said that my work was little more than "dime store" pictures. They said I should use them for picture postcards. Imagine that! I was told I had no artistic ability. I was told to become a commercial artist—to draw sketches, to sell tooth-paste or face cream! It was an insult. I was going to teach the art world a lesson. I was going to prove, once and for all, that I, Hans van Meegeren, was a great painter! I could do it only one way . . . to convince the so-called experts that I had a great talent.

If in the forger's trade the term *caveat emptor* (let the buyer beware) is the rule, one journalist was to observe that van Meegeren offered yet another: *peritis nec crede* (put not thy trust in experts).

The treason charge against van Meegeren was dropped by the court, and in 1947 he was convicted of fraud for forging Vermeer's signature. He was sentenced to one year's imprisonment, but frail and depressed, he suffered a fatal heart attack at the age of 57 before he could start his prison term.

VEGETABLE LAMB OF TARTARY *alleged lamb-bearing plant*

The plants could be found in the realm of the Cham of Tartary. On these strange vegetables were baby lambs that grew, matured and became fully independent living lambs. This bizarre belief, widely embraced in the Middle Ages, was based on the report of Sir John Mandeville, a notorious liar who wrote some of the most outrageous travel books of the time. In his day Mandeville's reportage was given much credence by folk raised in fervent faith and uncritical attitudes.

Mandeville was not the only one to spread the tale of the "Vegetable Lamb of Tartary." Many others spread further half truths about the plant, which was correctly identified in the 17th century as *Cibotium barometz*, a fern with a woolly rootstalk. It is not hard to understand why the medieval observer, examining this woolly covering could come to believe it was indeed some sort of hybrid plant and animal. The fern grew in certain areas of Asia, and its down was used in India for staunching wounds. We can only guess how many investors were taken in cons supposedly seeking to import and market these lambs from far-off exotic places.

VELLA'S HISTORY OF SICILY *six-volume fake*

The record for the most ambitious forging of an entirely bogus scholarly history may belong to Joseph Vella, who in the late 18th century produced a six-volume translation from the Arabic of 17 of the lost books of the historian Livy. Vella, chaplain of the Knights of Malta, visited the monks of Palermo in 1782 and listened to their hopes of some day finding some Arabic sources that could complete their histories. Seven years later Vella edited the first volume of *Codice Diplomatico di Sicilia sotto il governo degli Arabi, pubblicato per cura e studio di Alfonso Airoldi.*

Over the next four years the five remaining volumes appeared. Together these supposed books of

Above: Van Meegeren forgery of Pieter de Hooch. Opposite: Van Meegeren's *Christ at Emmaus*, allegedly by Vermeer.

Livy offered a definitive history of Sicily. Vella gained royal approval for his scholarship by dedicating all of the volumes to the king of Naples.

Then a German Orientalist named Hager visited Sicily and declared Vella's works to be fake. The king of Naples afforded Vella with the opportunity to clear his name by appointing a commission to examine him. Vella successfully got away with his hoax by reading off a number of passages he had memorized from his Italian translation of the alleged Arabic originals; since none of his inquisitors knew a word of Arabic, they were effectively conned.

In 1796 some Arabic scholars examined the so-called originals, which Vella had had printed from type he'd ordered from the typemaker Bodoni. They declared the originals were not a history of Sicily at all, but actually the tale of Mahomet. In an era when scholarly fakery drew stronger reprimands than today Vella was sentenced to 15 years imprisonment.

VENDING MACHINE SWINDLE

Mr. Davis is desperately in need of a decent income. A middle management employee of a large corporation undergoing a "restructuring" has let him go. At 56 Mr. Jones is in a quandry. He has become a member of the new middle-class unemployed, and whatever job he can get—especially at his age—is very near the minimum wage. Starting a new career isn't

really viable. Luckily, Mr. Davis has some savings planned for his retirement. He has enough money to invest in a vending machine business he has seen ads for.

He answers one describing marvelous money-making opportunities for a "reasonable" investment of several thousand dollars. The sales representative who shows up stresses that only half the money has to be put up immediately. The rest can be paid under an easy payment plan. He promises Mr. Davis he will get an exclusive territory, help in installing machines at outlets already available and, best of all, if Mr. Davis is dissatisfied with his investment there is a money-back guarantee.

The sales representative is selling a pipe dream. In most cases Mr. Davis never sees the sales representative or his money again. That so-called territory has already been awarded to dozens of other investors. If any machines are actually furnished, it turns out the locations that would supposedly take the machines are totally ignorant of the vending machine company and of any written or oral agreement to let the victim put vending machines on the premises.

Sometimes the so-called vending machine company simply vanishes by the time numerous victims are ready to start business. In other cases the swindlers continue to maintain contact with the victims, claiming that the vending machines have been held up because of manufacturing delays that will soon be remedied. Eventually the typical Mr. Davis becomes totally exasperated and asks for his money back as the contract states. He is staved off with lulling letters for a time until the swindlers decide it's prudent for the company to do its vanishing act.

Before postal inspectors ran down one gang of swindlers operating in a number of southern states they had cheated victims, many of them elderly, out of three-quarters of a million dollars for almond vending machines that they said could be operated on a part-time basis. Either cheap machines or none at all were furnished and the victims were left with only some nuts to eat.

VINLAND MAP   *historical forgery*

According to the Norse sagas, North America was discovered by Norse explorer Leif Ericson at the end of the 10th century. The Norse saga *Flateyjarbók* states, "When spring came they made ready and left, and Leif named the land after its fruits, and called it *Vinland*." However, definitive historical confirmation of the Viking legends was long missing. Then, in 1957 discovery was made of a map of the Northeast American coast that seemingly confirmed the Norse version. This was apparently the most exciting cartographic find of the 20th century.

Over the next eight years the map was subjected to intensive tests. In October 1965 Yale University Press published the findings in a study called *The Vinland Map and the Tartar Relation*. The map was said to have been part of a book, partly on parchment, that detailed a church mission to the Tartars during the Middle Ages. The map itself had been copied by an unknown scribe in about 1440 from earlier originals and was presumably prepared for a conference of religious scholars that took place in Basel about 1440. Since the date of this conference long preceded the voyages of Columbus and John Cabot, it appeared beyond dispute that the Vikings had been the first to reach North America. Every possible test was applied to the materials—the vellum, paper and ink—and all were consistent with a date in the 1440s. Also worm holes of the same type had passed through both of some pages of the manuscript and the map as well. Among the experts who confirmed the genuineness of the manuscript and map were R. A. Skelton, superintendent of the Map Room, British Museum; G. D. Painter, assistant keeper in charge of incunabula, British Museum; Dr. T. E. Marston, curator of medieval and Renaissance literature, Yale University Library; and Alexander O. Vietor, curator of maps, Yale University Library.

However, some scholars seemed dissatisfied with the study. In 1966 doubts were voiced at a forum sponsored by the Smithsonian Institute. Particularly upsetting was the fact that the rare book dealer who first approached Vietor and Marston refused to identify the source from whom he had purchased the map for $3,500. The dealer insisted it was common in the rare book field to promise anonymity to clients for legal and tax considerations.

One of the leading skeptics was Professor Armando Cortesao of Coimbra, Portugal, the only person to hold an endowed chair in the history of world cartography. Professor Cortesao insisted that without knowing the source of the map, falsification could not be ruled out, since the map could have been inserted at a later stage. Even the similarity of the papers did not impress him, as it was entirely possible that the manuscript contained a blank sheet of parchment. Still, the Cortesao thesis itself hardly constitued proof of forgery, only the possibility.

Nine years later Yale University announced that the Vinland Map had been a forgery after all. A new test for the age of inks determined that the inks in the manuscript were 15th-century materials, but that the ink used for the Vinland Map contained anatase, a derivative of titanium oxide not discovered until the 1920s.

VOIGT, WILHELM   See CAPTAIN OF KOPENICK.

VOLTAIRE'S MOST FAMOUS QUOTATION   *fabrication*

"I do not agree with a word you say, but I will defend to the death your right to say it." It is Voltaire's most celebrated statement. But did he really say it?

For years many scholars who searched Voltaire's writings for the quotation were always unsuccessful. The furthest back they got was 1907, when E. Beatrice Hall incorporated it in *The Friends of Voltaire* in the name of S. G. Tallentyre. Finally, in 1935 Hall confessed to Christopher Morley and the *Saturday Review of Literature* that she had invented the quotation, saying she had meant it "as a description of Voltaire's attitude to Helvetius—and more widely, to the freedom of expression in general. I do not think and did not intend to imply that Voltaire used these words *verbatim*, and should be surprised if they are found in any of his works. They are rather a *paraphrase* of Voltaire's words in the Essay on Tolerance—'Think for yourselves and let others enjoy the privilege to do so too.'"

Given that remarkable confession, the *Brooklyn Eagle* commented: "One might make a pretty sound bet that what M. Voltaire is mostly remembered for is a quotation he didn't make, which is an irony that François Marie Arouet would have cackled over in the full savage misery of his old age."

W

WADDELL, REED   *gold brick swindler*

A successful con man who operated on two continents and was never imprisoned despite operating two of the most audacious confidence games of all, Reed Waddell (1859–1895) was born into a wealthy Springfield, Illinois family. Although college-educated and groomed to take over the family business, young Reed seemed more interested in gambling and wild living and while still in his teens was disowned by his family. Reed relocated to New York City, whereupon he introduced the gold brick swindle (see entry) in 1880. Some biographers insist that Waddell invented that colossal scam, but the activity traces back at least to the 1850s in California. In any event, Waddell became its most prolific practitioner and was said to have made something like a quarter of a million dollars—an astonishing sum for the era—over the next decade.

The Waddell gold brick was made of lead, but was covered with three platings of gold and had a slug of solid gold in the center. It was marked in the manner of a regulation brick from the U.S. Assayer's Office, with the letters "U.S." at one end and below the letters the name of the assayer. Waddell would inform a potential sucker that he was forced to sell the brick to settle some very urgent gambling debts, indicating he had obtained it from his family's private hoard. If he gave the brick directly to the criminal gamblers, he said, he feared they would force him to loot more of his family's holdings. It was not a tale to touch a sucker's heart, but rather to whet his appetite for quick profits. Although the brick was worth much more, the sucker would beat Waddell's price down to about $4,000 or so.

Of course, the validity of the gold brick had to be determined and Waddell would guide the sucker—frequently a tough-minded banker or businessman—to what appeared to be a genuine assayer's office. In actuality it was operated by a Waddell accomplice. The bogus assayer would declare the brick solid gold. Usually that was enough to hook the sucker, but some insisted on a second opinion. Waddell would feign being insulted and with apparent impulsiveness and disdain he would dig out the slug of real gold in the center and dismiss the sucker to go in search of his own expert to test it. Naturally, that test also proved positive and now the sucker could not be stopped. Some haggled the price down to $3,500, but in other cases Waddell took his victim for as much as $7,000.

Waddell also developed a very profitable side con known as the green goods swindle (see entry). This involved selling counterfeit bills at a huge discount. Once the victim determined that the counterfeit was a superior product—and it was since he was shown genuine currency—he would agree to a big buy. At the time of the transaction he would again be shown genuine currency, but at the last moment the package containing the bills was switched to one packed with pieces of green paper. Waddell preferred the gold brick swindle (see entry) to the green goods version because of the time lag before the victim realized he had been cheated.

In about 1893 Waddell decided New York City had become too hot and he shifted operations to Europe, where European trust in gold was even more pronounced than in the United States. He teamed up with another gold brick artist named Tom O'Brien, who had netted about $100,000 over a five-month period working the World's Fair in Chicago. The pair were brilliant working swindles in Paris on both Europeans and Americans, but each thought his contribution was the most valuable and thus should be rewarded with a larger cut. In March 1895 an argument turned violent and O'Brien shot Reed Waddell dead.

WAGNER, JOHN F. *Robin Hood bank embezzler*

By any of the usual standards, John F. Wagner (1893–1950) was not the usual bank embezzler. He did not wench, drink or gamble, the three siren calls to embezzlers. Wagner was the cashier of the First National Bank in the hardly well-to-do coal town of Cecil, Pennsylvania. It became known that bank examiners would be coming to the bank one Monday morning in 1950. Wagner was the first employee to open the bank, and when the examiners arrived, Wagner lay dead on the floor next to the vault, gun in hand and a bullet in his brain.

A detailed audit revealed the reason Wagner had taken his life. He was short $1,125,000. The puzzling detail was what the lifelong resident had done with the money. He had never lived high on the hog and, in fact, had only two winter suits, one of which he was buried in. Then authorities found a note in Wagner's handwriting. "The reason for the shortage was because of paying checks that were not good." Attached to the note was a list of persons who had written scores of rubber checks or defaulted on their loan payments. Wagner had covered up all these transactions. Cecil residents offered an explanation for Wagner's behavior: He was a soft touch who could neither turn away a friend in need or dispute a sad story.

Authorities set up a program to try to get as many people as possible to meet their debts, but the question remained: Who was the scam artist, John Wagner or those who took advantage of him?

THE WALKAWAY *shortchanging technique*

This is a small dodge that some crooked cashiers pull 10 or 20 times a day. It works best at circuses, sporting events, carnivals, movie houses, subway token booths or just about any place where money is handled from a booth. The reason for the scam's success is that all change booths are built in such a way that there is a small area that the customer cannot see. Crooked cashiers call it the "blind spot" and they may even mark off the boundaries in some unobtrusive way. In New York City, new subway token booths recently installed have a larger blind spot than in the older models.

As a cashier makes change, he or she makes sure to shovel some of the change into the blind spot. The customer, often in a hurry, obligingly scoops up the ticket or token and the visible change and charges off. While this is going on the shrewd shortchanger manages to look away as though taking care of some special chore. If instead the customer holds his ground, counts his change and demands the rest, the cashier looks back innocently, then points coldly at the missing change. The customer isn't cheated and walks away feeling two feet tall.

WALSH, ELLEN   See MAYFIELD, IDA.

WAR OF THE WORLDS   See MEN FROM MARS PANIC.

WASHINGTON AND THE CHERRY TREE *historical myth*

The myth is a part of American history: Six-year-old George Washington chopped down the cherry tree (or at least "barked" it so that it died) and then revealed the deed because, as he said, "I can't tell a lie." From the time of its invention in 1806 for well over a century, the story has had a profound effect on boys and girls who had the "fact" drummed into them by parents and teachers.

The story appeared in the variously titled *Life of George Washington, With Curious Anecdotes Equally Honorable to Himself, and Exemplary to His Young Countrymen*, by Parson Malon L. Weems (1760–1825). Weems was a clergyman turned bookseller whose best-selling ware was the Bible. Weems turned author himself in search of the volume that could do as well as that Good Book. Some of his creations included: *Hymen's Recruiting Sargeant, or the New Matrimonial Tat-too for Old Bachelors; God's Revenge against Adultery; The Immortal Mentor, or Man's Unerring Guide to a Healthy, Wealthy and Happy Life;* and *Drunkard's Looking Glass.* In personally hawking this last opus, Weems would pop into a tavern in a haggard and drunken state, appearing in his own words, "A little on the Staggers or so." Thus attracting the attention of his clientele, he would produce his pamphlets, which he said sold "like hotcakes."

Weems lost interest in his other books when his *Life of George Washington* appeared in 1799, the year of the latter's death. Sales were enormous. By 1806 the book was going into its fifth edition, the version in which the cherry tree tale first appeared. It seems Weems decided to add "new and valuable anecdotes" to keep sales high. Nothing worried Weems more than a nonselling book. He wrote his employer, Philadelphia publisher Matthew Carey: "God knows there is nothing I dread so as dead stock, dull sales, back loads, and blank looks. But the Joy of my soul is quick and clean sales—heavy pockets, and light hearts."

To achieve this, Parson Weems saw no moral compunction engaging in what may be considered a flair for exaggeration. Indeed, it turned out he even lifted the cherry tree anecdote from a story by Dr. James Beattie, "The Minstrel," published in England in 1799. The good parson also appropriated from the same source an anecdote of cabbage seeds that grew up to form a person's name, and attributed it to Washington.

In any event, no one could accuse Weems of not knowing how to tell a good story. *The Life of George*

Washington afforded Weems a good life for the rest of his days. It was so popular that before 1850 a total of 59 editions were published, and not until well into the 20th century was Weems' veracity challenged to the point that few schools today teach his statements with any seriousness.

WATERED STOCK *bringing stuffed cattle to market*

When a person is said to have bought "watered stock," it means he has bought stock in a non-existent company, or if it exists, it has little or no value. However, the origins of the term are said to have evolved from a cattle country con practiced by stockmen for generations. As they drove their animals to market, they gave them all the dry feed stuff they could get down. Then just before arriving at the selling yards, the cattle would be permitted to drink all the water they wanted or, in fact, needed. Since cattle were sold by weight, this "watering" of stock significantly increased their price.

WE BOYS MOB *swindling newspapermen*

It is now a given in the newspaper field that obituaries of newsmen are more free from errors of fact than any other obituary. This is not due to professional courtesy, but can be traced to an audacious group of con men called the "We Boys Mob."

These scam artists specialized in hoodwinking the nation's supposedly shrewd and cynical journalists. Members of the gang would hit a newspaper city room with the sad report of the death of a "veteran newspaperman." The story would be untrue but profitable, precisely because the newspaper profession in the 1920s was not a well-paying one.

The swindlers' spiel went something like this: "We boys are getting together to see that he gets a decent burial and have something in the pot afterward for the widow, and knowing how all you guys feel about the boys in the business, we were sure all of you would like to make a small donation to build the kitty." The appeal always worked, and the con would not be discovered until some time later when the old-time newspaperman—alive and well—would saunter into a news room for a visit.

The con died out when newspaper publishers ordered much more fact-checking whenever the death of a journalist was reported.

WEEMS, PARSON MASON See WASHINGTON AND THE CHERRY TREE.

WEIGHT AND FITNESS CONS *quack treatments and devices*

Capitalizing on most people's desire to enjoy the benefits of exercise and weight loss without the ef-

fort, innumerable quacks have brought out all sorts of "body toning" devices such as electrical muscle stimulators. As the Food and Drug Administration has pointed out, "Such devices are, of course, worthless for 'body toning' and can even be dangerous, but they're advertised and sold as substituting for exercising."

Quack advertising offers such wonders as: NO MORE DIETING . . . NO MORE HUNGER . . . NO MORE CALORIE COUNTING . . . NO MORE PILLS (unless the sales pitch is for pills). Customers are assured they can make pounds and inches vanish with wonderful body belts while watching TV, while they sleep, while they work and even while they are eating. And Magical rolling pins are peddled to simply roll away fat.

The FDA warns:

> But quick weight-loss products aren't worth a try when they affect your health and harm you, and they can harm you if only by not helping you. Being overweight can lead to a number of health problems, including high blood pressure, heart attack, stroke, and kidney disease.
>
> The fact is that you cannot lose weight if you do not cut down on the amount of food you eat or exercise more to burn up calories. Any product claim that promises to trim you down and tone you up effortlessly is false. Consult your doctor before beginning any diet program, and remember, there are no medicines or devices that will let you lose weight effortlessly.

WEIL, JOSEPH "YELLOW KID" *great con man*

The greatest con man ever to operate in the United States? Some might say it was "Count" Victor Lustig (see entry), others Fred Buckminster (see entry), but most would tend to go with Joseph "Yellow Kid" Weil (1877–1976), who probably invented and practiced more swindles and con games than any other crook in history. He was the master of the "big store" (see entry) and, according to Illinois authorities, he alone suckered some 20 victims out of a half million dollars in the summer of 1924.

Weil was born in Chicago and started hanging around underworld dives as a teenager. He always carried a copy of the *New York Journal*, which contained his favorite comic strip, "Hogan's Alley and the Yellow Kid." Soon all of the underworld characters began calling him the Yellow Kid.

Weil married young, but he never let it interfere with his career in spite of his wife's attempts to reform him. For her sake, Weil often tried to become as honest as he could, which was not much. He once tried to make a living peddling a Catholic encyclopedia, using the name of Daniel O'Connell. He told a priest in Flint, Michigan that the Holy Father, Pope

Yellow Kid Weil: "I never cheated an honest man . . . only rascals."

Pius X, had expressed the hope that at least 2,000 copies be placed in Flint homes. The priest bought a set and, on the strength of that sale, Weil sold 80 more sets and made $1,600 in commissions before the priest learned of his imposture and canceled his order. Weil decided he had enough of honesty and went back to pulling phony boxing match and horse race cons.

In his early 20s Weil developed the earnestness and dignified air that always stood him well in his cons. Around the turn of the century he and Colonel Jim Porter, a former riverboat gambler, pulled off what became known as the Michigan "Free Land" Swindle (see entry). Weil guided Porter around Chicago, introducing him as an eccentric millionaire who was giving away free lots. The pair gave land to prostitutes, waiters, bartenders and even city policemen. The con men opened up a sales office showing the usual artist's conception of a huge vacationland being planned in Michigan.

Weil's supposedly big problem with the scam was trying to keep the colonel from giving away all the lots for free. Whenever his older partner gave away

some lots—purchased by the pair at $1 an acre—Weil would beg the happy recipient not to tell anyone else or everyone would be wanting free lots. The hook in the con was that he also advised the lucky person to make sure he had the transaction recorded at the county seat in Michigan. The recording fee had previously been $2, but Porter's cousin—who held the post—raised it to $30 with the understanding that he would keep half and give half to Porter and Weil. The pair made about $16,000 from the caper.

In another masterful con, Weil posed as a mining engineer named Pope Yateman, who had made a fortune in Chile. Yateman had been glowingly profiled in *McClure's* magazine under the title "$100,000 A Year," together with a large photo. A crooked printer (who otherwise specialized in "first editions" of famous books) substituted Weil's picture for Yateman's and, for a price, reprinted the required pages. Weil rebound the pages into a number of actual copies of the magazine and went on a triumphant tour of the Midwest. He and a confederate, usually Fred Buckminster, would locate a rich individual with money to invest in mining ventures and then Buckminster would happen to mention the article in *McClure's*, which could be found at the local library.

Of course, Weil and Buckminster had pinched the library copy and put a bogus magazine in its place. The victim would rush to the library, find the article sporting an impressive picture of Weil and be convinced he should invest money with such a genius. When the boys milked all the money they could from the sucker, they reswitched the library copies of the magazine and left town. As Weil often recalled, "You can imagine the victim's amazement, after being swindled, to go to the library and look up that article only to find the picture did not resemble me at all!"

On one occasion Weil and Buckminster rented a vacant bank in Muncie, Indiana, stocked it with con men and their lady friends acting as depositors and then talked investors into buying interests in the thriving institution. The bank later collapsed.

Despite his charm and glibness, Weil—like other con men—was arrested often. Usually, however, he beat the charge because he could fix the case, or because his victim would be put in a position of having been knowingly involved in a dishonest scheme. "I never cheated an honest man," Weil was to announce at Senator Estes Kefauver's famed crime hearings of 1950–1951. He charmed the interrogators by saying his victims were "only rascals."

Like most con men, Weil himself was not immune to being conned. Once, while working a transatlantic liner, he became enamoured by a beautiful countess and forgot all about his swindling duties. By the time the ship had docked, the countess had confessed to him she needed a fast $10,000 to take care of her alcoholic father's gambling debts. Weil gave her the money and she gave him her valuable pearls to hold until she could meet him in a few hours. She never came back, and the pearls turned out to be paste.

Weil took the scam with good grace, saying of his lost love: "What a team we would have made."

Many times Weil publicly proclaimed he was quitting the con, but he never did. In 1948 the Kid wrote his memoirs with Chicago journalist W. T. Brannon, again declaring he was going straight. That didn't last long, as he proceeded to sell Brannon the exclusive rights to make the autobiography into a movie. Then he turned around and sold the same rights to a Hollywood studio. Tied up in legal snarls, the movie never got made; but Weil did enjoy two payoffs.

One of Weil's last coups was to try to establish a little independent republic on a small island in Lake Michigan. He told Saul Bellow in a magazine interview that he would then make himself eligible under the foreign aid program.

Weil died on February 26, 1976. In his late years he said he was determined to live to 100. Weil told folks he had been born in 1875, but various records indicated he was really born in 1877. Until the very end Weil still had to try to pull an obituary con.

See also PEDIGREED DOG SCAM.

WEISS CLUB BROTHEL *great vice scam*

The Weiss Club was a luxurious brothel in Chicago in that city's golden days of harlotry. Operated by Ed and Aimee (born Leslie, a beautiful retired courtesan), it opened its doors in 1904 at 2135 South Dearborn. However, its chief claim to fame was that it was designed to be mistaken for the Everleigh Club, indisputably the most opulent whorehouse ever in North America.

The best that could be said for the Weiss Club was that it was literally the next best thing to the Everleigh Club, situated right next door. Oddly, the Weiss Club had relatively few patrons of its own, even though its rates (for regulars) were less than half the Everleigh's astronomical bill of fare. The idea for the club was born when Ed Weiss married Aimee, who was one of the top attractions of the Everleigh at the time. Aimee suggested buying up the brothel next door and converting it into an imitation of the famed vice resort.

The Weiss Club was done up with expensive appointments and stocked with women who would have at least made the final cut at the Everleigh and could thus command high fees. The success of the club was guaranteed by Ed's shrewd scam of putting most of the vice area's cabbies on commission. Whenever one of them picked up a fare who asked for the Everleigh Club and seemed too drunk to know where he was going, the cabbie would haul him to the Weiss establishment. Similarly, out-of-town free spending conventioneers were brought to the Weiss Club under false pretenses. Invariably, the customers entered the club, were properly entertained (at full Everleigh rates of course) and left all the while believing they had enjoyed the real thing.

The underhanded competition went on for seven years until both establishments were shuttered in an uncharacteristic crackdown by the city. Weiss later wanted to reopen, but the Everleigh sisters who ran the fabulous sex resort chose to go into genteel retirement; without that foil the Weiss Club was nothing. Poor Ed Weiss moved on in later years to handle a large portion of the Capone brothel empire in the 1920s, but somehow supervision of 50-cent, $2, $5 and $10 joints seemed a sad comedown from the sex scam of the century.

WELFARE CHEAT See MORENO, ANTHONY.

WELLS, CHARLES See MAN WHO BROKE THE BANK AT MONTE CARLO.

WEYMAN, STANLEY CLIFFORD *devilish impostor*

Brooklyn-born Stanley Clifford Weyman (1891–1960) was a fabulous fraud who bedeviled authorities with many identities and impostures. He was, among other identities, a diplomat, doctor, journalist and a draft-dodger adviser. He monitored sanitation conditions for an American firm in Peru, helped run a clinic at the New York Hospital for Joint Diseases and attended to the grieving actress Pola Negri at the time of her greatest tragedy—the death of her betrothed, silent-film star Rudolph Valentino. Weyman rarely carried out any of his impostures looking for financial reward. He was in the business of fooling people, often with hilarious results.

In his early 20s Weyman found working in a Brooklyn counting house was boring. He faced a future probably always limited to clerking. Weyman rebelled at the thought, quit his job and marched off to Manhattan, where he donned a purple uniform and declared himself to be the U.S. consul delegate to Morocco. He ran up enormous bills at plush hotels and restaurants as this mythical diplomat. Once, out of checks, he pinched an expensive camera and hocked it. This led to the unmasking of the consul delegate and he was sent to the Elmira Reformatory.

Here Weyman learned the secret of reforming; he resolved never again to engage in mere petty thievery. When he was paroled, he informed his parole officer he had a job. He actually had two "jobs." He obtained another impressive uniform and became a military attache from Serbia. He was also a lieutenant in the U.S. Navy. These two military men did favors for one another, setting up interesting situations for each. Then they both got caught and Weyman went back to prison. Paroled once again in 1915, he dressed as a lieutenant commander in the Romanian Navy as well as a Romanian consul general in New York. Weyman decided to pay his respects to the Navy Department and was invited to visit the USS *Wyoming*. Weyman bore a severe mein as he inspected the sailors standing in ranks, and he even reprimanded some of them. Later, this impressive officer in his dapper sky-blue uniform mellowed a bit, issued an invitation for an official visit to Romania's Black Sea ports and then invited the ship's officers to dine with him at the Astor Hotel.

Weyman arranged for a private dining room, with the bill to be sent to the Romanian consulate in Washington. Weyman might have pulled off the caper had the hotel's publicity department not been so taken with him and issued a press release on the upcoming affair that was reported in the *New York Times*. A sharp-eyed police officer noted the item and wondered if it could possibly be good old Stanley. A couple of detectives checked out the banquet and again took Weyman into custody. "You could have waited until after dessert," Weyman, a master of protocol, remarked.

During World War I, Weyman decided to do his bit. He commissioned himself a lieutenant in the Army Air Corps under the name of Royal St. Cyr. He was finally arrested at a Brooklyn armory while staging one of his usual inspections.

In 1921 Weyman scored his most impressive success when Princess Fatima of Afghanistan was visiting America and took a suite at the Waldorf Astoria. Lieutenant Commander Weyman showed up as the State Department's head of protocol to serve as her guide. This pleased the princess very much because up until then the U.S. government had ignored her. He told her that in America it was customary to distribute cash gifts to various junior officials who supervised her visit. He took $10,000 from the princess to handle the mundane distributions. It all seemed to pay off for the princess, for whom Weyman wheedled a visit to the White House. Fatima posed proudly beside President Harding for pictures. Weyman got more money from Fatima "to pay the hotel bill" and vanished.

In New York a newspaper photo editor saw pictures of Weyman's White House call and tossed the prints in the air, shouting, "That little S.O.B.'s done it again!"

The following year, Weyman was arrested for posing as a hospital official to take fees from patients of a visiting Viennese surgeon. He also served two years for his Fatima capers.

Despite prison, Weyman remained unrepentant. He showed up at Valentino's funeral and for a while became Pola Negri's personal physician. Then Weyman switched professions and was caught twice posing as a lawyer. He also became a visiting lecturer in both law and medicine at a couple of colleges. During World War II Weyman became a "selective service consultant," giving instruction in draft-dodging to pupils interested in how to simulate deafness or feeblemindedness. That unpatriotic scam earned Weyman seven years in the slammer.

Fresh out of prison in 1948, Weyman showed up at a spot that would surely appreciate his talents: the United Nations at Lake Success. Using phony credentials he went to work for a small news service and radio station. He was on a first-name basis with Warren Austin, the chief American delegate, and Andrei Gromyko, the chief Soviet delegate. When the Thai delegation, impressed with his fine work, offered him the post of its press officer with full diplomatic accreditation, Weyman was thrilled. It was what he had worked for all his life. Unfortunately, he made the mistake of writing the State Department inquiring if taking such a position would affect his U.S. citizenship. Someone there remembered Weyman's name from many past sad experiences, and Stanley's diplomatic career was dashed.

Late in Weyman's life a reporter asked him why he had lived such a life of trickery. "One man's life is a boring thing," he explained. "I lived many lives. I'm never bored."

After that Weyman was not heard of again until 1960 when he was working as a night manager in a New York hotel. He was shot to death by a thief he had tried to stop from robbing the hotel safe. Oddly, Stanley Weyman's last masquerade was that of a real-life hero.

WHIPLASH *accident claims abuses*

Whiplash is the most common fraud in automobile accident claims. A Los Angeles orthopedic surgeon named Dr. Harold E. Crowe, much to his own later regret, came up with the term in 1928. He used the term in an address to the American Academy of Medicine to describe the cause of the condition of eight patients who suffered difficult-to-cure neck injuries in car accidents. Since then whiplash has been the bane of motorists involved in accidents, their insurance companies and public and private mass transit systems.

Years later Dr. Crowe said: "The expression was intended to be a description of motion—not of a disease." But by that time it was widely used by doctors, patients and claims lawyers. By some estimates as many as nine out of every ten persons in rear-end car collisions contract this popular "disease," one that is most difficult to disprove.

Many medical experts, including Dr. Crowe, have contended that true whiplash is a rare occurrence. Out of 300 cases studied by Dr. Crowe, he turned up only 18 victims of "whiplash" who would have benefited from medical treatment. The rest, he declared, had only simple strains that would have disappeared if left unattended.

Needless to say, claims lawyers disagree. Accident victims tend to become convinced they must have a neck injury and think themselves into it. That became Dr. Crowe's view, which was readily seconded by psychiatrists.

In an address to the Western Orthopedic Association, Dr. Crowe recommended that the best cure for most whiplash cases was a "green poultice." By that, he said, "I mean a financial settlement. There's no question but that such a settlement has a high therapeutic value. Insurance claims adjusters have known for years the 'whiplash' victims get well with amazing rapidity after they receive their court settlements."

Over an eight-year period a Miami doctor handled no less than 3,000 cases of whiplash; about 90% to 95% of his cases turned out to be automobile accident victims. It was estimated that the whiplash medic earned $1,233,000 during this span. Legally there was no fraud involved, despite the contention of insurance experts that almost all whiplash claims are fake. Whiplash fraud scams simply remain above detection, if not suspicion.

WHISKEY RING   defrauding the government

In the 1970s similarities were pointed out between the Watergate scandal and the Whiskey Ring, another government scandal that occurred exactly one century earlier. Both scandals bore the same motivation of the politicians involved, namely the reelection of a president. However, the Whiskey Ring had more monies floating around, as the true motivation was a major defrauding of the government.

The plot was hatched by a group of Western distillers who bribed corrupt officials in what was then the Internal Revenue Service to avoid payment of the whiskey tax. The conspirators were all closely connected to President Ulysses S. Grant, and undoubtedly felt they were immune to detection and prosecution. However, when Benjamin H. Bristow, Grant's secretary of the Treasury, moved for the indictment of 230 persons in May 1875, he unleashed one of the century's greatest political scandals. Some observers said this was the one that most linked Grant himself to money taking.

A total of 110 defendants—including four government officials—were convicted, and the legal cases clearly demonstrated that part of the illegally avoided taxes were instead funneled to the Republican Party to help Grant's reelection to a second term in 1872. The conspirators had been busy setting up a slush fund for a prospective third run for office by Grant when the massive swindle was uncovered. At the time General Orville E. Babcock, Grant's private secretary, was indicted and there seemed to be strong evidence that the president himself was directly implicated. Fortunately for the president, General Babcock was acquitted and the interest in involving Grant evaporated—as did any plans for a run for the third term.

WHITE, E. J. "STROLLER"   See ICE WORM COCKTAILS.

WHITE DIAMONDS   coloring cheaper yellows

Generally speaking, white diamonds are more brilliant and more expensive than yellow ones; but in the fringe areas of the jewelry trade, a thin film is used to turn yellow diamonds white or at least whitish. A reformed operator in the field was once asked by bunco authorities how customers can avoid being fooled by the white diamond caper. "Always have the stones examined." And what if they have already bought them? "Have their heads examined."

WHITNEY, RICHARD F.   the wolf of Wall Street

As head of the New York Stock Exchange, Richard F. Whitney (1888–1974) was known as a financier of rockbed conservatism. In 1929 he was tapped by the Bankers' Pool to lead the intervention in the market to buy hundreds of millions of dollars in stock during the crash in an effort to buoy public confidence. For his efforts he gained the sobriquet "the Strongman of Wall Street." However, there was another side to Whitney, one that was to earn him a different nickname, "the Wolf of Wall Street." Whitney had invested heavily in the stock of Distilled Liquors, a manufacturer of applejack, and had used the stock to back bank loans. Facing a possible call by the banks on the loans, Whitney diverted securities of the clients of his bond firm into purchases of the stock to keep it from falling. Whitney's exposure in 1938 produced a mini-panic on Wall Street. He was convicted of fraud and sent to Sing Sing for five to ten years. He became an outfielder for the penitentiary's renowned baseball team.

On his release, Whitney did not return to Wall Street. He disappeared from sight for a number of years. Eventually he turned up managing a Florida fiber mill. He died in obscurity in 1974.

WHO'S WHO IN AMERICA   *fake entries*
While some reference works have carried inaccurate information either because of faulty research or lies supplied to them (see entry *Appleton's Cyclopedia of American Biography*), only one publication is known for deliberately planting false entries itself. It is *Who's Who in America*, published by A. N. Marquis Company. The publication's spokespersons in the past have admitted that fake biographies have been printed, although they much prefer the term "dummy sketches." Outsiders who know of the practice frequently assume *Who's Who in America* runs such hoaxes as a way of preventing copyright violations by other publications; but this is not even a significant factor in the procedure.

Tom Burnham in *More Misinformation* quotes Di-Anne Halenar, editorial director of the publication:

> We use these sketches (that contain false information but real addresses) to prevent any organization from using our publications as mailing lists. Although the sketches appearing in our publications are not to be reproduced without our permission, the information itself is available to be used as part of newspaper articles, etc. Since we rely on biographies to provide us with the majority of information contained in our books, we do not want them bothered by solicitations as a result of having their sketches appear in our publications. It is for this reason that we initiated the concept of "dummy sketches."

Thus in the past *Who's Who in America* once carried a biography of Samuel G. Hansell, an "Illinois lawyer." Everything in the biography was unreal save for the home address given. "Hansell" did not live there but Wheeler Sammons, Jr., then publisher of the publication, did. Any mailings to an address of an employee of the publication is immediately forwarded to the reference book's attorneys for action.

There is, of course, other fictitious information appearing in *Who's Who in America*, an inevitable situation since the subjects themselves are the chief source of all facts published. For that reason, subjects' ages can be viewed as quite often more a reflection of vanity than accuracy. As Burnham points out, American critic and historian Henry Adams "kept getting younger with every edition. His younger brother finally remarked that he could not very well be older than his older brother."

WILD ANIMAL HOAX   *false newspaper story*
On Monday, November 9, 1874 James Gordon Bennett, owner of the *New York Herald*, received the morning copy of his own newspaper in bed and promptly collapsed, to remain there the rest of the day. Many New Yorkers had similar or even more panicked reactions.

Under a headline "AWFUL CALAMITY" they read of ferocious beasts loose in the streets and stalking human prey after breaking out of the Central Park Zoo. "Another Sunday of horror has been added to those already memorable in our city annals," the *Herald* cried in what purported to be eyewitness accounts of the awful events:

> . . . We have a list of forty-nine killed, of which only twenty-seven bodies have been identified, and it is much to be feared that this large total of fatalities will be much increased with the return of daylight. The list of mutilated, trampled and injured in various ways must reach nearly 200 persons. . . . Twelve of the large carnivorous beasts are still at large, their lurking places not being known.

The mayor reportedly issued a "state-of-siege" proclamation that declared, "All citizens, except members of the National Guard are enjoined to keep within their houses or residences until the wild animals now at large are captured or killed."

An eyewitness to the catastrophe was quoted:

> There was evidently a fight over the body of Anderson (the keeper whose unfortunate poke at the rhinoceros had set off all the trouble). But I could see nothing more than a mingling, gleaming mass, whence arose the most awful cries. Near to me, where (Keeper) Hyland lay, the lioness, the panther, the puma, and presently the Bengal tiger, were rolling over and over, striking at each other with their mighty paws. The lioness tore the skin off the puma's flank with one blow. The coming of the tiger was something terrible. I shall never forget the awful, splendid look of him as he landed with a spring in the thick of them. I could not move. It was too awful for anything. Oddly enough, while the fight was going on . . . I could not help looking at Lincoln, the lion, who was standing behind them, pawing and roaring and lashing his sides with his tail, every muscle in uneasy tension. All of a sudden I had a flash.
>
> *"By God, he's looking at me!"* I said to myself. I saw him crouch. I turned and ran. . . .
>
> I saw a young man fall from a blow of the awful paw, and another crushed to earth beneath the beast's weight. . . .

There were more reports of horror and a vast hunt was being organized by armed men, including, said the *Herald*, Chester Arthur, Samuel J. Tilden and other leading citizens, patrolling up and down Broadway and Fifth Avenue and even inside cathedrals and churches. The celebrated war correspondent George W. Hosmer, a member of the Herald's staff, showed up at the office brandishing two big navy revolvers, shouting at the top of his lungs as he entered, "Well, here I am."

Earl Roseberry had his carriage bowled over by a mad buffalo in front of the Brevoort Hotel, which then rammed headlong into another one. A tiger jumped onto a departing ferryboat at the foot of 23rd Street and sent horses, wagons and petrified passengers plunging overboard.

"It would be impossible at this late hour to describe the numberless scenes of dismay and disaster," the *Herald* continued. "The hospitals are full of wounded. . . . A sentiment of horror pervades the community."

Much of the life of the city came to an abrupt halt and few ventured out, most cowering behind furniture that barricaded home doors and windows.

Other newspapers also fell for the story. Major George F. Williams, the city editor of the *Times*, lashed his horses to police headquarters to angrily condemn officials for giving a rival newspaper such a tremendous scoop.

Of course, it had all been a journalistic hoax, as the *Herald* took care to clarify in the final paragraph of the sensational story. Subheaded "THE MORAL OF THE WHOLE," the conclusion read:

> Of course the entire story given above is a pure fabrication. Not one word of it is true. Not a single act or incident described has taken place. It is a huge hoax, a wild romance, or whatever other epithet of utter untrustworthiness our readers may care to apply to it. It is simply a fancy picture which crowded upon the mind of the writer a few days ago while he was gazing through the iron bars of the cages of the wild animals in the menagerie at Central Park. Yet as each of its horrid but perfectly natural sequences impressed themselves upon his mind, the question presented itself, How is New York prepared to meet such a catastrophe? How easily could it occur any day of the week? How much, let the citizens ponder, depends upon the indiscretion of even one of the keepers? A little oversight, a trifling imprudence might lead to the actual happening of all, and even worse than has been pictured. From causes quite as insignificant the greatest calamities of history have sprung. Horror, devastation and widespread slaughter of human beings have had small mishaps for parents time and again.

While the *Herald* could insist the motive for the "huge hoax, a wild romance" was a call for improvements at the zoo, such as stronger bars, rather than anything so crass as the selling of newspapers, its tactic of burying the disclaimer at the end of five full newspaper columns was a guarantee that it would be read by very few people. In fact, the nervous caution of the vast number of New Yorkers continued for days, as average Gothamites showed less interest in stouter bars anywhere—save around their own homes.

WILD MAN FROM BORNEO *popular freak show performer*

A popular 19th century hoax was the California appearance of the so-called Wild Man from Borneo. The Wild Man first appeared in a Market Street freak show on San Francisco's Barbary Coast. He was presumably captured in the wilds of Borneo and was imported to San Francisco "at enormous expense" by show business entrepreneurs determined to impart new scientific knowledge to the gullible public.

Covered from crown to heel with road tar, the Wild Man was decorated with an enormous coat of horse hair and offered to the public as a most fearsome sight. An attendant, approaching the creature's cage with cautious respect, tossed the Wild Man large chunks of raw meat, which he devoured with ravenous gusto, pausing only long enough to rattle the bars and scream menacingly, "Oofty goofty! Oofty goofty!" The braver members of the audience shouted back to draw an even more howling response.

Record crowds for any freak show were thrilled and often sickened by the Wild Man's performances, a histrionic sensation. The creature, now dubbed Oofty Goofty, became the toast of the Pacific Coast. Until . . . tragedy struck.

Oofty Goofty could not perspire through his thick coating of tar and hair, and he became ill. When he collapsed in his cage, he was rushed to Receiving Hospital, where his problem was quickly discerned but doctors had great difficulties effecting a cure. For several days the medical men found it impossible to remove Oofty Goofty's costume without peeling off his true epidermis as well. The press reported on the medical dilemma until doctors hit on a solution. They poured tar solvent all over Oofty Goofty and deposited him out on the hospital roof until the sun finished the job of cleaning up the Wild Man from Borneo.

The entire episode did not dampen the public's affection for Oofty Goofty and he became a great draw at leading beer halls and variety houses on the Barbary Coast. His new act was singing a song with little more harmony than his oofty goofty calls in the Wild Man's cage. Then with great ceremony and to the applause of the audience, he was kicked out onto the sidewalk with considerable force.

Here Oofty Goofty made an important scientific discovery. He was largely immune to pain. Thus he was launched on a new, if perilous, career of allowing the denizens of the Barbary Coast to physically attack him—for a fee. A dime earned a citizen the right to crack Oofty Goofty with a walking stick. For a mere 50 cents a brutal-minded citizen could have the enjoyment of slamming Oofty Goofty with a baseball bat. Soon Oofty Goofty was a familiar sight all over San Francisco, carrying a bat into barber shops, saloons, or even amidst street corner congregations and announcing, "Hit me with a bat for four bits, gents?"

In 1890 Oofty Goofty was worked over by heavyweight boxing champion John L. Sullivan with a billiard cue, and suddenly he felt enormous pain. That ended his career and thereafter Oofty Goofty lost his ability to withstand even the slightest discomfort. When Oofty Goofty died in 1896 newspapers reported that doctors declared that the beating by Sullivan was not responsible for his death. The ertswhile Wild Man from Borneo was buried as Oofty Goofty, without ever having revealed his true identity.

WILSON, SARAH *Princess Susanna Carolina Matilda*
A 16-year-old village girl from Staffordshire, Sarah Wilson came to London in 1771 and became a servant to Caroline Vernon, a lady-in-waiting to Queen Charlotte. Working in "the Queen's House," she was in a position to steal royal possessions. She proceeded to do just that, taking a number of jewels, a dress and a portrait of the queen. The girl was caught and sentenced to death, but through the intercession of her mistress, the punishment was reduced to transportation to the American colonies for life.

Somehow Sarah contrived to smuggle the queen's dress, the portrait and even a few of the jewels aboard the convict ship bound for Maryland. In Baltimore Sarah was sold to a planter, William Devall, as an indentured servant. The cunning girl quickly escaped and headed south. There the daring Sarah dressed herself in her royal garb and jewels and declared herself to be Princess Susanna Carolina Matilda, the sister of Queen Charlotte, exiled to America for a court scandal she did not deign to discuss.

Well-versed in palace gossip, she had little trouble fooling wealthy Virginia families, who feted her and kept her in the style to which she was accustomed. Sarah played to the snobbery of the ladies and the business ambitions of the gentlemen, inferring she was still not without power back in England and could win them prize appointments. Of course, the finer the lodgings and the more gold that crossed her palm, the higher the potential appointments. The only murmur raised about Sarah was that she did not speak German, since her sister and obviously herself were German, having come to Britain from Mecklenburg-Strelitz. Sarah explained this by saying she most certainly did speak German but had vowed never to utter a word of that language until her sister returned her to favor at court. It was German-speaking foes at court, she said, who had caused her woes.

Sarah might have gone on for a long time soaking Southern society had her fame not spread so widely. It seems her old master, William Devall, heard tales of her and deduced she was Sarah Wilson. Devall

sent one Michael Dalton to pursue her; Dalton tracked her down at a salon of a plantation just outside Charleston, South Carolina, where she was holding court. Dalton, to the chagrin of "Princess Susanna's" hosts, took her away at pistol point.

Back in Maryland, Sarah was contrite and vowed to her employer that she would be a loyal servant. She was for almost two years until 1775 when her master was called into the militia. Sarah swapped identities with another indentured maiden and was on the loose again.

Posing as a Tory, she married a British army officer. After the Revolution, Sarah remained ineligible for return to England. As far as is known she and her husband moved to New York, apparently living quite well on the fruits of Sarah's past impostures.

WIMBLEDON MILITARY REVIEW RIOT *hoax announcement*
Swept up in the fervor of the Napoleonic War, the English public turned out 20,000 strong on the Wimbledon Common on June 12, 1812 for a grand military review. The crowd was in a merry mood until an announcement was made by a government official that there would be no review and the government had never intended to stage one—since the printed notices of the review had been forgeries.

The merrymaking character of the crowd changed, and the heath was set afire and talk circulated about attacking military personnel for failure "to do their duty." As the crowd's anger increased, the police proved unable to quell the disturbance. An urgent request went to London: Large detachments had to be rushed to Wimbledon to stage an unscheduled review and appease an angry mob.

WINCHELL, WALTER *gossip columnist hoax victim*
During the era of the Broadway columnist, Walter Winchell was in a class by himself as the King of Gossip. Within the journalism field he was never celebrated for his accuracy, and public relations people always knew he could be conned into publishing more phony items than any of his colleagues. It took Winchell some years to finally stop running items about celebrities traveling to Europe and their steamships docking in Paris. Despite his reputation as a knowledgeable insider on criminal matters, few journalists considered him so. In fact, many duped him with preposterous stories and then roared with laughter when they appeared in print. Clearly, some of this hostility toward Winchell was triggered by outrage at the huge salaries he commanded while most journalists labored for relatively meager wages.

One classic hoax pulled on Winchell (which he never learned about) concerned the unsolved murder of mobster Bugsy Siegel. Winchell considered this to be one of his greatest "exclusives," and he saved it for his autobiography, which appeared after he died. Some Hearst newsmen fed Winchell the "low-down" on the case, which they informed him had been determined secretly by Thomas E. Dewey [when he was still district attorney] and Frank Hogan [when he was Mr. Dewey's chief aide]. Winchell proclaimed to his readers that the killers were the notorious Happy Maione and Dasher Abbandando of Murder, Inc., who were assigned to make the hit because Siegel had squandered $4 million of the mob's money building the Flamingo, the first elegant hotel casino in Las Vegas.

Winchell was not about to start checking facts this late in his career. If racket buster Dewey had really solved the Siegel killing during his D.A. days, he had used clairvoyance since he left that office in 1943 and Siegel was murdered in 1947. And as for Winchell suspects Maione and Abbandando, they had gone to the electric chair for sundry murders in 1942, but certainly not for killing Siegel five years after their own demise.

Chalk one up for the boys in the city room.

WINTER WETLANDS SALES *vacation home scam*

The standard advice given to buyers of vacation or retirement home real estate is always to inspect the property before purchase. Even that is not always enough, especially during certain periods of the year. Recently in New England a high-pressure vacation property scam offered buyers bargain prices during a winter sale. Since the properties, mostly in Maine, were intended for snow vacations, it seemed logical for buyers to view the properties in their snow-topped glory, especially when prices were slashed during a wintertime sales extravaganza. With a big enough purchase, according to the promotion, it would even have been possible to build a house and have a huge area available for a family's private cross-country course.

Buyers by the hundreds fell for the sales pitch, only to discover that as much as 90 to 95 percent of their property could not be used as a building site since it was wetlands. In the winter it looked like a wonderland, as the ground was frozen and covered with snow; but by spring the wonderland turned to a sodden nightmare.

WISHING CORK TREE *endless heavenly supply*

The circulars come from Torquay, England. For a mere $5 or $10 or $15, depending on what the traffic will bear at the moment, you can have a piece of the famous Wishing Cork Tree at Coombe-in-Teighhead, Devon. It will be sent by mail with the special blessing of the Druids. The cork brings good luck, of course, for whoever is lucky enough to own it; indeed, it may even offer the same godly benefits as those who own a bit of the True Cross.

Naturally, if one wants a bit of the Devon cork tree, the circular advises quick action as the supply can't last forever. That pitch would be quite a surprise to the Better Business Bureau, which had come to the conclusion that Coombe-in-Teighhead must have an entire cork tree orchard available—considering the known level of sales—and would have to be in the process of reseeding the entire area.

WITCH DOCTORS (WHITE) *curse swindlers*

Witch doctors and their curses are a practice that goes back many centuries and endures to the present in the United States. The leading practitioners in this century were two audacious swindlers, Mrs. William McBride and Edgar Zug, the latter being plugged as the sole living white witch doctor in the United States. The pair, dressed in eery ceremonial costumes, sparked terror in hundreds of people and then bilked them for fortunes. Victims were told they were under evil spells as Zug intoned: "The only way to relieve this deadly spell is to buy your way out of it. These evil spirits respect cash."

In 1902 the white witch doctor and his accomplice put a curse on a rich Pennsylvania couple, Mrs. Susan Stambaugh and her palsy-ridden husband. Witch doctor Zug divined a terrible vision. He said he saw their profiles on a distant mountain and discovered that evil spirits had jammed long needles into the brains of these profiles. That was at the time of the original curse; the needles had since grown rusty. "When these needles break," Zug warned them, "you both will die."

The elderly Stambaughs fainted. When they revived, Mrs. McBride had some good news for them: Witch doctor Zug might be able to induce the evil spirits to remove the needles, but it would take a bit of money.

The Stambaughs grasped at that straw and, inside of a week, turned over their savings as well as deeds to many of their properties. Unfortunately, the evil spirits were not pacified. "You both will die," Zug announced with a beaten air. "Unless, that is, you can come up with another $5,000."

Happily there was an upside to this. If the couple produced the extra $5,000, the Stambaughs could get back all they gave the spirits and even a bit more from a hidden treasure that the spirits would reveal to them.

Desperate yet hopeful, the couple searched for more money, turning to friends for help. In doing so, Mrs. Stambaugh told one friend the reason they needed the money. The white witch doctor and his female aide were arrested and convicted of fraud. As he was being led from the courtroom, Zug cried, "That's what I get for being kind!"

WITCHES' SCALE   *life-saving hoax*
Today in the public square of the village of Oudewater in the Netherlands stands a weighing scale in memory of a benign hoax that saved the lives of many women accused of being witches during the hysteria that swept Europe in the 16th century. Unlike the town officials in other communities, the officials of Oudewater were an unsuperstitious lot and were determined to prevent the executions of "witches."

They erected a special scale in the town square. Suspected sorceresses were marched to the scale, weighed and then exonerated with the official determination that they were too heavy to ride through the air on a broomstick.

WOLF-MAN MANIAS   *fraudulent claims*
The belief in wolf men has a long, barbaric history and is replete with fraudulent claims. Sixteenth-century France was especially a center of *loup-garou*, or wolf-man mania. One of the most sensational cases occurred in 1588 in a village in the mountains of Auvergne. As summarized by Charles Mackay in his classic *Extraordinary Popular Delusions and the Madness of Crowds*:

> A gentleman of that place being at his window, there passed a friend of his who had been out hunting, and who was then returning to his own house. The gentleman asked his friend what sport he had had; upon which the latter informed him that he had been attacked in the plain by a large and savage wolf, which he shot at without wounding, and that he had then drawn out his hunting-knife and cut off the animal's fore-paw as it sprang upon his neck to devour him. The huntsman upon this put his hand into his bag to pull out the paw, but was shocked to find that it was a woman's hand, with a wedding-ring on the finger. The gentleman immediately recognized his wife's ring, "which," says the indictment against her, "made him begin to suspect some evil of her." He immediately went in search of her, and found her sitting by the fire in the kitchen, with her arm hidden underneath her apron. He tore off her apron with great vehemence, and found that she had no hand, and that stump was even then bleeding. She was given into custody, and burnt at Riom, in presence of some thousands of spectators.

In a less credulous and more cynical age as today, the deadly hoax becomes readily apparent. A husband cannot divorce his unwanted wife because of religious strictures or else he fears losing his wife's fortune. He solves his dilemma in league with a friend by cutting her hand off and accusing her of being a "wolfman."

WOODEN NUTMEGS   *Connecticut peddler con*
It was and is "the Nutmeg State," but in the early 19th century Connecticut was known derisively as the "Wooden Nutmeg State." The majority of the old-time Yankee peddlers came from Connecticut, and they traveled through most of the states by horse and cart peddling their wares, which were, alas, noted for their inferiority. They offered defective clocks and watches, leaky calf weaners, cigars that would not draw and wooden nutmegs. Housewives bought these ribbon-decorated wooden pieces as exotic East Indian spice mills, but the ground spice they got was unadulterated sawdust.

Weary of the bad name Connecticut had been saddled with for well over a century, the state legislature changed the official state designation to "The Constitution State" in the 1960s. But to most Connecticut citizens—as well as to the rest of New England, which still revels in tales of the old Yankee peddlers—Connecticut will always remain the "(Wooden) Nutmeg State."

WORLD WAR I ARMISTICE HOAX   *November 8, 1918*
On November 8, 1918 news of the end of World War I brought great joy to the United States from coast to coast. Newspapers put out extra editions with gigantic headlines. Church bells rang. Factory sirens sounded. Parades formed. Bonfires blazed. Speeches were made. Jubilant crowds cheered.

But none of this should have happened, as the war was not over. All of this had been—by most later deductions—a desperate hoax committed by German intelligence to prevent their government from agreeing to peace on unacceptable terms. A German secret agent apparently had telephoned American intelligence offices and declared that an armistice had been signed. The message was in turn sent out by American officials in Europe. A naval attache in the American embassy in Paris sent a telegram to Admiral Henry B. Wilson, commanding officer of the American naval force then stationed at Brest. Admiral Wilson showed the report to Roy W. Howard, president of United Press, who was about to sail back to the United States.

Howard was jubilant, realizing he had the scoop of the decade, and he cabled the story to America. As he started fleshing out the big newsbreak, Howard discovered he could not get any confirmation of the report. Within an hour of the first cable, Howard cabled off a "kill" of the story; but the lines were

Typical wolf-man attacks are depicted in a 16th-century German engraving and in a French news sheet c. 1660.

jammed at the time and it took 24 hours for the second cable to be transmitted.

Later investigations appeared to establish with relative certainty that the hoax report had been a plant by German Intelligence, in part to discourage the German government from agreeing to peace on unacceptable terms, since the celebrations the hoax produced showed that the people in the Allied nations and especially in America wanted immediate peace themselves rather than revenge.

In the field of journalism, the embarrassment suffered by the United Press was compounded by the subsequent distrust of the agency's "scoops." Thereafter the custom developed that whenever possible a U.P. story should be confirmed by the Associated Press before being printed.

WRIGHT, WHITAKER *swindler*

No British swindler has ever come close to the record take garnered by Whitaker Wright (1846–1904), who swindled both nobleman and commoner with

democratic impartiality. Starting in 1889 when he came back to England after a successful rags-to-riches business career in the United States, Wright floated no less than 42 companies, most allegedly involved in gold mining in Australia and South Africa. The key to Wright's success was his ability to cultivate British nobility and royalty, even entertaining the Prince of Wales, later Edward VII, aboard his luxurious yacht.

Wright made members of the nobility large stockholders and directors in his firms, duping them and the public with phony financial statements. His empire was most impressive—on paper; the total capitalization was put at $110,775,000, of which no more than $10 million was real.

Meanwhile, Wright lived the good life, residing in absolute splendor at times in a palatial home purchased from William Gladstone. He also built a magnificent country home in Godalming, in Surrey, 30 miles from London. The grand mansion sported a famous palm garden, many suites of reception rooms and a great ballroom, which was capable of accommodating several hundred persons. At one end of the room was a stage for theatricals; at the other a great organ, the whole crowned by an observatory containing one of the largest telescopes in England. The estate comprised about 2,000 acres in all and was adorned by gardens and terraces, a statuary, summer houses, pagodas, rare trees and a number of lakes stocked with trout. His guests were probably most awed by a billiard room set beneath a lake with a glass ceiling, so that the players could watch fish overhead.

In 1903 the Wright bubble burst because of a stock market slump induced by the Boer War. Even Wright's most inspired juggling of the books could not cover up his depredations from his noblemen associates, especially the Earl of Dufferin and Ava, former governor general of both Canada and India and Lord Loch. Dufferin himself lost his good name and his personal fortune as well. The public adduced that both gentlemen soon took to their sickbeds and died because of shame and shock.

Wright fled the country to the United States, but after considerable legal jockeying he returned to England. Tried and found guilty, Wright was sentenced to seven years imprisonment. While still in the court house he swallowed some poison pills and died on the spot.

The correspondent for the *New York Times* cabled from London: "The career of this man, who was known on three continents for his stupendous financial operations, closed in a startling tragedy. Even in his life, which with his rise from poverty to enormous wealth, was full of dramatic incidents, there was nothing that could compare with the manner of his death. All London to-night is thrilled with the news of it."

Among those most or least thrilled were Wright's investors, the luckiest of whom lost at least 90 cents on the dollar in a financial empire made of pure water.

X-RAY-PROOF UNDERWEAR HOAX

Within months of the 1895 discovery of x rays by German physicist Wilhelm Konrad Roentgen, a rumor spread among British women than an English company was intending to introduce x-ray glass that would permit the wearer to look right through clothing. Indeed, some reports indicated that such glasses were already being sold surreptitiously. Fortunately, at the same time as the surfacing of the preposterous rumor, a certain manufacturer brought to market "x-ray-proof" underwear that would thwart those devilish spectacles.

In time scientists successfully exploded the idiotic see-through theory. While it was never proved, the common belief is that the underwear manufacturer had been the father of the original rumor. The hoax had allowed him—and a leading department store of the period—to make a considerable fortune with his x-ray-proof undergarments. Needless to say, the evil maker of the x-ray glasses never actually marketed that visionary invention.

Y

YAZOO LAND FRAUDS *public land giveaways*
Dubbed by historian Paul W. Gates as "one of the most corrupt actions taken by any legislative body," the Yazoo land frauds involved the western lands of Georgia, which in the late 18th century extended to the Mississippi River and comprised the present states of Alabama and Mississippi. In 1789 the members of the Georgia legislature authorized the sale of more than 25 million acres of rich Yazoo territory to three land companies for a piddling $273,580. Six years later Georgia sold some 35 million acres to four more speculative land companies for a half million dollars. Thus all of the lands were essentially given away for less than $1\frac{1}{2}$ cents per acre.

The argument made by legislators was that the state might eventually be forced to cede that land to the U.S. government and should instead seek to enrich the impoverished state treasury. They were actually much more interested in enriching themselves, since the land companies in turn sold shares in the land for next to nothing to the legislators who stood to make enormous profits when the tracts were later sold by promoters to northern investors and eager farmers. One so victimized was merchant Robert Morris, a signer of the Declaration of Independence who was known thereafter as the "financier of the Revolution" for his fund-raising efforts. Morris eventually went bankrupt in his Yazoo investments.

Not only had the legislators virtually given away rich lands ideal for growing cotton for a pittance, but members of the legislature, it was later established, had bribed one another to effect passage of the various bills. In the resultant public uproar, there were serious calls for lynching of the politicians involved. In 1796 a newly organized "throw the rascals out" legislature was established and it rescinded the original Yazoo deals. This did not stop unscrupulous agents from continuing to sell tracts in New England and the Middle Atlantic states to the unsuspecting. Titles to the lands became confused, especially since the greedy earlier legislators had approved the sale of warrants to much more land than there actually was.

The whole problem was passed to the federal government in 1802 when Georgia ceded the entire disputed territories to the United States. The state stipulated that the United States had to assume responsibility for any claims arising from the earlier sales. However, Virginia Representative John Randolph fought to prevent Congress from granting relief to the holders of the lands, even though many were now innocent parties (called "widows and orphans" by the Yazooists). In 1810 the U.S. Supreme Court unanimously decided that the Yazooists were in the right and that the original land grants were valid contracts; the Georgia legislature's later attempt to rescind the deals was in violation of the constitutional obligations on contracts. In 1814 Congress finally passed a bill that awarded the shareholders $4.7 million in relief for the losses of their lands. In effect, the Court had ruled that the land had been originally stolen fair and square.

YELLOWSTONE PARK GEYSERS See GEYSERS ON COMMAND.

Z

0-INTEREST FINANCING PLANS *dubious sales pitch*
Some consumer advocates charge that a sales pitch by auto makers and big-appliance dealers about "0-interest financing plans" are at best misleading and misrepresentative. In reality, such plans do not really exist. Nobody will provide something for nothing, especially not money. When cars, appliances or jewelry are offered with no interest added for time payments, one thing is certain: The cost of the financing has been figured into the sales price. In the dickering, the car dealer or discount-store owner will simply cut the haggle area by limiting the price he'll drop. The same principle is involved when a car dealer offers to throw in a "free set" of snow tires if he arranges the financing. Obviously, the price of the tires is included in the interest charge.

ZINOVIEV LETTER *political dirty trick*
Few political campaign fakes have had as profound an impact on an election as the so-called Zinoviev Letter or Red Letter Scare in England in 1924. At the time, Britain's first Labor government, which had recognized Soviet Russia, was seeking to enter into a commercial treaty with that country. While it appeared that Labor would lose the upcoming election to the Conservatives, there is no doubt that the appearance of the bombshell Zinoviev letter four days before the election turned the contest into a debacle.

The letter, supposedly written by Gregory Zinoviev—president of the Third Communist International—summoned the British Communist Party to open violence, sedition and subversion of the British armed forces as the first move in a Communist revolution in Britain. The letter (published in the *London Mail* on October 25, 1924, four days before the general election) appeared too late to permit adequate response or disclaimers, and let a "red scare" loose in the country. Typical was the editorial comment of the *Mail* upon its printing of the forgery:

> That such a document should have been held back until the very last minute of the election campaign is another sign that the government has a bad conscience in the matter. And well it might have! The country now knows that Moscow issues orders to British Communists and they are obeyed by the Communists here. British Communists, in turn, give orders to the Socialist government, which it tamely and humbly obeys.

In succeeding years, leaders of the Labor Party and the Soviet government continued to denounce the letter as a forgery. Most historians came to agree on that point.

In 1966 the *Sunday Times* effectively established the fact that the letter was a forgery carried out by a group of White Russian emigres. The *Times* also suggested that although the average Tory party official and member considered it an honest document, some leaders of the Conservative Central Office were aware that the letter was a fake.

Selected Bibliography

It would be impossible to list all sources, especially of confirmatory detail, in this bibliography. While there are many celebrated scams, hoaxes and impostures, there are many others that can be documented only by fragmentary news accounts that must be pieced together with considerable care so that accuracy may be preserved. The so-called memoirs of con men are especially not to be trusted. They may well be reformed, but that does not necessarily prevent them from embellishing their recollections to make a good story better. Two magnificent rogues, Yellow Kid Weil and Fred Buckminster, often worked together, but in the twilight of their careers both claimed credit for each other's scams, and those of other con men as well.

The following bibliography therefore lists only those accounts that the author most relied upon and was able to verify independently.

Allen, Frederick Lewis. *Only Yesterday.* New York: Harper & Bros., 1931.

Ashbury, Herbert. *All Around the Town.* New York: Alfred A. Knopf, 1934.

———. *The Barbary Coast.* New York: Alfred A. Knopf, 1933.

———. *The Gangs of New York.* New York: Alfred A. Knopf, 1927.

———. *Gem of the Praire.* New York: Alfred A. Knopf, 1940.

———. *Sucker's Progress.* New York: Dodd, Mead & Co., 1938.

Beam, Maurice. *It's a Racket.* New York: Macfadden, 1962.

Bloom, Murray Teigh. *The Man Who Stole Portugal.* New York: Charles Scribner's Sons, 1953.

Botkin, B. A., ed. *A Treasury of Western Folklore.* New York: Bonanza Books, 1980.

Brannon, William T. *The Fabulous Drake Swindle.* New York: Mercury Press, Inc. 1955.

Brewer's Dictionary of Phrase & Fable. New York: Harper & Row, 1981.

Burnham, Tom. *The Dictionary of Misinformation.* New York: Crowell, 1975.

———. *More Misinformation.* New York: Lippincott & Crowell, 1980.

Chafetz, Henry. *Play the Devil.* New York: Clarkson N. Potter, 1960.

Durant, Will and Ariel. *Rousseau and Revolution.* New York: Simon and Schuster, 1967.

Ellison, E. Jerome, and Brock, Frank W. *The Run for Your Money.* New York: Dodge Publishing Co., 1935.

Emrich, Duncan. *It's an Old Wild West Custom.* New York: Vanguard Press, 1949.

Evans, Bergen. *The Natural History of Nonsense.* New York: Alfred A. Knopf, 1946.

———. *The Spoor of Spooks and Other Nonsense.* New York: Alfred A. Knopf, 1954.

Fishbein, Morris. *Fads and Quackery in Healing.* New York: Covici, Friede, 1932.

Gardner, Martin. *Fads and Fallacies in the Name of Science.* New York: Dover Publications, 1957.

Green, J. H. *Gambling Unmasked!* Philadelphia: n.p., 1847.

Green, Jonathan. *The Greatest Criminals of All Time.* New York: Stein and Day, 1982.

Hamilton, Charles, ed. *Men of the Underworld.* New York: Macmillan, 1952.

Hancock, Ralph, and Chafetz, Henry. *The Compleat Swindler.* New York: Macmillan, 1968.

Hecht, Ben. *A Child of the Century.* New York: Simon and Schuster, 1954.

Horan, James D., and Sann, Paul. *Pictorial History of the Wild West.* New York: Crown, 1970.

Horan, James D. *The Pinkertons: The Detective Dynasty That Made History*. New York: Bonanza Books, 1967.

Johnston, Alva. *The Legendary Mizners*. New York: Farrar, Straus & Young, 1942.

Kahn, E. J. *Fraud*. New York: Harper & Row, 1973.

Klein, Alexander, ed. *The Double Dealers*. Philadelphia and New York: J. B. Lippincott & Co., 1958.

———. *Grand Deception*. Philadelphia and New York: J. B. Lippincott & Co., 1955.

MacDougall, Curtis D. *Hoaxes*. New York: Ace Books, 1958.

Makris, John N. *The Silent Investigators*. New York: E. P. Dutton & Co., 1959.

Maurer, David W. *The Big Con*. New York: Pocket Books, 1949.

McLoughlin, Denis. *Wild & Woolly*. Garden City, N.Y.: Doubleday & Company, 1975.

Mendax, Fritz. *Art Fakes & Forgeries*. New York: Philosophical Library, 1956.

Milner, Richard. *The Encyclopedia of Evolution*. New York: Facts On File, 1990.

Phelan, James. *Scandals, Scamps and Scoundrels*. New York: Random House, 1982.

Quinn, John Philip. *Fools of Fortune*. Chicago: W. B. Conkey, 1890.

Roberts, David. *Great Exploration Hoaxes*. San Francisco: Sierra Club Books, 1982.

Rosefsky, Robert S. *Frauds, Swindles, and Rackets*. Chicago: Follett Publishing Co., 1973.

Sann, Paul. *The Lawless Decade*. New York: Crown, 1957.

Sharpe, May Churchill. *Chicago May*. New York: Maccaulay Co., 1928.

Sifakis, Carl. *American Eccentrics*. New York: Facts On File, 1984.

———. *Encyclopedia of American Crime*. New York: Facts On File, 1982.

———. *The Mafia Encyclopedia*. New York: Facts On File, 1987.

Silberberg, Robert. *Scientists and Scoundrels*. New York: Thomas Y. Crowell Company, 1965.

Sitwell, Edith. *English Eccentrics*. New York: Vanguard Press, 1957.

Tuleja, Tad. *Fabulous Fallacies*. New York: Harmony Books, 1982.

Wade, Carlson. *Great Hoaxes and Famous Impostors*. Middle Village, N.Y.: Jonathan David Publishers, 1976.

Whitehead, Don. *The FBI Story*. New York: Random House, 1956.

Wright, Richardson. *Grandfather Was Queer*. Philadelphia: J.B. Lippincott Company, 1939.

———. *Hawkers and Walkers in Early America*. New York: J. B. Lippincott, 1927.

In addition, the following standard news sources were consulted frequently: *Encyclopedia Britannica, Encyclopedia Americana, Facts On File News Digest, New York Times, New York Daily News, Wall Street Journal, Time* and *Newsweek*.

PHOTO CREDITS

INDEX OF PERSONALITIES

A

Abbandando, Dasher 286
Abrams, Albert 1
Abrams, Robert 8, 37–38
Adams, Caswell 94
Adams, John Quincy 137–138
Aelian 268
Ahlers, Cyriacus 220
Aislabie, John 182
Akst, Daniel 179
Alexander, John M. 170
Alexander II, Czar of Russia 123
Allen, Stephen 234
Aluys, Albert 2
Ames, Oakes 64–65
Amin, Idi 215
Ammon, Robert 177
Anderson, Bloody Bill 137
Anderson, Robert P. 150
Annbury, Miss Julia xi
"Antique" Smith 4
Arnold, Philip 108–109
Arnstein, Nick 160
Arthur, Chester 283
Ashby, James 5–6
Asher, Maxine 6
Ashkin, Julius 120
Augustus, King Stanislas of Poland 208
Aust, Hans 271
Austin, Warren 281
Australian Harry 258

B

Babcok, Orville 292
Babelon, Ernest 27
Bailey, James 25, 74
Bain, John 213
Baker, Bobby 20–21
Baker, Col. Jacob 21
Baker, Mary 47–48
Baker, Norman 45
Baldwin, Charles 158
Balfour, Jabez 21
Balsamo, Giuseppe 43–44
Bandeira, Jose 225

Barannikov, Gennady 151
Barnhart, John H. 4
Barnum, P.T. 25, 48, 61, 82, 88–89, 109–110, 118–119, 180
Baron of Arizona See Reavis, James Addison
Barrie, Paddy 23–24
Barrow, Clyde 34
Barry, Dr. James 24
Bateman, Mary 84
Baxter, Gen. H. Henry 83
Beam, Maurice 260
Beatles, The 200–201
Beatty, Warren 36
Beauregard, P.G.T. 158
Beazley, Sam 28–29
Beethoven, Ludwig von 55
Bellow, Saul 280
Bellow-Lowndes, Mrs. 198
Bennett, Alex 201
Bennett, James Gordon 119, 283
Bennett, Wallace F. 251
Bergen, Edgar, and Charlie McCarthy 173
Beringer, Dr. Johannes 27–28
Berryman, Clifford 259
Bigelow, Charlie 137
Bigley, Elizabeth See Chadwick, Cassie
Binney, Dr. Barnabas 232
Birdwell, Russell 146
Blackbeard 93
Blair, Hugh 163
Blinderman, Charles 206
Bliss, George 154
Block, Lazare 117
Blonger, Lou 31
Blood, Col. Thomas 65
Bluffstein, Sophie 225–226
Blum, Hans 151
Boatright, Buck 30–31
Bodinus 124
Boesky, Ivan 33–34, 152, 167
Bogle 262
Boguet 124
Bond, James 87
Boris, Czar of Russia 212
Bottomley 35–36

Bovar, Oric 36–37
Boy with His Fingers in the Dike 37
Brady, Mathew 101
Brandegee, Frank 195
Brandenburg, Elector of 254
Brannon, W. T. 280
Brawley, Glenda 37
Brawley, Tawana 37–38
Breadline Charlie 27
Bridges, Rev. Thomas 62
Brinkley, John R. 103–104
Brisbane, Arthur 143
Bristow, Benjamin 282
Britton, Nan 170
Brown, Frank 88
Brown, Pat 75
Brownlee, W.C. 183–184
Bryant, William Cullen 97
Byron, Gordon De Luna 40–41
Byron, Lord 40–41, 196
Byron's Illegitimate Son 40–41
Buckley, Christopher 151
Buckley, William F. 151
Buckminster, Fred x, 39–40, 113, 278–279
Burkett, J. H. 85
Burnham, Tom 233, 283
Burnett, Carol 36
Burns, Robert 4
Burns, William J. 148, 169
Bushman, Francis S. 122
"Butterbrod, Dr." 138
Butts, A. L. 102
Buxton, Anthony 60

C

Cabell, Gen. W.L. 158
Caesar, Julius 23
Cagliostro, Count Alessandro di 43–44, 72
Calhoun, John C. 97
Cameron, Lady Mary 23
Capone, Al 46, 98, 160–161
Caprara 26
Captain of Köpenick 46–47

Caraboo of Javasu, Princess 47–48
Carlyle, Thomas 220
Carnegie, Andrew 51–52
Carey, Matthew 277
Carter, Clifton 86
Caruthers, William 157
Catherine the Great, Empress of Russia 44
Caul, Rev. Mr. 125
Cavendish, Lord 199
Cazeau, Paul 178
Cerf, Bennett 80
Chadwick, Cassie 51–52
Chadwick, Leroy 51
Chafetz, Henry 211, 254
Chakhvashvili, "Professor" David 52
Chamberlain, Neville ix, 60
Chapman, Lucretia 178
Chapman, William 178
Charles I of England 149
Charles II of England 65
Charlotte, Queen of England 285
Chartes, Michael 158–159
Chatterton, Thomas 53–55, 163
Chester, Captain 93
Chesterfield, Earl of 108
Chicago May 56–57
Chiles, George V. 96
Christ 268
Christopher, Melbourne 147
Chung, Johnny 94
Church, Benjamin 226
Churchill, Charles 226
Churchill, Dal 56
Churchill, May See Chicago May
Cisco, John J. 141
Clarke, Charles Langdon 138, 142
Clemens, Samuel See Twain, Mark
Clermont, Ganneau 238
Cleveland, Grover 168
Cole, Horace de Vere ix, 60–61

Coleridge, Samuel Taylor 115
Colfax, Schuyler 64
Collier, Charlies P. 141
Collins, Dapper Don x, 161, 165
Collins, Douglas 80
Conlish, Pete 113
Constantine the Great 76
Cook, Dr. Frederick A. 62–63
Cook, Helene 62
Coolidge, Calvin 63
Cooper, James Fenimore 97
Coppola, Roberto 63
Cornell, George de 178
Corot, Jean-Baptiste-Camille 178
Cortesao, Armando 275
Costello, Frank 193
Coster, F. Donald *See* Musica, Philip
Coughlin, Father George 215
Coward, Noel 122
Cranston, Alan 140
Crichton, Robert 70
Crittenden, Gov. Thomas 137
Cromwell, Thomas 76
Crowe, Dr. Harold E. 281–282
Croy, Homer 137
Ctesias 268
Culhane, John 119, 224
Cullen, Richard 91
Cumanus 124
Cuomo, Mario 37
Currelly, Dr. C.T. 142

D

Dali, Salvador 5
Dalimier, Albert 249
Dalton Gang 56
Dalton, J. Frank 137
Dalton, Michael 285
Darsee, Dr. John 67
Darwin, Charles 180, 205, 241
Dashti, Ali 196
Daudet, Leon 67–68
Daugherty, Harry 170, 195
David, James R. 137
Dawson, Benjamin 205
Day, Benjamin 184–185
De Angelis, Anthony "Tino" 109
De Barle, Dr. 69
DeConcini, Dennis 140
De Cosque 86
De Courteville 69
Defenbach, Marie 88
De Hooch, Dieter 274
De Hory, Elmyr 68
De Loys, François 68–69
Delric 124
Demara, Ferdinand Waldo, Jr. 69–70
De Quincy, Thomas 115, 116
De Rougemont, Louis 70–71
Desmond, Beatrice *See* Chicago May
Devall, William 285

DeVoe, John 234–235
DeVoe, Thomas 234
DeWelles, Roy W. 4
Dewey, Thomas E. 286
Diamond, Legs 160
Diamond, Stanley 38
Dickens, Charles, 31, 117, 210–211
Dickenson, Mother 148
Diderot, Denis 163
Dietrich, Noah 134
Dillinger, John 73–74
Dirks, Ray 85
Dmitry Ivanovitch, Czar of Russia 212
Dmitrys, False 212, 213
Dodge, Mary Mapes 37
Doheny, Edward L. 257–258
Dossena, Alceo 76–77
Douglas, John 149
Downes, Olin 144
Doyle, Arthur Conan 206
Dragna, Jack 214
Drake, Ernest 78
Drake, Francis 77, 77–78
Drake, John 93
Draper, Shang 19–20
Drigo, Richard 193
Dropper, Kid 79

E

Earp, Wyatt 104, 169
Eaton, Charles 31
Eckhart, Georg von 28
Edison, Thomas A. 130
Edward VII, King of England 168, 288
Edwards, Herbert H. 81
Edwards, Robert 81
Eisenhower, Dwight D. 251
Eliot, Osborn 116
Elizabeth I, Queen of England 77, 78, 82, 213, 268
Elizalde, Manuel, Jr. 256
Ellsworth, Oliver 202
Emerson, Ralph Waldo 48
Estes, Billie Sol 85–86
Eulenspiegel, Till 86
Evans, Bergan 160
Evans, John 204

F

Fairbairn, Nicholas 155
Faisal, King 215
Falke, Otto von 167
Fall, Albert S. 195, 257
Fallon, William J. 88–89
Farouk, King 53
Fasoli, Alfredo 76
Fatima, Princess 281
Fawcett, Percy H. 6
Feller, John Quentin 90–91
Ferris, Danny 135
Fey, Dietrich 179–180
Fillmore, Millard 172

Fischer, Konrad 121
Fisher, Charles E. 105
Fitzgerald, Edward 196
Fleming, Ian 87
Foley, John P. 159
Fonda, Claudia 146–147
Forbes, Charles R. 195
Ford, Bob 137
Ford, Henry 214
Ford, Worthington Chauncey 171
Forepaugh, Adam 25–26
Fortunato, Nick and Tony 107–108
Fossil Willy 96
Foster, John W. 154
Fountenay, Father 216
Fowler, Gene 87
Fox, John Tobin 96–97
Fox, Kate 96–97, 122, 240, 255
Fox, Margaret 96–97, 122, 240, 255
Franklin, Benjamin 97, 177, 233, 248
Franlin, Charles B. 141
Friedlander, Eric 124
Frick, Henry Clay 76
Fuller, B. J. 102
Furguson, Arthur 99
Fyodor I, Czar of Russia 212

G

Galbraith, John Kenneth 181
Gallienus 100
Gambino, Carlo 113
Gannett, Benjamin 232–233
Gardner, Martin 6–7, 147
Gareau, Jacqueline 230
Garfield, James A. 64, 100–101
Gates, John "Bet a Million" 93–94
Gates, Paul 291
Gautier, Theophile 116
Genovese, Vito 87
Geoffroy the elder, M. 2
George I, King of England 220
George III, King of England 47
George IV, King of England 211
Ghengis Khan 180
Ghirlandajo, Domenico 175
Gladstone, William 284
Glenn, John 140
Godunov, Boris *See* Boris, Czar of Russia
Goering, Hermann ix, 121, 273
Goethe, Johann Wolfgang von 26, 162–163
Goetz, Karl 160
Goldberg, Rube 55
Golding, Mrs. 206–207
Golowinsky, Matthew 214
Gordon, Thomas F. 204
Gould, Jay 106
Gould, Stephen Jay 205
Graber, Roland H. 271
Grandier, Father Urbain 194

Grant, Baron Albert 84
Grant, Duncan 60
Grant, Ulysses S. 135, 282
Grantaire, Pierre 247
Graves, Philip 215
Gray, George 27
Gray, Thomas 55, 163
Greeley, Horace 97, 106, 110–111
Green, Hetty 53
Green, Jonathan, F. 110– 111
Green, Lester 111–112
Green, Ned 53
Greenbaum, Walter 142
"Gregor I, Prince" 211
Grin *See* De Rougemont, Louis
Gromyko, Andrei 281
Gronen, Jimmy 243
Guare, John 116–117
Guerin, Eddie 57
Guistaf, King of Sweden 145
Guzik, Jake "Greasy Thumb" 98

H

Hadfield, John 115–116
Hahn, Otto 251
Haldeman, "Bob" 75
Haldeman, Julius E. 103, 116
Hale, William K. 129–130
Hall, A. Oakley 266
Hall, E. Beatrice 275
Halley, Edmund 216
Halliburton, Richard 116
Hampton, David 116–117
Hanau, Marthe 117
Hancock, Ralph 211, 254
Harding, Mrs. Warren 170, 195
Harding, Warren 170, 195–196, 291
Harriman, Karl 198
Harrison, Benjamin 154
Hartzell, Oscar x, 78–79
Hassell, Blount 81
Hatzitheordorou, Stephanos 37
Hauptmann, Bruno 169
Hayes, Edward 81
Hayes, Rutherford B. 135
Hearst, William Randolph 39, 76, 174
Hecht, Ben 93
Heckethorn, C. W. 111
Heidemann, Gerd 121
Henderson, Dr. Alexander 186
Hennies, Gustav 225
Henry II, King of France 71, 133
Henry VIII, King of England 76
Herder, Johann 163
Herschel, Sir John 184–185
Hersey, John 172
Herzl, Theodor 214
Heth, Joice 118–119, 180
Hewitt, Marvin 119–120
Heydrich, Reinhard 223
Hickey, Michael 272
Hill, Susanna Mildred 156
Hilley, Audrey Marie 32

Himmler, Heinrich 223
Hitchcock, Alfred 198
Hitchcock, Ethan A. 148
Hitler, Adolf 223
Hockney, David 120–121
Hogan, Frank 219, 286
Holly, Lillian 74
Holmes, Oliver Wendell 48
Holmes, Sherlock 200
Homan, Robbi 32
Home, Daniel 122–123
Home, John 163
Homer 162–163, 240
Hook, Theodore 28
Hoover, Herbert 78
Hoover, J. Edgar 169–170
Hopkins, Matthew 124–125, 254
Hopper, Hedda 146
Hosmer, George W. 283
Houston, Temple L. 126
Howard, Don 213–214
Howard, John 220
Howard, Joseph 59
Howard, Roy W. 287
Howland, Alexander See
   "Antique" Smith
Hoyt, Rev. W. K. 183–184
Hughes, Brian G. 126–127
Hughes, Howard 68, 74
Hugo, Victor 116
Hull, George 48
Hull, Lytle 93
Humbert, Therese 127, 128
Hume, David 163
Hutchinson, Ann 188
Huxley, Thomas Henry 241, 255

I

Ingles, Robert T. 27
Innes, Rev. William 215–216
Insull, Samuel 130–131
Ireland, Samuel 133
Ireland, William 132–133
Irving, Clifford 68, 133–134
Isenburg, Prince Carl von 126
Iten, Oswald 256
Ivan the Terrible 212

J

Jackson, Fanny 248
Jackson, Perry 94
Jackson, Stonewall 248
Jacobson, Dr. Cecil B. 91
James VI, King of Scotland
   (James I, King of England)
   213, 254
James, Jesse 136
Janin, John 108
Jefferson, Thomas 170
Jeffries, Norman 136
Jenkins, Peter 168
Jernegan, Prescott Ford 105
Johnny on the Spot 221–222
Johnson, Alexander Arthur 149
Johnson, Alva 239

Johnson, Lady Bird 21
Johnson, Lyndon 20–21, 85–86
Johnson, Samuel 1, 55, 149, 163,
   216
Joly, Maurice 215
Jones, Canada Bill 238
Josedsche, Herman 215

K

Kames, Lord 163
Kammerer, Paul 139
Kaplan, Nathan 79
Keating, Charles H., Jr. 140, 167
Keating, Tom 140
Keats, John 40, 53, 55
Keeley, John E. W. 140–141
Kefauver, Estes x, 279
Kelly, Joseph "Bunco" 237
Kelly, Shanghai 141–142
Kennedy, Robert 86, 169
Kerr, Alphonse 152
Kerry, John F. 175
Keyte, Lou See Koretz, Leo
Kid DImes, 39–40
King, Clarence 109
King, Maude B. 169
King, Ralph 37
Kirk, Francis 81
Koch, Howard 173
Koretz, Leo 143
Kreisler, Fritz 144–145
Kreuger, Ivar 145
Kriegel, Glenn F. 7
Krupp family 6
Kujau, Konrad 121
Kyton, Elizabeth 268

L

Lady in Black 146
La Motte, Jeanne Countier
   71–72
Landon, Alf 103
Lange, Robert, Sr. 243
Langley, Samuel P. 136
Lankester, Edwin Ray 241
Lansky, Meyer 193
"La Reverte" 231
Lasseter, Harry 148–149
LaTour, Mademoiselle Octavie
   74
Lauder, William 149
Law, John 180–182
Lee, Robert E. 90
Leibl, Wilhelm 151
Leif Ericson 275
Lenin, Vladimir 151
Leonardo da Vinci 28, 182
Leslie, George 154
Levine, Dennis 33, 152–153, 269
Levy, Jay 153
Lewis, John 110
Liche, Carle 164
Li Hung Chang 153–154
Lincoln, Abraham 59, 101
Lind, Jennie 180

Linz, Herr 248
Livy 273–274
Loch, Lord 289
Locke, Richard Adams 22, 119,
   185
Longfellow, Henry Wadsworth
   1
Loomis, John S. 106
Lorenzo de Medici 175
Lorimer, George Horace 233
Louis XIV of France 71
Louis Philippe 226
Lozier 234–235
Lucas, Vrain 158–159
Luciano, Lucky 193
Ludendorff, Gen. Erich von 2,
   257
Lukas, the Baboon-Boy 159–160
Lustig, "Count" Victor x,
   82–83, 160–161, 183
Lutz, Philip, Jr. 74
Lux, Captain Charles 210
Lyman, Levi 119
Lyon, James 83

M

Maas, Peter 193
MacArthur, Charles 122
MacDonald, Ramsey 60
MacFadden, Bernarr 272
Mackay, Charles 61, 65, 148,
   205, 254, 287
McAvoy, J.P. 93
McBride, Mrs. William 286
McCain, John 140, 175
McCartney, Paul 200–201
McClelland, Kacy 105
McCutcheon, John 142
McDonald, Mike 36
McDonald, William 113
McDougall, Curtis D. 247
McGlue, Luke 169
McGregor, Gregor 211–212
McGregor, James 163
McKinley, William 52
McLean, Edward B. 257
McLean, Evalyn Walsh 170
McLoughlin, Denis 51, 187
McNally, Frank 156
McNally, Hazel 156
McNutt, Paul 74
McPherson, James 162–163
Maddox, Alton H., Jr. 37–38
Maelzel, Johann Nepomuk
   55–56
Mahomet 274
Maione, Happy 287
Makley, Charles 74
Malins, G.H. 25
Mallison, Francis A. 59
Malskat, Lothar 179–180
Mandeville, Sir John 273
Mann, Herman 232
Mann, James Robert 165
Manningham, Sir Richard
   220–221

Mannix, William F. 154
Marcos, Ferdinand and
   Imelda 250
Marcy, Louis 166–167
Margaret, Countess of Bath
   268
Margaret, Countess of
   Henneberg 188
Maria Theresa 71
Marie Antoinette 71–72, 152
Marks, Ben 75–76
Marsh, O.C. 48, 61
Marshall, Henry 86
Marston, T.E. 275
Martin, John S. 89
Martin, Tony 87
Marx, Zeppo 87
Marx Brothers 28
Maskeleyne, Neville 241
Mason, C. Vernon 37–38
Mason, William 55
Massaro, Jim 153
Masterson, Bat 50–51
Mather, Mysterious Dave 104
Maximillian, King of Bavaria
   123
Maxwell, Robert 167–168
Mayfield, Ida 168–169
Means, Gaston B. 169–170
Medawar, Sir Peter 252
Mellon, Andrew 170
Mencken, H.L. 1, 172
Mendax, Fritz 151
Menelek II, Emperor of
   Ethiopia 83
Merritt, Martyn 89
Michelangelo 175
Mihavecz, Andreas 89
Miles, Louisa 225–226
Miller, William F. "520%"
   175–176, 203–204, 209
Millet, Jean Charles 178
Millet, Jean François 178
Milner, Richard 47, 205, 255,
   259
Milton, John 149
Mina, Lino Amalia Espy y 178
Mines, Eddie 221–222
Minkow, Barry 179
Minnis, Horace 139
Minuit, Peter 165
Miranda, Mike 87
Mitchell, John H. 148
Mizner, Addison 92, 93
Mizner, Wilson 92–93, 93, 239,
   267
Mniszek, Marina 212
Moltke, Gen. H.J.L. von 47
Molyneux, Hon. Mr. 220
Monk, Maria 183–184
Montague, Duke of 108
Montague, Louise 25–26
Montague, Miss St. John 78
Moore, Ann 185–186
Moore, Clara Jessup 141
Moore, Lester 186–187
Moore, Odie 130

Morehouse, Homer 166
Moreno, Anthony 187
Moriarty, Professor 206
Morley, Christopher 275
Morris, Robert 291
Morris, Robert Tappan, Jr. 62
Morse, Charles W. 187
Mortison, C. Louis 111–112
Moseley, Oswald 186
Moses 238
Mozart, Wolfgang 193
Mullens, Rant 29–30
Musica, Philip 189–191
Mussolini, Benito 145, 209–210

N

Nance, John 256
Napoleon I, Emperor of the
    French 71
Napoleon III, Emperor of the
    French 123, 215
Nasser, Gamal Abdel 215
Nast, Thomas 267
Nation, Mrs. 115
Negri, Pola 280–281
Newburger, Morris 94
Newell, William 48
Newman, Ernest 144
Newton, Isaac 159
Nicholas II, Czar of Russia 193,
    215
Nick the Greek 87, 93
Nicotra, Tobia 193
Nikko the Laplander 237
Nilus, Sergei 214–215
Nixon, Donald 75
Nixon, Richard 74–75
Northbrook, Lord 129

O

Oakley, Kenneth P. 205
O'Brien, Tom 113, 276
O'Donnell, F. F. 199
Ogle, Nathaniel 208
Olmedo, Jose 196
Omar Khayyam 196
Oofty Goofty 284–285
Oppenheimer, J. Robert 120
Oppian 268
Orleans, Duchess of 226
Ort, Charley 92, 93
Orton, Arthur 262–263
Otrepvev, Grigory Boganovich
    212
Otto, Carl C. F. 48
Otto, King of Bavaria 201
Oxford, Earl of 83
Owens, Jesse 197

P

Paine, Ralph D. 154, 247
Painter, G.D. 275
Palgrave, Robert 41
Palmer, Stewart 140

Park, Trevor M. 83–84
Parker, Bonnie 34
Parker, Geroge C. 101, 198–199
Parkhurst, Charlie 199
Parkingson, Robert 149
Parmeggiani, Luigi See Marcy,
    Louis
Parnell, Charles Stewart
    199–200
Pascal, Blaise 159
Paterson, Gen. John 232
Peary, Robert E. 62
Peaston, Janet 213
Peck, John M. 248
Pelham, Henry 226
Pepys, Samuel 1
Perkins, Benjamin 202
Perkins, Elisha 202
Peruggia, Vincenzo 182
Peters, Bernadette 36
Peters, Frederick Emerson
    202–203
Peters, Rev. Samuel 33, 203
Phelan, James 134
Piccard, Auguste and Jean Felix
    188
Pierce, Mrs. Franklin 97
Pierpont, Harry 74
Pigott, Richard 199–200
Piquett, Louis 73
Pius X, Pope 268
Poe, Edgar Allan 1, 22
Poitier, Sidney 116
Poniatowski, Prince Stanislas
    208
Ponzi, Charles 143, 176, 208–210
Pope, Alexander 149, 220
Porter, "Colonel" Jim 97–98, 279
Post, George 113
Potemkin 44
Powell, Lord Chief Justice 213
Powhatan 6
Pressel, Milo 81
Price, Andrew 31
Prince, Albert 249
Psalmanazar, George 215–216
Puzo, Mario 193

Q

Qaddafi, Muammer el- 215
Quantrill, William C. 137
Quinn, John Philip 227–228

R

Rabbit Woman, The 220–221
Rachkovsky, Gen. Pyotr 214
Ralston, William C. 108
Ramirez brothers 221
Randolph, John 291
Rasputin 180
Raymond the Cleric 20
Reavis, James Addison 222–223
Reichenbach, Harry 93, 122, 265
Reis, Auturo Alves 224–225
Remigius 124

Remus, George 225
Revere, Paul 226, 233
Reynolds, Quentin 79–80
Rhine, Dr. J. B. 146–147, 153
Richardson, William John 211
Richebourg, M. 226
Richelieu, Cardinal 194
Richelieu, Duke de 2
Richmond, Rev. Leigh 186
Ridley, Guy 60
Riegle, Donald 140
Rines, Robert 155
Rising, Lawrence 198
Roberts, Edmund 163
Robinson, Anne 206–207
Robinson, Mary 115–116
Robinson, Young 148
Rochette, R. 208
Roderick, J. Ignatz 28
Rodriguez, Agustin 231
Roentgen, Wilhelm Konrad 290
Roger, Patricia 114
Rohan, Cardinal Prince de 44,
    71–72
Roosevelt, Franklin 63, 78
Roosevelt, Theodore 148, 203,
    259
Roseberry, Earl 284
Roselli, Johnny 87
Ross, Mrs. Hannah 229–230
Rothstein, Arnold 93
Rousseau, Jean-Jacques 152
Rowley, Thomas 53
Royall, Anne New Port 138
Ruark, Robert 137
Ruiz, Rosie 230
Russell, Charles 199
Russell, George 265
Rutland, Duke of 115

S

St Andre, Nathaniel 220–221
Salle, Edward 48
Salley, A.S., Jr. 170
Salomé, Maria 231
Salonina 100
Sampson, Deborah 232–233
Saxon, Arthur 82
Scarne, John 238
Scheible, Billie 160–161
Schellenberg, Walter 223
Schick, Robert 65
Schlesinger, T. Edward 177
Schliemann, Heinrich 6
Schliemann, Paul 6
"Schmierkase, Dr." 138
Schockley, Arnold 94
Schwanthaler, Ludwig von 58
Scott, Peter 155–156
Scott, Thomas A. 106
Scribner, John C. 44
Segretti, Donald 75
Sergeant, Henry S. 141
Sestini 26
Seward, William H. 59

Shabaka, Pharaoh 236
Shakespeare, William 132–133
Shapira, M.W. 237–238
Shapiro, Aaron 214
Shapley, Harlow 120
Sharpe, May Churchill See
    Chicago May
Sharpton, Al 37–38
Shelley, Percy Bysshe 41, 53–55
Sheridan, Richard Brinsley 133
Sherril, Avanana 239
Shuysky, Vasily See Vasily IV,
    Czar of Russia
Sidney, Philip 149
Siegel, Bugsy 87, 93, 193,
    285–286
Silliman, Benjamin, Jr. 83
Silvers, Phil 87
Simondes, Alcibiades
    Constantine 240
Simpson, Edward 96
Sinclair, Harry B. 257–258
Sinclair, Upton 1
Siolerwicz, Jack B. 150
Skelton, R.A. 275
Slack, John 108–109
Slade, Alcida 241
Slade, Henry 240–241
Sleigh, Dr. 184
Slocum, John J.L. 184
Smith, Jefferson Randolph
    "Soapy" 238–239, 240,
    242–243
Smith, Jess 195
Smith, John H. 132
Smith, Mrs. John H. 132
Smith, Thomas "Pegleg" 157
Smith, Whittam 168
Smith, William 31
Smith, William Cameron 21
Sober Sue 243–244
Solomon, Samuel 22
Sophia, Queen of the
    Netherlands 123
Southcott, Joanne, 245
Spelvin, George 246
Spelvin, Georgette 246
Spelvin, Georgina 246
Spelving, Gregor 246
Spiegelman, Jerome Louis 150
Sprenger, Jacob 124
Spring, Robert 248
Stagg, Harold 251
Stalin, Joseph 223
Stallings, Laurence 121
Stanton, Edward M. 59
Stavisky, Arletta 249
Stavisky, Serge 248–249
Stein, David 249–250
Stempel, Herbert 219
Stephen, Adrian 60
Stephen, Virginia 60
Stephens, Joanna 250
Stevens, Al 110
Stevenson, Frances 25
Stevenson, William H. 83–84
Strauss, Jesse L. 27

Strauss, Johann 51
Strauss, Richard 86
Stringfellow, Douglas R.
   251–252
Strosnider, John Henry 258
Sullivan, Mark 166
Summerlin, Dr. William T. 252
Sun, Mona 253
Susanna, Princess See Wilson,
   Sarah
Susskind, Richard 133
Swift, Jonathan 151
Swope, Herbert Bayard 93
Sylvester I, Pope 76

T

Taft, Charles 225
Taft, William Howard 148, 187,
   225
Tallentyre, S.G. 275
Tallmadge, N.P. 97
Taub, Sergio 150
Tausend, Franz 2, 256–257
Tear-off Arthur 258
Teilhard de Chardin, Pierre 205
Tennant of the Strand 96
Thompson, Adam 172
Thompson, Alvin "Titanic"
   260–261
Thompson, Augustin 188
Thompson, Dorothy 173–174
Thomson, Samuel 261
Thumb, Gen. Tom 117, 180
Tichborne, Lady 262–263
Tichborne, Roger 262–263
Tichborne, Sir James 262–263
Tiffany, Charles Lewis 109
Tilden, Samuel J. 168, 266, 283
Timberlane, James 137
Tnesba, Evael O.W. 263
Toddy, Ted 34

Toft, Mary 220–221
Toland, John 73
Tölken, E. 208
Toscanini, Auturo 193
Toscanini, Walter 193
Tottingham, Mrs. 28
Tourbillon, Robert Arthur See
   Collins, Dapper Don
Tournay, Jack 110
Townsend, Charles H. 62
Trammell, John 137
Troy, Hugh xi, 94, 272
Truesdell, J.N. 241
Truman, Harry 172
Tuck, Dick 75
Tukhachevsky, Marshal
   Mikhail 223
Tutankhamen 142
Twain, Mark, 24, 45, 56, 231
Tweed, William Marcy 266–267
Tyrrell, John 208

U

Underwood, Joseph 211
Unger, August M. 88
Urban VIII, Pope 85

V

Valentino, Rudolph 146, 272,
   280
Valla, Lorenzo 76
Van Doren 218–219
Van Gogh, Vincent 272
Van Meegeren, Hans ix, 273
Van Ysselveere, Karel Morang
   224–225
Vasily IV, Czar of Russia 212
Vella, Joseph 273–274
Vermeer, Jan 273
Vernon, Caroline 285

Vietor, Alexander O. 275
Virgin Mary 268
Voigt, Wilhelm 46–47
Voltaire (François Marie
   Arouet) 76, 275

W

Waddell, Reed 104, 113,
   276
Wagner, John F. 237
Wallace, Alfred Russel 241
Wallace, DeWitt 80
Wallace, Malcolm 86
Walker, A.W. 235
Walpole, Horace 53, 55, 163
Walsh, Ellen See Mayfield, Ida
Walsh, James 213
Walsh, Thomas J. 257
Walter, Paul 67
Warner, George F. 4
Warren, Jesse 34
Washington, George 90,
   118–119, 202, 232, 248, 277
Watkins, Arthur 251
Webster, Dan 272
Weems, Parson Mason L.
   277–278
Weil, Yellow Kid x, 6–7, 39–40,
   97–98, 113, 183, 229, 258, 267,
   278–280
Weiner, J.S. 205
Weiss, Ed and Aimee 280
Welles, Orson x, 25, 68, 172–
   174
Wells, Charles 166
Wells, H. G. 172
Wenham, Jane 213
Weyman, Stanley 280–281
White, William Allen 195
Whiteaker, Sudie B. 78
Whitman, Richard F. 282

Whitney, James T. 44
Whitney, Mrs. Payne 23
Wickersham, George W. 148
Wilde, Oscar 1, 30
Wild Man from Borneo 283–
   284
Wilhelm, Kaiser (Emperor of
   Germany, King of Prussia)
   46
Williams, Blind 211
Williams, George F. 284
Williamson, John N. 148
Wilshire, Hal 110
Wilson, Adm. Henry 287
Wilson, Henry 64
Wilson, Sarah 285
Winchell, Walter 285–286
Winslow, John 206
Winston, Steven 150
Witch of Walkerne 213
Wood, Benjamin 168
Woolf, Virginia 60
Woollcott, Alexander 198
Worrall, Samuel 47
Wright, Whitaker 288–289
Wurm, Ole 268

Y

Yamba 70
Young, Roby 201

Z

Zancig, Mrs. and Mrs. Julius
   178–179
Zingg, Prof. R. M. 159–
   160
Zinoviev, Gregory 292
"Zip, the What-is-it?" 180
Zug, Edgar 286–287

INDEX OF SUBJECTS

A

Abbey Road 201
Addressing Envelopes at
  Home 2
"Adonais" 55
Adulterated gas 8
Age of Uncertainty 181
Agincourt, Battle of 248
Air bag insurance overpricing 8
Aknahton 23
Alchemist Cons 2–3
All-American Soap Box Derby
  243
Alley treatment 8
American Academy of
  Medicine 281
American Circus, The 119, 224
American Journal of Psychology
  281
American Magazine 111
American Medical Association
  2, 103
American prison swindle 246
American Weekly, The 159–160
Animal Farming Rackets 3
A. N. Marquis Company 283
*Appleton's Cyclopedia of American
  Biography* 4, 283
Arcadia 149
Army Times 251
Arthritis Cure Cons 4–5
Arthritis Foundation 4
Art Fakes & Forgeries 5
Art Print Frauds 5
Aspirin 5
Associated Press 151, 288
Atahualpa Statue 6
Atlantic Monthly 247
Atlantis Searches 6–7
*Authentic Account of the
  Shakespearean Manuscripts*
  133
Auto-Bolide 74
Automatic choke cons 8–9
Automatic transmission con 9
Automobile Ploys and Scams
  7–18

*Awful Disclosures of Maria Monk,
  The* 183–184

B

"*Babylon Gazette*" 138
Bacon Waxing 19
Badger Game 19–20, 56
Bait and Switch 20
Baker Estate Swindle 21
Balloon Busters 21–22
Balloon Hoax 22
Balm of Gilead 22
Baltimore Gazette 56
Bank Examiner 23
Bank of Portugal 224–225
Bankers' Pool 282
Barbizon School 178
Barnum & Bailey Circus 74
Barnum's American Museum
  82, 89–90, 180
Barron's 179
"Battery Boiling" gyps 9
"Battery-Free" Flashlight 24
Battery test scam 9
"Battle of the Ancre and the
  Advance of the Tanks"
  25
"Battle of the Somme, The"
  24–25
Bayano Timber Syndicate 143
BBC-Riot Panic 25
Beauty Contest Fixing 25–26
Begging 26–27, 27, 32, 204,
  210–211, 250
Begging Counterfeit Racket
  26–27
Begging Scams 27
Belvedere 167
Beringer's Stones 27–28
Berliner Tageblatt 144
Berner Street Hoax 28–29
Better Business Bureau Cons 29
Biarritz 215
Bible Scam 29
Bigamy 29, 32
Big Ben 99
Bigfoot Fakes 29–30

Big 6-Big 8 30
Big Store 30–31, 278
*Billie Sol: King of the Wheeler
  Dealers* 86
Billies and Charlies 31
Bill Stump's Stone 31
Bird dogging 9
Blackboard Bowl 94
Black Sox Scandal Doublecross
  31–32
Black Widow of Marlow 32
"Blindmen's Dinner" *See*
  Eulenspeigel, Till
Blinkies 32
Blue Law Hoax 32–33
Bobbed Hair Tax 33
Boiler Room Operations 33–34
Bonnie & Clyde's Death Car 34
Book of Lismore 163
Book of Lists 133
Book of Psalms 221
Boot Hill 186
Border Jumping Scams 34–35
Boston Marathon 230
Boston Post 209
Bounty Jumping 36
Boxer Rebellion 110
Brake pedal con 9
Brazilian Card Smuggling
  Scam 38
Breather cap con 9–10
Brewster's Millions 246
British Association for the
  Advancement of Science 70
British Communist Party 292
British Museum 4, 27, 52, 71,
  99, 155, 167, 174, 205, 237, 239,
  275
Brooklyn Bridge 82, 198–199
Brooklyn Eagle 59, 275
Brothers and Sisters of the Red
  Death 39
Buckingham Palace Hunger
  March 39
Buckland Abbey 77
Burns Detective Agency 169,
  257
Bushel Basket Toss 40

Butcher shop rackets 19, 89,
  150–151
Byzantine 23

C

Cabbie Count 42
Cackle-bladder 31, 42–43
Caesar's Marble Head 43
Calaveras Skull 44
Calgary Herald 80
California Department of
  Corporations 113
Calistoga Springs Water Scam
  44–45
Campbell Soups 174
Canarsee Indians 165
Cancer Cure Cons 45
Canned Goods 45–46
Cape Fear Mercury 170–171
Capone Grave Hoax 46
Capone's Soup Kitchen Fraud
  46
Carburetor cons 10
Cardiff Giant 48, 60
Car insurance misclassifying
  trick 10
Car insurance trick policies 10
Carnival gyps 21–22, 40–41, 91,
  124, 167, 176, 187–188, 191,
  226–227, 227, 250–251
Car owners fraud protection 10
Car Resale Swindle 48–49
Cash Machine Scams 49–50
Catalog Cons 50
Cat and Rat Ranches 50
"Caterpillar invasion" 50
Cat-wanted Hoax 50
Celebrity Scams 50–51
Central Pacific Railroad 264
Central Park Zoo x, 283
Charity Cons 52
Chastity Belt Frauds 53
Chastity Frauds 53
Chattanooga Times 140
Check-passing "Drunks" 55
Chess-playing Automaton
  55–56

Chicago Journal 142
Chicago Tribune 142
Chincilla farming 3–4
Chinese International Growth Fund 253
Christ and the Adulteress 273
Christ at Emmaus 273
Christmas Card Envelope Scheme 57–58
Christmas Carol Killings 58
Church of England 78
Cigar-filled statues 58
Circus Grifting 58–59
City Inspector Scam 59
Civil War Gold Hoax 59–60
Cleveland Museum of Art 76
Cleveland Press 52
Cluny Museum 53
Cock Lane Ghost 207–208
Cockroach Exterminator 60
Cold Poking 60
Collier's 170
Colorado Man 61
Committee of 101 243
Committee of 303 243
Communist Academy (Moscow) 139
"Company for carrying on an undertaking of great advantage, but nobody to know what it is" 61
Compleat Swindler, The 211, 254
"Composograph" 272
Computer Fraud and Abuse Act 62
Computer Scams 61–62
Computer Viruses and Other Frauds 62
Comstock Lode 105
Confessions (Rousseau) 152
Confessions of William Ireland 133
Connell's Mystery Rhino 63
Considine's 57
Coolidge Hoaxes the Secret Service 63
Counterfeit Fake Scams 63–64
Counterfeiting 63–64, 64, 112–113, 221
Counterfeit Money by Mail 64
Counterfeit Passing Scams 64
Courtroom hoaxes 88–89, 126, 225
"Coyotes" 35
Credit Mobilier Railroad Scandal 64–65
Credit Scams 65
Crown Jewels Theft 65
Cunning Men 65–66

D

Daily Chronicle 70
Daily Mail 155
Daily Racing Form 265
Darwinian theory 205
Daudet's Escape 67–68
Daytop Village, Inc. 150

"Dead battery" 10
Dearborn Independent 214
Debt Consolidation Scam 68
Declaration of Independence 170
De Loys Ape 68–69
Demonologie 213, 254
Denver Post 110
Denver Republican 110
Denver Times 110
Detective Lessons by Mail 71
Detoxacolon 4
Detroit Free Press 198
Deuteronomy 237–238
Dialogue in Hell Between Machiavelli and Montesquieu 215
Diamond Counting Contests 71
Diamond Necklace Hoax 44, 71–72
Diamond Switchers 72–73
Dictionary of Misinformation 233
Dillinger Days, The 73
Dillinger's Wooden Gun Escape 77
Dip of Death 74
Dipstick dodges 11
Dirty oil dodge 11
Dirty Tricks 74–75
Distributor Frauds 75
Divers *See* Floppers and Divers
Dodge City 168
Dog Race Doping 75
Dollar Store 75–76
Donation of Constantine 76
Doomsday hoaxes 39, 84
Dossena's Genuine Fakes 76–77
Double Count 77
Double-trays 77
Drake Brass Plate 77
Drake Inheritance Swindles 77–79
Dreadnaught, H.M.S. 60
Drexel Burnham Lambert 33, 152–153
Driveway Scams 79
Drop, The 79
Drop Scams 79
"Dynamizer" 1

E

Edinburgh Journal of Science 184–185
Edwards Heir Association 81
Edwards Heir Swindle 81
Egg Sex Determinator 81–82
Egress 82
Eiffel Tower Sale 82–83, 160–161, 198
Eikon Basilke 149
El Camino Real 92–93
Electric Chair Immunity 83
"Electronic Reaction of Abrams" (E.R.A.) 1
Elevator Drop 83
Elizabeth I "Hag" Coin 83

Emma Silver Mine Bubble 83–84
Emory University 67
Encyclopaedia Britannica 62–63, 254
Encyclopedia of Evolution 48, 205, 255, 259
End-of-the-World Egg 84
Endymion: A Poetic Romance 55
Envelope Switch 84–85
Equity Funding Corporation 62, 85
Erie Railroad 106
Essay on Conversation 116
Essay on Milton's Use of an Imitation of the Moderns in His Paradise Lost 149
Evening Graphic 272
Everleigh Club 280
Extraordinary Popular Delusions and the Madness of Crowds 61, 66, 148, 205, 254, 287
Eye Bet 86
Eye-in-the-Sky Scam 86–87

F

Fads & Fallacies in the Name of Science 7, 149
"Fagin Prep" 27
Fake! 68
Fake Murder Fakes 88
False Messiahs 36–37, 39, 84, 245
Famine Frauds 89
Fannie Mae 123–124
Fanning 89
Farmer's Museum, Cooperstown, N.Y. 48
Fasting 89, 185
"Father of the Beauty Contest" 26
Federal Communications Commission 260
Federal House of Detention (N.Y.) 161
Feejee Mermaid 89–90
Fertility Frauds 91
Financial Times 35
Finding of Moses at Triepolo, The 247
Fine Arts Guild of America 178
Fingal 163
"Fire Injectors" 11
Fireplace Fixers 91
Fish Pond Carnival Scam 91
Flamingo 87, 186
Flat-rate Manual dodges 11
Floppers and Divers 91–92, 131
Florida Land Boom 92–93
Florida Pirate Gold Cons 93
Fly Bet 93–94
Flypaper Reports 94
Food and Drug Administration 4–5
Fools of Fortune 227
Football Hoaxes 94–95

Foot Race Con 95
Forbes 151
Foreign Currency Speculation Swindles 95
Foreign Job Scams 95–96
Forged Decretals of Isidore 76
Forgeries and counterfeits 4, 5, 22, 27, 27–28, 31, 40–41, 43, 53–55, 55–56, 68, 76, 76–77, 79, 96, 132–133, 133–134, 140, 149, 150–151, 153–154, 158–159, 162–163, 166–167, 170–171, 174–175, 175, 178, 179–180, 182, 192, 199–200, 205–206, 208, 214–215, 222–223, 223, 224–225, 226, 235, 237, 237–238, 239–240, 240, 246, 248, 249–250, 273, 273–274, 275, 292
Formosa 215–216
Four Deuces 98
Freedland Mortgage Company 124
"Free inspection" car repairs 11
Free Land Swindle 97
Freeway runners 11–12
Friar's Club 87
Friends of Voltaire, The 275
Frog-farming Cons 98
Frolics Club Hoax Murders 98
Funeral Chasers 98–99, 210
Fur-bearing Trout 99
Further Disclosures of Maria Monk 184
F.Y.I. 151–152

G

Gambling 5–6, 23–24, 30, 30–31, 39–40, 75, 75–76, 77, 86, 86–87, 93–94, 110–111, 165–166, 230, 238–239, 239, 241–242, 242–243, 247, 249, 260–261, 261–262, 263, 265–266, 267 (*See also* Carnival Gyps)
Gambling Unmasked 111
Garfield Engraving Scams 100–101
Gasoline brand hoax 12
Gas pump double dipping 12
Gas pump tumbler scam 12
General Dynamics 20
General History of Connecticut 33, 203
General Land Office 148
Gentle Tasaday, The 256
German Unification Scams 101
Gestapo 80
Geysers on Command 101
Ghost Hoaxes 102
Giant Grashoppers of Butts Orchard 102
Gift Family 102–103
Girard and Co. 190
Goat Gland Sex Rejuvenation 103–104
Godfather, The 193
Gold Brick Swindles 104

Gold Bullion Frauds 104–105
Golden Fleece 116
Gold Extraction Swindle 105
Gold Fakery 2, 44–45, 93, 104, 104–105, 105, 148–149, 156–157, 194, 202, 231–232, 256–257, 276
Goldfinger 87
Gold Mine Dirt 105–106
Gordon-Gordon, Lord 105–106
Grand Canal of Venice 92–93
Grand Central Station Information Booth Swindle 107–108
Grant's Tomb 198
Great Bottle Joke 105
Great Diamond Hoax 108–109
Great Impostor, The 70
Great in the Little, The 214
Great Mouthpiece, The 88
Great Salad Oil Swindle 109
Great Unknown, The 109–110
Great Wall of China x, 110
Green Goods Swindle 112–113
Greeting Card Charity Cons 113
Gruner & Jahr & Co. 121
Guarantee Prorating 113
Gulf War Scams 113–114
Guinness Book of Records, The 89
Gypsy Money Curse 114

H

Habeas Corpus Trick 115
Hammerstein's Victoria Theater 243
Hanover Trust Company 209
Hansard's Guide to Refreshing Sleep 117
Hans Brinker or the Silver Skates 37
Hargrave Secret Service 71
Harry Winston 73
Harvard Medical School 67, 202
Head gasket con 12
Height-stretching Cons 117–118
Heir-hunting Racket 118
Hereford Reformer 66
"Hidden Load" auto insurance 12–13
Highballing *See* Lowballing and Highballing
Highland, The 162
Historical and Geographical Description of Formosa 215
Historical Commission of South Carolina 215
History of New England, The 33
History of Pennsylvania, The 204
Hitler's Diaries 120–121
Hitler's Silly Dance 121
Hockney Forgery 121–122
"Hogan's Alley and the Yellow Kid" 278
Hollywood Career Hoaxes 122
Home Equity Scams 123–124
Honduras National Lottery 158
Honking 13

Honolulu Observer 154
Hoop and Block Carnival Gyp 124
Hoover Dam 233
Hotel Dieu nunnery 183–184
Houghton Mifflin 154
House of Nations 123–126
"House on 16th Street" 195
How I Filmed the War 25
How to Improve Your Conversation 116
Humbert Millions, The 127–128
Hypnotic Eye, The 70

I

Ice Worm Cocktails 129
Ignition wire switch 13
I Knew Jesse James 137
Illustrated London News 69
Imperial War Museum Review 160
Impersonators and impostors 24, 40–41, 43–44, 46–47, 47–48, 51–52, 52, 55–56, 69–70, 71–72, 85, 89, 94–95, 116–117, 119–120, 126–127, 127–128, 136–137, 159–160, 168–169, 178, 189–191, 196, 199, 210–211, 212–213, 215–216, 220–221, 222–223, 231, 232–233, 243–244, 246, 251–252, 256, 265
Independent, The 168
Indiana University 67
Indian Swindles 129–130
In Search of Omar Khayyam 196
Installment Payment Cons 130
Institute for Parapsychology 153
Insurance Frauds 131–132
Intelligence hoaxes 45–46
Internal Revenue Service 61
International Fur Trading 132
International Gift Shows, Inc. 205
International Jew, The 214
Internet Computer network 62
Interstate Appraisal Services 179
Investor Forecasting Swindle 132
It's a Racket 260

J

Jackass Notes 135
Jailhouse Shopping Network 135–136
Jersey Devil 136
"Jerusalem Times" 138
Jesse James Imposters 136137
Jesse James Museum 137
Jesse Owens Outruns a Racehorse 197
Jesus in the Temple 273
Job Report 137–138
John Blunt 36
John Bull 35

John Quincy Adams' Nude Press Conference 137
Jonah and the Whale Hoax 138
Journal of Abnormal and Social Psychology 146
Journal of Commerce 59, 185
Journal of Parapsychology 153
Journey to the Western Islands of Scotland, A 163

K

Kangaroo Monster Who Terrorized Tennessee 139–140
Kansas City Times 111
Keely and His Discoveries 141
Keely Motor Company 141
Kefauver Crime Hearings x, 279
Key clubs 189
Key Largo 93
"Key men" 189
Killer Hawk of Chicago 142
King Amuses Himself, the 116
King George Club 39–40
King Tut's Golden Typewriter 142
"Kiss-off" 31
Klondike 240
Klondike Nugget 129
Knife Sharpener Con 142
Knitting Machine Racket 142–143

L

Lady Ghislaine 168
Lady in Black 146
Lady Vanishes, The 198
Lady Wonder 146–147
Lancashire Witches 148
Land frauds 93, 93–94, 94, 97–98, 148, 193–194, 211, 228, 233, 253–254, 286, 291
Lasseter's Gold 148–149
Last Giraffe, The 149
Laundered Handkerchief Scam 150
Lawyer . . . Thief 150
Lead-headed Fowl 150–151
Leibl-Blum Paintings 151
Lemnian Athena 247
Lending gyps 68, 152–153, 154–155, 155, 269–270
Lenin-for-Sale 151–152
"Let Them Eat Cake" 152
Liberator Building and Investment Society 21
Lien Sharks 153
Life 133
Life of George Washington 277–279
Light-bulb con 13
Li Hung Chang Memoirs 153–154
Lincoln Savings and Loan of California 140

Lindbergh baby kidnapping 169–170
Lithographia Wirceburgensis 28
Little Blue Books 116
"Little Green House on H Street" 195
Little Joker 154
Loafing Along Death Valley Trails 157
Loan Churning 154–155
Loan Facilitators 155
Loch Ness Monster 155–156
London Daily Mail 198, 292
London Observer 154
London Times 140, 185, 199–200, 215
Lonely Hearts Queen 156
Long-term collision policies 13
Lorene and Lorene 156
Louvre Museum 182
Los Angeles Times 44, 179
Losing Horse Wins 156
Lost Mines 156–157
Lost Pegleg Mine 157
Lottery Con Games 157
Lottery Sidewalk Sales 157
Lottery Ticket Swindles 157–158
Louisiana Lottery 158
Lowball Home Repairs 158
Lusitania Medal Hoax 160
Lustful King Enjoys Himself, The 116

M

Madison Square Garden 198
Mafia 193, 223
Maharaja of Manchester 163
Mail-order Lab Test Scams 163–164
Maltless Malteds 164
Man-eating Trees 164–165
Manhattan Island x, 233–235
Manhattan Island Swindle 166
Mann Act Swindles 165
Man Who Broke the Bank at Monte Carlo 165–166
Marathon Dance Death Hoaxes 166
Marcos government 256
Marienkirche 179–180
Market Book, The 234
Marks 22, 167
Marriage Shakedowns 167
Marshall & Son 106
"Massacre at Palisade" 265
Maxwell Communication Corp. 168
Mayflower 238
McClure's 238
McGraw Hill 123–124
McKesson and Robbins 190–191
Mechanics and Handicraft 247
Mechanics lien 14
Mecklenburg Declaration of Independence 170–171

Medical quackery 1, 4–5, 22, 45, 103–104, 117–118, 165, 171–172, 197, 202, 231, 235–236, 236–237, 250, 255–256, 261, 270, 278
Mein Kampf 121
Memoirs of Li Hung Chang 153–154
Memphite Theology of Creations 237
Mencken's Bathtub Hoax 172
"Men from Mars" Panic x, 172–174
"Men from Mars" Panic (Ecuador) 174
Men of Emmaus 273
Mercury Theater of the Air 172–174
Mermen and Mermaids 174
Metropolitan Museum of Art 76, 198
Mexican Children Massacre Story 174
M.I.A. Rackets 174–175
Michelangelo virus 62
Middle West Utilities 131
Midnight Express 246
Milk Bottle Carnival Scam 176
Millet-Corot Art Fakes 178
Mind-reading Hoaxes 178–179
"Minstrel, The" 277
Miracle of Lübeck 179–180
Mirror Group Newspapers 167–168
Missing Link 180
Mississippi and South Sea Bubbles 61, 180–182
Moabite Stone 237
Modern Warfare 117
Mona Lisa Fakes 132
Money-making machine 182–183
Monster hoaxes 29–30, 48–49, 89–90, 99, 126–127, 136, 140, 142, 155–156, 174, 184–186, 235, 268
Moon Hoax 184–185
More Misinformation 283
Morning Chronicle 210
Mortar Mice Menace 187
Mother of Mankind Hoax 187
Mount McKinley, Scaling of 61
Mouse Game Carnival Gyp 187–188
Movietone News 121
Moxie Nerve Food 188
"Mules" 35
Multiple Birth Hoaxes 188
Mummy Fakes 188
Murder Inc. 286
Murphy Game 188–189, 236
Museum of Modern Art 272
Mushroom Raising Cons 189
Musical Times 144

N

Nail-hammering Carnival Scam 192
Nation, The 127
National Futures Association 132
National Geographic 256
National Institutes of Health 67
National Minority Protection Bureau 256
National Movement for Abolition of Theater Queues 26
National Police Gazette 137
National Student Marketing Corporation 192
Natural History of Nonsense 160
Nature 139, 155
Nelson's Column 99
Nessiteras Rhombopteryx 155–156
Nevada Control Board 230
New Jersey Division of Consumer Affairs 114
Newspaper and media fakes 6, 22, 50, 110, 111–112, 119, 129, 138, 139–140, 142, 151–152, 164–165, 174, 184–185, 194, 213–214, 233, 272, 283–284, 285–286
Newsweek 111
New York American 6, 174
New York Association for the Suppression of Gambling 110–111
New York Central Railroad 107
New York Daily News 37, 167, 168
New Yorker, The 239
New York Evening Mail 172
New York Evening Post 56
New York Evening Star 118
New York Herald 97, 247, 283–284
New York Herald Tribune 79, 94–95
New York Journal 278
New York Lighthouse 32
New York Marathon 230
New York Republican Chronicle 150
New York Sun 22, 64, 119, 154, 184–185
New York Times xi, 94–95, 123, 144, 174, 281, 284, 289
New York Tribune 119
New York World 59, 74, 93
Night at the Opera, A 28
"Nightly Business Report" 151
Night of the Sicilian Vespers 193
Nikko Securities Company 253
Nininger Daily Bugle 194
Nininger Swindle 193–194
Northern Pacific Railroad 106
North Ophir Claim 194

North Pole 62
Notre Dame 67
Nuns of Loudun 194

O

Odometer tricksters 14
Office of Strategic Services *See* O.S.S.
Ohio Gang 169, 195–196, 258
Ohio State Prison 74
Olmedo Statue 196
Omar Khayyam's Quatrains 196
Orphan Puldeca 126
"Oscilloclast" 1
O.S.S. 251
Ossian 162–163
Ossian and the Poetry of Ancient Races 163
Other Side of Hollywood, The 146
Otrano 53
Our Times 166
Over-Issue Con Game 196
Ozone Quacks 197

P

Padded insurance coverage 14
Pageant magazine 165
Palisade, Nevada 264
Panacea Society 245
"Pandiculator" 117–118
Paris Academy of Science 69
Paris Exposition Disappearance 198
Parnellism and Crime 199–200
Paste-up Money 200
Paul Is Dead! 200–201
Paul Pry 138
Peabody Museum 90
Peasant Shooter, The 201
Peat, Marwick, Mitchell & Co. 192
Pedigreed Dog Scam x, 201–202
Pennies Made of Gold 202
Pennsylvania Gazette 233
Pennsylvania Lottery 158
Pepperdine University 6
Perkins' Patented Metallic Tractor 202
Peter-to-Paul 203–204
Petroleum Producers Association 62
Phantom oil scam 15
Philadelphia Alarm 204
Philadelphia Press 247
Philadelphia Record 144–145
Phoenix Park Murders 199
Phony Crips 204
Pickpocketing techniques 60, 83, 204
Pick-up, The 230
Pickwick Papers 31
Pilgrimage Cons 204–205
Piltdown Inquest, The 206
Piltdown Man 205

Pitcairn's Records of Justiciary 213
"Placebo Wonder Pills" 236
Plainfield Teachers 94
Pocketbook Drop 206
Pollos 35
Poltergeist Hoaxes 206–207
Poniatowski Gems 208
Poole, J. P. 209
Poor Richard's Almanack 177
Pornographic Escape Ruse 210
Portrait Scam 210
Postal Impostors 210–211
Power steering garage gyps 15
Poyais Land Fraud 211–212
Precious Wentletrap 235
Prejudices 1
President's Daughter, The 170
Pretender Czars 212–213
Prickers 213
Privilege car 58
Prohibition Repeal Hoax 213–214
Protection con 214
Protocols of Zion 214–215
Ptan 247
Pullem Museum 242
Pyramid schemes 75, 216–217

Q

Quakers 204
Quest for a Blonde Mistress, The 116
Quill magazine 138
Quiz Show Hoaxes 218–219

R

Rabbit trick 221
Rabbit Woman, The 220–221
Radiator gyps 15
"Radiendocrenator" 236
Raleigh Register 170
Ramirez No-squawk Cut-outs 221
Random House 80
Raritan Indians 165
Reader's Digest 79–80
Realtors as Scam Victims 221–222
Receipt Racket 223
Red Army Officer Corps Plot 223
Red Dye Murders 223–224
Redlighting 224
Reetsa 126–127
Referral Rackets 224
"Reflexophone" 1
Reliquary Quarterly Architectural Journal and Review 96
Rented Flat Scams 225–226
Repair fixed price offers 15–16
Repair gadgets 16
Repair gyps 79, 91, 123, 158, 187, 260 (*See also* Automobile Ploys and Scams)

Repair shop invoice con 16
"Revolution No. 9" 201
Ring-a-Peg Carnival Scam 226–227
Ringling's Circus 58, 149
Rip, The 227
Robbins Bros. Circus 224
Rocks, The 227
Rock-weighing Swindle 227–228
Rocky Mountain News 110
Rolling Stone Colony 228
Ropers 31, 228
Rosary Game 229
Roulette Wheel Scams 230
Royal Academy of Sciences 2
Royal Geographical Society 70
Royal Ontario Museum 142
Royal Road to Romance, The 116
Rubaiyat of Omar Khayyam, The 196
Ruby Fakes 230

S

Safety Milk Con 231
Salting 231–232
Salt Lake City Telegram 213–214
Sand Swindlers 233
San Francisco Evening Bulletin 109
Santé Prison 67
Saturday Evening Post and Benjamin Franklin 233
Saturday Review of Literature 275
Savings and loan scandal 140
Sawing Off Manhattan Island 233–235
Scandals, Scamps and Scoundrels 133
Scientific American 141
Scientific hoaxes 27–28, 44, 48–49, 61, 68–69, 96, 99, 140–141, 153, 164–165, 184–185, 205–206, 220–221, 252–256
Sea Serpent of Silver Lake 235
Seattle Saloon and Dance Hall 189
Seawater Swindles 235–236
Second Continental Congress 170
Secret Band of Brothers, The 110–111
Secret Service 63
Secret Societies of All Ages 111
$75 Sony Trinitron Swindle 236
Sex Rejuvenator Aids 236–237
Sgt. Pepper 201
Shabaka Stone 237
"Shadow, The" 174
Sham 23
Shánghaiing Scams 237
Share-Expense Ride Scams 238
Shell Game 238–239
She Who Was Helena Cass 198
Shiner 111
Ship's Pool Swindles 239

Shock absorber tricks 16
Shopping scams 19, 20, 38–39, 89, 150–151, 252, 259, 292
Shortchanging gyps 42, 58, 77, 79, 227, 259–260, 277
Shrunken-head Forgeries 239–240
Siamese twins 58
Single-hand Con 240
Silent Investigators, The 157
Six Degrees of Separation 116–117
"Sixty Minutes" 5, 135, 153, 250, 269
Skagway Telegraph Con 240
Sleeping Beauty 175
"Slim-Twist Exerciser" 4
Sloan-Kettering Institute 252
Smack 241–242
Soap Box Derby Scams 243
Social Justice 215
Social Security Fake Claims 244
Social Security Scams 244–245
Society for the Diffusion of Christian Knowledge 183–184
Soldier of Fortune 95–96
Southern Pacific Railroad 65, 222
South Sea Bubble 61, 180–182
Sovyetskiy Soyuz 175
Spanish Inquisition Torture Chairs 246
Spanish Prisoner Swindle 246
Spectator, The 127
Spider Farm 247
Spinning-coin Game 247
Spiritualism 96–97, 122–123, 229–230, 240–241, 255
Split Masterpieces 247
Sports Betting 900 Lines 247–248
Sports Hoaxes 23–24, 31–32, 55–56, 74, 94–95, 95, 156, 197, 230, 231, 243, 247–248, 260–261, 265–266, 267
Sportsman, The 265–266
Spur of Agincourt 248
Spy Instructor Hoax 248
Star Route Scandals 248
Starter deception 16
Statue of Liberty 99, 198
Steerers 249
Stern 120–121
Sting, The 31
Stockwell Ghost 206, 207
Stone Soup 250
Strange Death of President Harding, The 170
"Strawberry Fields" 201
String Game 250–251
Stroller's Weekly 129
Stuffed Flat 252
Suing Insects 252
Sun, The 36
Sunday Times of London 121, 144, 292
Surprises of Love 245
Swag Hustlers 253

Swamp Swindlers 253
"Swedish Match King" 145
Swimming 254
Swindlers (major) 21, 35–36, 39–40, 51–52, 56–57, 97, 99, 106–107, 117, 127–128, 130–131, 140–141, 143, 145, 160–161, 169–170, 176–177, 179, 180–182, 189–191, 208–210, 222–223, 248–249, 278–280

T

Tacking 89
Taj Mahal 116
Talking Toe Tricks 255
Tammany Hall 266–267
Tapeworm Fakes 255–256
Tasaday Tribe 256
Teapot Dome 169, 195, 257
Tear-off Rats 258
Tear-up, The 258–259
Teddy Bear Origin Hoax 259
Telemarketing Frauds-on-Frauds 259
Temora 163
Ten-for-One Shortchanging Scam 259–260
Termite Scams 260
Third-party Telephone Calls 260
Thomson's Healing System 261
Three-card Monte 58, 75-76, 261–262
Tichbourne Claimant 262–263
Tiffany's 73, 108–109, 204
Till Eulenspiegel's Merry Pranks 86
Time 94, 252
"Time of Troubles" 212
Tip-the-Tee 263
Tire wear trick 16
Tishing a Lady 160, 263
Titanic 261
Tnesba, Evael O.W. 263
Tornado Alarm 264
Tornado-Taming Plutonium Generator 264
Toronto Mail and Empire 138, 142
Toughest Town West of Chicago 264–265
Tower of London 65
Tow truck thievery 16–17
Trade Fair Fakes 265
Transmission tricks 17
Trial-exchange car-buying hoax 17
Trilby 265
Trilby's Trance 265
Trodmore Races 265–266
Turk, The 55–56
Tweed Ring 267
"Twenty-One" 219
"20-20" 256
Two-horse Swindle 267

U

Ulenspiegel 86
Up-front Fee Scams 269–270
Unclaimed Merchandise Scam 268
Unicorn's Horn Fakes 268
Unillustrated Frauds 269
Union Pacific Railroad 64–65
United Nations 281, 194
United Press 287–288
University of Athens 240
University of Michigan *Daily* 200
Unordered Merchandise Racket 269
Uranium Quackery 270
Ursuline sisters 194
USA Today 135, 151
U.S. Postal Service 246, 269, 271
U.S. Senate Crime Hearings *See* Kefauver Crime Hearings

V

Vacation Scams 271
Vacuum Cleaner Recall Scam 271–272
Valachi Papers, The 193
Valentino Death Photo 272
Vampiring 272
Van Gogh's Ear 272
Vegetable Lamb of Tartary 273
Vella's History of Sicily 273–274
Vending Machine Swindle 274–275
Venice ix
"Vermeers" ix
Veterans Bureau frauds 195
Victoria and Albert Museum 167
Victory Bond Club 35–36
Vietnam War 174 –175
Vinland Map 275
Vinland Map and the Tartar Relation 275
Virgin Mary 180
Voltage generator dodges 17–18
Voltaire's Most Famous Quotation 275
Vortigen 133

W

Wadsworth Antheneum 90
Walkaway, The 277
Wall Street Journal 179
War of the Worlds x, 25, 172
Washington and the Cherry Tree 277–278
Washington Star 259
Waterbury Republican and American 111
Watered Stock 278

Watergate scandal 74
Waterlow & Sons 225
We Boys Mob 278
Weckquaesgeek Indians 165
Weight and Fitness Cons 278
Weiss Club Brothel 280
Wellington's Victory 55
Werther 163
Western Medical Repository
    172
Western Orthopedic
    Association 282
West Virginia Historical
    Society 31
What Really Happened 134
Wheel wobble con 18
Whiplash 281–282

Whiskey Ring 282
White and Case 192
White City Stadium 75
White Diamonds 282
White House bathtub 172
White House leasehold 99
White smoke trick 18
Who's Who in America 189, 283
Wide World 70–71
Wild and Wooly 186
Wild Animal Hoax 283–284
Wild Man from Borneo 283–284
Wimbledon Military Review
    Riot 285
Windshield wiper con 18
Winterthur Museum 90
Winter Wetlands Sales 286

Wishing Cork Tree 286
Witchcraft and similar subjects
    65–66, 102, 124–125, 148,
    206–207, 223, 254, 286–287,
    287
Witch Doctors (White) 286–
    287
Witches' Scale 287
Witch of Walkerne 213
Wolf-man Manias 287
Wooden guns 73–74
Wopoden Nutmegs 287
Works of Ossian, The 163
"World News Tonight" 151
World War I Armistice Hoax
    287–288
World Zionist Organization 214

X

X-ray-proof Underwear Hoax
    290

Y

Yale University Library 275
Yazoo Land Frauds 291

Z

Zero-interest Financing Plans
    292
Zinoview Letter 292
"Zip-the-What-Is-It" 180
ZZZZ Best 179